Reading in the
Elementary School

Reading in the Elementary School

FIFTH EDITION

George D. Spache
Evelyn B. Spache

Allyn and Bacon, Inc.
Boston   London   Sydney   Toronto

Photographic Credits: chapter 1, Stock, Boston/Susie Fitzhugh; chapter 2, The Picture Cube/Rick Friedman; chapter 3, The Picture Cube/Frank Siteman 1979; chapter 4, Stock, Boston/George Bellerose; chapter 5, Benji Jackson; chapter 6, The Picture Cube/Sharon A. Bazarian; chapter 7, Stock, Boston/Elizabeth Hamlin 1976; chapter 8, Benji Jackson; chapter 9, The Picture Cube/Rick Friedman; chapter 10, The Picture Cube/Frank Siteman MCMLXXXII; chapter 11, Benji Jackson; chapter 12, The Image Works/Alan Carey; chapter 13, Benji Jackson; chapter 14, The Picture Cube/Rick Friedman © 1981; chapter 15, Stock, Boston/Frank Siteman.

Series Editor: Susanne F. Canavan
Editorial and Production Services: TKM Productions
Cover Coordinator: Linda Dickinson

Library of Congress Cataloging-in-Publication Data

Spache, George Daniel, 1909–
  Reading in the elementary school

  Includes bibliographies and index.
  1. Reading (Elementary)   I. Spache, Evelyn B.
II. Title.
LB1573.S792   1985   372.4'1   85-13501
ISBN 0-205-08422-2

Printed in the United States of America
10 9 8 7 6 5 4 3 2 1 90 89 88 87 86 85

Contents

Preface to the Fifth Edition

In the eight years since the fourth edition of this book, several new approaches to instruction have had dramatic impact on classroom practices. State departments of education and teacher training institutions have increased their demands for preservice courses in reading methods. For example, Morrison and Austin's 1976 report[1] showed that 95 percent of the colleges surveyed offered a three-semester-hour course as compared to only 53 percent of those surveyed in 1961. About a third of these colleges required this basic course for all students. Other changes were an increased number of required courses, the introduction of competency-based courses, earlier field experiences, courses in diagnosis and correction, methods courses offered in school settings, and academic specialization in reading at the undergraduate level. However, the recommendations for a basic reading course for secondary teachers, a training and certification program for cooperating teachers supervising undergraduates in their classroom teaching, and prolonged apprenticeships were not adopted.

To aid our students in understanding more fully the implications of these trends, we have added brief chapters on computer and systems approaches to instruction as well as on reading interests and motivation. In addition, we have re-emphasized the parents' role in children's reading development by reviewing the increasing body of materials in this area. All the other chapters have been updated by citing current practices and recent research.

Note

1. Morrison, Coleman, and Austin, Mary C., "The Torch Lighters Revisited—A Preliminary Report," *Reading Teacher*, 29 (April 1976), 647–652.

Preface to the First Edition

This book offers what we believe is a different approach to the training of elementary teachers in methods of teaching reading. It is different in the sense that unlike many reading textbooks it does not simply present leading theories and methods and urge the teacher to formulate his or her own special combination of techniques. Without extensive classroom experience, the average teacher may find it difficult to make the judgments and choices of techniques and approaches which will be effective. Rather than exposing the teacher to a medley of confusing and contradictory ideas, we will analyze the leading theories, note their advantages and limitations as we see them, and then point out a specific combined approach.

This approach, drawing upon the proved strengths of older methods, will try to avoid their obvious shortcomings and failures. This eclectic method will enable the teacher to abbreviate the trial-and-error process of finding the most effective procedures for individualizing instruction to pupils' reading needs. It is true, of course, that some teachers will adopt our suggestions more readily than will others. However, through this approach some will achieve the flexibility, the insights, and the efficiency which are the foundations of successful reading instruction. We sincerely hope that these will be the outcomes for all who accept our approach.

This book was inspired by the shocking revelations of Mary C. Austin et al.'s study of tomorrow's teachers of reading.[1] Only seven of our states require a course in the teaching of reading for certification of elementary teachers. As a result, instruction in reading methods is most often embedded in a block course, or in one in the language arts. In 60 percent of these broad courses, the actual time devoted to reading methods ranges from *4½ to 11¼ clock hours;* 30 percent of these courses give reading even less time. This is hardly sufficient time to read, much less to digest and discuss, one of the leading textbooks unless, of course, the teacher has been trained in one of the new dynamic reading techniques which claims to teach reading such a book in two or three minutes.

Nowhere in Austin et al.'s summaries of the contents of the training in reading methods or student learning experiences is there mention of emphasis upon the diagnosis of pupil needs by means of observation or clinical tools. It is to fill this gap in particular that this book is offered, since in our opinion diagnostic skill is the heart of the reading program. At the base of all reading failures there is the contributing factor of the teacher's inability to recognize the pupil's peculiar needs and handicaps and to adapt procedures accordingly. Therefore, our approach centers around training in effective use of the teacher-pupil conference for observing significant reading behaviors, and planning appropriate developmental and corrective steps in the classroom. It will not cure or prevent all reading failures or supplant the need for remedial clinics. But this approach will help the elementary school teacher in diagnostic efforts.

To facilitate playing the diagnostic role, we have offered detailed suggestions for the conduct of the individual conference. We consider the diagnostic conference to be the most important skill that the teacher may bring to reading instruction. Second in importance is his or her knowledge of the proved values of basic approaches to reading. Thus this book attempts to build diagnostic and teaching skills upon a foundation of selected, proven methodological techniques.

Note

1. Austin, Mary C., et al., *The Torch Lighters: Tomorrow's Teachers of Reading*. Cambridge, Mass.: Harvard University Press, 1961.

PART ONE

Foundations of Reading

1 Ways of Defining the Reading Process

Reading is obviously a multifaceted process that, like a chameleon, changes its nature from one developmental stage to the next. At one stage, the major performances may be visual discrimination among forms and words, and the learning of sufficient common words to enable the reader to begin the true act of reading. Later, the process may shift to one involving a number of thinking processes—recalling, interpreting, judging, evaluating. During these stages, the reader's success is conditioned by such factors as language development, readiness for the school's objectives as determined by home background, and the accuracy of perceptual behaviors in both visual and auditory discrimination.

To some teachers, reading is simply a matter of drilling at different times on vocabulary, work attack skills, and a multitude of comprehension skills. Somehow or other, the reader is supposed to combine all these skills into a smooth, fluent processing of ideas in print. Other teachers recognize that skill drill may not result in an integrated process, and that hidden factors such as visual skills, perceptual discrimination, or lack of practice in a thinking activity may make reading a disjointed, fumbling effort. Only as this broad concept of the complex act we call reading is recognized can we be certain that our classroom practices are realistic and effective.

Although it is often avoided in books about reading, one of the major problems in reading instruction is a definition of reading. Without a clear-cut idea of the nature of the reading act and the reading process it is almost impossible to plan instructional goals. Without knowing what the process is, we cannot evaluate pupils' reading behaviors, nor can we distinguish an individual who is truly adept in reading from one whose skills are only superficially adequate. Without thorough knowledge of the process, we are prone to accept many reading tests uncritically and use their results naively, making faulty judgments regarding pupil progress, appropriate teaching materials, and proper teaching method. Because of our ignorance, we stress only the simplest and most obvious reading skills, conceiving these to be atomistic essentials, and ignore completely the changing relationships at different stages of development. Goals, methods, skills, and evaluation all depend upon our definition of the reading process.

A process that we stress throughout the student's entire school career obviously cannot be a simple act. Reading changes from what is considered primarily word recognition, through development of sight and meaning vocabulary and several methods of work attack, through different types and degrees of comprehension, to a mature act involving most of the higher mental

4

processes. Because of its complexity and the many stages of development, it is apparent that one simple definition will not suffice. For these reasons, we will describe or define reading in a variety of ways.

Reading as Skill Development

Paraphrasing Gray's description (*17*)* of reading in terms of skill development we might define reading in the following way. The reader directs his attention to the printed page with his mind intent on meaning. He reacts to each word with a group of mental associations regarding the word form, its meaning, and its sound. With the aid of these associations, clues of general configuration, distinctive characteristics of the shape, some of the letters or syllables, and the implications of the sense or pattern of the sentence, he discriminates each word from all others. Thus the reading process begins with word recognition.

As the meanings of successive words become clear, they are fused into thoughts or ideas. This implies that the reader holds in mind the meaning of the first words of the sentence as he reads those that follow. Similarly, the more mature reader retains the ideas of successive sentences, gradually modifying the total impression (main idea) as he reads through a paragraph or longer passage. Gray suggests that the reader achieves a literal meaning of the reading matter by attending to and anticipating meanings, relating ideas as they appear, and recognizing the author's organization of ideas. The reader evaluates the importance of the ideas offered, perhaps visualizing the events described, and adjusts his rate of reading to the difficulty of the material.

The reader may, in Gray's description, go beyond literal meanings in reacting to ideas implied but not stated by the author, and in identifying the author's purpose, mood, and attitude toward the reader. He may react to the occasion for the writing—the time and place setting, the writer's rhetorical devices, and the author's choice of words.

Some of the ideas gained from the reading material may be fused or blended with the reader's previous experiences, if they are not contradicted by these experiences and thus rejected. The new concepts may correct earlier ideas or be used to formulate newer, broader concepts. Thus the experiences gained from reading must, according to Gray, become part of the reader's associations to be used in future reading and thinking activities. All this, from one viewpoint, is the reading process.

William D. Sheldon (*38*) describes the reading process in terms of stages, somewhat as follows. The first stage is a transitional period which begins with listening and concept building, and proceeds through picture reading. Stage two is characterized by experience charts, picture story reading, and the gradual introduction to reading of words in preprimers. The third stage promotes

*Italic numbers in parentheses refer to the References at the chapter endings.

wide development of sight vocabulary, supported by training in auditory discrimination. A fourth stage introduces more careful discrimination by initial consonants, word endings, and the other phonic and structural details, as sight vocabulary continues to grow. The fifth stage in the primary period is, in Sheldon's words, a plateau during which the fundamental vocabulary is strengthened. The sixth stage introduces the intermediate-grade child to reading tasks in the content fields, to technical vocabularies and technical concepts. A seventh stage develops reading flexibility—the adjustment of rate and degree of comprehension to varying purposes. The maturing reader also begins to show the rudiments of critical reading involving judgmental, comparative, and inferential thinking, as well as creative ability to use reading as a tool for solving personal and group problems.

These definitions of reading in terms of skill development sometimes fail to convey the complete picture. The enumeration of stages and skills gives the impression that these are built upon each other or occur in some sort of sequence, but this is not realistic. Except for a few technical details which are introduced at certain stages in the process, practically all the skills enumerated are taught to the child almost simultaneously. For example, although the first few months of reading instruction may appear to be concentrated on teaching a few necessary words, other types of training are being offered. A background of experience to bring many associations and meanings to these beginning words is being built. Clues given by pictures, sentence patterns, and simple endings are pointed out to children, and they are urged to use these to aid themselves. The new ideas and concepts brought by the story are constantly compared and fused with the children's own experiences. Even at these primitive reading levels, the children are helped to do critical and creative reading. For example, they may be helped to tell their emotional reactions to the story content, to judge whether the story appealed to their sense of humor, sympathy, or realism. They may dramatize the story to portray their understanding of its action, the feelings of the characters, or the purpose of the author. As soon as they can, children are helped to use the ideas and vocabulary they are learning for creative purposes—in their own writing, speech, storytelling, reporting to the group, and similar activities. Thus word recognition, word meanings, some method of word attack, retention and reaction to new ideas, and critical and creative responses are all interwoven in the good reading program from the very first day. Learning to read is a complex process for which no one method or device is sufficient.

In our opinion the concept of reading as a skill development process is a very limited interpretation of what is really a very complex process. Belief in this concept is widespread and often leads to stereotyped drill with isolated reading behavior or skills. Many teachers utilize their own or commercial materials for repeated practice such as in "reading for main ideas" or "reading for details" or a group of four or five such labeled skills. There are two assumptions present in such practice; namely, that each skill represents a distinct way of thinking that is trainable, and that all these behaviors are eventually blended together into intelligent reading after sufficient practice.

However, readers hardly ever consciously read for main ideas or any of the types of facts teachers label. Only when they have been given specific prereading instructions, or are aware of the type of fact they are supposed to secure, does the process tend to be channeled. Most of the time they just read—processing the ideas they meet as best they can, combining them with their own—and later try to sort out and answer the facts demanded. In other words, repeated practice in answering a certain type of question does not necessarily fix a skill in readers' minds as a particular kind of reading they can do later upon demand. Reading is not a bundle of separate thinking skills.

What we are trying to say is that from the very beginning it makes sense to us to vary the types of questions, both before and after reading, to lead readers to think their way through printed matter. Certain types of questions may be emphasized from time to time (for example, as in more stress upon details in scientific, mathematical, and such materials). But too much emphasis upon one type of question will only handicap readers in future reading, which, of course, usually demands a variety of reactions. Certain experiments show that continued practice of one type of comprehension tends to prevent readers from securing a variety of ideas and facts, as they normally would. Thus the practice actually results in less depth of comprehension than is desirable. Only limited practice in securing any one type of fact seems justifiable. Reading is not a group of separate skills to be practiced in isolation and later blended together into the total act. It is rather a total act from the beginning, limited, of course, by the readers' reasoning capacities, experiences, and reading abilities.

This reaction to reading as a skill development process immediately raises questions about our definition of comprehension, and if we do not follow the skills-drill approach, what sort of training in comprehension we would offer.

Reading as a Visual Act

The definition of reading may be approached from an entirely different angle—as an almost purely visual act. This definition may seem to be a technical one that classroom teachers need not understand completely. Many teachers may feel that this facet of the reading process is not within their special area of competence—they are not vision specialists, nor directly responsible for visual training or the correction of visual defects. These opinions are not completely valid. Reading is, first of all, a visual act and it cannot ever be taught soundly if the functions of the eyes are not understood. Proper coordination of the eyes, the true eye span possible, the obstacles to successful reading in faulty movement patterns and various common visual defects must be understood by classroom teachers if they are to be successful.

Children's vision is tested more often by teachers than by any other adults they meet, vision specialists included. In this vision testing, teachers accept the responsibility for finding those children who may have academic difficulties because of visual defects. In accepting this responsibility, teachers owe it to themselves and to their pupils to understand the relations between vision and reading in order to do a better job of testing vision and teaching reading. Later chapters, particularly those on readiness, offer specific steps that teachers may follow to improve their effectiveness in both areas. But even before these, teachers must understand reading as a visual act.

The reading process may be described in visual terms somewhat as follows. As individuals read, their eyes hop or glide from one stop to the next from left to right. They do not read in a smooth sweep along the line but only when the eyes are at rest in each fixation. During the sweeps or swings from one fixation to the next readers see nothing clearly, for their eyes are temporarily out of focus. Each fixation during which reading actually occurs lasts from about one-third of a second in young children to about one-fourth of a second at the college level. In all probability most of the thinking that occurs during reading is done during this fraction of a second, for a number of studies show that the duration of the fixation often lengthens if the reading material is very difficult. The fixations are the heart of the visual reading act, for they occupy about 90 percent of reading time, while interfixation and return sweeps account for the rest.

If readers fail to recognize what they see in a fixation, or to understand the idea offered, they tend to make a regression. That is, they make another fixation at approximately the same place or swing backward to read again. They may regress several times until the word is recognized or the idea comprehended before resuming the normal series of fixations. Then near the end of each line they make one big return sweep to a fixation close to the beginning of the next line.

These facts are important to the classroom teacher because they explain the emphases in the reading program on controlled vocabulary, line length, building experiences with word meanings, and controlling the difficulty of concepts. To help children acquire a normal visual act in reading, the reading program must be planned to promote this pattern. An excessive proportion of unknown words, inadequate experiences with the multiple meanings of words, and reading matter which is too complex for the child's experiences all promote a faulty reading pattern and lack of progress in reading. Every teacher of reading recognizes the need for controlling these factors, but few realize the ultimate reasons for them.

Some self-proclaimed reading experts would have us begin reading with almost any book or, worse yet, by an alphabetic or spelling approach. "Start them with the Bible or the Constitution of the United States," they say. "What better material could they hope to read?" "Teach them the letters or the sounds first." "Stop babying our children with a controlled vocabulary." "Let them stretch their minds with something hard and challenging," they urge us. Picture what would happen to the normal pattern of eye movements if we followed this advice. Children might learn to read by these approaches, as many did in earlier periods in American reading instruction. But what sort of speed, fluency, or forward movement would be promoted by these methods? When would readers ever outgrow the process of deciphering or spelling letter by letter and achieve a normal pattern? When would they really learn to "read" in the appropriate pattern of eye movements we are describing here?

Almost from their beginning efforts, children vary in their reading speed. Some read painfully slowly, word by word, for what seems to be a long part of their primary years. Others read rapidly and smoothly, making it seem that to them "reading is really just talking written down." Because of these variations, reading teachers often try to urge children to read more fluently and naturally—in phrases or groups of words. But these practices, too, display ignorance of the visual components of the reading act.

The normal beginning reader makes an average of two fixations per word—seeing or recognizing less than one whole word at each fixation. This statistic was determined by photographing the reading of over a thousand first graders by "The Reading Eye," a camera made especially for this purpose (42). In this country-wide testing, each child read a selection of approximately 100 words. During the reading the average child made 224 fixations, about 2 fixations per word, or an eye span of 0.45 of a word. This average span of recognition increases very slowly to 1.11, or slightly more than one word per fixation, for normal college students reading at an average speed of 280 words per minute. The average number of words seen at each fixation does not reach one whole word until the eleventh grade.

Using a different technique of determining recognition span, that of reading through a small aperture, McConkie and Rayner (29) demonstrated that the length of a word can be distinguished for as far as 13 to 14 letters from the point of fixation. Actual shape of a word or letter was perceived no farther than 10 to 12 characters into the periphery. Identification of words was limited to a span encompassing 4 to 6 characters to the right of the fixation point. It is true, of course, that more can be read at a distance from a flash card or the chalkboard than at reading distance, as these two studies imply. As many as three or four words can be recognized in one brief exposure at distance. But, obviously, this span does not operate in reading a book.

Trying to teach children to recognize several words at each fixation by flash cards, pressure blackboard drills, or even mechanical training devices is a waste of time. It is particularly pointless to try to speed up the child's reactions when reading aloud at sight without having read the selection silently first. Children can be taught to phrase *mentally*, to try to read in a natural speech cadence, but this is not accomplished by the methods commonly employed. Natural reading, or reading which sounds like normal speech, can only be achieved with very simple material, or selections previously practiced or read silently. Furthermore, natural reading cannot be obtained until the child realizes that reading is really a kind of talking with the words printed on the page. Dramatizations using the book as the script, reading silently first and then trying to repeat aloud the words as one would in normal speech may also help. But natural reading is not achieved by trying to train children to read groups of words.

A second significant implication of the reader's true eye span is the degree of visual skill demanded. The young reader focuses, relaxes, focuses, relaxes almost 200 times per 100 running words. The eye must converge to a focus in perfect alignment over and over again, or word recognition is inaccurate and reading becomes faulty. When we realize the frequency and minuteness of the visual adjustments needed for the reading act we may appreciate our responsibility for development of the highest degree of visual skill in our pupils.

A few more facts about the visual behaviors of the reader will finish this description of reading as a visual act. Gilbert's eye-movement studies (11) led him to conclude that pupils do not naturally mature or improve in the pattern of eye movements simply because they have been exposed to a good reading program. Many who show apparently normal performances on ordinary measures of comprehension and rate employ ineffectual or even harmful visual patterns. They may, for example, consistently make excessive regressions, or have abnormal duration-of-fixation pauses or a very high number of fixations and a very small recognition span. Sometimes there are clues to this faulty development in the pupils' oral reading or in their very slow rate in silent or oral reading. However, some pupils compensate for a narrow recognition span and many fixations by a shorter-than-normal duration of fixation, and their gross rate of reading does not reveal their lack of a normal visual pattern. This compensatory adjustment may be accompanied by a high degree of tension, excessive energy demands with consequent rapid fatigue and dislike for sustained reading—common symptoms among poor readers. Moreover, these readers who unconsciously have the habit of too short and too many fixations are likely to have comprehension difficulties. They do not allow time for the brain to process each idea and thus fail to comprehend. Furthermore, because the durations of the fixations are so brief, successive word images on the retina of the eye may overlap, making perception and comprehension very difficult. All this occurs, of course, without the conscious knowledge of the reader.

Many pupils tend to develop a reading pattern which is relatively consistent, almost habitual. They do not necessarily alter this pattern in response to the difficulty of the material or to the purpose for which they are supposed to be reading. The visual pattern may be ineffectual and may interfere markedly with reading rate and comprehension, but the pupil unconsciously clings to the habits. Some pupils regress at certain points of every line. Others show an inaccurate return sweep, with visual fumbling at the beginning of each line. Poor directional attack may be shown by an excessive number of regressions in comparison with the total of fixations, or by excessive repetitions and a frequent tendency to lose the place. These disturbances in the visual pattern may or may not be manifest in a child's oral reading, but they will dramatically affect his or her comprehension and rate. Normally both eyes perform similarly in the reading act. But when coordination and good motility are lacking, the movements of one eye may be less pronounced than, or even different from, those of the other eye. One eye may not make the same sweeps between fixations as the other; it may overshoot on the return sweep, or the eyes may fail to converge at the beginning of each line. What do these facts mean to the classroom teacher?

These functional difficulties in the pattern of eye movements are reflected in such reading performances as loss of place, omissions, excessive repetitions, and slow rate. Defects in coordination or motility, directional attack, and form perception interfere with the development of a desirable pattern of eye movements. These problems can be approached by the classroom teacher in the way suggested in the chapters on readiness training. This visual training is not intended solely for beginning readers. The use of the eye camera reveals that many pupils of primary and intermediate levels manifest reading errors that reflect faulty or inadequate training in the visual components of the reading act. *We are not saying that training in eye movements is the basic method for improving reading or overcoming reading difficulties.* These problems may arise, as we have indicated, from inappropriate levels of reading materials, poor choice of method, and pressure to induce children to read in whole phrases. But in many cases poor reading is simply and directly a result of faulty visual habits which can be recognized and attacked by the classroom teacher.

As a further demonstration of the significance of vision in the reading act, Louis G. Hoffman (22) found highly significant relationships between the total score on the Metropolitan Readiness Test and binocular rotations, fusion at near and at distance, lateral phoria at near, visual efficiency of each eye at near, and accommodative flexibility. The tests Dr. Hoffman used sampled children's ability to follow a target with their eyes (binocular rotations) as they might try to follow a line of print, and their ability to focus and get a clear single image (fusion at near and far) as they must when focusing on printed words. The other tests measured the tendency of either eye to deviate horizontally from a normal position (wall-eye, cockeye); sharpness of vision of each eye at reading distance and the skill of adjusting focus from near to far as in shifting from reading at the desk to reading from the chalkboard. These visual skills are essential in ordinary classroom reading activities. Weakness in one or several of these visual skills could interfere with a child's learning to read. None of these functions are tested by the common Snellen Chart.

In the chapter on Reading for Young Children, we will discuss formal and informal vision skill tests that can be given by a teacher. Similarly, in the chapter on Readiness Training we recommend simple visual skill exercises that teachers can conduct for those children who are identified by testing as needing them.

Before leaving this subject we must mention the most dramatic outcomes in American reading instruction that arose from the early scientific studies of the visual facets of the reading act. Until early in this century the primary emphasis in our schools was upon oral reading. Skill in silent reading was of secondary importance. But early eye-movement studies demonstrated that the average individual could read up to twice as fast silently as he could orally. Moreover, as other studies accumulated it became apparent that silent reading often yielded better comprehension (5). As these facts were widely accepted by leading reading authorities, a complete reversal in the goals of reading instruction occurred. Classroom practices soon followed the new viewpoint and assumed the present pattern, in which silent reading is the major instructional goal—at least above the primary grades. Thus the study of reading as a visual act once caused a revolution in reading methods. Thorough understanding of this aspect of the reading process by classroom teachers should continue to guide their daily procedures.

Occasionally our stress upon the visual elements of reading is seen as a completely mechanistic interpretation of the process. Some readers believe that we ignore the comprehension or thinking aspects in favor of simply getting the child's eyes functioning properly for word recognition. Our true intention in this section is to provide sufficient background so the teacher can be acutely aware of this basic aspect of the reading process. By such understanding, we hope the teacher will make attempts to relate instructional practices, with machines and otherwise, to the facts about visual behavior in reading. The teacher should be concerned, we believe, about the maturity of the visual functioning of pupils, while trying to introduce them to a process which assumes highly developed visual skills.

We are *not* proposing that learning to read is furthered by the simple training of eye movements, and certainly not by vain efforts to increase visual span. There are devices such as the "Controlled Reader," the "Tach-X," and a few others which do help establish desirable patterns of visual behavior because they are specifically designed to simulate the natural reading act. But even these do not teach pupils to read, to think with symbols, or to react to ideas, which are the heart of reading. They simply aid children in achieving the visual skills which they must develop on the continuum toward true reading. We shall offer detailed suggestions later in this book of the ways and means classroom teachers may utilize to accomplish this goal.

Reading as a Perceptual Act

Perception may be defined, in psychological terms, as the preparation for a response, or as the processes which intervene between presentation of a stimulus and the ultimate response to it. In reading, this sequence includes the stimulus of the printed word, the processes of recognizing this word and attributing meaning to it, based on the reader's previous experiences. Thus, in its simplest form, reading may be considered a series of word perceptions. (This is a general definition of perception. The reader should be aware that perception may also be defined in terms of the sense modality involved, as visual perception, auditory perception, and so on.)

The process by which children of five or six learn to read may be likened to the ways in which children of one or two learn to perceive the world around them. In her excellent book, *The Psychology of Perception,* Magdalen Vernon has traced the development of the perception of objects in space (45). We will try to draw the analogy between these stages of perception, as described in Vernon's words, and the development of perception in the act of reading.

The Development of Perception

Perception in infancy*

"...about the end of the first year that he begins to realize that objects have an identity and a permanent existence...that this identity remains the same although they are shifted about in space" (pp. 18–19).

"...the same object may look different when it is seen from different aspects and at different distances...a large number of visual patterns which belong to the same object" (p. 19).

"...a toy which at a distance looks very small is the same as one which near to looks big" (p. 20).

"A further difficulty for the young child is that he tends to perceive situations as a whole" (p. 21).

"If a thing is hidden in one place and he finds it there, and then later hidden in another, he may go back to the first place to look for it; the reappearance of the object is associated with his movements in finding it, rather than with the actual position of the object" (p. 19).

"...children asked to group sets of meaningless drawings, called one set 'prickly' and another set 'mean.' Thus these emotional characteristics seem in some cases to look to the child more striking than do the shape characteristics, which appear more obvious to us" (p. 27).

Perception in reading

Words stand for objects, i.e., the label on the chair or table tells what it is. Although the tables and chairs may differ in size, shape and position, the label remains constant.

All these patterns are really the same word:

MOTHER
mother
mother

These are really the same word:

mother

mother
mother
mother

*Reprinted from *The Psychology of Perception,* by permission of the author, M. D. Vernon, and the publisher, Penguin Books Ltd., Harmondsworth, Middlesex, England, 1962.

The separate words of the familiar sentence, "We went home" are not readily recognized when viewed in isolation or in new arrangements, as "Then home we went" or "We went to our home." The base word *talk* may be read for any of its derived forms, as *talks, talked, talking.*

When rereading to correct miscalling of a word, the child's pattern of search may be inconsistent. He may begin the sentence again, or read the entire line again, or just reread several words, or read the word in reverse or transpose several words in rereading. He may even lose his place on the line and pick up with the line above or below.

Some words have pleasant connotations which speed up their learning, as *Christmas, mother, elephant.* Others that seem threatening may cause blocking and apparent forgetfulness.

What does this definition of reading as a perceptual act mean to the classroom teacher? Explored thoroughly, there are a number of implications here for our approach to the teaching of reading. First, perception of the same stimulus differs greatly from one individual to the next. The sight of a mountain has vastly different meanings for a painter, a geologist, a mountain climber, and a person whose birthplace it is. Printed words may have different meanings and connotations for each reader. For example, what is your first reaction to the word *fast?* Do you respond with "quick," or "attached to," or "strong, not yielding," or "dissipated," or "to abstain from food," or some other association? To be a fluent reader, the pupil must have a number of associations to each word to be able to select from among these the proper meaning for each context.

Second, the perceptual processes by which a word is recognized differ from one individual to another according to such factors as age, training, reading skill, and accuracy and maturity of visual discrimination. At one extreme we see preschool children, who don't know one letter or word from another, recognize or read the labels on products frequently advertised on television, and demand the purchase of these products when in the supermarket (*17*). At the other extreme, the perceptual processes of mature readers may involve a half-dozen such clues as common syllables, context or sense of the sentence, roots or base words and their affixes, as well as the general configuration. In the comprehensive reading program, maturation of perception must be promoted continuously by training in word recognition skills of gradually increasing complexity and variety, and by activities and experiences intended to broaden and deepen pupils' reading vocabulary. Teachers must never lose sight of the perceptual nature of reading or they will fail to emphasize it sufficiently. This perceptual process must be refined and its base in experience with words broadened, perhaps in the ways we will suggest in later chapters.

There is nothing vague about the perceptual process in reading, for it has been the subject of research studies for more than 60 years (*46*). Among the types of perception employed to recognize words, the following have been clearly identified:

1. Recognition solely by setting or context, as reading a sign by its shape, is one perceptive process. A middle-aged, almost illiterate client of the writers drove a car frequently, although she could not distinguish any of the words on road signs. We discovered that she discriminated by their shapes, colors, X-bars, and other features—a common perception among nonreaders.

2. Primary school children, or older persons beginning to learn to read, often perceive a word by some distinctive detail plus, of course, the general shape of the word. Some children readily discriminate *dog* from *boy* by the "curly tail" in the g of *dog.*

3. The general shape or configuration given by the ascending and descending letters is a significant part of the perceptual process for almost all

readers. The distinctive shapes of words such as *little* or *elephant* or *Christmas* promote very rapid learning of these words or quick perception among many young readers. In contrast, words such as *their, then* or *these, those* are difficult to discriminate by this particular perceptual process. Thus these words tend to persist as sources of confusion among readers who depend heavily upon perception by general shape or configuration.

4. The visual recognition of the sound of the first few letters of a word, plus its general shape and the context, is another type of perception. Many teachers and parents have observed that when a pupil hesitates over a word, giving him the sound of the first letter or the initial blend will trigger almost immediate perception of the complete word.

5. A few children trained in an ultraphonic approach to words may perceive a word by sounding it letter by letter. However, unless held to this laborious method, most readers discard a letter-by-letter analysis in favor of other perceptual approaches.

6. As early as 1908 Edmund B. Huey demonstrated the significance of the first half of a word for perception. His studies showed that this portion was much more helpful than the latter half of the words. Undoubtedly, the sense of the sentence, or the context, reinforces perception by the beginning of words. If you will slide a 3- by 5-inch card slowly along the first line of the next paragraph, stopping it after revealing only the first four or five letters of each word, you will recognize the potency of this type of perception. You will find that you do recognize many words before seeing the whole word.

7. Further studies by Huey also indicated the importance of the top halves of the letters in facilitating perception. In his early textbook, he contrasted several pages composed only of the top halves or the bottom halves of the printed words. Most readers find the reading of the upper portions much easier. If you will cover the bottom half of the letters in the first line of the next paragraph, and reverse this in another line, you may make this comparison.

8. The general shape or configuration of a word is determined in part by the pattern of lines and circles within the word. The image which strikes the retina is probably more of a grid of dark lines and light spaces than a simple outline of the word as created by the ascending and descending letters. In a sense, the image registered on the retina resembles a photographic negative of the word. One of the writers' daughters demonstrated this perceptual process while in the primary grades in much simpler terms than we have described it here. The writer noted that when she encountered the word *look* she read it correctly, despite the fact it had not occurred previously in her reading experiences. When questioned she explained quite simply, "Don't you see the two eyes (*oo*) there looking at you?"

9. In describing various forms of the perceptual process, we have noted several times that the sentence structure or pattern is often an important element. There is undoubtedly an anticipation of sentence structure, or of the appearance of certain words, in order for the sentence to make sense. This anticipation is based upon the reader's many reading and auditory experiences with similar sentences, and with familiar language patterns. A very simple example

of perception based on contextual clues is found in the last word of these two sentences. Can you supply the word?

"*This is a ball.* ⊘
It is a boy's _____."

10. Both beginning and mature readers employ a form of perception based on recognition of a base word and its endings. Many children who can read *walk* will probably recognize *walks, walked,* and *walking* in a context that leads them to expect such a word.

11. Compound words, composed of words already familiar to the reader, are quickly perceived, as in *milkman, houseboy.* Similarly, common syllables form convenient units to facilitate perception as in *con-fig-ur-a-tion.*

12. For some mature readers, word roots and their affixes promote word perception. If the reader is familiar with a root such as *aqua,* he may more readily recognize such related words as *aqueous, aquamarine,* and *aquatic.* Most readers recognize the effect of such prefixes as *in-, im-, en-,* or *un-* when these are affixed to a familiar word, as in *impossible, untruthful,* and *inaudible.* Similarly, the suffixes *-er, -or, -tion, -ance,* and the like speed quicker perception of such words as *translator, manager, construction,* and *appearance.*

13. Gibson and others[1] speak of distinctive features of letters, such as the directionality and nature of the lines forming them, as aids to recognition. The shapes and lines are significant aids to letter and word recognition because they are constant and invariant, according to these authors. Such distinctive features help children achieve automaticity of word recognition, which some claim to be an important element of reading development.

Our descriptions of various forms of word perception in the reading process have, we hope, emphasized several implications. Perception, or word recognition as it is more generally called, is not a single, simple process. It takes many forms, only a few of which are spontaneous or original to the reader. Most forms of perception must be thoroughly taught as the reader matures and is ready for them. The reader may discard certain primitive types of perception such as the use of distinctive details or simple configurations. But these must be supplanted by instruction in more effective perceptual skills. Thus the well-planned reading program continues to emphasize training in perception and word recognition throughout the school career.

Recent developments in the area of visual perception include several rather loose practices. It has become fashionable to label retarded or poor readers as "perceptually disturbed" or "perceptually handicapped." This label becomes a ready explanation for reading retardation, relieving children and their parents of anxieties about their own mental capacities, and relieving teachers of their guilt feeling in being unable to explain a child's failure. The corrective steps include outdoor, large-muscle exercises involving balance boards and other types of physical education apparatus; small-muscle activities with pegs, puzzles, blocks; seatwork materials for copying designs, matching forms, tracing, drawing from dot to dot, and the like. While these activities certainly do promote either large- or small-muscle coordination —which are not closely interrelated—and better hand-eye coordination, there is little evidence of their precise values for reading success.

With the tests currently available, we just do not know how to diagnose specific perceptual deficits, nor precisely what corrective training efforts to employ. We do not even know the composition of what is loosely termed visual perception, for only two factors—reproducing forms and matching forms —have been identified. There may be other factors present, but the research necessary to identify and validate them has not yet been done. A study conducted by one of the authors did seem to indicate that a variety of blackboard exercises for directionality and hand-eye coordination in conjunction with paper and pencil seatwork in matching and reproducing forms were valuable. When this training was substituted for reading instruction for periods from two to six months, according to pupils' needs as indicated by pretesting on the *Thurstone Tests of Pattern Copying* and *Matching Forms*, initially low scorers showed marked success in first-grade reading. Despite an average of four months less reading instruction, children in the experimental classes equaled the control classes, who followed the usual basal reading program in reading achievement. Moreover, children of low socioeconomic status, or in the lowest quarter of the population in intelligence, excelled their basal control groups in reading, implying that those with the greatest need for such training were most benefited by it. One obvious implication of this study, in our opinion, is that when valid facets of perception are measured and corrective steps taken, children are helped to greater success. But many other studies are needed to identify other components of visual perception, to determine their significance for reading, and to devise and prove the values of related corrective steps for beginning readers and retarded readers. When all this research has been completed, we may be able to form a concise operational definition of visual perception as it relates to reading and to deal constructively with each element of the process. (When we speak of visual perception we refer here only to that aspect known as visual discrimination of symbols. We must omit discussion at this time of many other facets of visual perception, such as physiological, mechanical, visual, attitudinal, and postural influences.)

Reading and Language

Recent literature in the field of reading strongly emphasizes the significance of language background and the development of reading success. One group of authors stresses that minority groups who speak in a dialect other than standard English are deficient in language development. They claim that their studies show these pupils to be lacking in range, level, and diversity of vocabulary; in the use of syntactic variations; and in such elements as clauses, infinitives, verbals, and linking verbs. When measured by the usual tests, their auditory discrimination is poor, final consonants such as *t*, *d*, *g* and *k* are weak or missing; final *th* becomes *v*; and unvoiced final *th* becomes *f*. As a result of these language deficits, these authors say, the child's cognitive ability, his skill in thinking with words, is underdeveloped. All these differences are a serious handicap to reading success, and must be corrected, perhaps even before reading instruction begins (9).

This concept that the bilingual or dialect-speaking child must be taught to use standard English to succeed academically is not a new idea. The belief has been accepted since before the beginning of the twentieth century in dealing with immigrants. Then, as now, the language problem was attacked by teaching pupils to speak the dialect of the middle-class school. The nature of the training has changed somewhat, to an emphasis upon auditory discrimination, use of proper syntactical endings and other emphasis upon auditory discrimination, use of proper syntactical endings and other conventions, and to practice with varying sentence patterns. But the goal of eradicating dialect and making the subject proficient in standard English has remained the same, and the acceptance of this as a primary goal is still very widespread in the American school system.

There are those who insist that bilingual children should first be taught to read in their own language or dialect. This approach, they claim, promotes success in early reading, despite its failure in trials in the Philippine Islands and Puerto Rico. Sooner or later reading matter in standard English must be introduced, and unless reading is thought of as a mechanical saying of words, the transition into standard English is very difficult. The vocabulary is totally different, many phonemes have different pronunciations, and sentence structure varies dramatically. Practice in reading in a language such as Spanish does not prepare the student to read in English. There is more logic in the argument that prereading training in oral English will help bilingual or dialectal children in early reading efforts. Those active in the English as a Second Language (ESL) programs have tried, with varying success, to teach English to bilingual children before or while they are learning to read. The results do not imply that there is a quick or easy answer to this problem.

In direct contrast, experts today from a number of disciplines completely reject the deficit theory that dialect users are in need of corrective language training or special attention in auditory discrimination, cognitive abilities, or even vocabulary development. They point out that black dialect, which is at the center of the present controversy, is a systematic, complete form of language that enables its users to deal with any mental process (15). The variations in oral enunciation of certain sounds does not interfere with obtaining meaning in reading. The supposed lack of vocabulary in speech does not prove that these pupils cannot understand ordinary language in reading or listening. Having a different syntax in speech does not prevent the dialect user from reading or listening to standard English; he readily translates the latter dialect into his own (47). Training programs directly intended to correct dialect do not effect reading progress (25), nor does instruction in sentence patterns or techniques of teaching language borrowed from the methodology of foreign language instruction (19).

The linguistically different child's primary problem is the attitude of the middle-class standard-English-speaking teacher. The teacher's judgments of the student's oral reading are depressed by the student's "errors"; the evaluation of thinking ability is lowered by the student's lack of fluency in expressing thoughts; and the teacher's reactions to the student's cooperativeness are negative because of apparent resistance to adopting the teacher's model of English. It does not occur to the teacher that these corrective efforts are perceived as a rejection of the child, the child's family, and the child's cultural background that will only be met with negativism and hostility, or passivity and withdrawal. As San-su Lin has expressed the situation, "To attack this dialect, whether directly or by implication, is to attack his loyalty to his group, his identity, his worth"(26, p. 753).

All of this is not to say that some aspects of language development do not directly affect reading progress. Retarded speech development does appear to create problems in early reading stages, as studies both in this country and England show (46). The evidence regarding articulatory disorders such as baby talk, substitutions, and lack of certain letter sounds is less consistent. Gaines (10) has shown that when these speech behaviors are judged by trained examiners, they are much less apt to appear a handicap to reading than when viewed subjectively by classroom teachers. Speech diagnosticians recognize that some of the defects reflect developmental stages that maturation will often eliminate, whereas teachers are prone to consider them as reading errors to be corrected.

Hammill and McNutt (20) have made an intensive review of the studies of the relationship of language abilities to reading. Based upon several hundred correlations, they do not find oral language tests in grammatical usage, contextual speech, or verbal reasoning to be good predictors. In contrast, listening comprehension, meaningful writing as measured by spelling, and writing mechanics were good predictors.

It is also true that cultural aspects of language, such as idioms, word meanings, word usage, and the presence of such variations as pidgin English in the home, are obstacles to reading progress for certain ethnic groups (31, 48). But these problems are readily overcome by appropriate materials and instruction within the classroom reading program if they are approached as contrasting or different modes of expression rather than as language deficiencies.

We have tried to summarize a great mass of publications on the interaction of language and reading. Just what may or should be done for pupils who differ in dialect or native language will be discussed fully later as we consider the stages of the reading program.

Reading as a Reflection of Economic Cultural Background

The reading process is undoubtedly based on sociological roots. Reading differs in its purposes, breadth, and quality among societies as well as among social classes within societies. Social factors such as education, cultural interests, income level, family stability, and vocational adjustment all affect the child's purposes and uses of the reading process. These factors determine the quantity and quality of reading materials available as well as the reading habits of the family and community—thus, in turn, influencing the reading behaviors of the child.

If we judge the statistics on book, newspaper, and magazine circulation in the United States, we receive a superficial impression that reading is a highly popular pursuit. Approximately 12,000 new books and new editions of old titles are published annually in this country. Of these, over 2000 are titles for children. Over 7500 magazines are published yearly, with a total circulation close to 175 million. Almost 1800 daily newspapers are printed in English, with a combined circulation of about 55 million readers. Media such as the paperback have grown tremendously in recent years, with total publication figures well into the millions. These figures suggest that there is wide distribution and use of reading materials.

Despite these impressive circulation statistics, there are a number of studies which show that reading is still not a widespread leisure-time activity. Three-fourths of the flood of paperbacks is purchased by about 10 percent of the population. Active readers, such as those who can truthfully claim to have read a book in the past month, seldom amount to more than 25 to 30 percent of any segment of the population. Between 60 and 70 percent regularly read one or several magazines, and 85 to 90 percent read a newspaper more or less regularly. Those who read to an appreciable degree are largely concentrated in the age group from twenty-one to twenty-nine and in the professional and skilled-worker categories. Those in the upper-income and higher-education groups form the bulk of the active readers in almost every comparison (1).

Approximately one in every four adults is registered with the public library, but only about 10 percent use the library as often as once a month. In other words, about three-fourths of the great bulk of reading is done by less than 5 percent of the adult population (1). Statistics on the reading of school children are not much more encouraging. Interest in reading, as recounted in many studies, gradually decreases from an initially strong position as children mature. After the freshman year of high school, interest in reading drops quite markedly, and this trend continues through the early college years. It has been estimated that use of the public library diminishes sharply in post–high school life, for some studies show that 90 percent of high school graduates let their library cards lapse soon after leaving school. College students, it is estimated, use about one book per month in free reading. But over half of this circulation from the college library is accounted for by about 20 percent of the students.

Studies of the reading tastes of college students, both during and after college, show them to be far below their potential reading levels. It would thus appear that, despite availability of a wide variety of reading materials, serious reading is confined to a small cross section of the adult population.

Economics and educational opportunities influence the extent of reading throughout the world. Of the approximately 500,000 books published in the world in 1969, the 13 percent of the world population in Europe had access to 45 percent of all the books. Asia, with 56 percent of the population, had only 20 percent; Africa, with 10 percent of the population, received only 2 percent; while North America, with 9 percent of the population, had 14 percent of the world's books. Four African countries have less than one copy of a daily newspaper *for every 1000 people* compared with one copy for every 2 persons in Sweden, 320 copies per 1000 people in Russia, 331 per 1000 in West Germany, and 305 per 1000 in the United States (52).

It has been suggested that our concern about worldwide literacy is pointless, for television will eventually replace the need for reading. But for the economically deprived, this millenium is hardly likely. Of the 1 million TV sets in Africa, for example, 79 percent are concentrated in the three relatively affluent countries of Algeria, Morocco, and Egypt. Thus we see the dependence of literacy upon the national and personal economy.

Perhaps the most ambitious attempt to identify the characteristics of economically poor children who tend to fail in reading in our country is the large-scale study of Metfessel and Seng (30). Over 3000 rural and urban poor children of five different ethnic groups were studied to identify the profile of the low achiever. Five major areas of traits were studied: learning style, value framework and self-concept, cognitive structure, modes of behavior, and home environment. The learning style of poor achievers was visual and kinesthetic rather than responsive to oral or written stimuli, and hindered by poor attention span to multiple stimuli, and poor perseverance in a single task. They responded to inductive approaches more readily than deductive. Moreover, these children were at a disadvantage in timed learning or testing situations because of lack of self-confidence and negative self-concept. Poor readers seldom receive approval for success, and consequently expect to fail to achieve. They are accustomed to home discipline by physical force and often fail to respond to the school's discipline through reason or loss of privileges.

Cognitively, these economically deprived children have uneven development and fundamental knowledge from lack of parental stimulation, family activities, or games. Language development is retarded in the sense of awareness of the concept that all objects or events or people have labels. Even more significant in their development, however, are the models of behavior to which poor children are exposed. Their parents seldom use a language model appropriate to the middle-class school, nor do they value intellectual development. The parents often work at jobs not requiring much education and convey to their children a low evaluation of school learning for vocational goals. The attitude is that the needs of the family are more important than school-attendance laws. School is thought of as a magic environment that teaches the child the basics of reading, writing, and arithmetic without requiring any parental approval or involvement.

Many contemporary writers reject the idea that children from low socioeconomic levels are necessarily deprived linguistically. They argue that the handicap lies in the differences between the cultural mores of the poor and those of the middle-class-oriented school. Some say that blacks, for example, have a dialect that is basically an ordered language, sufficient for communication in their group, and although different from the dialect commonly used in schools, is not inferior. These writers believe that the mismatch of value systems and cue systems and the variations in personal and school goals are responsible for the lesser achievement of some children of low socioeconomic status.

We have not been able to isolate the major cause of lower achievement by some economically deprived pupils. Obviously, it is not just the ramifications of lower income, for many of these families differ from the middle-class model in life style, child-rearing practices, language usage, personal goals, and social values. Moreover, many of these children do adjust to and achieve the school's goals for them. The shift from the term *disadvantaged* to *culturally different* in categorizing children who seem to have problems adjusting to school shows us the change in thinking regarding the nature and causes of their problem. We shall touch upon this problem again later in discussing a reading program for such pupils.

Of course, not all poor children fail in school or in reading. Those who do succeed tend to be opposite in their attributes to the low achiever. The greatest contrasts are in the area of values, self-concept, and behavior models. Successful pupils from the poverty culture tend to relate well to peers and adults. They and their friends receive strong approval which enables them to learn to defer gratification and to expect success. Since they are conscious of parental acceptance, they relate well to the values of their parents and teachers; in other words, they readily identify with the middle-class standards of the school. These achieving poor children become involved in schoolwork, and like their parents, see it as valuable to their future, as challenging and rewarding.

In his contrasting study of learners and nonlearners, Irving D. Harris also emphasizes the influence of social class upon learning problems (21). He finds a direct relationship between lower-class origin and low-average intelligence scores, repetition of grades, low familial values on education, and less intellectual stimulation. Other socioeconomic characteristics which he believes contribute to academic and reading failures are the mother's employment outside the home, large families, and father's occupation and education. Like a number of other writers in this field, Harris stresses the inherent conflict between the mores of the lower-class child and the middle-class values of the school and of teachers as a source of what appear to be learning problems.

Barton and Wilder (2) consider socioeconomic class to be the most important single factor in reading progress in school. Their national survey of elementary school teachers permitted the classification of classrooms according to parental income and occupation. The data of the study indicated that reading retardation below expected grade norms rises steadily through the first six grades for working-class children, markedly so for the children of the least-skilled, lowest-paid working-class parents. By the fourth grade about half of the classrooms of lower-class children show a degree of retardation as much as one year below grade level. The converse of this is also present in the Barton-Wilder study. Upper-class children tend to become advanced in reading from the first grade and to maintain this academic advantage. Some other observers of these trends would point out that they are reinforced by the differences among schools in upper- and lower-class communities in the training and skill of teachers, the supply of instructional materials, and, of course, teacher expectations.

We are not trying to imply that reading failures are concentrated in any one social class or stratum of society. Rather, it is apparent that because the public school clings to what are basically upper-middle-class ideals, the proportion of failures is probably greater among those children whose social backgrounds do not fit them to meet these standards. As Keshian's study (24) shows, reading success is found frequently in high, medium, and low socioeconomic groups. He also points out, however, that the families of good readers fostered success by such practices as reading regularly to their young children and placing high values on reading. These families also tended to remain intact and produce children who were basically well adjusted socially and emotionally.

As Wallace Ramsey shows in his survey of fifty-three school systems in Kentucky, reading achievement is also closely related to the economic situation of the school district. Systems in the highest quarter of achievement had significantly greater local and total revenue per child. They paid higher teacher salaries, used supplementary and informal materials and activities twice as much, and had slightly larger classroom and school libraries than other school systems. The more careful selection of teachers resulted in a staff with significantly more college credits and fewer years of teaching experience. These more successful schools spent more class time per day (eighty versus sixty-five minutes) in reading activities and used more innovations (such as interclass grouping and indivdualized reading) four times as often as the lowest quarter of the school systems (32).

Concern for the successful education of children who are economically deprived has increased tremendously in the past few years. In hundreds of federal and local projects, materials and means of aiding such children to succeed better in school are being explored. Typical of these is the extension of school services into the preschool years, as in Operation Head Start, which has shown the values of early attempts to stimulate language development and increase experiential background. Some researchers seem to think that the best program lies in simply beginning formal schoolwork earlier and offering lessons in reading, arithmetic, and spelling in a tightly scheduled program. Others point out that this earlier research in nursery education indicates that close scheduling at these ages creates resistance to authority and denies the individuality of child interest and development. Furthermore, the preschool specialists point out there is no evidence to show that the basic need of economically deprived children is met by formal schoolwork. Such children, they say, most need experiences with objects, people, and places to acquire the concepts and thinking which are expressed in language.

Other projects for these children have attempted to prepare special instructional materials, particularly in reading, which would reflect the living conditions and mores of groups other than the upper middle class. By presenting a picture of life closer to what culturally deprived children know, it is hoped that greater interest and success in reading will be stimulated. One serious question regarding the nature of the language to be employed plagues the producers of such reading materials. Should materials for children who speak only nonstandard English be presented in the language they use in order to facilitate easier reading? Or, in the hopes of improving the quality of usage, should materials be phrased only in standard English? Although it might seem more logical to offer stories in the children's own version of English, the variety of dialects seems to make such an effort impractical. It just would not be feasible to mass-produce books in a dozen or more versions. Besides, the argument is offered that such children must eventually learn to understand standard English if they are to communicate effectively. And there is evidence that children do eventually manage this more acceptable version of our language. In fact, some observers point out that by junior-high-school age, children have learned not only to use acceptable English in the classroom but also to communicate with their parents in their original dialect and with their peers in a jargon peculiar to present-day adolescents.

Reading as a Psycholinguistic Process

In the past decade a fresh view of the reading process has been offered by psycholinguists, those who study language from psychological grounds. To these specialists, reading is "a psycholinguistic guessing game" (13) involving a series of tentative decisions based on the reader's use of available language cues. In other words, the reader uses the graphic cues of letters, the semantic cues of word meanings, and the syntactic cues of word order to obtain the selection's message. Reading is often likened to a communication process, a direct interpretation of the printed symbol into the reader's thought processes. In this sense, the act of reading is not a word recognition act or a translation of words, but a fluent, almost instantaneous combining of words into complete thoughts. The whole process begins with the young child's first reactions to the symbols about her—on the TV screen, cereal boxes, street and store signs, in newspaper headlines, drawings in picture books, and the like. Young children also react in this interpretative process to other types of symbols, such as the shapes of road signs, the geometric shapes among toys such as parquetry blocks, puzzles, cutouts, and building blocks.

Thus the child reads or interprets many types of lettered and other symbols long before she begins to read in the usual sense. These early experiences with symbolic shapes and forms, in fact, are essential for the development of the visual discrimination, recognition, and interpretation behaviors of the reading act. We shall emphasize the primacy of this growth continuum in a later chapter, offering our suggestions regarding readiness training.

Although the beginning reader reads literally word by word, averaging no more than about one word per fixation until past the tenth grade, reading does not involve word-by-word thinking. Rather, even the young reader who tends to name or call words consecutively reacts to them collectively in terms of her familiarity with the structure and word order of the language. Partly because she has so often heard sentences with various patterns, she anticipates similar patterns in reading. In a sense, she expects sentences to fall into the familiar auditory patterns, and to make sense linguistically. This anticipation explains the high frequency of errors (as well as the unobserved successes) of omission and of substitution in an effort to produce a sentence which is meaningful, at least to the reader.

In fact, as speed and fluency in silent reading increase, this dependence upon context becomes more and more evident. It is probably the mature reader's basic aid to analysis of new or difficult words and phrases. This thinking, along with the flow of ideas from the printed symbols, may also result in many substitutions and omissions in the oral reading act, a behavior which is disconcerting to undiscerning teachers.

However, if we comprehend the nature of the reading act in its visual or mechanical sense, we realize the inevitability of these developments of dependence upon context and, consequently, toward the reader's combining his own vocabulary and concepts with those printed. As clarified in an earlier section of this chapter, the sole means of achieving rapid, fluent reading is not by increasing visual span but by speeding up fixations. This simply means reducing the time to process words. In effect, good readers must learn to react with gradually increasing speed of interpretation, which is equivalent to saying that they must learn to anticipate the flow of ideas presented more and more rapidly, if they are to read at their own thinking speed. The errors thus introduced into their reading are obviously an inescapable part of the increasing speed of flow of ideas and the strong tendency to read into the material. One does not simply read the printed word, but reacts to what it says, bringing to bear all his personal language-thinking experiences.

Robert B. Ruddell calls reading "a complex psycholinguistic behavior which consists of decoding written language units, processing the resulting language counterparts through structural and semantic dimensions, and interpreting the deep structure data relative to an individual's established objectives" (34). This definition adds two concepts in stressing the importance of decoding in word recognition and the fact that the reader extracts from the printed matter those ideas which match his previous experiences and his purpose in reading.

While he recognizes decoding as part of the process, Goodman (16) subordinates it to a minor role. To him, decoding is simply intended to move readers from the printed language to its meaning. Decoding is not primarily useful for aiding readers to say the word, to hear the word, or to recognize it, he says. The learning of sound-symbol correspondences is not decoding in Goodman's concept, for no written language is a one-to-one representation of the oral language. The correspondence is between patterns of letters and patterns of sounds. Teaching children to move from the graphic to the oral code is recoding, not decoding, and a process that short-circuits the obtaining of meaning, in Goodman's view of the reading process. While some letter-sound relationships may be useful in the very early stages of learning to read, children should be moved soon to reacting to the whole sentence, and to the meaning given to an unknown word by the context.

This view of reading has stimulated a number of research studies relevant to teaching methods. Goodman, for example, seemed to find that most of children's oral reading errors can be attributed to the attempt to make linguistic sense (14). Therefore, prompting and correcting oral reading errors may interfere with the normal self-corrective efforts of children by placing emphasis upon word recognition rather than obtaining meaning. Other studies support this argument in demonstrating that readers can recognize in context many of the words they cannot read in isolation. Similarly, trying to eliminate regressions or repetitions in oral reading, when these reflect self-corrective responses, is most unsound. Drill on isolated words out of meaningful contextual settings is pointless, and inimical to the true goal of reading for meaning.

These suggestions for teaching reading do not pretend to constitute a method, for there is no psycholinguistic method (40). What these specialists hope to accomplish is to move our teaching and testing techniques toward a broader understanding of the reading process. They are not suggesting, as some other linguists do, that children would benefit from instruction in linguistics or sentence patterns, for the rules for these areas could not be verbalized to children. Rather, readers need great experience with language, an opportunity to generate hypotheses about its structure, to test and modify these according to the unspoken rules about language that children generate. None of these can be expressed in behavioral objectives and programmed into children.

Psycholinguists tell us that comprehension is a process by which the reader progresses from the printed display of words to the deeper structure or meaningful interpretation of the material, utilizing his past experiences and his knowledge of language. Three cueing systems underlie the reading process. The first is the graphophonic system, using cues within words, such as letter-sound relationships, word parts or phonograms, phonics, and word shape or configuration. The second is syntactic cueing, which uses inflectional endings, grammatical relationships, and word order and punctuation. Finally, there is the semantic system, which employs what has commonly been called context. The values of these systems to the reader vary with his ability, for the highly proficient pupil uses a minimum of graphophonic cues to predict the syntactic structure and similarly increases his dependence upon semantic cues to support his expectations of what is to come on the printed page. The more control the learner has of oral language and the broader his experiences, the less visual information he needs from the text (45).

In interpreting Goodman's theory, Gollasch says: "Where should reading instruction begin? Not with letters or sounds but with whole real relevant language, we think.... What is the hierarchy of skills that should be taught in reading instruction? We think there is none. In fact, in learning to read as in learning to talk one must use all skills at the same time.... Why do some people fail to learn to read? Not because of their weaknesses but because we failed to build on their strengths as competent language users" (12, p. 113).

S. Jay Samuels counters with the viewpoint that reading is composed of subordinate units that must be mastered and integrated to form higher-order skills. Those who claim that reading can be mastered as readily as speech ignore the differences—length of practice time; difficulty of task; degree of reinforcement, which is great in speech and weak in reading; and degree of concentration required, which may turn a child off in learning to read (37).

Samuels continues: "...the importance of context in word recognition is overemphasized by Goodman and his followers because syntactic and semantic cues found in beginning reading materials are not very useful. Beginners' focus is usually on smaller elements than the word hence his short-term memory is filled with the non-meaning elements of a word and the meaningful context cannot be used."

John Downing says: "It seems quite unlikely that the learning to read process is directly derivable from the behavior observed in a fluent reader as is assumed in the theories of Smith and Goodman" (7, pp. 25–26).

Patrick Groff (18) has critically reviewed the concepts of psycholinguists and compared them with the available research facts. He points out the following claims by psycholinguists.

First, reading is not primarily a visual process, and word recognition, per se, does not play a very significant role. Yet we know there are high correlations between word recognition and sentence and paragraph reading, particularly at primary levels. A simple test of word recognition indicates fairly accurately the functional reading level of the child for at least the first three or four grades.

Second, the differences between good and poor readers often lies in their ability to deal with words and word analysis. But as we have said elsewhere, reading is first of all a visual act in word recognition and only secondly an interpretation of the writer's meanings.

Third, reading is best described as a cycle of sampling, predicting, testing, and confirming. However, there is ample evidence that children use context clues from the very first stages, as opposed to what psycholinguists assume (6). Training emphasizing context clues, as psycholinguists recommend, rather than letter clues results in poorer reading at the end of grade 1, according to Groff. Reading word-by-word is a normal developmental stage, as we have pointed out, and emphasizing the use of context clues and self-correction often "engenders feelings of indifference, frustration and/or even anxiety rather than the gratification psycholinguists claim" (6).

Beginning reading should teach children to use simultaneously three cue systems—graphic, syntactic, and semantic. Psycholinguists reject teaching any decoding skill beyond recognition of initial sounds, and the identification of the letters that represent such phonemes. Psycholinguists believe that the close scrutiny of words demanded by decoding, or what information processing experts call the identification of distinctive features of words, should not be stressed in beginning reading. However, Groff says that many reports show that teaching phonics as an aid to word recognition promotes good reading progress in almost any approach to reading instruction.

In later chapters we will further emphasize the implications of psycholinguistic research for the testing of oral reading, the learning of sight and meaning vocabulary, and the language problems of beginning readers. Also, in the later discussion of the so-called "linguistic" approach to teaching reading, we will contrast the views of the psycholinguists with those who produce what are called linguistic reading materials.

Reading as Information Processing

Many contemporary psychologists, linguists, and reading specialists are currently emphasizing the reading process as information processing. We have attempted to combine these ideas as offered by experts from the different disciplines (5, 28, 39). Their viewpoints do differ somewhat in their emphasis upon the importance of the child's language experiences, in terminology for information processing, and in other details. But we will try to merge these into a single interpretation of the reading process based on what we now know about the way the brain handles this situation.

Reading is conceived of as visual scanning directed by the child's general information store (or long-term memory, as it is called) and the information derived from the material being read (which is temporarily stored in short-term memory). According to this concept of reading, new material is assimilated into past experiences of related nature (passing from short-term to long-term memory store). The exact details of the new information may be lost, but basic concepts are retained. This result is evidenced by our inability to retain the exact words of a long statement (without considerable rehearsal) but our ability to paraphrase and summarize the ideas encountered in listening to or reading that statement.

Long-term memory operates by clustering, chunking, or organizing the material in some fashion. When this material is called upon for recall, the clues in the stimulus (the meaning, salient physical features, associations, contextual or temporal information present in the stimulus to recall) are guides to searching the long-term storage areas of the brain.

In reading (visual scanning), words are identified by a search of the associative word stores of high-frequency and low-frequency words. If a search of both of these storage areas is unsuccessful, the reader engages in more visual scanning. Input is in terms of pairs or groups of letters, then words, then phrases and larger units, according to some writers in this field. Letter and word identification and meaning are secured by testing a sufficient number of the distinctive features. This does not mean that reading occurs letter by letter, for it requires fewer distinctive features to discriminate a letter within a word than the isolated letter, and words can be recognized without identifying any of the letters, in many instances.

La Berge and Samuels (25) say that the information in printed material goes through codes or internal representations in visual memory (letter discrimination), phonological, episodic, and semantic memory systems. In other words, reading is processed through recognition of the distinctive features of words, the sounds within them, and the temporary and long-term understandings of their meanings. Not all of these levels are needed in all reading acts. Each level is learned by associative learning patterns, and is activated by attention. However, after being well learned, these levels or codes can be activated solely on the basis of the input stimulation; that is, they may become more or less automatic, not needing attention to direct them.

The beginning reader, La Berge and Samuels go on, may be able to identify single letters presented alone because of her attention to the task. But she may not be able to do this while other processes in reading are involved. For example, children may make reversal errors in words in reading, but not on single letters (such as *b* for *d*). The beginning reader has to devote a large part of her attention to the task; skilled readers do not. Hence poor readers have problems with the higher level codes or processes.

The beginning reader is handicapped by an empty letter store and no store of the visual patterns of either high-frequency or low-frequency words. Thus she has difficulty identifying letters or words directly and, some say, must map the word on to its sound pattern (which she often has already in storage) by using decoding or phonics as a means of mediation (handling the word recognition). Obviously, she must succeed in word identification in order to obtain some semblance of meaning, but these mediating behaviors tend to overload her visual information processing and memory systems; in other words, sometimes there are just too many new words for which she has no store of visual patterns to be able to read. To succeed in learning to read, she must soon learn to utilize the redundancies in the language of individual letters, patterns of letters (syllables), and sequences of words, or arrangements of words which impose semantic and syntactic constraints. She must learn the influence of word placement or word function in relation to the adjoining words upon the kind of word she is trying to read as well as upon its meaning.

To illustrate, "I stopped at the corner to read a sign which said Bus S_____." You can supply the missing word because of (1) the inherent meaningful message of the sentence, (2) the reproduction of the familiar visual pattern of a common sign, and (3) the additional clue of the first letter. Because of these clues (assuming you live in a country that has a bus system) you read the missing word as *Stop*. And because of the initial letter, you eliminated the possibility of *Change*, and the fact that the sign was on a corner eliminated *Station*. Or did it? The information processing you went through in using the message of the sentence, the constraint imposed by the phrase "at the corner," the further constraint of the initial letter, etc., were not conscious: they were never verbalized mentally or aloud, but they were part of the process of word recognition, just as they are for readers of all ages. Until the child acquires a store of visual patterns which permit quick identification of the parts of whole words, she is heavily dependent upon visual information, the graphic clues of the letters to their sounds. Thus for a long period of time for some children reading is slow and laborious, and allows little comprehension.

G. H. Bower (3) has summed it up well in saying: "No word is an island unto itself. It rather occupies the intersection of a vast number of classifying features." Would that some of this concept might penetrate the minds of teachers who "teach" vocabulary by rote memory, flash cards, machines, and other presentations carefully isolated from meaning!

Other experts point out the following implications of this concept of the reading process:

- Information transfer (from short-term to long-term memory storage) depends upon learners' strategies for encoding, their cognitive readiness or capacity for coping and integrating. Semantically or associatively meaningful materials and familiar items are retained better than single letters, nonsense groups, letter strings, or other meaningless materials. Advance organizers (prereading questions) emphasizing major concepts, principles, or relationships to be found in the reading are helpful to some pupils. However, some need to prepare their own advance organizers.
- Imagery is more easily evoked in older children (ages four to nine) and the profit from visual representation intended to evoke imagery comes later; for older children, simultaneous storage of imagery is more profitable if accompanied by verbal representation. In other words, verbal-symbolic presentation (talking plus reading) is better for sequential or related information.
- Items to be learned (words, signs, forms) should be presented as concretely as possible, probably in pairs in which a relationship can be recognized. Arranging such items in some sort of hierarchy also provides a retrieval scheme (a clue to searching long-term memory)—for example, size, part-whole, synonyms, opposites,

colors, action, common relationships (cars-people; pronouns for names; *cows* eat *hay*). Practice in shifting from one category to another, as recognizing that a father may also be a brother, a son, a cousin, or an uncle, is very desirable. Giving a set to look for certain attributes in a series (an advance organizer before presentation) facilitates scanning the series.

There is not a great deal that is brand new in this interpretation of reading as an information processing behavior other than perhaps a number of technical terms. A real contribution to teaching reading is the integration of scientific information from a wide variety of sources and the organization of these data into a coherent concept of reading which does further our understanding of how children read and how we might better help them.

Many would be tempted to see here a simple analogy between a reader attempting to find a meaning for a word or phrase and a computer searching its memory bank for a fact we have commanded it to find. In some respects this analogy is correct (although human brains can do some things computers cannot and vice versa), and it has led some experts to believe that reading can be taught by a computer programmed to anticipate and deal with most of the child's expected responses. As we point out later in our discussion of computer-assisted instruction, the analogy between the actions of a computer and those of a beginning reader is false in many respects. Learning to read does not occur simply as an isolated information processing act free from the dramatic effects of the child's emotions, attitudes, personality, motivation, attention, and cultural and language backgrounds. Information processing theory will bring us new insights into the learning process, but it does not yet deal with the human interrelationships present in the teacher-pupil interaction, which some of us believe are of paramount significance for the child's success.

The Role of Associational Learning

S. Jay Samuels of the University of Minnesota and a number of other educational psychologists have contributed markedly to our understanding of reading as an associational learning process. Deriving their insights from many studies of paired-associate learning or experiments in learning to associate pairs of words, symbols, or the like, this group has brought together a body of observations significant for the teacher of reading. Their theory, of course, does not encompass all facets of the reading process but rather is pertinent largely to word recognition, as Samuels points out (36).

Samuels emphasizes that reading is not a single-stage process of simply looking at a word and pronouncing it. First, there are the properties of the stimulus of letters and words. The child must discriminate among these stimuli and gradually acquire responses. These associations must be reinforced by a number of means we shall discuss later. A mediational stage is also involved;

that is, interpreting words and meanings by recognition of the syntactic relationships of the context, by categorizing, classifying, or reacting to them in various verbal ways.

Perception of symbols depends also upon the perceptual field, the set to match symbols and words and meanings, as well as the reader's short-term and long-term memory storage banks. The reading process also involves attention, distinctive feature learning, visual-recognition memory, mediation, and hookup, as well as auditory discrimination and auditory memory. When we combine all these components, it is apparent why associational learning specialists consider reading a multistage, complex act. Let us clarify this view of reading by exploring each of the components these experts attribute to the reading process.

Attention

Attention is essential for learning and is manifested by changes in galvanic skin response, heart rate, brain rhythm, pupillary dilation, and blood volume. The position of the head and eyes provides a clue with most pupils. In a sense, the whole body of the child is mobilized to the present task, if the child is really attending.

Since teachers are not in a position to keep records of the physiological changes in pupils that indicate their degree of attention, we must look elsewhere for pertinent suggestions for teachers from the field of associational learning. These experts confirm that attention distracters make tasks more difficult and that those pupils low in academic achievement appear more distractible than others. Older children, contrary to the general opinion, are as distractible as some much younger, in the presence of some disturbing stimuli. Most teachers are familiar with these facts and try to control attention and prevent distractions by a number of well-known practices.

A basic problem in attention is that the student may not know where to focus attention, particularly during his early learning experiences. He does not know whether or how to concentrate on letters, words, meanings, sounds of letters, or what. When he discovers the relevant dimension that matches the word with his store of memories, even the mental retardate can show normal curves of learning. Because of these observations, Samuels and his co-workers question the early presentation of whole words only, because their studies show that the transfer to new words (beginning with the same first or last letter or whatever cue the child was using) is poor, even among highly discriminable words normally recognized by their distinctive shape, length, and so on. These studies reemphasize the child's need for several realistic cues to word recognition early in the whole process to focus his attention.

Another example of the need for better cues to word recognition is present in experiments with the use of color in learning words. Color appears to be a help in learning new words, but the aid is soon lost because all future reading must be in black and white. Other studies indicate that when color in the letters or the backgrounds is used in learning words, the pupils may well learn the colors but fail to learn the associated words. This type of data can be interpreted as confirming the child's difficulty in knowing what to attend to. Despite the importance of directing a child's attention, Samuels points out that we have no studies yet of attention versus distractibility among first graders and the relationship to subsequent reading achievement, although almost every experienced primary teacher has an opinion on this subject.

Visual Discrimination

To the associational learning specialists, visual discrimination implies learning the distinctive features of visual stimuli. They show that much discrimination training, such as that in the Frostig program, does not promote the kinds of discrimination involved in letters and words. Moreover, the relationship between geometric form discrimination and reading is questionable to them, for in their studies it seems relevant only for the extreme cases, high or low in discrimination.

Distinctive feature training (as in matching given stimuli to a sample) utilizing memory has been shown to give better letter-name learning results than similar training which does not require memory. Other studies also support the need to emphasize discrimination from memory, rather than simple matching, as we often see in workbooks. Teaching like letters, such as *b—d*, in distinctive feature programs is more effective when these are presented separately and successively rather than at the same time. For unlike letters, such as *s—h*, simultaneous presentation appears efficient. Letters with alternative sounds, as *city—c*ow, are best taught concurrently, not consecutively or at widely separated times as they are commonly scheduled in many reading programs.

Some studies have shown that cross-modality training from blocks with raised letters to printed words, or from touch to vision, produces good transfer. Simultaneous discrimination with both touch and vision has also helped some pupils but appears to be most effective when memory is required. As a result of these latter studies, Samuels suggests touch training prior to visual training, as well as touch training on distinctive features to overcome poor readers' mistakes. Simultaneous training with touch and vision tends to lead only to distinctive feature learning, whereas successive training using these two media tends to help readers formulate schemata (draw conclusions about similarities and differences and combine both impressions into a clue) and learn distinctive features. The learning of letter names is facilitated and failure sizably reduced by training on the distinctive features of letters (by touch and then by vision) prior to introducing an association between the letter name and its symbol, unlike some current programs.

Some of these facts about learning the distinctive features of letters which will later serve as clues to word recognition, such as the value of touch or kinesthetic activities, have long been recognized by reading specialists. The procedure has often, however, been reserved for remedial work with poor readers. If we interpret him correctly, Samuels is recommending this type of training for most beginners, who appear to profit from it. His suggestions regarding like and unlike letters, those with alternative sounds, and the use of touch-vision successively rather than simultaneously, as well as the practice of both these presentations prior to introducing names for the letter symbols, do offer some fresh insights on the beginning program.

Visual and Auditory Memory

There is much attention to visual and auditory memory in many of today's "perceptual training" programs. But as we shall see, the terms are not synonymous with the concepts offered by educational psychologists. In their parlance there are three types of basic memory: the visual information store, in which images last for about a second; short-term memory, which lasts about fifteen seconds; and long-term memory, which persists over extended periods. An image flashed on the retina fades within a second, to be replaced by another image (the next letters or words or whatever). If this fading were not present, or, in other words, if our fixation pauses were not as brief as they are (about one-third to one-fifth of a second), a second image would compete with or superimpose itself on the first, with resulting confusion in perception.

The image in the visual information store usually passes to short-term memory. Because reading is basically a language act, and readers tend to articulate the words they are reading (obvious articulation or subvocalization is almost always present in the reading act, almost as though it were an essential, contrary to the ideas of those who think to increase speed of reading by eliminating subvocalization[2]), the visual information is encoded verbally and placed in short-term memory as an auditory image and perhaps then later stored in long-term memory through some mediating generalization. There is, to be sure, evidence of visually stored images among infants prior to speech, in animals, and in aphasics who have temporarily lost speech. But mistakes in reading often reflect misarticulation, auditory confusion, and verbal substitutions, thus supporting the belief in the storage of visual images in reading as auditory memories. These types of errors reflect the decay of memories stored in the short-term bank. In this line of thinking, both auditory and visual memory do seem to be related to poor reading, in the sense that such pupils first have trouble identifying the distinctive features of letters and words and then appear to fail to encode (process) these clues with an accurate verbalization.

We are offered facts here which agree completely with our knowledge of the role of eye movements in the act of reading. We are also led to believe that because the reader, any reader, tends to verbalize or say the words she is reading, the words or concepts that she is processing are stored as auditory memories. Again, we see the evidence that successful comprehension in reading demands mediation (comparing, classifying, etc.) in the act of reading; otherwise, visual images cannot move from the momentary visual information store to short-term memory and on to long-term memory. Similarly, since auditory stimuli likewise decay steadily in less than fifteen seconds, some method of manipulating these signals must be utilized to induce them to pass from short-term to long-term memory.

We believe that associational learning experts, like information processing specialists, are telling us over and over that learning the distinctive features of letters and words (word recognition) is not a rote memory process accomplished by sheer repetition. It must be attended with meaningful associations and cognitive strategies or schemata for generalizing about these symbols. Letters and words, we might say, are not learned as isolated items but in terms of their similarities and differences, their feel plus their visual images, and the organized meanings that children learn spontaneously or are led to recognize.

There would seem to be some support for using the following strategies in teaching letters:

- Emphasize physical similarities and differences by imitating shapes through bodily posture.
- Write the letters.
- Trace over letters in raised blocks or sandpaper forms or sand before stressing visual matching or comparison.
- Encourage or suggest verbalizations about the similarities or differences, such as tall versus short, fat versus thin, round versus straight.
- Verbalize the writing strokes.
- Draw simple analogies between the shapes of letters and common objects (e.g., *b* looks like a bat and ball).

Many of these mediating strategies are familiar to primary teachers. But our point is that although different strategies work better for different children (and perhaps best if they are spontaneously offered), they are an essential aid to storing visual images of letters and words as auditory (verbal) memories in the long-term memory bank.

Auditory Discrimination

Samuels appears to doubt the significance of auditory discrimination for beginning reading. As a number of studies show, the tests are of varying validity and often questionable reliability, particularly for nonstandard English speakers. In one study, in which children were tested on three successive days, the worst performance was on the first day. (Did the children have to learn what to attend to before the test could really function?) Repeated testing is thus a must for young school children for any real degree of reliability.

Some auditory discrimination tests are criticized for really being tests of intelligence and the child's ability to follow directions. The most common type, using discrimination of word pairs differing in a single initial or final sound, appears too difficult for many primary children unless the test is repeated several times, as we have already shown.

Among nonstandard English speakers, using a test demanding discriminations lacking in many dialects tends to give false results. Robinson's small-scale study (33) implies much lower reliability among economically disadvantaged children for what is considered one of the better measures involving word-pair discriminations. As a result of these observations, and in view of much evidence seemingly contradicting an emphasis on a meaningful linkage among dialect, auditory discrimination, and reading, many language specialists reject any causal interaction. As Samuels expresses it, the reading difficulties of dialectal groups could more readily be attributed to deficiencies in attention, language development, and cognitive development. The weight of evidence is against poor auditory discrimination as a cause of poor reading among dialect speakers according to such linguists as Venezky (43). Linguists offer the additional argument that such children can make the distinctions, even those they cannot evidence in the common test, from context in listening or reading. Moreover, these users of nonstandard English can understand both their own dialect and that of middle-class teachers, and as they mature they can answer in the teachers' own dialect if they choose.

We are also of the opinion that dialect and what appears to be poor auditory discrimination are not major contributors to reading failure. Upon occasion and for some pupils there is some justification for attempting to improve auditory discrimination. Since this would usually take place during the readiness period, we will reserve our further discussion until we treat that subject.

Although the technical terms may bother some of our readers, this interpretation of reading as an associational process is actually defining reading in much the same way as the psycholinguists, the language specialists, or those experts that emphasize the visual or perceptual aspects. Perhaps we can integrate these concepts of reading into a single description.

We have presented yet another group of scientifically based ideas about the nature of reading. This large body of studies has many implications for teaching children to read. We shall attempt to explore these implications thoroughly and to point out the teaching practices they seem to support as they are relevant to subsequent chapters of this book.

Top-Down vs. Bottom-Up vs. Interactive Reading

What are perhaps the latest models of the reading process attempt to encompass several of the viewpoints we have reviewed. Some call reading a *top-down* process—a guessing game in which the reader's knowledge of language and his world suggests several interpretations of the printed material. In this process, reading combines advanced organizers or prereading questions (printed or mental) and the reader's schemata to integrate textual and background information, to answer implicit questions rather than textually explicit (responses directly from the text) questions, as well as incorporate the use of pictures and textual adjuncts like titles, headings, etc. This is similar to the psycholinguistic concept.

Another model is *bottom-up* reading. In this model, the reader attends to letters, anticipates the words the letters will spell, and identifies the words with further expectations as to how they will be strung together and what they will mean when assembled into phrases and sentences. Children must be taught word meanings, to decode quickly, to interpret complex sentences and to apply reasoning strategies.

A combination of the two preceding models is the *interactive* model, which claims that both top-down and bottom-up processes occur at the same time, at least for skilled readers. Thus reading depends on the learner's knowledge as much as the information in the text. Top-down and bottom-up models when followed to the extreme present problems—the balance between the information brought by the reader and that of the writer may be lost. Moreover, guess piled upon guess is not really reading; also, too much attention to decoding takes away from meaning and rate of reading. Furthermore, training in rapid decoding does not effect comprehension unless the training is in context and extended for a year or more.

Reading concepts

The Word	is a very brief visual image recognized by distinctive features such as:
	letter groups or common phonograms
	translation of some letters into sounds
	the initial or final letter or two such letters
	a letter or two plus the configuration and the reader's anticipation as determined by the context
	is matched with an auditory memory and its associated ideas
	is accompanied by a meaning that is determined by:
	the reader's familiarity with or anticipation of syntax and word order
	the reader's previous reading and life experiences stored as auditory memories in his long-term memory bank (his schemata)
The Sentence	is interpreted as a rough approximation of the overall meanings of the words
	conveys a message which is not the sum of the words, but the reader's own interpretation or understanding

(continued)

The Paragraph	is a series of messages processed by the reader through inductive or deductive reasoning, in which the relationships among the messages (cause-effect, contrast, comparison, etc.) are recognized by the reader
	results in a final overall impression (main idea, conclusion, inference, etc.) or a message that is matched with and modified by the previous learnings of the reader, which may or may not agree with the writer's intentions

To put these same concepts in the negative sense:

The Word	is not recognized by the sheer act of saying it aloud or subvocally
	is not recognized because of repeated experiences simply in seeing and saying it
	is not recognized solely as a visual image that is familiar
	is not recognized letter by letter or phoneme by phoneme
The Sentence	does not require recognition of all the words to obtain the message
	is not the sum of all the meanings of all the words
	is not mentally classified as to type of structure (active, passive, negative, etc.)
	is not interpreted in terms of its exact phrasing or surface structure
The Paragraph	is not the sum of the facts presented
	is not comprehended exactly as presented

Endnotes

1. Gibson, Eleanor J., and Levin, Harry, *The Psychology of Reading.* Cambridge, Mass.: MIT Press, 1975.
2. Edfeldt, Ake W., *Silent Speech and Silent Reading.* Chicago: University of Chicago Press, 1960.

Discussion Questions

1. What faulty classroom practices reflect a narrow or single concept of the nature of the reading process?

2. What are some of the dangers in an oversimplified understanding of the reading process?

3. About when does reading begin to become largely a thinking rather than a word recognition act?

4. What are the limitations in treating reading instruction as simply successive training in one skill after another?

5. What evidence contradicts the concept of reading as the translation of successive letters into sounds and then into words?

6. Why did American schools gradually shift from an almost exclusive emphasis upon oral reading to a balance between oral and silent reading?

7. Does the present American reading program actually achieve a good balance between oral and silent reading? Between skill development and thinking? Defend your answers.

8. Why do most spelling and oral reading errors seem to be concentrated in the middle of words? What does this observation imply in terms of word recognition?

9. What types of thinking are not usually demanded by teachers' questions? How then does reading ever become a well-rounded thinking behavior?

10. What would be the characteristics of a reading program that integrated the various views of the reading process presented in this chapter?

References

1. *Albany Times Union*, "One in Four Reads 20 Books a Year, Survey Finds" (October 23, 1978), 14.

2. Barton, Allen H., and Wilder, David E., *Research and Practice in the Teaching of Reading: A Progress Report*. Study A-388. New York: Bureau of Applied Research, Columbia University, 1963.

3. Bower, G. H., "Organizational Factors in Memory," *Cognitive Psychology*, 1 (1970), 18–46.

4. Buswell, Guy T., "The Process of Reading," *Reading Teacher*, 13 (December 1969), 108–114.

5. Calfee, R., Chapman, R., and Venezky, R., "How a Child Needs to Think to Learn to Read," in *Cognition in Learning and Memory*, I. L. Gregg, ed. New York: John Wiley & Sons, 1971.

6. Deutsch, H., "The Role of Social Class in Language Development and Cognition," *American Journal of Orthopsychiatry*, 35 (1965), 78–88.

7. Downing, John, "The Child's Understanding of the Functional Processes of Communication," unpublished paper. Victoria, Canada: University of Victoria, 1977, 25–26.

8. Estes, Thomas H., "A Commentary on Reading and Understanding: Teaching from the Perspective of Artificial Intelligence," *Reading Teacher*, 36 (February 1983), 487–488.

9. Farnham-Diggery, Sylvia, *Information Processing in Children*. New York: Academic Press, 1977.

10. Gaines, Francis P., "Interrelations of Speech and Reading Disabilities," *Elementary School Journal*, 41 (April 1941), 606–613.

11. Gilbert, Luther C., "Functional Motor Efficiency of the Eyes and the Relation to Reading," *University of California Publications in Education*, 11 (1953), 159–232.

12. Gollasch, Frederick V., ed., *Language and Literacy: The Selected Writings of Kenneth S. Goodman.* Boston: Routledge and Kegan Paul, 1982.

13. Goodman, Kenneth S., "The Linguistics of Reading," *Elementary School Journal,* 64 (April 1964), 355–361.

14. Goodman, Kenneth S., "A Linguistic Study of Cues and Miscues in Reading," *Elementary English,* 42 (October 1965), 639–643.

15. Goodman, Kenneth S., "Dialect Rejection and Reading: A Response," *Reading Research Quarterly,* 5 (Summer 1970), 600–603.

16. Goodman, Kenneth S., "Decoding—From Code to What?" *Journal of Reading,* 14 (April 1971), 455–462, 498.

17. Gray, William S., "The Major Aspects of Reading," in *Sequential Development of Reading Abilities,* Helen M. Robinson, ed. Supplementary Educational Monographs, No. 90. Chicago: University of Chicago Press, 1960, 8–24.

18. Groff, Patrick, "Research vs. the Psycholinguistic Approach to Beginning Reading," *Elementary School Journal,* 80 (September 1980), 53–58.

19. Gunderson, Doris V., comp., *Language and Reading: An Interdisciplinary Approach.* Washington, D.C.: Center for Applied Linguistics, 1970.

20. Hammill, Donald D., and McNutt, Gaye, "Language Abilities and Reading: A Review of the Literature on Their Relationship," *Elementary School Journal,* 80 (May 1980), 269–277.

21. Harris, Irving D., *Emotional Blocks to Learning.* New York: Free Press, 1961.

22. Hoffman, Louis G., "The Relationship of Basic Visual Skills to School Readiness at the Kindergarten Level," *Journal of American Optometric Association,* 45 (May 1974), 608–614.

23. Huey, Edmund B., *The Psychology and Pedagogy of Reading.* New York: Macmillan, 1908; Cambridge, Mass.; MIT Press, 1968.

24. Keshian, Jerry G., "How Many Children Are Successful Readers?" *Elementary English,* 38 (October 1961), 408–410.

25. La Berge, D., and Samuels, S. Jay, "Toward a Theory of Automatic Information Processing in Reading," *Cognitive Psychology,* 6 (1974), 293–323.

26. Lin, San-su C., "Disadvantaged Student or Disadvantaged Teacher?" *English Journal,* 56 (May 1967), 751–756.

27. MacKinnon, A. R., "Insistent Tasks in Language Learning," *Toronto Education Quarterly,* 1 (Winter 1961–1962), 8–12.

28. Mackworth, Jane F., "Some Models of the Reading Process: Learners and Skilled Readers," *Reading Research Quarterly,* 7 (Summer 1972), 701–733.

29. McConkie, George W., and Rayner, Keith, "An On-line Computer Technique for Studying Reading: Identifying the Perceptual Span," in *Diversity in Mature Reading: Theory and Research—I,* Phil L. Nacke, ed., Twenty-second Yearbook National Reading Conference, 1973, 119–130.

30. Metfessel, Newton S., and Seng, Mark W., "Correlates with the School Success and Failure of Economically Disadvantaged Children," in *Reading for the Disadvantaged,* Thomas D. Horn, ed. New York: Harcourt Brace Jovanovich, 1970, 75–96.

31. Philion, William L. E., and Galloway, Charles G., "Indian Children and the Reading Program," *Journal of Reading,* 12 (April 1969), 553–560.

32. Ramsey, Wallace, "Which School System Gets the Best Results in Reading?" *Journal of Reading Behavior,* 1 (Summer 1969), 74–80.

33. Robinson, H. Alan, "Reliability of Measures Related to Reading Success of Average, Disadvantaged and Advantaged Children," *Reading Teacher*, 20 (December 1966), 203–208.

34. Ruddell, Robert B., *Innovations in Reading–Language Instruction.* Englewood Cliffs, N.J.: Prentice-Hall, 1974.

35. Rystrom, Richard, "Linguistics and the Teaching of Reading," *Journal of Reading Behavior*, 4 (Winter 1971–1972), 34–39.

36. Samuels, S. Jay, "The Psychology of Language," *Review of Educational Research*, 37 (April 1967), 109–119.

37. Samuels, S. Jay, "The Age-Old Controversy Between Holistic and Sub-Skill Approaches to Beginning Reading Instruction Revisited," in *Inchworm, Inchworm, Persistent Problems in Reading Education*, Constance M. McCullough, ed. Newark, Del.: International Reading Association, 1980.

38. Sheldon, William D., "Children's Experiences in Reading," in *Children and the Language Arts*, Vergil E. Herrick and Leland B. Jacobs, eds. Englewood Cliffs, N.J.: Prentice-Hall, 1955, 172–191.

39. Singer, Harry, and Ruddell, Robert B., eds. *Theoretical Models and Processes of Reading* (2d ed.). Newark, Del.: International Reading Association, 1976.

40. Smith, Frank, and Goodman, Kenneth S., "On the Psycholinguistic Method of Teaching Reading," *Elementary School Journal*, 71 (January 1971), 177–181.

41. Southgate, Vera, *Reading: Which Approach?* Mystic, Conn.: Lawrence Verry Inc., 1976.

42. Taylor, Stanford E., *Eye-Movement Photography with the Reading Eye.* Huntington, N.Y.: Educational Developmental Laboratories, 1958.

43. Venezky, R., *Nonstandard Language and Reading.* Madison, Wis.: Wisconsin Research and Development Center for Cognitive Learning, 1970.

44. Vernon, M. D., "The Perceptual Process in Reading," *Reading Teacher*, 13 (October 1959), 2–8.

45. Vernon, M. D., *The Psychology of Perception.* Baltimore: Penguin Books, 1962.

46. Warrington, Elizabeth K., "The Incidence of Verbal Disability Associated with Retardation in Reading," *Neuropsychologia*, 5 (1967), 175–179.

47. Weber, Rose-Marie, "Some Reservations on the Significance of Dialect in the Acquisition of Reading," in *Reading Goals for the Disadvantaged*, Thomas D. Horn, ed. Newark, Del.: International Reading Association, 1970, 124–131.

48. Werner, E. E., Simonian, K., and Smith, R. D., "Reading Achievement, Language Functioning and Perceptual Motor Development of 10 and 11 Year-Olds," *Perceptual and Motor Skills*, 25 (1967), 409–420.

49. Wheat, Thomas E., and Edmond, Rose Mary, "An Analysis of the Concept of Comprehension." Paper presented at the National Reading Conference, St. Petersburg, Fla., December 1975.

50. Wold, Robert M., *Vision, Its Impact on Learning.* Seattle: Special Child Publications, 1978.

51. Wolfram, Walt, et al., *Reading and Dialect Differences.* Washington, D.C.: Center for Applied Linguistics.

52. "World Education and Communication Seen Through Statistics," *Unesco Chronicle*, 18 (February 1972), 74–76.

PART TWO

Reading Practices Currently in Use

2 Using the Basal Reader Approach

Perhaps because of its almost universal use in America, the basal reading program is the target of much criticism and abuse. All self-appointed experts who appear on the educational horizon with their unique concept of the reading process feel obliged to attack this established approach in order to find some foundation for their own ideas. Some of these criticisms are undoubtedly justified, for at the hands of many teachers the program has become a stereotyped and discouraging experience for some pupils. Few teachers are conscious of the inherent limitations in submitting all pupils to basically the same group of reading experiences, varying perhaps only the pace of presentation. Even fewer teachers realize that the methods of learning emphasized in the program are not equally effective for all pupils, and that, in fact, their nature predestines some children to failure. How many basal teachers attribute pupil failure to their own disinclination to adapt their methods to differing pupil aptitudes? How many basal teachers attempt to discover through what medium—visual, auditory, kinesthetic, or multisensory—a failing pupil might learn more readily?

At the same time, there can be little doubt that if used intelligently, the basal program is relatively effective for a large proportion of pupils. Its highly complex structure represents the end product of more than one hundred years of experimentation, trial and error, and gradual improvement in materials and techniques of instruction. But since the basal program is not yet perfect nor any more effective than its users permit it to be, we believe that an objective, critical evaluation is needed.

The first series of what might be called basal readers appeared in America in 1790 under the authorship of Noah Webster. Prior to this time schools tended to use the same book, such as *The New England Primer* and similar books, at all grades. Soon other authors followed Webester's example, but it was not until 1840 that the idea of graded readers was developed in the McGuffey series. This author controlled the difficulty of his books, he believed, by the length of words in stories. The opening book used only two- or three-letter words and longer words were gradually introduced in later books. Supplementary readers were introduced about 50 years later, in 1890, and they took the form of alphabetic or phonic systems, sentence, or story methods, or literary readers. Little of the content of these early books had any relationship to children's life experiences. More often the books contained moralistic, religious, patriotic, or oratorical materials obviously intended to inculcate the proper values of life in the children.

Until about 1910 practically all classroom reading was oral, despite the criticisms of such observers as Horace Greeley that children were being trained to read without any real comprehension. But the discovery that silent reading rate and comprehension were definitely superior to that obtained in oral reading produced a dramatic change in teaching procedures. This new emphasis on silent reading necessitated such a different type of training for teachers that some sort of guide had to be devised for them. Thus, by necessity, teachers' manuals to accompany the readers were written to help teachers to present this new mode of learning. The emphasis on silent reading and, therefore, on independent activities demanded some means of assessing and directing children in seatwork. As a result, workbook exercises, first as single games and later in bound form, were invented. The woodcuts and reproduction of famous paintings common to the early readers were gradually replaced about 1890 by colored illustrations more closely related to the content.

Today the coordinated series of textbook, workbooks, and manuals known as a basal reading series undoubtedly forms the core of the American reading program. A survey of 1300 teachers sampled throughout the country indicates that 95 to 98 percent of primary teachers and at least 80 percent of intermediate-grade teachers use basal readers almost every school day. A survey in six states indicates that the manual for a basal series is used as the basis of the reading program in 95 percent of the classrooms. About 20 percent also use a guide developed within the school system as their basis.

In fact, in perhaps more than half of American classrooms the basal reader is the only instructional material. Nor is the extent of its use peculiar to American schools, for surveys in England indicate that 82 percent of the schools use a single basal, while the remainder use two or more such programs, as well as teacher-made materials. A group of instructional aids which receives such almost-universal acceptance certainly deserves our most serious consideration and evaluation.

Basal Reader Vocabulary

For the first 50 years, or until about 1965, vocabulary control took the form of repeating practically every word in any reader in all later books of the series. New words were severely limited by carefully counting the number of new words per page and the number of new words in the total vocabulary. Thus a high repetition of the "basal" vocabulary both in the readers and workbooks as well as any parallel materials was ensured. This vocabulary control showed a constant trend toward greater repetition and smaller vocabularies at every reading level until about 1965. By 1930–1931, the average primer had only 304 different words; by 1936–1937, the number had dropped to 247. By 1941 one of us reported that the range at this level had decreased to 225–335 (27). By 1965, estimates ranged from 113 to 173 words. Thus the emphasis upon vocabulary control had reduced the vocabulary burden in primary readers by 30 to 50 percent in three decades.

In 1976, an analysis of eight new primary reading series indicated that the average offered 551 words in the first grade. Only 103 words were common to all these basals, showing an average overlap of only 10 percent. What had happened to the "basic" vocabulary that was considered so all-important? In another study in 1974, the four most prominent series reported a first-grade vocabulary of from 305 to 675 words. There was a marked increase in the total number of words offered compared to the books of the same series a decade before. There was much less repetition of words (one book of 240 words presented 85 of them only once); and there was less common vocabulary among the four series. The study found a core vocabulary of only 134 words common to six new basal first grade programs (32).

It is undoubtedly true that the use of an excessive number of unknown or difficult words will prevent young learners from acquiring any fluency in reading. It will also interfere with development of the normal pattern of progressive eye movements which is the visual component of the reading act. On the other hand, what was the justification for this constant reduction of the vocabulary of primary readers? No one really knows precisely how often words must be repeated for the average learner or how simple the material must actually be in order to ensure ease of learning for most children. No one knows whether basals are now simple enough, or whether we had already passed this point in our efforts at vocabulary control, or whether the vocabulary should be increased.

It is probably true that slow learners need more repetition to ensure learning than do average learners, who, in turn, may need more repetitions than do rapid learners. Moreover, some early studies show that first graders who are introduced to a small, common vocabulary make better reading progress than do groups introduced to larger vocabularies. A small, controlled vocabulary tends to promote true reading in the sense that it is accompanied by meaning or reasoning, as opposed to a word-calling act. Very large, uncontrolled vocabularies tend to force children toward continual word analysis and word-by-word reading. These are a few of the sound justifications offered for the vocabulary control in basal readers.

Yet other studies we will discuss later raise some doubts about the use of highly repetitive materials. Is it the sheer repetition of a limited number of words which ensures success in reading above the first grade, or is this goal as readily accomplished by a variety of reading materials which includes a total vocabulary of reasonable size? Are the important beginning words of the primary grades learned best because they are repeated in the basal and supplementary basals, or are they learned because of the many associations built around them by a variety of visual, auditory, and language experiences? Is vocabulary control of great importance only at beginning stages and of decreasing significance at later primary- and intermediate-grade levels? Is vocabulary control closely related to children's learning rates rather than essential for most children? Perhaps it is significant to note that the latest editions of most basal reading series are increasing the breadth of the basal vocabulary, without answering these questions.

Some of the same arguments used to justify teaching reading in kindergarten are influencing the authors of the more recent basal series. They believe that children today are more verbal; more widely experienced because of family mobility, both in terms of residence and recreational travel; and have larger vocabularies due in part to televiewing experiences, and hence are capable of profiting from more broadly designed reading materials. As a result, newer series are lessening their vocabulary control dramatically. While aware of the limited learning capacities of young children, most authors are avoiding the carefully constructed, word-by-word count and substituting more original stories or those drawn from published children's literature. Control of the reading difficulty is ensured by readability formula analysis which enables monitoring the breadth of vocabulary and the complexity of sentence structure.

However, the increasing variety of words increases the concept load and, in a sense, decreases readability. Is this a desirable trend or one which may make the average basal reader too difficult for the child of average background and ability? The basal authors really do not know the answer to this question. Only trial and error in the use of the latest basal series will tell us.

There are at least three reasons which contradict the claim that a limited vocabulary is essential for the verbatim learning which is supposed to be the foundation of all future reading. First, certain studies show that average pupils who have advanced as far as the primer level spontaneously learn many words other than the basal vocabulary. Furthermore, the language facility and readiness of most pupils, as shown in their own speech vocabularies, are far in advance of the concept level of basal readers. It may be safely assumed that this spontaneous learning continues, and may even accelerate, throughout the child's school career. Second, except for a few hundred service words that recur frequently in practically all reading materials (mostly prepositions, conjunctions, verbs, and adverbs), there is hardly any such entity as an essential core or basal vocabulary.

As Patrick Groff points out, these service words are probably the only essential terms in any basal reader vocabulary (20). The lists of such words are available in a number of word counts, such as: John B. Carroll, et al., *American Heritage Word Frequency Book* (Boston: Houghton Mifflin, 1971); E. W. Dolch, *The Dolch Word List* (Champaign, Ill.: Garrard Publishing Co.); and Albert J. Harris and Milton D. Jacobson, *Basic Elementary Reading Vocabularies* (New York: MacMillan, 1972).

Our View

Because these words are so frequent in our language at all reading levels, quick recognition by beginning pupils (and all others) facilitates successful reading. However, we do not believe that such words should be taught by drill or repetition in isolation from their normal language contexts. In any training, the words should be presented in phrases or sentences, as suggested by the exercises in Chapter 13, Building Sight and Meaning Vocabulary.

Third, beginning readers seem to know many more words than the basic ones. Two research studies by Arthur I. Gates (*15, 16*) support this argument against extreme vocabulary control. In his first study, some 300 third-grade pupils, who were being taught by a basal reading method, were tested on their knowledge of the third- and fourth-grade vocabularies of their basal series. Gates discovered that on the average the pupils knew as many fourth-grade as third-grade words. Over half the pupils recognized practically all the third- and fourth-grade vocabularies. Even the poorest pupils recognized 90 percent as many fourth-grade words as they did third-grade. A second study by Gates (*16*) repeated this type of evaluation in two classes of average second graders. About 60 percent of the pupils knew 90 percent or more of the basal vocabulary to which they would be introduced in the first *four* grades. Seventy-five percent of the pupils knew at least 80 percent of this new vocabulary. Even the poorest 10 percent of the pupils had learned about half of the total vocabulary before the appropriate grades. Is it true that in order to learn to read successfully, most pupils must be exposed to only a very small vocabulary in a piecemeal or spoon-feeding fashion?

This emphasis upon vocabulary control or the learning of words by sheer repetition is, in our opinion, faulty in several respects. First, the actual need for repetitions probably varies from child to child. We grant that a degree of overlearning (overrepetition?) may be sound, but must all children overlearn to much the same degree? Second, it is obvious that words are not learned simply because of the number of repetitions. Certain errors of usage in words persist all through the pupils' school career, as *their* for *there*, *two* for *to*, and the like. These are examples of words introduced in primary grades which are still used erroneously by college students. We will discuss the true nature of vocabulary growth at length later. Perhaps it will suffice here simply to point out that, contrary to the vocabulary control theory of basal readers, words are learned only by the building of a depth of varied associations with their meanings, pronunciation, usage, and the like—not mainly by repetition in simple contexts.

In an attempt to keep the learning task reasonable, in terms of vocabulary and concept loads, some recent series offer "levels" of books in graduated steps. One series, for example, has six levels in the kindergarten-first grade program. Three levels offer readiness-reading training through the media of picture books, spirit masters, skill development workbooks, cassettes, and filmstrips. Following these introductory steps, three levels of readers and aids are used in the first grade. In the second, third, and subsequent grades, a collection of two levels per grade are offered and enriched with a reading development kit and a language enrichment kit. These kits function in lieu of supplementary readers in offering reading selections, skill development training, language development, listening training, and enrichment activities through printed matter, audiovisual aids, and games.

To aid in the use of these levels of books, or in other words, to translate them into terms the average teacher clearly understands, Greenfield, et al. have listed the approximate grade levels for the new "levels" in basals and supplementary readers (*18*). Of course, this listing may tend to defeat the intentions of the basal authors who want teachers to think of children's progress in small gradual steps rather than the gross steps from one grade level to the next.

Among the justifications offered for these dramatic changes in the basic instructional tool are the elimination of rigidly graded and labeled materials and the consequent lockstep progress fostered by that arrangement; the provision for smaller, more frequent, less obvious steps in development; and the provision for a multimedia, diversified body of instructional aids, each extending to a number of levels to permit individualized progress. In effect, these programs reject the former dependence upon word repetition to ensure learning to read, and are accepting instead the psycholinguistic emphasis upon obtaining meaning in reading and enriching children's experiences and language facility through a wide variety of approaches.

These newer developments in basals have not yet effected all the changes in method and use of materials that their authors intend, since many school systems cling to the use of the older, graded series and, of course, because of the lag in educational practice behind current knowledge and theory. For this reason, in descriptions of classroom procedures we are depending upon surveys and reports (*8*) that do not reflect the most modern arrangements. We shall describe, in general, what teachers are seen doing in the classroom and later comment upon the limitations of these practices which the newer series hope to eradicate.

The Method in First Grade

First Steps. Following the use of a readiness test, a week or two of teacher observation, or some combination of these means of evaluation, the children are divided into groups according to the teacher's estimate of their probable progress. One group, considered relatively unready for reading instruction, will receive perhaps one to five weeks of prereading training. For a second group the readiness training may be abbreviated to just several weeks, and mature groups may begin reading instruction after only a few days. Although a large number of first-grade teachers believe that some children would benefit from substituting a full-year readiness program for formal instruction, administrative and parental pressures seldom permit this. Initial reading experiences may take the form of an experience story—a group composition of a "story" describing an experience of the group—within or outside the classroom. Phrases or sentences are offered by various pupils and coordinated by the teacher, who then writes them in manuscript on a large chart or the blackboard. The choice of words and the sentence structure are manipulated by the teacher to ensure simplicity and comprehension by all members of the group. Words, phrases, sentences, and the entire story are read several times by various members of the group during the construction of the chart. The story may be used again on a number of occasions for individual or group reading.

Teachers vary, of course, in their initial approaches to beginning reading. Some may prefer to begin with the first preprimer in preference to experience charts, while others employ both types of materials in successive reading lessons. About half of first-grade teachers use the experience story approach at least once every two days, whereas another one-third claim to use charts many times during the year. These figures imply frequent use of the chart method by more than 80 percent of first-grade teachers. In addition to these more or less basic beginning steps, the average teacher will frequently incorporate some children's magazines or newspapers, and will ensure daily use of the basal workbooks and teacher-prepared exercises.

On the other hand, the average first-grade teacher does *not* usually employ any device for promoting development of a normal eye-movement pattern, even for the group of immature pupils. She is not likely to use the films or filmstrips made available by the basal series publishers despite their obvious relationships and values for reinforcement or motivation. Currently much emphasis is placed on phonics by a large proportion of teachers. At least three of every four teachers supplement the basal with phonics practice materials, and half of the teachers introduce materials of their own design.

When teachers are aware of the lack of development of directionality common to young children, they try to guide students to use a basic left-to-right eye movement when reading. They employ such techniques as pointing to the words they are reading or to those on the chalkboard with a flowing left-to-right movement of the hand, as the children follow along. Some workbooks provide practice in reading or writing guided by arrows, or green and red dots to indicate starting or stopping points. Other teachers use some of the directionality exercises outlined in the chapter on Readiness Training.

We have already noted the deemphasis on general configuration or details of the word outline at this level. First-grade teachers may avoid these obvious clues to word recognition for fear of being accused of using a whole-word or look-and-guess method, a current criticism of our public school reading methods. On the other hand, most first-grade teachers do stress word recognition techniques such as context and picture clues, reading words from letters or letter combinations, and noting similar sounds in words and relating these to their representative letters.

The time devoted to reading instruction is usually two hours in the morning and another hour in the afternoon in first grade. In about a third of the classrooms, this time allotment is reduced to an hour in morning sessions and another hour in the afternoon.

The Method in Second and Third Grades

Grouping. In the average second- or third-grade classroom, pupils are grouped presumably to permit greater recognition of individual differences, but actually, some would say, for convenience of the teacher. Despite the range of reading levels, which commonly extends over four or five grade levels, the almost universal practice is to form three reading groups: the *Blue-birds*, the *Redbirds*, and the *Buzzards*, or as one teacher frankly labeled this low group, the *Impossibles*. The low reading group usually includes about eight to nine pupils, while eleven to thirteen are placed in the middle and the high reading groups. All of these groups tend to remain approximately the same size throughout the school year (27). The groups allegedly are formed on the basis of reading ability, the three divisions probably corresponding to the teacher's belief that his pupils vary a total of three grades in reading levels despite the evidence in the available information. The results of standardized reading tests, the teacher's informal tests by having pupils read from various levels of materials, and perhaps the results of intelligence tests and last year's teacher's records, plus his own observations during the first week or so form the bases of the groupings which we find in about 90 percent of the second- and third-grade classrooms. Less than 5 percent of these primary teachers make any attempt to group children according to such recommended bases as social factors, interests, or need for specific training in important skills.

Several studies involving observation of teachers' practices and a comparison of pupil reading test scores with the reading levels of the instructional material they were offered provide additional criticism of how teachers group pupils. Judith Alpert noted that the reading materials used for high reading groups were often actually below their mean reading test scores, while the materials for low groups were well above the mean reading scores for the low reading groups (1). High groups were taught largely by a whole-word method; low groups were given supplementary training in phonics in addition to the whole-word method. Jorgenson (26) confirmed these facts by pointing out that reading materials were more often matched by grade placement than by the actual reading levels of pupils. Pupils reading above or below grade level were those most often mismatched. He also saw that classroom behavior tended to be poorer when pupils were grossly mismatched with their reading materials (26), as we might expect. Roslyn Rubin (32) repeated these observations in a sample of about 1500 pupils in 400 schools. She found that about 20 percent of the children who scored below their grade level, in other words only about one in every five poor readers, were assigned books at their low reading levels. Less than 5 percent in the first three grades and grade five were assigned books at advanced levels despite reading scores at or about the grade level above their placement. In the fourth grade, this figure was only 7 percent (34). Elfrieda H. Hiebert has made an excellent review of our grouping practices and their effects upon children (24).

Despite the many negative practices she observed, Hiebert is not anti-grouping. Her observations led her to suggest a need for more research on differences among teachers; teacher planning and interaction in lessons; the influence of teacher expectations upon these behaviors; teacher decisions regarding time allocation, pacing, and grouping placements; and the behaviors of pupils in different groups and their effect upon the teacher.

From these observations it is apparent that what appears to be the simple placement of children in groups according to teacher judgment of the pupils'

Grouping practices

Time. Teachers tend to spend more time with high-ability groups and to work with them when they are most alert, early in the morning.

Size of groups. Teachers give more directed time if the group is small. There are no studies showing the relationship between the size of a group, however, and its ultimate reading ability.

Management. There are variations among the groups in the different types of instruction they are offered, the difficulty of the assigned tasks, the time engaged in the reading task and the pace of presentation of new content. For example, about 17 percent of low-ability readers' time is spent on phonics, while high-ability pupils are required to spend only 7 percent of their time in such study. More than half of the time of high-ability students is spent on emphasizing meanings, but only one-fourth of instructional time for low-ability pupils is spent on this topic. High-ability pupils tend to have two to three times as much reading as low-ability students.

Oral vs. silent. High-ability students spend more time reading silently than reading orally. The opposite is true for low-ability pupils. Low-ability pupils are often required to reread orally some materials; high-ability pupils tend to be permitted to read new material.

Time on task. This is less among low-ability pupils because teachers spend more time dealing with behavior and attention than with high-ability groups. The more this kind of activity is demanded of a teacher, the less learning occurs among the group. This disciplining is not needed because low-ability pupils necessarily have short attention spans or behavior problems. Some teachers put children in the low-ability group because of behavior or attention problems. Also the overemphasis on oral reading permits children to become distracted more easily, which teachers feel they must correct. Moreover, low-ability groups are often required to try to read material that is relatively more difficult for them than what is given high-ability groups, hence more attention and behavior problems follow.

Pace of presentation. Teachers tend to maintain a constant pace with similar groups from year to year, regardless of the capabilities of the children within the groups. Children in low-ability groups are often required to complete worksheets and workbooks at a common pace. In fact, they are often told to wait for all in the group to finish. High-ability pupils are often allowed more flexible work patterns and independence.

Interaction. Teachers' question strategies for low-ability pupils give fewer opportunities to answer analysis type questions and less time to respond; also, less praise for correct responses is given by some teachers, more by others. High-ability pupils do better in small, peer-directed tasks; low-ability pupils do better in larger groups directed by the teachers.

(continued)

Responses to oral reading errors. Teachers tend to interrupt low-ability pupils more often than high-ability pupils who make similar errors, regardless of the semantic acceptability of the error. Teachers give information regarding graphemic and phonemic aspects of target words or simply pronounce them for low-ability students; semantic and syntactic information is stressed for high-ability students.

Teachers tend to stop the prompts from high-ability group members but not in low-ability groups, perhaps because the latter take longer to read, with more pauses. Encouraging more call-outs may be a way of maintaining the children's attention in the low-ability group.

Interruptions. Teachers permit fewer interruptions when working with high-ability students than when with low.

Teacher attitudes. The whole class is often told to watch the assignments being given to the high-ability group and are often told that sometime they would be able to do that work also. Teachers also tactfully point out that such assignments are made because the group is smart and their tasks are more difficult. Some teachers label the games or centers as exclusive materials for those of high ability.

Effects of grouping. Group membership accounted for 25 percent of the variation in reading achievement from the beginning to the middle of the first year. Performance of the low-ability group declined significantly compared to that of the pupils assigned to the high ability.

Self-concept. Low-ability pupils tend to be more derogatory about themselves and their group status. Many wanted to be in the high-ability group; none of the high-ability students wanted to be in the low group. There were lower self-evaluations among average- and low-ability pupils if they were members of such reading groups than if they were not grouped.

Feelings toward reading. Low-ability pupils have more negative feelings about reading and their group placement. Both high- and low-ability students felt they could read more books if they weren't in their respective groups; both desired to read more on their own; both wanted more chances to read silently than orally; both wanted more opportunities to choose their own readers. The low-ability students gave significantly lower estimates of their success, had less persistence on tasks, and attributed their failure to lack of ability and any success to factors beyond their control. They showed less expectancy of success following failure than did high ability.

Group dynamics. Members of the high-ability group are chosen significantly more often than average- or low-ability group members on a sociometric measure of children's liking for other members of the class. Even in the first few months of the first grade, group membership accounted for significant variation in social status of class members.

Reprinted with permission of Elfrieda H. Hiebert and the International Reading Association.

reading ability has significant impact upon the pupils' lives and personalities. In many cases, the placement conveys to the children what may be permanent impressions of their abilities and self-worth. Perhaps this is why it is possible to predict relative reading achievement as far as the sixth grade from pupils' first-grade accomplishments. To avoid the negative aspects of grouping, we believe in working toward individualized instruction using the naturalness of the language experience approach as first steps, as we explain in later chapters.

In our experience, we have seen some teachers make the serious error of underestimating the range of abilities in their reading groups. Often each reading group is given the basal reader of a particular level. The low-, middle-, and high-reading groups of a third grade may use, for example, second-, third-, and fourth-grade readers, respectively. If a fourth-grade reader is used with the best group, it is very likely to be a supplementary basal rather than the reader of the series used throughout the school. Many teachers fear the wrath of next year's teacher if they were to permit their good readers to complete the book intended for that grade.

The assumption in this practice is that a single level of instructional materials will suffice for each group. In reality, there is a range of reading abilities in each group, and particularly in the low and high groups. Bond and Tinker suggest that in the typical third-grade classroom the low group ranges from 1.4 to 2.7, while the high group ranges from 3.3 to 5.0 (12). If there are any real differences between a first- and a second-grade basal reader, then certainly the second-grade reader is not appropriate for some students in the low group. Similarly, a fourth-grade reader will fail to challenge a number of the high group. Thus, unless teachers recognize the range of reading levels in each group, they may only partially achieve their goal of providing for individual differences.

Another flaw in grouping practices is in the tendency to retain the size and personnel of the group throughout the school year. Groff's survey of grouping shows that in a 13-week period only about one-third of pupils are shifted from their original placement (19). Practically all these shifts occur in the first 2 to 4 weeks, indicating that they are due to quick revisions of the teacher's initial judgment rather than to any developmental changes in pupil progress.

During the daily one or two reading periods, the teacher works separately with each reading group, often in a circle reading situation. While the teacher is engaged with one group in this fashion, the other groups pursue a variety of activities. Most frequently these activities are related to the portion of the reader already reviewed by the teacher, such as completing the workbook exercises, writing an experience story, or rereading the basal story. These activities are almost always subsequent to their circle reading situation. Children are almost never allowed to read ahead in the daily lessons. Pupils incapable of such independent study activities may be told to complete a relevant drawing, engage in a picture word game, study their number work, or perform other such distantly related tasks. If we may judge from the usual classroom, the other groups' activities are not always closely related to their reading progress.

Perhaps the best picture of the basal reader approach may be conveyed by some description of the average, everyday reading activities which may be seen in classrooms using this method. Actual observation of the basal reader lesson is probably a more realistic way of recognizing all that is involved. But since this book cannot take the reader to such a classroom, we must adopt the second-best course. We have attempted to describe a typical basal reading lesson in a primary classroom by paraphrasing the procedures outlined in a number of teachers' manuals.

Most reading units are outlined in four or five major steps in the manuals. The first of these involves introduction to the new vocabulary and concepts of the unit or story. The purpose and nature of this step varies greatly in certain recent series, as the reader will discover. Following this introduction, most series go to the guided silent reading, based upon purposes for reading evolved by both teacher and pupils. A few series then suggest oral reading as a follow-up to the silent reading purposes. Recent series tend to play down the use of oral reading to this extent, preferring a guided thinking in silent reading emphasis. A third major step is the stress upon skill-building exercises which all series employ. The emphasis varies, of course, from one grade level to the next, but this step is an important segment of every plan. The final step includes supplementary activities for enrichment and motivational purposes.

Florence Pieronek offers what she considers an ideal reading lesson plan. She recommends: (1) concept development by discussion, new vocabulary, films, pictures, or relating first-hand experiences; (2) vocabulary recognition by the prereading study of word parts and reading words aloud without pictures; (3) meaning vocabulary clarified by discussion and emphasizing contextual analysis; (4) setting overall goals for comprehension by asking a global prereading question requiring children to read the entire selection, and putting this question on the blackboard; (5) directed reading and thinking activity—breaking the selection into segments, setting a single purpose for each section, then discussing answers and asking other questions to clarify answers; (6) purposeful oral reading by selecting sentences or words or a paragraph to respond to questions, to prove answers, to dramatize, or to interpret; (7) follow-up in independent thinking and problem solving by using the words and comprehension skills introduced earlier; and (8) enrichment to foster the love of reading, and time for silent reading of parallel themes to develop creative writing and oral expression (30).

In contrast to the first-grade reading program, a number of new trends or emphases appear in the other primary grades. Emphasis on reading skills is extended to the reading matter encountered in the areas of social science, science, and English by the average teacher. The use of experience stories, teacher-prepared worksheets, and supplementary basal readers is no longer usual in the average classroom. Use of the school or public library for recreational or supplementary reading becomes definitely more frequent. Emphasis upon recoding increases markedly, as shown by the frequent use of a special phonics workbook in almost 40 percent of the classrooms, and by increasing

Typical basal primary reading lesson

INTRODUCTION OF VOCABULARY (ESTABLISHING BACKGROUND, PREPARATION FOR READING)

The new words of the story or unit are presented by:

1. Using the word cards supplied by the publisher or writing them on the blackboard in a list or in sentences; having children read or point out words, phrases, sentences.
2. Reacting to their meanings by questions, prereading discussion of the story or children's related experiences; that is, weaving new words into contextual settings.
3. Pointing out their phonic, structural, or configuration characteristics, in keeping with the pupils' status in such skills, that is, by taking into account number of syllables, presence of phonic rule, the base word or root, and the affixes, differences in shapes, etc.
4. Reviewing briefly the familiar word recognition techniques or system of steps the pupils may employ with any unknown words they will meet in the story; that is, by distinguishing between long and short vowel sounds, recognizing a base word in a derived form, etc.
5. Establishing some experiential background when beginning a new unit or topic by a related film, filmstrip, or the pictures or selections read to or by the children; also weaving the ideas, words, and concepts to be read in the unit into the discussions of these background materials.
6. Reviewing old vocabulary by word cards or blackboard presentation, as in steps 1 and 3.

SILENT READING (GUIDED READING, GUIDING INTERPRETATION, DEVELOPING PUPIL PURPOSES)

1. Create prereading practice in:
   a. Locating information—finding title and page in table of contents; finding names of principal characters, or locale of story from title; for example, "Where does the title say this story took place?"
   b. Drawing inferences—about the nature of the story from the title; identifying facts about the setting, time, characters, dress, living conditions, habitat, etc., from inspection of the introductory picture.
   c. Setting a purpose for the reading—by raising simple questions about action, characters, sequence, etc., which will be answered by the reading of the first portion of the story; same for succeeding portions. Examples: "What is the name of the boy mentioned in the first paragraph? Who is he? Have you heard of him before?" or "Read the second paragraph and be ready to tell how to go from Bobby's home to his grandfather's farm."

(continued)

Varying the type of prereading questions to emphasize different skills, as gathering information, making judgments, finding a specific detail, summarizing a main idea, verifying an inference, seeing cause-effect relationships, visualizing action, and anticipating outcomes.

2. Read each portion of the story; wait for class discussion of the answers to the prereading question; listen to the next leading question; then read on. (Many teachers do not follow this practice of segmenting the material, each portion having a prereading question to be answered after the reading. They prefer to allow pupils to read almost the entire piece before answering the one general prereading question [assuming they have proposed one] and answering any questions raised by the teacher after the reading. Yet the research very definitely shows that this practice yields better comprehension than end-of-reading questions.)

3. If children request assistance in dealing with any words in the story, help them to apply their own word attack skills, rather than *simply telling them.* Urge them to use the context to derive a logical word, or to use the initial consonant sound or other phonic elements they already know, or a picture clue, or a structural clue.

ORAL READING (PURPOSEFUL REREADING, GUIDING INTERPRETATION)

1. Verification of facts: "Find and read the paragraph that proves Bobby's home was not far from his grandfather's farm."

2. Locating specific details: "Find and read each paragraph that tells the things Bobby saw on the way to his grandfather's farm."

3. Vocabulary review: "Whoever can read this new word (pointing to list on blackboard) may read page 86 for us."

4. Oral expression: "Find a sentence that asks a question. Read it aloud so that your voice shows the difference between a statement and a question."

5. Relating sequences: "Find and read the part of the story that tells what happened to Bobby at the top of the hill."

6. Dramatization: have children choose parts and read or dramatize the conversation between these characters.

7. Encouragement of expression and intonation: have pupils select and read various types of sentences: demands, requests, questions, exclamations, and poetry.

8. Preparation of pupils to read a story to the class: prepare a group of children for a presentation by stressing the need to "talk like real people, show how you feel by your voice, read in complete sentences rather than line by line."

9. Use of oral reading to answer any of the prereading questions proposed earlier in the lesson.

(*continued*)

SKILL BUILDING (WORD RECOGNITION TECHNIQUES, VOCABULARY ENRICH-MENT AND EXTENSION, EXTENDING COMPETENCE, RELATED COMPREHEN-SION AND VOCABULARY BUILDING) (See our extended discussion of comprehension instruction in a later chapter.)

1. Use new words of unit or previous story, review known phonic and structural elements. Use blackboard or word- or letter-cards for presentation.
2. Teach new phonic or structural elements, such as the long sound of *e,* as these occur in the new vocabulary, by blackboard exercises.
3. Use related pages in the workbook or activity book to practice or supplement the skills stressed in the daily lesson.
4. Give training in careful reading of pictures (picture clues) by asking a variety of questions about pictures in text and groups of pictures collected by teacher or pupils.
5. Try to build word associations to new vocabulary, and a variety of meanings for each, by discussion, blackboard exercises, and the like.
6. Give practice in using synonyms, homonyms, descriptive phrases (similes and metaphors) as related to new vocabulary. Use teacher's sentences or those drawn from the text as sources of practice at blackboard or desk.
7. Ask pupils for the meanings of any hard words they met in the selection. If they cannot identify such, choose several words you think were probably unknown. Ask "What meaning did you get for _____?" "How did you get that meaning?" Discuss children's answers.

SUPPLEMENTARY ACTIVITIES (ENRICHMENT ACTIVITIES, CULMINATING ACTIVITIES, EXTENDING INTERESTS)

1. Read selections related to the content of the current unit or story in parallel readers of the same series, other basal readers, trade books, literary readers correlated with the basal.
2. Use the sequentially arranged learning activities in a kit supplied by the publisher or made by the teacher.
3. Administer progress or end-of-unit test in the activity book or workbook. Or, use such criterion-referenced tests as supplied by the publisher. Evaluate child's oral reading errors in individual oral reading test. Check progress in sight vocabulary, word attack, and comprehension skills by other tests.
4. Use informal dramatization of a story, choral speaking, rhymes, jingles, and poetry to help develop normal expression in reading and to overcome the tendency toward word-by-word naming or word calling.
5. Use recordings, films, filmstrips, and other related materials as listed in the manual to enrich pupils' background for each unit or story. Teachers should visit the school librarian and the media center prior to a reading unit to arrange for related books and other materials.

(continued)

6. Expand the meanings of a story or unit, as one on pets, by an experience story composed by the group ("How to Take Care of a Pet"), or such stories composed by the individual pupils. Add drawings or cut-out pictures to these stories; construct clay or papier mâché models of the pets; make a class booklet on caring for a classroom pet. Extend by making murals or a frieze on "Our Pets"; arrange pictures and news articles about pets on the bulletin boards; invite a zoo attendant or a pet store manager to talk to the class. Other enrichment activities might include a trip to a pet store; making hand puppets to present a dramatization composed by the children; assembling a series of animal pictures to be displayed on a scroll (movie or TV show) to form the basis for discussions, storytelling and experience stories; making model animals of paper, yarn, pipe cleaners, and spools. (See our list of books describing learning activities in Chapter 12 for further suggestions.)

---

mention of stress upon letter sounds, phonic analysis of words, and phonic rules. Other practices found in marked frequency at these levels are the request to the children to write original stories based on experience or imagination, the study of synonyms and antonyms, and a questionable effort to induce children to look for small words within longer ones as an aid to recognition. Unfortunately, when common words seem to appear within other words, they seldom retain their original pronunciation. For example, the word *in* is no longer that word in such larger words as *ringing, line, ninety*, and *define*. In fact, one research study indicates that short, simple words more often than not vary from their usual pronunciation when combined in larger words.

Our View

The real degree of success of this primary reading program is a matter of acrid debate among various authorities (38). Estimates of the proportion of children failing to achieve sufficient reading skill to be able to meet the demands of the intermediate grades are around 15 to 25 percent. Whether it is possible under any circumstances for all children in any grade to be taught in such a manner that they would all meet the standards of the next grade level is, of course, highly questionable. But a great many critics of current reading instruction feel that, first, too great a proportion of children are unprepared for each successive year; second, many pupils, particularly those of greater intelligence, should be offered a richer, more challenging program; and, third, the primary program does not adequately prepare children to use their reading skills effectively in the content-field reading characteristic of the intermediate grades.

Many other criticisms really reflect the inadequate training and insecurity of some teachers rather than inherent faults in the primary basal program.

Among these are use of the basals not as the core but as the whole of the reading program, overdependence upon the workbooks and management systems for teaching skills, excessive oral reading without any real purposes, and a perfectionistic attitude toward learning the basal vocabulary. There is undoubtedly much to be done to improve both the basal program and teachers' application of it, as we shall point out.

The fact that a primary reading program centered around a basal series need not be stereotyped is shown in the existence of a wide variety of such programs. Among these are:

- Using the basal books from the very beginning.
- Using the basic text after initial instruction in teacher-made materials. The basal serves to test the development of skills and for practice in relatively easy material.
- Using the basals in exact consecutive order.
- Using the basals through the primer and then turning to a variety of preprimers from other basal series. Repeating the use of an easier level basal material for extended reading at the conclusion of the first, second, or third reader. There is little difference in final reading achievements, according to some studies, when broad supplementary reading is introduced at any of these levels.
- Centering reading around experience units or interest units with readings selected from a variety of basals and trade books.
- Continuing extensive use of experience stories throughout the primary period, as supplemental to the basals.
- Using basals for the low reading group and, perhaps, for the average but substituting individualized, self-selected reading in the high reading group.
- Allowing pupils of good reading ability to read ahead of their group in the basal and to do independent work in the workbook. Judgment of their progress may be made through small group sessions, the accuracy of their workbook responses, and individual conferences.

The Method in Intermediate Grades

Like the primary teacher, the intermediate-grade teacher frequently supplements the programs with magazines and newspapers, uses the school or public library with her pupils, and employs films or filmstrips a number of times for enrichment purposes, but does not use visual aids of these types that are specifically correlated with the basal series. The teacher gives much less attention to training in word recognition through phonic, context, or picture clues, emphasizing rather the structural analysis of words by syllabication and word parts such as roots and affixes. The average intermediate-grade teacher devotes less time to direct instruction in reading, averaging 6 to 10 hours per week or less, with a larger proportion of this instruction being given to reading in science, social science, and English textbooks. The teacher makes less use of the basal workbooks, although about 60 percent of these classrooms employ this tool every day or two. Teacher-planned exercise materials are used frequently in about one-third of the classrooms, but special workbooks for phonics training are discontinued in most (in about 70 percent). There are apparently conflicting opinions regarding the ways in which the reading program should be expanded in these grades. In about half of the classrooms children are introduced to a book club while at the same time the frequent use of trade books as part of the program increases slightly. This may reflect a tendency to regard recreational reading as an independent type of student activity rather than an integral part of the instructional program. For, actually, the average teacher allows less than an hour per week for library activities and a similar amount for independent reading or enrichment activities.

Dictionaries become a common aid to vocabulary building, and the intermediate-grade child is also introduced to a variety of other reference books, such as encyclopedias, almanacs, and yearbooks. Instruction in reading and study techniques such as outlining, summarizing, preparing book reports, and skimming is begun on a very simple level in the average classroom. However, little attention is given to improving such skills as recognizing bias or propaganda, reading or learning poetry, or choral reading. Oral reading from basals or trade books decreases a great deal, although it is still frequently used in about half of the intermediate-grade classrooms. Locational skills receive much attention, whereas only about half of the teachers give some attention to organizational skills, critical reading, or the use of graphic materials such as maps, charts, and graphs.

The three-reading group plan or, in some schools, the one- or two-group plan strongly persists in these grades despite the fact that the common range of reading abilities is often as great as eight grades or more. The bases for grouping by reading ability continue to be some combination of standardized, criterion-referenced, or informal reading tests, observation, previous reading records, and, sometimes, the result of a group intelligence test. Perhaps at these levels, experimentation with various forms of grouping for reading instruction is more widespread than in the earlier years. Both teachers and administrators may feel freer to modify the program because of the greater maturity of the pupils and their subsequent ability to work more independently for longer periods of time. Thus we find various grouping plans which attempt to solve the problems of class size and individual differences in homogeneous grouping of whole classes by reading ability or intelligence or both. Another effort involves intraclass grouping in which children of similar reading level are drawn from several classes of the same grade level or from several grade levels. These children receive their instruction in one large group and, usually, from some teacher other than their own. The merits of these various grouping ideas will be discussed in a later chapter on classroom organization.

Our View

Despite the absurd claims of some critics of the modern reading program, the average child does grow considerably in breadth and depth of sight and meaning vocabularies. Each intermediate-grade basal introduces the child to another 1200 to 1500 words beyond the primary reading vocabulary, which numbers approximately 2500 words.

Supporters of the basal reading program—a majority among prominent reading authorities—agree on the following advantages of the basal reading program. We may have some reservations about some of these claims, for in the hands of uncreative or uninspired teachers their value may be lost. But these are undoubtedly the outstanding features of the program, at least in the intentions of the authors.

The basal reading series tries to offer:

- Systematic guidance in the development of recognition, comprehension, and vocabulary skills by carefully planned sequential learning. Modern educational psychology tells us that such a system is superior to trial and error or to incidental learning, or, probably, to a program planned by the teacher.
- Materials based upon common child experiences and the well-known interests of children. Thus it provides for a common core of experiences for the entire group.
- A program that is greatly superior to any that an inexperienced teacher, in view of the breadth of professional preparation could possibly create.
- Techniques and materials for determining the readiness of the child to learn to read or to proceed from step to step by easy stages.
- Materials that are carefully scaled in difficulty, sequentially arranged to promote learning, and more or less controlled in vocabulary. Thus the program ensures enjoyable and successful growth of the child's reading abilities. No other available body of reading materials possesses these characteristics.
- Materials that follow the best knowledge in such aspects as typography, format, and physical readability.
- A well-rounded selection of reading experiences. It includes both recreational and work-type reading, poetry and prose, factual and fictional matter, and informational and entertaining materials that extend the child's ideas and knowledge in many fields.

Limitations of the Basal Reader Approach

Readiness Program

In Chapter 7 we raise a number of questions about the validity of the readiness program usually outlined in the basal series. We note the inadequacy of most so-called "readiness tests"—their lack of diagnostic information, their weakness in predicting reading success, their failure to evaluate the really significant readiness factors, and their overdependence upon intelligence and preschool learning as predictive elements. We accuse the basal readiness program of recommending superficial and misleading methods of visual screening and of ignoring the implications of recent research on the importance of visual perception. In addition, the basal readiness program has not succeeded in clarifying the direct association between auditory training and word recognition.

This misconception of the basic theory underlying reading readiness promotes a number of other faulty classroom procedures. As Heilman (23, p. 17) notes, "Teachers rarely withhold basal reading materials from the least ready for more than a few weeks after the rest of the class has started to use them." Thus the entire purpose of readiness activities to prepare children for reading and to facilitate the transition from a nonreading stage to beginning reading is defeated. For many teachers, readiness is simply a kind of workbook activity which happens to be employed prior to formal reading.

Even when teachers do comprehend the intrinsic purpose of readiness training, there is some doubt about the validity of the training materials currently offered. The experiments of Blakely and Shadle (10) agree in implying an inferior validity for common readiness workbooks. Other experiments that we have described on the types of visual perception training materials show no clear superiority for those in readiness workbooks. We have gone beyond the point of accepting the readiness materials common to basal series simply because they seem to give some help to some children. A reorganization of these materials in terms of the optometric and psychological research information now available appears to be demanded, perhaps in the manner offered in Chapters 7 and 8.

Content of the Basals

It is perhaps only human that any venture as widely accepted as the use of basal readers would be criticized by many who have not profited thereby. Moreover, much of the criticism of these books probably can be attributed to those who are simply chronic complainers against the status quo. On the other hand, there is an increasing volume of complaint from a wide variety of sources, even from within the ranks of those who have used or written basal reading materials. It is time that this criticism be listened to and evaluated.

Many of these comments are directed against the manner in which basal readers are used rather than against the basal approach itself. There are some weaknesses in current basal programs to be sure. But most authors of basals have not made the grandiose assumptions of which they are accused. Perhaps their major mistake was in preparing such highly organized bodies of materials that partially trained teachers using the system are incapable of recognizing its weaknesses as well as its strengths.

A primary focus in the criticism of basal readers is upon their content. The remarks of James M. Reid, formerly school editor for Harcourt Brace Jovanovich, made as a result of observations in classrooms and interviews with more than 100 persons concerned with this problem are sharply pertinent (*31*):

> A good many people wince over the lack of style in the writing of basal readers. Lack of a good writing style in itself kills interest. A good style helps to sweep a learner along. "So many of the stories are ridiculous," the pupils themselves say. And there is too much busy work in most of the basal readers. Even casual inspection of the readers reveals that they attempt to be all things to all pupils and rarely touch the hot spots of interest. Perhaps basal readers cannot be made exciting and interesting because of the many restrictions of vocabulary control, repetitions and fear of offending any group—responsibilities they have taken on themselves. But one wonders.
>
> It seems fair to say, however, that today's school readers are too much watered down and do not offer enough challenge to today's good pupils. At the very minimum, the basic reading series have sacrificed too much literary quality to the "necessities" of word control. As the poet Housman wrote, "Terence, this is stupid stuff."

Perhaps these are sharp words, but they are echoed around the country. By a noted child development specialist and author:

> The penalty the child pays for becoming Six is to be fed a two-year-old diet.

By a large number of college teachers of reading (*4*):

> Further changes in basal readers would include an overall upgrading of content so that the material would more nearly coincide with a child's speaking and listening vocabulary at the various stages of his development. In addition, it was pointed out that basal readers in the future should include more material designed to capitalize on boys' interests in the primary grades (p. 66).

From Jack A. Holmes, analyst of the substrata factors underlying reading ability (*25*):

> The basal program is weakest in reinforcing the child's range of information. The series merely repeats the homely concepts of vocabulary already known to the child. The series never stretches the child's mind, never prepares him

for the wide range of information he must know to read, to learn or to deal with the conceptualizations needed for power of reading. The child needs a wider vocabulary in his early reading, as well as more, deeper and wider concepts.

And, finally, from a noted reading consultant and researcher (40):

A growing body of professional opinion points out that we are in danger of producing skillful readers of basal reading series to the detriment of our larger aim. We may be handicapped, in other words, by the very virtues of these series—their carefully controlled vocabulary, their systematic attention to word attack skills developed through familiar words, their provision for spaced practice through basic reader, workbooks, and teacher's manual (p. 459).

British teachers surveyed in 1400 infant schools (primary grades) criticized their reading scheme (program) as dull, with uninteresting content and stilted or unnatural language. In their opinions, good reading systems have good clear print, attractive illustrations, carefully graded vocabulary, and strong repetition of vocabulary.

Over the years, there have been many other criticisms of the content of the average basal reading series from various sources. Among the faults decried are:

1. The distortion of reality of life not by invidious comparisons between cultures and classes but by the almost complete omission of any culture other than that of the upper-middle-class white group. The family is always presented as cheerful, prosperous, cohesive, harmonious, and as a complete unit. Father and mother have separate types of work (if, indeed, women at work are represented at all) and recreation. In fact, no recreational pursuits for women are represented since all are supposed to be very busy mothers, housekeepers, or teachers. Relations among children are friendly, subdued, and cooperative, with no racial interaction or conflict (25).

2. If present at all, blacks do not interact with whites; are engaged in unskilled labor or as servants; look more like suntanned whites than blacks; seldom occupy a major role in a story, and are often set apart from the milieu of the main characters by using dialect to represent their speech (7). The American Indian is only occasionally present, and then as a historical fact from past history rather than a living race. If portrayed in today's settings, the Indian male's activities completely parallel those of his white brothers, unless, of course, he is stereotyped as a chief or medicine man. The Indian woman is conspicuously absent. In fact, there are more animals than nonwhites in some basal series (36).

3. The world of work is unrealistically reflected in a number of respects. Professional and managerial occupations are markedly overrepresented; women are seldom portrayed in a variety of career roles; Asian Americans are

depicted in careers typical of centuries ago or as they might function in countries other than the United States; career roles for other minority groups are stereotyped and extremely limited in number (15).

4. The relative roles of males and females, boys and girls are greatly distorted. Males are main characters three times as often as women and are occupied outside the home four times as often as women, when actually women form more than 40 percent of the working population. Boys are the main characters 70 to 75 percent of the time and are represented as such in more than two-thirds of the illustrations (22). Six times as many occupations are mentioned for males as for women. Father is the family leader, mother, the housekeeper and shopper. In one analysis, in only one of 734 stories was the mother the breadwinner.

It should be noted that most of this criticism of sexism in basal readers is based on surveys of books published prior to the 1970s (18). The authors and publishers of several recent series have certainly been affected by this barrage of critical comments and many are attempting to make appropriate changes in this aspect of the content. It remains to be seen, however, how much real change will appear in the basals of the 1980s and 1990s.

5. The content of the stories in basals is in great contrast to studies of children's actual reading interests. Children prefer stories about pranks, peer interaction, animals, make-believe, nature, and science. Boys prefer boy-activity stories; girls show no sex preferences and would read both boy- and girl-centered tales. The major diet offered by the average basal is child and child-adult interactions, "good children," the activities of six- to seven-year-olds without older brothers and sisters, and too much personal adventure and historical adventure, all of which are low in children's own choices of books.

6. Basal readers are commonly lavishly illustrated with expensive four-color pictures. The use of color actually adds little or nothing to recall of information over black and white, nor does it have any interaction with race or economic status. But it does contribute substantially to the cost of the book. Pictures do help in initial learning, if they are also present in posttesting. But when pictures are omitted from the test, a group taught without pictures was superior. Pictures used in initial word recognition training should be dispensed with as soon as possible, particularly for poorer readers. In terms of comprehension, illustrations highly relevant to the text are helpful when students are reading materials well within their reading level, but not in difficult material. In the final analysis, the value of illustrations depends heavily upon the manner in which they are used to support the concepts underlying the vocabulary of the story by the pupils under teacher guidance.

7. Helen N. Rudie's study of poetry in basal readers confirms the criticism that this area of literature is not always adequately represented. Among eleven series examined, Rudie found that three had *no poetry at all*, although they did recommend that the teacher should provide poetry experience. In the

other eight series, one or two poems at least were presented in each unit of material. Rudie judged the quality of the poetry selections to be good and well illustrated in most instances (35).

The content of the basal reader has been criticized not only for these faults but also for its failure to provide an adequate foundation for the reading tasks of the content fields. Training in the reading of such materials as maps, charts, diagrams, and arithmetic problems is lacking in most basal series. Library skills—the proper use of reference materials, encyclopedias, almanacs, and the like—are hardly touched upon. Such organizing skills as summarizing, notetaking, and outlining are taught at so simple a level that they fail to function in the pupil's postelementary school life. The whole art of studying textbooks of various types and kinds with their varying demands for different rates of reading and degrees and types of comprehension is almost ignored. Similarly, because of the lack of training with samples of science, social science, natural history, and mathematical materials, the pupil is not helped to differentiate the kinds of thinking demanded and the varying purposes inherent in these materials, and to make the constant readjustments needed.

Some basal authors would probably answer these criticisms by pointing out that their series do not intend to supply training in applied reading in the content fields. They argue that this type of preparatory training is not a fundamental goal of the basal program but should be accomplished during classroom use of the content textbooks. The basal program, its authors say, cannot be expected to supply complete training in all aspects of the reading program—namely, in content field skills and in recreational reading. Its task is to supply the impetus for the development of what are called basic reading skills. This is perhaps a reasonable defense, but in our opinion it has one weakness. What skills are more basic for future academic success than training in content field reading?

The nature of the content of basals is not peculiar to the United States, however, for surveys of foreign beginning books give much the same picture. One analysis of the readers of seventeen countries found that their greatest emphasis was upon family life; happy child–child and child–family relationships; and love, joy, and respect for parents. The patriotic theme, so strongly stressed during the crisis of World War II, has disappeared in most European readers, except in the Soviet Union. A few emphasize their cultural heritage through legends, folk tales, and similar content, or through religious themes.

The Basal Workbook

The actual contribution of workbooks to reading achievement is more apparent in the minds of their authors and classroom teachers than it is in the relevant research studies. Two articles report a study in Los Angeles in thirty-six classes in eighteen schools comparing reading scores under instruction with workbooks versus those with teacher-made materials (*10, 13*). The basal workbook produced better vocabulary and comprehension scores in the second and third grades, on the average, and better comprehension in the fourth grade. In fifth and sixth grades there were no differences in reading skills with or without workbooks. In the first grade, as other studies also indicate, the nonworkbook classes were superior in both reading skills. When these studies are read carefully, however, most of the teachers did not like to prepare their own materials, including those who had to for the purposes of the experiment.

There is obviously truth on both sides of this question, for the crux of the matter is the way in which workbooks are used rather than the way they are constructed. For example, intelligent use would include varying amounts of teacher–pupil planning for the exercises and their evaluation. The true values cannot be achieved by routine, page-by-page use by all pupils. Rather, by using a variety of workbooks that are disassembled and rearranged according to the skills stressed in a teacher-planned box, and are labeled for ready use by pupils, the ultimate values of such materials for diagnosis, enrichment, or reinforcement may be secured.

Teachers' comments and experts' opinions regarding workbooks have been sampled in a number of studies, including those mentioned above. The strengths and weaknesses of these tools, as seen by their users and critics, are summarized next.

Methods in the Basal System

The Far West Laboratory for Educational Research conducted a study of the time spent doing various activities during reading instruction. They attempted to determine the "learning time" per day, or in other words, how long students work with materials suitable in difficulty for their reading abilities. The Laboratory estimated that about 50 percent of the time devoted to reading is learning time. When students had 52 minutes of learning time per day they increased their reading scores greatly. When the learning time was decreased by lack of attention to the task or by the use of inappropriate reading materials, the children's test scores fell far below the norm (*21*).

The study also provided data on the relative number of minutes spent doing various reading activities for two fifth-grade classes over a 90-day period. The two classes were fairly similar in time spent on word attack skills, verbatim comprehension and word meanings, and distinguishing fact and opinion in comprehension. But one class (Class A) spent as much as three to seven times as much time on paraphrasing, inferences, identifying main ideas, and other types of comprehension as did Class B. In the totals, one fifth-grade teacher of Class A spent more than four times as much instructional time on comprehension as did the teacher of Class B. The only type of comprehension stressed by the teacher of Class B was verbatim recall! Instruction in word at-

Evaluation of the basal reader workbook and basal management systems

STRENGTHS

1. Stress sequential learning, help develop skills.
2. Help to overcome effects of child absence.
3. Aid in diagnosing difficulties.
4. Help test achievement.
5. Offer opportunity for self-competition.
6. Provide record of progress.
7. Are more easily checked or graded.
8. Save teacher time for preparation.
9. Are prepared by skilled persons.
10. Provide for extensive, effective drill.
11. Permit pupil check on own progress.
12. Provide follow-up activities related to content of text.
13. Reinforce learning through repetition of vocabulary.

WEAKNESSES

1. Are boringly factual.
2. Are limited in variety of materials (little science, geography, or human relations).
3. Reflective thinking is sacrificed to unimportant objective responses (circles, lines, etc.).
4. Emphasize mechanics; word recognition more often than comprehension.
5. Often too hard for lower third of class, yet lacking in challenge for superior pupils.
6. Require much teacher time for checking, follow-up, and supervision.
7. May monopolize classroom time and leave none for creative activities.
8. Not conducive to independent work habits.
9. Poor in training of locational and organizing skills.
10. Often lacking in clarity of directions and in adequate explanation of purpose.
11. Tend to breed dependence on teacher.
12. Offer monotonous, piecemeal approach.
13. Disregard individual needs in attempting to provide material suitable to all.
14. Develop skills in isolation from the reading act, yet assume transfer.
15. Induce teachers to use in stereotyped, consecutive order.

tack skills in both classes seemed hardly adequate, for it occupied only 2 to 3 percent of the total instructional time.

Oral versus silent reading provided some striking contrasts. Class A devoted three times as much time to oral reading as did Class B, a seeming contradiction to their respective emphasis upon comprehension. Apparently, the teacher of Class A, who gave so much time to comprehension, believed that oral reading promoted that ability. There was very little difference in the attention to study skill training, the comparison being 1 or 2 percent. Yet the teacher of Class B spent four times as much class time with silent reading and reading in the content fields as the teacher of Class A, but without any real effort to improve the children's reading in these areas.

These comparisons illustrate the conflict between some teachers' concepts of the reading process and their instructional practices. The teacher who gave more time to comprehension gave students very little chance for application in silent reading and content areas. The teacher who gave little emphasis to comprehension encouraged more silent reading and work in the content areas, but without teacher direction.

In many schools, teachers employing the basal approach develop undesirable practices—for example, rigid structuring of three reading groups and excessive use of oral reading. These patterns are not necessarily suggested in the teachers' manuals nor are they inherent in the basal approach. But somehow a large proportion of teachers gravitate toward these habits.

A recent study of the content of teachers' manuals emphasized the current interest in comprehension instruction. An analysis of the manuals from four basal series found many fewer suggestions regarding comprehension than reviewing, application, assessment, and practice. The author concluded that the relationship between instruction and how to read is almost absent in present-day basal reader manuals (*14*).

Grouping

There is nothing unsound in the practice of grouping children for instruction. On the contrary, grouping economizes a teacher's planning and teaching time, fosters an *esprit* or group spirit among pupils, enables the teacher to work more intimately with a part of the class, and thus helps him to meet pupils' instructional needs. But in many classrooms there seems to be a belief in the magic of the number 3—three reading levels among the pupils, three reading groups, three levels of basal readers.

As we pointed out earlier, the average classroom above the first grade very likely has a greater range of reading levels than three grades. In fact, the higher the grade level, the greater the range of reading levels is apt to be. While the content of a second-grade basal reader may be reasonably suitable for a slow third-grade reading group, its structure and skill development may not be feasible for all the members of such a group. The slow reading group probably includes some pupils who read appropriately in high first-grade materials, as well as others who can perform adequately in beginning or high second-grade materials. If this range of ability is present, no one level of basal reader will suffice for all members of the group. First- and second-grade basal readers differ significantly in the rate of introduction of new words; the total number of different words; their demands for skill in phonic, structural, and contextual analysis; the complexity of the sentence patterns; the variety of alternative meanings of common words; and their assumptions about the children's experiential backgrounds. The pupils reading at the first-grade level and those at the second-grade level differ in these traits. Therefore, we conclude that the use of three reading groups using three levels of readers is not a satisfactory solution to the range of reading differences, particularly in the primary grades.

A survey of the reading practices in the six New England states indicates that over two-thirds of teachers group within the classroom on the basis of general instructional level, not individual needs. The placement of pupils is determined by their needs for specific skills in only 22 percent of the classes. Individualized instruction is used in only a minute proportion of classrooms. Grouping is commonly based, in order of frequency of use, on the previous book completed, skills tests, basal reader tests, and informal reading inventories. More than 70 percent of teachers in the New England area used one or several of these criteria in forming reading groups. This practice contrasts sharply with the expressed belief of the same teachers that informal inventories and skills tests were the more reliable instruments for the purpose.

The social effects of this magical use of 3's have other subtle effects upon pupil–teacher relationships and pupil self-concept. Teacher practices in grouping some 600 children were analyzed in terms of the pupils that the teachers preferred to teach (36). It became quite apparent that they preferred working with the better students, both boys and girls, in the top reading group. Poorer readers ranked lower in teacher preference, and thus tended to receive the least positive, inspiring lessons, despite their greater needs. These pupils soon become aware of the teacher's attitude, and their feelings of rejection and inadequacy are reinforced.

Perhaps the most significant social implication of the failure of the three-reading-group plan is its inadequacy for the training of superior or gifted children. Some experts deplore the tendency to underestimate gifted pupils' capabilities and needs for opportunities to do research reading, to develop reading maturity, and to find stimulating, challenging situations in reading (3). Another study adds strength to this criticism. The investigation suggests that most superior readers do not need basals to achieve desired reading skills, although some certainly need directed, planned training to achieve their full potentials. Other articles reinforce this criticism of basals by pointing out the special reading problems of gifted children that are not met by the three-reading-group plan.

In our opinion, the entire concept of grouping children by reading levels is often based upon a false premise—that the results of an informal or standardized reading test reflect an accurate, overall picture of a child's reading abilities. Even at the primary reading levels, where differentiation of various reading skills is less, the average formal or informal reading test may yield only a superficial classification of pupils. The reading test usually completely ignores such highly significant determinants of pupil progress as the rate at which the child can learn new vocabulary; the effectiveness of her structural, phonic, and contextual word analysis skills; the breadth of her sight vocabulary; the depth and efficiency of her comprehension; and the quality of her comprehension when she is reading at different rates of speed. The reading test upon which grouping is based almost never yields such essential information as the extent of the child's dependence upon sheer memory for acquiring sight vocabulary, as contrasted with her use of other perceptual or analytic clues; the depth of her meaning vocabulary and her needs in experiential background as a foundation for multiplicity of meanings; the types of reading materials which appeal strongly to her; her efficiency in using reading as a tool to satisfy academic demands or personal and social needs. Furthermore, reading tests do not predict individual variations in the learning process such as spurts, plateaus, periods of acceleration, consolidation, or regression, which ultimately determine the nature of the pupil's progress. Nor do they usually yield information regarding the reasons for any of a number of reading difficulties.

The most disconcerting truth about commercial reading tests, in general, is that they do not reflect the actual level of the reading materials that the pupil can handle most effectively. This level or, more accurately, these levels of efficiency are determined by the constellation of the very reading skills that most tests fail to consider. Perhaps the words of psychologist Grace Arthur may be appropriate to this critical evaluation of grouping practices in the basal system (2, p. vii):

> Group instruction presupposes similar intellectual needs among the members of the group to be taught. In order to profit from the instruction, all the members of the group must be ready to start at about the same point, be interested in the same type of material, and be able to learn by means of the same general methods.

Does the three-reading-group plan meet Arthur's criteria for group instruction or, indeed, any of the criteria we have suggested? Or it might be more truthful to say, as Heilman does (23, pp. 74–75):

> The curriculum of the school rests on the premise that children in a given classroom read at or near a particular level. Once the curriculum and graded reading materials have been determined, the tendency is to try to fit the learner to the materials. It is much easier to cling to an original false premise than it is to revise the curriculum and the grade level system to fit the facts of learner variability.

Some observers feel that while the teacher is engaged with a particular group, much time is wasted in the unsupervised groups. This apparent loss of efficiency may be due to the lack of maturity, or of training of the pupils in self-direction, or because of the omission of clear-cut directions by the teacher. Many teachers and pupils seem to believe that the oral reading done in the circle group is not only an essential procedure, but also the only true reading experience of the day. Perhaps this assumption explains the average teacher's lack of real concern about the learning value of the activities in which other groups engage (as shown by the rather casual planning of these supplementary activities).

The busywork of the unsupervised groups is seldom planned in detail by the joint action of the teacher and individual students or groups. The child's concepts of what he is trying to do, or exactly what he is supposed to be learning, are often quite vague. Most often he is not expected to maintain any records of his progress in a skill or of his independent reading. Nor is he given any means of self-evaluation of such progress. As some critics say, it appears that the teacher's only concern during this rather extended period of time is that the other groups keep themselves busy and quiet.

These descriptive generalizations regarding the ways in which group instruction functions in the daily basal reading lesson reflect, of course, the authors' interpretation of their firsthand observations in many classrooms. Certainly some teachers plan their groups' work more efficiently than this. On the other hand, others do not even pretend to divide their classes into groups. We have seen schools in a number of states where the use of a single reader for the entire class was not an isolated practice but common in every classroom in the system.

As we have admitted earlier, many of the criticisms of the basal reading program are really leveled at teacher practice more than at the series of books itself. At the same time, it must be recognized that some of these faulty practices are in a sense promoted by the nature of the system, and sometimes more directly by the authors. First, the very title of a basal reading series carries the implication that the material is almost absolutely essential for practically all children. Second, no series has ever attempted to provide for the actual range of reading levels within the average classroom, despite the fact that even authors of basals recognize this range. Some authors perpetuate the illusion that this range can be dealt with by using a three- or four-grade span of their readers, thus supporting the three-group practice. Although the manuals often speak of independent reading, and may even list some appropriate books, are these ever recommended as possible substitutes for the basal? How often is a teacher advised in the manuals to skip a portion of the reader with an advanced or rapidly learning group? Where is the suggestion that some of the children in almost any classroom need not read faithfully through a basal series story by story?[1]

Oral Reading

Oral reading, in the basal reader program, has developed a number of most undesirable aspects which are supported and abetted by the very nature of the basal series. We know of no manual for a basal series which suggests these practices, but believe they are a logical outcome of the overemphasis upon the importance of the basic vocabulary. One of these faulty practices is the round-robin or circle reading seen in most of today's classrooms. A reading group assembles in a semicircle around the teacher and the children take turns reading aloud to the group. All the children use the same book and attempt to follow silently as each pupil reads orally in turn. About the only real purpose for this practice is to permit the teacher to observe the accuracy with which each pupil reads the words of the text.

At worst, this practice violates the known fact that both oral reading and comprehension are superior when silent reading of a selection precedes oral. The relevant research indicates that this circle reading is probably one of the most effective devices yet discovered for practicing poor reading. What literally happens in this almost universal technique is that the listeners are forced to attempt to follow and imitate the halting reading of the leader. As a result, as Gilbert has shown, the children's reading performances are worse when reading in the circle than they would normally be (*17*). All the legitimate purposes of oral reading, which we will discuss in a subsequent chapter, are violated in the round-robin act.

Other critics of this practice point out that this faulty oral reading does not contribute to reading development, contrary to most teachers' assumptions. Oral reading, as commonly practiced in the basal program, is really a word-calling rather than a thought-getting process. In fact, its excessive use may well retard the development of good silent reading habits, which are the real goal of all reading instruction. Despite these pointed criticisms, this type of oral reading continues to be practiced, perhaps because it makes so little demand upon teacher planning.

Oral reading may have values in the reading program if it is conceived of as a communication skill—a way of delivering information or entertainment to listeners. If this view prevails, each act of oral reading must be planned for a specific purpose: sharing materials, proving a point, clarifying an idea, presenting a play or a poem, or for some other purpose. In this view, the listener must be prepared for the oral reading so she may realize its purpose, and the reader must be rehearsed so that she may be maximally effective. Constructive listening purposes will be clarified to the audience, discussion by them will be encouraged, and if information is the desired result, the questions will be addressed to the listeners, not to the reader. Within this framework of its function as a communication skill, oral reading is an essential part of the program.

Word Attack Skills

Areas of sharp debate regarding the basal reading system have been its success and methods in teaching effective word attack skills. The system has been criticized for failing to teach phonic skills, for promoting sheer guessing as the sole method of word recognition, for overdependence upon a visual or sight-word method, and for teaching practices which actually rob children of the opportunity of using the word attack skills that they have been taught or that they have developed spontaneously.

As we have pointed out, the bases for some of these criticisms are not only ill-founded and, in some cases, absurd, but they may also arise from personal rather than objective reasons. On the other hand, there are serious flaws in the basal program of word attack skills. Betts says (*8*):

Today there are too many first-grade classrooms in which the so-called "word method" of teaching *beginning* reading is used. When this so-called method is stripped of its "pedaguese," including the term sight words, it is merely a tell-the-child-the-word procedure. And telling isn't teaching! The word method, therefore, is a nothing-for-nothing proposition, emphasizing rote learning.

If words present in the material to be read are probably unknown to most of the pupils, previewing their meanings will certainly aid comprehension. The purpose of the preview is to foster understanding of the new words and hence of the reading material, and not just to add these words to the pupils' sight vocabulary.

The steps usually recommended in the manuals were mentioned earlier in our description of the typical basal reading lesson. However, we often see teachers abbreviate this preview. They seem more concerned with the correct decoding and pronunciation in oral reading than whether the meanings of the words are thoroughly understood. Some teachers don't bother to try to relate these meanings to the children's experiences and information (*schemata*, as they are now called). The amount of discussion of the children's relevant knowledge is subordinated to decoding and pronunciation practice in some classrooms. Such teachers are satisfied to begin the reading if the children can say the new word more or less as the teacher does.

In contrast, MacKinnon demonstrated that when primary school children were permitted complete independence of the teacher, they developed a high degree of word attack skill (28). In his experiment children in one group were never told a new word before they attempted the reading material, nor were they prompted by the teacher during the reading. Rather, they were constantly urged to attempt to recognize the word by their own efforts at structural, contextual, or phonic analysis. The result was that the children evolved a remarkable degree of independence and spontaneous word attack skill.

Beck, et al. analyzed two leading basal reading programs, the Houghton Mifflin program and the Ginn 720 (7). These authors were particularly interested in the purpose-setting directions given children, usually before their reading. They found misdirections that asked the children to search for information that wasn't in the story; that provided leads that conflicted with the theme of the text; or that established a line of reasoning that did not match the intent of the text. Other such directions were too narrow, thus inducing the recall of unimportant details; gave away the information that should be sought for in the text; focused on too small a portion of the story as in the beginning or end; or asked for some detail that was answered in the title or could be found by reading only a few paragraphs.

As we shall point out in our treatment of word attack skills, the basal system does appear to offer sequential training in word attack. But this program is sometimes introduced too late, divorced from its functional application to the act of reading, poorly related to the relevant research, dictated by the vagaries of the basal author's beliefs, and finally, taught by teachers who are woefully weak in their understanding and personal practice of good word attack skills. Certainly some new approach to these problems inherent in the basal approach seems indicated.

The later discussion of the primary and intermediate reading programs will point out possible improvements in classroom practices. It will offer specific suggestions for overcoming the inherent limitations of the basal readers and the current practices in grouping and oral reading.

Improving the Basal Program

In a second Carnegie study, Mary C. Austin and Coleman Morrison sent out questionnaires about reading programs to over 1000 school systems (5). Later these authors and their staff visited approximately 1800 classrooms in fifty-one communities throughout the United States. Some of their forty-five recommendations for the improvement of current reading programs appear to agree with our observations regarding the limitations of the basal program. They suggest:

- That schools should reassess current readiness programs by research efforts to determine the values of these programs for reading success.
- That greater emphasis must be placed on promoting comprehension rather than word calling in the reading act.
- That the oral reading circle be largely replaced by more functional oral reading practices.
- That teachers be trained in more intelligent use of basal readers.
- That the contents of basals should be carefully studied for the purpose of determining any need for their change.
- That teachers should be led to realize that basal manuals are to be regarded as guides or aids rather than prescriptions.
- That current uses of workbooks must be examined to determine whether they can be employed more constructively or should be abandoned.
- That flexible grouping determined by the nature and activities of the program be substituted for the three-group practice.

As we have noted earlier, authors and publishers of basal books have responded to criticisms by making major modifications in their most recent editions. Among some of the changes are increases in the vocabulary taught at each level; greater diversity of story material; deemphasis upon stereotyped middle-class settings and characters; greater emphasis upon earlier and stronger phonics programs; and provision for separate basal readers, games, and other materials at each grade level for children of high-, average-, or low-achievement levels.

More science materials have been added, even at primary-grade levels; stories with definitely masculine appeal are being featured; settings include apartment houses, trailers, and a variety of family backgrounds in addition to the little white house with the white fence around it; greater use is being made of stories drawn from good children's literature, and professional writers for children are lending their skills to the basal reading program. Other modifications are the inclusion of new aids, such as ditto masters, filmstrips, recordings and cassettes, programmed supplementary materials, and packages or kits of supplementary reading materials, rather than just listing aids, and a greater emphasis upon writing in the workbooks.

In choosing selections for the readers, the best of the minority literature by black, Indian, Mexican-American, and other such authors is also being introduced. Stories of urban, ghetto life as it really is are beginning to appear in our books. There is some evidence that use of this multiethnic material can help reduce the racial prejudice so common in our society. Children's attitudes toward other races do tend to improve as they gain information about the similarities and differences among groups. However, one author objects strenuously, and with merit, to our depicting the sordid life experiences of ghetto children as a perpetuation of the middle-class stereotyped concept of other children. Another investigator found that slum children preferred the usual family–pets–friends theme of basals to those in urban, multiethnic settings. Other analyses of the available multiethnic readers indicate that they fail both in illustrations and story line to convey the picture of a racially mixed, community-centered society, but are still overemphasizing young children in a family-centered theme. There are certainly still problems to be solved in these attempts to have our readers truly representative of American society.

Finally, by examining the current crop of basals we see a real recognition of the need for more mature, less repetitive language usage. No longer are primary children judged incapable of reading such structures as complex sentences, contractions, direct quotations, and the like (even though they speak in such terms). The manuals accompanying some basal series recognize this trend and aid teachers in providing a wide variety of experiences with sentence patterns and structures in keeping with a child's own language development.

Publishers and authors of basal reading systems have responded strongly to the widespread criticisms of sexism, racism, and lack of representation of minorities or the handicapped. Other improvements noted in recent basals are more training in study strategies, particularly at intermediate grades; more explanation of the structure of expository materials, such as the placement of main ideas in various types of paragraphs; and greater emphasis upon reading for enjoyment and more adaptations from trade or children's books.

Publishers and authors are paying careful attention to stories and characters representing the wide variety of races in the United States; to selections portraying women and girls in many different successful occupations and activities; to instructional materials such as supplementary kits that promote language development through listening, speaking, and writing; and to avoiding selections that present stereotyped concepts of other cultures.

Our View

In all fairness to the authors of basal readers, we must recognize the fact that they are "walking on eggs" when they attempt to include any material that may be controversial to some pressure groups. They dare not include content on one particular religion, culture, or political belief. To do so would at least bring action prohibiting the sale of the books in some areas of the country, if not a lawsuit. Many schools have been attacked by individuals or groups who want to censor the content of textbooks. These pressures are affecting the efforts of basal authors and publishers.

The Basal Versus Other Approaches

Several years ago, an invitation was offered by the Office of Education, Cooperative Research Branch, for the submission of proposed studies of the effectiveness of various instructional approaches in the first grade. Twenty-seven such studies were finally approved and completed. Many of these studies were comparisons among such methods as the basal program, Initial Teaching Alphabet (ITA), the language experience, and the linguistic and phonic systems. Fuller details of certain of the studies and their outcomes are presented in a later chapter.

It is pertinent to review briefly the results of the studies in which the basal method was one of the techniques employed. Fifteen of the first-grade projects used the basal and some other approach as experimental treatments. In all, five instructional systems were compared with the basal in typical populations.

The significance of the conclusions based on these studies may be judged by the quality of the research plans and the size of the populations involved. The entire plan for parallel research in tests—background data on pupils, schools, and teachers; evaluation of outcomes; control of pupil and teacher selection; and the other relevant variables—was evolved in a series of meetings of the project directors with the Coordinating Center at the University of Minnesota. Furthermore, to improve the values of the individual studies, it was agreed that method comparisons would involve at least twenty experimental and twenty control classes, about 1000 pupils in each study.

Combining the results of fifteen of the first-grade studies permits large-scale comparisons of five variations in reading methods.

Basal versus other approaches

BASAL VERSUS ITA

ITA was in most studies an American version of a British teaching scheme. A new alphabet that offered one symbol (letter or ligature) for each sound in our language was created, and primary reading materials were prepared in this system. The goal was to simplify learning to read by using this consistent grapheme–phoneme arrangement. The system has almost disappeared from the American school. It did not accomplish its goals because, in the American version, it placed too much emphasis upon letter–sound correspondence and used the simplified alphabet for only the first year.

Comparison with the contemporary basal systems gave no significant differences in tests of comprehension or accuracy or rate of oral reading. The ITA did produce superior scores in word-naming in three such tests, but in only one out of four studies in spelling.

BASAL VERSUS BASAL PLUS PHONICS

The basal plus phonics approach, when compared with basal alone, produced superior achievement in comprehension and word recognition, but not in rate or accuracy of oral reading. The actual differences were hardly educationally significant, averaging one or two months in achievement in a school year.

BASAL VERSUS LANGUAGE EXPERIENCE

Pupils taught by the language experience method tended to test superior in word recognition and comprehension and vocabulary, but the differences varied considerably from one study to the next. As explained in Chapter 5, this inconsistency may have been due to variations in the nature of the instruction under different directors.

BASAL VERSUS LINGUISTIC SYSTEMS

Linguistic systems of teaching reading are described in Chapter 4. Linguistic groups tended to be superior in word recognition, whereas basal groups were superior in speed and accuracy of reading. There were no real differences in measures of comprehension.

BASAL VERSUS LIPPINCOTT

The Lippincott basal reading series placed stronger emphasis upon decoding than other basal systems. A much larger vocabulary than common was used, and was justified in the minds of the authors and publishers

(continued)

by the letter–sound emphasis. Lippincott groups tended to be superior in word reading, comprehension, spelling and phonic skills, but not in rate or accuracy of oral reading. In only one of the three studies were these differences educationally meaningful. In the other two, the differences were as small as one month or less in a school year.

The general conclusion that may be drawn from this general review of the first-grade reading studies is that no one method seemed consistently superior to any other method. Some methods did yield higher test scores in certain skills, as the basal plus phonics or the Lippincott, but the differences were hardly educationally significant. There may have been other differences among these methods with respect to their effect upon boys or girls, on breadth of reading, on pupils of varying mental ability, and on attitudes toward reading that may be just as significant as the test scores. We will consider these other details in a later chapter.

Subsequently, the reports of the second year of some of these studies were released. Ten studies were concerned with normal pupil populations in the second grade of school who were studied in the original first-grade studies. Some of the same types of comparison between methods could be made from the results of these follow-up studies:

BASAL VERSUS ITA

The ITA groups were superior in word recognition skills and spelling, but not in comprehension, rate or accuracy of oral reading, language usage, or mechanics of writing.

BASAL VERSUS LANGUAGE EXPERIENCE

There were no real differences in spelling, word study skills, comprehension, or word recognition. There was some tendency for the language experience pupils to write longer stories with more varied vocabulary, as a result of their writing activities.

BASAL VERSUS LINGUISTIC SYSTEMS

In some projects, linguistic pupils scored higher in word recognition, but in other projects there were no such differences. No differences were found in comprehension in any project. Basal pupils generally scored higher in phonic skills.

BASAL VERSUS LIPPINCOTT

Lippincott pupils tended to achieve higher in reading, spelling, and general language ability, but these differences were not educationally significant.

READING PRACTICES CURRENTLY IN USE

Our View

If we were to believe, as some language specialists say, that a pupil's major task is to develop graphemic symbols into sounds, and by so decoding words he will understand their meaning, then the various teaching systems emphasizing sound–symbol relationships seem quite effective. The ITA, Lippincott, and linguistic programs do appear to produce generally greater skill in word recognition (although they do not necessarily produce better phonic skills). But this superiority in word recognition does not produce greater comprehension, or wider reading experience, or greater liking for reading—all of which are presumably primary goals of any good reading program. Nor do these systems consistently effect any superiority in the mechanics, fluency, or depth of children's writing and speaking abilities. It still remains to be seen whether a teaching system which emphasizes letter sounds as one of its major goals can do more than produce fluent word-callers. Can such systems really produce fluent, comprehending readers, as well as the basal system does? Can they provide the breadth of reading and writing experience that the basal or language experience approaches offer? Finally, we see that these letter–sound systems are often more effective than the basal with the brighter pupils and sometimes less effective with below-average pupils. Perhaps their proper future role in the reading program is as an adjunct to certain current practices, rather than as an approach offered for the instruction of all or even most pupils.

Management Systems and Basals

In a later chapter on technology in reading, we have critiqued management systems in general. But basal authors are adding to their programs what amount to their versions of management systems. Hence it is appropriate in this discussion of the basal system to react to this trend.

Programmed instruction and management systems are based on a detailed analysis of the reading act. Each step, as the authors identify it, is constantly reinforced and arranged for self-pacing. The systems are so detailed that the instructor need not know much about reading, because the system is so "complete." Some teachers are amazed at the intricacy of the steps which management systems authors find in the reading process. The claim is made that the nature of the material makes the most efficient use of pupil and teacher time by providing a wealth of specific tasks, frequent testing, and detailed assessments of pupil performance in the tasks.

These are the claims of the management systems authors, and now of basal authors who add such systems to their reading programs. Although both behavioristic and humanistic approaches to education are concerned with the issue of learning to read, there is strong disagreement on the appropriate techniques. The behavioristic tradition is built on animal study and laboratory experiments which, in the opinion of the humanists, ignore the social sources of human motivation. Humanists want to understand the human needs served by learning to read. In contrast, behaviorists wish to identify only what is to be learned and how the learner must be shaped toward that goal. The idea of manipulating humans and shaping their behavior for scientific purposes is abhorrent to humanists.[2]

Some believe that management systems give teachers a deeper understanding of the reading process, and that the worksheets offer supplementary practice in those elements of reading that form a hierarchy of skills, such as decoding. If we accept the skills theory of reading, these beliefs are tenable, and the management systems will then be helpful in the hands of a skills-oriented teacher—if such a teacher selects carefully in terms of student needs—and not just because the drill is present in the management system. An intelligent, selective use of a management system is, however, very difficult to implement because of the inherent implication that all the skills offered are essential.

Endnotes

1. See "Do Teachers Create Reading Problems?" in Spache, George D., *Investigating the Issues in Reading Disabilities.* Boston: Allyn and Bacon, 1976.
2. Blackford, Jean S., "A Teacher Views Criterion-Referenced Tests," *Today's Education,* 64 (March–April 1975), 36; Johnson, Dale D., and Pearson, P. David, "Skills Management Systems: A Critique," *Reading Teacher,* 28 (May 1975), 757–764.

Discussion Questions

1. What recent changes in basals are mentioned in this chapter? How would you explain these changes?

2. Discuss the question: Must beginning teachers use the basal reader approach because of their inexperience in teaching?

3. What defenses or criticisms of the basal reader can you offer based on your own experience?

4. What improvements in basals and basal reading instruction are essential if they are to deal realistically with individual pupil differences?

5. Discuss grouping practices in the average basal reading program, and suggest improvements.

6. For what types of pupils, under what circumstances, do you think basal readers might be the best possible program?

7. Answer the following questions after analyzing the teacher's guide for any basal reader available to you.

a. What provisions do you find for individual differences according to reading levels?

b. What resources, other than the workbook, are offered to aid in teaching skills?

c. What suggestions are given to aid the application of reading skills in independent work?

d. What are the steps of the typical reading lesson? Defend or criticize this arrangement.

8. Using the following guidelines, analyze the workbook accompanying a basal reader

a. for variety and depth of questioning used.

b. for provision for individual differences in pupils' need for skill training.

c. for relevance of workbook exercises to the content of the reader.

d. for the workbook's values in diagnosing pupil needs.

9. Visit a classroom in which the basal approach is being used. This will enable you to answer questions 7 and 8 more intelligently and accurately.

References

1. Alpert, Judith L., "Do Teachers Adapt Methods and Materials to Ability Groups in Reading?" *California Journal of Educational Research*, 26 (May 1975), 120–123.

2. Arthur, Grace, *Tutoring as Therapy*. New York: Commonwealth Fund, 1946.

3. Artley, A. Sterl, "Some Musts Ahead in Teaching Reading," *Reading for Today's Children*, Thirty-Fourth Yearbook. Washington, D.C.: Department of Elementary School Principals, National Education Association, 1955.

4. Austin, Mary C., et al., *The Torch Lighters: Tomorrow's Teachers of Reading*. Cambridge, Mass.: Harvard University Press, 1961, 66.

5. Austin, Mary C. and Coleman, Morrison, *The First R*. New York: Macmillan, 1963.

6. Barnard, Douglas F., and De Gracie, James, "Vocabulary Analysis of New Primary Reading Series," *Reading Teacher*, 30 (November 1976), 177–180.

7. Beck, Isabel L., McCaslin, Ellen S., and Mckeown, Margaret S., "Basal Readers' Purpose for Story Reading: Smoothly Paving the Road or Setting up a Detour?" *Elementary School Journal*, 81 (January 1981), 156–162.

8. Betts, Emmett A., "How Well Are We Teaching Reading?" *Elementary English*, 38 (October 1961), 377–381.

9. Black, Millard H., and Whitehorse, La Von Harper, "Reinforcing Reading Skills Through Workbooks," *Reading Teacher*, 15 (September 1961), 19–24.

10. Blakely, W. Paul, and Shadle, Erma M., "A Study of Two Readiness-for-Reading Programs in Kindergarten," *Elementary English*, 38 (November 1961), 502–505.

11. Bond, Guy L., and Dykstra, Robert, "The Cooperative Research Program in First-Grade Reading," *Reading Research Quarterly*, 2 (Summer 1967), 5–142.

12. Bond, Guy L., and Tinker, Miles A., *Reading Difficulties—Their Diagnosis and Correction*. New York: Macmillan, 1967.

13. Doctor, Robert L., "Reading Workbooks: Boon or Busywork?" *Elementary English*, 39 (March 1962), 224–228.

14. Durkin, Dolores, "Reading Comprehension Instruction in Four Basal Reader Series," *Reading Research Quarterly*, 16 (1981), 515–544.
15. Gates, Arthur I., "Vocabulary Control in Basal Reading Material," *Reading Teacher*, 15 (November 1961), 81–85.
16. Gates, Arthur I., "The Word Recognition Ability and the Reading Vocabulary of Second and Third-Grade Children," *Reading Teacher*, 15 (May 1962), 443–448.
17. Gilbert, Luther C., "The Effect Upon Silent Reading of Attempting to Follow Oral Reading," *Elementary School Journal*, 40 (April 1940), 614–621.
18. Greenfield, C. S., Greenlinger, S., and Lessen, Elliott L., "A Cross-Referenced Index for Choosing Reading Materials by Reading Levels," *Reading Teacher*, 33 (November 1979), 179–197.
19. Groff, Patrick J., "A Survey of Basal Reading Grouping Practices," *Reading Teacher*, 15 (January 1962), 232–238.
20. Groff, Patrick J., "The Problem of Vocabulary Load in Individualized Reading," *Reading Teacher*, 14 (January 1961), 188–190.
21. Guthrie, John T., "Time in Reading Programs," *Reading Teacher*, 33 (January 1980), 500–502.
22. Habecker, James E., "How Can We Improve Basic Readers?" *Elementary English*, 36 (December 1959), 560–563.
23. Heilman, Arthur W., *Principles and Practices of Teaching Reading*. Columbus, Ohio: Charles E. Merrill, 1977.
24. Hiebert, Elfrieda H., "An Examination of Ability Grouping for Reading Instruction," *Reading Research Quarterly*, 18 (Winter 1983), 231–255.
25. Holmes, Jack, in "Symposium on Viewpoints on Comprehension," in *Eleventh Yearbook*, National Reading Conference, 1961.
26. Jorgenson, Gerald W., "Relationship of Classroom Behavior to the Accuracy of the Match Between Material Difficulty and Student Ability," *Journal of Educational Psychology*, 69 (February 1977), 24–32.
27. Lyon, Rozeene E. A., "Comparative Analysis of Foreign Beginning Readers to Identify Values Emphasized in the Content," *Reading Quarterly* (Kansas State College), 3 (August 1970), 25–28.
28. MacKinnon, A. R., *How Do Children Learn to Read?* Toronto: Copp, Clark, 1959.
29. Miller, Harry E., and Hering, Steve, "Teacher's Ratings—Which Reading Group is Number One?" *Reading Teacher*, 28 (January 1974), 389–391.
30. Pieronek, Florence T., "Using Basal Guidebooks—The Ideal Integrated Reading Lesson Plan," *Reading Teacher*, 33 (November 1979), 67–172.
31. Reid, James M., "Report on Elementary Reading." Quoted by permission of the author and Harcourt Brace Jovanovich.
32. Rodenborn, Leo V., and Washburne, Earlene, "Some Implications of the New Basal Readers," *Elementary English*, 51 (September 1974), 885–888.
33. Rose, Cynthia, Zimet, Sara G., and Blom, Gaston E., "Content Counts: Children Have Preferences in Reading Textbook Stories," *Elementary English*, 49 (January 1972), 14–19.
34. Rubin, Rosalyn A., "Reading Ability and Assigned Materials: Accommodation for the Slow But Not the Accelerated," *Elementary School Journal*, 75 (March 1975), 373–377.
35. Rudie, Helen N., "Poetry in Basal Readers: Perished or Cherished?" *Elementary English*, 52 (January 1975), 136–140.

36. Samuels, S. Jay, "Effects of Pictures on Learning to Read: Comprehension and Attitudes," *Review of Educational Research*, 40 (June 1970), 397–407.
37. Spache, George D., "New Trends in Primary Grade Readers," *Elementary School Journal*, 42 (December 1941), 283–290.
38. Spache, George D., "Using Tests in a Small School System," *Educational and Psychological Measurement*, 6 (September 1946), 99–110.
39. Spache, George D., *Toward Better Reading*. Champaign, Ill.: Garrard Publishing, 1963, chapter 2.
40. Townsend, Agatha, "What Research Says to the Reading Teacher," *Reading Teacher*, 15 (May 1962), 459.

Supplementary Reading

Anderson, Richard, Osborn, Jean, and Tierney, Robert, eds., *Learning to Read in American Schools: Basal Readers and Content Texts*. Hillsdale, N.J.: Lawrence Erlbaum, 1983.

Aukerman, Robert C., *The Basal Reader Approach to Reading*. New York: John Wiley & Sons, 1981.

Aulls, Mark W., *Developing Readers in Today's Elementary School*. Newton, Mass.: Allyn & Bacon, 1982.

Burmeister, Lou E., *Foundations and Strategies for Teaching Children to Read*. Reading, Mass.: Addison-Wesley, 1983.

Cunningham, Patricia M., Moore, Sharon A., Cunningham, James W., and Moore, David W., *Reading in Elementary Classrooms*. New York: Longman, 1983.

Clay, Marie, *Reading: The Patterning of Complex Behavior*. Auckland, New Zealand: Heineman, 1980.

Durkin, Dolores, *Teaching Them to Read*. Newton, Mass.: Allyn and Bacon, 1982.

Durkin, Dolores, *Getting Ready to Read*. Newton, Mass.: Allyn and Bacon, 1982.

Farr, Roger, and Roser, Nancy, *Teaching a Child to Read*. New York: Harcourt Brace Jovanovich, 1979.

McNeil, John D., Donant, Lisbeth, and Alkin, Marvin C., *How to Teach Reading Successfully*. Boston: Little, Brown, 1980.

Southgate, Vera, *Beginning Reading*. Mystic, Vt.: Lawrence Verry, 1972.

3 Using the Individualized Approach

For the first time in American reading instruction an approach to teaching reading emphasizes the development of individual pupils rather than the importance of the materials, their sequence, and their absolute essentiality. Such a departure from long-established methods might be expected to meet with resistance and negative attitudes. The critics ask: How can teachers possibly plan and direct a completely different program for each pupil? How many teachers know enough about reading to depart from the teachers' guides of the basal system? Where will teachers find the time to offer individual instruction to each child (not to mention the obvious uneconomical use of time implied in such a practice)?

As we have tried to portray, these questions are based in part upon false concepts of the individualized approach, its organizational procedures, and its use of grouping. Hardly any teachers completely individualize all aspects of reading instruction. Most teachers move gradually toward this approach, using manuals and checklists to supplement their knowledge of the details of the reading program. Small-group, large-group, whole-class, and individualized activities all appear in the program. Progressing from large to small groups, then to individualized teaching, and back again to group work as the situation demands, teachers learn to meet individual differences among their pupils.

The realization that learners show individual differences that affect or modify the teacher's approach was probably a very early learning experience of the world's first teacher. Differences among pupils have been a constant source of concern for educators in all ages and civilizations. In this country, for example, this concern was shown in the title of the *Twenty-fourth Yearbook* of the National Society for the Study of Education, "Adapting the Schools to Individual Differences" (22). In the yearbook, many experiments and trials of individualized instruction were described as they were operating in such school systems as Winnetka, Illinois; Madison, Wisconsin; Detroit; Los Angeles; and San Francisco. However, these experiments in meeting pupil differences varied somewhat from the current emphasis upon individualized reading. For the most part, they were oriented to subject matter assignments that were short, simple, and sequential, and adapted to permitting the child to progress at her own rate of learning.

In contrast, individualized reading is concerned with the overall development of the child's reading skills and interests. This approach traces its origin not so much to the general theory of individual differences and the earlier experiments we have mentioned, but to a series of principles of child development—seeking, self-selection, and self-pacing. These principles are attributed by the leaders of the individualized reading movement to the research and observations of the child development specialist Willard C. Olson, who first suggested their relevance to the teaching of reading.

However, as Alexander Frazier has noted (6), several other influences, in addition to those we have suggested, have played a significant role in creating a possible foundation for an individualized approach to reading. Among these forces has been an increasing recognition of the importance of firsthand experiences in developing the child's background for obtaining meaning from reading (her schemata). Supplementary reading of all types has gradually been accepted as an integral part of the total reading program. School libraries, particularly in elementary schools, have increased in numbers and in adequacy in recent years. The supply of trade books that can be read by children with primary or limited reading ability has increased tremendously in the past decade. Finally, Frazier points out the obvious impetus toward an individualized approach created by contemporary educational concern with the impact of reading upon the learner's personal and social interests, values, and needs. In all probability all these factors have helped crystallize and support the individualized reading approach.

Objectives and Assumptions

Like most other reading methods, the objective of the individualized school is to promote the fullest development of the pupil's skills, capacities, and interests. The assumptions on which these goals are based differ, however, from those of any other school of thought. Olson's study of the variability in child growth patterns led him to suggest three major principles—seeking, self-selection, and self-pacing. It was his impression that each child carries within him the seeds of a drive for maturation and a pattern of development. Skills, habits, and attitudes, consequently, are not to be imposed from without but are acquired at the child's natural pace and in accordance with his readiness. According to this philosophy, the child, motivated by internal needs (seeking), will attempt to read those materials suited to his needs and interests (self-selection), and will progress in level and skills as his growth pattern and readiness for new learnings permit (self-pacing). By individualizing the teacher's approach to reading instruction, some means of dealing with these problems may be found: the range of individual differences, the creation of permanent reading interests and tastes, and the avoidance of the harmful effects of interpupil competition and rigid academic standards.

The Method

For the sake of convenience we shall divide the description of the individualized approach into the topics of (1) organizing procedures, (2) individual conference, (3) skills practice, (4) independent activities, and (5) record keeping. Pertinent research is also included.

Organizing the Program. *Organizing* an individualized reading program requires perhaps more detailed teacher planning than some other approaches. First there is the problem of securing a wide variety of reading materials, including magazines, newspapers, pamphlets, trade books, and basals drawn from a number of reading levels. The actual number of books and other materials needed by an average class of thirty pupils, assuming that all would engage in individualized reading, is quite large. Some writers have observed that as many as five hundred titles were used in a fifth-grade class, and over one hundred at the second-grade level. Individual pupils are reported to have read from five to one hundred books during a semester under this plan. Estimates of the number needed in the classroom at any one time range from two to ten books per child, of which perhaps a quarter should be multiple copies of the same books. Some teachers make a real effort to determine the readability levels of the materials and to familiarize themselves thoroughly with their contents. One teacher, for example, prepared specific summaries and exercises for each book, including a short description, a list of difficult words, and questions on comprehension. Other teachers have spent the entire summer in this type of previewing, grading, and identifying books with colored labels, and preparing comprehension checks in preparing for an individualized program.

The collected reading materials must be planned to appeal to a wide variety of common pupil interests ranging over a number of grade levels of difficulty, and to include information, reference, and recreational materials. Preparation of a large selection of spirit masters or mimeographed exercises in word recognition skills, word attack techniques, word meaning, vocabulary building, and other skills is often made at this time. Some teachers may substitute exercises drawn from a number of workbooks for their own devices but, in any event, a wide variety of these tools at different reading levels is most desirable. In addition to these basic materials, we suggest the preparation of work centers and other equipment such as bulletin boards, picture files, a science center, a puppet theater, a painting and clay center, the library corner or reading center, a worktable or center where a supply of exercises or worksheets is stored, a workshop or make-it table, a writer's table, and a supply of audiovisual aids such as records, films, and filmstrips. The preparation of a typical learning center and some of the resources for assembling this variety of materials are discussed in Chapter 11.

Some of the problems inherent in organizing individualized reading depend on the way to initiate the program, the influence of class size, preparation of pupils (and their parents) for the new approach, pupil maturity in habits of independent work individually and in small groups, in-service training and supervision of teachers inexperienced with this method, selection of pupils for this method, and suitability of the approach for pupils of varying mental abilities. Administrative problems include judgment of the teachers' readiness and flexibility, their degree of personal organization and planning skill, their overall efficiency and rapport with children, their need for further in-service training and supervision, and the strength of their authoritarian leanings. There are no easy answers to these organizational and administrative questions, for very little expository or research material on these is available. We simply do not know the maximum class size for which this approach is feasible, whether it is wiser to begin with the fast reading group and later extend the procedure to other pupils, whether this approach is best for high-, medium-, or low-ability groups or equally effective with all, or what the characteristics of those teachers best suited to the method are. Partial answers to some of these questions are offered here and in this chapter's list of supplementary readings.

In striking contrast to the common belief that individualizing becomes too difficult for teachers with classes of thirty or more pupils, some teachers' experiences with so large a group have been very positive. With a large class, it becomes necessary to conduct four or five or perhaps more reading groups, but there just is not enough instructional time for that many daily reading lessons. Besides, the preparation time for these lessons would become excessive. The individualized program with its elements of whole class, large- and small-group instruction, individual conferences, and record keeping is more readily fitted into the available instructional time and less demanding of formal preparation time, some teachers tell us, than a formal five-group plan.

The Individual Conference. The *individual conference* as a substitute for group instruction in basal reading materials is probably the unique element in this approach. Occasionally, a small group of children may read the same basal or trade book under direct teacher supervision, but the reading circle of the basal method is taboo according to most supporters of the individualized school. Instead of reading in the circle, the child usually selects a portion from the book and orally reads it to the teacher. During the oral reading, the teacher observes the child's reading errors and other behaviors, and checks comprehension by improvised questions or questions prepared beforehand. The teacher also discusses the book with the child and may suggest another to be read next (although the extent to which this guidance is extended is a question of sharp debate among different sects of the individualized reading school). The teacher makes plans with the child for future small-group work on the skills that appear to be weak, gives definite assignments in a workbook or worksheet intended to provide skill training, or suggests follow-up activities related to the content of the reader. The teacher may also suggest ways that the pupil may share his or her enjoyment or learning with class members.

Oral reading to the teacher is *not* an essential part of every conference. Some teachers make use of the conference to observe silent reading, to check the pupil's comprehension and ability to use context to derive word meanings, and to look over the pupil's reading records. Discussing the student's choices of reading materials, the reasons for the choices, and ways to select future readings may also be included. The conference may be extended to a small group of children, who gather around the teacher and read silently while awaiting their turn for the conference. In some classes children volunteer for the conference or sign up on a schedule sheet as they feel the need for teacher help or wish to share the book they are reading. A few teachers hold conferences throughout the school day upon request from pupils, but most hold only as many as can be scheduled during that part of the regular reading period when they are not otherwise engaged. The length of time given to each individual conference varies from as short as two or three minutes to as long as ten minutes (10). Two to four conferences a week for each pupil are recommended, if the teacher can accomplish it. Class size, proportion of the reading period devoted to small-group work, teaching of the whole class, sharing periods, follow-up activities, and other elements of the program obviously limit the possible number and the length of the individual conferences. Individual pupils' need for support and guidance also determines to some degree the number of conferences given weekly. Some children need almost daily brief conferences, whereas once or twice a week may suffice for others. The maturity of the child as well as her ability to work independently, either alone or in small groups, must influence the teacher's judgment of the child's needs for conferences.

Skills Practice. Skills practice for small groups, usually with teacher direction, arises directly from the observations made during the individual conference. Some teachers who have described their experiences with individualized reading are quite vague about the details of the materials or content of the small-group skills practice. Other leaders of the individualized reading school are, however, more emphatic in demanding skills training. Young (23) notes the words that the children misread during the conference. After a number of conferences she uses the list of words as a basis to instruct the whole class in word attack techniques. One teacher used basal readers two days a week as the basis of her training in skills, but substituted a variety of follow-up activities for the basal workbooks. Darrow and Howes (5) recommend that the teacher prepare a detailed plan for skills training based on such available sources as courses of study, workbooks, basal manuals, and textbooks on reading. Some teachers offer the entire class a short lesson in skills at the close of the reading period, but most teachers, according to their reports, are more likely to offer this instruction during the individual conference or to a small group called together for that specific purpose (21).

In some cases, skills training is based almost entirely upon basal workbooks, but more commonly, teachers use the worksheets they have devised plus a wide variety of individual group follow-up activities, such as we will describe later. In a few classrooms skills training under teacher direction may be as infrequent as once a month, while most teachers emphasize skills almost daily either in a special lesson for a group or the entire class, in conjunction with spelling lessons or language periods, or during social studies, science, and literature lessons.

In many individualized programs it is apparent that the pupils assume a larger part of the responsibility for their own skills development. They are frequently expected to work independently, with a helper, or in teams, on assignments in workbooks or worksheets, follow-up activities, or committee work. They may also work preparing reading materials for the teacher–pupil conference or the sharing period, demonstrating reading skills in content field books, and carrying on various types of group projects and self-expressive activities. Many of these activities in reading skills self-improvement are conducted with what appears to the casual observer to be a minimum of teacher supervision, although, of course, they are initiated and monitored by the teacher.

To develop vocabulary, for example, the child is often expected to keep a list of the unknown words he encounters, to study these independently or with the aid of a child helper, and to be ready to demonstrate his understanding of them in the teacher–pupil conference. From the list, a "word bank" box (words on cards) for varied practice in learning new words is kept in the pupil's desk. In any event, the pupil's independence and self-direction are important elements in his eventual skill development.

Independent Activities. We have alluded to a number of the *independent activities* that seem to be an integral part of the individualized approach. For some teachers these provide a way of applying reading skills and relating them to language development in its many facets. One teacher achieves an interrelationship among the independent reading materials and language arts by stimulating the children to write letters to authors, book reviews, a class newspaper and a magazine, poetry or free verse, and by planning a Book Week show. In addition to the skills practice we have mentioned, Darrow and Howes speak of the following independent activities as preparation for sharing reading: reading a notice on a bulletin board, making posters and book jackets, dramatizing part of the story, and practicing for the oral reading of a portion in an audience situation (5). Project work involving the construction of models, dioramas, murals, or play properties is often related to independent reading. Self-expressive activities that may grow out of reading include displays of hobbies and collections, science experiments, poetry or stories, committee research work to prepare reports, oral reporting to the class, and artwork in paint, clay, or crayon.

As is true in the area of skills practice, pupils are expected to display a significant measure of independence, motivation, and persistence in these follow-up activities. Groups of children must learn to function together effectively—as helpers, teams, or committees—in following their special interests, preparing projects, and in sharing the ideas gained from their independent reading, often with a minimum of teacher direction and supervision.

Perhaps, before discussing other facets of the individualized program, it is appropriate to introduce an actual description of the daily activities in one classroom. This diary may serve to show how one teacher integrated the individual conference, skills practice, and independent activities (10).[1]

Monday: All children read individually. Worked with Mary, Tom...on comprehension—had group read and discuss selection from _____. Held reading conferences with Joe, Sara, and Afaf.

Tuesday: Worked with Susan, John...on double vowel sounds. Helped small-group planning of St. Valentine's Day with their play to share with class. Other children worked on independent activities or read individually. Had reading conferences with George and Willie.

Wednesday: Taught proper names to children using Book 2. Helped Carl prepare a story to read to class. Worked with small group on dictionary skills. Several children worked on creative activities; others read individually.

Thursday: Had children read to each other in small groups while I circulated; each child kept record of unfamiliar words. Had Tom, Larry, and Ella read orally to class from their self-selected books.

Friday: Worked with group of eight children on word recognition—asked them to make a list of words beginning with *r*. Other children read or worked on independent activities. Had class evaluate the week's reading.

Monday: Had short class phonics drill. Individual reading conferences with six children—others read silently at seat. Worked with a group of four on word games. Had all children tell what they read over weekend. Made class summary sheet of time spent on reading. Plan to use this summary for making graphs.

Tuesday: Had twelve children read silently at my desk while others engaged in independent activities. Asked three children to read orally in class. Worked on comprehension with Becky, Larry, and Sue.

Wednesday: Circulated while children read independently at their seats. Had children bring news items for our reading bulletin board—small group arranged the display. Partners worked on graphs.

Record Keeping. The individualized reading classroom's informality, the pupils' freedom to select their own reading materials, and the amount of time given to independent activities make careful *record keeping* essential to a successful program. Pupil records may take a variety of forms and include:

1. A daily log of reading accomplishments, plans, and projects.
2. A file of cards giving such facts as the date, title of book read, plans for sharing, and results of this plan.
3. A list of the new or unknown words met in reading, giving the title of book, page, and context for each word.
4. A brief summary of the book, giving its type, title, author, pupil's reactions or recommendations, and a brief description.
5. A small chart listing types of books. Pupil indicates the variety of his or her reading by inserting titles of books read.

A sample of a summary record written by a sixth grader is:

Wibberly, Leonard *Deadman's Cave*
  This is an exciting adventure story about a runaway servant, Tom Lincoln and his experiences with pirates. The story takes place toward the end of the 1600's and is mostly a sea story. This book was so exciting I missed my favorite TV program.

Ronald

Some teachers also keep additional records of the pupils' independent activities, written work, projects, and participation in sharing. This record can serve to indicate both the teacher's suggestions given during the conference and the actual outcomes of the child's follow-up. Samples of these records are given in Chapter 11.

Teacher Reactions

Our description of the individualized reading program scarcely does justice to the tremendous enthusiasm with which some teachers greet this method. Most of the teachers' self-reports in the recent literature are enthusiastic. Among the outcomes such teachers seem to see are the following:

1. Great increase in the volume of children's reading.
2. Growth in skill in sharing the pleasure of reading, interests, and tastes.
3. Marked increase in the range of reading test scores, particularly at the upper end.
4. Increase in feelings of security and self-sufficiency due to the absence of pupil competition and comparison.
5. Growth in independence, planning ability, and persistence in follow-up.
6. Real enjoyment and interest in reading and in self-improvement.
7. Constant encouragement and support derived from the repeated experience of success.
8. Marked progress in the breadth and variety of reading in informational, reference, and recreational materials.
9. Opportunity to progress in reading in accordance with child's own pace and interests, to be informed of own progress, and to play a significant role in determining this development.
10. Marked increase in level of social studies and science achievement due to wide reading in related areas, observed by some teachers.

At the conclusion of their large-scale questionnaire and observation study, as reported in *The First R* (New York: Macmillan Publishing Co., Inc.,

1963), Mary C. Austin and Coleman Morrison made these recommendations regarding the individualized concept:

1. That all pupils be permitted to cross grade lines with all reading materials, including basals, in order that intelligent adjustments would be made in terms of children's progress.
2. That certain aspects of the individualized approach, such as self-selection of reading materials, individual conferences, and written records of pupil progress, be used as integral parts of all elementary school reading programs.

Problems of Individualized Reading

As Frazier has suggested, the significance of the principle of *self-selection* is much overemphasized in the literature of individualized programs (6). The principle assumes an almost endless variety of books from which to choose and a minor role of both the group and the teacher in influencing the selection of reading materials. The philosophy of individualized reading does not imply that the teacher must abandon guidance or supervisory function over children's reading. Frazier points out that teachers must continue to help the reader "find satisfying experiences in keeping with his interests, purposes, and ability, all at the same time" (6, p. 60). We would add that the teacher continues to play a significant role in stimulating and shaping these interests and purposes, and in helping the child realistically evaluate her abilities. Like so many of the terms characteristic of the school, *individualized*, *self-selection*, and *seeking* are misnomers, for in actual practice they do not mean what they seem to mean. The approach does not completely individualize instruction, for grouping remains present in many contexts; basal reading is often still present in the program. Self-selection does not mean that children have complete freedom or independence of choice, nor does seeking mean that all have an instinctive drive to read more and more.

In the individualized program, children are not constantly taught in a one-to-one setting with the teacher. While the teacher does spend more time with individual children than in other approaches to reading, much of the instruction in skills will be done in small groups. These groups will be formed for a specific purpose, will perhaps use the same book or skill development material for a time, and then, when their needs have been met, will disband. Thus, from time to time a child may be a member of a group for word analysis training, because of a special interest, to plan the sharing of reading with the rest of the class, to plan a play or a puppet show, to practice choral reading or role playing, or for any of a dozen reasons. Like other teachers, individualized practitioners are aware that the teaching of a group is more economical of their time, and that working in a group that shares a common purpose produces better learning than does solitary work or instruction.

Organizational Planning

In a recent article, Jerry L. Abbott, an elementary school principal, enumerated fifteen reasons why individualized reading will not work. His article was written with tongue in cheek, for he soon points out that none of his reasons are really barriers to successful individualization. Actually, they are simply inherent conditions such as class size, book supply, teacher competencies, cost, record keeping, and the like. These problems are numerous in individualized reading, perhaps even more than in other approaches, because this method depends so heavily upon the organizing ability of the teacher. Many teachers who try this approach discover that they are unable to schedule their time efficiently for sufficient conferences with pupils—conferences that are long enough and really private or free from interruptions. Other teachers feel the need for more planning time, perhaps as much as one free period before each reading period, to prepare materials, complete records, and plan for individual pupils. In many classrooms the question of logistics—or an adequate supply of reading materials, exercises, and seatwork activities, workbooks, and other tools—is a difficulty. Where do teachers find the time to preview all these books, to familiarize themselves with their significant meanings, to prepare adequate checks upon pupil comprehension, to identify and label books according to their difficulty of vocabulary and sentence structure? Even the most simple but objective methods of determining grade levels of books, such as the readability formulas, take from twenty to sixty minutes per book, depending upon the size of the book. Or, as some writers seem to imply, are we to believe that this approach does not necessitate teacher familiarity with the contents of the books that the children will read, that it is not essential that she know the approximate grade level of each book?

We disagree with this line of reasoning. We believe that teachers should preview the books they place in the class library to become somewhat familiar with their content and difficulty. However, as will be shown in Chapter 11, it is quite feasible for teachers to discuss a book and gain some idea of what students' comprehension of the book is even though the teachers have not read the book in its entirety.

The teacher obviously must have some scheme for scheduling herself and her pupils. This may take the form of posted sheets on which children sign up for conferences, and a checklist of the children's names, the dates of their conferences, and the outcomes. Time for conferences must be part of the teacher's daily schedule. She must certainly become familiar with the books of the classroom library and try to keep up with those obtained at intervals from the school or public library. This does not imply that she must have read all the books, prepared specific comprehension questions on each, or even listed the new vocabulary (a pointless task in view of the diversified reading experiences of the pupils).

An inherent difficulty in the individualized approach is that of the high teacher effectiveness and skill demanded. There are no manuals to dictate each day's lessons, or to tell the teacher what skill-reinforcing materials to use, or what story a group should read next. Each individualized reading practitioner must know a good deal about the way children usually develop in the reading process, know how to detect deviations or gaps in this development, and know how and what to prescribe for these needs as they are revealed during conferences or group work. The teacher is likely to need experienced help and supervision during the early stages of development of this approach. Appropriate in-service training through grade conferences, teacher–supervisor meetings, and exchange of ideas with fellow staff members is as essential here as it would be in approaching any other new way of teaching reading.

The teacher faces several administrative tasks in effective management of the class. The pupils often need training and direction in assuming the responsibility for their independent work. They must be able to act in a self-directing, responsible manner. They must understand the program, their own reading abilities and difficulties, and be able to organize their own efforts accordingly. If the pupils are unable to function efficiently without constant teacher supervision, the teacher must take the time and make the effort to teach them how to work independently. Most teachers have found that a gradual introduction to individualized reading, with considerable supervision at first of pupils during independent work, makes the program more feasible. Another successful variation of these beginning steps is to start with a small number of pupils, perhaps those of better reading ability, and then gradually extend the program to other pupils.

Some teachers encounter frustration in introducing this approach in a traditional school system. Principals and other teachers who have long been accustomed to the regimentation often characteristic of the use of a basal reader program often look askance at the whole idea of individualizing. They are apt to be very skeptical that pupils will develop the necessary skills without using a basal every day. Judging from their own shortcomings, they refuse to believe that such a degree of individualizing in instruction and materials is even possible. Often teachers may recognize the inherent criticism of their stereotyped approaches and resent the implications (without admitting the comparison, of course). If the teacher attempting individualized reading is young or new to the system, the task is sometimes made even more difficult by the attitudes of colleagues and administrators.

Obviously, it requires a good deal of self-confidence to initiate the individualized approach under such conditions. The teacher must first convince the supervisor or principal that the method is not a hare-brained notion but a widely accepted classroom practice that produces pupils as competent in reading as any other method. It would be wise to offer some of the resource materials listed in this chapter, such as the Veatch text or even this book, to permit the administrator to become familiar with the concept. If administrative approval and support can be thus obtained, the situation will be much less complicated. As for fellow teachers, there is no need to attempt to convince them of the merits of this approach. Let the test results and the actual reading progress of the pupils be the evidence of the soundness of the method.

Another personal challenge to the teacher employing the individualized approach is the demand upon his personality and interpersonal skill. He is constantly attempting to work closely and intimately with different children. He must continuously adjust himself to the pupils' needs for support, encouragement, correction, guidance, constructive criticism, and directions for the use of materials. He must combine some of the attributes of therapist, teacher, librarian, parent, counselor, and reading specialist. Needless to say, not all teachers can fulfill these demands.

The ultimate success of an individualized program is, of course, influenced by the adequacy of the solutions to the organizational and administrative problems. But of even greater significance is the teacher's skill in *record keeping* and the *individual conference*. The whole program rests upon the cornerstone of teacher diagnostic skill in the conference in identifying children's needs in the areas of reading skills and selection of materials, and in evaluation of the pupils' progress.

Individual Conference

We have already noted that one author has observed that many individualized reading teachers have not solved the problem of finding sufficient time for the number of conferences they feel are really needed. These teachers feel that the conferences are not only too infrequent but also too brief and superficial. The majority of Sartain's second-grade teachers had similar feelings of frustration after a three-month trial of the approach (*15*). These teachers frankly admitted that their diagnostic skills were inadequate to enable them to note and understand pupil needs for skill training. Several writers speak out strongly against depending upon the individual conference as a reliable means of evaluation of pupils' skill development and instructional needs. They consider the conference as usually practiced in the individualized program as an opportunistic, catch-as-catch-can method of assessing pupil needs and planning for instruction. Perhaps there is good reason for these negative reactions to the merits of the conference, unless it is carefully planned and the teacher is adequately trained.

All the information that a teacher might want to accumulate about each child certainly cannot be obtained in casual two-minute conferences. There must be different purposes for conferences and different types of conferences, as we shall illustrate later in this book. Some conferences may serve for diagnosis, others as progress checks, and others as motivational contacts with the pupil. Some conferences will be brief, whereas other conferences may be much longer. Some conferences will be with an individual child, as for diagnosis or progress checking, and others may involve several pupils, as for instruction, sharing, planning, or motivation.

One of our students, Mary Beth Erb, wrote a term paper describing her experiences in learning the individualized approach. Among her comments are statements such as these:

First and most important to the success of my program is that I realize my record keeping is not detailed enough....I have found I need to take better inventories of each child's overall reading development. I also need to do more recording during the diagnostic conference time. I see now that I need to follow the suggestion in our text, *Reading in the Elementary School*, for recording oral errors and interpreting these errors.

Another big problem has been that I do not know the reading level of many of the books in my room library....Actually I have been able to get along very well without this information, but I know it would be easier for me if I could quickly pick out a book for a specific child.

I found that I was putting too many books out at one time for the children to select. Now I choose about twenty-five books and put them on our library table and change them often.

When we first started using the reading record some of the children were so delighted with putting the names of the books in the notebook that they read all the picture books and easy books to get a long list of books recorded. I did not say anything about this to the children and the novelty wore off!

Miss Erb goes on in her paper to describe her learning experiences in adjusting to the individualized approach. Like most practitioners, she discovered that skill in organizing her instructional time, scheduling conferences of different types, and helping children to learn to work independently were among her major tasks. She also learned that individualized reading does not quite function in the manner implied by some authorities who speak for it. Conferences are not as frequent or as brief as some imply; each child does not always have a completely individualized program, for much activity occurs in small groups; and when the planned skill training of the basal program is discarded, the teacher must formulate a new checklist of skills and related diagnostic measures.

Skills Training

Numerous studies show that many teachers are not very knowledgeable in the area of word analysis skills (*17*). If teachers are to approach individualized reading, they must familiarize themselves with the facts about phonics (decoding), phonic principles, and contextual and structural analysis, with the aid of some recent review of the literature, as we have provided in a later chapter. They should also help themselves to learn more about this area with the aid of a detailed guide, such as Heilman's (*10*), or a self-teaching device, such as that offered by Marion A. Hull (*11*). Teachers attempting individualized reading cannot wait to learn something about word analysis from use of the teacher's manual, as so many teachers do. They cannot depend on being told what to teach and when to teach it, as in the usual manual, for individualized instruction does not necessarily progress in the structured pattern of basals.

In this area of skills training, it is apparent that many teachers would experience marked difficulty in shifting from a basal to an individualized approach. These are teachers who have simply followed basal manuals because of their own lack of professional knowledge or creativity in teaching. If, as research studies show, professional education may not have supplied adequate knowledge of skills and their principles, such as phonics, syllabication, and word recognition techniques, a teacher may not be ready to begin a program of individualized diagnosis and small-group instruction without further study in this area.

In this area of skills development Frazier raises a number of questions (6): How much training in word analysis do our children really need at primary, intermediate, and other levels? Just how much sight vocabulary is needed to enable children to begin to read on their own? Is it possible that many of these skills will develop spontaneously as a result of broadening reading experience? Can vocabulary be extended more rapidly when children use a variety of materials? Should not some of the performances thought of as reading skills be taught as study or learning skills in content texts and lessons? Or, as some recent authors express it: Cannot children learn to read by reading?

These are indeed decisions to be made by teachers who attempt individualization. Rather than taking each child through a preplanned skill development sequence (commonly known as a workbook), teachers will be devising a tailormade developmental sequence for individuals and groups. Some children will need a great deal of help in this or that skill, whereas others may develop these spontaneously. Still others will succeed in reading by using some but not all of the skills. Individualization demands a true recognition of individual differences in learning rate, learning modalities, and the child's actual functioning in the act of reading.

If used selectively and critically, some parts of management systems and similar skills-drills commercial materials can be used; not as consecutive worksheets, but as they appear relevant to teacher judgment of specific pupil needs.

The Research

Objective observers of the outcomes of the individualized approach are still somewhat cautious in extending wholehearted approval. Irene W. Vite has reviewed seven carefully controlled comparisons of the individualized approach versus ability grouping (21). Four of the control studies showed significant test results favoring individualized reading, but three yielded conclusive results in favor of ability grouping. Reading test scores are quite inadequate in measuring many of the outcomes of a reading method, for most of the results of individualized reading that we have noted above cannot be evaluated in this fashion. Yet test results are highly valued by most educators as fundamental, objective methods of comparison, and their equivocal nature in these studies leaves many administrators in doubt.

Safford compared reading gains with both local and national norms in seven classes using individualized reading (14). All the experimental classes made less than the expected gains, and there were no significant advantages for average or superior readers. Johnson conducted a twenty-eight-class, three-year study that favored individualized reading at the end of the first and third grades in several measures of reading (12). Two of the Cooperative First-Grade Studies obtained no significant differences at the end of the first grade (2, 13). However, use of an attitude scale measuring the pupils' feelings about reading in these studies showed a very positive advantage for individualized reading.

After a two-year study, Cyrog reported that there were still some pupils reading a year or more below their expected levels, although the great majority of pupils equaled or exceeded their mental age in reading achievement (4). Greenman and Kapilian's results indicated a better-than-average gain in test scores but showed that the greatest gains were present among the best pupils and some poor readers failed to show significant gains (7). Several other experiments in the primary grades showed that many children accustomed to a basal program made less than normal progress when shifted to the individualized one. Sartain's results indicated a marked spurt in progress during the first few months of either basal or individualized method in comparable classes, thus perhaps demonstrating the marked significance of teacher enthusiasm or experimental conditions upon pupil reading achievement (15). His final results did not indicate any real difference in achievement for average or superior pupils under either method. Poor readers, in fact, made greater growth in word recognition in a basal program.

A distinct problem in interpreting the mass of studies claiming to test the value of individualized reading is the extreme variation from one study to the next in the experimenter's definition and implementation of this approach. For example, in another of the Cooperative First-Grade Studies, Doris U. Spencer used a group commercial phonics program, teams of pupils working together, individual conferences, and group instruction in language arts (18). With this "individualized reading" program, she obtained results that were superior to those found in the use of a basal reading series. Another report considered individualized reading to be the distribution of worksheets to be placed in the child's folder (although no free time to work on these was scheduled), plus providing cardboard carrels for small-group work. Still another experimenter used a reader in an individual conference program versus a small-group plan (using the same reader).

Perhaps these variations are the reason why reviews of the research indicate that outcomes differ from one experiment in individualized reading to the next (9). Certainly there will and should be variations among the ways in which teachers implement the concept of individualized reading. This approach depends heavily on the personal organization, planning ability, and classroom management skills of the teachers. And teachers differ in these characteristics. But we must be careful not to be misled by those who think that any program that moves away in the smallest degree from constant teacher pacing through a reader is therefore an "individualized" program. We must also beware of entrepreneurs who try to capitalize on the term, and offer us programmed materials, sequential worksheets, or management systems to be done in solitary seat work—all the activities to be done by all the pupils, in the same sequence, and employing only a single learning modality—in the name of individualized reading. There are, of course, a number of sound book collections, skill development kits, and other aids for an individualized program. We will explore these later in a chapter devoted to ways of implementing such a program.

Some proponents of the individualized approach argue for its adoption because of certain conclusions that might be drawn from the comparative studies. They suggest that since test scores do not clearly show inferior results for the individualized program, it is justified on the basis of its other accomplishments in the areas of enjoyment, interest, breadth of reading, independence, and the like. Opponents are likely to point out that, despite its claims, individualized reading does not completely solve the range of differences in the classroom or produce increased rate of progress for all types of pupils at all levels of mental abilities, and that the program makes extraordinary demands upon teacher preparation and skill. These opposing viewpoints do not exhaust the arguments pro and con, but they suffice to show the distinct cleavage of opinion regarding this particular approach to the teaching of reading.

Advocates of individualized reading emphasize a number of subtle advantages in this approach. They point out, for example, that the self-selection feature avoids teacher pacing, with its leveling and retarding effects upon pupil progress. Present-day schools are strongly criticized for promoting mediocrity and failing to challenge individual potential, a condition which the individualized approach certainly does not foster. Motivation is thought to be greater in this program, for children tend to realize their own goals of interest and information, rather than teacher goals, which may be artificial. Self-selected reading provides a wide vocabulary in material on the child's level, thus stimulating marked growth in concepts, ideas, and facts, as well as words. Skill training is planned for each pupil or small group when it is appropriate rather than being offered in a set sequence to all pupils, regardless of their needs. Competition among children is diminished, greater socialization is promoted, and more pupil–teacher interaction on a one-to-one basis is present. Even though it may not be possible to show that the individualized program necessarily accelerates children in reading levels or test scores, these mental hygiene advantages remain highly significant.

Individualized reading, to be sure, has certain ideas and practices that might be incorporated into the total reading program, as we shall illustrate later. Adopting these practices will make definite demands for better teacher training and practice—in diagnosis of pupil needs, in preparation and evaluation of a wide variety of teaching materials, and in detailed planning. But these demands can be met, and the values of these individualized practices realized, by interested teachers.

As a follow-up to this overview of individualized reading, in Chapter 11 we will offer detailed suggestions regarding organizational steps, scheduling, record keeping, and conducting various types of conferences.

Endnote

1. Adapted from Darrow, Helen Fisher, and Howes, Virgil M., *Approaches to Individualized Reading*, Copyright © 1960. By permission of Appleton-Century-Crofts, Educational Division, Meredith Corporation.

Discussion Questions

1. When a teacher or school is committed to using a basal reader, how may a greater degree of individualization be introduced?

2. Are all teachers capable of moving gradually toward individualization? If not, why not?

3. How do the demands upon teaching skills differ in the individualized approach and the basal program?

4. Is it feasible to use basal readers in the individualized program? If so, how might they be used, and to what degree?

5. What types of pupils are likely to benefit most from individualization? Can most pupils learn to function in this framework under appropriate teacher direction?

6. Is an individualized reading program possible only for the experienced teacher? Justify your opinion.

7. How might the handicap of an inadequate classroom or school library be overcome by the teacher who wishes to individualize?

8. What factors in many school systems militate against adopting the individualized approach by a teacher? How can these be overcome?

9. Try to arrange to visit a classroom in which individualized reading is being used. Make notes of your observations of the teacher and the children and share them with your class.

References

1. Aaron, Ira E., "What Teachers and Prospective Teachers Know About Phonic Generalizations," *Journal of Educational Research*, 53 (May 1960), 323–330.

2. Bond, Guy L., and Dykstra, Robert, "The Cooperative Research Program in First-Grade Reading Instruction," *Reading Research Quarterly*, 2 (Summer 1967), 5–142.
3. Caldwell, Jay S., and Shnayer, Sidney W., "The Truth About Readiness," *School Library Journal*, 16 (May 1970), 39–40.
4. Cyrog, Frances, "The Principal and His Staff Move Forward in Developing New Ways of Thinking About Reading," *California Journal of Educational Research*, 27 (February 1959), 178–187.
5. Darrow, Helen Fisher, and Howes, Virgil M., *Approaches to Individualized Reading*. New York: Appleton-Century-Crofts, 1960.
6. Frazier, Alexander, "The Individualized Reading Program," in *Controversial Issues in Reading and Promising Solutions*, Supplementary Educational Monographs, No. 91. Chicago: University of Chicago Press, 1961, 57–74.
7. Greenman, Ruth, and Kapilian, Sharon, "Individual Reading in the Third and Fourth Grades," *Elementary English*, 35 (April 1959), 234–237.
8. Groff, Patrick J., "Materials for Individualized Reading," *Elementary English*, 38 (January 1961), 1–7.
9. Groff, Patrick J., "Comparisons of Individualized and Ability Grouping Approaches to Reading Achievement," *Elementary English*, 40 (March 1963), 258–264, 276.
10. Heilman, Arthur W., *Phonics in Proper Perspective*. Columbus, Ohio: Charles E. Merrill, 1976.
11. Hull, Marion A., *Phonics for the Teaching of Reading*. Columbus, Ohio: Charles E. Merrill, 1976.
12. Johnson, R. H., "Individualized and Basal Reading Programs," *Elementary English*, 42 (December 1965), 902–904.
13. Macdonald, J. B., Harris, T. L., and Mann, J. S., "Individual vs. Group Instruction in First Grade Reading," *Reading Teacher*, 19 (May 1966), 643–647.
14. Safford, Alton L., "Evaluation of an Individualized Reading Program," *Reading Teacher*, 13 (April 1960), 266–270.
15. Sartain, Harry W., "The Roseville Experiment with Individualized Reading," *Reading Teacher*, 13 (April 1960), 277–281.
16. Spache, George D., *Good Reading for Poor Readers*. Champaign, Ill.: Garrard Publishing, 1978.
17. Spache, George D., and Baggett, Mary E., "What Do Teachers Know About Phonics and Syllabication?" *Reading Teacher*, 19 (November 1965), 96–99.
18. Spencer, Doris U., "Individualized vs. a Basal Reader Program in Rural Communities, Grades One and Two," *Reading Teacher*, 21 (October 1967), 11–17.
19. Thiel, Norma, *An Analysis of the Effectiveness of the Teaching of Reading by Individual Prescription*. Newark, Del.: ERIC/CRIER ED 690, 1972.
20. Veatch, Jeanette, *Reading in the Elementary School*. New York: John Wiley & Sons, 1978.
21. Vite, Irene W., "Individualized Reading—The Scoreboard on Control Studies," *Education*, 81 (January 1961), 286–290.
22. Whipple, Guy M., ed., "Adapting the Schools to Individual Differences," in *Twenty-Fourth Yearbook*, Part II, National Society for the Study of Education. Chicago: University of Chicago Press, 1923.
23. Young, Elizabeth, "Individualized Reading," *Baltimore Bulletin of Education*, 35 (May–June 1958), 29–32.

Supplementary Reading

The reader will note that most of the research studies of the individualized approach were completed in the decade of the 1960s. This was the period of peak interest and exploration of this approach. Apparently proponents of the scheme were satisfied with the outcomes of the early research, for very few significant experiments have appeared in the literature since then. However, the books that expound and elucidate the system have continued to appear throughout the 1970s, indicating the extent of the continued interest and practice of this approach.

Atwood, Beth S., *Building Independent Learning Skills*. Belmont, Calif.: Pitman Learning, 1975.

Barnes, Ellen, Eyman, Bill, and Engolz, Maddy Bragar, *Teach and Reach*. Syracuse, N.Y.: Human Policy Press, 1977.

Bechtol, William, *Individualizing Instruction and Keeping Your Sanity*. Chicago: Follett Publishing, 1975.

Blackburn, Jack E., and Powell, W. Conrad, *One at a Time: All at Once*. Santa Monica, Calif.: Good Year Publishing, 1978.

Cunningham, Patricia Marr, et al., *Classroom Reading Instruction, K–5: Alternative Approaches*. Lexington, Mass.: D. C. Heath, 1977.

Harris, Larry A., and Smith, Carl B., *Reading Instruction: A Handbook*. New York: Holt, Rinehart and Winston, 1980.

Holdaway, Don, *Independence in Reading: A Handbook on Individualized Procedures*. Auckland, New Zealand: Ashton Press, 1972.

La Pray, Margaret, *Teaching Children to Become Independent Readers*. Washington, D.C.: Center for Applied Research in Education, 1972.

Learning Centers: Children on Their Own. Washington, D.C.: Association for Childhood Education International, 1970.

Marcus, Marie, *Handbook for Individualized Reading*. Gretna, La.: Pelican Publishing, 1974.

McNeil, John D., *Designing Curriculum: Self-Instructional Modules*. Boston: Little, Brown, 1976.

Musgrave, Ray, *Individualized Instruction: Teaching Strategies Focusing on the Learner*. Boston: Allyn and Bacon, 1975.

Noar, Gertrude, *Individualized Instruction: Every Child a Winner*. New York: John Wiley & Sons, 1972.

Shiman, David, ed., *Teachers on Individualization: The Way We Do It*. New York: McGraw-Hill, 1974.

Smith, James A., *Creative Teaching of the Language Arts in the Elementary School*. Boston: Allyn and Bacon, 1973.

Stahl, Dona, and Anzalone, Patricia, *Individualized Teaching in the Elementary Schools*. Englewood Cliffs, N.J.: Prentice-Hall, 1970.

Weiner, Bluma B., *Periscope: Views of the Individualized Education Program*. Reston, Va.: Council for Exceptional Children, 1978.

Weisgerber, Robert A., *Perspectives in Individualized Learning*. Itasca, Ill.: Peacock Publications, 1971.

"The linguist is carrying on his proper function when he advances linguistic generalizations that he believes apply to the teaching of reading. He is also performing a fitting and useful function when he criticizes the teaching of reading from his linguistic vantage point. But he is not on firm ground when he produces reading programs that are based solely on linguistic criteria"(16). This quotation from Kenneth S. Goodman, a psycholinguist, sums up our judgment of the present relationship of linguistics to reading instruction.

Reading is certainly a use of language, and reading specialists need to have a broad background in the scientific facts of language. But some of the popularizing linguists who have rushed into print with contradictory reading programs have done the field of reading a disservice. By propounding conflicting and naive theories of the reading process, by producing programs that often are not discernibly different from approaches discarded many years ago, by refusing to accept that much of current reading instruction is based on psychological and physiological principles unfamiliar to them, many linguists have failed in their role of advisers to the reading specialist. If linguistics is to make a contribution, it will probably be in the study of language development of children, how language conveys meaning, and the relationships between language and reading development.

Since the early 1960s, a group of language scientists, popularly known as linguists, have been proposing a variety of approaches to reading instruction that differ markedly from other methods. This group of materials offering a linguistic theory is proving to be somewhat confusing to the average classroom teacher. Without identifying their particular sphere of interest in linguistics, these authors offer quite conflicting explanations of the inadequacies of present teaching methods and how they might be improved by adopting their linguistic principles.

One linguist may attack the whole word or sight method (3, 4), another concentrates on criticizing popular methods of phonics instruction (25, 26), and a third finds fault with both these criticisms as well as any present procedures (13). Each critic offers a different substitute method of beginning instruction, and yet all these substitutes are called the linguistic approach.

Schools within Schools

The confusion lies in the fact that there are at least two kinds of linguists talking about reading instruction, each from within his own frame of reference in language research. These are the phonologists, and the structuralists.

The Phonologists' Definition of Reading

The phonologists concern themselves with the analysis of the sounds of spoken (and written) language. Leonard Bloomfield is credited by most of his fellow linguists with the identification of the various phonemes that are the basic sounds of our language. As early as 1942 Bloomfield (3) attempted to outline the implications of his research for reading instruction. Later, in 1961, Bloomfield offered instructional materials based on his phoneme-grapheme studies (4). Bloomfield (4) and Soffietti (45) recommend that reading be taught as a process of translating phonemes (basic sounds) into words. Working first with groups of letters, the child gradually learns words and later proceeds to larger units of sentence structure. Or, in the words of Goldberg and Rasmussen's article (13, p. 24):

> The main task in learning to read appears then to be able to produce the sounds of language when one sees the written marks which conventionally represent these sounds. . . . Even though one might insist that the derivation of meaning is a necessary element in the reading process, we feel that a separation of the skill of associating sound with symbol from the aim of deriving meaning is important for the reason that the presentation of the subject of reading is made much less complicated by concentrating on the skill rather than the promotion of understanding.

In effect, their concept of the act of reading is a translation of the sounds for which letters stand, first into spoken sounds, then into words, and possibly later into sentences. Whether the process deals with meaningful units seems unimportant, or at least subordinate, to the translating into sounds. At first glance this seems like an ultraphonic approach, but the phonologists deny the similarity, as we shall see.

Fries enlarges this definition of the reading process, as he sees it, in such statements as: "Letters must be recognized as they appear in sequences. The order of the letters in the directional sequence of left to right acts as a fundamental marker for the discrimination of lexical units" (12). Fries points out, however, that he is not referring to the recognition of individual letters as they stand alone. To promote this type of learning, Fries insists that the words must appear in regularly arranged spelling patterns and repetitive sentences, but never with any pictures that might lead the child to react to clues other than the sequence of letters.

The Structuralists' Definition of Reading

A second school of linguists, sometimes called grammarians or structural linguists, has investigated the structure of language. They point out the essential elements of language that result in the communication of ideas, such as word order or word position, word function; word groups that modify, expand, or change simple expressions; and the signals of intonation, such as pitch, stress, and pause. Other areas of structural linguistic research include the identification and frequency of types of sentences (simple statements, demands, requests, questions) and grammatical inflections or word changes to indicate tense and number. It is quite apparent that this approach to language would result in a quite different group of implications for reading instruction than would the work of phonologists. As yet there are no teaching materials offered for reading instruction exemplifying the ideas of the structuralists.

According to Warfel and Lloyd, the reading process is a recognition of the structural principles of word order (51). A few hundred structure words link words into groups that must be read as such. Lefevre and others stress recognition of larger speech patterns (simple statements, requests), or structural elements (noun groups, verb groups, phrases, clauses), or function words (articles, auxiliary verbs, prepositions), and grammatical inflections as the basic teaching material (25, 26). Eye movements in reading must therefore be related to structural elements of sentences rather than to words. In another article, Warfel enlarges upon this definition by stressing the fact that good reading requires an accompaniment of vocal sounds, at least during the primary stages (50). Only after wide oral reading experience is silent reading, as we commonly understand it, feasible or desirable.

Thus it appears that in the beginning, the child is to read by relating large units and patterns of speech to their graphic or symbolic representatives, the printed words. Children would be taught to react to signals such as capitals and periods; to the order and grouping of words; to the importance of such modifiers as articles, adverbs, and the like; and to the grammatical inflections of number, tense, and possession. Children would be alerted to the normal sentence order of subject, verb, and "completer" (direct object complement, or the like). Children would learn also to read the great variety of variations upon this normal sentence order possible through the use of function words (*the, into, when*) to signal additional elements. Just how this approach is to be implemented we will point out later.

Lefevre, a leading exponent of this particular linguistic approach to reading, has criticized the present authors for offering what he considers the most naive statement of the "simplistic word-perception theory" of reading. Lefevre believes rather that the sentence, not word perception, is the unit of meaning (26). He would have us teach reading by much listening to stories and by attention to sentence order, word order, and most important of all, intonation of sentences. Presumably, after such training the child would begin by reading whole sentences.

The Materials

There are currently a number of materials that appear or claim to follow linguistic principles. Among these is the text *Let's Read,* prepared by Bloomfield and published after his death by C. L. Barnhart, the famous lexicologist (*4*). The Bloomfield–Barnhart text follows these authors' version of a linguistic approach to teaching reading by presenting first a carefully controlled vocabulary of isolated words. Each list of words stresses a particular group of sounds of high consistency in the manner in which it is spelled. Thus a number of words containing the *an* spelling is presented, followed by another group containing the *at* spelling, etc. For the most part, each group of words with a common phoneme is composed of real or nonsense monosyllables. A second group of words varies only in vowel pattern (*mad–mid, hot–hut*). The progression continues from three- to four-letter words, from regulars to irregulars, and finally to polysyllabic words. Later lessons introduce the reading of unrelated sentences and brief stories in which words illustrating a certain sound are inserted. This is the approach endorsed by Hall (*18*), Fries (*12*), and a number of linguists who share Bloomfield's theoretical beliefs.

Other linguistically oriented series include *The Linguistic Readers* by Henry Lee Smith, Jr., Clara G. Stratemeyer, et al. (Benziger Corp.); *The Merrill Linguistic Readers* by C. C. Fries et al. (Charles E. Merrill); *The Basic Reading Series* by Lynn Goldberg and Donald Rasmussen (Science Research Associates); Frances Adkins Halls's *Sounds and Letters Series* (Linguistic); the *Miami Linguistic Readers* (D. C. Heath); Catherine Stern's *The Structural Reading Series* (L. W. Singer); the *Basic Reading Series* (J. B. Lippincott); and the new *Distar Program* (Science Research Associates).

Although all these readers are supposed to follow the tenets of linguistic science, there are interesting differences among them. Fries insists on no pictures; most of the other series are profusely illustrated. Fries insists on presenting words in sentences; Barnhart offers nothing but lists of words for almost half of his text. Fries depends upon regularly spelled words; Goldberg and Rasmussen introduce both regular and irregular words. Smith and Stratemeyer utilize story and poetry content from the beginning, while Barnhart and Fries deemphasize meaningful content by using nonsense words and sentences. If all these readers are supposed to be based on the same fundamental principles of linguistics, the contradictory practices are puzzling, to say the least.

Certain other reading materials are sometimes referred to as representative of the linguistic theory, but in actuality differ from each other in content and rationale. The *Royal Road Readers* by J. C. Daniels and H. Diack (Chatto & Windus, London) are an example of such pseudolinguistic materials. They differ fundamentally in employing a contextual setting—a story thread—to introduce their vocabulary. The sentence patterns used in this material are not closely controlled or varied systematically, as the structuralist school suggests they should be. Second, although a majority of the words used in any story or booklet present a particular group of sounds, many other words, and hence sounds, are also introduced as needed to tell the story. It is probably more accurate to designate the *Royal Road Readers* as a type of phonics system, as the authors do, rather than a true linguistic approach.

A second group of materials loosely labeled as linguistic in orientation is the Richards–Gibson *First Steps to Reading* (Washington Square Press). These booklets control very carefully the introduction of letters and attempt also to offer a very simple group of sentence patterns. Furthermore, the vocabulary is highly concrete and profusely illustrated by simple drawings and stick figures. Richards and Gibson, and A. R. MacKinnon, who made an intensive study of the value of this material (29), apparently share Bloomfield's belief that reading occurs letter by letter and that the letter controls they used simplified this process. MacKinnon's study did show that under certain grouping conditions the Richards–Gibson materials produced significant reading growth. But he, like Richards and Gibson, ignored the fact that the control of letters did not extend to the control of letter sounds, for many of the letters used varied widely in the sounds they represented in various words. Thus the material violates one of the basic principles of linguistic theory—consistency in the presentation of basic phonemes (sounds).

The *Merrill Linguistic Reading Program* has probably had the widest acceptance of series of this type. It is supposed to be based on the concepts of Dr. Charles C. Fries, a noted linguist, but in the twenty years since the first edition the content has moved far away from his philosophy. The 1980 edition, for example, varies from Fries's opinion in many ways. In fact, except for the rigid sequence of phonogram introduction that controls the nature of the reading material in the primary grades, it is almost indistinguishable from other basal series. It now includes picture word cards as well as pictures in the intermediate grade books; pattern pages or lessons that present the words of a certain spelling pattern in isolation for prereading drill, and yet, as it must, the story content contains sight words that do not follow the basic patterns. All of these aspects violate Fries's theories (but make the series more teachable).

The *Merrill* readers introduce thirty-four pattern words all containing the short *a* sound in a medial position in the beginning book; sixteen others in the second book, etc., for a total of seventy-seven in the first grade. Of course, to accommodate this plan "stories" are contrived to repeat each patterned word (*Dad, sad, had, van, ran, cap, lap, cat, mat*, etc.) As Aukerman notes, this rigid restraint results in no use of anything resembling standard children's literature (1) or, as some say, anything resembling natural language. In the intermediate grades, the content is quite similar to other basals in illustrations, stories, articles, poems, and informational material.

Later editions have gradually added reading activities other than the unit "story" and reading enrichment materials (written within the restrictions of the word patterning), and have slightly broadened the content of the very limited teacher's manuals. The 1980 edition also includes a Placement Test and criterion-referenced Mastery Tests for each reading Level.

A typical unit lesson from a beginning *Merrill* reader is:

Pat Nat

Dan, look at the cat.
Look, at fat Nat.
Can Dan pat the fat cat?
He can pat Nat.
Can Jan pat Nat?
Jan can pat the cat.

Aukerman raises several obvious questions regarding the validity of this linguistic program (*1*, p. 250):

> By what magic do children cope with the irregular features of our language when they are not provided in this program?
> How can such a dismal primary program suddenly blossom into such a beautifully conceived intermediate reading program?

Tom Nicholson of the University of Waikato, New Zealand, comments (*32*):

> Stories of the fat cat variety seem to require children to use a magnifying glass in order to get to the words.

Assumptions of the Linguistic Approaches

The phonologists offer the following as linguistic principles that should be incorporated into or determine the nature of reading instruction.

1. Speech is the primary language function, and writing and reading are secondary or derived from oral language. Hence any child with normal speech is ready to begin reading.

2. Learning the names of the letters of the alphabet is of primary value in beginning reading (*3, 4*).

3. Words offered for beginning texts must include only those regularly consistent in the grapheme–phoneme correspondence. Simple regular words and nonsense syllables are most appropriate.

4. Interpretation of the meaning of printed words is quite secondary to the process of sound–symbol recognition (*12*).

5. Words of similar pattern (called spelling patterns) should be introduced simultaneously so that the child will be led to emphasize the sound–symbol relationship rather than other possible clues to recognition.

6. Pictures tend to give clues to word recognition and hence should be omitted (*3, 4*).

7. As presently taught, phonics should be eliminated because it teaches children (a) to sound words when they already know the sounds of their lan-

guage; (b) that each letter has a sound (but letters do not make sounds—they stand for sounds); (c) that a letter makes a sound (people make the sound); (d) that there are silent letters (it is impossible for a letter to make a sound or a silence); (e) children are taught how to pronounce words when they should be reading them (*43*).

8. Word recognition occurs by the successive decoding of graphemes, not by recognition of word form, word length, or configuration, context clues, or the like (*4, 5, 12*).

9. It is a fallacy of the whole-word method to confuse reading and understanding. One may learn to read without being able to understand or comprehend (*4, 5, 12, 25*).

In contrast, the structuralists offer these ideas, which are also supposed to be linguistic principles relevant to reading instruction.

1. Comprehension is based on auditory memories; hence readers' ability to hear the written word in its normal spoken inflection and to respond to the stress, tone, pitch, and junctures of the sentences as they read *silently*.
2. Language patterns of the text should be as varied and complex as those present in the child's spoken language (*48*).
3. A conscious learning of syntax or sentence patterns is a significant aid to comprehension (*37*).
4. Early emphasis upon recognition or reading of structural units might help solve some of the problems of eye span (*37*).

Let us examine critically these linguistic principles offered by the various schools of language science.

The Phonological Approach

Reading Versus Speech. The idea that reading is the mirror of speech is rejected by many reading and linguistic writers (*33, 50, 54*). They point out that the intonation patterns and tempo of spoken language, the pauses between ideas, and the meaningful silences, gestures, and grimaces of conversation are all lacking in the printed page. Other differences are the fewer phonetically different sounds in speaking (words and phrases are often run together), as well as the repetitive but structurally incomplete nature of spoken language. Book English just does not resemble the spoken word any more than the written composition of children or adults mirrors their own speech.

Moreover, as Weaver points out (*52*), reading is not a one-to-one translation of graphic symbols to verbal signs to mental interpretation, as some linguists seem to think. Decoding or translating graphemes into phonemes requires only recognition, not recall or interpretation. Interpreting reading has a higher information load, for the reader must incorporate the ideas he reads with his recall of previous ideas stored in his mind. Oral language, as in reading aloud, actually interferes with mental interpretation, and as a result oral reading produces weak comprehension.

Although we utilize language experience charts and the like to make children believe that reading is talking written down, reading and talking just are not parallel mental processes and the possession of normal language does not ensure success with reading.

The Alphabet. Some believe that we read by the recognition of letters or even by spelling words mentally rather than by the recognition of whole words (*3, 4, 12*). They would begin with the names of the letters, some assuming that this learning even reveals the sounds of the letters. Alphabetic methods are ancient in the history of reading instruction and have never proved effective. The shapes, heights, and position of letters do contribute to word recognition, but they do this by providing a clue to the Gestalt, the overall pattern of the word. No reader in any alphabetic language recognizes words letter by letter, or by spelling. No reader is really conscious of the letters in a word, unless he or she fails utterly to recognize the word. If we were conscious of the order of letters in words, how would we explain the tendency for errors in reading and spelling to cluster in the middles? Why does a reader read groups of words presented tachistoscopically in a tenth of a second, but only recognize strings of five to six letters?

If reading is a direct decoding of the letters of a word into sounds, how did the early Egyptians read their nonphonetic alphabet? How did Phoenicians manage to read an alphabet with no vowels? Many others reject the identification of words by the letters present in pointing out that word identification is too fast for letter-by-letter recognition (*46*). Also, words cannot be identified if letters are presented one at a time; the reaction time for a word is scarcely longer than that for a single letter; and, finally, words can be identified when the component letters are not individually discriminable.

Regular Versus Irregular Words. According to Bloomfield, the primary vocabulary should be carefully controlled in the regularity of the sounds the words contain (*3, 4*). He would include both real and nonsense words, provided they are regular. But nonsense words are not an aid to reading, for as Goldberg and Rasmussen found, such units are meaningless and unlearnable despite their phonemic consistency (*13*).

Our language is hardly phonetic, except in consonant sounds, and it is misleading to represent it in consonant–vowel–consonant (*CVC*) monosyllables. In Clymer's data, *CVC* introduces a short vowel sound in primary reading only 62 percent of the time (*8*). Of other favorite units of the linguists, *CVCe* (silent *e*) is consistent 63 percent of the time, and *CVVC* (with a long and a silent vowel) is true only 45 percent of the time. The sounds of the vowels, as Venezky's analysis shows (*48*), are determined by the order of letters and by phonological habits, and the variations are great. Moreover, polysyllabic words are seldom combinations of these monosyllables, except in true compound words.

There is an element of logic in the phonetic consistency of the Bloomfield–Barnhart and Fries teaching materials. Grouping words according to the sounds composing them seems a sensible way of promoting the growth of phonic generalizations and word attack skills. But like many of the other linguistic principles, this concept is not a new discovery. Note the marked similarity between the materials offered by Bloomfield–Barnhart and those from the *Gradual Primer*[1] of 1853.

Bloomfield–Barnhart (*3*, p. 63)	The Gradual Primer
cap gap lap map nap rap sap tap	Pen led Let Bell
pap yap Hap	men bed pet tell
a cap a gap a lap	ten red yet well
a map a rap a tap	I met ten men.
Dan had a tan cap.	I have a bad pen.
Hap had a nap. Dad had a nap.	Let men set a net.
. . . .	
. . . .	
. . . .	
Nat had a cap. Nan had a hat.	
cap gap hap lap map pap sap tap	
cad gad had lad mad pad sad tad	

Even in 1853, the fallacy of teaching the entire alphabet before beginning reading, as Bloomfield–Barnhart materials do, was recognized. Letters and words illustrating their sounds were introduced gradually in a realistic recognition of pupil limitations in learning capacities, an area in which linguists appear to be inexperienced.

This pseudo-logical approach to beginning reading was finally discarded in America after exhaustive investigation proved it ineffective for modern reading goals. The artificial vocabulary divorced from its inherent meaningfulness and the overemphasis upon letter sounds produced overly cautious, slow, and uncomprehending readers. American children of the past eventually learned to read by this method, and many European children are still taught in this fashion. But, unfortunately for the linguists' goals, the phonic method is most effective in preventing the development of a sentence sense or a habit of responding to the structural elements of language. Probably more than any other method, the highly phonic system promotes the tendency to unintelligent word-by-word reading without the consequent recognition of the total significance of the context.

Spelling Patterns. The phonologists prefer to use a reading vocabulary of monosyllables spelled in a particular pattern, such as *rat, hat, fat*. Such a list is what the educational psychologists call a minimal contrast arrangement and it has been the subject of many studies. Levin and Watson demonstrated that these lists are easier to learn than those in which sound–symbol correspondence varies, as *come, go, hot* (*27*). But the learning of other words later was less successful with minimal contrasts. Rothkopf (*36*), Hartley (*19*), and others have also shown that the learning of vocabulary is better when initial materials offer maximal contrasts.

There is, of course, the very relevant question of how and what kinds of words children learn most readily. To mention only a single study, Bickley showed again that in a list of words of equal frequency and commonality, pupils learned best those organized in terms of their own meaningful associations, not those grouped by class, by logical order, or by spelling patterns (*2*). Frequency counts by computer lead linguists to teach such items as *dd, gg, ft* (left), *lf* (half), *ndk* (handkerchief), *nd* (handsome), *pb* (raspberry), and *di* (soldier) as significant clues to word recognition. The logic of this mathematical derivation of instructional units escapes most reading authorities, such as the present writers.

Decoding Versus Meaning. To emphasize decoding as the heart of the reading process is consistent, we suppose, with the phonologists' preoccupation with reading by letters. We have already pointed out the fallacy in attempting to define reading as simply decoding letter sounds. Such a concept of the reading process leaves us without any understanding or explanation of comprehension.

One additional study may serve to make our point. Kolers asked adult bilingual speakers to read mixed passages in their two languages (*23*). They tended to mispronounce and wrongly accent words of their native language, translated some words into the other language, and changed syntactic arrangements as they read. Obviously a lot more goes on in reading than just translating graphemes into phonemes, as Goodman would have us believe (*15*).

No Pictures. It is true that there is some question whether the pictures used in readers make a contribution to comprehension. But, on the other hand, pictures related to words, as nouns and verbs, do help in word recognition, as MacKinnon and others have shown (*21, 29*). The decision to ban pictures in beginning reading is completely arbitrary, not based on any linguistic principles.

No Phonics. The type of phonics training in distorted letter-by-letter sounding decried by linguists is also deplored by most basal authors and reading experts. For this, and any other current phonics approach, linguists would substitute learning sound–symbol relationships in a series of words varying only in the initial and final consonant. Long vowels are usually presented later in the questionable *CVCe* unit, and vowel combinations in the *CVVC* pattern. Thus, by repetition of words of certain patterns children presumably learn the grapheme–phoneme correspondence.[2]

Most linguistic series do not teach the generalizations about these sounds that basals do; they stress initial consonant substitution as the only phonic skill, omitting such others as blending syllables, the effect of the accent, and the multiple spellings possible for vowel sounds. Some teach consonant blends, digraphs, or trigraphs; others do not. Prefixes and suffixes are apt to be taught as letter combinations rather than as elements modifying the meaning of the root word.

Some psycholinguists consider this phonological approach limited in its failure to integrate the facts from psychology, sociology, and even some linguistic fields as semantics (meanings of words), structural linguistics, and morphemics (combinations of sounds).

Word Recognition Clues. To accept the premise of those linguists who claim that word recognition occurs only by decoding, we would have to ignore all word recognition research of the past half-century. Even the recent psycholinguistic studies of children's word recognition errors refute this argument. Analysis of children's errors over an entire year indicates that something like 90 percent of the substitutions are related to the contextual or syntactic nature of the material (55). Children tend to substitute words that make sense semantically and syntactically, as a noun for a noun, a verb for a verb. Goodman has also shown that the average pupil corrected most of his or her errors in reading a list of words (two-thirds in first grade, three-fourths in second, and four-fifths in third grade) when reading the same words in context (14). Children do try to make use of the semantic and contextual information in sentences when reading.

Reading and Meaning. Although some deny it, it is apparent that the authors of some linguistic readers do not believe that reading is a meaning-getting process. This is evidenced by their presentation of words in lists; of nonsense as well as true words; the emphasis upon decoding words of similar patterns, ignoring whether or not the words are common in children's backgrounds; their deemphasis of readiness for reading; their omission of follow-up language activities to add depth of meaning; the overemphasis upon oral reading; the tendency to equate fluency in oral reading with comprehension; and, in some series, the use of materials never longer than a programmed frame or at best a sentence or two.

The Structural Approach

Auditory Memory. No reading specialist questions whether reading is part of the language process and is strongly related to auditory memories of spoken words. Teachers of reading show their understanding of this relationship daily in using children's spoken words as a source of reading materials in experience charts, stories, and records. Teachers strive to help children read aloud with normal intonations so that the reading will resemble familiar speech and the children will realize the inherent parallelism (48).

However, because of classroom experience with both normal and deaf children, teachers do not believe that success in reading is completely dependent upon auditory memory for speech. They teach deaf children to read who have no auditory memories as a source of constant reference. They see that even beginning readers can read silently, without having to hear every word in order to read it, as the linguists seem to feel they must. Auditory memories are helpful for beginning readers in the act of word recognition or word attack, but they are not absolutely essential.

This school of linguists tells us that children must learn to read by attending to the structural elements of sentences, to signals, modifiers, and inflections. Experienced reading teachers would not refute this principle, for they know that comprehension depends upon the correct interpretation of these structural components of language (25). Inability to deal with complex combinations of structures interferes markedly with a child's reasoning while reading. But no linguist has yet explained or illustrated how this is to be implemented. How can a child learn to read large sentence elements or complete sentences without a sight vocabulary? The teaching of word recognition is strongly decried by some linguists, for it destroys sentence sense and the recognition of the greater significance of the complete element or sentence, they say. Are we then to return to the rote sentence method of the last century, which failed because it neglected to recognize the word as the basic unit of reading? This school of linguists has failed to read the message of our earlier failures and to learn that no reader can develop without an ever-growing stock of sight words and skill in attacking new words. Reading is first a word recognition task and only secondly a process of interpretation of word combinations.

Language Patterns. By comparing the sentence patterns in children's speech with those in their readers, Strickland has declared that the readers should present sentence patterns as varied and complex as any of those used by children (46). Her definition of a sentence is an utterance that ends only when the speaker shows by silence or falling intonation that he or she has finished (or has run out of breath). With this unique definition of a sentence, Strickland, of course, found that children speak longer sentences than those in readers. She concluded that the simpler sentence structure of readers handicaps the children's language development.

It is true that many basal readers employ very short, simple, and repetitive sentences (and so do some of the linguistic readers). But this situation has changed markedly in recent editions. However, it does not follow that children are ready to process sentences in reading as long or complex as those they sometimes speak. The two processes differ, as has been pointed out, in terms of information load and retrieval of ideas. Besides, early reading is complicated by the constant task of word recognition, which interferes with comprehension—a problem completely absent in children's own speech, and present only occasionally in listening to others.

Syntax. Structuralists contend that a knowledge of syntactic patterns would improve reading comprehension at all levels. When we remember that children do use syntactic clues to aid word recognition, as shown earlier, this contention seems logical. However, experiments in teaching linguistic structure as a means of improving comprehension have been complete failures, according to O'Donnell (33) and Devine (11). As Sauer's study indicates (39), children vary in ability to handle sentence patterns at different rates, and a gradual gradation in sentence patterns in readers would meet children's developing skills more effectively.

Practice in manipulating sentences, distinguishing kernel sentences, combining kernels into longer sentences, and the like has shown some value in a few studies, although not all those reported.

Weaver denies that structure of the sentence is the vehicle controlling word choice (52). Word choice is controlled by the message of the sentence, he contends. Moreover, children's short-term memory is not good enough to deal with sentences in a verbatim fashion (any more than adults can). Rather, the reader reacts to the message received, plus previously stored ideas, not only to the syntactic structure of the sentence, in obtaining comprehension.

Structural Units and Eye Span. The emphasis on reading by structural units rather than by words is, of course, based on linguists' naive interpretation of the reading process. They believe that we read by groups of words—by structural components such as phrases, clauses, noun groups, and verb groups. Or, at least if we don't read in this fashion, we certainly should. We must stretch our eye span to encompass whole elements or sentences. The linguists are obviously unaware of the human visual limitations in the act of near-point reading, which make it impossible for us to see clearly letters much more than a half-inch from the point of fixation. As Hall does (18), some linguists ignore the studies on eye movements or the psychology of reading and consequently urge us to do the impossible in the act of reading. It is undoubtedly true that the meaning of a sentence is greater than the significance of the separate words composing it. But this sentence must be read practically word by word and processed mentally before its total meaning is apparent.

Even punctuation does not have a significant influence upon comprehension when reading orally or silently, for its absence in the material read by college sophomores affected only rate of reading in Johnson's report (21). Eye-movement studies indicate that readers' pauses do not correspond either to the structure or the punctuation of the sentence. Ancient Greek contained no interword spaces or punctuation, and no indication of the boundaries of words or sentences, yet some of the world's masterpieces were written and read in this style.

Pikulski points out that linguists object to synthetic phonics, since parts of words should not be isolated (34). Many reading experts from other disciplines would agree that the whole word should be the unit while dealing with phonic elements. But some linguists are willing to have these words be nonsense words, devoid of meaning. Others insist that the sentence is the proper unit of instruction.

In oral reading, many linguists emphasize the necessity of achieving proper intonation and avoiding of word-by-word reading in order to promote comprehension. However, they fail to recognize that word-by-word reading is probably a basic developmental stage while the child is growing toward fluency, and that it does not necessarily interfere with comprehension in very simple materials such as those used in the beginning reading program (7). Linguists would instruct teachers not to waste time in correcting oral reading errors, but rather to ignore them unless they cause a change in the meaning, a recommendation with which we agree.

Poor oral reading causes poor comprehension, according to some linguists who fail to recognize that oral reading does not yield good comprehension under most circumstances. According to them, the form of the sentences should match the syntactical form of the sentences of the reader. This, of course, is most unlikely when the reader is bilingual or uses a dialect. Like the present authors, some linguists stress that the materials should reflect the language skills and background experiences of the readers, which, they too agree, is most readily achieved in language experience writings.

Linguists have helped teachers gain a better attitude toward children's dialect and to ignore it in making evaluations of children's reading. However, despite the validity and relevance of some of these linguistic suggestions, Pikulski points out, there is a growing disenchantment with that field because the common problems in instruction still persist (34). Also, as we have noted, many of these linguistic principles are not new.

The Research

DeLawter compared second graders who had been taught by a linguistic decoding approach (the Miami and the Merrill readers) with those using a basal system (the Chandler Language Experience readers) (10). After two years of instruction, the meaning-oriented children tended toward oral miscues that were real words, whereas the linguistically trained pupils produced mostly nonword miscues. DeLawter concluded that the linguistic approach tends to produce a high percentage of mispronunciations or nonwords, errors that show graphic similarity to the printed word but are semantically inappropriate much of the time. Self-corrections by these pupils were made largely on the basis of graphic cues (letter sounds), not contextual or semantic cues. As the psycholinguists would say, these pupils had been trained to respond mainly to the graphophonemic cues, which are the least significant printed cues for obtaining meaning.

Ruddell compared basal, basal plus language structure, a programmed linguistic series, and the programmed plus language structure (37, 38). The results varied at the end of the first and at the end of the second year, but in summary it appeared that there were hardly any real differences between the effectiveness of the four approaches. The linguistic programmed series was improved by the language structure training, but the basal program was not. On the whole, the students utilizing linguistic programs tended to show greater skill in word recognition than the basal.

One study compared basal and linguistic programs plus dialect training among four classes of rural black children. It found no advantages for the dialect training under either reading method, and no differences in reading performances with either approach. Using the Fries readers versus a basal, Schneyer reported the basal groups superior in paragraph meaning, spelling, and phonic skills in the total comparison (40). In comprehension, the basal produced superior results for average pupils only, and superior phonic skills for high-ability pupils only. In oral reading, basal pupils were superior in both rate and accuracy. The advantages of better writing mechanics, spelling, and total number of words in a writing sample among first-grade linguistic pupils disappeared in the second grade.

In a follow-up study at third grade with the same pupils, Schneyer found the only significant difference to be in favor of basal pupils in phonic skills (40). In writing, linguistic pupils used more running words and they were superior in rate but not in accuracy in oral reading.

William D. Sheldon et al. also continued their first-grade comparative study through the third grade (42, 43). They contrasted a basal versus a modified linguistic (Stern's *Structural Reading*) versus a true linguistic (Bloomfield's *Let's Read*). At the end of the first grade, basal pupils were superior in rate and accuracy of oral reading only. In second grade, the two linguistic systems resulted in better word meaning, spelling, and oral comprehension. No differences in any reading skills appeared at the end of the third grade, and, as Sheldon pointed out, regardless of the system used, some pupils from each group were still disabled in reading.

Wyatt compared three linguistic systems, *Royal Road Readers*, the *Linguistic Readers* (Benziger Corp.), and the *Lippincott Basic Readers*, with a multibasal program (55). At the end of the first grade, the linguistic systems gave superior results in word recognition only, and this difference was true just for girls.

J. Cayce Morrison contrasted structural patterns versus vocabulary training versus both among Puerto Rican pupils in New York City (31). All three approaches produced gains in writing and speaking, but none affected reading scores. In fact, the structural patterns and the vocabulary plus structural groups showed losses in reading.

Davis contrasted a basal supplemented by modified Bloomfield materials versus a basal (8). For a small number of first graders, the dual system produced better scores in word recognition only. Davis concluded that the linguistic materials did not retard reading development, but neither did they make much of a contribution.

Other studies of this type are reported by Wardhaugh, with quite similar results (49). Although all the results are not consistent, it does appear that linguistic systems tend to produce better word recognition only. In contrast, the same systems tend to produce inferior oral reading in both rate and accuracy than do common basal systems. The emphasis upon sound–symbol correspondence produces inconsistent results in current phonics tests and no differences in the ability to read regular or irregular words. The emphasis upon structural language knowledge does not produce any measurable improvement in comprehension. And despite the almost violent objections of the phonologists to current phonics teaching, their systems produce just about the same results—better word recognition.

At the moment we can see several possible contributions of linguistics to reading. After the research has been done, perhaps we will discover the proper learning sequence and the most effective method to present the basic sounds of our language. We hope, as Constance McCullough has suggested (28), the linguists may help us in teaching the relativity of language—the variants in sounds because of adjoining letters and the influence of context upon word and sentence meanings. Perhaps they too will recognize the logic of simultaneously teaching sounds, words, and forms that are grossly different, for this is obviously the most effective approach. We may hope that linguists will cease trying to superimpose adult logic upon children's learning, for as Constance McCullough says, "We don't sound the whole sentence before we utilize clues to structure, sense some possible clues to meaning and relationship, formulate hunches about the total meaning, and see possible applications of this meaning to past and future ideas" (28, p.189).

Since children's ability to deal with inflected words, as plurals, past tense, etc., seems to be related to reading, at least by the second grade (6), linguists might help us explore appropriate ways of conveying this information to children. Since both reading and language specialists believe that children's language development is significant for reading success, perhaps they will enter into joint research to discover why certain studies seem to deny this relationship (5, 54). Are the measures of language we are using inappropriate or is this really a tenable assumption? Doris Gunderson says that reading specialists need information from linguists regarding the significance of dialect and context clues (17). She also questions why linguists do not try to help with studies of how language is learned, in relating this development to learning theory, in finding principles of learning language, and in determining the interaction of learning style, racial and ethnic backgrounds, and language development. Some reading experts, such as Arthur W. Heilman, are pessimistic about such future possibilities, as expressed in his statement, "While every linguist is entitled to hypothesize as to how reading should be taught, there is nothing in the body of linguistic science which relates to the issue of *how children learn to read*" (*20*, p. 104).

Bill Martin, Jr., author of the delightful *Sounds of Language Series* (Holt, Rinehart and Winston), has said all this about linguistics much more entertainingly:

> Even the new linguistic materials that gave us so much hope that children would have a chance to respond to the dependable and variable parts of language patterns are scarcely more than re-done phonics programs. They, too, seem to be trapped by their focus on individual words. The repetitive reading of similarly constructed syllables such as *ham, gam, bam, sam, pam, ram* and *dam* may trigger visual recognition of structure, but it leads no further than phonic programs which give children a meager and unwarranted picture of our language.
>
> This does not deny the potential contribution of structural linguistics to children's reading materials once someone finds a way to translate linguistic insights into wholesome language patterns. But sentences such as "Nat has a fat bat" have been floating around in our readers since readers began and the fact that they are now paraded under the label of linguistics does not camouflage their weakness.[3]

Endnotes

1. After Tower, David B., *The Gradual Primer*, Boston: Sanborn, Carter, Bazin and Co., 1853, as cited by Smith, Nila B., *American Reading Instruction*, New York: Silver Burdette Company, 1934, 110–111.
2. See Emans, Robert, "Linguists and Phonics," *Reading Teacher*, 26 (February 1973), 477–482.
3. Reprinted from Martin, Bill Jr., "Literature, Linguistics and Reading," *Florida Reading Quarterly*, 1 (March 1965), 9–22. By permission of the author and the editors of the *Quarterly*.

Discussion Questions

1. Compare a basal reading series and a linguistic reading series using the guide outlined in the discussion questions at the end of Chapter 2.

2. How do linguistic concepts of the reading process differ from those believed by the authors of basals? From those offered by other reading experts? (See Chapter 1 for various definitions of reading.)

3. Discuss your understanding of the parallelism between speech and reading, and the ease with which children may make the transition.

4. What is your reaction to the tendency by some linguists to equate the act of reading with spelling by controlling the reading vocabulary according to spelling patterns of words? In such an approach, how do you think those words which do not fol-

low common spelling patterns would be taught? How does such an approach deal with the influence of word meaning upon learning?

5. Arrange to visit a classroom using a linguistic system. Share your observations with your class.

References

1. Aukerman, Robert C., *The Basal Reader Approach to Reading.* New York: John Wiley & Sons, 1981.
2. Bickley, A. C., "Categorization Constraints on Beginning Readers," Nineteenth Yearbook, National Reading Conference, 1972.
3. Bloomfield, Leonard, "Linguistics and Reading,"*Elementary English,* 19 (April 1942), 125–130, 183–186.
4. Bloomfield, Leonard, and Barnhart, C. L., *Let's Read.* Detroit: Wayne State University Press, 1961.
5. Bougere, Marguerite Bondy, "Selected Factors in Oral Language Related to First Grade Reading Achievement," *Reading Research Quarterly,* 5 (Fall 1969), 31–58.
6. Brittain, Mary M., "Inflectional Performance and Early Reading Achievement," *Reading Research Quarterly,* 6 (Fall 1970), 34–48.
7. Clay, Marie M, "Emergent Reading Behavior." Doctoral dissertation, University of Auckland, Auckland, New Zealand, 1966.
8. Clymer, Theodore, "The Utility of Phonic Generalizations in the Primary Grades," *Reading Teacher,* 16 (January 1963), 252–258.
9. Davis, David C., "Phonemic Structural Approach to Initial Reading Instruction," *Elementary English,* 41 (March 1964), 218–223.
10. DeLawter, Jayne A., "The Relationship of Beginning Reading Instruction and Miscue Patterns," in *Help for the Reading Teacher: New Directions in Research,* Wm. D. Page, ed. National Conference on Research in English, 1975, 42–51.
11. Devine, T. G., "Linguistic Research and the Teaching of Reading," *Journal of Reading,* 9 (March 1966), 272–277.
12. Fries, Charles C., *Linguistics and Reading.* New York: Holt, Rinehart and Winston, 1963.
13. Goldberg, Lynn, and Rasmussen, Donald, "Linguistics in Reading," in *Explorations in Reading,* Albert J. Mazurkiewicz, ed. Lehigh University Conference Proceedings, 2 (June 1962), 22–27.
14. Goodman, Kenneth S., "A Linguistic Study of Cues and Miscues in Reading," *Elementary English,* 42 (October 1965), 639–643.
15. Goodman, Kenneth S., "Decoding—From Code to What?" *Journal of Reading,* 14 (April 1971), 455–462, 498.
16. Goodman, Kenneth S., "The Linguistics of Reading," *Elementary School Journal,* 65 (April 1964), 355–361.
17. Gunderson, Doris, "Are Linguistic Programs Different?" in *Some Persistent Questions on Beginning Reading,* Robert C. Aukerman, ed. Newark, Del.: International Reading Association, 1972.
18. Hall, Robert A., *Sounds and Spelling in English.* Phildelphia: Chilton, 1961.

19. Hartley, Ruth Norene, "Effect of List Types and Cues in the Learning of Word Lists," *Reading Research Quarterly*, 6 (Fall 1970), 97–112.

20. Heilman, Arthur W., "Research Findings Concerning Phonics in Beginning Reading," in *A Decade of Innovations: Approaches to Beginning Reading*, Elaine C. Vilscek, ed. Proceedings of the International Reading Association, 12, Part 3, 1968, 100–106.

21. Johnson, David C., "The Effect of Reading and Punctuation Variations upon Reading Comprehension," in *Reading: The Right to Participate*, Twentieth Yearbook, National Reading Conference, 1971, 304–311.

22. King, Ethel M., and Muehl, S., "Different Sensory Cues as Aids in Beginning Reading," *Reading Teacher*, 19 (December 1965), 163–168.

23. Kolers, Paul A., "Reading Is Only Incidentally Visual," in *Psycholinguistics and the Teaching of Reading*, Kenneth S. Goodman, and James T. Fleming, eds. Newark, Del.: International Reading Association, 1969, 8–16.

24. Langman, Muriel Potter, "What Other Magazines Say About Reading," *Reading Teacher*, 15 (March 1962), 379–384.

25. LeFevre, Carl A., "Language Patterns and Their Graphic Counterparts: A Linguistic View of Reading," *Journal of Developmental Reading*, 4 (Spring 1961), 147–158.

26. LeFevre, Carl A., "The Simplistic Standard Word Perception Theory of Reading," *Elementary English*, 45 (March 1968), 349–353, 355.

27. Levin, Harry, and Watson, J., *The Learning of Variable Grapheme to Phoneme Correspondence: Variations in the Initial Consonant Position.* Cornell University Cooperative Research Project, No. 639, 1963.

28. McCullough, Constance M., "Applying Structural Linguistics in Beginning Reading: Vital Principles in Need of Application," in *A Decade of Innovations: Approaches to Beginning Reading*, Elaine C. Vilscek, ed. Proceedings of the International Reading Association, 12, Part 3, 1968, 180–191.

29. MacKinnon, A. R., *How Do Children Learn to Read?* Toronto: Copp, Clark, 1959.

30. Marquardt, W. F., "Language Interference in Reading," *Reading Teacher*, 18 (December 1964), 214–218.

31. Morrison, J. Cayce, *The Puerto Rican Study.* New York: Board of Education, City of New York, 1958.

32. Nicholson, Tom, *Anatomy of Reading.* Sydney: Martin Educational, 1982, 41.

33. O'Donnell, Roy C., "The Relationship Between Awareness of Structural Relationships in English and Ability in Reading Comprehension." Doctoral dissertation, George Peabody College for Teachers, Nashville, 1961.

34. Pikulski, John J., "Linguistics Applied to Reading," *Language Arts*, 53 (April 1976), 373–377, 384.

35. Pival, J. G., "Stress, Pitch and Juncture: Tools in the Diagnosis and Treatment of Reading Ills," *Elementary English*, 55 (May 1968), 458–463.

36. Rothkopf, E. Z., "Stimulus Similarity and Sequence of Stimulus Presentation in Paired Associate Learning," *Journal of Experimental Psychology*, 56 (1958), 114–122.

37. Ruddell, Robert B., "Reading Instruction in First Grade with Varying Emphasis upon the Regularity of Grapheme–Phoneme Correspondence and the Relation of Language Structure to Reading," *Reading Teacher*, 19 (May 1966), 653–660.

38. Ruddell, Robert B., "Reading Instruction in First Grade with Varying Emphasis on the Regularity of Grapheme–Phoneme Correspondence and the Relation of

Language Structure to Meaning—Extended into the Second Grade," *Reading Teacher*, 20 (May 1967), 730–739.

39. Sauer, Lois E., "Fourth Grade Children's Knowledge of Grammatical Structure," *Elementary English*, 47 (October 1970), 807–813.

40. Schneyer, J. Wesley, "Reading Achievement of First Grade Children Taught by a Linguistic Approach and a Basal Reader Approach—Extended into Third Grade," *Reading Teacher*, 22 (January 1969), 315–319.

41. Seymour, Dorothy Z., "The Difference Between Linguistics and Phonics," *Reading Teacher*, 23 (November 1969), 99–102, 111.

42. Sheldon, William D., Nichols, Nancy, and Lashinger, Donald R., "Effect of First Grade Instruction Using Basal Readers, Modified Linguistic Materials and Linguistic Readers—Extended into Second Grade," *Reading Teacher*, 20 (May 1967), 720–725.

43. Sheldon, William D., Stinson, Frange, and Peebles, James D., "Comparison of Three Methods of Reading: A Continuation Study in the Third Grade," *Reading Teacher*, 22 (March 1969), 539–546.

44. Smith, Frank, and Holmes, Deborah Loft, "The Independence of Letter, Word and Meaning Identification in Reading," *Reading Research Quarterly*, 6 (Spring 1971), 394–415.

45. Soffietti, James P., "Why Children Fail to Read: A Linguistic Analysis," *Harvard Educational Review*, 25 (Spring 1955), 63–84.

46. Strickland, Ruth G., "The Language of Elementary School Children in Relationship to the Language of Reading Textbooks and the Quality of Reading of Selected Children," *Bulletin of the School of Education*, Indiana University, 38 (July 1962), 1–131.

47. Veatch, Jeanette, "Linguistic Instruction in the Teaching of Reading: Kill or Cure?" *Elementary English*, 39 (March 1962), 231–233, 243.

48. Venezky, R. L., "English Orthography: Its Graphical Structure and Its Relation to Sound," *Reading Research Quarterly*, 2 (Spring 1967), 75–105.

49. Wardhaugh, Ronald, "Is the Linguistic Approach an Improvement in Reading Instruction?" in *Current Issues in Reading*, Nila Banton Smith, ed. Proceedings of the International Reading Association, 13, Part 2, 1969, 254–267.

50. Warfel, Harry R., "A Bag with Holes," *Journal of Developmental Reading*, 3 (Autumn 1959), 43–50.

51. Warfel, Harry R., and Lloyd, Donald J., "The Structural Approach to Reading," *School and Society*, 85 (June 8, 1957), 100–201.

52. Weaver, Wendell, W., "Linguistic Assumptions and Reading Instruction," in *The Psychology of Reading Behavior*, Eighteenth Yearbook, National Reading Conference, 1969, 107–112.

53. Weber, Rose-Marie, "A Linguistic Analysis of First Grade Reading Errors," *Reading Research Quarterly*, 5 (Spring 1970), 427–451.

54. Winter, Clotilda, "Interrelationships Among Language Variables in Children of First and Second Grade," *Elementary English*, 34 (February 1957), 108–113.

55. Wyatt, Nita M., *Reading Achievement of First Grade Boys vs. First Grade Girls Using Two Approaches: A Linguistic Approach and a Basal Reader Approach with Boys and Girls Grouped Separately*. Project 2735, University of Kansas, 1966.

Supplementary Reading

Aukerman, Robert, C., *Some Persistent Questions on Beginning Reading*. Newark, Del.: International Reading Association, 1972.

Fries, Charles C., *Linguistics and Reading*. New York: Holt, Rinehart and Winston, 1963.

Goodman, Kenneth S., ed., *The Psycholinguistic Nature of the Reading Process*. Detroit: Wayne State University Press, 1968.

Goodman, Kenneth S., and Fleming, James T., eds., *Psycholinguistics and the Teaching of Reading*. Newark, Del.: International Reading Association, 1969.

Gunderson, Doris V., comp., *Language and Reading: An Interdisciplinary Approach*, Washington, D.C.: Center for Applied Linguistics, 1970.

Henry, Nelson B., ed., *Linguistics in School Programs*, Sixty-Ninth Yearbook, National Society for the Study of Education, Part II. Chicago: University of Chicago Press, 1970.

Lamb, Pose, *Linguistics in Proper Perspective*. Columbus: Charles E. Merrill, 1977.

Lefevre, Carl A., *Linguistics and the Teaching of Reading*. New York: McGraw-Hill, 1964.

Postman, Neil, and Weingarten, Charles, *Linguistics: A Revolution in Teaching*. New York: Dell, 1977.

Ruddell, Robert B., *Innovations in Reading-Language Instruction*. Englewood Cliffs, N.J.: Prentice-Hall, 1974.

Savage, John F., *Linguistics for Teachers: Selected Readings*. Chicago: Science Research Associates, 1973.

Smith, Frank, *Psycholinguistics and Reading*. New York: Holt, Rinehart and Winston, 1973.

Smith, Nila B., *Current Issues in Reading*. Proceedings of the International Reading Association, 13, Part 2, 1969.

Vilscek, Elaine C., ed., *A Decade of Innovations: Approaches to Beginning Reading*. Proceedings of the International Reading Association, 12, Part 3, 1968.

Waller, T. Gary, and Mackinnon, G. E., *Reading Research: Advances in Theory and Practice*. New York: Academic Press, 1979.

Weaver, Constance, *Psycholinguistics and Reading: From Process to Practice*. Englewood Cliffs, N.J.: Prentice-Hall, 1980.

5 Using the Language Experience Approach

More than any other approach to the teaching of reading, the language experience approach conceives of learning to read as part of the process of language development. It alone recognizes the close relationship among reading, speaking, writing, and listening. It alone realizes that progress in reading is determined by the extent of the child's experiences in all these language media, prior to and during his or her early school years. Proponents of this approach clearly see that children cannot be expected to deal with ideas or language in reading that are much farther advanced than those they can speak or write.

Within such a philosophical framework, books become a resource tool rather than a basic device to teach children to read (or, as they really function, a device to help children memorize printed words). Books and readers help supply the vicarious experiences, the depth of meanings for the words which the child needs to express his or her ideas in oral and written work. Many other classroom and extra-classroom activities, plus teacher instruction and demonstration, further this development of concepts that will be translated into words. Learning to read then, in the language experience method, is interpreted as development in thinking and in expression of language.

In this approach to reading, the level of language at which the beginner functions is not highly significant. He or she may be weak or facile in the use of words. Progress becomes an individual matter with each child gradually developing a broader and deeper skill with words and moving toward more complex language patterns that help convey thoughts.

The language experience approach is unique among all other approaches in its rejection of the dichotomizing of language development into separate and unrelated learnings. It declares that speaking, listening, writing, and reading are interrelated and interdependent. It recognizes that children learn to read out of his present and past experiences with language, not only by perusing the pages of a book. Only the language experience method begins where children are in terms of their ability to think with words and simultaneously stimulates their language development in all media of expression and reception, in the hope of leading toward the ultimate goal of reading the writings of others.

Language experience maximizes the correspondence between the printed word and children's language, since it is often their own language they are reading. Moreover, the parallels between their speech and the reading matter provide for optimum success, as recent studies of the importance of using familiar oral sentence patterns in reading matter show.

Because of the current widespread attention to the language experience technique and the recent appearance of some commercial instructional materials, many teachers are under the impression that the practice is quite new and probably was invented by those authors. Actually, as Hildreth has shown in her historical review (14), it was used in several experimental schools before 1900, and discussed at considerable length in a yearbook on new materials of instruction in 1920. The term "language experience" was used first in 1934, by which time most of the basic practices of the method had been evolved. For example, the significant relationships of learning to read to writing, oral fluency, and the development of other language abilities was recognized. The use of children's own stories was considered a real reading experience at a pre-book stage, not simply readiness training or preparation for the vocabulary of basal readers. A wide variety of charts and stories was used for many learning activities as well as being the medium for teaching phonic and other skills. The values of the approach were widely recognized, for Hildreth mentions its use in England, France, Central and South America, Turkey, and New Zealand prior to 1960.

Objectives and Assumptions

The language experience approach attempts to bring reading and other communication skills together in the instructional program (4). No sharp distinction is made between the reading program and other language activities. In other words, the plan for reading instruction is based not on some series of books but on the oral and written expression and identified needs of the children. The basic motivation is approached through the child's realization that oral language, based on his or her thoughts and experiences as well as the ideas of others, can be written and thus read. This self-realization may be expressed, as Allen has phrased it (2):

> What I can think about, I can talk about.
> What I can say, I can write.
> What I can write, I can read.
> I can read what I write and what other people can write for me to read.

The assumption here is, of course, that reading is a by-product of children's thinking and oral expression. Progress in reading is therefore directly dependent upon their growth in experiences, which is translated into oral language and written expression. Our present knowledge of the significance of their experiential background, language development, and understanding of spoken language for reading progress would seem to support these assumptions.

MaryAnne Hall offers what she terms a linguistic rationale for language experience as follows (8):

- The beginning reader must be taught to view reading as a communication process.
- The beginning reader is a user of language.
- The beginning reader should understand the reading process as one of consciously relating print to oral language.
- The beginning reader should incorporate the learning of writing with the learning of reading.
- The beginning reader should learn to read with materials written in his language patterns.
- The beginning reader should learn to read meaningful language.
- The beginning reader should learn to read orally with smooth, fluent expression.

Hardly any reading expert would disagree with the general implications of Hall's statements, although many would question their exact meanings. In support of using writing as an aid to reading, Gertrude Hildreth (13) emphasizes the wide use of this procedure in other countries. She also believes that simultaneous training promotes reading growth by aiding memory of letter forms, directing attention to structural elements and other details of words, helping to form the habit of left-to-right direction in dealing with words, and providing an overt activity for restless pupils. Other advantages to the program, according to Hildreth (which we would certainly recognize as present in this approach to reading), are its tendency to strengthen association between word forms and meanings and to promote familiarity with sentence patterns.

Marie Dionisio gives us some idea of the results of integrating writing into the reading progam (6). These include: students sharing their writing, discovering the need for revision and more care, rereading, reacting to others' writings, expanding their reading to find facts and new writing topics, trying to acquire or imitate writing styles (poetry, plays, etc.), and learning to edit with the aid of dictionaries, grammar books, etc.

Methods and Materials

From the first day of school each child is encouraged to share his or her ideas and experiences with others through oral expression and the pictures he or she creates. As the child paints, works with clay, conducts science experiments, and looks at books, the teacher helps him or her to summarize ideas and discoveries. The child dictates, and the teacher writes the ideas on the child's drawing or elsewhere. The charts that result are then shared with others as the child reads (tells) his or her recorded stories. During the writing of the chart the teacher discusses word choice, sentence structure, and the sounds of letters and words. But the teacher does not censor or elaborate the story other than by preparing it in the proper experience chart manner.

In some classrooms the child dictates his or her material into a tape recorder. The tape is then given to the teacher or an aide to type and return to the child (*31*). This approach would, of course, precede the time when the child begins to write stories. If this procedure were allowed to continue through the year, it would deprive children of the marked advantages that accrue to their reading progress from the reinforcing writing experiences. Other teachers organize a group story on the blackboard and then copy it and distribute it to the children after making copies on a primer typewriter. Other teachers use flannelboard or a large chart to write the first version of the group story, after which the large chart or children's copies of it are used in various ways.

As Russell G. Stauffer has pointed out, the language experience approach makes a strong contribution to beginning reading. He suggests that after several weeks of experience with group-composed charts, small groups be formed within the class. These groups are organized on the bases of language facility, social maturity, and the children's interests and compatibility. By the grouping, the teacher will have more opportunity for stimulating small-group or individually dictated stories. A rotating schedule for teacher-group conferences should be arranged, and as each group meets, individual charts on group stories are dictated to the teacher. Since the stories should be quite brief, perhaps only two or three sentences at this stage, these activities are not as time-consuming as they might seem (*32*). The small groups also provide more opportunity for frequent exchange or presentation of children's own stories to other children. Small-group reading, learning to read one's own story independently, preparing illustrations for a story, practicing with individual word cards, and using picture dictionaries or other related resource books for additional ideas or words are activities promoted even at this early reading stage.

Soon each child manifests the desire to write his or her own stories, and is immediately encouraged and helped to do so. This breakthrough from oral to written expression marks the beginning of the child's efforts to produce written material and the beginning of instruction in reading and writing. Devices such as lists of service words, picture dictionaries, labels on classroom objects, lists of interest or topical words, and other children's charts help pupils rapidly extend their writing (and reading) vocabularies. Each child's charts are illustrated and bound into his or her book. Other books are created by collections of science, social science, and other content materials contributed by various pupils. Each child's charts and books, as well as the communal books, are shared freely and contribute to the writing and reading growth of the other children.

In the beginning months, the children's stories about their drawings, cut-outs, or easel paintings take such forms as these, when written by the teacher:

> *This here is an alligator.*
> *He eats fish and golf balls.*

Later, the children may begin to label their own drawings:

See me Tommy.
See Mary fish.

The children are encouraged to read and write with the aid of model sentences. These are examples:

Something I like is _____.
I don't like _____.
I ran to the _____.
Here is a big _____.
I can help _____.

Some groups prepare a class newspaper and place it on a bulletin board just outside the room for passersby to read, as:

Fire!

Did you see the fire?
It was at the A & P store.
It was a big fire.
Joan's daddy works there.
He didn't get hurt.

Rhyme and other phonic characteristics of words are emphasized by encouraging children to illustrate and write about such word groups:

tail–mail   *red–bed*
kite–bite   *A goat in a coat.*
fun–done   *The bean is green.*

Model sentences emphasizing initial consonants and context as clues to word meaning are to be completed by the children:

I caught a big f_____ on my line.
Do you want s_____ for your lunch?
Boots is a black-and-white c_____.

These experiences lead rapidly toward increased development of written expression, resulting in such efforts, halfway through the first grade, as:

Mother went to the store to buy a pumpkin. She saw all kinds of pumpkins. Some were big and some were little. She bought a little pumpkin and made a pumpkin pie. I made a halloween mask out of the shell.

Once upon a time I jumped into a pool and I drowned, I had to come up for breath. I came up and I got out of the pool. I went home and went to bed. I ate some fish.

Once upon a time there were two little boys. One was Cliff and one was Scott. They threw pie all over the school. They were bad.

Two little girls wanted to go trick or treating. The larger girls and boys went with them. They were frightened by a large flower. They all held hands and ran. Most of the children lost their trick or treatings. They all ran home.

A year later in the second grade some children are producing stories such as these (in their original spelling):

How We Got Our Canery

In first grade Mrs. Bankhead's room we wanted a canery, so we went to Woolworth on a bus. The other first grade went too. We all got us a bird and we were very happy, but it was funny. She never sang. We called her tweety.

Once Mrs. Zabcik said that who ever broght a note to school first would get to take the bird home for the summer. And I got to take the bird home. When I got the bird home it wouldent moov. The first day we washed it. It splashed and it got me all wet. The birds body was yellow and there was a little white spot on his head. Her name was Tweety. The summer was almost over and Tweety died.

Are you my mother. One day a mother bird felt a little tap from her egg. She sead I will go and get some food for my Baby. So she set off. Then pop out came a Baby Bird. It sead where is my mother he sead. He sead do I have a mother oh yes I do or I would not be here.

Various simple readers, trade books, science books, and so forth, are available to the class. These are constantly used as resource materials for ideas, for vocabulary, for enrichment, for spelling, and for other purposes. Each child, to a degree, learns a personal writing–reading vocabulary suitable to his or her needs for self-expression. No artificial controls are placed on the vocabulary any child employs. The service words that are significant for almost all reading and writing are given special attention by the teacher in charts available to all.

Phonics instruction is developed on a "say it–see it" basis, in which the child gradually learns how to represent by letters the sounds he or she wishes to record on paper. If generalizations or rules appear, they do because of spontaneous generalization by the pupils, not by deductive teaching. Phonic elements may be emphasized by the teacher in working with an individual or a small group, but the emphasis is purely on translating sounds of oral language into written form.

Emphasis is not placed upon separate periods for instruction in phonics or spelling. Rather these skills are based on the vocabulary used in the children's own stories. The sequence of instruction in phonics is similar to that of many basal programs, but the instruction is usually in small groups and related to the words and spelling in a particular composition by the children. Phonics, structural analysis, contextual analysis, and vocabulary are introduced as children appear to need them in writing and reading their own and other children's materials. There may be assigned or suggested reading but, again, this is related to the purposes and needs of the children in producing their material. Dictionaries, charts of words grouped by common phonic elements or themes or spelling, and other sources of words are offered freely. Recreational or free reading in class and at home is encouraged by providing a wide variety of books and children's booklets.

In the language experience approach, evaluation of pupil progress is not based primarily on standardized or informal reading tests, for these would sample only one facet of the language development being stimulated. Rather, pupil growth in ability to express ideas in oral and written form and to comprehend the writings of peers and to react actively to these is constantly observed. Growth in clarity and depth of thinking, in sentence sense, mechanics, and spelling is revealed in the child's own productions.

A group of stories written by a child may be bound in an attractive folder decorated by the child and taken home to display reading ability to his or her parents. Many teachers duplicate a collection of their pupil's stories and send this home with appropriate explanation and comments. Children are also encouraged to read from these booklets in class and at home, as well as to compose additional stories, book reports, and the like at home. See Chapter 9 for ideas on instructional techniques using children's stories.

Other Applications of the Approach

Russell G. Stauffer has reacted to our reviews of the language experience method in other writings by reminding us that there are a number of versions of the technique. Perhaps because of these variations, the research results of his and other trials we will cite later differ in their outcomes. Hence we should certainly point out some of the different applications of this system.

Working with black children of low-socioeconomic background, Margaret Irish evolved an introduction to the method which is particularly relevant to these children (17). She chose a local black college basketball player who had achieved national recognition, as well as a $1 million contract upon entering the professional ranks. She supplied the children with photographs, drawings of his hands and feet, taped interviews, biographical and personal history information, and the like. A school day was designated in his honor and the food he liked was served. Stories were composed by individuals or groups first about their hero, later on other sports figures, themselves, book characters, etc. Thus she led the children from an intensely interesting figure with whom they readily identified to other more personal themes. In other ethnic groups, Irish has employed a different hero, suited to the nature of the children involved.

A number of other writers, including Shuy (29), have emphasized the desirability of the language experience approach for culturally or linguistically different pupils. As Shuy suggests, using the child's own language avoids the types of sentences that give trouble to these children and minimizes the child's errors in omitting inflections and word endings and his or her problems with other aspects of standard English grammar.

Platt has her own version of this technique for use with culturally or linguistically different children (27). She labels the objects each child draws. Later she puts each child's drawings together into simple books, using the child's own words as the basis for simple stories that she writes in relation to each of the drawings. After a total vocabulary of 230 or so words has thus been learned, she moves the children into the basal first reader. We wonder why, if the method is satisfactory for the very beginning stages, Platt finds it necessary to drop it and move toward a structured system (which is often not really suitable for such pupils in its content).

Another version which has received wide attention is that termed "Organic Teaching," devised by Sylvia Ashton-Warner in her teaching Maori children in New Zealand. She recognizes four movements or periods in the child's development. The first is called the Output Period. Each day of this period, in a one-to-one session with the teacher, the child selects one word to be learned, out of the discussion of personal feelings. He or she receives help in tracing and noting the distinctive features of the word as it is printed by the teacher on a small card. The next morning all the children's words are placed in a pile, from which each must pick Key Words. Those they do not remember are discarded as unrepresentative of their own inner feelings. During the daily Intake Period, new words are gathered from the activities in the classroom and at home, and added to the pile of Key Words (37).

Later stages of Ashton-Warner's system include the use of small chalkboards instead of paper, and instruction in letter formation to aid children in writing their Key Words (which are gradually expanded into phrases on new cards, presumably to introduce the essential function words). Small books are composed by the teacher from each child's word and phrase cards. Finally, small books are written by the children and these gradually progress to collections of the children's stories.

The use of a Key Word method of teaching word recognition, which probably follows at least in part Ashton-Warner's ideas, has been the subject of several evaluations. Packer used this idea in four cities and discovered that the vocabulary learned by most of the children had little similarity to basal word lists (26). This must have been disappointing to him if, like Platt and others, he expected the Key Word approach to prepare children for a basal reader.

Roach Van Allen directed one of the earliest large-scale studies of language experience in a three-year trial in San Diego (1). On the whole, the results of this experiment indicated support for the system as a basic way of teaching beginning reading. On the basis of this experience, Allen and his wife prepared teachers' manuals and pupil activity books presenting their version of the technique (2). The manual is an extensive presentation of the rationale and a guide to skill development and the use of the pupil books. These latter offer space for a child's drawings and writing centered around a theme presented by poetry, stories, discussion, and other teacher or class activities. Each theme is followed for two to five days with a variety of language and firsthand experiences. Some observers would question the structured, whole-class aspects of the Allen materials, whereas others might approve of the detailed assistance in skill development for the teacher who is new to this system, as well as the fact that the themes go beyond everyday events and children's experiences to include science, nature study, and other informational areas. Like other writers, the Allens recognize the need for personalized attention through individual conferences, thus moving gradually toward an individualized reading program.

Mary A. Cain describes practices in British primary schools that emphasize the contribution of writing to learning to read (3). Materials for reading, both child-produced and commercial, are in prolific supply. If children cannot read the material themselves, another child or an adult will read it to them. The books by the children are first planned by the children, then reviewed by the teacher, who helps add sources of information or point out gaps in the plan. After the first draft, the child reviews and corrects it for mechanics, spelling, and the like, often with some guidance from the teacher. Handwriting is also important in the rewriting of the initial version. Structural organization is not emphasized to the detriment of the pupils' expression; content and accurate, good-looking copies are stressed as more important at this time. Word cards drawn from the children's picture captions or stories are used for review and for beginning phonic training. Individual reactions to even a group experience are fostered, and children's books on every aspect of the event are promoted. Individual conferences are held to read with each child two or three times a week, to note the books he or she has read and suggest others, and to assess the skills the child needs to practice. Cain attributes much of the mature literacy of these five- to eleven-year-olds to this stimulating environment and teaching approach.

Russell G. Stauffer offers another version of the language experience approach (33, 34). He begins with the child-composed stories but shifts to basal reading materials as soon as the child's reading vocabulary permits. Thereafter, basals taught by his directed reading technique form the basic reading program.

Current Applications

Since language experience stresses total language development at the child's rate of progress, it has been very appealing to those who deal with children with special problems. We find reports of its use with mentally retarded (40), with teenagers in need of remedial work (30), and with economically disadvantaged children (8). The present authors served as consultants to a project utilizing the language experience systems in content fields with junior high school students who were economically and academically handicapped. Five middle schools in Tampa, Florida, under the guidance of Erwin Franco, presented the content of science, social science, English, and mathematics through this medium. The procedure was to assemble all the information about each day's theme from textual materials, demonstrations, visual aids, and the informational backgrounds of the pupils in an organized manner on the chalkboard. These notes were then duplicated, as phrased by the pupils, and read and discussed the following day. Tests at the end of the project's first year showed significantly greater gains in reading, language usage, study skills, and social science than these pupils had shown in previous years. Decreases in school dropouts and absences were also noted.

In a review of the literature on the language experience approach with socioeconomically deprived and linguistically different persons, Hall cites more than a half dozen additional research studies (8). These ranged from the readiness level, first grade and seventh grade, to job training programs for functionally illiterate adults. When control groups were used, there were no differences in word recognition, comprehension, and other reading skills between the language experience groups and those elementary pupils taught by various basal systems. Superior readiness, creative writing, and oral language abilities seemed to develop from this method in various studies. Literacy and communication skills were dramatically improved for the adults.

In a clinical situation, we have employed language experience as the basic instructional approach in several very difficult cases. Severely brain-damaged (aphasic) patients were led by this method to recover their academic and vocational skills to the point where they were able to resume their schooling or work. One was a 14-year-old who has been able to complete high school in a private school setting with tutoring aid; a second case was an automobile mechanic who is now back at his job despite continuing partial paralysis and Jacksonian epilepsy stemming from the scar tissue of his brain tumor operation. The third case was a physician stricken by an embolism. He regained his reading skills by the approach and is now functioning as a medical technician. In less than a year, with concurrent speech and physical therapy, these cases were helped to recover their language abilities, particularly their reading skill, to almost their original educational levels.

In other reports, Miller and Johnson emphasize the practicality of language experience for Navajo children on a reservation where cultural differences and lack of a written language make ordinary instructional materials utterly inappropriate (24). Curry used this approach to teach blind children to read Braille, the system which demands learning different combinations of raised dots for letters, whole words, parts of words, abbreviations, and contractions (5). Learning the code became less a matter of rote memory for these handicapped children. Other advantages were the inherent verbal reality because the stories were the children's own, and the degree of independence in composing stories so essential to such restricted pupils.

Don Holdaway, formerly of New Zealand, offers a modification of the language experience approach that he terms "shared book experience" (*15*). The teacher reads a normal text to the children, sometimes pausing to permit them to supply a word. The same story is enlarged by an overhead projector or copied on large chart paper. The teacher reads the story with the children, pointing to words as they read. If a word is not recognized by the children, the teacher points to the picture or asks a leading question. The system can be adapted to teaching punctuation, sentence structure, masking words (as in cloze), showing only the initial letters to induce use of context and letter clues, decoding, and other skills. The story can also be put on tape for children to listen to and read many times.

Susan P. Homan tries to tie the language experience approach (LEA) to the use of basals (*16*). She lists the new words of a forthcoming basal story on the blackboard; builds a story around these words; reads (tells) the story to the group; the members of the group tell the story back to her; she then writes it on the board or chart. Children read the story in unison several times, reading individual sentences or the whole story. Homan underlines the new vocabulary words on the board or chart to emphasize them. The next day after a choral reading of the LEA story, children read the basal story and are "surprised and delighted at knowing the new words."

Norman R. Wetzel et al. extend the practice of children's writing throughout the elementary grades by sponsoring a Young Authors Conference (*38*). Awards are given by some prominent person in school assembly to the best book produced in each grade. The books are placed in the class or school libraries. The activity is supported by workshops for parents and aides in bookbinding and operating a school publishing center. Parents and aides work closely with teachers throughout the school year to help the children's writing, rewriting, editing, etc.

Teachers read each manuscript to the class, organize writing clubs, and form committees to name the award book from each grade. Winners are recognized by a handmade certificate and plaque mounted in the school lobby. The winners then enter the districtwide contest, and if successful, go on to a statewide contest.

Our View

This variety of current applications of the language experience approach certainly broadens the assumption of the technique as solely a tool for basal reading development. Obviously, it is effective at almost any age in stimulating language and reading skills, in difficult situations involving culturally or otherwise handicapped persons, as a remedial technique in which the student cannot fail to read successfully, and even in teaching content matter to those who are academically retarded.

In the second edition of his excellent book, Ronald Morris strongly supports the language experience approach because of its "context support," as he terms it (25). Because they have just dictated or written their stories, many of the cues present in oral language (and usually missing in written matter) are present for the children. Thus the readers do not depend so much on word recognition for obtaining the message. Raven I. McDavid, Jr., the linguist, stresses the importance of presenting reading materials, at any stage in the student's career, that employ language habits similar to those that the student has acquired in speaking, particularly for those for whom standard English is an alien idiom (22).

Limitations of the Language Experience Approach

Despite its many other applications, language experience is thought of as basically a way of introducing beginning reading. It has been broadened beyond its original concept of a brief preliminary experience intended to convince children that reading is really talking written down, as it was used early in this century. It has grown beyond the limited use implied in the Key Word approach described above to be recognized as a total system for teaching reading. Although it may have motivational or remedial applications with older pupils, in the hands of many teachers it remains largely a way of teaching beginning reading.

It is true that children's vocabularies in speaking, writing, reading, and listening differ in breadth, depth, and fluency. At primary ages, the listening vocabulary is normally the greatest, the speech next, and reading and writing very small. These differences in facility with words in various media vary as the children mature, with listening excelling that in reading until about the sixth grade, when the trend is reversed. Meanwhile, their reading vocabulary grows apace, while their speaking and writing store of words grows quite slowly. Perhaps more than any other approach to reading, language experience capitalizes on the differential between listening and reading vocabularies and facilitates transfer of words (and ideas) from listening and speech into writing and reading. Some of the evidence of superior breadth and diversity of vocabulary in the writing of children trained by language experience cited later supports this viewpoint.

Another frequent question raised about language experience concerns its inherent lack of structured guides for teachers and its problems of organization. As in individualized reading, teachers do not have daily lesson plans outlined for them, nor do they deal with instructional materials in which, presumably, there are planned sequences of activities for skill development. Their time is divided among individual, small-group, and whole-class activities. Their criteria for evaluating children's progress are largely their own observations rather than the progress that is assumed in the children's completion of successive stories in a reader or pages in a workbook. Casual observers of language experience in action receive the impression that skill learning is largely incidental. There appears to be little anxiety about the nature of the words children learn and use in their stories. These observers ask "Where are the checklists of skills to guide the teacher? In what sequence are interdependent skills taught? Where is the basic word list?"

In the earlier editions of this book, we, too, raised these questions about language experience. But because we believed in the approach and tried to train a large number of teachers in its use, we have found some answers to these doubts.

It is argued that, if language experience as the basic instructional procedure were continued much beyond the primary years, there is the possibility that it would retard the full development of reading ability. Children's reading and writing experiences would be too limited to permit them to deal with the more difficult materials of the content fields. Unless a transition to reading textbooks is somehow made, children's learning would be limited to the informational backgrounds of their peers, and no planned sequence of introduction of factual learning would be possible. There are those who doubt that use of language experience for the entire primary period would prepare pupils for textbook interpretation, or introduce them to adequate content matter. These critics ignore the fact that the program uses many sources of reading other than the children's own productions. In fact, as the studies we will cite later show, children trained in this technique often show above-average learning in science, social science, and other content areas.

The books of Maryanne Hall, Braun and Froese, and Nessel and Jones listed as supplementary reading to this chapter offer many pertinent suggestions. The versions of language experience offered by these authors differ, but they do assist the teacher in record keeping, evaluation, planning for skill development, and the other essentials of a reading program.

There are other problems in the language experience method mentioned by Stauffer (32). There is the tendency for some teachers to use the experience charts in the same stereotyped fashion in which they use basal readers. They go over the chart time after time, obviously expecting the repetition to fix the words in the children's brains. They may constantly correct the spontaneous expressions of children in grammar, usage, and punctuation. They may not permit individual words that may fit the story, but are not "basic" words, to be used, believing that these words are not important or essential to children learning to read. They treat the charts as a temporary activity to be dropped as soon as the children can be introduced to book reading. These teachers fail to recognize the wide variety of charts that could function in the classroom, limiting them instead only to contemporary incidents or to colorless descriptions of class activities. All of these are, of course, criticisms of the manner in which the language experience approach may be employed rather than of the technique itself.

Like individualized reading, language experience is not an easy way to teach reading. It demands flexibility in classroom management, recognition of individual differences in language development, personalized record keeping, and teacher skill in diagnosis and evaluation. Children must be helped to acquire the ability to work independently and cooperatively in small groups in this method, too.

The Research

An example of the widespread interest in language experience is its inclusion in six of the large-scale First-Grade Reading Studies. To contrast the results in these comparisons with the basal program, we have prepared charts of the outcomes in the first-grade and the follow-up second-grade experiments.

In Table 5.1, *LE* signifies a superior result for the language experience method; *basal*, for the basal reading program. A blank space indicates no significant difference between the two methods. Kendrick and Bennett (*20*) separated their results for high socioeconomic (*HSE*) and low socioeconomic (*LSE*), as well as for boys (*B*) and girls (*G*).

In Stauffer and Hammond's study, the language experience pupils excelled in nine of the ten areas in which significant differences were found. They would probably attribute this to the use of Stauffer's Directed Reading–Thinking Activities, in which the children were introduced to the basal reader after a vocabulary of about 150 words had been acquired. However, without this type of training in the use of a basal, the results of Vilscek and colleagues are just about as positively in favor of language experience. The

Table 5.1. Language Experience Versus Traditional Method in First Grade

	Stauffer and Hammond (33)	Hahn (7)	McCanne (21)	Harris and Serwer (12)	Vilscek et al. (36)	Kendrick and Bennett (20) HSE B	G	LSE B	G
Word meaning	LE	LE	Basal		LE				
Paragraph meaning	LE		Basal	Basal	LE	Basal		Basal	
Vocabulary		LE	Basal		LE				
Spelling	LE (girls)								
Word study (phonics)					LE				
Arithmetic	Basal						LE		
Oral—rate	LE								
Oral—accuracy									
Gates Word List	LE				LE				
Fry Word List	LE								
Karisen Word List	LE				LE				
Attitudes			Basal	Basal	LE			LE	
Writing mechanics	LE								
Spelling									
Number of running words	LE		LE			LE	LE	LE	LE

economically disadvantaged pupils in McCanne's study (Spanish-speaking or bilingual) and Harris's black, inner-city pupils did not respond favorably to this system, although Harris's experimental pupils scored higher than many comparable classes in the same schools, both types of classes being below national norms.

The results of the follow-up second-grade studies, with the same pupils, are presented in Table 5.2. Again, the results of Stauffer and Hammond, Hahn, Vilscek et al., and Kendrick and Bennett are in favor of the language experience approach. In the case of this last study, language experience seems less effective among pupils from high-socioeconomic groups and more effective among low-socioeconomic groups. Harris's trial with inner-city blacks, in contrast, yielded no significant differences at all, which is the reason for its omission from the chart.

Some of the results favoring basal students in the first-grade Kendrick–Bennett study, such as total words in speaking, favored the language experience in the second grade. Other advantages of the basal, as the number of different words in speaking, persisted into the second grade. In writing, the advantage of the language experience in number of running words persisted into the second grade only for boys in the low-socioeconomic group.

Table 5.2. Language Experience Versus Traditional Method in Second Grade

| | Stauffer and Hammond (33) | Hahn (7) | Vilscek et al. (36) | Kendrick and Bennett (20) | | | |
				HSE B	G	LSE B	G
Word meaning	LE	LE			Basal		
Paragraph meaning	LE	LE		Basal	Basal		
Spelling		LE	LE				
Word study		LE					
Vocabulary							
Arithmetic computation	Basal (boys)				Basal		
Arithmetic concepts			LE				LE
Science		LE	LE			LE	LE
Social studies concepts		LE	LE			LE	LE
Language usage		LE					
Oral—rate							
Oral—accuracy							
Gates Word List		LE					
Fry Word List		LE					
Karisen Word List		LE					
Attitudes					Basal		
Writing mechanics	LE	Basal		Basal			
Number of running words	LE	LE				LE	
Number of different words	LE					LE	
Spelling	LE					LE	
Number of books read		LE			Basal		

Stauffer and Hammond (*33, 34*) employed several unique measures in their experiments, such as originality of content, consistency in story sequence, and total polysyllabic words, and found language experience pupils consistently superior in these writing qualities.

Several of these studies continued their methods comparisons into the third grade. At that time Stauffer and Hammond (*34*) found language experience pupils superior in paragraph meaning (girls only), spelling, science, social studies concepts, oral rate and accuracy, two oral word lists, writing mechanics, number of running words, and number of different words. Basal boys continued to show superiority in arithmetic computation, however.

After three years, Harris and Morrison continued to report no significant differences in any test scores (*11*). As side effects of their experiment, however, they noted that after their trial with language experience, teachers were more permissive and creative and less rigid, and they tended to continue with language experience as an adjunct to their basal method.

In addition to these first- to third-grade cooperative studies, there are a few research reports from other sources. Cramer explored the effects of language experience upon spelling and writing (*4*). He discovered that language experience pupils learned to spell both irregular and regular words equally well, and better than basal pupils. They were also significantly better in the number of running words and different words in their compositions.

Keith used a 200-day language experience program, taught in both Spanish and English, with a group of bilingual children (*18*). The themes in their stories were centered around the Spanish-American-Anglo heritage of the New Mexico area. She found that the language experience children excelled the basal in word discrimination, and were also superior in this ability to a control group given a special oral language program in English. There were no differences among the groups in word knowledge or paragraph reading at the end of the first grade. Unfortunately, Keith did not evaluate the effect of bilingual instruction or the emphasis upon the cultural heritage of the children in her use of language experience. Hence her study cannot be considered as evidence in favor of the language experience per se.

In summarizing these one- to three-year studies, there do appear to be definite advantages for language experience. These results are not identical in all the experiments, since the implementation of the idea varied from study to study. It is apparent, however, that in terms of various reading, phonic, and spelling skills, the evidence in favor of language experience grows stronger after the first grade. Moreover, the approach does seem to make a contribution to the length and breadth of vocabulary in children's compositions and to their spelling in these creative efforts. In the development of informational background, as in science, social science, and the like, language experience again makes a significant impression, as shown in the second-grade reports of Hahn, Vilscek et al., and Kendrick and Bennett, and again in the three-year report of Stauffer and Hammond.

Several more recent studies continue to offer positive support for the language experience approach. Kelly's retarded readers gained significantly more sight words in 15 weeks than matched basal pupils (18). Sinatra used language experience for pupils with severe reading deficits in a three-week summer camp for Title I students (30). Vocabulary tests showed significant gains for the campers. Smith and Morgan reported on three studies in primary grades (31). In all three, the primary pupils given language experience in addition to a basal program showed superior gains in comprehension and vocabulary over those for pupils in a basal-only program. After this experience, the teachers had less preference for the basal and greater preference for the language experience and individualized approaches. Almost all of the parents of the children in the experiments approved the technique and the interest among their children. Mallett found superior gains in writing and attitude toward reading among junior high American Indian students (23). Their gains in vocabulary and comprehension were equal to a control group.

Our View

These various studies would seem to support amply such statements as the following about language experience:

- It must be recognized as an independent, effective method of teaching reading during primary levels of development.
- It is not just an adjunct to or a preliminary stage to other methods, although it may be so used.
- It is as effective in stimulating skill development among middle-class children as the basal approach.
- Among low-socioeconomic or bilingual children, the supporting evidence is weak in the first grade, but grows to equal, at least, the basal method after two years of such instruction for these atypical pupils.
- In measures of quantity, quality, and diversity of vocabulary in writing, the language experience appears to be superior, even in the first grade.
- By the second grade, children trained by the language experience approach begin to evidence broader backgrounds in science and social science, and better spelling than basal pupils.
- Teachers who have been trained in the language experience method tend to modify their classroom climate toward less authoritarian relationships. Even though test results in their populations may be inconclusive, these teachers tend to realize the advantages in this approach by continuing to use it, even if they return to using the basal also.

- Successful applications of the technique have been made in a variety of situations ranging from early elementary grades to adults. These include initial language and reading development, clinical cases, remedial training, teaching content subjects, and in meeting the problems of students with cultural or language differences.

Discussion Questions

1. How does the authors' concept of the language experience approach differ from the Key Word method? From other versions of the language experience approach?

2. What do you consider to be the greatest strengths of the language experience approach? The greatest weaknesses?

3. How would the language experience approach prove advantageous in remedial work with severely retarded readers of almost any age? Why would it be very useful?

4. Offer suggestions that might improve the effectiveness of the language experience method with bilingual, inner-city, migrant or immigrant pupils. What particular aspects of language development should be emphasized for these groups?

5. Why do you suppose results have varied so much from one large-scale study to the next? Is the approach still being defined?

6. What possibilities do you see for using the language experience approach above primary grades in having children prepare some of their own reading and study materials?

7. If you are teaching or have access to a classroom, present a topic to a small group for them to prepare jointly a summary of ideas or reactions. Among the suitable topics might be: a trip to the zoo, farm, seashore, or grandparents; "What Parents Ought to Do"; "My Most Exciting Day"; or "My Favorite Pet."

8. Compare the Allen Manuals with a basal manual for the same grade and prepare to present your analysis to your college class.

9. Visit a language experience classroom and then share your notes with your classmates.

References

1. Allen, Roach Van, *Report of the Reading Study Project*. Monograph No. 1. San Diego: Department of Education, San Diego County, 1961.
2. Allen, Roach Van, and Allen, Claryce Van, *Language Experience Activities*. Boston: Houghton Mifflin, 1982.
3. Cain, Mary A., "The Literate Children of British Primary Schools," *Elementary English*, 52 (January 1975), 84–87.
4. Cramer, Ronald L., "An Investigation of First Grade Spelling Achievement," *Elementary English*, 47 (February 1970), 230–240.

5. Curry, Rebecca G., "Using LEA to Teach Blind Children to Read," *Reading Teacher*, 29 (December 1975), 272–279.

6. Dionisio, Marie, "Write? Isn't This the Reading Class?" *Reading Teacher*, 36 (April 1983), 746–750.

7. Hahn, Harry T., "Three Approaches to Beginning Reading Instruction: I.T.A., Language Experience and Basic Readers—Extended into Second Grade," *Reading Teacher*, 27 (May 1967), 711–715.

8. Hall, MaryAnne, *The Language Experience Approach for the Culturally Disadvantaged*. Newark, Del.: International Reading Association, ERIC/CRIER, 1972.

9. Hall, MaryAnne, "Linguistically Speaking: Why Language Experience," *Reading Teacher*, 25 (January 1972), 328–331.

10. Hall, MaryAnne, *The Language Experience Approach for Teaching Reading: A Research Perspective*. Newark, Del.: International Reading Association, ERIC/CRIER, 1978.

11. Harris, Albert J., and Morrison, Coleman, "The Craft Project: A Final Report," *Reading Teacher*, 22 (January 1969), 335–340.

12. Harris, Albert J., and Serwer, Blanche, L., "Comparing Reading Approaches in First Grade Teaching with Disadvantaged Children," *Reading Teacher*, 19 (May 1966), 698–703.

13. Hildreth, Gertrude H., "Early Writing as an Aid to Reading," *Elementary English*, 40 (January 1963), 15–20.

14. Hildreth, Gertrude H., "Experience-Related Reading for School Beginners," *Elementary English*, 42 (March 1965), 280–284, 289.

15. Holdaway, Don, *Foundations of Literacy*. Sydney, Australia: Ashton Press, 1979.

16. Homan, Susan P., "LEA and Basals Unite," *Reading Teacher*, 36 (March 1983), 693–694.

17. Irish, Margaret, "Role Playing for Reluctant Readers," *Florida Reading Quarterly*, 7 (January 1971), 20–22.

18. Keith, Mary T., "Sustained Primary Program for Bilingual Children," in *Reading Goals for the Disadvantaged*, J. Allen Figurel, ed. Newark, Del.: International Reading Association, 1970, 262–277.

19. Kelly, Ann Marie, "Sight Vocabularies and Experience Stories," *Elementary English*, 52 (March 1975), 327–328.

20. Kendrick, William M., and Bennett, Clayton, L., "A Comparative Study of Two First Grade Language Arts Programs—Extended into Second Grade," *Reading Teacher*, 20 (May 1967), 747–755.

21. McCanne, R., "Approaches to First Grade English Reading Instruction for Children from Spanish-speaking Homes," *Reading Teacher*, 19 (May 1966), 670–675.

22. McDavid Raven I., "Dialectology and the Teaching of Reading," *Reading Teacher*, 18 (December 1964), 206–213.

23. Mallett, Graham, "Using Language Experience with Junior High School Native Indian Students," *Journal of Reading*, 21 (October 1977), 25–28.

24. Miller, D. D. and Johnson, Gail, "What We've Learned about Teaching Reading to Navajo Indians," *Reading Teacher*, 27 (March 1974), 550–554.

25. Morris, Donald, *Success and Failure in Learning to Read* 2d ed. Baltimore: Penguin Books, 1973.

26. Packer, Athold B., "Ashton-Warner's Key Vocabulary for the Disadvantaged," *Reading Teacher*, 23 (March 1970), 559–569.

27. Platt, Penny, "Teaching Beginning Reading to Disadvantaged Children from Pictures Children Draw," in *Reading Goals for the Disadvantaged*, J. Allen Figurel, ed. Newark, Del.: International Reading Association, 1970, 84–90.
28. Ross, Ramon Royal, "Fran and Frank and the Flannelboard," *Reading Teacher*, 27 (October 1973), 43–47.
29. Shuy, Roger W., "Some Considerations for Developing Reading Materials for Ghetto Children," *Journal of Reading Behavior*, 1 (Spring 1969), 33–44.
30. Sinatra, Richard C., "Language Experience in Title 1 Summer Camping Problems," *Reading Improvement*, 12 (Fall 1975), 148–156.
31. Smith, Lewis B., and Morgan, Glen D., "Cassette Tape Recording as a Primary Method in the Development of Early Reading," *Elementary English*, 52 (April 1975), 534–538.
32. Stauffer, Russell G., "The Language Experience Approach," in *First Grade Reading Programs*, James F. Kerfoot, ed. Newark, Del.: International Reading Association, 1965.
33. Stauffer, Russell G., and Hammond, W. Dorsey, "The Effectiveness of Language Arts and Basic Reader Approaches to First-Grade Reading Instruction— Extended into Second Grade," *Reading Teacher*, 20 (May 1967), 740–746.
34. Stauffer, Russell G., and Hammond, W. Dorsey, "The Effectiveness of Language Arts and Basic Reader Approaches to First Grade Reading Instruction— Extended into Third Grade," *Reading Research Quarterly*, 4 (Summer 1969), 468–499.
35. Vilscek, Elaine, Cleland, Donald, and Bilka, Loisanne, "Coordinating and Integrating Language Arts Instruction," *Reading Teacher*, 21 (October 1967), 3–10.
36. Vilscek, Elaine, Morgan, Lorraine and Cleland, Donald, "Coordinating and Integrating Language Arts Instruction in the First Grade," *Reading Teacher*, 20 (October 1966), 31–37.
37. Wasserman, Selma, "Aspen Mornings with Sylvia Ashton-Warner," *Childhood Education*, 48 (April 1972), 348–353.
38. Wetzel, Norman R., David, Lorri, and James, Elizabeth, "Young Authors Conference," *Reading Teacher*, 36 (February 1983), 530–532.
39. Yerkes, Marie, "We're Helping Johnnie Read," *National Retired Teachers Association Journal*, 23 (January–February 1972), 27–28.
40. Young, Virgil A., and Young, Katherine A., "Special Education Children as the Authors of Books," *Reading Teacher*, 22 (November 1968), 122–125.

Supplementary Reading

Allen, Roach Van, and Allen, Claryce Van, *Language Experience Activities*. Boston: Houghton Mifflin, 1982.

Ashton-Warner, Sylvia, *Spinster*. New York: Simon and Schuster, 1971.

Ashton-Warner, Sylvia, *Teacher*. New York: Simon and Schuster, 1971.

Braun, Carl, and Froese, V., *An Experience Based Approach to Language and Reading*. Baltimore: University Park Press, 1977.

Clay, Marie M., *What Did I Write?* Exeter, N.H.: Heinemann Educational Books, 1975.

Cunningham, Patricia M., et al., *Reading in Elementary Classrooms: Strategies and Observations.* New York: Longman, 1983.

Cypress Publishing, *Make-A-Books.* Glendale, Calif.

Cypress Publishing, *Write It Yourself Books.* Glendale, Calif.

Darrow, Helen Fisher, and Allen, Roach Van, *Independent Activities for Creative Learning.* New York: Teachers College Press, 1961.

Flood, James, and Lapp, Diane, *Language–Reading Instruction for the Young Child.* New York: Macmillan, 1981.

Ganes, Roma, *Guiding Children's Reading Through Experience.* New York: Teachers College Press, 1979.

Hoy, James F., and Somer, John, *Language Experience.* New York: Dell, 1979.

Lee, Doris M., and Allen, Roach Van, *Learning to Read Through Experience.* Englewood Cliffs, N.J.: Prentice-Hall, 1966.

Moe, Alden J., Hopkins, Carol J., and Rush, R. Timothy, *The Vocabulary of First Grade Children.* Springfield, Ill.: Charles C. Thomas, 1982.

Nessel, Denise, and Jones, Margaret, *The Language Experience Approach to Reading.* New York: Teachers College Press, 1981.

Spache, Evelyn B., *Reading Activities for Child Involvement.* Boston: Allyn and Bacon, 1981.

Vacca, Richard T., and Meagher, Judith A., eds., *Reading as a Language Experience.* Storrs, Ct.: Reading-Study Center, University of Connecticut, 1978.

Webster, James E., *Combining Reading and Writing.* Dubuque, Ia.: Kendall-Hunt, 1977.

PART THREE

Teaching for Maximum Success

6   Technology in Reading

Technology or applied science began to enter the field of reading instruction in the 1950s. The first evidence of the application of engineering to reading was the appearance of various machines intended to increase reading rates. By projecting words, phrases, sentences, or even portions of complete stories at controlled speeds, these devices tried to induce readers to process at ever increasing rates. In the same decade, programmed instruction and teaching machines were introduced. These followed new theories of learning derived from animal psychology, and combined printed material with teaching devices. At the same time, a movement to hold teachers accountable for their pupils' achievement led to the concept of behavioral objectives. Hundreds of reading skills were identified and defined in terms of what the pupil would be able to do after appropriate instruction. Obviously, the next step was the preparation of instructional materials that would test, teach, and drill children in efforts to attain the behavioral objectives. These massive collections of largely worksheet matter are called *management systems.*

Since the corpus of reading skills was now so finely described, and instructional materials for each skill were available, the management systems were soon declared to be diagnostic and prescriptive programs. After sampling each child's performance in a number of behavioral objectives, it was thought possible to identify the precise skills the child needed to succeed and to provide the appropriate drill and practice.

The use of computers in schools was also growing at this time. The instruction put into the computer is really programmed materials and follows the concepts of the programmed learning theory. Recently microcomputers and minicomputers serving a single pupil at a time have become available, and instructional materials have been created for these devices.

From the very beginning of this technological movement, many teachers and reading specialists have been prejudiced against applying engineering and management principles to reading instruction. They have resented the tendency for technology to displace teachers and to take over many teaching functions. Our detailed review of each of these developments will enable you to form your own concept of the value of what some call "scientific" reading instruction.

Rate-of-Reading Devices

Objectives and Assumptions

Some of the manufacturers of rate-training machines made a number of claims for their devices. They said the machines would increase pupils' rate of reading without diminishing comprehension. The machines were also supposed to lead to improvements in eye movements by eliminating regressions, reducing the number of fixations and increasing reader's perceptual span. It was also claimed that the training would decrease vocalization or whispering because the reader would be trained to read faster than he or she could possibly mouth the words. (There is no doubt that an individual can learn to increase his or her rate of reading in time. The question is which training procedures will truly help accomplish this goal.)

Inherent in these claims was the belief that if eye movements were improved, then reading ability would increase. Pupils would be able to handle more difficult matter at faster speeds if their eye movements could be changed.

Some instructors recognized a possible motivational value in that pupils would believe that the machines would help them. With the machines, students could do what they couldn't do on their own. Other teachers saw the machine as contributing to attention reinforcement and to a mind-set for faster reading.

The Method

The first of the rate-training devices, the tachistoscope, was borrowed from psychological laboratories. This machine projected letters, words, or numbers on a screen in exposures of a fraction of a second. Repeated drill would, it was claimed, result in quicker word recognition and the ability to see increasingly wider spans of material during the act of reading.

Other machines employed films in which portions of a line would be highlighted in succession, thus inducing the reader to follow. The rate at which the lighted portions were projected would be gradually increased, and were to influence the students' rate of reading. A few devices allowed words or phrases to be projected from a slide projector. The number of words or the size of the phrase was gradually increased to widen the reader's perceptual span.

One of the prominent devices is the Controlled Reader, which employs filmstrips and complete stories moving across the screen from right to left. Another, the Tach-X, uses filmstrips to expose words, letters, and numbers. More recent versions of these two are the Guided Reader and the Tach-Mate. (The makers of these devices, Educational Developmental Laboratories and Instructional Communications Technology, never made claims that their devices would change eye movements, as other manufacturers did.) A third, the Reading Rate Accelerator, moves an opaque slide down over the reading material at a controlled rate, thus forcing the reader to read more rapidly. A fourth, the Craig Reader, projects ever-increasing phrases, presumably to increase the reader's span.

Limitations of Rate of Reading Devices

The attempt to modify eye movements in hopes of changing reading habits is based upon several faulty concepts. First of all, good eye movements do not cause good reading, but rather reflect the fluency of the reader and the difficulty of the material. The late Miles Tinker of the University of Minnesota spent much of his academic life studying eye movements. Although aware of the differences between good and poor readers, Tinker emphatically denied that modifying eye movements, assuming it were possible, would improve reading.

Second, attempts to eliminate all regressions and vocalization are either unwise or impossible. Regressions serve the useful purposes of allowing the reader to analyze a word, to clarify a concept, to find his or her place on the line, and sometimes to find the next line. If they were eliminated, the result would be very superficial reading and poor comprehension. Vocalization is a normal accompaniment of the silent reading act. Although not all readers whisper or mouth words or move their tongues as if to say the words, all are being told to move their tongues by the brain and the nerves. Reading cannot be entirely divorced from speech.

Changing perceptual span by practicing with increasing widths of material is not possible. The retina, with which we see the reading matter, is about the size of a pinhead. It works at its maximum all the time, and its size cannot be increased by training. Moreover, the perceptual span at distance, when our eyes are parallel, is much larger than the span when our eyes converge on the page of a book. Transfer of this wider span at distance isn't physically possible in reading a book.

Fixations are shortened minutely by training with quick exposures or in accelerated reading. In effect, readers are trained to react more quickly and to use fewer clues to word recognition. Since fixations occupy about 90 percent of the reading time, practice that results in lessening their duration does tend to increase reading speed. The quicker fixations probably reflect readers' mindset induced by the teacher's exhortations and possibly by students' belief in the efficacy of the machine. Because of this psychological reaction to the training, some readers respond with faster reading even when the training is given at far point or when it emphasizes increasing span (which we know to be unsound).

The Research

There are almost as many reports of negative results in the literature as there are positive reports. The same devices produce different outcomes with different teachers. Other informal means of increasing speed of reading are often equal or superior in their results (21). (Informal rate training usually takes the form of repeated practice with comparable units under timed conditions.) But there is undoubtedly some degree of permanency with maintenance of comprehension when using those devices that more effectively simulate the actual reading act. When the readers are exposed to continuous material and allowed to use their own perceptual spans, rather than trying to follow a predetermined span, they may well respond with gradually increasing reading rates in material that is within their reading levels and comprehension abilities. The Controlled Reader and the Guided Reader are probably the most efficient in meeting these criteria. The Tach-X and the Tach-Mate are near-point devices that have the unique function of blurring after each exposure to prevent false recall based on an after image. These machines are useful in promoting quicker word recognition after the meanings and uses of the words have been clearly established.

Programmed Instruction

Objectives and Assumptions

The early experiments of Pavlov, a Russian physiologist, demonstrated that dogs could be trained to salivate in anticipation of a meal when a bell was rung. More recently, B. F. Skinner, an American psychologist, extended this type of training to pigeons—teaching them to perform various tasks by what is called *operant conditioning*.

Very briefly, this theory of learning in animals, and now in humans, involves these concepts (as applied in reading):

- The desired behavior is carefully analyzed and all of its major and minor components that must be acquired are identified.
- These preliminary learnings are translated into very small, repetitive steps. These steps require an active answer by learners. The answer is most frequently the insertion of a word or letter in a context. The sequence of steps is called a program.
- As learners complete each step or frame, they must receive reinforcement, or the reward of being told or shown that they are correct. If they are wrong, some programs tell them so; some direct them to another step to repeat the task. Some programs neither correct nor offer corrective steps in the learning.

The Method

The first attempt to translate this learning theory into a classroom application occurred in the 1950s. Programmed workbooks and teaching machines with programs in them appeared in great variety from book publishers, test publishers, and systems development companies. Programmed workbooks are a series of many simple frames intended to lead students gradually toward major learning. The steps were printed in a workbook with the correct answer on the back of the same page, or farther down the page so that learners could check their responses. The pupils' responses were usually written as a single letter or word to fit in a given sentence.

To illustrate:

It's _____ for the movie to start.
    tim   time

The multiple choice answers were deliberately limited and the correct choice was a very simple one to ensure the learner's success.

Teaching machines were small devices designed to hold a program printed on a roll. By turning a handle, one task or frame at a time was exposed. Students would insert their responses and turn the handle to advance the frame, and to expose the correct answer. Their responses were still visible so that they could compare them with the correct answers, but since their answers were now under glass, they could not change them.

Advantages of Programmed Instruction

According to its proponents, the advantages of this programmed instruction theory of learning are:

- The program individualizes instruction about as well as a teacher or aide can.
- The program relieves the teacher of record keeping, testing, workbook marking, and many other clerical responsibilities.
- Learning is efficiently managed, constantly reinforced, evaluated at each step, and self-pacing.
- The completeness of the program compensates for any lack of teacher preparation or knowledge of the reading process.
- Some pupils respond better to the impersonal independent study than they do to traditional instruction.
- The program makes the most efficient use of both teacher and pupil time by providing specific tasks, by providing guidelines for the teacher, and by providing detailed assessments of pupil needs and progress.
- Other claims emphasized the motivation inherent in the programs, as well as the instant feedback or corrections.

Limitations of Programmed Instruction

Of the advantages in the preceding list, the first is strongly disputed. Pupils do progress through the program at their own rate. However, each one pursues learning in exactly the same manner as every other pupil that works through the program. All students follow the same sequence of steps, learn the very same skills to the same degree as all other students, through the same modality. Ultimately, they all are expected to show the same behaviors in reading as the others. Unfortunately for this belief, all children and adults do not read alike, and do not employ the same skills to obtain comprehension. Some use context clues to unlock word meanings, others substitute phonic or structural analysis with similar results, and still others use all three types of clues. Some read slowly to obtain their degree of comprehension, whereas others get the same degree by reading more rapidly. Good readers are not perfect in all or most skills, nor are poor readers necessarily lacking in many subskills.

Our View

After a few years of experimental use in schools and colleges, teaching machines virtually disappeared from use, while programmed workbooks suffered great losses. Some of the reasons for this negative reaction were:

- Teachers felt that their instructional role was being invaded by the programs. They resented the monopolization of instructional time.
- Pupils tended to react positively at first to the new devices. But the highly repetitive nature and the extreme simplicity of the learning steps proved boring to average and bright pupils.
- Teachers and curriculum specialists objected to the mechanistic practice with minute details of the reading act. By the very nature of their format, most programs dealt only with letters, letter sounds, or single words, and not any paragraph-sized reading samples.
- The lack of actual practice in any form of sustained reading was questioned by many reading authorities. How could one-sentence practice promote the comprehension that is expected in stories, chapters, or other large portions of reading?

Typical of the programmed learning approach to reading is Sullivan's "Programmed Reading Series." This series includes twenty-four programmed workbooks with a strong linguistic emphasis. The publishers claim that children would be reading at sixth-grade level when they finish the series. The present authors were among the consultants asked to observe this series in the classrooms of two New York City districts in a year-and-a-half project. Our observations and reports were collated by the Educational Records Bureau of Stamford, Connecticut(6).

The publisher's claims that the pupils would reach the sixth-grade reading level, and that on standardized tests the pupils, who were largely Puerto Rican and blacks, would show two years gain after one year's use of the program, were not fulfilled. Rather, the learning proved to be transitory and greatly diminished over the intervening summer vacation. The usual rate of progress was one workbook per month. After the summer vacation, most pupils regressed as much as five or six workbooks. This sort of regression is common in first or second grade, but not in intermediate grades. The posttraining test composed of actual pages of the workbooks showed no significant gains for most of the pupils. All eight of the reading specialists that acted as consultants concurred with these observations.

The Research

A number of studies are cited in an earlier review of this subject by the authors (22). Of eleven studies reviewed, only three were clearly in favor of programmed reading materials. Two others found that programs produced better word naming but inferior results in sentence or paragraph comprehension. The other six studies found no advantages for programmed instruction. In a later group of studies reviewed by the authors, four yielded superior results for programmed reading in the elementary grades (24). But in one of these four, the advantages disappeared after four months in the next grade, implying again that the gains were transitory. Four more studies showed no advantages over other approaches. One final study found the program superior in word recognition tests and a list of irregular words, but inferior in paragraph or sentence meaning, vocabulary, phonic skills, and a regular word list in the first grade (21). Above the elementary grades, three studies found no advantages for programs versus traditional methods.

Our View

As an adjunct to traditional methods, not as a substitute, programmed learning can be useful in areas where drill and practice are desirable. Programs in phonic skills, structural analysis, and perhaps dictionary skills may be profitable. The research is also more positive in mathematics areas. But most reading authorities do not prefer programs for initial instruction in any of these areas, nor do they accept the claim that the programs can teach comprehension or critical reading, particularly at elementary grades.

Accountability and Behavioral Objectives

Recently there has been great interest in the accountability of teachers for their pupils' achievement. An outcome of this trend was the task of carefully describing every skill and subskill teachers would teach. These descriptions are called *behavioral objectives*, and are simply statements of the behaviors that should be acquired by pupils in learning to read. In many school systems, teachers were required to frame these objectives. In some instances teachers gained better understanding of the reading process when they made the detailed analysis of all the components of the reading act. Sometimes the schools purchased a number of behavioral objectives from a researcher or a commercial source. In these cases, the application of the objectives to the curriculum was superimposed upon teachers' ongoing practices.

David N. Campbell says that many teachers viewed the behavioral objectives that they were required to state as yet another burden on the same level as washroom, corridor, or playground duty (2). Furthermore, he adds, "these objectives disregard contemporary research which indicates that effective learning requires a highly individualized and flexible mode of instruction." He continues:

> "As always the real victims are the children who must now endure the spectacle of teachers attempting to meet the new requirements and being forced in the process to ignore their experiences, the needs of the children, and indeed their common sense as they organize classroom instruction into segmented fragments of information which can be easily observed and measured. In short, accountability—as it is generally described and applied —is the final triumph of that mediocrity which so infects professional education, especially at the higher levels. . . . What is so distressing is that so many people involved with children on a daily basis could even begin to accept such a simplistic and indeed intellectually naive notion about the learning process" (2, p. 43).

Our View

In our opinion, overemphasis upon behavioral objectives encourages lockstep learning because it penalizes creativity and limits educational goals to what can be easily stated and readily measured. The practice fractionates the reading process into hundreds of bits and pieces without attempting to show that these bits are truly related to reading success.

Management Systems

A natural outcome of the compiling of behavioral objectives was the need to collate educational materials that could be used in achieving each of these objectives. (We have not mentioned the studies of Edward Coleman of El Paso and Eleanor Gibson of Cornell University on the learnability of letter combinations and words. This work suggested the sequential arrangement of management systems even though its details were never implemented.)

The Method

In general, systems or management systems have these characteristics:

1. The behavior desired is defined by a behavioral objective that describes exactly what the learner should be able to do at the conclusion of the related training.
2. Hundreds of behavioral objectives are written to outline the many subskills the program will cover.
3. For each objective, activities are provided or recommended for practicing each subskill. Usually a pretest is offered to determine children's readiness for the practice or whether they have already acquired the subskill. After completion of each period of practice, a posttest assesses students' attainment of the objective.
4. Pre- and posttests are called "criterion-referenced" tests, implying that they are not standardized instruments, but are graded according to a standard set by the authors, such as 80 percent correct. If students meet this criterion, they may proceed to the next portion; if not, some programs suggest or offer other sources of practice. Some offer no materials or teaching strategies to overcome pupils' failure, but simply direct them to go on to the next step.

Perhaps a very brief description of several programs will convey a more complete picture.

Criterion-Referenced Reading (Random House) offers about five Progress Tests for each of 380 Outcome Skills, extending from kindergarten to sixth grade. After successfully completing the Progress Tests, the children's success with a subskill is assessed in the Outcomes measure. Parallel practice materials from the publisher are listed for the teacher. The worksheets and tests are bound like workbooks.

Croft Inservice Reading Program (Croft Educational Services) opens with an eight-session training program for teachers. Initially, pupils are tested through the levels until their performance falls below the 50 percent level. At this point, children begin to work the five tests for readiness, seventeen phonic skills, and ten structural analysis skills, and are expected to show a perfect score to show their mastery except in the readiness level, where 80 percent is acceptable. A parallel program for comprehension involves thirty-one skills in the areas of oral language readiness, written language readiness, interpretive reading, analytic reading, and critical reading. Each skill test is available in a hand-scored spirit-master. A large wall chart enables the teacher to record every pupil's progress in each skill. A teachers' guide offers models for the one or two recommended teacher presentations of each skill, plus a few suggestions and activities.

Fountain Valley Teacher Support System (Richard L. Zweig Associates) stresses 428 skills for the first six grades. Seventy-seven self-scoring tests for which directions are recorded on cassettes assess pupil mastery. Pupils are to be grouped for instruction with the aid of a large list of basal and supplementary materials keyed to the skill sequence of the program.

Prescriptive Reading Inventory (CTB/McGraw-Hill) offers 172 skills for the first six grades derived from a survey of basal reader programs. Color-coded test booklets at four levels, each spanning a grade or two, are to be computer scored by the publisher. Student profiles indicating each child's needs are then returned to aid the teacher in grouping for instruction. The areas covered include comprehension and study skills, sound-symbol correspondence, visual discrimination, structural analysis, and phonics. Program Reference Guides list textbooks and other materials related to each specific objective. Extensive testing was undertaken to determine the suitability of the items and the objectives for the various grades.

Read-On (Random House) is a boxed kit of tests, cassettes, and scoring keys for sixty reading skills in auditory and visual discrimination, word attack, and comprehension for use in grades one to four. The tests are administered by recorded directions on spirit masters, and are scored by cardboard masks. The test results are recorded on a wall chart as the child progresses. Materials paralleling the objectives are bound in booklets to be purchased separately from the basic kit.

Wisconsin Design for Reading Skill Development (National Computer Systems) emphasizes 309 skills for the first six grades in such areas as word attack, study skills, comprehension, self-directed reading, interpretive reading, and creative reading. These groups of skills are arranged in sections spanning four to seven grade levels. Machine or hand-scored tests and informal testing procedures are outlined in an accompanying teacher guide. Thirty-nine file folders contain commercial materials for instruction as well as suggested ideas on successful teaching techniques for presenting the skills.

Cathy Stallard has made a detailed comparison of sixteen management programs (25). The programs differed in their methods of identifying essential skills, the number of skills they identified, the range of the program (kindergarten to adult), and the very skills themselves. Some programs offer specific instructional lessons, others do not; some offer in-service training for their users, others do not. Even major components of reading—i.e., readiness skills, study skills, applied reading skills, vocabulary, etc.—were absent in some. Only comprehension and word attack skills are included in all sixteen programs, and these are defined differently by various authors. Each program also has unique elements not found in any other program.

Because of the different sources and criteria used to identify desirable behavioral objectives, the programs have from 31 to 1,100 such goals. In the first six grades plus kindergarten, the objectives range from 31 to 450, with an average of 358. The average number of test items per skill range from 2–3 to 25 with 60 percent of the programs using 5 or fewer test items to assess mastery in each skill. Only one-third of the programs offer specific activities for teaching each skill. As a result, the brief tests often became the instructional material in the hands of naive teachers. Standards for the children, or the proficiency level, vary from 50 percent to 100 percent according to each author's beliefs, with 60 percent of the programs expecting performance higher than 75 percent in all tests. All except one program will make in-service training of teachers available, at extra cost. In five of the programs, the school may pick and choose whatever objectives it desires from the publisher's catalog, and thus build its own peculiar program (25).

Stallard did not point out, as she might have, that the sequence of skills in any major component of reading differs from one program to another. Yet apparently each publisher is quite certain that its program has the right and best learning sequence.

Advantages of Management Systems

Among the advantages claimed for these approaches to reading are that they are systematic sequential materials based upon analyses of the entire spectrum of reading behaviors. Learning is efficiently managed, they say, is evaluated at each step, and is self-pacing. (Can you imagine trying to keep track of a class in which each child may be working on any of fifty to one hundred different skills?) Deficiencies in teacher preparation or knowledge are compensated for by the programs' completeness. Teachers learn more about the intricacies of the reading process subskills than in using any other approach. The nature of the program makes the most efficient use of pupil and teacher time by (1) providing specific tasks keyed to frequent testing, (2) giving guidelines to the teacher, and (3) replacing global diagnostic evaluations with detailed assessments.

Stollard claims that these programs are intended to be only a segment of the total program, and that their use provides time for other aspects such as enjoyable activities (implying that these programs are not enjoyable?) and for exposing children to a broad base of literary and writing experiences. She concluded that when used as a portion of the reading program these management systems will help teachers maintain a balanced experience for all children.

Our View

The Criterion Reading system was given a trial in Florida early in its history. Eight reading specialists acted as consultants to the use of the program in seventeen counties. They visited every classroom where the system was employed to observe and to interview teachers, pupils, and administrators over a two-semester span. The consultants' consensus was quite negative. They found that the program monopolized the time for reading instruction, frustrated and confused teachers, bored pupils, and did not materially increase reading ability. The management of the system required giving hundreds of tests to the children and then going back perhaps several grade levels to repractice earlier skills, even when the pupils were reading at or above grade level.

There are inherent in management systems, as in behavioral objectives, a number of questionable assumptions, such as:

- All children learn to read by working through a certain series of skills in the order planned by the program's author.
- All children need training in these hundreds of skills to read with success.
- There are definite hierarchies of subskills that underlie each of the behavioral objectives.
- These skills must be real since they can be described in the behavioral objectives (*31*).
- The identity and independence of the subskills has been established (*31*). Taking tests on these subskills constitutes a diagnosis of needs.
- The tests are valid and reliable samples of the subskills (*31*).
- Normal or acceptable standards of performance in each subskill test can be established by the author's *a priori* judgments.
- Identifying deficiencies in subskills in this fashion and then teaching to eradicate these deficiencies has been shown to be the most practical way of conducting reading instruction.

Dale D. Johnson has raised other questions about this approach to reading instruction (*12*). He points out that the program authors

- think of learning as a reaction to stimuli, not as interaction (as between a teacher and pupil, a book and a child), imitation, or discovery
- believe reading involves mastering hundreds of fragmented skills
- imply or even insist on specific hierarchies for which there is no research basis
- assume validity for their tests
- believe in mastery, the meaning and significance of which are not really known (How many items or what proportion of a given group should be mastered? Are these performances essential or related to reading success?)
- believe that skills should take precedence over interest, reading as work, reading as pleasure, or even any reading at all.

Moreover, Johnson points out that the problem of logistics in handling a management system is terrific.

Robert Hillerich believes that if a commercial management system is used, it behooves the staff to eliminate some of the items to be tested, since many of these skills are doubtful contributors to success (*10*). "To use the entire package is likely to turn teachers into testers and bookkeepers who have little time for teaching" (*10*, p. 120). Hillerich feels that at least 45 to 50 percent of the time allotted to reading should stress appreciation and use of newspapers, magazines, and study materials.

L. C. Taylor, a New Zealand educator, warns against the dangers of "paralysis by perfection" or the "cramp of completeness" (*29*). The perfect, complete curriculum, he says, does not exist, yet the projects of recent years influenced by the theories of behavioral objectives and mastery learning often give the impression that their particular package is the only way in which reading can be taught.

Children probably can learn to read as measured by standardized tests when exposed to management reading programs. But the program authors have not yet offered any comparisons with other reading approaches that show any superiority of their particular systems. Nor have they said anything about the breadth of the reading experiences that children using their programs enjoy, nor what such programs do for the pupils.

Computer-Assisted Instruction

Computer-assisted instruction (CAI) began in the 1960s. By 1974, 11.6 percent of secondary schools and 3.9 percent of elementary schools were using some form of this approach. Williams claims that the National Center for Educational Statistics has evidence that there are 50,000 computers in our schools today, and that the number is multiplying rapidly (*32*).

The Method

When we reviewed an early CAI program for the first grade (*22*), the curriculum it offered contained six strands:

1. Letter discrimination and identification—matching single and multiple-letter strands.
2. Initial vocabulary—words with matching pictures chosen in terms of the vowels and consonants present, as VC, CVC, CCVC, CVCe, CVCC, and CCVCC. The presentation was limited by the use of only those combinations containing a certain vowel. Fourteen lessons of 30 minutes each were given with words containing *a*, as *at*, *cat*, *chat*, *came*, *fast*, and *trash*. The next series of lessons introduced words of these patterns containing the vowel *i*; later, *e*; and so on. No attention was paid to the familiarity or meaningfulness of the words or the fact that word recognition may be related to physical or language experiences of the children. It was assumed that words such as *id*, *ad*, *em*, *od*, *roc*, *pip*, and *rep* (all of which are true words) were more simple and meaningful than such irregulars as *mother*, *father*, *brother*, etc.

3. Word decoding—activities involved comparing and contrasting monosyllables arranged in such lists as bag, rag; bat, rat; ban, ran, etc. (an approach used in Noah Webster's *American Spelling Book* of 1790).

4. Syntactic and intonation practice in sentences arranged in varying patterns—sentences were completely unrelated to each other.

5. Syntactic and semantic practice—involved practice in recognition of word functions, subjects, and predicates, presumably as a foundation for comprehension.

6. Informational processing tasks—listening to and reading simple stories and answering questions. This portion occupied the last few weeks of the first grade.

The skills listed on page 170 are typical of items in CAI programs, and are labeled according to the reading skills they intend to emphasize. They are drawn from a computer program entitled "Reading—Grades 3–6" of the Computer Corporation of Palo Alto (*15*).

Advantages of Computer-Assisted Instruction

Since CAI is really programmed material inserted in a computer, its advantages are synonymous with the earlier programs and management systems. (One present computer program is actually the Fountain Valley Teacher Support System, mentioned earlier.) It claims to be efficient, individualized, complete, and superior to traditional methods. Dennis A. Williams claims that children learn math twice as fast with CAI as from the blackboard (*32*). But Williams thinks the basic reason for CAI is to teach computer literacy, for in his opinion, 75 percent of all jobs in 1985 will involve computers. Williams gives no source for his statistics nor does he clarify how children will learn to operate computers when about all they do in CAI is to insert letters or words.

In the Education Newsletter of the University of Texas (*3*), statements are made that the computer (a large IBM model) has great flexibility and can offer concentrated drill, tutorial instruction, or individualized review, as well as game-like interaction with analytic questions for the student. This large computer can interface with as many as ten typewriter terminals, although not all can be used at the same time at all times. Moreover, the Newsletter goes on to say, the computer can be used to study how pupils learn and thus perhaps to formulate a new theory of learning.

Frank B. Baker, on the other hand, believes CAI has failed for the following reasons (*1*):

- It approaches learning as "Here is technology: What educational procedures can be implemented using it?" In other words, here is the machine, now how do we sell it to education? And are we getting a hard sell!

Typical CAI sequence of reading skills

Compounds
A sunburn is a burn caused by the _____.
sun   moon   heat

Prefixes
The color of your hair is determined before you are born.
The color of your hair is _____.
prejudiced   predetermined   precooked

Suffixes
We had a lot of snow here last winter.
Last winter was very _____.
foggy   snowy   rainy

Vocabulary
The lofty building blocked out the sun.
"Lofty" means _____.
very high   made of glass

Literal Comprehension
Our school was struck by lightning.
_____ struck our school.

Sequence of Events
Barbara woke up _____. Then she woke Albert up.
last   while   first

Primary Inference
Patricia likes to run in the snow. She likes _____.
time   winter   spring

Cause and Effect
A big dog scared Phyllis out of the park.
Phyllis left the park because _____.
her father told her to   she is afraid of the big dog

Alphabetizing
_____ comes first alphabetically.
Lounge   Mercy   Prairies

From Kenneth Majer, "Computer Assisted Instruction and Reading" in *Reading Process and Pedagogy*, W. E. Blanton and J. Jaap Tuimann, eds. *Viewpoints, Bulletin of the School of Education*, Indiana University, vol. 48, no. 5 (September 1972): 77–98.

- Communication between the user and the machine remains a typewriter device that can now produce a printed copy or the typewritten material on a video display. A few computers have added slide projectors and audio capability. (Is this really an improvement on O. K. Moore's talking typewriter?)

- There is no overwhelming evidence of the superiority of CAI over other modes of instruction, although it may be effective in some kinds of drill.

The cost of CAI is almost prohibitive. It costs from $5 to $7 per pupil hour, not counting the total cost of the computer, the cost of developing software, or the high cost of maintenance and repairs.

Baker goes on to say that all that is measured are the test results, the units completed, and the lesson assigned. The programs follow a "school as factory" model in which teachers have the role of seeing that pupils complete instructional units (and the children are piece workers on an assembly line). "Because of this trend toward scientific management, school administrators, school boards and the public evaluate educational innovations in terms of student achievement. Such gains are the educational equivalent of profit in industry" (*1*, p. 17).

Furthermore, the argument that our children must learn to use computers in order to fit into the business world of tomorrow is false, according to Baker. The great majority of computers in business are used to perform repetitive functions. They keep inventories, produce paychecks, maintain bank balances, print mailing labels, and validate credit cards. All these are conceptually and mechanically simple, and not very imaginative. This reality is not reflected in the ways CAI is being used in schools.

Teachers often raise questions about CAI; these questions are directed to the items of the computer program described:

1. How are basic concepts of prefixes, suffixes, and roots taught?
2. What evidence is there that the affixes and roots taught are essential or even functional in learning to read?
3. What are the sources of these items of word analysis—the program author's opinion, their frequency in instructional materials or reading matter, or some other source?
4. What research indicates that children read better because they are taught any of these items?
5. Is reading vocabulary really learned and retained by most children because of simple exercises such as these? Or are vocabulary terms really learned by acquiring a variety of related associations gained from meeting the words in speaking, writing, listening, and reading?
6. How does practice in such reasoning as cause–effect, sequence of events, and inference transfer from these one- or two-sentence exercises to reading in large units?
7. When should such programs be used for greatest effect—after basic teacher instruction, before such instruction, as the sole method, or as a supplement to the teacher's efforts as needed?
8. For which children—average, bright, dull, advanced, or retarded—are these programs most effective?

9. What do detailed analyses of the field trials say about the efficiency of these programs in helping children progress in reading?

10. How do teachers integrate this type of program with their instruction in the total language arts program?

11. What do teachers do with children who don't like or are bored with the program?

Williams cites examples of children teaching the computer to do certain tasks, such as monitoring electricity use, producing report cards, etc. (32). But he also recognizes that the software (discs and cassettes) varies considerably in value and that the production of this software can hardly keep up with the hardware boom or the model changes.

Our View

In our opinion, the creators of CAI programs tend to have these misconceptions of how children learn to read:

1. The reading process begins basically as a letter recognition act.

2. Analysis of language in terms of hierarchies of letter, word, and sentence structure yields a functional teaching sequence.

3. The words to be learned can be divorced from any depth of context, and the firsthand experiences that give meanings to these words can be ignored.

4. The learning of reading can be divorced from classroom reinforcement. (See the Stanford Project reviewed earlier, which was conducted in a little private building apart from the usual classroom and with no adult present.) The interactions that effect learning such as teacher–pupil dialogue, social climate of the classroom, pupil–pupil interaction, group dynamics, and punishment and reward can be eliminated.

5. The multiple clues to word recognition that pupils must learn need not be integrated in computer programs. These clues include word shape, context, phonics, and the sound of the whole word as an auditory memory.

6. Reading in a CAI program can be largely learning to name or call words presented (often in almost meaningless contexts). Memorization of word lists and simple repetition of word-drill exercises are supposed to result in pupils' ability to read.

7. All pupils are presumed to be ready for CAI. The needs for any readiness training in ocular motility and hand–eye coordination can be ignored. Auditory discrimination and sound–symbol correspondence are taught only in a visual modality.

8. CAI programs are able to divorce learning to read from children's language development and their attention to the learning modalities (all are presumed to be visual learners), and can ignore children's language back-

ground or whether the children are bilingual, monolingual, or partly bilingual.

Despite the claims of a psycholinguistic basis in some systems, the content with its emphasis upon minute skills fractionates language rather than recognizes the psycholinguistic concepts that reading is one facet of language development and that reading is a meaning-oriented act, not simply a decoding process.

Other writers on this subject express somewhat similar views. For example, Hoetker warns against systems that present solutions, such as "all children will learn to read by this system" without having first defined the problems of learning style, modality preference, rate of learning, individual differences in need for repetition, and the effect of varying degrees of motivation (11). Summers points out that the issues computer programmers do not address include: whether there is a need for different programs for different children, how to deal with the boredom that often occurs, and the difficulty inherent in learning to read from a program that demands reading ability (28).

Stolurow, a widely recognized expert on programmed instruction, stresses that such programs lack one of the major components of the tutorial process, namely attention to the learner's characteristics as manifested in attitude and personality variables (26). To this criticism can be added that these characteristics can be recognized only by teachers, but teachers cannot change the computer program to make the adjustments they see necessary.

In speaking of the word-processing computer, Dorothy Grant Hennings recommends it for teaching writing skills, for writing group experience stories with primary children, and for teacher-guided group writing in upper elementary and junior high school (9). She feels that this type of computer has the advantage of providing fun and combining speaking, listening, writing, and editing. However, she points out that some machines are nothing more than workbooks in a new format: "Students who spend their classroom hours with the machine in this way interacting with the machine have little opportunity to listen, to speak and to compose meaningful sentence and paragraph patterns" (9, p. 22).

Andrew Pollack, a newspaper reporter, points out that "Fully half, if not more of all computer users suffer some frustrated expectations" (19). He cites 185 suits that have been filed against the Burroughs Corporation by purchasers of several models of small computers sold in the late 1970s. Similar claims have been made against National Cash Register and IBM, makers of other models. Among the complaints are that computers are being oversold with promises they cannot fulfill; that they have mechanical flaws and errors in the software; and that the companies make false claims as to the kinds and extent of functions computers can perform (19).

In a speech delivered to the San Mateo County Reading Association, Michael Kamil suggested that prospective users of classroom computers should look very carefully at the programs' course content and their relevance to present curricula; the organization of the programs; their documentation and research; and probable maintenance costs, which may prove more expensive than the machines themselves. Kamil went on to point out that the computer cannot diagnose or listen to oral reading, nor can it test use of the children's efforts at contextual analysis or their use of other word recognition clues when they are reading silently or orally. The machine cannot contribute to fluency, expression, or reading rate. Moreover, the computer makers have learned from the comparative basal reading studies that they should not attempt to make comparative studies between their programs and traditional methods. Obviously they would not fare well in these studies, for CAI almost totally ignores the primary catalyst in children's progress—the teacher.

Kamil cited the cost of a program lasting 10 minutes a day, or a total of 20 hours, averaging $8000 just for the software. A quality microcomputer and printer may cost several more thousand dollars.

The Future of Computer-Assisted Instruction

At the Florida State Reading Association meeting in October 1981, Barbara Buys spoke of using microcomputers to create individual instruction plans. All the skills in a basal reading program were identified, and related preparatory and reinforcing activities were listed. These data were fed into the computer so that when the mastery tests of the reading program indicated deficiencies for certain children, individual instruction plans could be worked out on the computer. The children's record of progress and their reevaluation with respect to the missing skills were also recorded in the computer.

The basic objective of this adaptation is to relieve teachers of the task of writing the plans for all children as they progressed through the reading program. Of course, such plans would not have to be made for all the class, and in fact the teachers said that only a third of the class would need this type of treatment.

Other possible uses of the computer in a small school are storing records, children's grades, and school budgets. Keeping an inventory of school supplies, books, and attendance records are other possible applications.

One question that arises in our minds regarding this use of a microcomputer is whether the goal could have been accomplished without a computer. Having assembled a master list of the training materials available in the school for each reading skill, why weren't these plans put on skill-masters and duplicated as needed? All the teachers would have had to do was to tell the main office the number of remedial plans for any particular skill that they wanted. Does relieving teachers of planning individual remedial programs promote or retard teacher–pupil interaction or actual instruction by the teacher?

There is no question that the computer-assisted developers are most optimistic about the growth of their field. They foresee that most American homes will have a $5000–$6000 microcomputer before 1990. This machine, they claim, will do all sorts of tasks as well as providing academic instruction for adults and children. They also foresee schools having computers in every classroom connected to a larger computer that will serve an entire school district. Some schools, they say, will also supply pupils with personal computers to carry back and forth to school. The assignments given in school will be stored in the machine, with the work done at home and rechecked when the children return (17). Computers will also be used, according to some writers, to teach such mechanical skills as reading a telephone directory or index (27) and spelling (by using the typewriter that activates the computer) as a supplement to workbook activities (31); to make counts of words in various segments of reading materials and thus produce lists of words to be learned (5, 18); and to study pupil eye movements during reading (?) (7). As Mason and Blanchard say, "One thing is sure, educators will be bombarded by sales representatives and brochures, etc." (17).

Schools are being threatened by such statements as: "The failure of schools to make a major commitment to computer literacy now can have disastrous consequences for the public and for public education."[1] Typical of the unsupported claims are those made by Donahue (4): that computers can be used for drill and practice, tutorial programs, diagnosis and remediation (better than the comprehension section of the Stanford Reading Test), and teaching aids such as games, class records, word searches, puzzles, etc.; that computers can help content area teachers to determine the readability of their materials; that they can correct or overcome specific learning problems by color cuing, animation, underlining, arrows, etc.; that they give children extra time to respond; that they correct impulsive answers by the command "Stop and think before you answer." But Donahue does not refer to any software exemplifying these uses, except for drill and practice.

George E. Mason would use computers for writing prescriptions based on test scores (tests of subskills?); to overcome student hostility; to let students act as tutors to build their self-esteem; as conversationalist; as accuracy trainer; as game partner; and as provider of repetition (16).

Our View

Despite CAI's marketing agents, an objective observer may question this optimism. Teaching machines, which offer the same pattern of instruction as computers, were introduced to the educational world with equal enthusiasm and similar claims. Today, few if any teaching machines are being manufactured and most of those already sold to schools have been stored in closets or junked. There was no resale value for them.

Jongsma warns:

Unlike more traditional software, most software publishers do not allow prospective customers to preview computer programs before purchase. Furthermore, most companies do not allow return privileges if you are dissatisfied with a product after buying it. And finally, the expense involved may make consumers even more wary. The axiom of *caveat emptor* (let the buyer beware) may never have been more true than in purchasing educational software (*13*).

Could the same series of events that took place with teaching machines and programmed instruction occur in the case of CAI? Some publishers' experiences with software may be germane. Addison-Wesley, primarily a textbook publisher, tried producing a computer system for reading instruction, but eventually withdrew it from the market. Harcourt Brace Jovanovich, a book and test publisher, marketed two programs in the late 1960s. After a five-year period, the programs were withdrawn. The high costs of production, software, and maintenance were the reasons for termination.

Can today's schools afford this ultra-expensive instruction mode that, in the author's opinion, is as yet unproven in the area of reading? Furthermore, if a program is adopted but fails to produce the claimed results after the several years trial needed for evaluation, how does a school recover any of the extraordinary costs?

Endnote

1. Quotation in Watt, Daniel H., *Instructor and Teacher*, October 1981.

References

1. Baker, Frank B., "Computers and the Classroom," *New York University Education Quarterly*, 9 (Summer 1978), 13–19.
2. Campbell, David N., "Behavioral Objectives: The Grand Charade," *Today's Education* (March–April 1976), 43–44.
3. "Computer-Assisted Instruction," *The Education Newsletter*, College of Education, University of Texas, 8 (Spring 1966), 6–7.
4. Donahue, Barb, "Improving Reading Comprehension: Will Computer Assisted Instruction Be the Answer?" *The Reading Professor*, 9 (Spring 1983), 9–14.
5. Durr, W. K., "A Computer Study of High Frequency words in Popular Trade Juveniles." Paper read at the conference of the International Reading Association, May 1970.
6. Educational Records Bureau, *Final Evaluation of Project Read in New York City Schools*. Greenwich, Conn.: Educational Records Bureau, 1971.
7. *Educators Handbook and Software Directory for Microcomputers*. Overland Park, Kan.: Vital Information.

8. Hawley, T. T., Stern, J. A., and Chen, S. C., "Computer Analysis of Eye Movements During Reading," *Reading World*, 13 (1974), 307–317.

9. Hennings, Dorothy Grant, "Input: Enter the Word-Processing Computer," *Language Arts*, 58 (January 1981), 18–22.

10. Hillerich, Robert L., "Continuous Assessment of Instructional Needs in Reading," in *Making Reading Possible Through Effective Classroom Management*, Diane Lapp, ed. Newark, Del.: International Reading Association, 1980, 116–145.

11. Hoetker, James, Fichtenau, Robert, and Farr, Helen L. K., *Systems, System Approaches and the Teacher*. Urbana, Ill.: National Council of Teachers of English, 1972.

12. Johnson, Dale D., "Skills Management Systems," *Language Arts*, 54 (May 1977), 511–516.

13. Jongsma, Eugene A., "For Classroom Use," *Reading Teacher*, 36 (March 1983), 724. (The NEA Educational Computer Service, 4720 Montgomery Lane, Bethesda, Md., 20814, will examine and evaluate computer software.)

14. Levine, Jane, "Let's Debate Programmed Reading Instruction," *Reading Teacher*, 16 (March 1963), 337–341.

15. Majer, Kenneth, "Computer Assisted Instruction and Reading," in *Reading Process and Pedagogy*, W. E. Blanton, J. Jaap Tuinman, eds. *Bulletin of the School of Education*, Indiana University, 48 (September 1972), 77–98.

16. Mason, George E., "The Computer in the Reading Clinic," *Reading Teacher*, 36 (February 1983), 504–507.

17. Mason, George E., and Blanchard, Jay S., *Computer Application in Reading*. Newark, Del.: International Reading Association, 1983.

18. Pennock, C. D., "Quick Word Lists for Canadian Readers," *Alberta Journal of Educational Research*, 20 (1974), 8–14.

19. Pollack, Andrew, "Disenchantment Surfaces Among Computer Buyers." *The Sarasota Herald Tribune*, November 11, 1981.

20. Rankin, Earl F., and Bryant, P. G., "Use of Prediction Equations and Computer Simulation for Identifying Preferred Sensory Modality for Training in Reading," in *Reading, Convention and Inquiry*, Twenty-Fourth Yearbook National Reading Conference, G. H. McNinch and W. D. Miller, eds, 1975.

21. Ruddell, Robert B., "Reading Instruction in First Grade with Varying Emphasis on the Regularity of Grapheme–Phoneme Correspondences and the Relation of Language Structures to Meaning—Extended into the Second Grade," *Reading Teacher*, 20 (May 1967), 730–739.

22. Spache, George D., "A Reaction to 'Computer-Assisted Instruction in Initial Reading: The Stanford Project,' " *Reading Research Quarterly*, 3 (Fall 1967), 101–110.

23. Spache, George D., "Mechanical Methods of Improving Reading," in *Diagnosing and Correcting Reading Disabilities*, 2d ed. Boston: Allyn and Bacon, 1981, pp. 365–383.

24. Spache, George D., *Investigating the Issues of Reading Disabilities*. Boston, Mass.: Allyn and Bacon, 1976.

25. Stallard, Cathy, "Comparing Objective Based Reading Programs," *Journal of Reading*, 21 (October 1977), 36–44.

26. Stolurow, Lawrence M., *Essential Principles of Programmed Instruction*. Technical Report No. 8. Urbana, Ill.: Training Research Laboratory, University of Illinois, June 1965.

27. Strang, H. R., "The Automated Instruction of Practical Reading Skills to Disadvantaged Sixth Grade Children," *Improving Human Performance*, 4 (1975), 43–52.

28. Summers, Edward G., "Programmed Learning and Reading Instruction," in *Conference on Reading*, University of Pittsburgh, 20 (1954), 67–76.

29. Taylor, L. C., "Educational Materials: Their Development, Supply, Use and Management," in *Commonwealth Conference on Materials for Learning and Teaching*. Wellington, New Zealand, 1975.

30. Thompson, M. D. Jr., "The Effects of Spelling Pattern Training on the Spelling Behavior of Primary Elementary Students: An Evaluative Study." Doctoral dissertation, University of Pittsburgh, 1976.

31. Thompson, Richard A., and Dziuban, Charles D., "Criterion-Referenced Tests in Perspective," *Reading Teacher*, 27 (December 1973), 292–295.

32 Williams, Dennis A., "Classroom Computers," from *Newsweek*, as reprinted in *Eastern Review*, May 1981, 44–49.

Supplementary Reading

International Reading Association, *Guidelines for Evaluating Computerized Instructional Materials*. Newark, Del.: International Reading Association, 1982.

Wedman, Judy, "Reading Software: What's Out There", *Language Arts*, 60 (April 1983), 516–517. (Categorizes software from numerous sources.)

7 Reading for Young Children

Widely different definitions of readiness persist in current textbooks as well as in instructional materials. These concepts and practices range from a trusting belief in the ultimate effects of simple maturation or the passage of time to highly developed programs based on diagnosis of pupil needs. A great variety of instructional materials and devices are appearing on the market. Many of these purport to provide perceptual training, to improve visual and auditory skills, or to promote hand, eye, and body coordination. Wide experimentation is occurring in efforts to enhance significant factors in early reading success, such as language development and teacher–pupil relationships. At the same time, school systems are beginning to experiment with a number of organizational patterns, such as preschool groups, prekindergarten classes, and transitional kindergartens or first grades extending such an experience for another year, and even nursery school classes.

It is apparent that these developments imply a growing concern for the success of the beginning reader. These experimental school arrangements and teaching materials are all intended to provide developmental training that will foster early adjustment to the school's demands. As this trend progresses, it moves us toward that day when preschool children and school entrants will really be carefully evaluated. They will receive training of proven value keyed to their needs and of sufficient duration to facilitate early school progress.

During the past few years, practices in reading instruction in the United States have shown a truly innovative trend—that of starting reading during the nursery or preschool years or kindergarten. The arguments offered for this downward extension of the school system are varied. Some point out that today's children are more mature and have greater vocabularies and wider experiences than the last generation or two. Because of their superior development, it is argued that children should be introduced to schoolwork earlier. Other writers have expressed their opinion that if school training began earlier, children could be accelerated through their entire school career. One or two experts offer the weak rationalization that since it has not been shown that early schooling actually harms children, it should be initiated.

At the Preschool Level

At the preschool level, we see such reactions to early reading programs as this:

A growing number of children are enrolled in prekindergarten classes in which highly structured pre-reading and reading programs are being used. Decisions related to schooling, including the teaching of reading, are increasingly being made on economic and political bases instead of our knowledge of young children and of how they best learn. In a time of diminishing financial resources, schools often try to make "a good showing" on measures of achievement that may or may not be appropriate for the children involved. Such measures all too often dictate the content and goals of the programs. In attempting to respond to pressures for high scores on widely used measures of achievement, teachers of young children sometimes feel compelled to use materials, methods, and activities designed for older children. In so doing, they may impede the development of intellectual functions such as curiosity, critical thinking, and creative expression, and at the same time promote negative attitudes toward reading. A need exists to provide alternative ways to teach and evaluate progress in pre-reading and reading skills.[1]

These educational groups are properly concerned when they see nursery or kindergarten teachers utilizing a structured reading program (like Distar) or one obviously written for first- or second-grade children. Moreover, the pressure from public opinion and from such media as television in favor of early reading programs has upset some educators. They are concerned that many early childhood workers seem to believe that reading instruction means drill on skills—not actual reading. And they object to such instruction because as it is commonly practiced it is not consistent with their beliefs as to how children learn or what is important for such children to learn (57).

There has been a great deal of praise for the television programs *Sesame Street* and the *Electric Company*. Undoubtedly children who watch these programs frequently learn some reading and prereading skills, such as sound–symbol correspondence and other phonic skills. However, the tendency to overemphasize the alphabet and the distorted sounds of single letters in isolation is deplorable. The Sesame Street Library of books has been seriously criticized for sexism (the ratio of male to female pictures is six to one); for males outnumbering females as main characters; and for portraying females in stereotyped roles. Even though many characters are animals, examples of racism were noted. Furthermore, the books were criticized for incorrect grammar, oversimplification of the learning tasks, and the pointlessness of the stories.

Observers of such preschool programs as the nationwide Head Start note the growth in vocabulary and in cognitive or thinking skills of the children given special attention in some of the centers. This stimulation presumably helps many children from lower socioeconomic groups to deal with the school's highly verbal demands. The fact that some Head Start programs have been successful in these areas is now used as another support for early schooling. Trials with a "talking typewriter" and with a highly scheduled formal school day for preschoolers have shown certain types of success. Some of the young children have learned to read and write a few words and to do simple arithmetic. They also showed some gain on a reading readiness test after the training, indicating, perhaps, that they were better prepared for school entrance.

As is typical in American industry, as soon as the trend toward early schooling became obvious, many manufacturers and even some reading specialists offered a variety of materials and programs for young children. Among these are collections of large flash cards to be attached to objects in the home or to the family members; books on how to teach a baby to read; and readers, workbooks, games, and puzzles—usually emphasizing learning the alphabet—specifically designed for this early instruction. Federal and local projects were designed to train parents in tutoring their children or to employ parents as aides to teachers so that they might learn to reinforce the school's program by parallel coaching at home (54).

Some school systems have built new facilities for four- and five-year-olds; others have begun to require children to attend school during the summer prior to their formal school enrollment. A few schools have experimented with a twelve-month arrangement or with enrichment programs during the summer vacation. Special oral language programs, often based on practices used with adults in teaching English as a second language, have been used prior to or early in the school years in many places. Several school systems have extended the kindergarten program to as long as three years by admitting the younger children to a prekindergarten program, followed by a transitional kindergarten and a traditional kindergarten of a year each.

The evidence regarding the effectiveness of such programs as Head Start, Title I, and Upward Bound, as well as individual efforts initiated by various school systems, is very ambiguous (38). The Head Start program for preschool children did not concern itself with what is needed to produce good readers in families in which the children typically do not learn to read well. Rather, it attempted to see how much good could be done in a predetermined time with a specific amount of money per child. The emphasis was upon medical, dental, nutritional, emotional, and cognitive improvement. Naturally the children profited from this massive treatment, and gains in the areas stressed in some cases were quite spectacular at the end of a year. But these gains in cognitive growth, alertness, general health, and the like were not sustained in the next four years, unless the program was constantly reinforced. Groups of untreated children, once they were exposed to a stimulating school experience, readily overtook the Head Start pupils. Perhaps the only significant outcome of these preschool and early school programs was the slowing down of the usual downward trend of intelligence and academic performance commonly present among socioeconomically handicapped children. To a sociologist, these ultimate outcomes would seem to have justified such programs, but, from their viewpoint, educators, in general, were disappointed in the lack of results more specifically related to early reading.

All these activities and programs tend to lead us to believe that early school instruction is being established on a wide and firm basis. But few of those promoting this new development have asked what research really tells us about its value. There are at least three sources of information regarding the merits of early schooling. Comparative studies of British and American children's school progress are one source. These studies indicate that although British children begin formal school a year earlier, they are no farther advanced in the curricula and content they can deal with in comparisons three or four years later with American pupils. A second clue to the outcome of formal programs for young children is given in the research studies of various child welfare research centers, such as that at the University of Iowa. Their reports show that routinized or structured programs for preschool children stimulate aggressive behavior among the children and negative feelings against the teacher. Highly directed training of preschool children does not appear to transfer to greater school achievement as well as imitative, incidental social learning in an atmosphere of warmth, acceptance, and encouragement. Moreover, the routinized day for preschoolers ignores their differences in attention span, their needs for activity and freedom of movement, their inability to share the attention of an adult with their peers, and their needs for self-identification.

The two groups of studies just mentioned would certainly lead us to question the claims for early schooling. But research by Dolores Durkin on children who were reading well before entering school is directly relevant to this new trend (14). Durkin found forty-nine children in a total population of over 5000 school entrants whose performance on a formal reading test proved their reading ability. By interviews with their parents, she established that the children were of two types: those who had been tutored by their parents and those who had learned to read spontaneously and independently, often as a result of playing school with their older brothers and sisters. As one such child interviewed by the present writer said, "My sister brings her book home and tells me the words. The next day I know them. That's all!"

These forty-nine early readers were, on the average, quite superior in intelligence, very curious, and interested in words and letters. Follow-up studies of this group were made over a six-year period, while a second group of 156 early readers was studied over a three-year span. The longitudinal test results showed that, on the average, these children continued to be markedly accelerated in reading at the third and the sixth grades. However, those children tutored by their parents *did not maintain* the initial degree of acceleration. In the sixth grade their reading test scores were not as far accelerated as their generally superior intelligence would warrant.

Perhaps the implications of Durkin's studies should be considered before rushing into early formal schooling. It is apparent that only a very small proportion, perhaps less than 1 percent, of preschoolers, even with superior intelligence, readily learn to read before first grade. It is true that the proportion might be greater in a planned program, but since we do not know how many children failed to learn to read despite their parents' efforts, we cannot be certain that the proportion would increase. What happened in this select group of interested, bright youngsters cannot readily be generalized to most preschoolers, either. While early progress in reading is accelerated, direct instruction apparently does not permanently affect reading skill, interests, and attitudes. Certainly, if we can identify them, some of the bright children of four and five should be offered an opportunity to learn to read. But from Durkin's results it appears that this should be an informal program directed largely by the children's growing interest in words and letters rather than by parent or teacher scheduling.

Several studies have followed the implications of Durkin's research in offering unstructured, informal reading activities to those children who were interested in such a program. About half of the children, mainly those of better-than-average intelligence, learned to read. The other half, who were of average ability, did not. Those who learned to read early exceeded the others in testing at the end of the second and third grades, with both groups being markedly above national norms. By the third grade, a control group of kindergarten children exceeded those who had failed to learn to read. In effect, these results tell us that some children, whether average or above-average, even when exposed to a self-paced informal reading program in kindergarten, do not learn to read either then or in later primary grades as well as other groups matched in ability. Thus the individual differences among young children continue to argue against early schooling for some—whether it is informal or formal in nature.

Other observers of early reading programs have noted that boys who are taught reading tend to develop less acceptable classroom behavior than girls, or than boys and girls in a nontutored group. Jean E. Robertson of Alberta, Canada, offers several other cautions about early school programs (50). Since a number of speech sounds are not usually completely developed even by the age of eight, and because of the lesser auditory discrimination among boys, she doubts the advisability of the common programs emphasizing decoding or phonics. Robertson also emphasizes the difficulties of young children in dealing with successive sounds in words (that is, in auditory sequencing, synthesis, or blending) as another argument against the formal phonics programs so widely offered for this type of program.

Undoubtedly, more children are receiving some kind of early school experience in reading today than even ten years ago. Such early childhood education is definitely becoming more widely accepted by parents and school administrators. Whether we like it or not, or whether the research shows ultimate profit for the children's reading progress, we will witness most preschool children being subjected to some form of reading program based largely on teachers' own ideas, since few nursery teachers receive any formal training in reading instruction.

In the Kindergarten

At the kindergarten level, the dramatic rise in public acceptance of early school is shown in the indications of Robinson's survey (53). She found that kindergartens are now offered for all children in forty-four states. Most of these kindergartens are supported by tax money, further indicating the public's willingness to support education at this level.

Bailey's report on the preparation of kindergarten teachers for reading instruction (5) is disturbing to say the least. Ninety-one percent of teacher training colleges require a course in reading, but only one-third of these courses are designed for early childhood teachers. The courses are usually offered in elementary education departments. Less than two percent of the reading courses are offered in early childhood education departments or such combined with elementary education.

As a result we see such approaches to the problem as that found in a survey of six New England states (43): 62 percent of the teachers used published readiness materials with *all* their pupils in addition to informal readiness activities. Most of these teachers expressed the belief that, whether they can already read or not, all children need the formal program. Even the amount of time for the program, one to four weeks, was the same for average, below-average, and above-average pupils in these schools. Apparently, a readiness workbook is an absolute essential in the minds of some teachers. Certainly, this survey shows that the present-day kindergarten is moving in the direction of instruction in what we formerly thought of as readiness or beginning reading skills.

According to another survey, 31 percent of teachers regularly teach reading using a readiness workbook, language experience charts, a classroom library, and dittoed worksheets, yet only 2 to 5 percent report using preprimers or primers. Only 19 percent of the kindergarten teachers refuse to teach any of these skills. A third survey of 354 kindergarten teachers in Virginia (56) indicated that 40 percent were in favor of teaching reading but only 25 percent saw a need for a planned readiness program prior to the introduction to reading. Among those who offered reading instruction, use of the language experience approach was most frequent, phonics programs second, and basal readers third.

Judi Lesiak points out that the research does not tell what methods or materials should be used in the kindergarten (34). Nor does it suggest that books and workbooks should be used, or tell how long any instruction should be or what achievement should be measured. She questions whether early reading instruction really makes a difference, for although such children appear accelerated in primary grades, the acceleration soon disappears. What are the social and emotional effects of early reading? Which children are likely to benefit from early instruction? All of these questions are unanswered.

Research on Readiness: Factors Influencing Success in Beginning Reading

Age at School Entrance

Despite the hope of many school administrators that raising school entrance age will reduce the number of early reading failures, there is practically no research support for this practice. Prescott's study of over 14,000 beginning first-grade pupils showed no significant differences in readiness between "overage" pupils of seven years and two months and above, and "underage" pupils of five years and eight months and below (46). Many other earlier reports confirm the fact that the nature of the program offered and its flexibility and provision for individual differences are what determine the percentage of reading failures. Chronological age alone has very little significance in determining children's readiness for reading or subsequent success in reading achievement.

For example, for the past thirty years the public schools of Brookline, Massachusetts, have been admitting to kindergarten children with a minimum chronological age of four years and nine months (24). During the first fifteen years of this admission policy children as young as four were admitted on trial. In 1948 a study of the success of the underage children showed that average marks and achievement test results, except in the kindergarten, were higher than those of other children in every grade in the schools. The margin of superior academic success actually increased as these underage children progressed through the eight grades of elementary school.

Because these children were admitted only after physical and psychological examinations, they were probably of superior mental ability. However, their success demonstrates that age is not a highly significant factor in school success. When special instructional efforts are made, and children are screened for physical and mental readiness, the Brookline results show that many children as young as four years and three months when admitted to kindergarten make good school progress.

Austin and Postlethwaite used data from an international study of reading comprehension and found that an earlier age of school entry was associated with high scores in math at age 13, but lower scores in reading at age 10 (4).

In reviewing international practices in primary reading, Malmquist also pointed out that the optimum age for beginning reading has not yet been determined by research, for it is relevant to a number of other factors (37). Some research he cites indicates that the earlier children go to school, the more negative their attitudes toward school become. Because of these findings, most European schools are continuing their current practices regarding the age of admission and rejecting early instruction in reading.

In American schools, however, age at school entrance continues to be practically the only criterion of readiness for school, perhaps for political or economic reasons. In a survey of six New England states, 88 percent of admissions to kindergarten were based on the single criterion of chronological age. Only 8 percent of the schools employed other criteria, such as intelligence tests, evaluation of the child's social maturity, or teacher judgment.

Sex

Several large-scale studies comparing the readiness of boys and girls confirm the widespread impression of the superiority of girls. Prescott's investigation, for example, concurred in this finding even when the groups were matched for chronological age (46). Despite the general greater readiness of girls, few schools, if any, differentiate early reading instruction on this basis.

It probably would not be feasible or necessary to offer a different type of instruction to the sexes or, as some might suggest, to have them enter school at different ages. The great mass of boys and girls entering school show a similar, average readiness. But at the lower extreme there is a real need for exploring the specific needs of the boys who are unready for reading instruction.

Some authors interpret the differential success of boys and girls in American schools as reflecting some natural hereditary differences in physiological development. Girls are credited with a more rapid rate of physical maturation, and this is interpreted as the reason for their more frequent successes in reading and other types of schoolwork. But the failure ratio is reversed in certain other countries, such as Germany (47). This observation denies the importance of any sex-linked hereditary factor in school success, and implies that the explanation for the difference in failure rate must be sought elsewhere. We believe it may more accurately be attributed to such factors as the attitudes of women teachers toward boy pupils, the socially conforming attitudes of American girls, and the proportion of male teachers in primary schools (as compared with Germany). What is thought to be a sex difference may well be simply a reflection of the pupil-teacher relationships and the climate of the classroom.

Dale D. Johnson confirmed this interpretation by comparing the sexes in eighteen aspects of achievement in Canada, United States, England, and Nigeria (27). The differences favored girls in the United States and Canada, which have a majority of female teachers; and favored boys in England and Nigeria, where the sex ratio of teachers is less predominantly female. Boys and girls in these countries achieved exactly as the bulk of their teachers thought they would in the comparison of the sexes. Recent studies definitely support these inferences in pointing out that boys receive more negative comments and fewer opportunities to read in mixed classes. Furthermore, some studies indicate that when boys are separated into groups for reading instruction, their reading achievement is greater.

Physical Development

Measures of physical characteristics such as height and weight show some relationship to readiness in certain studies (41). Height in particular reflects nutrition and general health, which in turn reflect parental knowledge of hygiene and principles of physical health. Thus in a general sense, children whose parents provide appropriate diet and adequate medical care tend to enjoy greater success in school. However, the relationship between these factors and reading is not great enough for anything like individual predictions.

Vision

Although reading is first and foremost a visual act, and literally hundreds of studies show the importance of certain visual skills for successful reading, most readiness programs ignore these facts completely. The visual skills of young children are, in our opinion, one of the most significant factors in their early reading success. But in most schools vision is tested, if at all, by a Snellen chart, which measures nothing but visual acuity or keenness of vision. This test is given at a 20-foot distance, thus determining visual acuity at that point—a measure which is comparatively unrelated to vision at the reading distance. In fact, the Snellen test only reveals the nearsighted child, who, as the research shows, is *most likely to succeed in reading.* Because of the stage of their visual development, most young children are farsighted and can readily pass the distance test. Yet they may be suffering any of a half-dozen undetected visual defects that affect their near-point vision and limit their success in reading (61).

Studies conducted in California, in an attempt to devise a better vision screening program that would be feasible in schools, revealed the shocking inadequacy of the Snellen Test (45). A careful examination of the results of testing with the Snellen alone showed that 60 percent of the first-grade children needing professional vision care would be entirely overlooked if the usual standard of 20/30 were used. When the standard of 20/40 was used, as some authorities recommend for this grade, 70 percent of the visually defective children were missed. These results are not peculiar to California, for a study in the New Haven schools (68) indicated that the Snellen Test detected about half of the elementary children who needed visual care. It is particularly interesting to note that, probably because of the tendency to farsightedness at this age, all the New Haven kindergarten children were found normal by the Snellen Test when actually 46 percent were found defective in vision by more careful testing. This indictment of the Snellen Test might be summarized in the words of one of the authors of the Orinda study in California, who pointed out that, in all, more than one-half of all children with real vision problems will pass this so-called test of vision (45).

A more recent study cited by Theodore Grosvenor indicated that the Snellen Test using 20/40 or worse or 20/20 (the usual standard) with 1.50 diopters sphere to improve the testing missed three times as many children needing referral for a complete examination as it found. In other words, the Snellen Test found only about one-fourth of the children who had defective vision. The Massachusetts Vision Test and the Telebinocular in its original form were just about as bad.

Complete testing of vision is obviously a professional task and cannot be attempted by a teacher. But under the leadership of teachers and administrators who are concerned about vision screening, many schools are introducing significantly better methods (68). In most such communities these efforts are actively supported by the local Lions Clubs and optometrists, and occasionally by interested medical specialists. Some nurses and physicians seem to fear that teachers who are interested in better vision tests are attempting to usurp their medical functions. But dissemination of the facts about the Snellen Test to parents, which can be accomplished by distributing informational literature obtainable from the American Optometric Association and other sources, often helps obtain favorable action.

It is obvious that schools must use better vision screening programs than the Snellen Test if they are to find the 20 to 40 percent of children whose visual difficulties may hinder reading success (51). Most schools concerned about this problem, like those in New Haven, have formed committees composed of interested parents, local ophthalmologists and optometrists, school doctors and nurses, and teachers. When they approach the problem with open minds, they can arrange simple screening programs to be administered by school nurses assisted by parents to find those pupils who need professional vision care. Although these screening programs can be simple enough for a parent or teacher to administer, they should certainly include the skills of binocular acuity at near-point, binocular coordination, accommodation, and convergence. Many studies show these skills to be essential to successful reading (26, 45).

There are a number of informal vision tests that teachers can conduct to find children who need referral to professional eye specialists or who can benefit from training activities teachers can direct.

Visual Perception

Visual discrimination or perception is derived from or based upon physical handling of objects. In other words, children tend to explore objects in space—to learn shapes and spatial relationships first with their hands (and mouth), later with their eyes. During the preschool ages when vision is developing, children learn to explore, recognize, and discriminate objects or forms by tactile and visual approaches, with a gradually greater dependence upon visual clues (*19*).

Those children who have had little experience with objects or forms at near-point have difficulty with the ultimate visual discriminations among words necessary for reading. We describe these difficulties in various ways: (1) they lack visual discrimination or perception; (2) they lack hand–eye coordination; (3) they lack orientation to left and right (reversals, inversions, letter confusions); (4) they cannot sit still long enough while working at near-point tasks; (5) they cannot concentrate or they have a short attention span; (6) they cannot read without pointing or using a marker (they still need tactile clues or fingers to lead their eyes in reading). These are some of the familiar descriptive phrases used by teachers in pointing out the difficulties of slow learners or poor readers. They all refer to the same basic problem—lack of sufficient tactile and visual experience with objects, forms, and spatial relationships. Related symptoms that teachers commonly observe but do not recognize as part of the syndrome are inability to identify verbally right or left in space or in parts of their own or others' bodies, difficulties with cross-identification of a facing body, and inability to reproduce simple two-dimensional forms or designs (unless these are first named verbally, as the square or triangle, in which case the children produce a stereotyped model).

Despite the beliefs of some writers, these symbols of disturbances of visual perception are not readily explained by handedness, cerebral dominance, crossed-dominance, mixed eye–hand dominance, and similar theories. These theories completely fail to explain visual perception or the most irritating symptom, reversals in reading. Nor is there any reason to believe that these behaviors have a neurological basis in average normal or non-brain-damaged children. Poor visual perception is found among children with any and every combination of preferences for hand, foot, and eye. Moreover, recent extended brain surgery research shows that cerebral dominance has nothing to do with language functions or visual perception. Reversals in reading are a common reading behavior among beginners in reading in any language or even among older persons who are learning to read for the first time. The simplest proof that reversals arise from immaturity in visual discrimination or perception is the fact that, without any special attention, they spontaneously disappear among successful readers as the accuracy of word discrimination increases or, in other words, as perception improves. The fact that some of these symptoms persist among ineffectual readers is a better argument for perceptual training than for classifying such pupils as ineducable, or as having neurological problems.

Barrett has made a careful review of the available studies involving tests of visual perception and discrimination (*6*). He concluded that the best tests for predicting early reading ability have not yet been identified. He therefore recommended that the assessment include measures of discrimination among words, letters, and geometric designs as well as tests of letter names. We will examine this recommendation more carefully later.

Teachers generally recognize the perceptual limitations of grossly brain-damaged or mentally retarded children, children with cerebral palsy, or even posttraumatic aphasic children (those who have lost certain language functions as a result of cerebral injury), although they see very few of this last type outside the reading clinic. At the same time, teachers fail to recognize that similar handicaps may hinder the reading success of apparently normal pupils. The assumption is often made that since children are now of school age, they must have passed through all the stages of neuromuscular development that result in visual perception. Fortunately, as we learn more about perception and improve our diagnostic abilities, we are recognizing that this assumption is often false.

With the current increasing interest in visual perception, there has come a distinct looseness in the use of the term. All sorts of tests are being called measures of visual perception, including copying letters, numbers, words, and geometric forms; matching these same symbols; and drawing or reproducing letters or forms while viewing or from memory. Figure–ground perception, as it is called, is measured in many ways—pictures embedded in a loose or highly structured background, intersecting geometric forms or other figures, marble board figures against a background. Tests involving part–whole relationships, hand–eye coordination in a tracing task, tests of arranging cutouts or marking pictures by size, tests involving memory for geometric forms, and such tests free of the memory factor, discrimination and memory for single letters, bigrams, and trigrams—all are considered tests of visual perception. And the concept is also broadened by some to include left–right orientation in space and in relation to one's own body. Some writers link this left–right orientation to laterality and handedness, to cerebral dominance, and to reversals in reading, with very little research justification.

Visual perception obviously means different behaviors to different authors; furthermore, they often do not bother to discover the influence of memory, drawing skill, coordination, and intelligence upon the results of the tests they create. Often several tests are thrown together into a battery, à la Frostig and de Hirsch, with little concern for duplication, overlap, or intercorrelations between subtests as great as their reliability.

Table 7–1 offers comparative information on the eight most widely used standardized tests of visual perception. Briefly, they may be described as follows.

The Bender Visual–Motor Gestalt Test requires the reproduction of nine complex geometric forms from memory. It is interpreted by some as a test for brain injury, emotional problems, perceptual handicaps, immaturity, or general intelligence. Still others consider it a test of the child's personality or ego strength. It was originally designed to detect organic pathology among adults and was later adapted for use with children by employing various scoring systems. It does seem to yield results somewhat similar to readiness tests in some populations but it is a poorer predictor of reading achievement than such tests, particularly when the intelligence factor is removed from the correlation.

Table 7-1 Scoreboard on Visual Perception Tests

Test	Validity for reading	Reliability	Control of		
			Speed	Memory	Intelligence
Bender	−.16 to −.17	.54 to .71	None	None	None; .48 to .79
Frostig	.32 to .615 total; −.03 to .49 subtests	.69 to .98 total; .29 to .74 subtests	Yes	Yes	None; .318 to .460
MPD	Uses cutoff scores: r's not known	.74 to .85	Yes	Yes	Yes (?); norms corrected for IQ
Graham–Kendall	Unknown	.72 to .90	None	None	Yes (?); −.60
Winter Haven	.24 to .44	Unknown	Yes	Yes	None
Beery	.33 to .50	.80 to .90	Yes	Yes	None; .37 to .70
Benton	Unknown	ca. .85	Yes	Yes	Yes; norms corrected for IQ
de Hirsch	.55, .63		Yes	Yes	None

The Frostig Test of Developmental Perception includes subtests of motor coordination, figure–ground, constancy of shape, position in space, and spatial relationships. It was standardized in southern California with middle-class white children exclusively. There are several questionable aspects in the battery; for example, subtest V does not function when it is used to test children under the age of five, but the instructions are to score children as succeeding at this level even when they achieve a zero score. This same arbitrary scoring for zero scores is also used in the other subtests. The reported reliability of the test drops markedly when it is given by teachers or others who are not highly trained in its use. Subtest III is more reliable than any others and, in fact, is more reliable than the entire test. Intercorrelations among the subtests are higher than their reliabilities in some cases, implying that the various subtests resemble and duplicate one another more closely than two administrations of the same subtest.

Summaries of the studies on the validity of the Frostig tests in predicting reading achievement show that in most populations this relationship is very low. Several researchers have seriously questioned whether there is any justification for the subtest labels, or in fact for use of any of the tests in predicting reading success (44).

Predictive Index Tests are a battery of tests tried out on fifty-three kindergarten children to eliminate the less discriminative subtests. Ten of the thirty-seven tests assessed in this fashion seemed desirable to the authors. They include measures of pencil use, the Bender, the Wepman auditory discrimination, the number of words used in a child's story, a categories and a reversals test, a word matching test, a word reproduction test, and two-word recognition tests. The procedure has been severely criticized for the minute size of the population and the faulty assumption that given a large number of tests we can select out a few with any certainty that the present relationship is anything more than chance. The tests appear to predict about as well as the readiness tests except in overpredicting failures. It is also an error to assume that the subtest correlations or their predictive abilities cited by the authors would be equally effective in all populations, until they have been so tested.

Other available tests of visual perception include the *Graham–Kendall Memory for Designs,* the *Beery Developmental Tests of Visual Integration,* the *Revised Visual Retention,* and the *Minnesota Perception-Diagnostic Test.* In content these instruments are all very similar to the Bender in requiring the reproduction of two to twenty-four geometric forms, usually from memory. Like their parent, none of these has shown strong relationships with reading success, although some seem relatively efficient in identifying brain-damaged children, which was the original purpose for their creation (2).

The *Winter Haven Perceptual Forms Test* was designed for teacher use and interpretation and, if hand–eye coordination is believed to be relevant to beginning reading, does help to identify those pupils likely to have problems in handwriting, letter formation, and word recognition because of this factor. Its value is not specifically in predicting reading failure but rather in finding pupils who would benefit from coordination training.

It is quite clear that most of these published tests of visual perception leave a great deal to be desired. Of these eight, none is entirely satisfactory in its ability to predict readiness or reading achievement; in reliability, which should be .90 or above for individual diagnosis; in control of the speed, memory, or intelligence factors; or in the possibility of alternative administrations to analyze children's performances. We need a test that consistently predicts reading as well as the Bender sometimes does, a test with the higher reliabilities of the Beery, Benton, or Graham–Kendall, none of which relates well to reading achievement, or a test that can be scored for several different ways of testing, in the manner of the Benton. Only then could we distinguish children's ability to trace, to match, to copy at sight, and to reproduce from memory, and perhaps thus determine whether a perceptual difficulty was present or whether children simply lacked basic visual–motor abilities. In our opinion, these popular tests of visual perception, most of which were built for the different purpose of detecting brain damage among adults, are not ready to make a real contribution to teachers' attempts to decide which of their pupils need visual–motor training.[2]

Intelligence

Children's mental age and intelligence quotient are often considered among the most important factors in their significance for reading success. Many early studies of the intelligence of beginning readers led to the conclusion that a mental age of approximately six was essential before children could be successfully introduced to reading. Under most classroom conditions this is probably a reasonably accurate statement. A mental age of six is highly desirable because the teacher is unable or unwilling to differentiate instruction according to pupil needs. Under optimum classroom conditions, as Gates' almost forgotten study shows (18), children of much lower mental age can learn to read adequately. Gates's classroom studies indicated that the necessary mental age for successful reading was related to the size of the group and the flexibility of the program. In small groups and with differentiated procedures some children with mental ages of four-and-one-half to five may well learn to read. At the other extreme, some teachers operate in a manner that makes it very difficult for pupils of even seven years of mental age. Like these authors, Gates considers statements regarding the necessary mental age for beginning reading to be meaningless, unless we state the prevailing classroom conditions and methods of instruction. Schools in other English-speaking countries commonly admit children as young as five and experience no great difficulties in teaching them to read. It is the stereotyped, inflexible, and mass-oriented reading program that demands a higher mental age, and makes intelligence so important a factor in reading success, in our primary classrooms. The demands of the average or poor classroom in effect create a condition in which only the fittest (the brightest) can survive and meet these demands. This is why intelligence seems to be an important factor in early reading success.

Many other research studies on school beginners show that intelligence test results are not highly predictive of early reading success. If pupils are arranged in the order of their reading test scores after a period of training, the order just does not neatly parallel a ranking based on mental age or intelligence quotient. Only the extreme cases, the very superior and the mentally retarded pupils, tend to agree in their ranks in reading and intelligence. The degree of reading success for most pupils is determined not by their exact level or rank in intelligence but by other, more influential factors.

In these writers' opinion, altogether too much dependence is placed upon mental test results as predictors of reading progress. First, mental tests are not per se very accurate predictors of reading achievement, particularly at primary levels. Any broad intelligence test samples facets such as concrete reasoning, spatial relations, and quantitative thinking, which have little relationship to reading. The broader the sampling of intellectual abilities, the less accurate is the test for specific reading predictions.

Second, the test results represent a sort of average of the child's cognitive abilities. This average could not be equally related to such diverse abilities as handwriting, spelling, language usage, and arithmetic fundamentals. These school subjects require different mental abilities and, besides, they develop dissimilarly as the child grows. The variation in both mental and school abilities constantly increases for both individuals and groups. One test offering an average estimate of mental ability cannot possibly predict accurately in these varying school abilities. *The mental age obtained from a test does not indicate the level of school performance to be expected, for the test just is not that good a predictor.* Nor does the intelligence quotient show the probable rate of learning of new material, since those behaviors depend upon the nature of the task in many instances.

Practically all intelligence tests currently available for classroom use, particularly those that emphasize verbal intelligence, are keyed to the middle-class culture in the language development, information, and experiences they assume the students have. Many minority children tend to test low, thus reducing teacher expectations and often underestimating their actual potential for learning. The intelligence test result ignores the very potent factors of pupil and parental aspirations, which are often more significant in academic success than actual level of ability. Even if the test items did reflect the backgrounds of minority children, such elements as negativism, lack of drive, poor response to timed tasks, and the possible effect of an examiner from a different race or culture militate against accurate results in many cases. The cultural bias in most intelligence tests has led to their discontinuation in many school systems.

Some indication of relative strengths and weaknesses in attention, informational background, verbal ability, and nonverbal ability can be derived from certain individual intelligence tests when interpreted by trained examiners. But pattern analysis of the test results is often overworked and based on very subjective grounds in attempts to detect brain damage, dyslexia, educational disabilities, and the like. At best, the intelligence test is a crude estimate of the child's learning abilities, divorced from consideration of cultural and language background, self-concept, family attitudes, the method of instruction, the attitudes and competence of the teacher, and the other factors that tend to influence the child's school progress. If used, the implication of the results must be combined judiciously with other measures, such as auditory comprehension and learning style, and the possible effects of the influential elements mentioned.

Language Facility

Many parents and teachers believe that the early development of language skills, such as breadth of speaking vocabulary and fluency in using it, are a strong indication of readiness. Observations of first-graders indicate that the development of these and other language skills follows individual patterns and that they are unrelated to each other, to readiness, or to early reading achievement. A child's total number of words used in oral communication, his or her average sentence length as well as grammatical usage, and the number of different words he or she uses have negligible significance, according to one comprehensive review (23).

This is not the observation of many other writers, who have emphasized the positive relationships between language and speech development and reading success. Group data tend to conceal the true relationships. Children at the lower end of the continuum in language development—those with very limited vocabularies, poor articulation, and poor ability to communicate—will obviously have difficulty with reading. At the upper end, children with advanced language skills will probably experience success. But the great number of children with average language skills do not show a marked relationship of these abilities to reading.

In other words, these language abilities are most significant when they differ greatly from the average. Most school beginners probably show sufficient language development to be ready or to achieve success in the average early reading program. Most beginners will succeed reasonably well in reading without extended or intensive language training in the readiness program. In the average American community retardation in language abilities will be a crucial factor for only that small number of children who have had a bilingual or dialectal background or extremely isolated environment, and who thus deviate markedly in language development.

We have already mentioned the disagreement among language specialists regarding the nature and extent of the handicap among economically disadvantaged children. Since it is at the readiness level that the reading teacher begins to become concerned about these language differences, it is appropriate to review some of the studies that describe and evaluate the differences.

In a population of Mexican-American pupils, one study claims to have found minimal attention span, auditory and visual discrimination, and experiential background for early reading materials; fear, apathy, or insensitivity toward school; inadequacy in simple cognitive abilities such as directions, labeling, classifying, and discrimination of differences among objects; and marked nutritional deficiences. Several studies have shown that average length of sentence and range and diversity of vocabulary were slightly related to reading tests of word recognition and comprehension but not to measures of vocabulary or oral reading. Ralph claimed that economically disadvantaged children are deficient in range and level of vocabulary, use of syntactic variations within sentences, and such structures as clauses, infinitives, verbals, linking verbs, and complete sentences (49). These children tended to use a restricted code, as in fast speech, reduced articulatory clues (wat-cha-dn?), and confused word meanings. These differences vary with geographical regions of the United States, but are present in parallel studies in England. Another study compared the oral language with that of upper-social-status groups and found that children of the poor used shorter sentences, fewer words, less variety, less mature and complete sentences, and showed more syntactical errors. The children apparently used only about 50 percent of the words in basals for the first two grades and a similar proportion of the words in common vocabulary lists. The pertinent question, of course, is whether these differences are as general as these authors imply, and whether they must be treated before we can expect children to succeed in early reading.

Other samples of economically disadvantaged children indicate that these apparent handicaps may not be as great as claimed. Sherk has found, for example, that poor black children used about 75 percent of the Dolch list, a list considered to contain most of the basic vocabulary of beginning reading (59). There were differences in types of words in using fewer adjectives and adverbs, comparatives, animals, flowers, and foods, which is perhaps an indication of lack of richness in experiences and vocabulary rather than a real lack in high frequency words. Several studies have shown that the variety of sentence types or structures among these pupils is not significantly different from the usage of middle-class whites (35, 59).

Sheperd's study of the relationship of children's language to pictures used a correlation with the Metropolitan Readiness Test. Assuming that this test really measures readiness, only one of the 36 correlations between the length of the children's sentences and the listening subtest was significant (58).

One of the problems in interpreting the studies of these pupils' language is the nature of the testing instruments and the manner in which language is analyzed. These pupils' sentences may be shorter, but are as varied in type and structure as those of other children. We see that the variety of words may be limited in some categories, yet most of those essential to beginning reading are present. Syntactical variations are interpreted as a handicap by some, and by others as simply characteristic of a dialect that is not really an interference with reading success at all. Moreover, the use of unstandardized measures of various language aspects for which there are no norms, the use of test items that are unfamiliar to poor children, the lack of knowledge of what really is an adequate vocabulary for a first-grader, plus the possible effects of being tested by a person of another race or culture in a school setting that is strange and threatening, tend to yield confusing and contradictory observations.

Perhaps the best conclusion we can reach is that there are differences between the language of economically disadvantaged children and the standard English of the school. These differences must be carefully observed and evaluated, perhaps in the manner described later and, where it can be justified, training instituted as suggested in a later chapter.

The child's articulation, or his or her tendency to use baby talk or to make substitutions for certain sounds, relates to the child's early reading because these difficulties affect oral reading. Since oral reading is commonly used to such a great degree in beginning programs, children with articulatory defects suffer constant comparison, embarrassment, and correction. Their early reading experiences at the hands of unsympathetic teachers and classmates are often unhappy and frustrating.

Auditory Factors

Certain other language skills, however, have shown greater relationships to reading in several studies. Iver Moe's dissertation study found that a first-grader's ability to answer questions based on standardized reading selections read to him or her, or in other words, a child's auditory comprehension was more efficient in predicting early reading achievement than several common readiness or intelligence tests (40). Earlier studies confirmed the importance of this language ability as a predictor. Auditory comprehension is a far more complex ability, of course, than other simple skills. Therefore, it is not easy to isolate the reason for its predictive value. The relation of auditory comprehension to intelligence is quite high and probably reflects the intellectual stimulation and the level of oral communication in the home (44). If early reading is presented as a thinking process, it is obvious that the child who has been previously stimulated to employ his or her reasoning abilities in verbal contexts and to listen thoughtfully will show greater progress in reading achievement.

In our opinion, a measure of auditory comprehension is superior to a general group or individual intelligence test in indicating children's readiness for reading or, in other words, predicting their degree of success in early reading. A measure of auditory comprehension makes a particular demand upon the intellectual processes of memory, cognition, and reasoning as well as the verbal factor of intelligence. Skill in auditory comprehension probably reflects more faithfully the language factors and the intellectual factors in the child's background that influence his or her readiness and early reading success.

Auditory vocabulary, or the breadth of words that a child recognizes when he or she hears them, is significantly related to readiness. Measures of this language skill are often included in readiness tests and, in some instances, comprise the entire test. The degree to which a test of auditory vocabulary precisely predicts future reading success varies from one test to another, and also according to the nature of the readiness training and the early reading program. In his review of readiness tests, Starr found a wide range of correlations between various auditory vocabulary tests and reading (67). Overall, these correlations imply a moderate tendency for children with good auditory vocabularies to show high reading scores.

Auditory acuity refers to the ability to hear sounds of varying pitch and loudness. We are not referring here to the condition of being hard-of-hearing, which implies loss of acuity over a wide range of tones, or extreme losses. The various research studies indicate that losses in auditory acuity, particularly of high tones, are related to reading success in the primary program.

Such losses in acuity affect the child's ability to hear such consonants as *p*, *b*, *s*, *t*, *k*, *v*, *c* and such blends as *fl*, *ch*, *th*. The child hears most of the vowel sounds, however. Losses of acuity in the high tones have obvious implications in the phonics training involving consonants and in word discrimination by auditory means.

Auditory discrimination refers to the abilities to hear likenesses and differences among letter sounds as they occur in words. Pupils with normal auditory discrimination are able to detect that words begin or end with the same sound, that words rhyme, that they contain a given sound, and that they are composed of a sequence of sounds in a certain order. These abilities enable a normal pupil to match his or her pronunciation of an unknown printed word with his or her auditory memory of the word. Good auditory discrimination helps the beginner to match words he or she is learning with previous auditory experiences with the same words.

Auditory discrimination may, in a few cases, be poorer because of actual hearing losses for certain tones or pitches. Because of loss in auditory acuity, a child may be unable to discriminate, for example, between several sounds that vibrate at similar pitches. He or she may not be able to hear any difference between *t* and *d*, *s* and *z*, *m* and *n*, or other sounds that are close together on the scale of pitches. However, in most cases of poor auditory discrimination the problem is not an obvious hearing loss.

Poor auditory discrimination is most frequently related to musical abilities such as pitch discrimination, recognition of auditory rhythms and beat, discrimination of tonal quality, timbre, and loudness. Various research studies differ in their identification of the most important of these auditory skills, probably because they are interrelated or interdependent. Children with weak auditory discrimination tend to be unskilled in several or most of these abilities rather than simply defective in one. Observing such children, the primary teacher notes that they seem to lack an alertness or awareness of the auditory characteristics of words. They seem unable to hear small differences between words, to recognize rhyming, and even to distinguish differences in loudness or pitch in everyday sounds. They readily miscall or mispronounce words, substitute or transpose sounds or syllables in words, and have trouble with complex or polysyllabic words. Sometimes these same auditory errors appear in a child's speech and spelling. These auditory difficulties assume lesser significance as pupils above the critical level become less dependent upon relating their auditory vocabulary to word recognition, are less needful of phonic clues, and develop other word recognition clues such as word form, context, and structural analysis.

A research study conducted by one of the writers gave some evidence of the importance of auditory discrimination in early reading. Some six tests of visual discrimination, auditory discrimination, and auditory vocabulary were used in this study. Each of the tests was repeated four times at two-month intervals. Thus data for predicting first-grade reading success were gathered on what amounted to twenty-four tests. In these predictions, the measures of auditory discrimination were the best single predictors in sixteen out of the twenty-four possibilities. This observation reinforces the significance of auditory discrimination in some first grades using the basal reader approach or a highly phonic method (64).

Several problems, however, cloud our interpretation of the exact significance of auditory discrimination in reading. Dykstra, for example, found seven such tests, each of which claimed to measure auditory discrimination in a different manner (16). The tests varied greatly in their intercorrelations and in their relevance to reading. In fact, combinations of five or six of these tests had only a moderate relationship with reading (multiple coefficient of about .60). As a result of his data, Dykstra concluded that auditory discrimination was not a highly significant factor in beginning reading. Perhaps his conclusion should have been tempered by relating it to the kind of test and reading program offered to the children. Auditory discrimination undoubtedly varies in significance according to the demand for phonic analysis in the program and the teacher's attitude toward accurate pronunciation in oral reading, as well as the nature of the test.

In testing with the common measure of distinguishing pairs of words that differ in a single sound, many studies report the inferior performance of minority or economically disadvantaged children. As a result of their findings, most of these researchers recommend intensified training for extended periods in auditory discrimination for these populations (1). In contrast, Venezky and other language specialists feel that auditory discrimination is not a cause of poor reading among dialect users (70). Their poor reading might just as readily be due to other lacks in attention and in cognitive and verbal development, Venezky argues. Besides, the common discrimination of pairs of words demands distinctions not commonly present in dialectal speech, and not really necessary in reading because of the clues supplied by the context. Moreover, the test is quite unreliable in these populations. Thus, although auditory discrimination may be poorer for dialect speakers, their inferior performance is largely due to the nature of the test and does not affect the pupils' reading comprehension.

There is also the evidence that such sounds as *l*, *sh*, voiced *th*, *v*, *s*, *z*, *j*, and *r* are not yet fully developed in the average primary child's speech, but continue improving spontaneously during this period without speech therapy. Since this is so, overemphasis upon correct discrimination of these sounds would seem pointless. In other words, articulation and auditory discrimination are related and are not completely developed until the age of eight or nine, or perhaps later for some children, and thus reflect their development rather than a defect to be corrected. Perhaps the best we should say for auditory discrimination training is that a child probably needs no more than he or she has to have to deal with the phonics or decoding aspect of a reading program. We should also recognize that there is a difference between teaching children to make the sounds of letters and apparently to recognize differences—and the ability to use these learnings in obtaining meaning from the printed page by phonic analysis.

Further evidence of this interpretation of the lack of auditory discrimination was presented when Karlsen and Blocker tested black children on the final consonant blends in the Stanford primary test (31). They found that the pupils who were drawn from the upper lower class and lower middle class equaled the norms for the test. It appeared that, although they may not say these final consonant blends in speech or oral reading, these pupils could hear and discriminate among them. This ability to discriminate was further shown in Williams's study in the pupils' success with initial phonemes in a common test, although not with finals (72). Groff also argued strongly against a significant relationship between auditory discrimination and reading, repeating these same criticisms of the tests used and their low relationship with early reading, and he pointed out the very small proportion of children for whom this ability is really a problem (21).

It is essential to recognize that the use of a test of auditory discrimination does not neatly divide pupils into those who need training and those who do not. Among the relevant facts that affect the interpretation of the test are:

1. The child's performance may reflect a hearing loss among high tones—certain consonants and their blends—or among low tones—the vowels, *m, n, b, h,* and their blends.

2 The child's articulatory development: the sounds of *z, zh, s, sh, r, th* (thin or the), *wh,* and *l* are not commonly mastered by the age of six or seven. If this is the explanation for the test result, what is the point in training the child to discriminate sounds not yet present in his or her speech? Seek the advice of a speech therapist.

3. If the errors are due to dialect, as in final consonants in particular, is training really essential for the reading program because of its emphasis upon phonics? Or, will the teacher accept the child's dialect and recognize that he or she can read and comprehend without modifying speech?

4. Auditory discrimination is not an independent ability; it is linked with auditory span and intelligence. Is it possible that these account for the test results? Perhaps repeated testing and some observation of the apparent attention span are needed to obtain a more meaningful assessment. All three of these traits will effect the child's progress in a heavily phonic oriented reading program, in the negative sense if they are less than average. What modification of such a program will be made for this type of pupil? What alternatives to discrimination and phonics training can be used with this pupil? (See Chapter 12.)

Preschool Learning

Under certain circumstances children's preschool learning seems to be an important factor in their readiness and early reading success. Some upper-class homes provide a wealth of experiences with language and books. Beginning as early as twelve months of age, some children develop important concepts of books. Among these are the following: books contain pages to be turned; pictures resemble familiar objects; pictures and books have a top and bottom, a front and a back; books give information and pleasure; and language adults use in reading is constant for each page; this language can be remembered and related to specific pages or pictures; the printed symbols tell the reader what to say. These concepts facilitate the gradual development of children from a nonreading status to that of actual reading.

Many different tests are included in readiness tests in an attempt to sample these preschool learnings. Among these are matching or naming letters, giving sounds of letters, writing letters, matching beginning and ending sounds in words, and speed in learning words, to mention just a few. Some of these tests give a fair prediction of reading achievement at the middle or end of the first grade, and thus their use tends to persist in common readiness tests. The assumption is that they are measuring children's status in developing readiness for reading. Because the tests seem of some use in predicting early reading success, some of their authors jump to the conclusion that these skills with letters and letter sounds should be greatly emphasized in the reading program of the first year (15). Actually, these tests merely sample bits of information that some children, particularly the bright ones, have acquired. Careful review of these readiness studies shows that the tests of preschool learning are loaded with the intelligence factor. In a roundabout way they are simply measuring mental ability, which, as we have pointed out, tends to be an important factor under the conditions present in the average or the poor classroom. Moreover, it is fallacious to insist that the skill involved in a certain readiness test should be highly emphasized in the reading training as an essential part of the reading process. By the same logic it would be wise to train intelligence, if this is conceivable, because in many classooms this factor seems to affect ultimate reading achievement. Many reading programs put very little emphasis on letters, and yet their pupils learn to read adequately. Like John Downing, the British researcher, we refuse to believe that knowledge of letter names is very important in first-grade reading, until it has been shown that this ability is not merely a reflection of intelligence and socioeconomic status (12).

The long process of preschool learning of concepts about language and books is certainly helpful in creating a readiness for reading. But its lack can be readily overcome by a competent teacher in a first-grade program. This is shown by the comparable reading success of pupils who vary widely in their preschool learning and experiences. Unless there are other significant handicaps, most of these pupils learn to read as well as the average when the readiness program is keyed to their needs.

Another aspect of preschool learning that assumes importance in some studies of beginning readers is the child's range of information. A few commercial readiness tests include a measure of this range. Like the other tests of preschool experiences, this random sampling of the child's information is, in all probability, another test of his or her mental ability. Tests of general information have been used to distinguish degrees of intelligence ever since the first so-called intelligence test was built. In fact, it is one of the basic assumptions in intelligence testing that the retention of information is a major evidence of intelligence.

It is probably true that the child's range of information assumes real significance as the content of his or her reading material broadens in the intermediate grades. But, at the primary levels, the reading materials are so simple and the demands for background so slight that the extent of the child's informational background is not often a crucial factor. The average child has sufficient informational background to understand the usual basal reader program, with the exception perhaps of a few children from bilingual or particularly isolated or barren environments. Furthermore, the few concepts the child may lack are readily supplied by direct instruction or the exchange of ideas and information in classroom discussion.

As we have pointed out earlier, good nursery school or day care experiences do contribute to early reading success. The boost comes not from formal reading training but from the experiences in socializing, routinizing, learning to handle books, learning to listen and to follow directions, and learning to work in a group.

Emotional Adjustment

All experienced primary teachers have taught children whose lack of emotional adjustment to the classroom has hindered their reading success. They have seen excessive timidity or fearfulness, hyperactivity, overaggressiveness, and such personality traits constantly handicap these children in their attempts to function in the group. Teachers do the best they can to meet the needs of maladjusted children, sometimes with success, sometimes without avail. Unfortunately, the research on personalities of beginning readers has not contributed very much to this situation. We do not know which traits are most handicapping or conducive to reading failure; nor do we have any simple, effective tools to aid the teacher to make this judgment. In fact, the best diagnostic tools for teacher detection of the emotionally maladjusted child are still in the research stage. We know very little about the appropriate corrective or preventive steps for teachers to take in dealing with personality problems. Thus, despite its importance for reading success, this is one area still highly dependent upon the individual teacher's subjective judgment. This is not exactly a hopeless situation, for many research studies of beginning readers show that teacher appraisal is still the most effective predictive tool. Apparently, the average teacher can identify and help children whose maladjustments predestine them to failure even if the psychologists have not been able to teach the teacher how to prevent this failure.

When Is a Child Ready to Read?

Readiness to read does not occur at a certain point in a child's development in the sense that a child is ready to read one day but not the day before. The child is not necessarily ready for reading instruction the day he or she completes a readiness workbook or when he or she finishes a readiness program offered to the class as a whole. Readiness is a gradual development from nonreading to beginning reading. Or, as Wilson et al. phrased it, readiness is, in reality, *reading progress in the initial stages of learning to read* (73). The child gradually develops interest in words as meaningful symbols that resemble the words he or she hears. The child shows increasing ability to make accurate discriminations among these symbols and to relate them to words in his or her auditory vocabulary.

These visual and auditory learnings gradually result in the act of reading and writing letters and words. The sequence often proceeds from scribbling to copying (inaccurately), to writing, and to naming written words (9). Several writers also recognize the continuity of this developmental process and suggest that perhaps the best way to determine readiness is to try reading instruction at intervals until children begin to show regular progress. This trial process is probably a fair description of what occurs in many first-grade classrooms.

Most teachers, however, feel the need for some guidelines to help them judge readiness. This is perhaps a more realistic viewpoint than simply deciding in the negative when children show a poor response to repeated attempts to teach them to read. Some teachers will use these guidelines to initiate active readiness training related to a child's individual needs. Thus checklists and readiness tests have a twofold value—to suggest the type of readiness training that will promote a child's development and to suggest that a child is about ready to profit from formal instruction in reading.

As we have pointed out, teachers' judgments of their pupils' readiness status are usually quite effective. In many studies, teachers have demonstrated their skill in differentiating between children who would succeed in reading and those who would not. In some cases, after only a few weeks with their kindergarten or first-grade classes, teachers can predict the probable reading success of their pupils with about as much accuracy as a readiness test. However, this is not proof that teachers can substitute their global judgments or ranking of pupils for readiness tests, as one writer suggests (32). In our opinion, definitely not (32). The purpose of teacher judgment of each child's readiness is not, as some seem to think, a global, overall judgment—"This child is ready, this is not." "This one is an excellent risk, this is not." Both teacher observation and readiness tests are supposed to yield detailed information regarding the child's specific instructional needs during the readiness period. Global judgments of pupils imply that readiness is a thing, a specific stage the child reaches on a certain day, or that at a certain time he or she is mentally, visually, auditorily, and linguistically ready to begin reading. Such an interpretation of readiness is nonsense.

Perhaps first-grade teachers evolve some standards of readiness of their own or depend on an intuitive feeling about when a child is ready for instruction in reading. But it is also essential to enumerate a number of behaviors that readiness research indicates are characteristic of this stage of reading development. The most efficient way to use this checklist would be to make a chart listing the items to be observed in the left-hand column. Draw three or four vertical lines about a half inch apart on the chart. Reproduce one of these charts for each child in the class. The three or four spaces enable the teacher to record observations (check if positive, cross if negative) at intervals during the school year. Or, make one large chart with the children's names inscribed at the head of the column. Some items, of course, need only one recording, as the results of the vision and hearing screening tests; whereas others, such as the speech, listening, and other areas, will need repeated observations. Plans for corrective attention can be made for each child as soon as a negative recording

Readiness Checklist

Vision

Good binocular acuity, near
Good binocular acuity, far
Able to shift focus easily and accurately
Good binocular coordination
Good visual discrimination
Good hand–eye coordination, near

Speech

Free from substitutions and baby talk
Able to communicate in conversation and with group
Reasonable fluency and sentence structure

Listening

Able to hear and respond in class or group situation
Normal hearing indicated in screening test
Able to attend to and recall story
Able to answer simple questions
Able to follow simple directions
Able to follow sequence of story
Able to discriminate sounds of varying pitch and loudness
Able to detect similarities and differences in words
Sufficient auditory vocabulary for common concepts

Social and emotional behavior

Able to work independently or in group
Able to share materials
Able to await turn for teacher's attention
Able to lead or to follow

Interest in learning to read

Shows interest in signs and symbols
Is interested in listening to stories
Can tell some stories and recite some poems or rhymes
Likes to look at the pictures in books
Can attend to the continuity in a sequential picture book
Makes up stories about a picture
Asks to take books home; brings some to school
Tries to identify words in familiar book

(continued)

appears on the chart. Group corrective efforts can be begun as soon as the records for a half dozen or fewer children indicate an area of need.

A few minutes spent writing the observations made during each day's activities will suffice for keeping the record. Observations of incidents that raise doubts in the teacher's mind can be very briefly summarized on the back of a child's chart. To illustrate, on Johnny's chart, "Seemed withdrawn and tense in group" might appear (with the date). This type of entry would alert the teacher to make subsequent notes on Johnny's group behavior and thus reach a decision regarding the approach to use in the future. If similar statements appeared as the year progressed, a clearer idea of the seriousness of the problem or the child's positive progress would become possible. Anecdotal records of classroom incidents and pupil behaviors, as these are called, stimulate the teacher to action and to seek the advice or help of other school personnel, such as counselors, school psychologists, and principals. In parental interviews, these brief descriptions of unusual behavior enable the teacher to explore specific areas of a pupil's adjustment and progress, both positive and negative. This exploration will be intended to elicit parental reaction, to determine whether similar behavior is present at home, whether home conditions are contributing, how such incidents are handled by the parents, to suggest steps that might be taken by the parents to aid or reinforce the teacher's approach, and to decide jointly on a course of action to help the child.

These suggestions for follow-up on the observations based on the checklist may be interpreted as though we were expecting each first-grade teacher to function like a guidance counselor or school psychologist. We do know that many teachers are concerned about the 20 percent or so of school entrants who show problems in school adjustment and that children's overall adjustment and achievement during the first grade is highly predictive of their success for a number of years. We know that this aid will be rejected by some and adopted and improved upon by others. It is offered solely because it draws attention to the significant factors likely to influence a child's success in early reading. It is offered as a diagnostic aid during the entire first grade, not as a series of criteria to determine when a child is completely ready for formal reading. As we illustrate in Chapter 8, a child's experiences with reading do *not* have to be delayed until all factors in the checklist are positive. The checklist items are not absolute standards, but are the needs of beginning readers that the teacher will try to fulfill.

In evaluating pupil readiness, the experience of having attended nursery school or kindergarten is usually interpreted as a favorable factor. Children without this previous training are often expected to perform more poorly in beginning reading. But Morrison and Harris have shown that the effects of kindergarten vary with the method of instruction (*41*). Kindergarten or no kindergarten made no difference for pupils taught by a basal or language experience approach. Only when an ultraphonic method was used were children without kindergarten experience handicapped, evidencing again the greater demands of this type of program. Of course, whatever value kindergarten experience has for progress in early reading is related to the extent that its program is keyed to that goal in providing language and experiential stimulation in terms of pupil needs. Kindergarten or no, each child's readiness will have to be assessed by the teacher on an individual basis.

Learning Disabled

There has been a surge of interest in the past few years in attempts to identify "learning disabled" or "at risk" or "high risk" children; as they are dubbed, prior to school admission, and in some instances even during nursery school ages. The theory is offered that if we identify children early who will later experience severe difficulties in school learning we could prevent many school failures. The concept is certainly laudable, but the possibility of implementation is presently very dubious.

Florida has mandated a program called PREP, an approach to diagnostic-prescriptive instruction for kindergarten through third grade. Screening is conducted during the first eight weeks of school. The state of confusion is shown by the fact that some 80 different tests are used in various districts, many of these being keyed to the local basal or math program. Health screening is done by the County Health unit, probably including the pointless Snellen Test. The program assumes that such screening and consequent related instruction (assuming there is such in existence) will prevent "learning disability." This condition is defined as a discrepancy between what a child is learning and his or her capacity to learn. The pretesting is also intended to identify promising or talented learners who, presumably, will receive some form of accelerated instruction (*48*).

Early prevention programs usually involve giving preschoolers a battery of tests of visual, auditory, and cognitive abilities, often including the Illinois Test of Psycholinguistic Abilities. Specific deficits supposed to be fundamental to school learning are thus presumably found, and the "at risk" children are given training programs intended to repair each deficit and thus ensure their success in school in subsequent years. Critics of these programs point out that (1) there is little or no research indicating that the abilities tested are really significant for predicting early school success; (2) the tests and instruments used, including the Illinois Test of Psycholinguistic Abilities, are of dubious relationship to later success, and often have very low reliabilities because of the immaturity of the children or the construction of the tests themselves; (3) there is very little evidence that the abilities can be developed by training at these ages, or by the programs in common use. Shipe and Miezitis, for example, tested a number of five-year-olds, offered apparently appropriate training programs, but found no substantial improvement related to either of two types of training (62). Like Stott (68) and Clark (8) and others, these authors concluded that large-scale preventive programs as a prophylactic educational measure have, as yet, no solid research foundation. Stott believes that the factors to be identified, at about the kindergarten level, are inappropriate learning style, impulsivity, and lack of self-confidence.

Carol and James Beers point out and dispute the following assumptions of these early testing programs (7):

1. "Learning disability" is a relatively easy to define category because we know the characteristics of the learning disabled child. Yet there is no clear-cut line between a learning disorder and a behavior disorder. Many so-called learning disabled children could be emotionally disturbed or educably retarded. Some labels have been neurological—brain injury, minimal brain damage, minimal brain dysfunction, etc. Others are perceptual—learning disability, auditory impairment, etc.—or behavioral—learning disorder, dyslexia, etc. Yet no one child would have all these traits, nor would all learning disabled have *any one* of these traits. As the Beers's say, "The term learning disabled has become a dumping ground for reading problems, emotional problems, management problems, intellectual problems, speech problems, handwriting problems and others."

2. Identification can readily be done by trained professionals and paraprofessionals. Yet standardized tests used are not highly valid; e.g., visual perception and auditory perception tests are based on vague definitions and show little relation to subsequent academic performance. Reliability of tests at preschool ages is particularly poor (2). The same may be said for the informal tests, checklists, scales, and observation schedules employed. It is extremely difficult to separate learning disability from immaturity. Yet the percentage of "learning disabled" continues to increase each year. Why? Some say to get money and jobs for the special

programs, and because of lack of familiarity with the variability of normal development and the rising school expectations.

3. Prevention in the form of intervention naturally follows identification. But the prescriptions are based on the theory of the examiner, and the processes that the programs are based on don't have strong relationships to academic success. How can such programs help children in later school years? Where is the evidence that the types of programs prescribed prevent academic failure? Not much is known about why children fail, not even why many teaching techniques are incompatible with children's learning.

A. Sterl Artley, a nationally recognized authority in reading, decries the almost impossible task of discriminating between "learning disabled" and "reading disabled" (3). He finds that the labels are often used for the same child, depending upon who is doing the labeling. The definition of "learning disabled" does not help in specifying treatment, for in actual practice these children are often given the same programs as "retarded readers." Many teachers of the learning disabled shifted from remedial reading positions because of the added salary and publicity. As for others, most states do not offer any training in reading methods, or even require such training of the "learning disabled" teachers, even though reading is one of the greatest problems faced by such teachers.

The problems of hyperactivity, visual perceptual dysfunction, right–left discrimination—all often attributed to brain injury—are highly suspect as indicators of learning disability. According to Wallace and McLoughlin, studies show that some children with normal achievement show some of these disturbances and that some children with "learning disabilities" show no evidence of any of these traits (71).

Diane Divorsky cites the federal Department of Education surveys that found "unexpectedly high rates of minority, particularly black children participating in special education." Black pupils were twice as numerous as nonminority pupils. She remarks that as money becomes available, more and more children seem to be handicapped. In Texas, when "minimal brain injury" was funded, many suddenly had that problem; then when funds for "learning language disabled" became available, many children lost their minimal brain damage and suddenly had language disabilities. In California there was an epidemic of aphasia, when such programs were funded, among children who formerly were "educationally handicapped" or "learning disabled" (11).

Robert Karlin extends these criticisms of the identification of the learning disabled. He points out that there is not much hard evidence of these conditions as being basic to reading or learning disabilities (30). In most of the children supposed to exhibit learning disability there is no evidence of brain damage. As for minimal brain damage, there are no consistent symptoms that distinguish such children, for even those with known brain damage often cannot be identified or differentiated from those without brain damage. As for perceptual handicaps, we have already pointed out the extreme weakness of most such tests in predicting reading failure. If children with known brain damage cannot be readily identified, how can we find those with minimal brain damage or brain dysfunction? As for dyslexia, which is also supposed to be related to inherited brain damage or dysfunction, many reading authorities question any use of the term or its supposed symptoms in referring to retarded readers.

The treatment of disabled children is largely borrowed from remedial reading practices (and not necessarily the best ones). Treatment most often consists of teaching letter–sound associations, which are then blended in some programs to form words. Teaching to the suspected modality of the child is also popular. Other writers stress teaching by a whole word method; still others by a kinesthetic approach. There is little agreement among learning disability "experts" regarding treatments.

As the research cited earlier, and a great deal more in England, Sweden, and other countries shows, handicaps in visual, auditory, language, and cognitive abilities can be discovered and ameliorated at the readiness level. High-risk children can be identified and their needs met in the ordinary classroom with subsequent positive results in reading achievement. But there is very little evidence that prevention of failure programs can be profitably or rationally begun in the preschool years.

Testing for Readiness

Vision Tests

Until better vision tests are universally available in schools, some of the responsibility for detecting pupils' visual difficulties falls upon teachers. It is possible to improve the results of the present inadequate vision testing by careful teacher observation of pupil behavior and posture. Several authorities have suggested rather long lists of visual symptoms to be noticed by teachers. These impractical lists represented only opinions and until recently were unverified. A study by Gertrude Knox has attempted to evaluate the symptoms shown by elementary school children that may indicate visual difficulties that are verified by complete professional examinations. She found that both observation and screening should be used to refer pupils to an eye specialist. This combined method resulted in referring some children who were not in need of visual help, but, on the other hand, no child needing such help was overlooked (33).

The significant symptoms that were found to indicate probable visual difficulties fell into definite patterns such as these: (1) facial contortions and forward thrusting of head, (2) facial contortions and tilting of head, (3) facial contortions and tension during close work, and (4) forward thrusting of head and holding book close to face.

Other significant symptoms that may be observed by teachers are these: (1) tension while looking at distant objects, (2) posture that may indicate strain, (3) excessive head movements while reading, (4) rubbing eyes often, (5) avoiding close work, and (6) tending to lose place in reading. A number of other symptoms were investigated but they were not found to be closely related to true visual difficulties.

None of the commercial vision screening batteries available are complete tests of all important visual skills. Some of these tests omit measures of near-point visual acuity, farsightedness, depth perception, and convergence difficulties at near-point. Many of the commercial tests are based upon, and are no better than, the Snellen Test. Because of this situation, we shall point out the specific limitations of the various vision screening tests.

Schubert and Walton have made an adaptation of the Keystone Telebinocular Test that yields comparable results with a modified clinical technique used by optometrists (56). Several new tests are added and some of the present tests are revised to correct the tendency to overrefer.

We would recommend these tests:

- *Keystone Visual Survey Tests*, Keystone View Company, Meadville, Pa.
- *Orthorater*, Bausch and Lomb Optical Company, Rochester, N.Y.
- *Professional Vision Tester*, Titmus Optical Company, Petersburg, Va.
- *Spache Binocular Reading Test*, Keystone View Company, Meadville, Pa. This is a necessary supplement to measure the child's use of both eyes in the binocular act of reading.
- *Stereotests*, Titmus Optical Company, Petersburg, Va. This test of depth perception at near-point is a necessary supplement to the batteries listed above, since none of them includes such a test.

We would not recommend the following batteries because they are largely simple imitations of the Snellen Test. This medically approved instrument tests only far-point acuity, and has almost no relationship to the near-point task of reading. Hence it fails to identify children whose near point visual problems hinder reading success (perhaps as many as 25 percent of the reading disabled).

- *American Optical School Vision Screening Test*, American Optical Company, Southbridge, Mass.
- *Eames Eye Test*, Harcourt Brace Jovanovich, New York, N.Y.
- *King Sight Screener*, King Sight Screener, Quincy, Ill.
- *Massachusetts Vision Test*, Welch Allyn, Inc., Auburn, N.Y.
- *New York School Vision Tester*, Bausch and Lomb, Rochester, N.Y.
- *School Vision Tester*, Titmus Optical Company, Petersburg, Va.

There are a number of informal vision tests that can be used in the classroom. These are not substitutes for professional examination, but rather serve to indicate whether such an examination is needed. In these authors' opinion, these informal tests are preferable to the useless Snellen Test, for their indications are much more relevant to school work.

Fusion or Binocular Function[3]

The String Test. Hold one end of a two-foot string on the bridge of a child's nose, making sure that your hand does not block the child's vision of the string. Ask the child to focus on a knot in the string 16 inches away from the nose, while you hold the extended string. Ask, "How many strings do you see? What do they do?" If necessary, have the child show you with his or her hands what is seen. The child should see two strings forming a V at the knot. If the two strings appear to meet before the knot, the child is overconverging. If the strings appear to meet past the knot, the child is underconverging. If the child sees only one string, he or she is suppressing vision in one eye. If one string appears to be higher than the other, he or she has a vertical imbalance.

Cover Test. Hold a small card over one of the child's eyes while the child focuses on a shiny object at eye level about arm's distance away. Remove the card quickly several times to see whether the covered eye moves. Repeat for the other eye. If the covered eye jerks when the card is removed, it indicates that the child is not focusing with both eyes.

Pursuits Test. Move a shiny object slowly in a vertical half-circle about 16 to 18 inches from the child's head. Repeat, moving the shiny object in horizontal and oblique semicircles in front of the child's head. Ask the child to follow the object with his or her eyes without moving his or her head. The child should follow smoothly, not jerkily, if your movements are smooth. The child's head should not have to move and there should be a reflection of the shiny object in both eyes at all times. Both eyes should move evenly in all directions.

Motility Test (H Test). Have the child follow a penlight or a small shiny object with his or her eyes. Move the object to the right and have the child look up and down. Move the object to the left and ask the child to look up and down. Watch both eyes, or even more reliably watch first the right eye and then the left, to look for limitations in the movement of either eye.

Binocular Test. Have the child hold up one finger at arm's length, and looking past the finger focus on something beyond. The child should see two fingers. Cover each eye alternately to see whether one of the fingers disappears. Repeat by having the child look at the extended finger in the same direction as before. The distant small object should now appear to be double. Seeing only one object at distance or only one finger indicates that the child is suppressing vision in one eye.

Accommodation–Convergence

Pencil Test. Slowly move a pencil or small flashlight horizontally toward the child's eyes at eye level. The child is to say when he or she sees two images. Watch also to determine whether one eye suddenly diverges. Repeat the test several times. If the pencil doubles or the child's eye diverges before you are 3 to 5 inches from the nose, the child has failed the test. As the pencil is gradually withdrawn, the single image should appear again at 5 to 6 inches away. The child should be able to converge and maintain single image until about 4 to 5 inches from the nose, and regain the single image as the pencil is moved back. When you have reached the nearest point at which the child can maintain focus, one eye will move away to break from the converging posture.

Point-to-Point Test. Have the child hold a book and focus on the first word in the first line. Then ask the child to jump his or her eyes to a card containing a well-known word mounted on a distant wall of the classroom. Uncover this card as you ask the child to look at it. (Be sure that the letters are large enough so the word can be easily read.) Repeat the test in reverse, having the child jump from a word on the wall to the first word in the second line in the book. Repeat the test several times. The child should be able to read the distant word almost instantly, or read the word in the book without hesitation, if his or her eyes can make these accommodations or changes from far to near.

Visual Acuity. It is essential to test children's vision at reading distance, since the Snellen Test does not include this measure. The School Vision Card of Dr. Marvin Efron, 1205 D Avenue, Columbia, S.C., 29169, is a very simple instrument for assessing visual acuity at near-point. Reading from the card is alternated with reading from the blackboard to measure the accommodation–convergence function, also. The first three of the recommended commercial batteries also have tests of visual acuity at near-point.

Visual Discrimination

True tests of visual discrimination, which do not simply measure the child's previous knowledge of letters and words, are offered in the *Harrison–Stroud Reading Readiness Test*, the *Murphy–Durrell Reading Readiness Analysis*, and the *Reading Aptitude Tests* by Marion Monroe. It is important to note, moreover, that these visual discrimination tests show significant relationships with later reading achievement in a great many research studies.

The simplest visual discrimination test to administer and interpret is probably the *Winter Haven Perceptual Achievement Forms* (74). It reveals those children who are likely to have difficulties in writing and reading letters and words, and it can be used by the teacher without special training. More-over, it leads directly to a corrective program of definite effectiveness in promoting better hand–eye coordination.

Commercial Readiness Tests

There are several basic limitations in most reading readiness tests. First, most are limited in the sampling of abilities included. Some measure only au-ditory vocabulary; others omit any evaluation of such significant factors as visual or auditory discrimination, articulation, or auditory comprehension. A second common limitation in readiness tests is the tendency to depend upon measures of preschool learning such as matching or even reading words and letters. Because of this content, many readiness tests are not much more than concealed measures of intelligence determined by sampling the child's pre-school learning. Finally, most readiness tests do not yield very accurate predic-tions of later reading success. Their correlations with reading are usually about .5 or .6, a relationship which gives a prediction 25 to 30 percent better than sheer chance. Is it surprising that careful teacher observation and judg-ment often yield predictions just as accurate as any readiness test?

Several studies indicate that, like other commercial instruments, readi-ness tests are not so reliable nor as effective in predicting future pupil achievement when used with minority pupils as their standardization data imply (39). When analyzed item by item, only 35 percent of the tasks in the Metropolitan Readiness test had acceptable levels of difficulty and validity in predicting reading in one study. This is the same type of problem discussed earlier in the use of intelligence tests with minority pupils. Another analysis of the Lee Clark Readiness and the Metropolitan did not find that the various subtests were measuring different abilities, nor that they were assessing facets unlike those in a common intelligence test.

Some of these inherent difficulties in using readiness tests could be over-come by more intelligent planning for interpretation of the results. The norms or standards given by the publisher are seldom appropriate to the particular class being tested. Norms based on many classes drawn from both rural and urban areas, from industrial and agricultural communities, from large and small school systems, and from high and low socioeconomic groups are seldom meaningful in any one particular class. Predictions based on these general norms are more inclined to predictive error the more individual the class is. One solution to this problem is the accumulation of local norms based on all the first grades or kindergartens in the local school system or, if the number of classes in one year is very small, on the accumulation of norms based on succes-sive years. This type of norm, like all others, assumes that the different groups are sufficiently similar in intelligence and socioeconomic background to warrant combining the scores.

Sometimes the major differences in the backgrounds of different classes, or the small number of cases that can be accumulated, make the formation of local norms unfeasible. Even then, however, it is possible to use the reading readiness test scores for the maximum accuracy in prediction despite the inherent weakness of the test in this respect. Scores in the various portions of the test as well as the total score may be used, as the items of the *Readiness Checklist* are employed, to make separate and combined judgments regarding the children's readiness. If the scores of the children are arranged in rank order from lowest to highest, those in serious difficulty are identified, and necessary corrective steps are implied. It is not essential to compare each child's score with the hypothetical standard which is supposed to apply to all children, the test norm, in order to discover those pupils in need of a particular type of readiness training.

Furthermore, by accumulating scores from successive years for classes that are offered a program that is consistent in its methods and philosophy, predictions of pupil success may be further refined. Both by teacher observation and by noting the ranked scores of pupils, cutoff scores or minimum scores in the various parts or the total test can be established. These cutoff scores will be the next highest scores above those achieved by children who failed to learn to read successfully. The cutoff scores separate the successful pupils from those who may fail. Thus without falling into the errors induced by the use of national norms, it is possible to find the individual needs of pupils in the readiness program, and, as scores accumulate, to increase the predictive accuracy of the tests by using cutoff scores.

With these possibilities of overcoming the common limitations of readiness tests, let us review the major characteristics of the leading tests.

Gesell Institute Readiness Tests (see *School Readiness* by Ilg and Ames, Harper & Row) are a series of readiness tests employing a developmental schedule rather than standardized norms for evaluating pupil readiness among children from five to ten years in the areas of visual perception, directionality, and language (25).

Clymer–Barrett Prereading Battery (Chapman, Brook & Hart) is a diagnostic battery of six subtests in reading letters, word matching, discrimination of beginning and ending sounds in words, form completion, and copying a sentence. The test is intended for use at the end of kindergarten or the beginning of first grade. A checklist of readiness behaviors is also included. Continued study of this test supports its validity as a reasonable predictor of first-grade reading (28). However, like the other readiness tests it is influenced by the socioeconomic status and intelligence of the pupils. Children tend to score in keeping with their social ranking, from upper middle class to lower class, and their relative intelligence. In this and other readiness tests, there is still a significant relationship between socioeconomic status and visual discrimination—even when the intelligence factor is held constant—reflecting the preschool experiences of the children (38). This is not an argument against their use, for the results can still be interpreted at face value as indicating children in need of some specific training to ensure their success in early reading. Unlike most of the others, the subtests of the Clymer–Barrett are reliable enough for individual prescriptions.

Harrison–Stroud Reading Readiness Test (Houghton Mifflin Company) has subtests of (1) visual discrimination, (2) using the context, (3) context and auditory clues, (4) auditory discrimination, and (5) using symbols. No data are offered by the authors to support the validity of this test. A study by Spaulding showed a correlation of the total score with achievement on a later reading test of .46, indicating poor predictive value (66). The visual discrimination test and the context and auditory clues were least effective; the remaining tests were fair to poor in predicting reading success.

Lee–Clark Reading Readiness Test (California Test Bureau) includes measures of (1) discrimination of letters, (2) selection of pictures according to verbal descriptions, and (3) discrimination of printed word forms. Various reports of validity studies by Starr (65) indicate a range of correlations between this test and later reading success from .43 to .68. Correlations with intelligence tests as high as .65 have been reported for this test. This is also a weak test.

Metropolitan Readiness Test (Harcourt Brace Jovanovich) measures (1) general reading readiness, (2) number readiness, and (3) total readiness. One study reports various validity correlations of this test, with a later reading test ranging from .27 to .69, with the majority in the .5 to .6 level. Spaulding (66) reported a correlation of .59, while Karlin (29) found only .36 when chronological age and intelligence were held constant. As Starr noted (67), and Karlin's data indicate, many studies of this test show that scores on it are highly related to intelligence.

An analysis of the current research on this test indicated that (1) users did not use the test results to choose an instructional approach (assuming, of course, that the test would give such indications); (2) the time of testing, in kindergarten or early or later first grade, did not influence the predictive validity; (3) multiple regression equations include the Metropolitan average .65, a moderate relationship with reading, but insufficient for individual predictions; (4) no study has attempted to relate the predictive validity of the test with the subsequent method of instruction (20). Greenlaw and Moore also found correlations from .34 to .72 with reading achievement, relationships good enough only for group predictions (20). Although this may be the most widely used readiness test, it is apparent that it is not very helpful in indicating the method of instruction to be used or the instructional needs of the pupils, nor in predicting the probable future reading achievement of individual pupils.

Murphy–Durrell Diagnostic Reading Readiness Test (Harcourt Brace Jovanovich) purports to measure (1) auditory discrimination, (2) visual discrimination, and (3) learning rate. No data on the reliability or validity of this test are reported by the authors. The learning rate test is unique in that it requires twenty minutes of group instruction and three individual retests of the child's retention of words during the same day. Although there is other evidence of the significance of visual and auditory discrimination for reading success, there is no indication of the value of these tests as they appear in this battery. Nor is the significance or true meaning of the learning rate test known.

Reading Aptitude Tests (Houghton Mifflin Company) by Marion Monroe includes eight tests of (1) motor coordination, (2) perception of forms, (3) visual memory for forms, (4) auditory discrimination, (5) maze tracing, (6) blending of sounds, and (7) auditory vocabulary. In addition, individual tests of articulation, auditory memory for a story, and name writing are used. Starr's review of studies (67) of this test shows validity coefficients in predicting later reading success of .38, .41, and .75. These tests sample significant readiness factors more widely than any other available readiness test, thus yielding more diagnostic information for the teacher. Unfortunately for the validity of the norms, the test was standardized over twenty-five years ago and the norms are relatively meaningless today. However, the test can be utilized intelligently if local norms or cutoff scores are established. As Starr remarks, the broad sampling of readiness factors in this test and the consequent diagnostic advantages appeal to many teachers.

Gates–MacGinitie Readiness Skills Test is an eight-subtest battery of listening comprehension, auditory discrimination, visual discrimination of words, following directions, letter recognition, visual–motor coordination in completing letters, auditory blending of word parts, and word recognition. The emphasis upon beginning reading skills as compared with readiness skills is apparent here.

The coauthor of this test, MacGinitie, has severely criticized other readiness tests for (1) low subtest validity; (2) failure to provide diagnostic information; (3) lack of factor analysis to discover the true components of the test, as opposed to just labeling its parts; (4) subtest reliability too low for individual prescriptions; (5) using weights in scoring subtests that are not applicable from one population to another, and (6) ignoring that the predictive validity of any readiness measure will depend upon the particular reading method, and hence will vary from one class to another (36). These are certainly accurate criticisms of many readiness tests. But they were apparently conceived after the Gates–MacGinitie test was constructed, for most of them apply to this test also. The authors of this test have not given sufficient information to determine whether their subtests are very valid or reliable enough for diagnosing individual needs.

Other readiness tests are, of course, available but have not yet had sufficient use for us to judge their merits and include them here. Some publishers of reading series also offer their own readiness tests for use with their instructional system. Usually, these are unstandardized and unnormed, which means that no one knows what levels of performances are normal for any particular type of children. They tend to lack the basic elements of good test construction, such as item analysis for validity and difficulty, field trials to establish overall validity in predicting later reading performances, and analysis of the subtests to determine their values in discrimination, prediction, and validity. These criticisms are particularly relevant in view of the flaws even in the better-constructed tests described above.

One other aspect of the use of readiness tests, or indeed of any other standardized test, must be emphasized. The testing of young children is obviously more fraught with error than is the testing of older children. The reliability of the measures is often quite low because tests are administered in groups larger than four or five children, which is about as large as any adult can carefully monitor. Young children are more disturbed and their responses more inhibited or distorted by a cold testing atmosphere. Sometimes teachers recognize these problems and think to ease the situation by ignoring test timing limits or changing the directions, or even by helping or coaching young children in the hopes of stimulating their best performances. Although the test should be presented as a game situation, in a very small group, using several settings if fatigue or distractions intervene, it must be given exactly as the manual dictates. The only legitimate variation is in providing pretest explanations or examples to be certain that the pupils understand each task clearly. After being certain that each pupil understands what the "game" is and what needs to be done, the teacher should move among the group to be sure that they are moving along from one item to the next, are keeping their place, and are working on the correct item. Quiet comments such as, "That's good. Go on with the next one" are permissible. Comments indicating recognition of a poor performance or attempts to correct these are not permissible. Timed limits may not be ignored simply because the pupils seem to have done only a small portion of a subtest, for that may be all they can be expected to do. Following these suggestions, if the test is well made, will result in obtaining some accurate indications of the pupils' needs to ensure their reading success.

Informal Readiness Tests

Mark W. Aulls is severely critical of commercial readiness tests and workbooks. He points out that testing and teaching letter recognition, for example, has no significant effect upon success in beginning reading. Similarly, measures of auditory discrimination, auditory blending, and rhyming are probably too difficult for accurate results before the age of seven or eight. Instead of commercial tests, he recommends the following informal tests:

The Metalinguistic Inventory, by Evans, Taylor and Blum (*17*) tests children's acquaintance with books and letters. Children are asked to show that the terms *alphabet* and *ABC's* refer to letters; to identify a single letter, a single word and a single sentence on a page; to show where one starts to read a page and a book; and where one reads when a page is finished.

The *Aural Consonant Closure Test,* by the same authors, samples the child's ability to predict the last word in ten printed sentences (when the sentence and word are visible to the child). The authors give one point for a response that makes sense; three points for a response that makes sense and has the same initial consonant. A score of twenty or more indicates a performance equal to the end of first grade.

The *Naming and Matching Letters Test* requires a child to find a matching letter in a random list when shown a letter on an index card. Aulls mentions this test despite his criticism of such a measure.

The *Sight Word Instruction* samples what high frequency words (from the Dolch List or Johnson's First Grade List) the child can read. The students are taught five nouns from flash cards by a sight–word method of repeated telling and testing. Later a row of pictures corresponding to the five nouns taught are to be matched with the word cards. The matching is repeated after an interval of 10 or 15 minutes for a final assessment. Aulls says that children who learn two or less words are not ready to be taught sight words.

Marie M. Clay devised a test of concepts about reading composed of twenty-four items asking the child to identify parts of a book and a story; to show orientation to left and right and top and bottom; to match words; to recognize line sequence and punctuation; and to identify a letter and a word (*10*).

The *Test of Linguistic Awareness in Reading Readiness* has three parts: Recognizing Literacy Behavior (the child's conceptions of the reading and writing acts); Understanding Literacy Functions (the child's understanding of the purposes of reading and writing); and Technical Language of Literacy (the child's concept of such terms as *letter, word, number, top line*). These tests should help to alert teachers to their children's strengths and weaknesses in understanding the concepts they need for reasoning about the tasks of reading (*13*).

Auditory Tests

Auditory Acuity. Identification of children with mild to severe hearing losses can be done by teacher observation with some small degree of accuracy, according to some studies. But when hearing loss is suspected or the child's behavior raises some doubt in the teacher's mind, it is wisest to refer the child for a professional hearing examination. The average medical practitioner is not equipped to perform this examination. The best referral is to a medical hearing specialist, an otolaryngologist or otologist, a speech or hearing clinic, or, if it is properly equipped, a reading clinic in a nearby college. If there are no such sources of help, the teacher may seek advice from the Volta Bureau, 1537 35 Street, N.W., Washington, D.C., or from the state or National Society for Crippled Children or Adults, 11. S. LaSalle Street, Chicago, Ill.

Auditory Discrimination. One or two simple tests of auditory discrimination are suitable for use by the primary teacher, such as the *Auditory Discrimination Test* by Joseph M. Wepman of the Department of Surgery, University of Chicago. A similar test could be constructed by the teacher using twenty-five pairs of monosyllabic words with some of the pairs differing in a single sound, such as the beginning consonant. The test words may be real or nonsense words composed of a consonant or consonant blend, a vowel, and a final consonant, as *pin–tin, kate–gate.* The pairs of words are read to each child while he or she is seated with back to the teacher. The child simply tells whether the pair of words sounds the same or different. In such a test, the child with normal auditory discrimination is likely to make no more than two or three errors. The most reliable way to handle the scores on an unstandardized test like this would be to make further careful observation of those children making the greatest number of errors to watch for the speech and hearing errors that would confirm the test results.

It must be remembered that this type of test is quite unreliable with young children and may need to be repeated several times. Also, it may demand discrimination of sounds that are not normally present in the child's dialect, and thus it is testing the child's ability to hear discriminations he or she does not naturally make. It may also be testing sounds that have not yet appeared in the child's speech development. As we pointed out earlier, accuracy in a test of auditory discrimination is not significant for dialect speakers, for if they can recognize and interpret a word, it does not really matter whether they pronounce it differently. Reading orally with a dialect produces as much comprehension as reading in standard English. Perhaps auditory discrimination tests have their best use in detecting middle-class children whose poor performance would militate against their profiting from the phonics instruction of the reading program. Since there are alternative methods of instruction for these cases that we will discuss later, the test results may not really be significant for this group either, unless a heavy phonics program is mandatory.

There are a number of group tests of auditory discrimination in the commercial readiness tests listed above. A study that analyzed and compared seven of these tests yielded some very interesting insights. Auditory discrimination is measured in a half-dozen ways in these batteries, and these tests obviously do not measure the same factor. The discrimination between spoken words that may or may not begin with the same sound, as in the Harrison–Stroud battery, was consistently effective in predicting reading achievement. Monroe's subtest of selecting the correct pronunciation of a word from among three versions was also relatively good. At the same time, the *Gates Rhyming Test*, the Monroe blending, and the Harrison–Stroud measure of context and auditory clues were poor predictors. The two Murphy–Durrell samples of discrimination of beginning and ending sounds were the poorest of all. The conclusions were that girls were better than boys in initial discrimination ability, as well as learning this skill, and in reading achievement; various tests do not measure this ability similarly, for some were good, some poor, and all less efficient than the intelligence test used. Further research seeking the most effective tests, the values of specific training, and the true nature of the components of auditory discrimination is needed (*16*).

Auditory Comprehension. The child's abilities to listen to, understand, and react to story material may be sampled by an auditory comprehension test such as that included in the *Spache Diagnostic Reading Scales* (California Test Bureau) or the *Durrell Reading Capacity Test* (Harcourt Brace Jovanovich). Or teachers may construct their own test in the manner used in the authors' *Diagnostic Reading Scales* (*63*). Short units of story material, ranging from 100 to 200 words in length and offering a relatively complete story, may be selected from a basal reading series. Selections are chosen and graded by formula to represent each reading level, as preprimer, primer, first reader, low second, high second, low third, high third, etc. Don't take the basal author's grade designations at face value, since it is impossible to write a book in which all passages are at a certain grade level. One portion of a book may be three or more grade levels harder than another. If you are selecting among primary materials, use the Spache formula (65), or the close procedure of determining readability. This technique is described later in this book.

After the story has been read to the child, he or she is asked eight to ten questions previously prepared on the story facts, the sequence of events, and the characters. These questions should be phrased so that they must be answered in the child's own words rather than by a simple yes or no. At this level it is advisable to avoid questions involving interpretation of the motives of the characters, the purpose of the author, or others demanding any depth of interpretation. The purpose of the testing is to discover the level of the material the child can recall and comprehend. Adequate comprehension is indicated by the ability to answer 60 percent or more of the questions. Most children will do much better than this cutoff score, which represents a minimum acceptable level of comprehension.

A third way of measuring auditory comprehension is by giving one form of a standardized reading test in the usual manner, followed a few days later by a second form of the same test. The second testing is administered by reading the selections and the questions to the pupil (repeating the latter if necessary). The pupils will record their answers in the usual fashion. A difference of two stanines on the tests is considered significant, or a difference of one year or more at primary and two years at intermediate grades. When the auditory test score is significantly below the silent reading score, consider using the training strategies mentioned in the next chapters.

The higher the level of the selections for which children can answer with at least the minimum degree of comprehension, the greater their auditory comprehension and, all other things being equal, the more favorable the prediction of their later reading achievement. Most middle-class pupils can listen to and show comprehension of selections scaled more than a year or two above their school or reading status. But any successful performance much above a child's grade level is a favorable sign.

Summary

In this chapter we have reviewed present knowledge about factors that influence readiness for reading instruction and current testing practices. Theories of readiness, the values of the training, and readiness activities not yet in common use are presented in Chapter 8. We intend that Chapter 8 will introduce readers to the truly significant influences upon early reading success insofar as available research clarifies them. Review of these factors will demonstrate the necessity for a diagnostic approach to children's needs, an approach which may then be implemented by later suggestions.

Endnotes

1. This statement is endorsed by the American Association for Elementary/Kinder-garten/Nursery Educators, Association for Childhood Education, Association of Supervision and Curriculum, International Reading Association, National Association for the Education of Young Children, and others.
2. For complete evaluations of these tests, see Spache, George D., *Investigating the Issues of Reading Disabilities*. Boston: Allyn and Bacon, 1976.
3. These informal tests are adapted from Spache, George D., *Diagnosing and Correcting Reading Disabilities*. Boston: Allyn and Bacon, 1981.

Discussion Questions

1. Define your concept of readiness. Has it been modified by reading this chapter? How has it changed?
2. In view of the somewhat contradictory research, why do you suppose schools continue to justify their demand for a certain chronological age for admission to school?
3. What is your reaction to the evidence that early language development of the average child is not very significant for early reading success? How do these facts apply to bilingual children?
4. Why do you suppose there is such a strong debate over beginning reading in kindergarten or nursery school? What are some of the arguments pro and con? What do you believe?
5. Do you believe reading readiness should begin at the nursery school level? If not, why? If so, explain your concept of a good readiness program for that level.
6. What is your reaction to the section on testing for perceptual difficulties? Is such testing practical?
7. What do you think is the reason for sex differences in reading success?
8. Secure one or two of the readiness tests mentioned and prepare an evaluation for presentation to your class. Include any research data on the tests that you can find.
9. Would you use the Readiness Checklist? If so, how?
10. Try to observe several kindergarten and first-grade classes at the beginning of the school year to study their teachers' readiness practices. Share your notes with your classmates.

References

1. Arnold, Richard D., and Wist, Anne H., "Auditory Discrimination Abilities of Disadvantaged Anglo- and Mexican-American Children," *Elementary School Journal*, 70 (March 1970), 295–299.
2. Arter, Judith A., and Jenkins, Joseph R., "Differential Diagnosis and Prescriptive Teaching: A Critical Appraisal." University of Illinois, Technical Report 10, 1978.

3. Artley, A. Sterl, "Learning Disabilities vs. Reading Disabilities: A Vexing Problem," in *Inchworm, Inchworm, Persistent Problems in Reading Education*, Constance M. McCullough, ed. pp. 119–124. Newark, Del.: International Reading Association, 1980.

4. Austin, Gilbert E., and Postlethwaite, T. Neville, "Cognitive Results Based on Different Ages of Entry to School: A Comparative Study," *Journal of Educational Psychology*, 66 (December 1974), 857–863.

5. Bailey, Mildred Hart, et al., "Preparation of Kindergarten Teachers for Reading Instruction," *Reading Teacher*, 36 (December 1982), 307–311.

6. Barrett, Thomas C., "The Relationship Between Measures of Prereading Visual Discrimination and First-Grade Reading Achievement: A Review of the Literature," *Reading Research Quarterly*, 1 (Fall 1965), 51–76.

7. Beers, Carol S. and James W., "Early Identification of Learning Disabilities: Facts and Fallacies," *Elementary School Journal*, 81 (November 1980) 67–76.

8. Clark, Richard M., "The Risk in Early Identification." Paper presented at the National Reading Conference, St. Petersburg, Fla., December 1975.

9. Clay, Marie M., *What Did I Write?* Exeter, N.H.: Heinemann, Educational Books, 1975.

10. Clay, Marie M., *The Early Detection of Reading Difficulties: A Diagnostic Study*. Auckland, New Zealand: Heinemann Educational Books, 1980.

11. Divorsky, Diane, "State of the Art," *Learning*, 5 (August–September 1976), 21, 23, 25, 27.

12. Downing, John, "Specific Cognitive Factors in the Reading Process," in *Reading: The Right to Participate*, Twentieth Yearbook, National Reading Conference, 1971, 38–45.

13. Downing, John, Ayers, D., and Schaefer, B., *Test of Linguistic Awareness in Reading Readiness*. Windsor, Berkshire, England.

14. Durkin, Dolores, *Children Who Read Early*. New York: Teachers College Press, 1966.

15. Durrell, Donald D., et al., "Success in First Grade Reading," *Journal of Education*, 140 (December 1958), 1–48.

16. Dykstra, Robert, "Auditory Discrimination Abilities and Beginning Reading Achievement," *Reading Research Quarterly*, 1 (Spring 1966), 5–34.

17. Evans, M., Taylor, N., and Blum, I., "Children's Written Language Awareness and Its Relationship to Reading Acquisition," *Journal of Reading Behavior*, 11 (Spring 1979), 1–19.

18. Gates, Arthur I., "The Necessary Mental Age for Beginning Reading," *Elementary School Journal*, 37 (March 1937), 498–508.

19. Gesell, Arnold, Ilg, Frances L., and Bullis, Glenna E., *Vision: Its Development in Infant and Child*. New York: Harper and Row, 1949.

20. Greenlaw, M. Jean, and Moore, David, "An Analysis of Current Research on the Metropolitan Readiness Test and First Grade Reading Achievement," in *Reading Research Studies and Applications*, Michael L. Kamil and Alden I. Moe, eds., Twenty-Eighth Yearbook, National Reading Conference, 23–28.

21. Groff, Patrick, "Reading Ability and Auditory Discrimination: Are They Related?" *Reading Teacher*, 28 (May 1975), 742–747.

22. Grosvenor, Theodore, "Vision Screening in Schools, Part I," *Optometric Weekly*, 28 (May 12, 1977), 500–512.

23. Hammill, Donald D., and McNutt, Gaye, "Language Abilities and Reading: A Review of the Literature on Their Relationships," *Elementary School Journal*, 80 (May 1980), 269–277.

24. Hobson, James R., "Scholastic Standing and Activity Participation of Underage High School Pupils Originally Admitted to Kindergarten on the Basis of Physical and Psychological Evaluation." Presidential Address, Division 16, American Psychological Association, September 1956.

25. Ilg, Frances L., and Ames, Louise Bates, *School Readiness*. New York: Harper and Row, 1978.

26. Jones, R. R., and Lee, D. N., "Why Two Eyes are Better Than One: The Two Views of Binocular Vision," *Journal of Experimental Psychology, Human Perception and Performance*, 7 (1981), 30–40.

27. Johnson, Dale D., "Sex Differences in Reading Across Cultures," *Reading Research Quarterly*, 9 (1973–74), 67–86.

28. Johnson, Roger E., "The Validity of the Clymer-Barrett Prereading Readiness Tests," *Reading Teacher*, 22 (April 1969), 609–614.

29. Karlin, Robert, "The Prediction of Reading Success and Reading Readiness Tests," *Elementary English*, 34 (May 1957), 320–322.

30. Karlin, Robert, "Learning Disability and Reading: Theory or Fact?" in *Inchworm, Inchworm, Persistent Problems in Reading Education*, Constance M. McCullough, ed. Newark, Del.: International Reading Association, 1980, 102–110.

31. Karlsen, Bjorn, and Blocker, Margaret, "Black Children and Final Consonant Blends," *Reading Teacher*, 27 (February 1979), 462–463.

32. Kermoian, Samuel B., "Teacher Appraisal of First Grade Readiness," *Elementary English*, 39 (March 1962), 196–201.

33. Knox, Gertrude, "Classroom Symptoms of Visual Difficulty." Master's Thesis, University of Chicago, 1951.

34. Lesiak, Judi, "Reading in Kindergarten: What the Research Doesn't Tell Us," *Reading Teacher*, 32 (November 1978), 135–138.

35. Levy, Beatrice, "Is the Oral Language of Inner City Children Adequate for Beginning Reading?" *Research in the Teaching of English*, 7 (Spring 1973), 51–60.

36. MacGinitie, W. H., "Evaluating Reading for Learning to Read: A Critical Review and Evaluation of Research," *Reading Research Quarterly*, 4 (Spring 1969), 396–410.

37. Malmquist, Eve, "An International Overview of Primary Reading Practices," *Journal of Reading*, 18 (May 1975), 615–624.

38. McDill, Edward L., McDill, Mary S., and Sprehe, J. Timothy, *Strategies for Success in Compensatory Education: An Appraisal of Evaluation*. Baltimore: Johns Hopkins Press, 1969.

39. Mishra, Shitala, and Hart, M., "The Use of Metropolitan Readiness Tests with Mexican-American Children," *California Journal of Educational Research*, 21 (1970), 182–187.

40. Moe, Iver A., "Auding Ability as a Measure of Reading Potential Among Pupils in Primary Grades." Doctoral dissertation, University of Florida, 1957.

41. Morrison, Coleman, and Harris, Albert J., "Effect of Kindergarten on the Reading of the Disadvantaged Child," *Reading Teacher*, 22 (October 1968), 4–9.

42. Mortenson, Paul, "Selected Pre-Reading Tasks, Socioeconomic Status and Sex," *Reading Teacher*, 22 (October 1968), 45–49.

43. Niedermeyer, Fred C., "Parents Teach Kindergarten Reading at Home," *Elementary School Journal*, 70 (May 1970), 438–448.

44. Olson, Arthur V., "School Achievement, Reading Ability and Specific Visual Perception Skills in the Third Grade," *Reading Teacher*, 10 (April 1966), 490–492.

45. Peters, Henry B., "Vision Screening with a Snellen Chart," *American Journal of Optometry and Archives of American Academy of Optometry*, 38 (September 1961), 487–505.

46. Prescott, George A., "Sex Differences in Metropolitan Readiness Test Results," *Journal of Educational Research*, 48 (April 1955), 605–610.

47. Preston, Ralph C., "Reading Achievement of German and American Children," *School and Society*, 90 (October 20, 1962), 350–354.

48. Puryear, Ada P., "Reading Statewide," *Florida Reading Quarterly*, 17 (March 1981), 28–30.

49. Raph, Jane Beasley, "Language Development in Socially Disadvantaged Children," *Review of Educational Research*, 35 (December 1965), 389–400.

50. Robertson, Jean E., "Kindergarten Perception Training: Its Effect on First Grade Reading," in *Perception and Reading*, Helen K. Smith, ed. Proceedings of the International Reading Association, 12, No. 4, 1968, 93–98.

51. Robinson, Helen M., "Vision Screening Tests for Schools," *Elementary School Journal*, 53 (December 1953), 217–222.

52. Robinson, Helen M., and Huelsman, Charles B., "Visual Efficiency and Learning to Read," in *Clinical Studies in Reading—II*, Helen M. Robinson, ed. Supplementary Educational Monographs, No. 77. Chicago: University of Chicago Press, 1953, 31–63.

53. Robinson, Sandra Longfellow, "Educational Opportunities for Young Children in America," *Childhood Education*, 59 (September–October 1982), 42–45.

54. Rosen, Carl L., and Ohnmacht, Fred, "Perception, Readiness and Reading: Achievement in First Grade," in *Perception and Reading*, Helen K. Smith, ed., Proceedings of the International Reading Association, 12, No. 4, 1968, 33–39.

55. Rystrom, Richard, "Caveat Qui Credit (Let the Believer Beware)," *Journal of Reading*, 16 (December 1972), 236–240.

56. Scherwitsky, Marjorie, "Reading in the Kindergarten: A Survey in Virginia," *Young Children*, 29 (March 1979), 161–169.

57. Schickendanz, Judith, *Using Symbolic Props in Play: A Curriculum Guide and Discussion for Preschool Teachers.* Boston: Boston University, 1977. ERIC/CRIER ED 142 292.

58. Schubert, Delwyn G., and Walton, Howard N., "Visual Screening: A New Breakthrough," *Reading Teacher*, 34 (November 1980), 175–177.

59. Sherk, John E. Jr., "A Word Count of Spoken English of Culturally Disadvantaged Preschool and Elementary Pupils." Kansas City, Mo.: University of Missouri, 1973.

60. Sheperd, Richard C., "Oral Language Performance and Reading Instruction," *Elementary English*, 51 (April 1974), 544–546, 560.

61. Sherman, Arnold, "Vision Screening of School Children: Time for a Change," *Optometric Weekly*, 66 (September 4, 1975), 817–819.

62. Shipe, Dorothy, and Miezitis, Solveiga, "A Pilot Study in the Diagnosis and Remediation of Special Learning Disabilities in Preschool Children," *Journal of Learning Disabilities*, 2 (November 1969), 579–592.

63. Spache, George D., *Diagnostic Reading Scales.* Del Monte Research Park, Monterey, Calif.: CTB/McGraw-Hill, 1981.

64. Spache, George D., Andres, Micaela C., Curtis, H. A., et al., *A Longitudinal First Grade Reading Readiness Program.* Cooperative Research Project No. 2742, Florida State Department of Education, 1965.

65. Spache, George D., *Good Reading for Poor Readers.* Champaign, Ill.: Garrard Publishing Co., 1978.

66. Spaulding, Geraldine, "The Relation Between Performance of Independent Pupils on the Harrison-Stroud Reading Readiness Tests and Reading Achievement a Year Later," in *1955 Fall Testing Program in Independent Schools and Supplementary Studies.* Educational Records Bulletin, No. 67. New York: Educational Records Bureau, February 1956, 73–76.

67. Starr, John W. III, "Analysis of Reading Readiness Tests," *Curriculum Bulletin* 13, No. 180 (December 10, 1957). Eugene, Ore.: School of Education, University of Oregon, 1–10.

68. Stott, D. H., "A Preventive Program for the Primary Grades," *Elementary School Journal,* 74 (February 1974), 299–308.

69. Sweeting, Orville J., "An Improved Vision Screening Program for the New Haven Schools," *Journal American Optometric Association,* 30 (May 1959), 657–677.

70. Venezky, R. L., *Nonstandard Language and Reading.* Madison, Wis.: Wisconsin Research and Development Center for Cognitive Learning, 1970.

71. Wallace, G., and McLoughlin, J., *Learning Disabilities: Concepts and Characteristics.* Columbus: Charles E. Merrill, 1975.

72. Williams, Peggy E., "Auditory Discrimination: Differences vs. Deficits," in *Help for the Reading Teacher: New Directions in Research,* W. D. Page, ed. National Conference on Research in English, 1975, 91–99.

73. Wilson, F. T., et al., "Reading Progress In Kindergarten and Primary Grades," *Elementary School Journal,* 38 (February 1938), 442–449.

74. *Winter Haven Perceptual Achievement Tests.* Winter Haven, Fla.: Winter Haven Lions Research Foundation, 1963.

Supplementary Reading

Aulls, Mark W., *Developing Readers in Today's Elementary School.* Boston: Allyn and Bacon, 1982.

Beck, Jean, *How to Raise a Brighter Child: The Case for Early Learning.* New York: Trident Press, 1967.*

Downing, John, and Thackray, Derek, *Reading Readiness.* London: University of London Press, 1972.

Durkin, Dolores, *Getting Reading Started.* Boston: Allyn and Bacon, 1982.

Emery, Donald C., *Teach Your Preschooler to Read.* New York: Simon and Schuster, 1975.*

Give More Children a Head Start: It Pays. Washington, D.C.: CDF Publications.

*We are not recommending these books as guides for parents or teachers. They are mentioned simply because they present contrasting viewpoints.

Hillerich, Robert L., *Reading Fundamentals for Preschool and Primary Children*. Columbus: Charles E. Merrill, 1977.

Hughes, Felicity, *Reading and Writing Before School*. New York: St. Martin's Press, 1972.*

Jobe, Fred W., *Screening Vision in Schools*. Newark, Del.: International Reading Association, 1976.

Kuzma, Kay, *Teaching Your Own Preschool Children*. New York: Doubleday, 1980.

Ollila, Lloyd O., *The Kindergarten Child and Reading*. Newark, Del.: International Reading Association, 1977.

Preschool Breakthrough: What Works in Early Childhood Education. Washington, D.C.: National School Public Relations Association, National Education Association, 1970.

Smethurst, Wood, *Teaching Young Children to Read at Home*. New York: McGraw-Hill, 1975.*

Spache, George D., ed., *Reading Disability and Perception*. Newark, Del.: International Reading Association, 1969.

Strickland, Dorothy, et al., *Reading and Pre-First Grade*. Newark, Del.: International Reading Association, 1977.

Tinker, Miles A., *Preparing Your Child for Reading*. New York: McGraw-Hill, 1976.

Vernon, Magdalen D., *Visual Perception and Its Relation to Reading*. Newark, Del.: International Reading Association, 1973.

8 Readiness Training

Theories and training materials offered to promote readiness for beginning reading differ widely in philosophy and in effectiveness. Some would dispense with any readiness program in order to speed up, they think, the introduction to formal reading. Some teachers place their faith in a whole class use of a readiness workbook. After all, if the authors of this workbook are to be believed, the pupils will now be ready to proceed successfully with learning to read—or so some teachers interpret the use of this device. Currently, a few writers are emphasizing the learning of the names of the letters of the alphabet as an essential, and sometimes, a complete, readiness preparation. Just how this knowledge actually affects the word recognition act has not yet been demonstrated. But after all, these writers say, the alphabet must be important, for children who tend to succeed in reading have learned some letters before entering school. But is this the reason for their success, or is it simply a reflection of their intelligence and socioeconomic background?

The present authors' concept of readiness needs, while not unique or original, is based on attention to those factors found significant in the research literature. Few would dispute the fact that visual perception is based on such visual-motor skills as form perception, directionality, and ocular motility. Some might question the nature of the training programs recommended here. But this criticism would be based on unfamiliarity with their effectiveness, not on any negative research results. After more than five years of trial with these procedures in about 150 first-grade classrooms, the authors are quite convinced of their efficacy, when the programs and their duration are fitted to individual pupil needs.

There are a number of views regarding the proper type of readiness training. One view is that such training is wasted effort. Regardless of mental test results, which some do not believe in anyway, and without any pretense of grouping for individual differences, they would have the teacher begin reading instruction with the total class. Some years ago, Glenn McCracken had his teachers sit the first-graders in front of a few frames of a filmstrip for forty minutes, while they memorized the story. In the afternoon, the children read the same pages in the basal reader. Although he has since dropped the filmstrip session, early editions of the Lippincott readers offered no readiness program. And they still emphasize whole-class instruction in one reader as well as the same brief readiness workbook for all the children. This concept of how to begin reading instruction is unique among those current today.

A second concept of readiness might be entitled the "do nothing" school. Sheer maturation of first-graders will take care of all their needs and deficiencies, according to this view. If we just wait, all the problems will disappear, and if they do not, we'll just raise the entrance age a bit higher next year, or we'll let the children repeat the first grade. After all, everyone knows that children need time to grow and mature before they will be ready for reading. It never seems to occur to the followers of this school that those characteristics of children that might interfere with their early progress could be overcome by instruction or some adaptation of teaching procedures.

The third and largest school of thought regarding readiness has found a complete answer to all the problems in the readiness workbook. These are purchased for every child and appear to provide all the necessary training preliminary to beginning reading. Most basal reading series offer such a workbook presumably directly keyed to future needs during the early reading program. Or, similar workbooks are available in bound or ditto form from other publishers. After completion of this workbook, practically all children except the most immature will be ready to begin the basal program, the authors of some of these imply.

Despite the widespread dependence upon readiness workbooks, there has been extremely little research demonstrating their supposed values. For the most part the exercises they contain have been selected empirically because they seemed related to significant readiness factors. Most contain activities such as the following, in order of their frequency: (1) language development through the medium of sequential pictures; (2) visual discrimination (matching) involving pictures, common objects, geometric forms, letters, and words; (3) motor training through tracing, copying, drawing, dot pictures, and mazes; (4) auditory training with common sounds, rhyming, and initial consonants; and, in a very few cases, (5) discrimination of outlines of word shapes.

In his three-volume review of the literature on early reading instruction, Blanton has summarized the evidence regarding commercial readiness materials in this fashion: "...there is no definitive evidence attesting to the fact that readiness for learning to read can be facilitated by using commercially published readiness materials at the preschool level" (7).

Definitions of Readiness

Some attempts have been made in this area of conflicting philosophies to define what it is that we call readiness. Here are several definitions of readiness and reading:

1. *Readiness:* Word reading strategies rely on previous knowledge and picture cues.
   Reading: Strategies shift to use of the sound–symbol relationship or whole word memorization.

2. *Readiness:* Involves knowledge of the alphabet and some high frequency words. The prereader has book orientation but reads from memory.

    Reading: The child attempts a letter–sound correspondence and word-by-word reading.
3. There is no real difference between these stages since readiness is a task-to-task phenomenon; i.e., a child may be ready for sound–symbol instruction yet be a reader of whole words.
4. *Readiness:* Oral language emphases are appropriate, though the child can be approached with reading preparatory activities.

    Reading: Instruction underscores the realization that sounds are predictable and can be the basis for word identification.
5. *Readiness:* Means a slow and gentle introduction to reading itself—often gamelike, often hidden in other activities. The younger the children the less they are able to understand rules; it is better for them to learn by example and practice (42).

The distinction between readiness and reading as distinct stages in learning to read is rather blurred in these definitions, aside from the fairly general belief that reading involves instruction in and use of sound–symbol correspondences. Readiness seems to slide into reading, and indeed it seems to in recent naturalistic approaches. As Hoskisson expresses it, "Perhaps one of education's greatest delusions is that we really teach children to read. All that may really occur is that materials are presented to a child in one form or another and he uses them to solve the reading problem" (33, p. 446).

In effect, Hoskisson, Butler and Clay (11), Don Holdaway (32), Tom Nicholson (47), and a number of other reading specialists (24, 41) are saying that children practically learn to read on their own. The teacher becomes a facilitator, provider of materials, arranger of experiences, rather than an instructor. Let us look at the manner in which these experts approach readiness and beginning reading.

Learning to Read by Reading

Don Holdaway calls his technique "Shared Book Experiences" and it is intended to be modeled after the way in which some children learn to read at home (32). His method involves these five steps:

1. Being able to see the print and follow along as a book is read. In a classroom this is accomplished by reproducing a story on large charts (or displaying it by an overhead projector or on trans-

parencies). The illustrations are added by the teacher, as best he or she can on the large charts. (Some "Big Books" can be obtained commercially.)

2. The story is read repeatedly with children pointing to words, letters, and sentences as requested (and reading these aloud). The group is encouraged to ask for parts to be reread or to ask questions during any reading.

3. The children store in their memory a model of the language structure. This is essential, Holdaway says, to permit predicting words and phrases and correcting their own mistakes when they read the story. Nicholson implements this step by using a picture book or one with the print covered (47). The children offer sentences describing or interpreting the pictures. Nicholson writes these down, the children and he read them, continuing in this fashion until the picture story is complete. Then the children take turns in rereading *their* story with the teacher pointing to the words as the child or group reads.

4. Children become increasingly more active in participating in reading new books. They are asked to predict a concealed word in a sentence. Their answers are written on tagboard and attached to the Big Book (or written on masking tape on the transparency, or on small cards attached to the book when using the overhead projector). The children's responses are discussed, the sentence is reread by the teacher, who takes off the tape or card to show the original word, and continues reading the story.

5. Children are encouraged to try out their reading behavior with old favorites, predictable books, and easy reading books.

The entire Big Book process is repeated with many books and follow-up activities. For example, Slaughter lists key words on index cards to form each child's word bank (59). These word banks are consulted for spelling when children compose their own stories, are used to form phrases or sentences, and are used for many other types of language practice. See Garton (26), Gillet (27), and Evelyn B. Spache (65) for description of such activities.

The natural process of learning to read is broadened by a number of basic procedures by some teachers. Alphabet books are used to teach young children the names and sounds of letters and to help them identify objects, animals, concepts, etc., thus fostering language development and providing the schemata (stored background information) for reading. Children may make their own Alphabet Books by cutting out pictures for each letter (with the same initial letter), or by composing sentences such as "A is for the apple I eat for my snack." Children's alphabet books may cover countries, things to ride, occupations, things on a farm, foods, etc. (38). (Appendix 2 lists titles of additional books of these various types.)

ABC books

Azarian, Mary, *A Farmer's Alphabet.* Boston: David R. Godine, 1981.
Brown, Marcia, *All Butterflies: An ABC.* New York: Charles Scribner's Sons, 1974.
Baskin, Leonard, *Hosie's Alphabet.* New York: Viking, 1977.
Burton, Marilee Robin, *Aaron Awakes: An Alphabet Book.* New York: Harper and Row, 1982.
Farber, Norma, *As I Was Crossing Boston Common.* New York: E. P. Dutton, 1973.
Geisel, Theodore Seuss, *Dr. Seuss's ABC.* New York: Random House, 1963.
Harrison, Ted, *A Northern Alphabet.* New York: Tundra Books, 1982.
Kraus, Robert, *Good Night Little ABC.* New York: Scholastic Press, 1972.
Lobel, Arnold, *On Market Street.* New York: Greenwillow Books, 1981.
Mmeling, Carl, *Riddles, Riddles from A to Z.* Wayne, N.J.: Golden Press, 1972.
Provenson, Alice and Martin, *A Peaceable Kingdom: The Shaker Abecdarius.* New York: Viking, 1978.
Wildsmith, Brian, *Brian Wildsmith's ABC.* New York: Franklin Watts, 1962.

Wordless Books or picture books are utilized in this naturalistic approach for language practice in elaborating about the picture contents, in interpreting the pictures, in contrasting the experiences of the characters depicted with the children's own, and for role playing or reenacting what the characters did or might do, as well as in the manner described by Tom Nicholson above.

Picture books

Bahr, Robert, *Blizzard at the Zoo.* New York: Lothrop, Lee and Shepard, 1982.
Barton, Byron, *Elephant.* Boston: Houghton Mifflin, 1971.
Carle, Eric, *Do You Want to Be My Friend?* New York: Harper and Row, 1971.
De Regniers, Beatrice Schenk, *Going for a Walk.* New York: Harper and Row, 1982.
Goodall, J. S. *Shrewbettina's Birthday.* New York: Harcourt Brace Jovanovich, 1971.
Hutchins, Pat, *Changes, Changes.* New York: Macmillan, 1971.
Keats, Ezra Jack, *Clementina's Cactus.* New York: Viking Press, 1982.

(continued)

Krahn, Fernando, *Sebastian and the Mushroom*. New York: Delacorte, 1976.

Lisker, Sonia O., *Lost*. New York: Harcourt Brace Jovanovich, 1975.

Mari, Lela *The Apple and the Moth*. New York: Pantheon Books, 1970.

Mari, Lela and Enzo, *The Chicken and the Egg*. New York: Pantheon Books, 1970.

Mayer, Mercer, *Ah-Choo*. New York: Dial, 1976.

Mayer, Mercer, *Frog Goes to Dinner*. New York: Dial, 1977.

Mayer, Mercer, *Frog on His Own*. New York: Dial, 1973.

Shimin, Symeon, *A Special Birthday*. New York: McGraw-Hill, 1976.

Taylor, Mark, *Henry the Explorer*. New York: Atheneum, 1976.

Turk, Hanne, *Max, the Mouse*. New York: Alphabet Press, 1982 (a three-book series).

Wright, Betty R., *I Want to Read*. Chicago: Western Publishing, 1965.

Yaffe, Ruth, *A Winter Place*. Boston: Little, Brown, 1982.

Spatial and relational concepts of size, shape, bodily concepts, and the like are developed through a selection of books in these areas, used for group reading with teacher-led discussion, or for indendent reading.

Spatial and relational concepts

Borten, Helen, *Do You Move As I Do?* New York: Abelard- Schuman, 1963.

Hutchins, I., *Hunter*. New York: Greenwillow Books, 1982 (a number book).

Kohn, Bernice, *Everything Has a Size*. Englewood Cliffs, N.J.: Prentice-Hall, 1966.

Kohn, Bernice, *Everything Has a Shape*. Englewood Cliffs: Prentice-Hall, 1966.

Krauss, Ruth, *I'll Be You—You Be Me*. New York: Harper and Row, 1973.

Palazzo, Tony, *The Magic Crayon*. New York: Lion Books, 1967 (creative experiences with common shapes and forms).

Perkins, Al, *Hand, Hand, Finger, Thumb*. New York: Random House, 1969 (finger play).

Shapp, Charles and Martha, *Let's Find Out What's Big and What's Small*. New York: Franklin Watts, 1975.

Srivasta, Jane Jonas, *Spaces, Shapes and Sizes*. New York: Crowell, 1980.

Reading to children is an integral part of this introduction to reading. Just as children would for oral reading, teachers rehearse the books they are going to read by reading them to themselves. When reading, teachers try to convey tone and mood and to dramatize significant parts with their voices. By practicing the pacing of their reading, and planning where or when and what types of questions they will ask to initiate discussion, they give an improved performance. While reading to their groups, teachers try to maintain eye contact to hold the children's attention and increase their involvement. They hold the book so that all the children can see the illustrations and the print. They point to the print as they read, if the group can really see the words (*12, 13*).

Storytelling is an integral part of the daily program. It is a skilled performance that requires careful planning, according to some experts. Here are some of the suggestions of Ramon R. Ross (*58*):

1. Start with short, simple stories that you enjoy.
2. Some stories need to be memorized, at least in part, because the children are familiar with some of the key phrases.
3. Practice the story aloud.
4. Think about the characters and how they would talk. Try to vary your voice accordingly.
5. Choose certain phrases or sentences that you will repeat because of their effect. Practice their intonation.
6. Plan gestures; the fewer, the better.
7. Plan a lead-in and a closing to your story.
8. Practice the entire story, gestures, special phrases, sequencing, and the like.

If you do it well, the children will want to hear it again and again. They may want to enact it in costume, use puppets, or even write their own short versions or adaptations. One of the characters may become a class mascot to be pictured, consulted, played with, etc.

Some teachers use a flannelboard for storytelling (*58*). They use cutout felt figures and objects to illustrate the characters and events and setting. Paper cutouts with sandpaper glued to the back, cotton balls, pieces of yarn and sponge are useful and will adhere to the flannelboard. The children will want to repeat the entire process again and again, perhaps with their own bits and pieces to illustrate as they retell their versions. You can get materials for the flannelboard from Teachers Publishing Corp. of Darien, Conn., or any large school supply house.

Aulls mentions two interesting learning activities suitable at beginning reading stages. One involves a stool or reading chair placed in a corner of the room. When a child has learned to read a story of his or her own or a book or whatever, he or she may take the stool and read to another child. If no one comes to listen, he or she should read it silently several times before relinquishing the stool.

A second activity is the preparation of several photocopies of a cartoon with the words deleted. Several children take turns trying to reassemble the pictures in a sensible order and to make up the dialogue. The best version may be chosen by mutual consent.

Predictable books or those having repetitive, patterned language have been shown to produce distinctly favorable attitudes toward reading and greater ease in handling the context to derive unfamiliar words. Bridge et al. employed such books in the following manner (9):

> The teacher reads the book to a group and then again inviting the children to join in. She will read part of a sentence and have the children predict what comes next. Next the children take turns in reading the story or in choral reading. Then the story is written on a large chart without the picture cues. Teachers and children take turns reading from the chart.

Sentence strips are matched to the chart. Word cards are arranged in the story sentences and matched to the chart. The group reads the whole story chorally from the chart and then matches the word cards to it.

Some of the children may wish to add certain of the word cards to their word banks. Others will want to copy the story for their books of stories. The word cards may be placed in an envelope pinned to the chart as it is mounted on the wall. Children may practice forming sentences or the entire story as they wish.

Bridge et al. found that their procedures, which are paraphrased above, resulted in the children learning significantly more of the words of a preprimer than the control group did. The researchers concluded that using patterned, predictable books was most desirable as a resource in writing, using patterns, changing them, improving them, etc. They also found that (1) rhyming helped children learn common phonograms and syllables; (2) the books helped children to recognize some of the rules of letter–sound correspondence and to recognize unfamiliar words by analogy with known words; (3) the activities provided opportunities for children to compose their own language experience charts on basic societal information (day, numbers, etc.) as well as themes (circus, farm, city) and facilitated learning-related vocabulary and concepts. Rhodes offers another list of these books (52).

Most of the following books are cited by Bridge et al. (9). See Appendix 2 of this book for other titles.

Rhythmic verse or repetitive patterns (predictable books)

Barrett, Judi, *Animals Should Definitely Not Wear Clothes.* New York: Atheneum, 1970.
Battaglia, Aurelius, *Old Mother Hubbard.* Wayne, N.J.: Golden Press, 1972.
Berenstain, Stanley and Janice, *The B Book.* New York: Random House, 1971.
Brooke, Leslie, *Johnny Crow's Garden.* New York: Frederick Warne, 1968.
Burningham, John, *Mr. Gumpy's Outing.* New York: Scholastic Press, 1970.
Carle, Eric, *Do You Want to Be My Friend?* New York: Crowell, 1971.
Carle, Eric, *The Very Hungry Caterpillar.* Cleveland: Collins-World, 1969.

(continued)

Carle, Eric, *The Rooster Who Set Out to See the World.* New York: Four Winds Press, 1972.

Charlip, Remy, *Fortunately.* New York: Parents Magazine Press, 1971.

de Paola, Tomie, *Pancakes for Breakfast.* New York: Harcourt Brace Jovanovich, 1978.

de Regniers, Beatrice, *Willy O'Dwyer Jumped in the Fire.* New York: Atheneum, 1968.

Einsel, Walter, *Did You Ever See?* New York: Scholastic Press, 1962.

Emberly, Barbara, *Drummer Hoff.* Englewood Cliffs: Prentice-Hall, 1967.

Galdone, Paul, *Henny Penny.* Boston: Houghton Mifflin, 1975.

Galdone, Paul, *The Three Billy Goats Gruff.* Boston: Houghton Mifflin, 1973.

Hutchins, Pat, *Good Night, Owl.* New York: Macmillan, 1972.

Hutchins, Pat, *Rosie's Wall.* New York: Macmillan, 1978.

Keats, Ezra Jack, *Over in the Meadow.* New York: Four Winds Press, 1972.

Kesselman, Wendy, *There's a Train Going By My Window.* New York: Doubleday, 1982.

Mars, W. T., *The Old Woman and Her Pig.* Chicago: Western Publishing, 1964.

Martin, Bill, Jr., *Brown Bear, Brown Bear, What Do You See?* New York: Holt, Rinehart and Winston, 1967.

Martin, Bill, Jr., *The Haunted House.* New York: Holt, Rinehart and Winston, 1970.

Martin, Bill, Jr., *Freedom Books.* Los Angeles: Bowmar/Noble, 1965 (series).

Martin, Bill, Jr., *Instant Readers.* New York: Holt, Rinehart and Winston, 1975 (series).

Martin, Bill, Jr., *Little Owl Series.* New York: Holt, Rinehart and Winston, 1965 (series).

Martin, Bill, Jr., *Sounds of Language.* New York: Holt, Rinehart and Winston, 1966 (series).

Martin, Bill, Jr., *Wise Owl Series.* New York: Holt, Rinehart and Winston, 1967 (series).

Martin, Bill, Jr., *Young Owl Series.* New York: Holt, Rinehart and Winston, 1964 (series).

Patrick, Gloria, *A Bug in a Jug.* New York: Scholastic Press, 1970.

Peek, Merie, *Roll Over!* Boston: Houghton Mifflin, 1981.

Petersham, Maud and Miska, *The Rooster Crows: A Book of American Rhymes and Jingles.* New York: Scholastic Press, 1971.

Preston, Edna M., *The Temper Tantrum.* New York: Viking, 1969.

Tolstoi, Alexei, *The Great Big Enormous Turnip.* New York: Franklin Watts, 1968.

Waston, Clyde, *Father Fox's Pennyrhymes.* New York: Scholastic Press, 1971.

Westcott, Nadine Bernard, *I Know an Old Lady Who Swallowed a Fly.* Boston: Little, Brown, 1980.

Withers, Carl, *A Rocket in My Pocket.* New York: Scholastic Press, 1967.

Zemach, Margot, *The Judge.* New York: Farrar, Strauss and York, 1969.

Our View

Although we accept this naturalistic approach to beginning reading, we recognize that some children may not learn to read by this technique. Some will still need visual, auditory, oral language, or visual motor experiences if they are to succeed in the reading act. Let us consider some of these readiness needs.

We have referred several times to the research study conducted by one of the authors, but it is most appropriate to repeat its description again here, for it is a dramatic demonstration of the values of an extended, intensified readiness program. Thirty-two first-grade classes in which the usual basal reading program was employed served as the control group. In an equal number of classes, reading instruction was supplanted by small-group training in visual discrimination, auditory discrimination, or auditory vocabulary. The children's needs were determined every two months by repeated use of six readiness tests, two in each area. Special training was offered each child for periods of two, four, or six months as test results warranted. Children performing in the upper quartile of scores on all tests were introduced to basal reading at the beginning of the year or after each retesting.

The training materials in visual discrimination employed the chalkboard exercises described later in this chapter and the seatwork *Visual Discrimination* and *Visuo-Motor Skills* workbooks of Continental Press. The auditory training included a wide variety of group activities selected from Russell and Russell—*Listening Aids Through the Grades,* and for seatwork, the *Blending and Rhyming* workbooks of Continental Press. The auditory vocabulary training was drawn largely from Russell and Russell and other standard sources.

Some of the significant results of the experiment were as follows (*61*):

1. Growth in visual discrimination was significant during four months of the special training, and greater after two months than that present among control groups after six months in the basal program.

2. Growth in auditory discrimination was significant but similar in both experimental and control groups. Only among older black boys was the experimental training more effective than that present in basal programs.

3. Growth in auditory vocabulary, as measured by tests of auditory comprehension, was significantly greater in the experimental classes among white pupils.

4. There were no significant differences in the overall reading achievement of the control and experimental groups (despite the two to six months' less reading instruction in experimentals).

5. Reading achievement was greatest among the white pupils in the control classes, but also among black pupils in the experimental classes, evidencing the marked advantages in the experimental training for black children, particularly those of lower mental ability.

6. Level of mental ability was significantly related to reading achievement, for (a) at upper levels of ability, the experimental training en-

abled white boys to equal the achievement of girls; (b) black experimentals of lower mental ability exceeded white experimentals of similar ability; and (c) white pupils of upper mental ability profit more from the basal program than do black pupils of similar ability.

Our readiness experiment emphasized a number of significant readiness factors. Both training programs enabled economically and language-handicapped children, those obviously most in need of such experiences, to exceed the achievement of matched control groups. In our study, black children given extended readiness training and the pupils of the lowest quartile in intelligence profited most, and surpassed in reading the control basal reader groups. Surely readiness training seems profitable for those with the greatest needs.

Since readiness is not a simple global trait such as maturation, the training program must be multifaceted, and its application differentiated to the pupils' needs as determined by readiness tests, teacher observation, a checklist of behaviors, and the responsiveness of the child to training. The overview of the readiness program given in the following table does not, of course, mention all the procedures and materials which the teacher may utilize. Space does not permit such a complete listing. But we know that interested teachers will extend these few suggestions as their judgment dictates, and from the discussion of the rationale and results of various programs that follows the chart.

Overview of the reading readiness program

Perceptual–motor

Body image	Jointed dolls, Simon Says, mirror, rhythmic activities to music, movement games, skipping rope, Angels-in-the-Snow, trunk and leg lifts, sit-ups
Laterality and directionality	Etch-A-Sketch, balance beam and balance disc, chalkboard exercises, creeping obstacle course, walking obstacle course, stepping games
Hand–eye coordination	Templates, chalkboard exercises, coloring, cutting, pasting, jacks, marbles Swinging ball, finger play, straight line and rotary pursuits with flashlight or eyes, eye-movement charts, Space Masks, Space Sighters

(continued)

Form perception
Three-dimensional

Puzzles, nested cubes, pegboards, parquetry, mosaic tiles, pattern boards, block designs, clay

Two-dimensional

Ditto masters, tracing and reproducing forms, matching forms, likenesses and differences, desk templates, drawing

Coordination
Small-muscle coordination

Bead stringing, paper and pencil activities, tracing, dot pictures, pick-up sticks

Large-muscle coordination

Bean bags, dart games, ball throwing, catching and bouncing, nail pounding, ring toss, rhythm bands, Lummi sticks, hoops, jump board

Discrimination
Word and letter discrimination

Sandpaper letters, magnetic letters, flocked letters, ditto masters for matching and reproducing

Sensory discrimination

Identifying by feel, taste, smell, and sight, describing sensations, as in Feel Box, Smell Box

Auditory awareness

Identifying sounds of the earth, animals, human-made sounds; imitating and responding to inflections; distinguishing intensity or loudness, pitch, duration, and sequences of sounds; What Is It Game

Auditory perception

Expressing sounds as in dances, marching, rhythmic activities, finger snapping; alliterative play with rhymes and jingles; games such as Sound of the Day

Auditory memory

Echo game, reproducing tapping patterns, following one-, two-, and three-step directions, Whispering Game, Restaurant Game, You Must Game, Bring Me Game

Auditory discrimination

Identifying sounds, words, rhymes on records; anticipating words or sounds in storytelling; imitating ani-

(continued)

mal noises as in *Billy Goats Gruff, The Three Bears;* identifying sounds or number of syllables in names and other words; practicing rhyming in poetry, songs, and jingles

Language and thinking
Receptive language

Listening to stories, dramatizing antonyms, following directions, detecting omissions or absurdities in stories, rhymes, or jingles, categorizing pictures, matching pictures and story sequence, enacting action words.

Expressive language

Telling Time, Sharing Time, social games, interpreting pictures and picture sequences, telling rote or cumulative tales, talking games such as Gossip Game, I Am Thinking of a Word That Tells Game, composing group experience charts, retelling stories, composing original stories, rhymes, and riddles

Adapted from *The Teaching of Reading* by George D. Spache (Bloomington, Ind.: Phi Delta Kappa Educational Foundation, 1972), by permission of the publisher.

Training in Visual Perception

In the words of G. N. Getman, the prominent optometrist, "the concepts of our world are learned.... Visual perception, which should become the supreme skill for more complete and adequate concepts of our world of people, objects, words, pictures, direction, distance, size, shape, color and texture, develops out of the sensory-receptor mechanisms of actual contact." As suggested earlier, visual perception grows out of visual–tactual experiences. These experiences are multitudinous and require four to six years for sufficient development to levels permitting children to read. They begin with the first visually directed reach and grasp of infants, their first visual–tactual learning. Their number and variety determine most of the children's nonverbal or kinesthetic learning and also form the basis for their verbal learnings, speech or reading.

Visual–tactual experiences eventually are substituted for by visual movements, communication and speech patterns, which in turn yield to visualization and symbol manipulation (reading). Restriction of these experiences retards children's entire physical and intellectual development to a point below their inherited potential.

In view of these facts, it is not surprising that we emphasize teacher observation, diagnosis, and training of visual–tactual development, visual perception, and functional visual skills as absolute prerequisites to reading instruction. Space does not permit adequate treatment of this subject, but the readers should fill this lack by consulting some of the resources mentioned in the bibliography.

The act of reading demands such visual discriminations and perceptions as an orientation to left and right, up and down, front and back; accurate binocular shifts from point to point; accurate focus and accommodation to distance; and a fine degree of parallel or coordinated action of both eyes, or binocular coordination. To read, children must be able to note similarities and differences among words by the clues given by the shapes of their beginning and ending letters, by letters that ascend and descend above and below the line, and by the patterns or outlines formed by combinations of these elements of words. The children must learn to make quick, accurate discriminations among a host of words, perhaps a more demanding visual task than any other they have experienced. Reading is first and foremost a visual task for beginning readers and almost impossible for them to accomplish without the perceptual and discriminative abilities we have stressed. (See the discussion of reading as a visual and a perceptual act in Chapter 1 for a complete description of the visual skills demanded by reading.)

Therefore, when children's behavior and quality of performance during near-point tasks indicate lack of visual perception or hand–eye coordination, developmental training should be given. In fact, the research on perceptual training shows that the entire third of the class which is lowest in general ability, readiness, or reading progress will probably benefit from this training. The values of developmental work in visual perception and hand–eye coordination are attested by many optometric and educational studies. Office records of hundreds of optometrists who specialize in visual training, and of orthoptists, their medical counterparts, show that training such as we will outline results in greater comfort and success in near-point activities as well as in reading and other academic tasks. Lillian Hinds's longitudinal study showed that first-graders receiving this training were decidedly more successful in reading than might have been expected by reason of their intelligence or readiness. First-grade pupils showed improvement in discrimination after training given in the second semester, if they were already reading well in the first semester. In other words, tachistoscopic training with geometric forms and digits was not very helpful for the less successful perceivers and readers either in improving discrimination or reading. Cox and Hambly employed a variety of training procedures, such as we shall describe later, with low achievers (17). The trained pupils showed significantly greater gain in tests of visual skills given a year and a half after the three-month training period. The interdependence of the visual skills was shown by the fact that those children who improved in all three skills stressed showed the greatest gain in learning rate or achievement quotient. Improvement of only one visual skill did not produce greater learning ability. Halgren gave training to both ninth-graders and first-graders, although he gives detailed results only for the older group (30). Since the training procedures are very similar to those we will describe, the marked gains in academic achievement for low achievers are significant to the primary school teacher.

Space does not permit a detailed review of all the evidence pro and con on visual-perception training experiments, for there are dozens and dozens of studies. For those who feel a need to evaluate this area more in depth before accepting some of our later suggestions, intensive reviews of the outcomes of perceptual training programs are offered in the senior author's most recent books (61, 62).

One approach to this area in the readiness program is the use of commercial programs advertised for the development of visual perception or discrimination. Two popular programs of this type are the Frostig Visual-Perceptual Program based on the test by the same author, and the Delacato neurological organization training (18, 19, 25). Because of their wide use and, in our opinion, questionable results, we have tried to find as many studies of the outcomes of these two programs as a search of the literature would reveal. Those relevant to the Frostig program are summarized in Table 8.1.

It is apparent that using the Frostig program in the hopes of improving pupil readiness or reading is not likely to succeed. Four of the five studies testing the effects of the program on a readiness test gave nonsignificant gains. Six of the seven studies testing the effects of the Frostig training on reading again gave insignificant gains in reading. The only result of this visual perception program appears to be in raising scores on the Frostig test, a finding in three out of five experiments. In other words, when children are practiced in materials patterned on the Frostig test, they improve in that test, but there is little or no transfer to readiness or reading achievement. In the only study in which the training produced gains in reading, two other perceptual training programs were also used, so that the good results cannot really be attributed to the Frostig.

The Delacato program is supposed to be based on a theory of neurological organization, or developing complete sidedness in the child. The brain, presumably, is retrained and the sidedness induced by a variety of creeping and crawling exercises. Glass and Robbins reviewed twelve reports from schools which adopted this program but found that all of them lacked careful research designs and the usual scientific controls of a true experiment (28). O'Donnell (48), McCormick et al. (41), and Stone and Pielstick (66) used the program, but only McCormick claimed any favorable results. Unfortunately, his study was faulty in selecting children from a larger group, and failing to control the teacher inspiration or in-service training variables.

Robbins studied the program under Delacato and applied it to second-graders in comparison with one group given unpatterned physical activities

Table 8.1   Scoreboard on the Frostig Perceptual Training Program

Source; grade level; number of cases	Gains on Frostig test	Gains in readiness test	Gains in reading test	Frostig versus
Beaupre and Kennard (5); kindergarten; N = ca. 75		Not significant		Five other programs all superior to Frostig
Buckland (10); grade one; 16 classes	Not significant		Not significant; controls superior	Listening to stories and discussion
Cohen (15); grade one; N = 155	Significant		Not significant	
Cohen (16); grade one; N = 120			Not significant	
Faustman (21); kindergarten; 14 classes			Significant	Frostig plus Winter Haven plus Kephart programs
Fortenberry (23); grade one			Not significant	Frostig plus usual readiness
Jacobs el al. (36); prekindergarten, kindergarten, and grade one; N = 300		Not significant		
Jacobs et al. (36); prekindergarten to grade three; N = 300		Not significant	Not significant	
Pumfrey and Anthony (51); physically handicapped; N = 24	Not significant			Frostig training keyed to initial subtest vs. total Frostig vs. none
Rosen (57); grade one; N = 637	Significant		Not significant	
Wingert (69); kindergarten; N = 54	Significant	Not significant		

and a control group given no training (54). The results did not support the neurological reorganization theory or its relationship to reading or its effect upon sidedness of children. Like the American Academy of Pediatrics (19), Robbins rejects completely both the theory and the treatment program as being relevant to reading or any other type of language difficulty.

On the positive side of visual perception training experiments, there are many other studies. We cannot possibly review all the individual studies here, but we will attempt to categorize them into types of programs and summarize their results. One group of studies emphasizes training with letters and words. In toto, these seem to indicate that using color in letters or backgrounds, letter names or letter discrimination, or matching geometric forms or words seems to contribute little to eventual skill in word recognition. Another group indicates that it is possible to stimulate whatever is measured by popular perception tests, like the Bender or the Frostig, but these results do not seem to transfer to readiness or reading. Among brain-damaged or mentally retarded children even these gains are only temporary and not much greater than the effects of mental maturation.

Readiness training intended to facilitate word recognition should move toward the meaningfulness of words rather than word form, or sound, or both, and toward training in letter discrimination without stressing letter names. Pretraining trials should probably be conducted to discover the individual differences among children so that perceptual training can be matched to their development and aptitudes. One group of studies has emphasized the chalkboard and template exercises we will describe later. This training seems profitable for children in low socioeconomic groups or those of low intelligence rather than those of the middle or upper class. In fact, used as tests to predict reading achievement, the form perception, the chalkboard, and the walking beam programs show good relationship to reading through the second grade.

Other experiments that failed to influence reading achievement include those stressing tachistoscopic training in form recognition, noting likenesses or differences in words or pictures, tracing textured word forms, matching word forms, and rearranging plastic letters. These activities do not readily transfer to the act of word recognition.

There are three major types of visual training for perception and discrimination that any teacher can conduct. These include (1) directionality, or orientation to direction; (2) ocular motility, or promoting coordinated movements of both eyes; and (3) form perception, or discrimination of similarities and differences in designs, figures, and wordlike forms. A few children may also need more fundamental training in body coordination or motor development. These exercises and tests for general physical fitness of children are widely accepted by physical educators and other experts. This basic body conditioning is highly desirable for brain-damaged and cerebral-palsied children, and also for a small proportion of grossly uncoordinated normal children. It is not highly related to success in reading; hence the exercises and tests will not be reviewed in detail here. But every primary teacher should be thoroughly familiar with this gross coordination training program.

Directionality

A well-developed sense of directionality to left–right, up–down, front–back, as well as to curves and angles in both three-dimensional and two-dimensional representation, is fundamental to successful reading. Although reading is only a two-dimension task, with words having length and height but not thickness, visual skill in depth perception is still highly important for reading. (Depth perception is the visual recognition of thickness, depth, or solidity of objects arising in part from a blending of the images received by the separate eyes, and organizing in visual–actual experiences.) Many careful studies of child vision show that loss of depth perception is a significant symptom of subsequent academic difficulties (39). The relationships of other types of directionality skill must be quite obvious. Children must stabilize a constant left-to-right movement and an accurate return sweep for successful word recognition and forward progress along the lines of print. They must recognize and retain the patterns made by the curved and straight lines of letters and whole words. For fluent reading, the recognition of these shapes or patterns must constantly increase in speed and accuracy. Without adequate development of these directional skills, children's reading is retarded by frequent reversals, inversions, word confusions, and substitutions.

Working with five-year-old New Zealand children, Marie M. Clay found that after the first year of schooling, 4 to 10 percent (varying according to the ethnic composition of the group—white, Maori, or Samoan) have no firm understanding of the left-to-right directionality of reading (14). After the first six months of school, 2.5 percent still had not learned to move from left to right or to return to the beginning of the next line.

The research study conducted by one of these authors employed a number of chalkboard exercises in directionality as part of the training for the first graders who were lacking in accurate visual perception. About fifteen minutes per day of this training, accompanied by seatwork in similar discriminations offered by the Continental Press workbooks, was offered. The training in the experimental classes was substituted for the usual reading instruction for periods ranging from at least two months to as long as six months. Despite the shorter time for reading training, the experimental classes equaled in reading achievement the classes not receiving such training. Moreover, the experimental children in the lowest quarter in intelligence and those in the lowest levels of socioeconomic status benefited most from this training, for both these groups excelled their matched control groups in the regular basal reading program (64).

In the area of directionality, the chalkboard exercises used in this study were as described below. These practices were drawn from the recommendations of Getman and others and are adapted from the description in the leaflet *Proper Chalkboards Properly Used* (49).

Chalkboard exercises in directionality

When child is facing the chalkboard at a distance of about ten inches, an X is placed on the board at a point directly in front of the tip of his or her nose. The child is to fixate on this mark while doing these preliminary exercises:

SPACE ORGANIZATION
The child holds the chalk between the thumb and the inside of the first finger (inside the palm, not like a pencil) and scribes with both hands back and forth from the X, as far as the arms will extend. The child scribes repeated

(continued)

lines at points about as high as the hairline, at the level of the X, and again opposite the hips. When scribing at or above eye level, the thumbs are opposite each other, the back of the hands up; below eye level, the hands are rotated with the thumbs outward and the back of the hands underneath.

The teacher draws a vertical line through the X, and draws horizontal lines through the center of the child's lines. If the child's lines deviate or slant upward or downward, he or she should continue practice until appropriate bimanual control is achieved.

MOTOR EQUIVALENCE

The child scribes bimanual circles with both hands, at the same levels on the chalkboard, as above. Circles are scribed with both hands simultaneously, first outward from the X, then inward with both hands, and then alternately with both hands scribing toward the right and then the left.

BIMANUAL STRAIGHT LINES

The teacher places a large circle of dots on the chalkboard (with a felt-tip pen) with a large center dot opposite the child's nose. The dots around the circle are lettered or numbered, or if the child cannot read these symbols, the teacher indicates the two dots for the starting points. Using both hands, the child tries to draw from the opposite dots on the edges of the circle to the center dot, or from the center dot to the two opposite outer dots. Extend this training so that the child can scribe simultaneously from any two dots to the center or the reverse. In this exercise, as in those above, the teacher should continue with short daily practice sessions until the child's movements become comfortable and fluent, and the performances with both hands are relatively similar.

Unimanual training procedures

A. Make a vertical row of dots on the chalkboard with a felt-tip pen at about ten inches to the right of the center position and a similar row of dots to the left of the center position. Label each dot on the same horizontal line similarly and the vertical spacing between the dots should be about three inches. (If the child is unfamiliar with letters or numbers, use stars or asterisks to mark the points in each pattern.) Your chalkboard would have this type of pattern:

```
A  ·                         ·  A
B  ·                         ·  B
C  ·                         ·  C
```

About five pairs of dots are sufficient. The child is given his piece of chalk and told to place it on the dot by the letter A on his left. He then scribes a chalkline from the left A to the right A in a straight line *without stopping.* When he has completed drawing the lines, erase the lines, and have the

(*continued*)

child continue the training. If these lines can be drawn easily, continuously, and accurately (start precisely from one dot and end right on the other dot), begin using the next exercise.

B. Construct two rows of horizontal dots with a vertical spacing of about twelve inches apart. In the horizontal row the dots should be about three inches apart. The chalkboard pattern will now be:

The child is asked to start with his chalk at the dot below the letter A and draw a *continuous* line to the lower A. This is done for all the different letters, so that you end up with a series of vertical lines. Now have the child reverse the procedure and again make a series of vertical lines starting with the lower dots and going upward to the top dots. When the child can perform adequately on the horizontal and vertical lines, we advance to the oblique lines.

C. Again two rows of dots are constructed and labeled but placed at an oblique angle:

A •
   B •
      C •
         D •
           E •

                  • A
                • B
              • C
            • D
               • E

The child scribes lines from a left-to-right, upward direction.

         A •
       B •
    C •

                • A
              • B
           • C

The child scribes from left to right downward. The child must make a continuous line, quickly and easily, starting from one dot and ending at the other dot before it is considered that he or she has developed adequate performance ability.

D. Combining straight and oblique lines. Using the rows of dots as in exercises *A, B,* and *C,* ask the child to draw both horizontally (as in *A*), and obliquely, from the dot at the right to the second dot at the left.

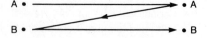

(continued)

Repeat using the vertical spacing of dots, as in exercise *B,* and the oblique spacing as in *C.*

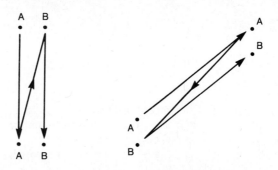

The child should make a continuous, rapid line from each dot to the next. Please note that these lines are drawn straight, quickly, and with a single free motion, *not* painstakingly, slowly, with only hand or wrist movement.

E. Repetitive forms. This technique develops rhythm, shape, or form, and the ability to maintain constancy of size. Two parallel lines are constructed across the board with a separation of about six inches and at the nose level of the child. The child starts with the chalk about four inches from the left edge of the lines and makes circles in a counterclockwise direction moving slowly toward the right. It looks as follows:

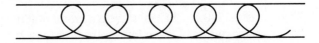

As a variation of this, have the child scribe vertical lines in the same manner.

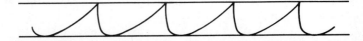

When the child can perform these visual-kinesthetic procedures with ease and accuracy, proceed to Chase the Leader.

F. Chase the Leader. You construct a series of three dots or more on a chalkboard and label them A, B, C . . . M. The child must go in the proper direction and continuously scribe a line from A to B and on to the last letter on the chalkboard. This develops ability to rapidly scribe lines in all directions. It teaches the child to be able to make a rapid shift in direction (to draw angles) and it also enables the child to develop the ability to stay on his primary target in spite of the distraction of other lines in his field of view. Start with three dots, then increase to five, seven, etc.

(continued)

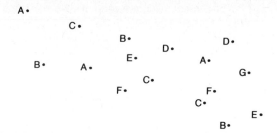

G. Dot Pictures. Drawing from dot to dot to form the outlines of objects is another directionality exercise found in some readiness workbooks and children's playtime or coloring books. These are desirable near-point unimanual exercises only if the child is held to a standard of straight, fluent movements.

H. Visual projection. Directionality training should be extended to include visualization of objects, distances, and directions. Games of describing his route to and from school, to the store or church, or while on a common auto trip, which require the child to visualize and describe direction, are excellent. Other variations include describing the directions necessary to complete an errand at school or home, or the contents of a room or a store.

Almost any teacher can devise variations of these basic directionality exercises. The teacher must keep in mind that the primary purposes are to produce recognition of directions, pursuit of these directions by coordinated hand and eye movements, and, eventually, the ability to verbalize directions or translate directions into words.

These exercises, as well as those that follow, are not designed exclusively for beginning readers. Many poor readers, of all ages, show their need for directionality training by excessive regressions or repetitions and losing their place.

We cannot expect complete control of left–right discrimination or laterality until somewhere between the ages of eleven to twelve. Nor can we really expect very efficient eye movements along the line or in a return sweep until these visual skills are well learned.

Ocular Motility

Many children entering school have not developed coordinated eye movements. Their eyes do not follow an object in motion with equal binocular movements. One eye may lag behind the other, or overreach, or even remain still while the other is reaching out in space. Visually speaking, because of lack of binocular coordination children may not receive exactly the same images from both eyes since they may not bear upon the same object. These conflicting images are reflected in inaccurate perception and discrimination and if persistent or severe, lead to a tendency to suppress or ignore one of the images. To accomplish this children may permit one eye to drift or turn away almost constantly in what is called strabismus, cockeye, or walleye. Practically every thorough study of child vision indicates that these various difficulties in binocular coordination are highly significant in reading failure for children at almost all ages. Parallel studies of school children by the senior author and by Helen M. Robinson, formerly of the University of Chicago, indicate that 27 to 28 percent of the children tested lacked two-eyed (binocular) reading (55, 60).

A study of the coordination of kindergartners emphasizes this point. Seventy-five percent could not look at a card with three stars in a line, fixate on the first star, jump to the second, then to the third, and return to the first. Their eyes kept straying away from the targets in this task that simulates the act of reading. How many first grade teachers ever suspect that their children may have this difficulty with coordination?

Among the exercises commonly employed by visual training experts to improve ocular motility are these:

1. *Swinging ball.* Suspend a small rubber ball (or any similar object) from a doorway, light fixture, or the hand, at the child's eye level. Gently swing the ball to and fro, in a circle, and from side to side a foot or two from the child's face, while he or she watches. To vary this exercise, hang the ball about three feet from the floor, and have the child watch it while lying directly beneath it. Or, have the child try to follow movement of ball with a jar four or five inches in diameter, without hitting sides of jar. This can be varied by asking child to reach out with a forefinger to touch the ball in flight, from beneath or the side.

2. *Finger play.* Have the child jump his or her eyes back and forth to the tip of each of your forefingers, held a foot apart at a foot from the child's face. If the child needs assistance, pace his or her eyes with your finger swinging slowly between the tips of his or her forefingers.

3. *Flashlight.* To vary these straight line and rotary pursuits, use a small flashlight or other bright object in place of the ball or fingers. Or, have the child point with a flashlight to crosses on the blackboard arranged in a large circle. The child holds flashlight at side, points on signal.

4. *Point to point.* Hold a pencil twelve to fourteen inches from the child's face, and have the child look from the pencil to a picture on the wall. Be sure that the child sees each clearly when his or her eyes are at rest on either target. As this exercise becomes easier, move the pencil closer to the child's face. Or, using primer or pica

typewriter, prepare two sheets of capital letters in rows, five spaces between each letter. Hold the sheets in each hand, and have the child jump his or her eyes back and forth from letter to letter without moving his or her head. Have the child move along the lines and down the page in this fashion.

The Informal Vision Tests described in the preceding chapter, particularly those assessing fusion, will enable the teacher to select the children in need of this training.

The purpose of these ocular motility exercises is to promote equal, coordinated, and quick binocular movements. If the child shows any difficulty in these activities after a half-dozen ten-minute practice sessions, the wisest course would be to recommend a complete professional examination, preferably by an optometrist or ophthalmologist who is interested and trained in visual training. The classroom teacher should realize that this training is not intended as a substitute for professional care, and it is not intended to correct or repair severe visual problems. It simply provides practice in several visual functions that are essential to the act of reading for all pupils.

Some children may need the reinforcement of hand action in these exercises in ocular motility. They may need to follow the swinging ball or the flashlight at first with their pointed finger as well as with their eyes. Thus they may lead their eyes with their fingers or hands, as a small child does in exploring space. Some children show this dependence upon tactual contact by using their finger to point as they read. If so, they should be permitted to use this method of reinforcement or be supplied with a marker until they spontaneously discard it because of increasing visual coordination. It is unnecessary to note that this reading behavior is strong evidence of the need for training in directionality and ocular motility.

Since children are most experienced in ocular control in a restricted central area, it is highly desirable to extend the action gradually into periphery. Children should learn both to cross the midline of their bodies to the opposite side with accurate movements and to extend this binocular coordination outward in all directions. Most children and adults show better control in an area opposite the center of the body and extending toward the preferred right or left side. On the other side of the body and toward the outer edges of our visual or manual reach, more training may be necessary for accuracy.

In ocular motility training the children have no real way of judging whether they are following the target accurately and binocularly. The teacher should watch closely to be certain that children are fixating constantly on the target. If there is any doubt that they are seeing the target sharply and clearly, check by asking them to point to it or touch it. If it appears that they are following with only one eye, cover that eye and ask them to look again at the target. When the wandering eye has fixated, uncover the other eye and resume the exercise. By these two checks children can be helped to maintain binocular fixation in the training exercises.

A team of optometrists worked with sixty-eight second- and third-grade children who tested below the fortieth percentile on the Metropolitan Reading Test and who were deficient in the ocular pursuits test of the Purdue Motor Survey. In other words, they showed difficulties in binocular coordination in tracking a target. Training similar to that outlined here produced significant gains on the ocular pursuits test and better reading than in the control group (*31*).

Alleman and Bescopy matched pairs of children in two first-grade classes (*1*). The experimental class was given visual tracking training. This resulted in significantly better reading than in the control group. Since none of the children were originally poor readers, the authors suggested that this type of training might well be used in the usual reading program for normal children rather than being thought of only as a remedial effort.

Although it is not always recognized as such, practice on the walking beam or rail is an extension of the training in ocular motility and control. It is based on the fact that binocular control of one's own vision while in motion is related to reading progress. Thus fixation on the target during these exercises is an essential part of the training. The specific exercises are adapted from the program outlined by Getman and his collaborators. The various exercises possible with the walking beam, and the construction of the beam and its supports, are described in Evelyn B. Spache's *Reading Activities for Child Involvement* (*65*).

A class record sheet listing the eight types of exercises on the walking beam at the top of the page and spaces for each child's name in a vertical column at the left will be useful to keep track of pupil progress. The exercises are arranged in order of increasing difficulty. As each can be performed comfortably by children, perhaps after related brief trials scheduled daily, they may progress to the next exercise. To save the teacher's time, an aide or a parent can direct other children through the sequence, judge their performances, and record their progress by check marks on the record sheet, as each exercise is accomplished.

Form Perception

Discrimination of wordlike forms is, of course, desired as the ultimate outcome of all visual training, as well as all readiness training. But, like the other visual skills, form perception is a complex, learned act that has not yet been completely analyzed by vision and reading specialists. Training materials that are supposed to increase accuracy of form perception are commonly found in readiness workbooks. Children are asked to detect slight differences among a series of drawings of common objects, geometric forms, designs resembling objects or words, and actual letters and words. Frequently, the training begins with large drawings and continues through a series that is gradually reduced in size. There is some evidence that this logical arrangement aids some beginning readers to achieve greater reading success. But it is not clearly understood why and how this training is helpful. We are not certain how to identify the pupils who need the training, the amount needed, or the most effective types.

Several rather brief experiments on kindergarten children have been attempted to discover the best type of form perception training for learning a few words. Muehl gave a short training period in discriminating geometric forms, letters, or words (45). One control group had no discrimination training. The letters or words used as practice material were identical with those found in the final test of word recognition. All groups, including the controls, showed learning of a similar degree in the test. There was only slight evidence that practice in discriminating words was most effective for immediate learning. Final retention of the test words was similar for all types of discrimination training. These are rather inconclusive results for a number of reasons. They seem to support the logic that form perception training should involve the discrimination of words or wordlike forms. But they give no explanation for the variations in learning among the individuals in these groups. Do some children need more of this particular type of training, or do they need some other more basic type? Some of the children undoubtedly began the experiment with good form perception, while others were quite undeveloped in this skill. Which of these children profited from the training? A study involving tachistoscopic training with geometric forms and gradually increasing groups of numbers again showed marked individual differences, with the greatest benefit being shown by pupils whose pretraining form perception was high. What type of form training do the poor perceivers need to prepare them for accurate discriminations among words? Perhaps these are the only tentative conclusions we may draw from these experiments: (1) pupils will vary a great deal in the amount of form perception training they need; (2) the training should probably proceed from gross discriminations to fine; (3) the more closely the final perceptual tasks resemble word forms, the more effective they are likely to be; and (4) emphasis upon speed in discrimination should probably occur late in the training process, after a high degree of accuracy has first been developed.

We have attempted to list a sequence of form perception activities that observes these tentative conclusions drawn from the research.

1. Tracing around simple pictures, coloring within the lines, and cutting out simple forms are basic types of form discrimination. But they are certainly not as necessary for all children as the extent of their use in readiness and reading workbooks would imply.

2. Practice with tridimensional objects such as puzzles, nested cubes, and peg boards is highly desirable. Pegboard play can be varied by varying the picture the child tries to produce or by reducing the number of pegs used for each object or form.

3. Tracing geometric forms, designs, words, or the child's own name on a magic slate or carbon paper fosters comparison and discrimination.

4. Using templates of geometric forms aids in perception training. Templates can be made from Masonite, plastic, pressed board, or artist board with cutouts of the geometric forms: circle, square, rectangle, diamond, triangle. The template should be 10 by 12 inches and the cutout extend to 1 inch of the edges on three sides. The cutout is centered in the upper two-thirds of the template. This allows a solid portion of about 4 inches for the child to hold the template with the nonwriting hand. Some teachers fix a wooden spool to the solid portion to provide a more positive grip.

The template is held against the chalkboard with the nonwriting hand below the cutout. The X placed on the board opposite the child's nose should appear through the cutout slightly above the center of the opening. The child traces around inside the form, continuously for five to six times, with the chalk constantly touching the edges of the shape. The tracing should be done smoothly and rhythmically. Practice may be scheduled daily for 5 to 10 minutes with a number of children at the blackboard.

The order of difficulty is from circle, square, rectangle, triangle, to diamond. When the child can repeatedly trace within the template fluently, he or she should progress to making the same shape on the board without the aid of the template, and then go on to the next-most-difficult form.

5. Having the child attempt to draw forms, patterns, or shapes you put on the blackboard is helpful. After he or she has seen these for a few seconds, erase them and let the child reproduce your drawing. Use simple geometric forms at first, then reduce size and increase complexity.

6. Encouraging the child to make line drawings of persons, objects, and common events (and to tell the story of the drawings) is a useful training procedure.

7. As actual introduction to reading begins, pencil or chalk outlines of common words, emphasizing the ascending and descending letters and cued by context and initial letters or blends, should be used. Begin with pupils' names, your name, and objects in the classroom.

8. See also such sources as Evelyn B. Spache's *Reading Activities for Child Involvement* (65).

Another possible extension is by the use of small-size templates for seatwork on blank newspaper sheets and later paper of ordinary sizes. This approach has been intensively studied in the Winter Haven (Florida) schools as a means of helping poor achievers acquire patterns and freedom in hand–eye coordination. Results are reported to show that trained first graders exceeded matched controls by six to nine months in reading, four months in arithmetic, three to four months in spelling, and seven months in vocabulary (38). The differences were greatest between matched low socioeconomic groups but also marked in high-socioeconomic groups. One of the obvious values of this template training is the relationship to children's learning to write. They are, in effect, practicing the strokes that comprise written letters as well as learning to direct their hands and eyes in tracing and reproducing basic shapes. The value of learning to write as an aid to progress in early reading was redemonstrated in the results of the Cooperative First-Grade Studies (8). If extended training seems necessary for some children, as shown in the research study of one of the present authors (64), the Continental Press ditto masters entitled *Visual Discrimination* and *Visuo-Motor Skills* are relevant.

Another basic effort to improve perception would consider the child's posture during the act of reading and writing. Faulty posture will distort the child's perception of objects in space or, more significant for our concern, result in faulty interpretation of printed symbols. Tilting of the head, or shoulders, improper distance from the printed page, partial suppression of the vision in one eye because of these postural distortions—all may cause distorted perception despite our training efforts. To aid the child to secure the proper posture for reading, the desk should be tilted at approximately 15 degrees. This slant tends to promote a balanced, bilateral approach to the reading and writing task.

The proper working distance from the paper or book is approximately equal to the distance between the ridge of the middle knuckle of the child's clenched fist resting on the cheekbone and elbow joint, measured on the outside of the arm. In other words, both of the child's eyes should be about as far from the working task as the length of the child's forearm and the back of his or her hand combined. The paper may be turned slightly to the right or left to favor the preferred writing hand, but this turn should not be so exaggerated as to force the child into one-eyed reading.

The most healthful relationship between children's desks or tables and the height of their chairs can be readily determined. The child bends his or her arms vertically toward the head (without raising the elbows). The child should be able to slide his or her elbows forward onto the working surface without raising or lowering the elbows. In other words, the proper height for a table or desk is opposite the child's elbows. This relationship prevents the build-up of muscular tension and fatigue in the neck and shoulders.

The obvious questions in using these exercises in improving visual skills are which children need the training and how long they should continue to receive it. In the absence of any standardized tests of these visual skills other than those employed in a professional optometric examination, these decisions must be based on the observations and judgment of the teacher or on the Informal Vision Tests offered earlier. The exercises themselves and some trained observations offered by the staff of the Gesell Institute of Child Development of New Haven, Connecticut, will be helpful in selecting children for training and deciding when to terminate the exercises. Try the first few exercises in directionality, ocular motility, and form perception with each child or group of children. When the child can do each exercise readily with speed and accuracy, progress to the next exercise. If the child evidences incoordination or any other type of difficulty in an exercise, continue to repeat it in varied ways until his or her performance shows distinct improvement.

From their many observations of reading and visual behaviors under controlled conditions, Ilg and Ames suggest that the child's visual skills show a sequential development (35). These stages may be observed during some of the exercises or in a teacher-pupil conversational setting or while looking at a book together:

1. Eye movements are more circular than direct, more disorganized than orderly or methodical.

2. The eyes tend to make wide horizontal sweeps from one side to another, rather than many small disorganized movements. (See particularly the first three ocular motility exercises.)

3. The eyes can make planned oblique movements upward and downward.

4. The child can combine both oblique and horizontal movements into a single coordinated movement.

5. The eyes can move quickly and accurately from point to point horizontally, vertically, or obliquely. They can also repeatedly shift focus from near point (reading distance) to far point (any distance greater than three or four feet) with speed and accuracy.

6. The child can trace, copy, match, reproduce from memory, discriminate differences among outlines of simple geometric forms, designs, symbols, or word forms. Do not, however, expect reproduction of the diamond or other forms involving oblique lines or complex internal diagonals or other details until about seven years of age.

Visual Perception Training Materials

The current interest, and confusion, regarding training materials for improving visual perception demands special treatment. We cannot define visual perception simply here, if at all, for it is still in the process of being identified in laboratories, clinics, classrooms, and research centers. However, despite incomplete definition, it is possible to suggest activities and devices that will contribute to the ability to make the discriminations which underlie word recognition and writing.

Visual perception represents, in our opinion, an ultimate performance in the acts of reading and writing, at the end of a long continuum of bodily, hand, and visual experiences. In Gesell's terminology, we might say that the child learns to recognize abstract symbols first with the mouth and hand; later with the hand and body; then with the hand and eyes; and only eventually with the eyes alone. In this long development, the learning of finger, hand, and bodily coordination, of directionality, of the properties of objects in space or depth perception, and of tridimensionality form foundations for the child's functioning in the two-dimensional media of reading and writing.

Although the research evidence is not entirely clear, it is possible that development of rhythmic bodily movements, of bodily balance, of auditory rhythms, and of orientation to laterality in one's own body or in that of other bodies may be significant steps in this development of visual perception. In the belief that future research may give some support to these latter experiences, some related training materials have been included. As this research appears, this eclectic list will be refined accordingly.

These perceptual training materials are offered without reference to special types of children exhibiting learning difficulties. We are not concerned here with such meaningless categories as the "minimal brain damaged," "slight cerebral dysfunction," "dyslexic," "incompletely lateralized," "poorly neurologically organized," or the like. We are concerned here only with children (or adults) who show marked difficulties in discriminating among forms, letters, or words despite exposure to ordinarily effective instruction. In our opinion, the job of teachers, clinicians, and reading specialists is to find appropriate developmental tasks, no matter what diagnostic labels are offered by this or that cult or school.

In our judgment, the logical sequence in the testing-training program in visual perception extends from hand–eye and bodily coordination, to spatial relationships, to three-dimensional and later two-dimensional form discriminations, and finally to word and letter discrimination. In addition to the specific training suggestions offered earlier, we would offer a list of readily obtainable materials. Included are trade books that offer experiences with physical and/or verbal concepts of size, directionality, spatial relationships, self-concepts, and the like.

Visual perception training materials

HAND AND BODILY COORDINATION

Chalkboard Templates. Manchester, Mo.: Webster. Opaque templates of geometric forms to be used at the chalkboard.

Creative Playthings, Inc., Princeton, N.J. Rubber pegboard and pegs; rhythm band set; balance blocks and boards; pegboard tiles; kikit.

Desk Templates. Manchester, Mo.: Webster. Similar in form to those for chalkboard use, but smaller in size.

Developing Body–Space Perception Motor Skills. Freeport, N.Y.: Activity Records. Offers two albums and activities to improve sense of form, structure, laterality, and directionality.

Eye Movement Charts, Space Masks, and Space Sighters. Manchester, Mo.: Webster. These charts and masks enable the child to develop control and accuracy of eye movements.

Judy Clown Bean Bag Set. Minneapolis, Minn.: Judy. Large wood clown and bean bags intended to improve hand–eye coordination.

Listening and Moving. Freeport, N.Y.: Activity Records. A pair of LP records provide a training program in development of body awareness and position in space; perceptual-motor skills involving body balance.

Perceptual-Motor Development Kit by Fairbanks and Robinson. Boston: Teaching Resources. This kit includes a number of training materials for

(continued)

improving hand–eye coordination, as (1) lines-movement exercises; (2) coloring exercises; (3) cutting exercises; (4) spatial relations, which involves drawing from point to point.

Tootie-A-Go-Go. Hawthorne, Calif.: Creative Ideas Co. A game of toss and catch with small bean bags and a hand-operated net catcher.

Walking Beam. Manchester, Mo.: Webster. A wooden beam on blocks, for developing bilateral balance, peripheral awareness, and related abilities. Targets for visual fixation are also available.

Webstermasters and Movable Melvin. Manchester, Mo.: Webster. Melvin is a doll character with movable parts. Its use plus the two-dimensional duplicating masters are intended to aid children in exploring movement patterns.

Words and Movement About Myself. Dansville, N.Y.: F. A. Owen. A record for relating physical movements and language concepts of directionality, laterality, and the like.

SPATIAL RELATIONSHIPS

Creative Playthings, Inc., Princeton, N.J.: Geometric metal insets; parquetry blocks; graded circles, squares, and triangles; rubber oversized parquetry; geometric mosaic tiles; pattern boards.

Parquetry Design Blocks. Chicago: Beckley-Cardy. Forms in smooth wood for making designs in color.

Stick-O-Mats. Minneapolis, Minn.: Judy. For discrimination of geometric forms at the flannelboard. Another set, *Color-Shapes,* provides experiences with both forms and colors.

Sticks for Laying. Chicago: Beckley-Cardy. Sticks from one to five inches long in separate or assorted sets. For spatial relationship development.

Visual-Perceptual Exercises. Boston: Teaching Resources. This group of exercises and a *Perceptual Bingo* game are part of the *Erie Perceptual-Motor Kit.* Offers variety of exercises in form and color discrimination.

WORD AND LETTER DISCRIMINATION

Creative Playthings, Inc., Princeton, N.J.: Magnetic letters and board; sandpaper letters; kinesthetic letters on board; word building box.

Cut-Out Letters and Figures. Darien, Conn.: Teachers Publishing Corp. Sets of letters and numbers in two-, three-, or four-inch sizes for flannelboard or kinesthetic use.

Flocked Assortment. Darien, Conn.: Teachers Publishing Corp. Over 200 pieces of card stock for flannelboard or kinesthetic use. Includes forms, pictures, letters, etc.

Geake, R. Robert, and Smith, Donald E.P. *Visual Tracking.* Ann Arbor, Mich.: Ulrich's Books Inc., 1962. A practice book in visual discrimination among letters of decreasing size.

Judy Manuscript Letters. Minneapolis. Minn.: Judy. Heavy stock letters, manuscript capitals or lowercase, for flannelboard or kinesthetic use.

(continued)

Magnetic Assortment. Chicago: Beckley-Cardy. Plastic letters, assorted capitals or lowercase, with built-in permanent magnets for use with metal chalkboard or bulletin board.

Smith, Donald E. P. *Symbol Tracking.* Ann Arbor, Mich.: Ulrich's Books Inc. Supplementary to the *Visual Tracking* noted above.

Stolpen, Beulah Harris, et al., *Linguistic Block Series.* Chicago: Scott, Foresman. Plastic blocks engraved with letters or words can be arranged to form words or sentences.

A Footnote to Training in Visual Perception

Some reviewers of the results of perceptual-motor training programs, including Helen M. Robinson (56) and Stephen E. Klesius (40), are disturbed by the poor and contradictory research, and the unproved nature of the tests in this area. These reviewers agree in concluding that a direct effect upon reading achievement or readiness has not been shown for such programs. Even when the more careful research studies only are considered, as by Klesius, the evidence is about equally positive or negative. In some experiments, readiness is improved or reading is increased or both results appear. In almost as many other studies, only the scores on some perceptual-motor test or other are increased, and there are no observable effects in readiness or reading.

Thus research on perceptual-motor programs is often inconclusive or doubtful. Is it possible that this is due to the confusion in defining the basic elements of perceptual-motor development, the extreme variations in the types of training given, the unproven validity of many of the tests of perception offered, as well as to the lack of careful control of many of the studies? Are the indefinite results also influenced by the fact that the experimenters try to isolate the effect of perceptual-motor programs from other normal readiness activities with which they are interrelated? It is apparent that the field of perceptual-motor training is in a very early stage of evolution. We do not really know all the skills that are significant, how to test their development, what types of training produce the most valuable results, or what influence the skills we should train will have on school success.

If perceptual-motor training constituted the entire readiness program, it would certainly be difficult to justify it in the reading program, at this stage of our knowledge. But the same could be said of other readiness factors, such as auditory discrimination or language development. If one of these were the sole content of readiness activities, the results would be just as inconclusive. Success in early reading, as pointed out earlier, is not based entirely upon the child's development in just one of these areas, but rather depends upon overall development in all of them. To say this another way, we could ignore visual perception or auditory discrimination or language-development entirely in the beginning reading program, and yet some children would learn to read. At the same time, many would fail because of deficits in directionality, visual discrimination, auditory confusions, inadequate speaking or listening vocabulary, or the like.

It may not yet be possible to show a direct impact of perceptual-motor training on some aspects of readiness or reading. On the other hand, we do know that these activities are appropriate in early childhood education to increase body awareness, balance, locomotor, and manipulative skills. We all acknowledge the relationship between hand–eye coordination and handwriting, which in turn influences letter formation, letter and word recognition, and early reading success. We know that this type of training is developmentally sound for many children as a preventive program, or as a remedial program for some with "learning disabilities." Perceptual-motor programs that more closely resemble classroom tasks do tend to transfer to academic performances. Moreover, the programs have a positive influence in developing attention, impulse control, and self-concept, probably more so for younger than older children. These values are reiterated in the publications of a number of national organizations of optometrists, physical educators, and early childhood specialists. These specialists firmly believe that a sequential perceptual-motor program integrated with the other important readiness activities, and emphasized only for those children who appear to need such training, will make a greater contribution to child development than the prevailing free play or game-oriented programs now used in many kindergarten, nursery, or primary-grade classes (29, 50, 53).

As implied in the preceding section, the exercises in directionality, ocular motility, and form perception will contribute to the overall development of the children who need such training. In the absence of very valid tests, the exercises themselves can function as screening devices to identify children lacking in each area. Thus we would give intensive practice beginning at the point of the child's failure in any series of exercises, and no training to any child who can successfully perform the entire sequence. Five years of experience in several hundred classrooms in the schools of Jacksonville, Florida, in training teachers in these techniques and observing the results has convinced these authors of the values of these specific exercises. They do not prevent all reading failures, nor do all the children given extensive training always score high in reading. Reading success or failure is not determined by any such single factor in the child's experiences or backgrounds. But, like our colleagues in the other disciplines, we see young disadvantaged children given a better chance of school success when aided in this fashion, if they show need.

Training in Auditory Discrimination

The purpose of auditory training in the readiness program is the development of the child's ability to hear similarities and differences in sounds. The ultimate goal is, of course, preparation of the child for the auditory discriminations present in the word recognition process. Such discriminations are essential for effective use of letter sounds in word attack or phonics. Because of the obvious relationships of auditory training to the child's early training in phonics, some authors assume, logically enough, that the training should begin with attention to letter sounds as they occur in isolation or in whole words. This approach ignores the fact that there are auditory discriminations basic even to these that some pupils cannot make when they enter school. Some children cannot discriminate (although they may hear) differences in common sounds of widely varying pitch and loudness, much less make the fine distinctions among letter sounds.

The values of auditory training for reading achievement are demonstrated particularly by the experiments of Helen A. Murphy (46). All groups given training showed superior reading achievement, on the average, throughout successive tests in the first grade, except for one very low ability class which did not exceed its matched controls. In one study this superior reading achievement attributed to the auditory training was still present at the end of the second year in school. Training continued throughout the first year, as contrasted to that during the first semester only, showed very small differences in average reading achievement at the end of the first or second grade. Other outcomes noted by the teachers were greater success in sight reading early in the reading program, better listening skills, and increased comprehension. Murphy noted that sex differences in reading achievement were lessened among trained groups. In neither experiment, however, did all children benefit from these particular exercises, nor did all the trained children react with increased reading achievement.

As was pointed out in the discussion of auditory factors, discrimination training is probably essential only for programs that emphasize sound–symbol associations as the primary word recognition technique. The experiments of Murphy cited above appeared to be successful mainly because the reading programs stressed this auditory skill. The auditory training programs, it should be noted, were heavily loaded with phonics training. The senior author's finding that auditory discrimination tests were apparently good predictors of first-grade reading success similarly reflects the nature of the reading program rather than the inherent value of such training for all primary children (63).

Another chapter questions the belief that intensive auditory discrimination training is so essential for dialect-speaking pupils who appear to lack this ability. Because of the variations in their enunciation of speech sounds from standard English, such children may not respond to or need the usual phonics program. Because they speak the dialect of their families and communities, they have perhaps not learned to hear the differences between sounds commonly demanded in phonics training. Nor is there strong evidence that dialect users really cannot learn to read well, or even to use some phonics as a minor aid to word recognition. In fact, there is the contradictory evidence that children from the white majority groups in various parts of our country also speak dialects, such as the Bostonian, the New England, the Southern, the Midwestern, and others. Yet most of these children learn to use phonics sufficiently for their purposes, even though they vary greatly in the enunciation of vowel sounds.

In our opinion, the most practical steps to help young children who speak any sort of dialect likely to interfere with reading, and who test poorly in auditory discrimination because of the dialectal variations, are as follows:

1. Accept the child's dialect just as you do other individual traits, without criticism or constant correction. You are not trying to make the child over in your image.

2. Provide alternatives in standard English for dialectal expressions casually, as you would in writing the language experience chart. Speak of these as simply other ways of saying a thought. Elicit these alternatives (as during a group language experience chart) from the rest of the class as often as you can. If they cannot supply any that approximate standard English, then offer several from which they may select one. Treat this activity as a game, not as an instructional procedure.

3. Provide as much opportunity for oral composition, playing roles, telling stories, and engaging in real or make-believe conversation as you can to build auditory memories of language. Play an active part yourself in these activities so as to provide a constant model of standard English (if you speak it) that the children will hear and, perhaps, imitate. Keep your language spontaneous and natural, not stilted and formal.

4. If the dialect does not greatly interfere, teach children the sounds of initial consonants and digraphs. Skip the endings, the inflectional forms, and the vowel sounds, all of which are often affected by dialect. Children can read and understand sentences containing these forms, even though they do not repeat them in their own speech or oral reading.

5. Teach your children, if they seem to be able to profit from it, to use the context and the sound of the initial letter or digraph as basic clues to word recognition. Do not attempt to teach blending or synthesis of sounds, or letter-by-letter phonic analysis, for all of these demand good auditory discrimination.

6. Remember that most of your pupils can learn to read to the limits of their potential, even though they speak a dialect, if you provide a reading program that emphasizes getting ideas from the printed page—not just letter sounds and word calling.

Provide other types of auditory training as outlined below for all your beginning pupils, omitting only those in auditory discrimination that are too demanding for pupils with dialectal speech and poor auditory discrimination.

Don't expect great gains with children who have poor articulation or immature speech. They may not have reached the developmental stage at which they hear and speak clearly such sounds as *l, sh, v, s, z, j,* or voiced *th.*

Auditory Training Exercises

Dorothy B. Butt, formerly adjunct professor of Jacksonville University, made a detailed outline of auditory training activities. Space does not permit the reproduction of the entire outline, but the sequence that Butt has evolved and the auditory aids she recommends are described briefly below.

Auditory training activities

AUDITORY AWARENESS
1. Sounds of the earth—wind, thunder, rain, waves. Records: *Spook Stuff for Halloween,* MP-TV Services, Inc. *Spotlight on Sound Effects,* Pickwick International, Inc. Long Island City, N.Y. *Sounds Around Us,* Scott, Foresman. *Auditory Training,* Greystone Corporation. *Sounds for Young Readers,* Educational Record Sales.
2. Sounds of animals—birds, dogs, cats, ducks. Records: *Muffin in the City; Muffin in the Country; Noisy Book; Muffin at the Seashore,* E. M. Hale Company, Eau Claire, Wis. Pete Seeger—*Bought Me a Cat; Frog Went A Courtin; Jim Crack Corn; All Around the Kitchen; American Folk Songs for Children,* Folkways Records and Service Corp., New York. Burl Ives—*The Fox; Woolie Boogie Bee; Bluetail Fly,* Decca. Josef Marais—*Songs of the South African Veld; Steilenbosch Boys,* Decca. *Warbler's Serenade,* Victor Records. *The Whistler and His Dog,* Victor.
3. Man-made sounds—bouncing ball, crunching, cars, planes, trains, bells.
4. Varying inflections of a single word—*PLLLL-ease! PIEEEase! PleaSSe! Oh! OOOOh! OOOOOhhh!* Use also the story of the little engine, *Little Toot.*
5. Intensity of sounds—stamping versus tiptoe; loud and soft sounds of bell, clapping, closing door.
6. Pitch—contrasting high and low tones to show monotony and variation, alarm–reassurance, anger–pleasure. Use such stories as *Three Bears, Billy Goats Gruff.*
7. Duration and sequence—how successive sounds make music or words or sentences; contrast staccato rhythm with legato time; keeping time in skipping, marching, galloping; contrast short and long notes on piano; same with two or three syllable words exaggerating the accented syllable.
8. Quality—contrasting same tone on different rhythm instruments; resonance of tuning fork versus piano; using natural and disguised voices in games such as Who Said That?
9. Recognizing rhythm and rhyme—use a wide variety of poems, limericks, jingles, and rhymes from any good anthology of children's literature. See *Riddle-a-Rhyme,* Eye Gate House.

(continued)

AUDITORY PERCEPTION

1. Expressing sounds—provide opportunities for children to express the ways sound affects them in dances, rhythmic activity, tapping, finger snapping.
2. Alliteration—play with rhymes and jingles—*Lucy Locket; Hickory, Dickory, Dock; Baa-Baa Black Sheep;* use pictures cut out or drawn to show alliteration—pig in a pen, house on a hill, boy on a bike; composite pictures to use for finding similarities and differences in sounds; games as Sound of the Day—children listen for or offer words with the sound of *b* as in *baa.*

AUDITORY MEMORY

1. Play echo game—children attempt to reproduce three tones (words or numbers) given by child behind screen.
2. Children repeat tapping pattern given by teacher.
3. Children attempt to follow one-, two-, and three-step directions.
4. Have children think sounds and tell or reproduce what they hear.
5. Play gossip game—one child whispers a sentence to another, who whispers it to another, who whispers it to another, etc.
6. Play the restaurant game—children choose foods from picture display, give orders to waiter, who must remember them and pretend to serve.
7. Play store—clerk must remember orders.

AUDITORY DISCRIMINATION

1. Draw attention to common sounds in and around the classroom, such as children walking or running, bells ringing, dogs barking, and the like. Encourage descriptions and comparisons by the children. What do you hear? What is happening?
2. Have short listening periods for the pupils to identify sounds they hear. Use recordings such as *Sounds Around Us* (Scott, Foresman), *Listening Time Albums* (Webster), and recordings of poetry and children's stories. Or read selections to the group. Ask pupils to anticipate sounds in the records or words in the story.
3. Pronounce children's names, names of common objects, and actions letter by letter or syllable by syllable. Have children identify and indicate number of separate sounds.
4. As discrimination of pitch and loudness increases, introduce sounds of initial consonants. Draw attention to beginning sounds in pupils' names, classroom objects, pictured objects. Ask children to note similarities and differences and to make discriminations. Stress commonly recurring consonants such as *b, k* or hard *c, f,* hard *g, h, j, l, m, n, p, r, s, t, w;* speech blends *wh, ch, sh, th;* and consonant blends *fr, tr, br, st, pl, gr,* etc. Identify letter sound by its name (*m* has sound of the beginning of *Mary*) in dealing with single consonant sounds, but do not

(continued)

emphasize an isolated letter sound such as *muh.* Introduce blends by analogy with common sounds (*drip, splash, pulp, gr-r-r,* etc.) Use recordings such as *Let's Listen* (Ginn), *Listening Time Albums* (Webster).

5. Continue with auditory exercises on letter sounds as outlined in readiness workbooks or other easily available sources, such as Spache (*65*).

6. Introduce concept of rhyming by riddles, jingles, nursery rhymes, and poetry. Permit children to suggest rhyming words for such selection.

7. Ask children to supply a rhyming word for a given word or to choose one of a given group that does not rhyme.

8. To sharpen discrimination, ask children to listen for similar sounds in the beginning, middle, or end of words. Again, use children's names, common objects and actions, and pictured objects. Proceed slowly, asking for discrimination of similarity or difference in only one area, as beginnings, at a time. Then move to a different area of a word as task is consistently accomplished correctly by group.

9. As the introduction to reading begins, emphasize the use of sounds to derive the word implied by the story, as in guessing the word you omit or the word that rhymes.

10. Use the McKee–Harrison technique of having children identify words beginning with the same letter before you say them while reading a story to them. For example, let them guess any word in the story that begins with *b.* Stop reading as you reach each such word (which they already know begins with the sound of *b* as in *boy*).

Lest we be swept away by the enthusiasm of some for auditory training, Terence J. Bailey found no effects upon reading of a nine-hour training program in auditory discrimination, auditory memory, auditory analysis and synthesis and auditory-visual integration (*3*). Scores on tests of these functions improved, but reading did not. Of course, the brevity of the program and the multiplicity of the skills stressed may have defeated Bailey's purpose. On the other hand, his study may have shown that a shotgun approach to auditory factors does not work.

Language Training

A number of reports on the vocabularies of children entering school imply that average children are familiar with at least several thousand words. They do not necessarily employ this number in their speech but recognize them when they hear them, and have meaningful associations for them. Since children have this relatively large auditory vocabulary, it is apparent that they are auditorily familiar with most of the words, and hence the concepts, that are introduced in the vocabulary of the beginning readers. Their primary language needs in the readiness period are not those of introduction to the words and concepts presented in the readers. Rather, they may need help in developing fluency, depth, and facility in the language patterns in which the basal reader concepts are to be presented. If children speak and think in monosyllables or fragments, they may have difficulty with the sentence and paragraph structure of beginning reading materials. Although basal readers are not noted for the depth of their content, children must have more than rudimentary understanding of the words of the basal vocabulary if they are to become more than mechanical word callers. The children's own output and language usage must be comparable to that found in the beginning reading materials or their intake may be severely limited.

Basically, language training in the readiness and early reading stages is based upon firsthand experiences with words and ideas through the medium of pictures, trips and excursions, story material, and games. A wide variety of such experiences broadens and deepens children's language skills, thus ensuring a greater degree of success in the verbal task of reading. Many of the daily activities such as storytelling, reading to and with children, using picture books to compose stories, reading predictable books, and the composing of the children's own language experience stories promote language development.

Concepts (schemata) essential for comprehension are fostered by the varied language experiences and others such as classifying objects and labeling them as, sea shells, coins, flowers, foods, animals. Similar activities in classifying the words alone that stand for these objects are excellent.

Several authors have suggested an activity called mapping to promote vocabulary growth. Children are led to offer all the associated words they can think of related to a picture, word, or topic. The basic word is centered on the chalkboard (or preferably on a large chart for permanence) and all the associated words are written around it. For example:

Stripes		Dangerous		Indian
	Fierce		Cubs	
African		**TIGER**		Meat eating
	Jungle		Zoo	
Paws		Circus		Cat
	Claws		Beautiful	

An approach still being explored for its values is that of combining or extending sentences. Several simple (kernel) sentences are combined into a longer one or several kernel sentences are extracted from a long, complex sentence. This practice is intended to enable children to deal with the increasing complexities of the writings they will eventually deal with. The practice also helps develop children's understanding of word order and word function, which some experts feel must be strengthened. Some of those teaching this activity claim that it also improves children's comprehension.

Fluency

School beginners may exhibit a number of levels of fluency or expressiveness ranging from practically no response to a veritable flood of ideas. When teachers use such stimuli as a story, picture, or conversation, they may observe these variations in fluency:

1. Monosyllabic words, simple pointing or naming of objects in the picture, or even no response at all. Example: "Boy," "There's boy," "That's me."
2. One or two short sentences, offering a simple description of the picture. Example: "Boy and girl are running. That's all."
3. Response to prompting questions, simple interpretation. Example: "The boy and girl are running a race."
4. Free, fluent response, perhaps with own story. Example: "One day a boy said, 'I can beat you.' . . ."
5. Reaction to teacher as well as the stimuli offered; evaluation of the picture or story, morals or conclusions. Example: "You know, girls shouldn't race boys because boys always win."

School beginners' output and expressiveness can be stimulated in many ways by alert teachers. They can ensure ample opportunity for the children to speak or take turns in small-group work. Talking games, in which children take turns finishing a sentence or a story, played in a group of lesser fluency, provide excellent practice. Talking with the teacher about their own art work or some other familiar topic provides opportunity for the children who are not sufficiently fluent for group games, or for participating in "Telling Time" or other audience situations. Face-to-face work with the teacher or a very small group may be preferable and less threatening for the child lacking in fluency.

Children who are reluctant to talk to an adult will often talk to a hand puppet. With this aid, they may be led to retell a story that has been read to them, or to offer an original playlet or dramatization of an actual incident they have experienced. Acting out the meanings of words, as verbs; labeling and classifying objects, pictures, and action; talking about the attributes, such as color, size, and use, are stimuli to growth in dealing with words or, in other words, with ideas (67, 68). The primary purpose of this training is to promote children's ability to express their own thoughts and thus to grow in power of handling ideas. Many games and activities which will contribute to these language skills may be found in Russell and Russell, Spache, and other sources.

Sentence Structure

Children differ not only in the quantity and content of their language but also in the complexity of the patterns in which it is expressed. They may employ any of the following:

1. Monosyllables, simple nouns: "Boy."
2. Simple sentences with subject and one verb: "Boy runs."
3. Simple sentences with compound subject or predicate: "The boy and girl are running," or a run-on sentence: "The boy is running, the girl is running."
4. Compound or complex sentences: "The girl is running but the boy is beating her."
5. Complex sentences with more than one dependent clause: "The girl is running but I think the boy will win because boys can run faster."

Auditory Comprehension

To a large degree, children's use of more mature language patterns reflects the quality and complexity of the language to which they are exposed. We have already pointed out the significance of auditory comprehension as a predictor of early reading success. Growth in auditory comprehension can be markedly promoted by persistent teacher efforts. The sentences the teacher uses in speaking with them, the directions offered, the stories read to them, the reasoning demanded by the questions asked—all help children to grow in comprehension of and development of sentence structure. Whereas it is true that reading involves learning to recognize many words, success in word recognition is strongly dependent upon children's sentence sense, their feeling for or expectation of the appropriate words for each idea or thought. Success in contextual analysis, as it is called, demands a sentence sense—a familiarity with the language patterns through which ideas are expressed. Children who truly read do not simply name words as they meet them, but having read the first few words, anticipate the rest of the thought. They logically expect certain words to occur next because they would follow the train of events or ideas. In anticipating the sentence pattern they help themselves to read unknown or unfamiliar words because they sense the word that would be most logical. They have heard and reacted to similar patterns of language many times and, once they have acquired a reasonable sight vocabulary, readily make the transition from listening to sentence patterns to reading sentence patterns.

The extent of thinking or reasoning children do in listening is based upon the facts and relationships they are asked to report. In other words, depth of auditory comprehension is determined by the questions the teacher proposes before reading to the group, while reading, and after reading. It is important here to stress the significance of the pattern of comprehension established by the demands upon the child listener. One of the frequent criticisms of current early reading instruction is that it fails to promote creative, critical thinking among children. Teachers are apparently satisfied when children can simply parrot back the facts given. Seldom are children asked to answer such questions as "Why? What will happen next? Why will it happen? What will he do? What would you do? Why?" Or reactions to "Why did the author write this story? What did she want to tell you? How did she expect you to feel? How did you feel?" are not demanded.

There is ample evidence that training in auditory comprehension interacts with reading success. Practical training steps that parallel reading behaviors are:

1. Listening to and answering questions based on expository or narrative materials. (See our Chapter 14 for suggested types of questions.)

2. Listening to and executing a series of two or three simple directions regarding movements about the room, paper cutting, paper folding, using an index or table of contents, etc.

3. Listening to material offering a sequence of acts or events and trying to recall the sequence.

4. Finding facts on a given page or in a portion of reading matter in answer to questions. Have answers read aloud and discuss the accuracy and relevance of the answers.

5. Trying to retell short, simple stories.

6. Rearranging a series of pictures related to a known story to show the proper sequence of events. Explaining one's own choice of arrangement.

The aim of auditory comprehension training is not only to provide experiences with words, to deepen and broaden children's knowledge of words or their auditory vocabulary. It provides these stimuli to language development, but even more significantly the training promotes children's verbal reasoning, memory, critical thinking, and other intellectual processes. These are the processes they must employ in dealing with ideas encountered later in reading. These are the processes which underlie that rather vague ability, comprehension. Training in auditory comprehension is, in effect, training to think with words. For this reason, early skill in auditory comprehension is a good predictor of children's later success in reading. For the same reason, training in auditory comprehension is one of the essential facets of the prereading and beginning reading stages of children's development.

Articulation

Several aspects of the child's speech may militate against his or her success in reading if they are not corrected. Substitutions of one sound for another as *w* for *l*, and *d* for *th* (*dat* for *that*), baby talk, and stammering are among these handicaps. Correcting these speech difficulties is properly the work of the speech correctionist or therapist, but there is much teachers can do in the absence of professional help. The pattern of speech that teachers exhibit to the children is an important influence. Individual help in correct formation of the proper sounds, the placement of the tongue and teeth for correct sound formation, is of primary value. These children will also need assistance in hearing the differences between their enunciation and the proper models. Simple recordings by tape are useful in this effort. Then with correct use of speech mechanism and a proper auditory image of the desired sound the child is prepared for individual or small-group work. This may include such devices as choral reading and listening to and imitating jingles, poems, and rhymes that emphasize the sounds.

Since a number of speech sounds usually do not appear to be used correctly by many six- and seven-year-olds, but do develop later, speech correction efforts by teachers should be approached cautiously. The advice of the school speech therapist should be used as a guide to the nature and amount of any training offered. Sometimes auditory training in hearing the differences among these late-appearing speech sounds, without much emphasis upon reproducing them, may be all that is desirable. As we have repeatedly pointed out, this type of training is necessary only if letter–sound discrimination is going to be stressed in subsequent reading lessons. Persistence of articulatory substitutions beyond primary ages is, however, a cause for concern and treatment, perhaps not so much for reading success as for social communication and self-concept.

Reading Concepts

There are fundamental concepts about books and pictures that children must acquire if they are to be successful in reading. Many of these concepts may be established early in the preschool years if children are given sufficient experiences with books. Among these concepts, the following are the most significant:

- There is a directional orientation to book and pictures. The flow of ideas is from left to right, from top to bottom, or from the beginning of the book to the end.
- Pictures and books tell stories. They suggest action and events that occur sequentially. The action seems to move from one picture to the next, from one page to the next. The action often evokes emotions in the reader or listener.
- When reading, adults constantly use the same words or the same language patterns for each particular picture or page. They say the same thing each time they read the story. This story often may be remembered, particularly if it has rhythm or rhyme.
- Sharing pictures and books with others is a pleasant experience. Stories can be told about the picture sequences. Other children react to these stories as the storyteller did.
- Pictures and books stimulate users to suggest ideas of their own, to react to the pictures and books, to ask questions, and perhaps even to compose similar stories.

- The words used to tell the story in a picture sequence or book are natural and familiar. They resemble the oral language one would be likely to use in telling the story. The words on the page are, in effect, talking written down.

Marie M. Clay discovered that, after the first six months of schooling, 10 percent of New Zealand five-year-olds were still confused whether the picture or the print was the source of the story. At six years, or after a full year of school, 16 percent still could not recognize the boundaries of a word, and 19 percent could not locate the "first letter" of a word (14). While observing in kindergarten and first grade, Anne D. Forester saw that teachers' explanations about words or sentences frequently failed to elicit a response or a sign of understanding (22). Jerry L. Johns found that the ability to distinguish among words, phrases, sentences, phonemes, and syllables was significantly related to reading placement in primary grades (37). W. D. Barney studied New Zealand four-year-old kindergartners. Fifty percent said that a book was "pictures"; 10 percent said "words or writing"; only 4 percent said "a story." When asked what part of a page is usually read, 34 percent roamed vaguely over the page, while 4 percent said "the pictures." Sixty-three percent indicated the print (4).

These reading concepts can be built by the following firsthand experiences with books and pictures:

- Ample opportunity to handle books in a library corner.
- Helping to assemble a picture file organized under various headings; using this as a source for portraying stories, cartoons, and action sequences.
- Making scrapbooks of pictures selected by the children to illustrate topics of interest to them; to tell a story; to use on the flannelboard.
- Listening to stories and following the story by seeing the accompanying pictures.
- Pictures on the bulletin board, changed each day or two after directed discussion.
- Picture sequences (or picture books) which illustrate nursery rhymes.
- Small-group discussion of pictures, books, and stories read by the teacher or a child.
- Picture study as outlined in various readiness books and manuals.
- Using films, filmstrips, or slides as a basis for storytelling and class discussion.
- Sharing books from home by leaving them in the library corner, by telling or reading a story from them, or by lending them to other children.

- Drawing picture sequences to illustrate a class trip or experience. These may be made into simple movies and used as a basis of sharing with other classes or to review together a pleasant group experience.
- Labeling or writing on children's artwork the interpretation they offer for the material.

A significant warning about training in reading concepts is implied in the studies of John Downing (20), Meltzer and Herse (44) in this country, and parallel studies in Canada. Interviews and observations of first graders show that these children often do not comprehend the terms the teacher uses. In listening to a tape or cutting up a sentence strip, many could not demonstrate that they understood what a letter, a sound, a word, a phoneme, a phrase, or a sentence really was. Teachers use these terms glibly, often assume that their pupils comprehend their meanings, and then attribute irrelevant or incorrect answers to inattention or mental dullness. Certainly teachers must ensure that children have concrete experiences with materials that represent these abstract terms (matching cutouts of letters, words, sentences, composing from letter or word cards, writing and editing their own stories, etc.) if the child is to understand this process of learning to read.

Downing has stressed the need for child understanding of the reading act in pointing out the marked relationship between confusion in these concepts and reading failure even beyond the primary levels (20). Of course, clarification of all these concepts will just be begun during the readiness period, for many of them become relevant only as the reading program advances. We are not suggesting teaching technical terms, such as word, sound, and the like, for this only leads to verbalism, parroting back to the teacher what she has just said. Rather, it is through actual experiences with reading materials, as suggested above, that beginning concepts of the reading act are conveyed.

Our View

We suggest means of identifying the children who are in need of the training activities described here. It is apparent, however, that available tests and observation procedures do not always completely reveal each child's needs. For this reason, trials with the exercises outlined here, particularly in visual perception and auditory discrimination, may be necessary for further diagnosis and final determination of individual and group needs. The time consumed by these trials may appear to be considerable, and some teachers (or administrators) may be concerned about the effects of the delay of the introduction to reading. But the ultimate success of children trained by these methods, and the elimination of reading failures caused by too rapid introduction of the reading act more than compensate for any initial loss of time due to careful diagnosis and planning of the readiness program. Moreover, using the training exercises as supplementary diagnostic tools eliminates the obvious inefficiency inherent in offering all types of training to all pupils suggested by so many workbook-oriented readiness programs.

Discussion Questions

1. How do the readiness program concepts offered here differ from those with which you are familiar?

2. Why do you suppose that it is suggested that the emphasis in readiness training should be given to visual perception, auditory abilities and language? Do you agree? What would you emphasize?

3. In your opinion, what would be an ideal readiness program?

4. Why do you think that the authors do not suggest a variety of outdoor large-muscle activities as essential to readiness?

5. What types of training outlined here do you believe might be helpful for primary pupils who make very poor progress in reading? Why?

6. Visit several first grade classrooms early in the school year. Try to select those with contrasting readiness programs. Share your observations and comments with your classmates.

References

1. Alleman, K. G., and Bescopy, W. A., "Ocular Motility Training and Its Relationship to Reading Readiness and Achievement." Unpublished senior thesis, Southern College of Optometry, Fullerton, Calif., 1981.

2. Alley, G., et al., "Reading Readiness and the Frostig Training Program," *Exceptional Children*, 35 (September 1968), 68.

3. Bailey, Terence J., "Effects of Auditory Perception Training on Reading Achievement," *Journal of Research and Reading*, 2 (February 1979), 24–43.

4. Barney, W. D., "Kindergarten Four-Year-Olds Concept of Reading, Knowledge of Books and of Prints." Paper presented at the New Zealand I.R.A. Conference, Christchurch, New Zealand, 1974.

5. Beaupre, R. G., and Kennard, Ann, "An Investigation of Pre- and Post-Metropolitan Readiness Scores for Differing Motor Education Programs," *Illinois School Research*, 5 (1968), 22–25.

6. Bernetta, Sister M., "Visual Readiness and Developmental Visual Perception for Reading," *Journal of Developmental Reading*, 5 (Winter 1962), 82–86.

7. Blanton, William E., *Preschool Reading Instruction: A Literature Search, Evaluation and Interpretation*. Urbana, Ill.: ERIC/ED 069 347.

8. Bond, Guy L., and Dykstra, Robert, "The Cooperative Research Program in First Grade Reading," *Reading Research Quarterly*, 2 (Summer 1967), 5–142.

9. Bridge, Connie A., Winograd, Peter N., and Haley, Darlene, "Using Predictable Materials vs. Preprimers to Teach Beginning Sight Words," *Reading Teacher*, 36 (May 1983), 884–891.

10. Buckland, Paul, "The Effect of Visual Perception Training on Reading Achievement of Low Readiness First Grade Pupils." Doctoral dissertation, University of Minnesota, 1969.

11. Butler, Dorothy, and Clay, Marie M. *Reading Begins at Home: Preparing Children for Reading Before They Go to School.* Exeter, N.H.: Heinemann Educational Books, 1982.

12 Chan, Julie M. T., *Why Read Aloud to Children?* Newark, Del.: International Reading Association, 1974.

13. Children's Book Committee, *Reading with Your Child Through Age Five.* Washington, D.C.: Child Study Association, 1976.

14. Clay, Marie M., *Reading: The Patterning of Complex Behavior.* Auckland, New Zealand: Heinemann Educational Books, 1972.

15. Cohen, R. R., "Remedial Training of First Grade Children with Visual Perceptual Retardation." Doctoral dissertation, University of California at Los Angeles, 1966.

16. Cohen, S. A., "Studies in Visual Perception and Reading in Disadvantaged Children," *Journal of Learning Disabilities,* 2 (October 1969), 498–507.

17. Cox, Brian, and Hambly, Lionel R., "Guided Development of Perceptual Skills of Visual Space as a Factor in the Achievement of Primary Grade Children," *American Journal of Optometry and Archives of the American Academy of Optometry,* 38 (August 1961), 433–444.

18. Delacato, Carl H., *Neurological Organization and Reading.* Springfield, Ill.: Charles C. Thomas, 1966.

19. "The Doman–Delacato Treatment of Neurologically-Handicapped Children," *Journal of Pediatrics* (May 1968), 750–752.

20. Downing, John A., "Children's Developing Concepts of Spoken and Written Language," *Journal of Reading Behavior,* 4 (Winter 1971–1972), 1–19.

21. Faustman, Marion N., "Some Effects of Perception Training in Kindergarten on First Grade Success in Reading," in *Perception and Reading,* Helen K. Smith, ed. Proceedings of the International Reading Association, 12, No. 4, 1968, 99–101.

22. Forester, Anne D., "Learning the Language of Reading," *Alberta Journal of Educational Research,* 21 (March 1975), 56–62.

23. Fortenberry, Warren Dale, "An Investigation of the Effectiveness of the Frostig Program upon the Development of Visual Perception for Word Recognition of Culturally Disadvantaged First Grade Students." Doctoral dissertation, University of Southern Mississippi, 1968.

24. Francis, Hazel, *Learning to Read: Literate Behavior and Orthographic Knowledge.* Winchester: Allen and Unwin, 1982.

25. Frostig, Marianna, and Horne, David, *The Frostig Program for the Development of Visual Perception.* Chicago: Follett Publishing, 1964.

26. Garton, Sharon, Schoenfelder, Paula, and Skriba, Patricia, "Activities for Young Word Bankers," *Reading Teacher,* 32 (January 1979), 453–457.

27. Gillet, Jean Wallace, and Kite, M. Kane, "Words, Kids and Categories," *Reading Teacher,* 32 (February 1979), 538–542.

28. Glass, Gene V., and Robbins, Melvyn F., "A Critique of Experiments on the Role of Neurological Organization in Reading Performance," *Reading Research Quarterly,* 3 (Fall 1967), 5–52.

29. Greenspan, Steven B., "Research Studies of Visual and Perceptual Motor Training," *Optometric Extension Program,* 44 (October 1971–August 1972). Duncan, Ok.: Optometric Extension Program Foundation.

30. Halgren, Marvin N., "Opus in See Sharp," *Education*, 81 (February 1961), 369–371.
31. Heath, Earl J., Cook, Patricia and O'Dell, Nancy, "Eye Exercises and Reading Efficiency," *Journal of Optometric Vision Development*, 9 (September 1978), 16–27.
32. Holdaway, Don, *Foundations of Literacy*. Sydney, Australia: Ashton Press, 1979.
33. Hoskisson, Kenneth, "Successive Approximation and Beginning Reading," *Elementary School Journal*, 175 (April 1975), 442–451.
34. Hurst, W. A., "Vision and the Retarded Reader," *Canadian Teacher's Guide*, 10 (Winter 1960), 3, 7.
35. Ilg, Frances L., and Ames, Louise, "Developmental Trends in Reading Behavior," *Journal of Genetic Psychology*, 76 (June 1960), 291–312.
36. Jacobs, J. N., "A Follow-up Evaluation of the Frostig Visual–Perceptual Training Program," *Educational Leadership Research Supplement*, 26 (1968) 169–175.
37. Johns, Jerry L., "The Growth of Children's Knowledge about Spoken Words," *Reading Psychology*, 1 (Spring 1980), 103–110.
38. Jones, Marian, "AB (by) C Means Alphabet Books by Children," *Reading Teacher*, 36 (March 1983), 646–648.
39. Kelley, Charles R., *Visual Screening and Child Development: The North Carolina Study*. Raleigh: Department of Psychology, School of Education, North Carolina State College, 1957.
40. Klesius, Stephen E., "Perceptual Motor Development and Reading—A Closer Look," in *Some Persistent Questions on Beginning Reading*, Robert C. Aukerman, ed. Newark, Del.: International Reading Association, 1972, 151–159.
41. Lass, Bonnie, "Portrait of My Son as an Early Reader II," *Reading Teacher*, 36 (February 1983), 508–515.
42. McGinitie, Walter H., "When Should We Begin to Teach Reading?" *Language Arts*, 63 (November–December 1976), 878–882.
43. McCormick, C. C. et al., "The Effect of Perceptual Motor Training on Reading Achievement," *Academic Therapy Quarterly*, 4 (1969), 171–176.
44. Meltzer, N. S., and Herse, R., "The Boundaries of Written Words as Seen by First Graders," *Journal of Reading Behavior*, 1 (Summer 1969), 3–13.
45. Muehl, Siegmar, "Effects of Visual Discrimination Training on Learning to Read a Vocabulary List in Kindergarten Children," *Journal of Educational Psychology*, 51 (August 1960), 217–221.
46. Murphy, Helen A., "An Evaluation of the Effect of Specific Training in Auditory and Visual Discrimination on Beginning Reading." Doctoral dissertation, Boston University, 1943.
47. Nicholson, Tom, *An Anatomy of Reading*. Cammeray, Australia: Martin Educational, 1982.
48. O'Donnell, F. A., "The Effects of Delacato Training on Reading Achievement and Visual Motor Integration." Doctoral dissertation, Stanford University, 1969.
49. "Optometric Child Vision Care and Guidance," *Optometric Extension Program*, 37 (December 1964), Series 9. Duncan, Okla.: Optometric Extension Program Foundation.
50. Porter, Lorena, *Movement Education for Children*. Washington, D.C.: American Association of Elementary-Kindergarten-Nursery Education, 1969.

51. Pumpfrey, P. D., and Anthony, D. A. S., "The Use of the Frostig Programme for the Development of Visual Perception with Children Attending a Residential School," University of Manchester, England. Personal communication, 1972.

52. Rhodes, Lynn K., "I Can Read: Predictable Books as Resources for Reading and Writing Instruction," *Reading Teacher*, 34 (February 1981), 516–518.

53. Robb, Margaret D., *Foundations and Practices in Perceptual Motor Learning: A Quest for Understanding.* Washington, D.C.: American Association for Health, Physical Education and Recreation, 1971.

54. Robbins, Melvin Paul, "The Delacato Interpretation of Neurological Organization," *Reading Research Quarterly*, 1 (Spring 1966), 57–78.

55. Robinson, Helen M. and Huelsman, Charles B., "Visual Efficiency and Learning to Read," in *Clinical Studies in Reading II*, Helen M. Robinson, editor. Supplementary Educational Monographs, No. 77. Chicago: University of Chicago Press, 1953, 31–63.

56. Robinson, Helen M., "Perceptual Training—Does it Result in Reading Improvement?" in *Some Persistent Problems in Reading*, Robert C. Aukerman, editor. Newark: International Reading Association, 1972, 135–150.

57. Rosen, Carl L., "An Experimental Study of Visual Perceptual Training and Reading Achievement in First Grade," *Perceptual and Motor Skills*, 22 (1966), 979–986.

58. Ross, Ramon R., "Franme and Frank and the Flannelboard," *Reading Teacher*, 27 (October 1973), 43–47.

59. Slaughter, Judith Pollard, "Big Books for Little Kids: Another Fad or a New Approach for Teaching Beginning Reading?" *Reading Teacher*, 36 (April 1983), 758–760.

60. Spache, George D., *The Binocular Reading Test.* Indianapolis: Mast Development, 1943.

61. Spache, George D., *Investigating the Issues of Reading Disability.* Boston: Allyn and Bacon, 1976.

62. Spache, George D., *Diagnosing and Correcting Reading Disabilities.* Boston: Allyn and Bacon, 1981.

63. Spache, George, D., *The Teaching of Reading.* Bloomington, Ind.: Phi Delta Kappa Educational Foundation, 1972.

64. Spache, George D., Andres, Micaela C., and Curtis, H. A., et al., *A Longitudinal First Grade Reading Readiness Program.* Cooperative Research Project No. 2742. Tallahassee, Fla.: Florida State Department of Education, 1965.

65. Spache, Evelyn B., *Reading Activities for Child Involvement.* Boston: Allyn and Bacon, 1981.

66. Stone, M., and Pielstick, N. L., "Effectiveness of the Delacato Treatment with Kindergarten Children," *Psychology in the Schools*, 6 (1969), 63–68.

67. Vukelich, Carol, and Matthais, Margaret, "A Language Process for Use with Disadvantaged Children," *Elementary English*, 51 (January 1974), 119–124.

68. Yawkey, Thomas D., Aronin, Eugene I., Street, Michael A., and Hinjosa, Olga N., "Teaching Oral Language to Young Mexican-Americans," *Elementary English*, 51 (February 1974), 198–202.

69. Wingert, Roger C., "Evaluation of a Readiness Training Program," *Reading Teacher*, 22 (January 1969), 325–328.

70. Young, Lula Mae, Kane, Burton M., et al., *Marion Hill School Motor Coordination-Visual Perception Study.* Duncan, Okla.: Optometric Extension Program Foundation, 1971.

Resources for the Teacher

Aulls, Mark W., *Developing Readers in Today's Elementary School.* Boston: Allyn and Bacon, 1982.

Bennett, J., *Learning to Read with Picture Books.* South Woodchester, England: The Thumble Press, 1979.

Chan, Julie M. T., *Why Read Aloud to Children?* Newark, Del.: International Reading Association, 1974.

Children's Book Committee, *Reading with Your Child Through Age Five.* Washington, D.C.: Child Study Association, 1976.

Cratty, Bryant, *Perceptual and Motor Development in Infants and Young Children.* Englewood Cliffs: Prentice-Hall, 1979.

Duane, Drake C., and Rawson, Margaret B., *Reading, Perception and Language.* Baltimore: York Press, 1975.

Durkin, Dolores, *Getting Ready to Read.* Boston: Allyn and Bacon, 1982.

Getz, Donald, and McGraw, Lora, *Vision Training for Better Learning.* Johnstown, Pa.: Mafex Associates, 1981.

Lerch, E., *Perceptual–Motor Learning: Theory and Practice.* Mountain View, Calif.: Peek Publications, 1974.

MacCann, D., and Richard, O., *The Child's First Books: A Critical Study of Pictures and Texts.* New York: H. W. Wilson, 1973.

McQuarrie, Charles W., and McQuarrie, Charles Warren, *How Parents Can Help a Child Learn to Learn Using the Optometric Care Form.* Duncan, Okla.: Optometric Extension Program Foundation, 1975.

Ross, Ramon Royal, *Storyteller.* Columbus: Charles E. Merrill, 1972.

Van Witsen, Betty, *Perceptual Training Activities Handbook.* New York: Teachers College Press, 1979.

Ziskind, S., *Telling Stories to Children.* New York: H. W. Wilson, 1976.

Training Materials

Balance Beam Activities. Long Branch, N.J.: Kimbo Educational. (Two LP records and a teacher's guide to promote balance, body image, and ocular control.)

Braley, W. T., et al., *Daily Sensorimotor Training Activities.* Freeport, N.Y.: Educational Activities.

Capon, Jack, *Perceptual Motor Development Series.* Belmont, Calif.: Pitman Learning, 1975. (Five books on various types of activities.)

Capon, Jack, and Hallum, Rosemary, *Perceptual–Motor Rhythm Games.* Freeport, N.Y.: Educational Activities. (An LP record for movement activities.)

Carr, Dorothy, and Cratty, Bryant J., *Perceptual Motor Development Programs.* Freeport, N.Y.: Educational Activities. (Ten LP records and a teacher's guide.)

Casebeer, Beverly, *Casebeer Program Developing Motor Skills for Early Childhood Education.* Novato, Calif.: Academic Therapy Publications, 1978.

Coordination Skills. Long Branch, N.J.: Kimbo Educational. (An LP record for patterned movement activities.)

Daily Sensorimotor Training Activities. Long Branch, N.J.: Kimbo Educational. (A handbook of lessons to improve balance, body image, form perception, auditory discrimination, etc.)

Experience in Reading Readiness. Palo Alto, Calif.: Creative Publications. (A kit and guide for verbal, visual, and auditory training.)

Getting to Know Myself. Freeport, N.Y.: Educational Activities. (An LP record or cassette to promote awareness of body image and position in space.)

Lev, L. Jay, *Lev Perceptual Motor Development Program.* Novato, Calif.: Academic Therapy Publications. (For developing hand–eye coordination.)

Mulac, Margaret E., *Perceptual Games and Activities.* New York: Harper and Row, 1977.

Stewart, Georgiana L., *Bean Bag Activities and Coordination Skills.* Freeport, N.Y.: Educational Activities. (An LP record and guide.)

Stewart, Georgiana L., *Developmental Motor Skills for Self-Awareness.* Freeport, N.Y.: Educational Activities. (Two LP records and a guide for rhythmic games, body identification and spatial relationships.)

Werner, Peter H., and Rini, Lisa, *Perceptual Motor Development Equipment: Inexpensive Ideas and Activities.* New York: John Wiley and Sons, 1976.

9 A Program for Primary Grades

It is apparent that the authors' concept of a reading program is not one that is carefully prescribed with daily plans that are supposed to fit all situations. If we believed this, we would have spent our time in preparing a basal reading series. Rather, we believe that the effective reading program is a flexible instrument based on what is clearly demonstrated by the research on reading instruction.

A good reading program shows that a degree of individualization that is possible within the framework of the teacher's planning and organizing capacities. It is not determined by the materials provided by the state, nor can it be prescribed exercise by exercise, skill by skill, as many reading experts believe. The variety of learning activities and teacher-made materials, the possibility of differentiation into small groups, and the needs of the particular class are the true determinants of a reading program.

Good teachers bring to bear everything they know about child development, learning, and materials. They combine these elements into a program that meets the needs of every pupil, insofar as their experience and skill in teaching permit.

Constance M. McCullough has said (33):

> Much of the knowledge we now have about the teaching of reading has been developed by a curious and—in terms of the lives of students—wasteful pattern of extremes. We learned a great deal about oral reading by having too much of it, about silent reading by neglecting oral reading, about extensive reading by neglecting intensive reading, about sight vocabulary by neglecting phonics, about phonics and speed by neglecting comprehenson. . . . One would think that it should finally have dawned on us that all of these practices have value and that the sensible, most efficient program encompasses them all.

The purpose of the earlier reviews of various approaches to beginning reading was to point out their strengths and weaknesses. Now we shall presume to offer a combined approach that will avoid the flaws and build on the advantages of each. As the reader will soon recognize, ours is not, strictly speaking, a new approach but an attempt to capitalize on the strengths of other methods and to avoid their weaknesses. All the techniques that we shall suggest have been used before by teachers who were prone to experiment. Our contribution consists of the emphasis, rationale, and justification we shall offer for these techniques, as well as an organizational plan within which they may operate.

Readiness for Reading

Our concept of readiness implies a pacing of the introduction to beginning reading according to children's abilities to profit. By observation, readiness tests, and evaluation of children's development in vision, speech, listening, and social and emotional factors, teachers decide when an introduction to formal reading is appropriate. Depending upon their diagnostic judgments, teachers delay reading instruction for varying periods of time for different pupils. Meanwhile they offer preparatory training in directionality, ocular motility, form perception, auditory discrimination, language fluency, oral language, and auditory comprehension as well as articulation and reading concepts, as pupils evidence their needs. With repeated observations they note the increasing skill with which various pupils handle these fundamental exercises and their decreasing need for continued readiness training. At intervals they permit these rapidly developing pupils to participate in the reading activities of the class, and note their successes. With these observations as a basis they arrange for some of these pupils to join the type of group reading for which they appear ready. For certain pupils they will continue to offer visual, auditory, language, or speech training because of their needs and in order to ensure their success in beginning reading. Thus, as they demonstrate the ability to participate successfully in simple reading activities, first graders will be introduced to beginning reading.

The reader will note the lack of reference to a formal readiness program such as that commonly offered in readiness workbooks. Such workbooks do not, and cannot, accomplish their avowed purpose of providing essential prereading training for most pupils. Their treatment of the important readiness traits is too brief, too superficial, and too stereotyped to serve the needs of any large number of pupils. As we have pointed out earlier, there is little evidence of the validity of the workbook, even if readiness for most pupils could be achieved within a set period of time. Readiness implies development, and development differs significantly among individuals.

Rather, a wide variety of workbook-type exercises, whether drawn from commercial sources or teacher-made, will be an essential aid in several readiness areas, as well as later development of reading skills. There are a number of collections or kits of these materials available mentioned in the chapter bibliography. If desired, the expense of these can be avoided by the construction of the teacher's own kits of materials, an approach we think permits more flexibility and relevance to the teacher's own goals and procedures. The construction of this kit is described in detail in *Reading Activities for Child Involvement* by Evelyn B. Spache (Boston: Allyn and Bacon, Inc., 1981). Briefly stated, the kit is made by selecting exercises from a variety of sources and other collections. Exercises of different types or workbook pages which, preferably, present a single exercise are collected, collated in a rough order of difficulty, color coded according to their type, and placed in a convenient box. Acetate folders are made available in which the exercise is placed, as children indicate their answers by crayon or felt-tip pen. If desired, pages may be mounted permanently in the acetate folders. After children have completed an exercise, they check it with an answer key in the file, remove their writing from the acetate by a moist tissue, and replace the material in its proper place, as indicated by color coding. With this approach, a teacher can provide training in depth for any specific skill for any children in accordance with their needs.

Beginning Reading

We suggest that the introduction to reading occur through the medium of experience charts. For those unfamiliar with this term, an experience chart is an original composition arising from children's common experiences. With the help and guidance of the teacher, the group or child composes materials based on a trip, the weather, a holiday, a greeting, a message, classroom rules, and the like.

We suggest that experience charts should constitute the beginning reading program for at least several months, or until the pupils demonstrate sufficient reading vocabulary to read independently. Some pupils, of course, are ready to read when they enter school and should be permitted to do so. But they should also participate in the group work in composing experience charts. Experience chart work would continue throughout the primary grades.

In addition to providing reading materials of timely and interesting nature, the chart approach serves a number of other functions. The children's first experiences in composing and learning to read a chart provide opportunities for judging their readiness for reading instruction. Their difficulties with directionality, word discrimination, recall of words, their fluency and sentence structure, and their concepts of the reading act are manifest in these early trials at reading.

It is also probable that by its very nature the language experience technique makes a real contribution to clarifying children's concepts of the reading process. It may thus help avoid the confusions about such terms as *word, sentence, letter,* and *sound,* and about what goes on when one reads that Meltzer and Herse (34) have shown to be so prevalent. The act of composing, writing, editing, rewriting, and arranging stories in book format, followed by the use of these materials for a variety of word recognition and word analysis activities—all of which are part of this approach—should obviate these difficulties that arise from other methods of instruction.

When the reading materials are the children's very own experiences, the concept that written or printed words convey meaning is inherent. This approach may be able to avoid the naive interpretation of the reading act present in these quotes from intermediate-grade children about reading (25):

a book. If you don't know the words, sound them out.

when you see a group of words in a sentence

something you do from books

words have names and they have certain letters you look at the letters and you put them together and you read a whole bunch of words together

when you say a whole bunch of words

Some idea of the nature and composition of these charts may be gained from the following samples.

OUR GOLD FISH

Our first gold fish died. We had three fish and three of them died. But after the three died, Mrs. B. got two more fish.

The fish needs special food. The water needs to be changed every week. If you give gold fish too much food they will die, and you will not know until you look and change the water.

These fish are funny because one stays down at the bottom and he floats back up. The other one stays on the top. WATCH! The other one floated up to the top and goes back down.

This one is too fat. He is too heavy to get up to the top. The fish go to the sides and they blow bubbles.

THE REASON I LIKE MY BEST FRIEND

I like my best friend because she is very nice. She has a good talent. You would like her if you saw her because she is like a sister.

She has a nice mom. I love her. I forgot to tell you her name is Jeanine.
Diedre

WHAT I THINK HEAVEN IS LIKE

I think it is a wonderful place where you fish for golden fish in a silver pond and you get to see all of the famous people and even Jesus and the Wright Brothers, too, and there is gold and silver. And I think that Heaven has God as a leader.

THE RESTROOM

*The restroom smells
like a skunk when it has
been disinfected. But when
it has worn off it
smells better.*

*Two little monkeys, jumping on a bed.
One fell off and hurt his head.
The other called the Doctor
And the Doctor said.
"That's what you get for jumping on beds."*

Once upon a time
I found a shiny dime.
I tried to make a rhyme
About my shiny dime.
But before I made this rhyme
I lost my shiny dime.

MY FISHY

I have a little fishy.
And her name is Mishy.
She swims around
in a little dishy.

Children's stories are a natural source for skill development. Most compositions contain word endings, compound words, descriptive words and phrases, action words, long and short vowels, and the like.

As you read the charts with the children (and even as they are written at the children's dictation) stress why you use certain punctuation marks, and point out the difference between a word with an ending, such as *s*, *ed*, *ing*, and one without endings (tell the children what the ending does to the word, and which word is better for their story). After the charts have been completed and the children have copied them on smaller paper, use the charts for group activities in finding compound words, looking for descriptive words or phrases, and looking for words with long or short vowels and other graphemic characteristics, if you have already introduced them to these phonic elements.

There was a little wild canary outside who flew into our room because it was raining. It fluttered around the room in two circles then flew straight into the blackboard. Down he went! Our teacher put him in a box to keep him warm. When we were at reading she let him fly far away. The canary was green, yellow, and it had orange feet, too.

Elizabeth

Other compositions are rich in words that tell what, how, when, and name substitutes (*I, his, mother, him, she, my*), and words to express feelings (*scared, sorry*).

MY THREE WISHES

I hope Santa Claus gets more money than he had this year. I wish everybody had homes. I wish that Santa Claus does not get sick this year.

Robert

I wish that there won't be much school this year. I wish that everybody had a beautiful life and could live a long time until they have to die. I wish I didn't have to work in the house or the store my grandfather owns.

Brian

THE FIRST THING I REMEMBER

When I was three years old my mom and daddy owned the pier. My dad brought some of his friends to go fishing. I went to go get some food. I put my pole down and got something to eat. Then a fish got on my hook. Then the fish pulled my pole in the water. Then I went running to my dad crying because I thought I would get in trouble.

Kathy

The first thing I remember I was walking and I went in the bathroom and I hid in there and when my dad walked in I said, "Boo" at my dad and then I said, "Be quiet. I am going to scare my mom."

I hit John with a rock
yesterday.
Blood came out of his
head.
Boy was I scared!
His mother said I had
to tell him I was sorry.
Shucks. She didn't have
to do that.
John's my best friend.
I WAS sorry!

Charts are composed in connection with special days or seasonal changes.

AN EASTER BUNNY

Once there was an Easter bunny,
He came out when days were sunny.
Long pink ears and funny legs.
He delivered Easter eggs.
Around the bushes and in the trees,
And around the houses where nobody sees.
Some are pink and some are blue.
And some are even just for you.

WALKING THROUGH THE WOODS

When we were walking thru the woods we took our magnifying glass and our butterfly net. We looked at some berries under the magnifying glass. We saw different kinds of tree bark under the magnifying glass too. When we were walking through the woods a black cat kept following us. Her name was Muchacha.

THE ORANGE CITY

The sun was shining in the blue sky. An old witch and a cat came and sat on the boat. The bats started to fly around them. A ghost spreaded his arms and legs out and frighten the witch. The witch banged her pumpkin down, and everything turned orange, even the dog. From that time on everything was orange.

A group composition fully explains the recipe for preparing the Thanksgiving turkey.

> *Kill the turkey.*
> *Chop off its head.*
> *Take out the blood, guts and heart.*
> *Pull out the feathers.*
> *Put him in a pan.*
> *Pour on salt, pepper and sauce.*
> *Put him in the oven.*
> *Take him out.*
> *Carve the turkey.*
> *Put it on the table.*
> *Pour the Kool-Aid.*
> *Say a prayer of thank-you.*
> *Then eat!*

A graduate student, observing in a fourth-grade class, found this note left for her:

TO THE NICE LADY

I hope you will come back before school is out because I like you a lot you is very nice. I like it when you said I can read well because no one never said I can read well I don't think and I love everybody and I hope to see you soon again.

yours Iruely,

Children collaborated on this story:

> *How old is Miss Pippin?*
> *Joan says she's 15.*
> *But Mark says "No!*
> *My sister is younger and*
> *she's 15."*
> *"She's not married so she*
> *can't be very old" says Alan.*
> *"I think she's 79," said Mark.*
> *"Ha-ha-ha," we all laughed.*

A first-grade repeater who could seldom remember any written word read this personalized story to his principal two days after it was recorded on the back of his drawing of a hot rod.

I brung my toy.
I brung my hot rod.
And I don't want nobody
to touch it!

Simple charts for following directions:

To feed the fish we:
   1. Get the food from the shelf.
   2. Open the box.
   3. Shake it 3 times over the fish.
   4. Close the box.
   5. Return the box to the shelf.

To feed the birds we will bring:
   Apple—Maryanne
   Raisins—Margaret
   Chopped nuts—Carl
   Corn—George
   Stale bread—Jane and Nancy
   Pumpkin seeds—Nina

We will:
   LISTEN for their kind of talk
   WATCH what they do
   SEE what kinds come
   LOOK UP pictures of them

Classification charts (may be illustrated):

Words for Halloween
   pumpkin
   jack-o-lantern
   black cat
   witch
   broomstick
   trick-or-treat
   costume

Observation charts:

Watch our beans grow
   Mar. 2—We planted the seeds in cups.
   Mar. 10—We can see the sprouts.
   Mar. 12—The sprouts have leaves.
   Mar. 16—We planted them outdoors.
   Now we must care for them every day.
   Soon we will have beans to eat.

Kaper charts:

We all do our share
   Messenger—Jean
   Librarian—Ann
   Gardener—Stephen
   Aquarium—Della
   Host or hostess—George

Mr. or Miss Tidy Clean
   1. See that all chairs are put on the desks at 3 P.M.
   2. Wash the desk tops on Friday.
   3. Clean the sink daily.
   4. Dust shelves and counters daily.
   5. Erase the board.

Librarian
   1. Stamp the book card and keep the cards in alphabetical order in the box.
   2. Go to the library on Monday at 2 P.M. and return five of our books and select five new ones.
   3. Keep time during USSR. At the end of 15 minutes, tell Mrs. B.
   4. You are in charge of our class library. Please keep the books in order.

Lunch Tickets
   1. Pass out the lunch tickets at 12 o'clock.
   2. Collect tickets in the cafeteria.
   3. Go to the cafeteria each morning, write down the menu, and report this to the class.
   4. Wipe the tables and chairs after lunch.

Instruction for duty charts like these may be mounted in easy view, or typed on cards and placed in a folder labeled "Jobs."

Display charts (with realia attached):

THE MYSTERY TOOTH

This tooth was found by Ray.
He found it at Sandy Bluff.
What kind is it?
How can we get more information?

The following story was painstakingly typed by a sixth-grade eleven-year-old from a Mexican-American family.

THis IS for when I get my check.
I am to post to do this with my check.
Pay 7 dollers on my tapereqrter. That leves

$$\begin{array}{r} 12 \\ -\ 7 \\ \hline 5 \end{array}$$

IAM going to spen 2 dollers on my family.
I have left.   5
               − 2
                 3

I will give my Ma Ma 1 doller. And I will give my Daddy 50¢. And I will give baby 25¢ each.
Buy Mrs. Mc something. And spen the writ for me. Andy Maybe buy my Mama a bannan spit.
xx xxandx
By Angel Flores

To aid this very poor family, the principal had arranged a job for the boy with specific duties around the school. This plan, the boy's first real attempt at composition, was typed in the office in anticipation of his first weekly check. Unfortunately for the boy's progress in English, this school did not employ the language experience method.

The Method

Components of the Program

Among the major elements of a language experience program are:

1. Dictating to teacher.
2. Listening to stories and content material daily.
3. Discussing common experiences.
4. Sharing personal versions of common experiences.
5. Constructing group charts (with labeling by child's name in color of each child's contribution).
6. Writing stories independently.
7. Compiling individual stories on a common topic in a book to be placed in the classroom library.
8. Compiling a child's own stories in a book, suitably inscribed to be read to other classes or to parents or to be taped for others to listen to while they attempt to read.
9. Using resource books, pictures, and other audiovisual aids for information to be incorporated in one's own stories; include books on animals, other lands, nature study, simple science, picture dictionaries, etc.
10. Supplying art and construction materials for preparing charts, murals, dioramas, models, etc., to illustrate a story.
11. Providing charts of words to aid in spelling—on current themes, holidays, hard words, interesting words, and the like.
12. Preparing collections of narrative and informational books, poems, records, filmstrips, word recognition games, and constantly replenishing the classroom library.

13. Arranging work centers in the classroom for art, library, music, construction, science, and nature study materials.

14. Using the vocabulary of the stories as a basis for training in many significant skills.

15. Promoting individual vocabulary development by use of a card file word bank.

The younger child's first compositions are usually told to the teacher, who writes or types them directly. This is to prevent the mechanics of writing or typing from hindering the fluency of the child's contribution. Later, the material is often written by hand or typewritten by the child, unless it is apparent that these methods of reproduction interfere with the child's expression. Best results are obtained if the processes of composition and reproduction are distributed over a number of sessions and alternated with varied uses of the child-made materials.

The experience charts may be the initial reading materials supplanting the usual basal readers. This program is distinctly preferable for a number of reasons. Unlike most preprimers, charts provide interesting, varied reading materials that resemble the language forms and structures already known to the children. The direct connection between reading and other forms of language activity is made obvious to the children, for they see the very words they have spoken written on paper. The chart approach makes realistic use of the pupils' auditory memories for speech, and promotes the set toward thought-getting from printed words. A feeling for sentence structure and sequence is fostered as well as the habit of reading from left to right. Word recognition, comparison, and discrimination are promoted by the fact that the children see their words take form as they are written. In contrast to the content of the basal reader, the experience chart is real, familiar, concrete, and spontaneous.

This approach to beginning reading through the experience chart capitalizes upon the strongest value of the technique. It equates reading progress with the children's verbal skills in a realistic fashion. Certainly children cannot learn to read faster than their own auditory and speaking vocabularies permit. This limitation is truly recognized most clearly in the experience chart or language experience approach. The reading materials the children use are created out of their own language backgrounds and daily experiences. The children learn to read the very words they know best from their auditory and speaking experiences.

The experience chart approach is functional for average children and is particularly appropriate for children with language handicaps. Bilingual children who may have heard and spoken a language other than English during much of their preschool years; children with delayed language development because of isolation, timidity, or cultural difference; children who come from homes that employ nonstandard English or a marked dialect—all these benefit markedly from the realism of the experience chart approach to reading. As studies show when taught by this approach, these children show increased reading achievement and interest, more rapid development of vocabulary in speaking, reading, writing, and listening, and early development of independence in using such aids as the dictionary and reference books.

As children mature in their ability to compose independently, a number of other values appear in the use of the language experience chart. A graduate student of the authors', Carolyn Hendrix, has offered a number of observations on her employment of the child's compositions in understanding their personal problems. These are the provocative titles for such efforts, and some of her pertinent comments:

"What I Think Heaven Is Like"—seems to be a subject that draws out the child's wants and needs; and often the thing he misses most in his home life will be present in his description of heaven.

"The Way I Feel on Dark, Rainy Days"—a subject to find causes of moodiness (on an appropriate day).

"The First Thing I Remember"—brings forth some very interesting memories.

"The Reason I Like My Best Friend"—helps children realize the qualities they like in others and want to develop in themselves.

"Why I Am Happy"—often reflects a picture of home life.

"Why I Am Sad"—is also often a picture of the child's home life.

"Ten Rules for Mother and Daddy"—may provide a very interesting insight into parent-child relationships.

"What I Want Most To Do When I Grow Up"—a discussion before this paper can lead it to be more than a simple description of occupational goals, for there are other aims in life than simply vocational goals.

"If I Were a Turkey"—is usually done at some time near Thanksgiving, again to reflect child's needs and wants.

"What Makes Me Bad?"—an obviously leading subject.

"My New Year's Resolutions"—excellent for revealing children's feelings about right and wrong, and their consciousness of their own shortcomings.

"The World I Live In"—may be used following a discussion of moon, stars, and space, as an imaginary conversation with one we might find on another planet. Also reflects the child's view of his world.

Other story starters for late primary or older children are:

"People should remember that . . ."—many show insight into actions of people which bother the child that may not fit into a particular category.

"If I could go to . . ."—may lead to some research on places of interest locally or perhaps foreign countries.

"I was calmly waiting for my friend, when suddenly . . ."—opens the mind to try an action-packed account of an imaginary event.

"If I had only known . . ."—may release some guilt feelings, or help him (or the teacher) to make better plans for future events.

Other story starters are:

How I feel when...
When I go to...
What happens at my house...
The people in my neighborhood...
This summer I...
Sometimes I dream about...

Another aid for stimulating use of descriptive terms is to introduce metaphors, explaining that a metaphor makes something more real by giving it live action, even though it is not alive. Children can supply the nouns or objects, then supply some action words. These words can be combined into sentences or incorporated into stories.

Inanimate Nouns	Metaphors
furnace	licked, burped, belched, gobbled, ate, sizzled
truck	leaped, skid, skipped, purred
light	blinked, flitted, danced, bounced
limbs	clawed, snapped, scratched, tore, clung
floor	jerked, swam, slanted
shoes	skipped, danced, stumbled, pinched

Examples:
The limbs clawed and scratched at me as I ran. The old truck burped, leaped, and slid, then purred down the road.

The ability to react to these provocative story titles will, of course, reflect the maturity of the pupils. We would not expect first-graders, for example, to offer very long compositions or to show deep self-insights as a result of these stimuli. Second- or third-graders, or older children, are more likely to react in depth in their compositions. But subjects dealing with the feelings about self, the family, friends, one's future, and the like can be used with children of any school age to help gain insight into the child's self-concept. This is another way of learning more about children as individuals in order to relate to them more effectively.

The language experience approach has many mental hygiene advantages often lacking in other reading methods. It fosters an informal, helping relationship between teacher and pupil, as we aid children to get their ideas on paper. Working this closely together promotes personal, physical contact with the pupil, again reassuring the child of our liking for him or her as a person. The frequent use of children's stories by other pupils strengthens the child's positive self-concept as a worthy member of the group, because of the peer recognition of his or her contributions. Hence, our emphasis upon the constant sharing of each child's compositions with others has many different advantages. Through the child's stories and drawings, we gain insights into the child's likes, dislikes, fears, family, and sibling relations. The child's feelings of restriction or freedom are also manifest in the size and placement of the drawings on the page, and the length and fluency of the stories. Sharing of one another's chart stories, working together in pupil teams, using children of other races and other lands as subjects of compositions about such topics as homes, schools, and families around the world have mental hygiene implications. Feelings about other races, prejudices, and misconceptions can be affected through the language experience medium to a far greater degree than in most other methods, if teachers provide the appropriate resource materials, stimulating story titles, and classroom climate.

The curiosity of the child is increased by his or her participation in the firsthand experiences arranged by the teacher in nature study, science, social studies, community life, etc. This observation is supported by the results of studies showing the superior test performances of these pupils in these areas by the third grade. Also, the teacher does not constantly dominate the classroom with lecturing at children, thus reducing their opportunities for learning by discovery as well as their ultimate academic achievement. Other strengths are the actual transcription of talking into writing, an essential realization by pupils for true progress in reading, and the strengthening of recall of words by the feedback through auditory and visual media, as the chart story is read aloud to others.

General principles to guide the teacher in the preparation of experience charts are:

1. Charts should be done in manuscript with words clearly spaced. A dark crayon or felt-tip pen is probably best for visibility.

2. The chart can be any size. If the story is only a sentence or two, 12- by 18-inch drawing paper is sufficient. For longer stories 24- by 36-inch chart paper is best.

3. Lettering should be large—capitals double-spaced (two inches) and lowercase single-spaced (one inch).

4. The actual story may be written on anything, as chart paper is not often handy when a spontaneous story erupts; later the story can be rewritten on chart paper.

5. The story should be written as the child relates it. In the beginning stages of this approach, errors in grammar or sentence structure should not be corrected.

6. The words should be visible to the child, or children, as the teacher writes them. A left-to-right direction should be emphasized by moving the pointer or hand to guide the pupil's rereading. The return sweep to the next line should be similarly pointed out. In this manner, the association between the spoken and written word becomes apparent to the children.

7. When rewriting the story, the teacher may want to question the child as to which event happened first, next, or later and rearrange some sentences to show sequence of events.

8. The teacher should help the child realize when good stopping points arrive in the story to complete a sentence, and take advantage of natural breaks in phrasing.

Manuscript

In the 1930s there was considerable debate about the values of manuscript versus cursive writing for beginning readers. Eventually, the research both in this country and England demonstrated the superiority of manuscript for legibility, for promoting reading because of its similarity to printed words, for individuality in writing style, and its lesser demands for fine coordination in the writing act. The arguments that it was slower than cursive, unacceptable in business as a legal signature, or that it prevented children from learning to read cursive were readily disproved. Manuscript writing has persisted in use in the early grades in many school systems (23). But the tendency to discard it in favor of cursive as soon as possible, as after perhaps only a year or so, is quite common. To remind school systems of its basic values, Eve Malmquist has reported a series of studies in the schools of Sweden (31). He shows that when introduction to cursive was delayed until the latter half of the third grade, children using manuscript were superior in silent comprehension, clearer and more legible in handwriting, and better in spelling for the whole three-year period. The delay until the second half of the third grade, instead of the current practice of changing the mode in the latter part of the first or second year, did not interfere with learning to write in cursive as well as that done by those who changed over earlier.

Harrison emphasizes some significant facts for the teacher dealing with left-handed children's handwriting (19). She recognizes that children tend to take teachers (aides) as models and to imitate their writing hand when they are beginning to write in the classroom. To deal with these tendencies, some practices she suggests are:

- Group the left-handed children for their writing instruction.
- Give these children directionality training.
- Provide a good model in the teacher, aide, or parent.
- Use the blackboard for practice to promote fuller movement. (See blackboard exercises in our Chapter 8.)
- Have pupils hold the pencil one-and-one-half inches from the point so that they can see what they are writing without twisting their wrists. (See your school supply house for rubber guides to slip over the pencil to direct the proper grip.)
- Have the children slant the paper to the right and turn their bodies to the right slightly when writing, enabling them to write almost vertically or with a backhand slant.
- Provide a model alphabet showing left-handed writing (made by the teacher?).

Anne H. Dipon helps us to understand children's beginning efforts at writing (8). As they begin to write, more or less spontaneously, they ask us, "What does that spell?" That is a jumble of letters. "Can't you read it?" or "Whose name is that?" (a letter or two). Later, children label their drawings with a few odd letters. Much later they begin to spell their names, those of their parents, classmates, and siblings. They write letters to classmates, parents, and others, not to give a message but to create something—odd letters, words, names of the sender and recipient, and the like.

In experimenting with letters, they create words—*cot, pop, no, mom, man*, etc. Sometimes they write letters and by listening to their names, can decide what word they made: *PEVN—then, EVEV—Yvonne, PFDIRFP—flip*.

In trying to write their language experience stories, they write "How do you spell _____? Yah? Wow? He likes swings. He says Wow cuz he likes swings and he says Oh." "How do you spell boy? He says Oh boy." Using writing to convey a message is a relatively late development. Writing is apparently its own gratification.

Applications

Earlier, many types of experience charts were illustrated, but this list may serve as a quick reminder of the variety possible.

Chart of charts

Picture story	Child draws picture, dictates one or two sentences about it. Teacher writes sentences and attaches them to picture.
Sharing	One of the sharing stories told by the children is selected by group and retold for chart. Group may jointly or alternately contribute to this story.
Seasonal	Rhymes, slogans, greetings appropriate to holidays or season are used; may include short stories about the weather, season, calendar.
Instructions	Lists children's rules for lunchroom, for listening behavior, for fire drill, etc.
Kaper	Includes step-by-step directions for classroom duties, as care of chalkboard, feeding fish or animals; to be read by child chosen for each duty.
Classification	Employs vocabulary lists of concrete (not abstract) words children need for their stories; spelling words needed, etc.
Informational	Centers around steps in science experiments, nature study; social science materials (with context).
Phonics	Key words for consonant or vowel sounds, supplied by the *children,* with or without illustrative pictures; same for blends, phonograms, syllables, roots, and affixes.

(continued)

Display	Shells, rocks, insects, leaves mounted and accompanied by identifying words, phrases, or labels.
Letters	Letters written to another class, an absentee, an author, to express thanks, regrets, or other communication; may be composed in individual or group session. For older children, provide model of letter noting address, salutation, body, close, punctuation, etc.
Maps	Includes maps of playground, school, home, classroom, community, town, state, appropriately labeled.
Time lines	Uses listing of school holidays, children's birthdays, school events, or those related to social science units.
Phonics	Words in stories containing any designated phonic element may be identified; copied in classified lists; read aloud to another pupil to demonstrate control of the phoneme or morpheme; used in initial consonant substitution exercises or as illustrative words in the teacher's lesson on an element.
Structural analysis	Compound words, words with specific endings, prefixes or suffixes, syllables or phonograms, may be identified by the children and used as the material for a variety of exercises and teaching approaches.
English mechanics	Before transferring handwritten stories from the paper to a large chart that others may also read, or before binding them into a book of stories, the children should be helped to edit punctuation and spelling. They can gradually learn to do much of this editing themselves with the aid of a picture dictionary, a buddy or helper, or a word bank. Children's stories are at first written exactly as dictated without censorship. However, in the writing, endings, spelling, and punctuation are used as in standard English, without particular emphasis. Later, alternative expressions and appropriate idioms are offered as "other ways of saying that," inserted in the dictated stories between lines to be read or not by the children, as they choose. This editing is not present in children's initial efforts, since it may interfere with spontaneity and the recognition that you are writing exactly what they say.

These are a few of the activities by which experience charts may be directed toward skill development.

Some ways of using experience charts

Small-group reading	Each child may read a part of the chart (that portion the child contributed or another part). In the group, a child may share his or her chart with the others by reading to them.
Individual reading	Charts may be read to oneself, to a buddy or helper, or to the teacher during a conference.
Sequence strips	Cut copy of chart into strips, each one line long. Child reassembles chart by arranging strips in sequence, then reads.
	Draw sentences from large, illustrated shopping bag. Use strips from different charts. Child goes to chart and matches strip, then reads it. Child separates strips and assembles them in proper story sequence for each story. Use also sentence strips depicting action: "Roar like a lion, cry like a baby." Child reads and enacts action.
Word discrimination	All the words of a chart are written on small cards. Child reassembles entire chart, word by word, then reads. Words may be filed by placing them in an envelope stapled to the chart. New stories may be made using the word cards.
	Draw words from a large pumpkin, Santa's sack, etc. Match each word to those in a chart nearby. Group takes turns drawing cards.
Copying charts	Small-group or individual charts may be recopied by the child, with an illustration. Chart should be one composed by the children, not one phrased by the teacher for handwriting drill.
Storybook	Collections of child's or group's charts are brought together into a booklet with illustrations. This storybook may be read by child to himself or herself, to group, to another class, to teacher, to parent. Stories may be duplicated and copies of books placed in the classroom library.
Movies	Series of related charts depicting the events of a story are taped together in one long strip. The strip is mounted on dowels and drawn past

(continued)

	opening in a large box, while group takes turns narrating story.
Computer	Type children's stories into the computer, keyed to each child's name. A disc can be devoted to the activity and expanded throughout the year, to be recalled and reread at any time.
Flannelboard	A child may use the chalkboard or flannelboard to rewrite or reenact his or her individual story for the rest of the group.

Children will use a wide variety of picture books, children's books, and picture collections as sources for their ideas for writing charts and books. Thus this approach is superior to all others in promoting breadth of reading experiences and enjoyment of reading, elements sadly lacking in many contemporary programs.

It is apparent from the variety of activities suggested above that a primary goal of the language experience approach is the development of the child's language by speaking, writing, and reading. We firmly believe that progress in early reading is promoted by exercise of all these media of expression, not by reading alone.

Because the language experience technique includes instruction in many aspects of language, it should be apparent that it will require a larger block of time in the day than is usually devoted just to reading instruction. This need not be a continuous period of writing stories, correcting mechanics, learning phonic, structural, and contextual clues from the stories, practicing manuscript, listening to the teacher read, and all the other adjunctive classroom activities that characterize the method. Rather, teachers may schedule these as they choose in terms of the maturity of attention span of the pupils, and the periods of time needed for other curricular areas and for school routines. Because it is child-centered and small-group-oriented, the technique can be scheduled much more flexibly than methods that tend to demand set periods.

Some object to the extended use of experience charts because, they claim, the compositions lack vocabulary control, repetition of the basal vocabulary, and depth and variety of organized content matter. As a result, these critics recommend that experience stories be employed for only a short part of the beginning reading program, or only as an interesting supplement to the basal reading program, or for occasional lessons in creative writing. It is apparent that our concept of the language experience approach is as a relatively complete method of teaching early reading through the primary grades.

As for the lack of repetition of the basal vocabulary, if there is such a group of words, it is probably no more than the 200 or so most frequent words in our language (and as we have pointed out earlier, these words are not necessarily present in basal readers). These few most frequent words (largely prepositions, adverbs, conjunctions, and such structure words) are important, but it is also true that they are present even in children's stories (see earlier samples of chart stories). In fact, one cannot form English sentences without using these words, which mark the structure of such sentences. To manipulate children's compositions to include some list of "basal vocabulary" in preparation for the use of a certain reader is self-defeating and a distortion of the true purpose of the language experience approach. Overconcern about these service words will destroy the meaningfulness and vitality that characterize experience charts. The appropriate methods to ensure learning of this list of words are illustrated later in this chapter, and do not include censoring or editing children's spontaneous material.

The child who is a poor reader is asked to underline the words he or she knows in the written story. Then teacher and child read together, with the child reading those words that are underlined. With children lacking in fluency or self-confidence this supportive variation should be very helpful. Smith and Morgan have shown that simply having children record their stories on tape, which were then typed and placed in their folder to be read a number of times later, produced superior reading for groups of pupils in a basal program in both first and second grades (45). In our opinion, the obvious contribution of the language experience strengthens basal programs. The novelty effect of using a recorder could be retained by having children also read them into the machine for other children to listen to while following a typewritten copy.

As for experience charts lacking organized content material, the same criticism could be made of most primary reading materials. In contrast, as we have stressed several times, children taught to read by language experience do learn more organized content matter than other pupils.

In fact, using various types of instructional charts can strengthen the teaching in content areas a great deal. A few of the ways of reinforcing learning in these fields are time lines; directions for class or individual routine activities; classification of products, rivers, cities; collections of leaves, rocks, and shells mounted and labeled; reports on animal life—food, habitat, life cycle; and information on community workers.

Another point made by those who object to language experience is that the charts often include words of only immediate value, such as *satellite, astronaut,* or *antimissile.* The critics say children should not be exposed to these mature terms. However, this thinking reflects the common basal author's overconcern with spoon-feeding vocabulary. We know better than this today, for we have finally realized that when given any skill in word attack, children learn hundreds of words beyond those presented in the reader. If these difficult words are significant to the child's composition, why shouldn't he or she learn them, even if only temporarily? Knowledgeable language experience teachers do not expect pupils to learn these technical terms permanently, knowing that the context, the unusual lengths and shapes will suffice for temporary reading of the charts. In a word, we believe the chart should reflect truly the child's thoughts, vocabulary, and feelings, without undue adult manipulation.

Children's Strategies

Today's researchers in reading are very interested in comprehending the strategies that children use in learning to read. Nicholoson has pointed out that some relate to the picture in a story but invent a story as they attempt or pretend to read it (37).

Text
    Had illustration of a snake coiled on a rock.

Story
    A snake was on a rock.
    Then he saw a mouse.
    "SSS—SSS," he said.
    The mouse wanted to run away.
    But the snake was too fast.
    Zip—crunch. Where is the mouse?

Child
    The snake is looking for a mouse.
    "SSS—SSS." Zip—crunchy.
    Poor mouse.

Some use the first letter of a word as the only cue for recognition (30):

Text
    See the aeroplane fly.

Child
    The aeroplane can fly fast.

Sometimes children use both beginning and ending of words as cues (30):

Text
    Look at the boat.

Child
    Look at the basket.

A child may use the preceding context as a cue (30):

Text
    See the kittens, Janet.
    One little kitten.

Child
    See the one little kitten.

Previously learned words are sometimes substituted for the text (37):

Text
   Come and see.

Child
   Come up here.

In the early stages of learning to read, children may make partial reversals in words or word order:

big *for* pig   was *for* saw
play *for* day   no *for* on

They may ask the teacher, parent, or another child for help.

Child: "I am going. Is that going?"

Parent: "Going"

Child: "Going. But it doesn't begin with a g. (Now getting parent's attention.) I mean that word there (pointing).

Parent: "Taking."

Child: "I am taking a walk."

Some knowledge of decoding may end up in errors:

show-ess *for* shoes
mendow *for* meadow

Stress upon reading for meaning tends to prolong the inventive reading behavior. After a year, children still show many reading errors reflecting the dependence upon memory for the text or picture clues (37). On the other hand, emphasis upon learning the sounds of letters tends to produce mistakes of nonwords created by the child's efforts at decoding, as illustrated above. Such mistakes are often accepted by the child or the group, if the word is unknown, as though they had forgotten that reading is supposed to make sense.

After two years in school, most errors are single-word substitutions and are usually graphically similar. Children are apt to say *pasture* for *panther* or *shredded wheat* for *stewed prunes*, substitutions that at least begin with the same letter or show some relationship to the sense of the text.

Children who make good progress in the early years make few mistakes, are able to use letter and meaning cues, self-correct about a third of their mistakes, and read about four times as much as slower learners. Marie Clay says they have experimented with writing (often inventing spellings), tend to copy labels, and write messages to their friends and parents (which only they can read). Some have learned to read from television commercials, or by listening to stories or cassette recordings while looking at the printed words. In other words, they have learned to make the connection between the alphabet and its sounds and the links between the print and what it says.

Oral Reading in the Primary Program

Despite the criticisms of reading authorities and the trend in basal reader manuals away from oral reading, this activity still occupies much of the class time in primary classrooms. Over two-thirds of the first- and second-grade teachers observed or questioned by Austin and Morrison (3) admit to spending "considerable" time on this form of reading. Although there is a shift in emphasis to silent reading in the third and fourth grades, 30 percent of such teachers still devote *most* of their instructional time to oral reading. As observers note, these teachers are aware of some of the objections to oral reading as they employ it, but persist in overemphasizing and misusing the practice, perhaps because of inertia or simple resistance to change. Others cling to the habit with a sincere but mistaken belief in its effectiveness as an instructional technique.

Few reading experts would argue that oral reading has no legitimate functions or goals in the total program. Rather, their objections center on the manner in which oral reading is conducted in the average classroom. In many schools, the most frequent oral reading activity consists solely of round-robin recitations of pupil after pupil reading a small portion aloud to a group or the entire class. This practice is used not only in the basal reader but also in many other schoolbooks, particularly in intermediate grades.

Virginia G. Goldsmith severely criticizes the oral reading circle (16). She asks, "Have you disabled a potential reading dropout lately?" by subjecting the child to the embarrassment of reading poorly before teacher and peers. As one child phrased it, "She gits you so mixed up that I can't read a word. Then the other kids laugh or show off when I make a little mistake. I hate read'n in a circle. I hate read'n. I hate it, hate it!" (16).

Even the child who reads well can read no faster than the group. The child must slow down to keep the place, for fear he or she may be called on next. Perhaps the only children who really pay attention during the circle reading are the eager little fellow who raises his hand to tell the word as soon as the oral reader stumbles, and the other is the kid sitting next to the one reading who expects to be called on next, when the teacher gets bored listening to the reader.

As Goldsmith says, children learn the following things from reading in turn around the circle: to tune out the poorest readers, to pretend to be following the reader, to try to read as slowly (and, in a sense, as poorly) as the poorer readers of the group, to pay so much attention to getting the words correct during his or her turn that the reader never gets the message of the story.

Some teachers make the oral reading more functional by using it largely to permit children to answer questions or substantiate their answers. A few utilize oral reading in play acting, asking children to assume roles and to read only the dialogue. Occasionally one sees oral reading functioning in choral reading of poetry or prose in which groups of children enact roles or the contrasting voice levels of boys and girls are used to add enjoyment to the story. And, of course, oral reading is sometimes used in the classroom to convey messages and to share selected portions of the children's recreational reading. All of these oral reading activities are justifiable and they actually accomplish the aims teachers attribute to them.

The following chart presents as objectively as possible the usual claims made for or against oral reading. These pros and cons arise from many sources, including classroom teachers and reading authorities. Each claimed advantage or justification for oral reading is contrasted with a contradictory statement attempting to question each claim. The reader should keep in mind that the point of discussion is oral reading as it is commonly practiced, not oral reading per se. A discussion of each pro and con is offered following the chart to clarify the antagonistic viewpoints.

Pros and cons of oral reading

ASSUMPTIONS	REFUTATIONS
1. Reinforces the child's effort to recognize words by their sounds.	1. Assumes that reading vocabulary, particularly the new or unknown sight words, are within child's auditory vocabulary.
2. Permits teacher observation of child's knowledge of reading vocabulary.	2. Emphasizes word calling at the expense of comprehension.
3. Permits teacher observation of error tendencies in pupil's reading (i.e., confusion of word form, failure in semantics, etc.).	3. Assumes that teacher hears and records most of child's errors for subsequent analysis.
4. Permits observation of pupil's word attack habits and techniques.	4. Assumes that teacher analyzes errors and plans corrective steps for each pupil from his or her written notes.
5. Provides repetitive practice for rest of the group or class, thus strengthening their reading development.	5. Actually requires children to follow closely a pupil who often reads worse than they do.
6. Centers attention of group upon the reader and the teacher; promotes group esprit and identification.	6. Promotes boredom and inattention among the better readers of the group.
7. Provides opportunity for practice in listening skills for the rest of the group.	7. Promotes inattention, for unless questions are used to focus attention of the other members of the group, no real training in listening occurs.

(continued)

8. Gives child practice in proper phrasing, pitch, inflection, and other speech habits, thus promoting skill in oral communication.

8. Assumes that the teacher actually directs and corrects speech habits; rather it emphasizes oral reading at sight, thus promoting what is basically an inferior and unnatural oral performance.

9. Promotes attention to punctuation, phrasing and other linguistic features of the language.

9. Actually the reader does not pay close attention to phrasing or to punctuation in order to comprehend.

10. Offers opportunities for role playing, dramatization, choral reading, and other practices leading to oral communication skill.

10. Overemphasizes the learning of the reading vocabulary and thus provides little practice in individual or group communication situations.

11. Helps emphasize the relationship between the printed word and normal speech—that "reading is talking written down."

11. Assumes that printed prose and normal speech are quite parallel.

12. Provides opportunity for personal contact between the pupil and teacher, thus strengthening his or her ego and social adjustment.

12. Offers basically a threatening, anxiety-producing experience for the poor reader or even the child with slight speech handicaps.

13. Provides foundational training for present and future development of silent reading ability.

13. Assumes that silent and oral reading are similar processes and mutually supporting.

The Pros and Cons of Oral Reading Reviewed

Auditory Reinforcement. As a child reads aloud, assuming that the words are pronounced in a manner natural to him or her, the sounds the child says help to reinforce the visual impressions of the words. In a sense, the child strengthens his or her visual recognitions with auditory memories for the same words, thus promoting a multisensory impression. However, this reinforcement occurs only when (1) the child has previously heard and understood the words, (2) the child analyzes the words correctly and pronounces them the same way he or she has usually heard them. If the words are not in his or her auditory vocabulary, or are not ones the child remembers from the classroom or normal conversation, he or she may not be able to say it correctly, and certainly will be unable to deduce its meaning just because he or she can pronounce it.

For example, you can probably read and pronounce *Deltamatic*. But what does it mean? Does the ability to say it clarify that this word refers to the electronic system of handling reservations on Delta Air Lines? Teachers often justify a great deal of oral reading in and above primary grades by claiming that it helps word recognition and even comprehension. Unfortunately, this assumption is true only in material that is easy for the reader, with very few unfamiliar words and few technical terms. The claim is entirely true perhaps only at the beginning stages of reading and then only if the material resembles normal conversation in its selection of words (which it seldom does). When does an oral reader have any time to make judgments, to reach conclusions, in fact, to do any real thinking about the ideas behind the words he or she is trying to say?

Others who insist that early reading is highly dependent upon auditory memories for speech forget that reading is taught successfully to many without such memories, as the deaf, hard-of-hearing, bilingual, and foreign born. In fact, in some experiments, children have been taught to read for as long a period as the first six years without any practice in circle reading. Many types of oral reading were permitted, but only for obvious communication. At the close of the experiment, these children read as well as any others in every respect. To paraphrase Constance McCullough's remarks, "How moral is oral?"

Learning Basal Vocabulary. Teachers often believe that oral reading permits them to determine children's command of the basic vocabulary in the basal reader or their understanding in content field books. It is obvious, however, that first, the ability to read a sentence (that is, to pronounce all the words correctly) does not prove anything about comprehension. If we could be certain that readers understood the material because they read it aloud reasonably well, we would never have to ask questions testing their comprehension. But every experienced teacher recognizes the falsity of assuming understanding of material just because it is read aloud well. In fact, practically all research studies on the subject indicate that comprehension is relatively weak in oral reading. Readers have too many other demands to meet in delivering the sentences well to be able to listen comprehendingly or to spend any time really thinking about what they are saying.

What we see in most classrooms in the oral reading circle is really a worship of word calling, with the implicit belief that if children read the words correctly, they have learned these words and they are comprehending. We cannot assume that saying the words correctly once, twice, or a dozen times proves that children really understand them, or even that they can now easily recognize them. Words are learned as sight words or in terms of their various meanings quite gradually in a process that extends over a long time, perhaps a lifetime. Learning sight words (and their meanings) is not a simple additive process accomplished by so many repetitions per new word. Words are known some days and forgotten others; their command is irregular and almost unpredictable. No teacher could guarantee which of the basic words overemphasized in this type of oral reading the pupils really know on any single day.

Every experienced teacher probably knows that the words read correctly one day, or on one page, may be forgotten on the next.

Furthermore, the stress is upon saying the words precisely in this circle reading, as shown by the fact that in many classrooms the teacher's main effort is spent in correcting children's word-naming efforts. Children are not permitted to substitute words despite the fact that such words might convey the same sense or meaning as the original words. They are not supposed to think their way through the material, calling on their previous learning or associations to aid in interpreting the ideas. They are simply supposed to call the words correctly and that act, of course, is supposed to result in comprehension. We know that teachers try hard to build a mental bank of ideas or words in children's minds. Yet in this type of oral reading, pupils are not permitted to call on these memories, integrate them with the concepts offered by the printed page, and, in reading, present a mixture of both. Obviously, the practice of circle oral reading as usually practiced promotes word calling rather than comprehension.

A recent study required children to read orally under two conditions: reading without any interruptions or corrections, and with the teacher correcting all word recognition errors (39). The correction of errors, as most teachers might do, actually produced slower rate and poorer comprehension. Even when simply asked to "pay closer attention to the words," these trends were present. Thus this common practice acts as a deterrent to oral reading progress.

A much sounder practice would lead the children to read each portion silently first, in order to answer leading questions. This usage would provide opportunities in independent word attack in keeping with the training given previously and would emphasize comprehension rather than word calling. Later, if oral reading still seems desirable, it might be used in answering the prereading questions or in some of the other ways, such as play acting, choral reading, or sharing selected portions mentioned earlier.

Correcting Errors. Oral reading is often justified as an opportunity for the teacher to observe the child's word error tendencies and thus to plan corrective steps. It is claimed that the teacher will note whether the child readily recognizes the basic vocabulary or whether the child's errors involve word form, meaning, or both. However, as most observers of classroom practices know, few teachers follow through on this opportunity. Few teachers ever keep any records of pupil reading errors in the circle or do any more than correct the errors orally as the child reads. Most teachers apparently depend upon their overall impressions of the child's oral reading and use these to make whatever readjustments in materials or instruction seem indicated.

Diagnosis. Circle reading is also supposed to provide the chance for the teacher to diagnose the child's abilities in word attack—in phonics, or in structural or contextual analysis (2). If this were true, two conditions would have to be present. First, teachers would have to be skilled in analyzing the child's reading, and second, they would have to make some type of detailed record of the child's errors that would later be analyzed. Unless the teacher is well practiced in recording errors and has a duplicate copy of the selection on which errors can be marked, no adequate record is possible. Few teachers have such training, and fewer still actually attempt to record and analyze the child's word attack habits. Most commonly, what really takes place is that the teacher notes mentally a few errors, draws a quick conclusion, and proceeds to take some corrective measures that seem appropriate. The proportion of retarded readers who exhibit poor word attack techniques is evidence that this particular value of oral reading as an aid to diagnosis is very doubtful in the ordinary classroom.

Most teachers would frankly admit that in group reading the necessity for the teacher to supervise the group, try to maintain the attention of the members, direct questions, and the like precludes any real possibility of carefully analyzing the reader's errors. Such diagnosis is probably feasible only in a one-to-one situation of teacher and pupil.

Following a Model. Most teachers assume, almost without question, that oral reading in a group with each pupil reading in turn provides some sort of helpful practice for the entire group. Presumably it helps the others when they read along with the child reading aloud. As a matter of fact, this group practice results in requiring children to follow and imitate someone who often reads more poorly than they. Gilbert's eye-movement studies of children reading in this fashion indicate that they actually read with many more errors, poorer phrasing, and excessive fixations while following another child (*15*). The type of reading done in this situation is much worse than that done by children reading similar material silently and independently.

Requiring other children in the group to read along silently as each child reads aloud is *not* a sound instructional technique. It obviously does not provide training in quick, accurate word recognition (even though children are permitted to call out a word on which the reader stumbles). It does not provide a helpful repetition of the basic vocabulary, for all the fumbling, mispronunciations, or miscalling that the child hears certainly do not reinforce a correct impression of the words. This type of oral reading practice does not strengthen children's word analysis techniques since the context, which should assist such analysis, is often distorted by the fumbling oral reader. How, then, can it contribute to the development of better oral or silent reading? Perhaps the only result is to strengthen the child's impression that the most important goal in reading is calling the words correctly, a view apparently shared by many teachers.

A much sounder approach would substitute listening for reading along silently as the group activity. All books would be closed except for that of the child reading aloud. Then the questions on the content would be addressed not to the reader, but to the listeners. Any benefits in following another reader are achieved only when the reader is a superior, fluent performer or when the teacher, a tape recording, or record provides the model.

In recent studies, having children read along with a tape, either orally or silently, has been tried. In fact, the market is being flooded with cassettes paralleling trade books. It is claimed that this experience makes reading an enjoyable activity, promotes better comprehension, and overcomes the obstacle to fluency that decoding causes. Laffey and Kelly have carried this idea a step or two farther by having children engage in repeated readings of taped literature (29). In a small-scale year-long study with nine retarded readers from the fifth and sixth grades, these authors asked the pupils to read along with the tape silently twice before trying to follow it aloud. The oral reading was repeated two to six times until they could read the story fluently.

The pupils needed a marker, a piece of cardboard held on the line above where they were reading. After mastering a story, they could read it to the teacher, the reading group, or another class in the school. The gains in comprehension were significant at the end of the year.

Laffey and Kelly attribute the gains to the repeated readings. It is also possible that the reading growth was due, in large part, to the enriched instructional procedures offered the pupils. They engaged in oral discussion with the teacher, retold the story to her upon occasion, discussed and compared the various stories, answered written questions, and were stimulated to engage in creative writing based on their reading. These activities were presumably done to test the children's comprehension, but it is quite likely that all these additional activities, which would not be common in the basal program, greatly stimulated their interest in reading and thus fostered growth. Much more research needs to be done on these multisensory modes, as they are called, of practicing reading before we can know their true value.

The present authors have observed a number of groups engaged in listening to a taped presentation. When the members around the listening post are asked to indicate exactly where the speaker is reading, they are very apt to give widely different answers. They point to different places on a page, or simply say they don't know. We question whether children, particularly those who are poor readers, can really follow the oral reading of a professional, unless the tape can be run at a very slow rate. Tapes made by the teacher or a good child reader would be preferable to commercial tapes. Repeated listening and reading, á la Laffey and Kelly, may eliminate this discrepancy and prove more effective.

Attention. Some say that the oral reading circle helps to center the attention of the group upon the child reading; to give the child a sense of importance and strengthen his or her ego. It also serves to build a group esprit among the members, a sense of belonging. However, when we see the group in action, it is apparent that only a few actually listen to or read along with the reader; the others appear bored and inattentive because of the poor performance of the reader. The majority sit apathetically (or impatiently) waiting their turn. Only one or two follow the reader carefully enough to note errors and to flap their arms for a chance to call out corrections. Even the teacher's efforts to focus their listening by calling on those deemed inattentive seldom suffice to maintain more than sporadic listening.

Yet children seem to want this type of reading activity, to feel neglected or disappointed if they do not get a turn at reading. They may complain to their parents that "they didn't get a chance to read today," although they have read silently several times during the day in other lessons. This attitude implies that there is a moral or ego-building value to be found here, if we could only eliminate some of the wasted time. Perhaps the answer lies in a smaller reading group and better selection of children of equal abilities to compose a group. Other arrangements preferable to the usual practice include more opportunity for reading to the teacher alone, or to another child, or to a small group that simply listens to and enjoys the story without attempting to follow silently. Reading to an audience that is attentive is a highly gratifying experience, but teachers must try to ensure that the situation is truly rewarding and not a farcical imitation.

Listening Skills. Group oral reading may be intended to provide an experience in listening while one member reads aloud. As we have pointed out, this experience is seldom realized, for most of the listeners tune out the reader or only pretend to listen while they wait for their turns. If listening training is to occur, it must be planned and directed. Leading questions should be presented to the group before the reading to direct their listening toward the types of ideas to be gained from the material. Meanwhile, they are not required to follow the oral reader by reading silently. After the reading, or at intervals during it, if it is a long selection, the prereading questions should be answered and discussed. At the end of the reading, questions may be answered either orally by the group or in the accompanying workbook material. These pre- and postreading questions should parallel the type of questions used to direct reading comprehension.

Such a listening activity provides practice in the kinds of thinking that are supposed to occur in the act of reading—various types of reasoning, memory or recall, evaluation, and the like. There is ample evidence that this activity helps children to read (and to listen) more effectively when it is carefully directed, somewhat as we have suggested.

Speech Training. Oral reading in turn in a group is claimed to offer practice in acquiring good speech habits, such as proper inflection of sentences, modulation of the pitch of the voice, and correct phrasing of the elements of sentences. If this is true, then this type of reading would have value in improving the oral communication abilities of children. But do most teachers use the situation for these constructive purposes? Do they even know very much about improving the children's reading habits? Are they really concerned that the reading sounds like good, natural speech, or do they spend most of their time correcting word recognition errors?

Phrasing. If we photograph the eye movements of a good reader (or a poor one) we find that his or her fixations do not closely correspond to the structural aspects of the passage. Fixations occur every word or two, sometimes in the middle of a phrase, sometimes part way into the next sentence. When reading rapidly, the skilled reader obviously does not fixate each word, but skips over many. The fixations do not correspond to the punctuation with stops at periods, commas, etc.—most of the time the eyes carry over into the next group of words.

Pupils read literally word by word, with an eye span of less than a word, until they are at secondary reading levels. Obviously when they read rapidly they must be skipping words and moving along rapidly to pick up related facts. Despite the claims of some linguists, we read for ideas, assuming many words without reading them, mentally grouping the meanings of the words (not the phrases), and reading for associated or relevant ideas.

If oral reading is to result in speech improvement, the teacher's instructional activities will have to change a great deal. Except among superior readers, oral reading at sight is apt to be a halting, unnatural activity. The teacher should first ask the children to read the material silently so that their later oral reading will be a better, more fluent performance. The teacher may also stress playing roles by various children with each child reading only the appropriate dialogue of the character represented. After having practiced each bit silently, the oral reading of the part of each character will tend to resemble natural speech with its intonations, inflection, pitch, and rhythm. Frequent use of simple plays as a substitute for the basal stories, or employing recreational materials selected by the members of the group (and practiced silently and orally before presentation), are superior ways of promoting better and more natural speech habits in oral reading. Oral reading can contribute to improve speech habits in other oral communication acts, but if it is to do so the group reading must be structured to achieve this goal.

Communications Skills. We have emphasized several times in the preceding discussions of the claims for group oral reading that it can indeed contribute to speech habits and oral communications skills. If the modifications in the usual procedures are made, and if the more appropriate oral reading activities are frequently substituted for round-robin reading, then these particular values certainly can be achieved. On the other hand, when teachers persist in pointless reading in turn around the circle, it is very doubtful that there is ever any such value.

Reading and Speech. Some reading specialists and some linguists insist that oral reading strengthens the relationship between reading and speech. It is supposed to help children realize that printed matter is simply speech written down, and thus foster the transition from speaking to reading. This assertion depends strongly on several assumptions that are seriously questioned by other reading and language specialists.

The first and most obvious of these assumptions is that printed prose and normal speech are parallel, or at least sufficiently parallel to promote easy transition to reading. However, as Marquardt, a language specialist, has pointed out, these media are more different than parallel or similar (32). They differ in these ways:

1. Printed material is not a complete representation of spoken matter, for these are oral sounds for which there are not possible printed symbols.

2. Speech is accompanied with a variety of exclamations, grunts, sighs, and other sounds that help communication but are seldom present in prose.

3. Facial changes, silences, gestures, shrugs, and many nonverbal signs clarify speech and are completely lacking in print.

4. Sentence length and structure differ markedly in the two media, for those in speech are often fragmentary, run-on, faulty in grammatical features, monosyllabic, and the like. These characteristics are absent in prose. Moreover, printed or even handwritten sentences are longer, more formal, and more complex, even in children's writings from about third-grade level on.

5. Pitch, intonation, and inflection help carry the meaning of the speaker, as well as volume and tone of the voice. None of these can be produced in prose.

6. In appropriate settings, accent, dialect, and regional variations help convey the speaker's meanings. Each group of listeners tends to understand and react to these familiar nuances more readily than to standard English. These differences in speech either cannot be or seldom are conveyed in print.

7. As critics of basal readers indicate, the content seldom resembles normal speech as children know or use it. The sentences tend to be artificially short, stilted, and limited in variations of their patterns when compared with the oral language most children hear and use. The authors of recent basal reading series are trying to avoid the artificial, stilted language (imposed by the miniscule vocabulary) that has so long characterized primary books.

For all these reasons, spoken and written language differ, and we cannot assume that the reading of written prose is simply a type of speaking or the reading of "talking written down." If children are ever to read intelligently, it may be essential for them to recognize that written prose and speaking involve the same kinds of thinking and processing of ideas. But to assume that children are ready to read because they can speak reasonably well, or that they move easily from speaking and listening to reading because of the parallelism, is manifestly absurd, as almost any primary teacher can testify.

Perhaps the only situations in which prose and spoken language are really alike are those in which the material is actually composed by the children, as in experience charts. If the chart follows faithfully what the children are saying, it comes as close to being "talking written down" as it is possible for prose to be. Yet it still lacks the gestural, facial, and inflectional signs of spoken language.

Ego Building. As we have said, oral reading can be a gratifying, ego-strengthening experience. But for some children it may be a threatening, anxiety-producing task. When children who know they read poorly are required to read aloud before others, the results may well be tension, fear, and other types of unwholesome emotional reactions. Pupils who suffer from minor speech difficulties, such as baby talk, substitutions, lisp, or stuttering, may also react badly to required oral reading. The unsympathetic laughter or ridicule of classmates, or sometimes even of the teacher, makes oral reading a nightmare for some children. Need we point out the obvious necessity for teachers to prevent these disturbing experiences for such children by permitting them to read silently whenever possible? Sometimes the morale-building effects of oral reading may be better achieved by extending to these children the privilege of reading aloud to the teacher alone, or permitting them to read aloud to an audience only when they have had ample previous practice with the material.

Unwholesome, frightening experiences in oral reading are not uncommon among children. Experienced reading clinicians can recount the stories of such children whom they had later almost vainly tried to help recapture some enjoyment in reading. On the other hand, alert, sympathetic teachers can capture the positive values for the child's personality in the oral reading situation and help build self-confidence and a strong foundation for future academic success.

Oral Versus Silent. Perhaps the most frequently repeated justification for group oral reading is that it is the essential experience upon which future silent reading activity is based. Unfortunately, this is an almost completely mistaken belief, for the two ways of reading are not interdependent but rather almost antagonistic to each other. Some of the common basic goals of oral reading are (1) correct pronunciation of the words; (2) delivery in a proper speech manner; (3) communication with the listeners; and (4) proper use of pitch, volume, inflection, rhythm, and enunciation. In contrast, none of these goals for which we practice oral reading functions significantly in the silent reading act. Silent reading training is intended to produce (1) adequate comprehension; (2) an integration of the reader's background of information with the content of the reading; (3) a rate of reading comparable to the reader's capacity for speed in associating ideas; (4) an intelligent use of the context to help derive the meanings of new or difficult words; and (5) successful use of a variety of methods of word analysis resulting in the deduction of word meanings (not necessarily their pronunciation).

There are, of course, other goals for both types of reading that stress enjoyment; growth in use of reading as a tool for personal, social, and academic needs; reading tastes and interest; and so forth. But we are emphasizing the dissimilarities between silent and oral reading rather than their common goals.

None of the aims of oral reading function in silent reading. In fact, if we try to transfer some of them, such as the need for careful reading of each word, we would block silent reading development. Silent reading must involve the skipping of words, the omissions of unimportant words, and an emphasis upon the basic ideas of the sentence or the paragraph. A careful word-by-word emphasis, characteristic of good oral reading, would destroy comprehension in silent reading. If children were to read this slowly and carefully, their comprehension as well as their concentration would be minimal. Silent reading demands a thinking act, a reaction to ideas, at the rate of thinking and associating of which readers are capable. If they move through the material at a slower rate, their minds wander; they deal with words and not ideas, with consequent loss in comprehension.

Furthermore, studies of the errors in reading indicate more omissions and substitutions among sixth-graders than at beginning levels. These errors reflect pupils' attempts to read more rapidly and fluently—a normal developmental trend beginning at about high-third-grade level—and to associate their knowledge with the ideas of the material. They are typical behaviors in the silent reading act and, moreover, essential to it. But when children use these same behaviors in oral reading, they are likely to be considered poor readers. They cannot transfer the behavior characteristics of each type of reading back and forth—slow word reading from oral to silent, or rapid idea gathering with little attention to the exact words from silent to oral.

Practice in oral reading promotes that type of reading but, except for the development of sight vocabulary, tends to retard the development of silent reading ability. Practice in silent reading may interfere with good oral reading if silent habits are carried over. Perhaps each type of training has its place in the total reading program, but it is obvious that oral reading, if justified in the early stages, must be greatly deemphasized at later levels if eventual development of silent abilities is to be promoted. This trend is present in most surveys of classroom practices.

Yet we see the confusion of the two processes persisting in many classrooms. For example, intermediate-grade as well as middle school and high school teachers show lack of complete understanding of this problem. They often ask students to read materials aloud at sight, such as difficult textbooks, under the impression that they are promoting comprehension. Such oral reading is supposed to make it easier for the reader to understand the content when, as a matter of fact, it benefits only those listening carefully (not the reader or necessarily those following him or her in their own book). Any gain in comprehension from this approach arises from the discussion of each portion, not from the oral presentation, which could, therefore, be entirely omitted.

In this and other classroom practices, and in their attempts to judge probable silent reading ability from oral informal or formal tests, teachers and even some reading clinicians demonstrate their confusion over the two processes. When oral reading is accompanied by many errors or weak comprehension, it is assumed that the silent reading of the pupil is similarly poor. As many reading clinic personnel can testify, a large number of pupils are referred to reading centers because of this assumption of parallelism between the two reading behaviors. However, as we have tried to point out, oral and silent reading are not very similar performances in rate, comprehension, use of word attack or word recognition techniques, or thinking processes.

Using a standardized oral–silent reading test, Rowell showed that a large sample of third- and fifth-grade boys showed higher reading performance in oral than in silent reading (*41*). The reading level was higher also in whichever ability was tested second. Rowell justly raises questions about the validity of judging silent reading behavior from an oral test, and is concerned with the implication in his data that oral reading is apparently being emphasized at the expense of silent in many of our schools, despite the general acceptance of the opposite goal in most reading programs.

Our View

We are sure that by this time some of our readers are certain that we are most antagonistic toward oral reading. Perhaps we can dispel this illusion by repeating that there are many legitimate types of oral reading and that a small degree of this practice is necessary in a good reading program. But we differ strongly with common oral reading practices and the manner in which this skill is fostered in the usual basal reading program. Rather, we see many possible uses of oral reading for functional purposes, as in the following list.

Substitutes for the oral reading circle

1. Read story to children. Discuss its ideas, new words, its meaning, and the children's reactions. Have them relate their own parallel experiences. Let them read aloud their favorite portions.
2. Plan and write together an experience chart about a recent common experience or happening. If children can, let them copy the chart and take it home to read to their parents.
3. Ask children to select a story from a supplementary or basal reader. Let them read it silently, then ask questions. Use oral reading, if necessary to prove answers.
4. Ask children to bring their library books to the reading circle. Permit each child to tell something about his or her book and to share an interesting portion (that the pupil has already read silently).
5. Ask children to think of the most exciting or frightening thing that ever happened to them. Let several tell their experience. Make a group experience chart on the story that the children think is most interesting. Let each child read aloud the portion he or she contributed.
6. Allow children to read a chosen selection from the basal reader silently. Use oral reading to illustrate certain facts elicited in the discussion, to share interesting portions, etc., and *not* just for rereading the story.

(continued)

7. Let children who have progressed to the first reader level choose the next story to be read from the basal reader. Read it silently first, then use oral reading to clarify disputed facts, to prove answers, etc.
8. Have children bring their spontaneous drawings to the reading circle. Let them tell the story of the drawing. Select one story, with the children's help, for a group experience chart. Let each child read the bit he or she offered.
9. Construct mobiles of book characters from such materials as clothes hangers, pipe cleaners, and colored paper. Have children describe the characters they are portraying.
10. Children can compose sentences with several interpretations based on the emphasis on different words. They can read them aloud using different patterns of emphasis, such as:

This is <u>my</u> book.
This <u>is</u> my book.
<u>This</u> is my book.

11. Children may search the library for books with dialect. After practicing until they feel comfortable with the oral interpretation, they can read portions aloud to interested listeners.
12. A team of two students can preview and practice reading a filmstrip that is relevant to a content area topic. Then they may read the captions to the class at an appropriate time.
13. Have the children use the flannelboard cutouts to tell part of a story or to show the action while they take turns in reading selected portions to the group. One may handle the board while the other tells the story.
14. Upon completion of a story, make a list of the various materials referred to; i.e., cloth, wood, paper. Ask children to list all the things they can think of that could be made from one of these materials. Read lists and discuss.
15. Use clay to make small models of story characters, to stimulate discussion of the action and to initiate creative suggestions from the group of alternate actions or outcomes of the story. Let each child tell or enact the story of the model he or she constructed. If they can, encourage a group to write and enact a play based on their models.
16. Dramatize a library book or basal story with homemade hand puppets of cloth or paper bags. Let various children use the puppets to reenact portions of the story, using their own dialogue.
17. Each pupil writes a description of a popular person in sports, politics, or entertainment. Then the pupil reads it to the others, who try to name the person.
18. Have children study parts and act out scenes from the story they are reading. Practice by reading dialogue over several times silently and orally. Permit children to use books during the play, if they are needed.
19. Simulate a radio play with sound effects based on a story familiar to the group. Have different children play the roles in depicting various parts of the action. Don't forget the sound effects.

(continued)

20. Children collect various greeting cards and practice reading the verses aloud. You can expand this basic idea and use the verses on many occasions during the school year (holidays, birthdays, illnesses, etc.).

21. Let one child silently act out a part of a story just read. The other children look for the place in the story where that action occurs. The one who first finds the correct portion may read it to the group to prove his or her choice. Repeat at various places in the story, with different children.

22. Help children to write rhymes or poems expressing or paraphrasing a story. Ask several children to read their contribution to the group.

23. Let children read only the dialogue in a story, with each child reading a particular part. Let one child act as narrator to read any necessary description of the setting.

24. Have children bring their ''book'' of original experience stories to the circle to share with the others. During the school year, these books will be placed in the class library for anyone to read. At the end of the year, they will be taken home to be shared with parents and friends.

25. Let children who have read a certain poem prepare for choral reading. Assign parts to various children or groups. Contrast high and low voices, try to simulate various emotions—anger, joy, enthusiasm, etc. After several practices, visit other classes to present this effort.

26. Have a well-prepared child read a story onto tape for others to hear at a listening station. Some teachers make a copy of the story available while children are listening to the tape.

27. Have ''Today's Reporter'' or ''Town Crier'' read aloud the notes that come from the central office, such as the daily menu, after-school activities, new bus schedules, etc. Alternate this assignment among various pupils.

28. Make up riddles from reading materials and read them to the class. Ask children to guess what the riddle is saying. Let children make their own riddles to share with the others.

29. Start a pen pal activity with children in other cities or countries. Your pupils can read their letters or those they receive to the group for comments and suggestions.

30. Allow children to read the daily comic strips to the group. Have them take turns reading from day to day. You will notice that they really use expression when reading these.

31. With mature children who can compose complete stories of several pages, sharing can be made easier by constructing a ''movie.'' Paste the pages of the illustrated story in a long vertical strip. Pass the strip through a box with a large opening in the side facing the class. As the strip is moved, each page becomes visible through the opening. The story can be read to the group by the author, if necessary.

32. Have two children tape two person plays from *Plays for Echo Reading* (Durrell and Milia, Harcourt Brace Jovanovich). The children may make puppets for a presentation while the tape is playing.

Conducting Oral Reading

Other techniques have been suggested for helping children improve their oral reading, or their ability to communicate information to others. One of these, for no apparent reason, is called the Neurological Impress Method. Despite its beguiling name, this is not a new practice. It was used in the Dames Schools of England one hundred or more years ago in which the untrained "teacher" worked individually with each child. In its latest form, the teacher reads to the child, sitting next to him or her. The child follows in the text, then rereads each portion aloud. Eventually the child takes over the initial reading, while the teacher listens. Presumably the child learns to memorize the words because they are told to him or her by the teacher.

Another approach has been called Echo Reading. In this the teacher reads a part first and the child simply repeats it. Still another idea has been called Assisted Reading. A parent, a teacher, or an older pupil reads aloud to the child, who then repeats the passage. Later, the adult begins to leave out words so that the child can supply them. As a final stage, the child reads most of the passage, while the adult supplies an occasional word that the child does not know. Again, the assumption is that learning to read is largely a memory stunt.

Henk offers another version of this ancient technique (22). Before reading with the child, he suggests discussing the last story read, and what might happen in the new story as implied in the title, captions, and illustrations; and asking about any parallel stories or experiences of the child that would help in predicting the events of the current story. He recommends reading in unison with the child for only ten minutes before discussing the questions raised in the prereading stage, and making further predictions. Apparently he would tell the child the unfamiliar words, for he recommends his technique for materials that the child could not read independently.

Repeated Readings is another method some teachers prefer. In this the child reads easy materials to herself or himself several times, then to the teacher. Earlier in this chapter, in discussing the practice of reading orally in a circle, another type of repeated readings was mentioned in which the child follows a taped presentation with repeated readings.

Our View

We think these approaches would have some value in a one-to-one relationship of a child with a remedial teacher, a parent, or an aide. It would be particularly acceptable in the latter instances since it demands no technical knowledge of the reading process. However, we do not see any great value for children who are past the very beginning stages of learning to read. The sheer memorization that is the basic learning accomplished would be undesirable beyond this initial stage.

We think these rather naive techniques could be much improved by allowing the child to skip the too-difficult words while reading orally. Then when the child is finished, the adult and the child should return to those words and together try to deduce them from the context. Practicing using contextual clues in this fashion prevents the method from becoming a pattern of telling children the words they don't recognize (which isn't teaching anything). Supplying the difficult words while the child reads is not actually helping the child develop reading vocabulary, for the child has only a momentary association with the printed word.

Most of the teachers who use these various techniques believe strongly in their efficacy. There is no doubt that they convey a sense of accomplishment to children when they can reread what the adult has just read to them. But there is more to learning to read, orally or silently, than one simple type of practice. Children learn to read well only when they experience a wide breadth of reading experience, not only in reading along with an older person, but also in listening, speaking, writing, and interacting with their classmates. There is a real danger that these practices may induce the teacher to have an oversimplified concept of the learning to read process. Used as a supplement to broader instruction, these methods can help to individualize the program and increase teacher–pupil interaction, however.

Jenkins and Larson have studied and evaluated teachers' error correction procedures while children are reading orally (25). Among the habits they saw practiced with children were:

- Word supply: Teacher tells the child the miscalled word.
- Sentence repeat: Teacher tells the word but asks the child to reread the entire sentence.
- End of page review: The words told to the child are reviewed at the end of the page by asking the child to repeat them.
- Word meaning: The word is told to the child; then the child is asked for its meaning. The teacher assists by giving a synonym or definition.
- No supply: The child is just told to skip the word and go on reading.
- Drill: The unfamiliar words are told and after the reading session are written on index cards. The child is to practice pronouncing them. If the child is incorrect when reciting to the teacher or a classmate, he or she is given the correct word. The child continues the drill until he or she gives two successive correct answers for each word.

Jenkins and Larson tested seven students after five sessions each by presenting the list of miscalled words and the original sentences in which the errors had occurred. The children were not corrected during the testing. The researchers found that the word meaning practice as well as the drill technique were superior on both test measures. The other practices varied in their effectiveness from pupil to pupil and in their relative efficiency compared with the other practices. Jenkins and Larsen made the point that the very popular word supply practice does *not* have a good effect upon word recognition growth, as we have implied many times.

Silent Reading in the Primary Program

Because of the widespread overemphasis upon oral reading that they have witnessed, many interns and beginning teachers are at a loss to know how to move toward stressing silent reading. If the language experience approach is used as the initial method, there are many opportunities for practice in silent reading. Among these are: searching one's own stories for words containing a specific phonic element, reading the charts or books composed by other children, reading resource materials to provide facts for a story, reading in the classroom library corner, reviewing material that is to be read aloud later to peers or the teacher, reading in a group to answer and discuss prereading questions proposed by the teacher, and practicing a part to be read aloud in a play or dramatization or in choral reading. If these activities are used frequently, they will help promote the silent reading habit and convey the concept that this, too, is true reading. Many of these silent reading practices can also be employed when the basal reader is the medium of instruction.

Ganz and Theofield offer many suggestions for teachers and administrators who wish to promote silent reading (*11*). Basically, the practice consists of setting aside a specific time of the day when everyone in the school reads—teachers, pupils, administrators, and clerks. Some call this SQUIRT —Student Quiet Uninterrupted Reading Time. Others call it SSR—Sustained Silent Reading, or USSR—Uninterrupted Sustained Silent Reading, or SSRT—Sustained Silent Reading Time. Whatever it is called, the research doesn't show very significant gains in silent reading comprehension (*38*). However, the technique is favored because it promotes certain ideas among pupils, namely (1) voluntary reading can be enjoyable; (2) adults and (some) children like to read; (3) silent reading is the real mode in which reading is practiced.

Berglund and Johns would use USSR (1) to overcome excessive paperwork (often called instruction); (2) as an opportunity to practice reading since so little is done at home; (3) to promote comprehension; (4) because silent reading is more important in the long run than oral; (5) to give a greater freedom of selection and practice in choosing appropriate materials and setting purposes (*5*).

Southgate et al. also emphasize the value of silent reading for eventual growth. Their four-year study of primary classrooms revealed that the most successful children were in those classes where the teacher placed the least emphasis upon oral reading and a greater than average amount of time was spent in uninterrupted personal reading and in discussing the children's books (*46*).

Despite the largely negative results from comparative studies (38), Berglund and Johns see these possible outcomes for USSR: (1) power in silent reading and higher levels of concentration; (2) increasing security in reading; (3) more responsibility in selecting one's own materials; (4) gradual increase in the difficulty of the material selected; (5) increased use of the library; (6) greater sharing of books and magazines, which can help promote reading since peer selections have strong impact upon children (5).

At the same time, some problems have been encountered in implementing the USSR program: (1) the teacher does not read, thus failing to set the proper model; (2) troublesome students do not (or cannot) read; (3) the aide does not read; (4) there are too few books; (5) too long a period is used in beginning trials of the system; (6) sessions may be too short; (7) students are not helped to formulate ground rules; (8) it is not made clear that the children do not have to know every word while reading, and that they must not frequently ask for help.

In initiating the program, Berglund and Johns recommend publicizing it by teacher modeling, reading to children, offering books, making posters, assembly announcements, and describing the system at parent-teacher association meetings. Teachers should ask for donations of books, and make some out of old basals and magazines to insure a wide variety. The system should start with brief sessions that are gradually lengthened. Daily reading to children could be part of the sessions. The time of the USSR period should be fixed in primary grades and varied in intermediate grades or with older children so as not to interfere with one certain subject matter area.

Essentials of the Primary Reading Lesson

Understandably, inexperienced teachers will find it advisable or almost necessary to follow the basal manual until their self-confidence and teaching skills enable them to develop the techniques we are promoting. However, even inexperienced teachers will want to take some steps toward meeting individual needs from the beginning. Hence, some of the knowledge about the primary reading lesson is outlined here.

Anderson et al. tried to induce teachers to follow some twenty-two principles in their instructional practices (1). The purpose of the study was to establish the most essential practices and their effects upon pupil achievement. The researchers were not successful in getting teachers to follow all the principles. But the results can be interpreted to indicate that the following are most important for pupil growth:

1. Efficient transitions from one lesson to the next. This implies adequate teacher planning for the distribution of materials, for the review of earlier, related lessons, and for the training of children in knowing their groups.

2. The teacher should be seated facing the class, while the group being taught has their backs to the class. At least two results are obtained by this arrangement. First, the teacher can overview the rest of the class and possibly prevent disruptions. Secondly, the members of the groups are not likely to be distracted by non-group members' actions.

3. The teacher provides an overview of the concepts (schemata) of the story before the group reads. The teacher may, á la Henk, discuss the last story read, encourage predictions of the story action from the title, captions, and illustrations and from parallel stories or experiences the children have had, and raise prereading questions.

4. The teacher provides practice for individual pupils in taking turns in the group activities.

5. The teacher minimizes or discourages choral (whole group) responses.

6. The teacher minimizes or discourages call-outs from the eager beavers of the group.

7. The teacher provides positive feedback to help when children make errors (perhaps by the word meaning or drill techniques suggested by Jenkins and Larson) or fail to respond. By giving more time to slow responders, by changing or simplifying questions and by giving children the right answer or explaining it as needed, the teacher encourages their active participation.

8. The teacher omits feedback when an answer is correct. (Since there are dozens of ways of saying "Good," we think there could be a positive feedback in this instance).

9. The teacher uses praise moderately as encouragement without exaggeration.

10. The teacher addresses praise or criticism specifically to the child, not generally to the group.

11. The teacher discusses the clues children used in deducing unfamiliar words.

12. The teacher spends time in a postreading question-and-answer session with the group.

13. The teacher's corrections of the behavior of the members of the group are subtle and quiet because he or she has anticipated the disruptive behavior and tries to forestall it.

14. The teacher does not strive to cover all the basals possible. Perhaps he or she realizes that better progress in reading development arises from a broadened enrichment program than simply following the basals for the grade.

Our View

If we were in favor of a reading program based almost exclusively on a basal reader system plus perhaps a management system, we could stop discussing primary reading at this point. However, we believe there is a great deal more to primary reading than just formal reading lessons in a basal reader. The teacher of primary children should continue the practices described in Chapter 8. In our opinion, the teacher should continue daily storytelling periods (27)—reading to children, which could be an alternate use of the USSR period; persist in helping children with their experience charts, which will gradually be based more and more on content area matter; and carry on the follow-up activities and the use of predictable books.

Big Book or shared book experiences should be continued for at least the first five to six months of the first grade. Readiness training in visual perception, auditory alertness, language, auditory comprehension, and growth in the children's concepts of the reading process should be continued as long as some of the children show need for a particular type of training. Our study of an extension of this training for as long as six months showed that the eventual reading progress of the children was as great as their classmates who had been receiving reading instruction rather than the prereading training for part or all of this period. Teachers need not fear that attention to the readiness needs of children prior to or during the learning to read stage will delay ultimate reading development.

The Primary Program with Gifted Pupils

Some teachers use experience charts simply as an introduction to the basal reading materials. Others regard the charts as supplements that add spice and variety to the basal program. Very few teachers regard chart reading as a complete substitute for basals. We suggest that the charts are most intelligently used in these three ways—as a substitute for basal reading among gifted children and as an introduction to and supplement to the basal among average and slow learning groups.

The individualized approach has shown us the fallacy of following a basal program written for average learners when dealing with gifted pupils. These are the fortunate children who learn to read earlier and more easily than the average. These are the pupils of high verbal ability, strong vocabularies, and quick learning aptitude. These are the pupils who can and do read more widely and deeply when the reading program is stimulating and challenging. Therefore, we suggest that the reading program for the fastest-learning third or quarter of the class follow the individualized approach, after introduction to reading through experience charts. These children may be permitted to read the basal materials, if they choose them. But formal instruction in the basal in the usual manner would be eliminated in order to permit the rapid progress of which these pupils are capable. They may function as a group for chart reading and writing, project work, special reports, training in skills, and many other purposes. But the content of their reading program would be determined basically by self-selection under the guidance of the teacher in individual and group conferences.

Despite their superior learning aptitudes, the fast learners, like other children, need help in planning and organizing their reading efforts. They should not simply be turned loose in the classroom or school library to fumble their way toward satisfying reading materials. They will need help in developing discrimination, purpose for reading, criteria for selecting books they can read and enjoy, and instruction in how to organize their reporting on books and record keeping. As several studies have shown, children permitted to do individualized reading do not necessarily read easier books first and then progress directly to the harder. Their reading records are more likely to show a kind of alternation between easy and hard books, not because they cannot discriminate, but perhaps because of their motivation to reach out for more challenging materials or because of their interest in the content. Children spontaneously evolve such clues to the reading difficulty of a book as familiarity of vocabulary, details of format such as size of type or book, amount of text on page, and the relevance of pictures to text. Some teachers make a definite attempt to facilitate the child's discriminative ability by pointing out these differences early in the individualized program. Children may be trained to judge the vocabulary difficulty of a book by practice in previewing or sampling it before attempting to read it completely.

Early in the individualized program for gifted pupils, the teacher must help the children evolve some methods of record keeping. These will differ, of course, from class to class in terms of the teacher's philosophy and goals. But the teacher must decide on the types and kinds of child records that will enable him or her to observe pupil progress, guide and develop reading interests, and permit observation of growth in skills. Is a running record needed of the titles of books students are reading, their reactions to these, a list of the vocabulary they encountered, or other facts? Should children keep a notebook for these facts, or report them verbally in the conference, or demonstrate their learning by projects reported to the group or class? These decisions must be made before individualized reading begins, and the details must be worked out with the children so that they understand the procedures they will follow. Other preliminary steps in organizing for individualized reading are suggested in another chapter.

The different types and purposes of individual conferences, and the inventorying and diagnosis of pupil reading skills that may be attempted in certain of these conferences will be discussed at length elsewhere. In our opinion, the effective conference is the heart of the individualized approach and must be studied most carefully. Other problems inherent in individualized reading, such as planning, use of conferences, judgment of pupil readiness for this method, planning follow-up, and the keeping of pupil and teacher records will be discussed in detail.

It is obvious that we are attempting to capture the peculiar values of the individualized approach in our suggested program for fast-learning pupils. This method is most feasible with children capable of rapid, individual progress. These children, in our opinion, do not require the measured pace of the basal program, the cumulative repetitions, and the careful doling out of new words. With adequate teacher support and guidance to ensure well-rounded development of word recognition skills, of sight and meaning vocabularies, and of comprehension, these pupils may grow at their potential accelerated rates. Avoidance of the basal program with these pupils does not imply that they do not need diagnosis of their skill development and appropriate training. The syllabi of skills offered are intended for these pupils as much as for the slow and average groups.

The Primary Program with Average Pupils

The second large segment of the class is composed of pupils of average verbal skills and learning capacities. For these pupils we suggest a modified basal reader approach, involving introduction to reading by the experience chart, followed by the use of basal materials, and later, individualization. There are a number of sound reasons for this type of program, in our opinion. These are the pupils for whom the basal program has primarily been devised. The controlled vocabulary is offered at a rate commensurate with the learning capacities of average pupils. Yet most of these children can reach out toward individualized reading after completion of the basals, if given the opportunity. During the period that is needed to complete the basal books, teacher skill in individualizing will grow because of experiences with the fast reading group. For the average group, individualization can begin gradually with recreational materials and, as children grow in independence and reading skill, can be extended to their entire reading program. The exact point at which extended, individualized reading is begun is not critical in the children's reading development. This decision can well be a matter of teacher judgment and experience.

Individualized reading may be introduced to the average readers in a variety of ways: by releasing individuals from the group work, by special reading assignments, by urging children to prepare themselves for sharing time by special reading, by substituting individualized reading on the topic for a basal unit, by using the parallel readings suggested in the basal as a substitute for a basal lesson, by using the group lesson as an occasion for sharing best-liked books, and most of all, by providing ample time, motivation, and materials for self-selected reading. All average pupils will not necessarily be ready for individualized reading at the same time. Despite their gross similarities in capacity, average pupils will differ in the breadth of sight vocabulary, in the rate with which they can learn new words, and in their independence in word attack and other important reading behaviors. Teacher judgment based on observations of group work and of children's success in their first trials in self-selected materials will indicate when the children are ready for some degree of individualized reading. Detailed suggestions for making this judgment of pupil readiness for individualized reading are offered later.

We would depart drastically from several of the common practices in using basals. First, we would not repeat the mistake in some manuals of coaching the children in pronunciation of the new vocabulary prior to their reading of the story. Children will grow much more in independence in word attack when their spontaneous efforts are not stifled by prereading coaching. A setting for the main idea of the story and a structuring of children's purposes for reading should certainly precede actual reading. If desired, the new vocabulary may be woven into this discussion, but it should not be written on the blackboard or chart for memorization. Children should be permitted and urged to attempt independent word attack and given assistance only when this is unsuccessful, or when it is apparent from their answers to questions on the material that their techniques were inadequate to the task.

It is currently popular to call the prereading activities a way of establishing schemata, or a group of ideas about the story drawn from the children's background information. Relevant child experiences, predictions of the probable content of the material gleaned from the title, subheads, captions, and illustrations, relevance of the story to the preceding ones in the unit, and discussion of the main idea of any parallel stories the children have read are all employed to prepare the pupils for comprehension.

These schemata are certainly desirable, for they help to provide a set, an attitude toward the meanings of the story, as well as to stimulate the children's thinking while reading. Some believe that it is essential to preview all the new or difficult words that will appear in the reading material. We disagree with this coaching. First, unless the children are at the very beginning stages of learning to read, teachers may be coaching on a number of words already known to some of the children. If the reading program has any breadth at all, there is little doubt that pupils learn many "new" words as they grow in reading ability. Second, this prereading coaching, as it is often done, deprives children of essential practice in applying their phonic, structural, or contextual clues to deduce the "new" words. Lack of skill or practice in word attack is one of the prominent characteristics of retarded readers. Coaching in the "new" words in every bit of group reading material may contribute to this deficiency among pupils who are not really good readers, since very often it is not much more than telling the children how to say the words, and not always a preview of their possible meanings or structural or phonic characteristics.

Our View

We prefer to use postreading questions to ask pupils to define the "new" words, explain how they derived the meanings, and defend their definitions. If they cannot do this, we help by giving a synonym or definition. In this way, pupils are constantly impelled to use their word attack skills as well as semantic and syntactic clues rather than depending upon the teacher to tell them what the words are and what they mean. If the prereading preview of the "new" words involved all this, we would accept it; but it does not make any use of contextual cues, since they are encountered only while reading the story. Using contextual (semantic and syntactic) cues is the commonest mode of word attack used by mature readers, and we believe it is most essential to take every means to promote its development.

In content material, our practice will not suffice, for many of the words are technical, unknown, or foreign to common child experiences. In such instances, a few minutes' discussion prior to the reading will reveal that these words are truly unknown. They can be clarified by the teacher and reviewed again after the reading, in the manner we have suggested.

Follow-Up Activities

In many classrooms, using the workbook or management system is the primary type of follow-up activity, whether or not the children really need to do these exercises. Child progress in reading is judged by the number of worksheets or pages in the workbook completed in some schools. Certainly every child does not need to do every exercise that is supposed to parallel a basal story. The teacher must be selective in using these basal tools in terms of his or her observations of children's need for further practice in some particular behavior. Reinforcement of learning with workbook or management system worksheets can be ensured by selecting only the exercises related to children's needs in an area such as word recognition, word attack, and interpretation. This matching of exercises and child needs should be based upon the teacher's observation of children's answers and reading behaviors during the basal lesson, small group activities, and teacher conferences with individual children or small groups. Further reinforcement of schemata, vocabulary growth, and experiential background may be achieved by continued supplemental use of experience charts, thus adding some degree of spontaneity and creativity to the learning.

The selective use of workbook materials can be readily effected within the average school budget for such items. Instead of ordering multiple copies of a workbook to parallel each basal, we suggest buying a few copies each of a half-dozen workbooks from different series or levels. After all, there is no definitive evidence showing that following the parallel workbook in detail produces greater achievement than a more eclectic approach. Complete directions for making kits of these workbooks are offered in Evelyn Spache's *Reading Activities for Child Involvement.*

The sheets and unbound pages of the workbooks can be collated into related groups of exercises for each fact of the reading. If teachers place each sheet in a heavy acetate folder obtainable from most school supply houses, the children can indicate their answers in crayon or marking pen on the acetate. Thus the worksheets may be used again and again, for each child will wipe off his or her markings after checking with the group leader or neighbor. This arrangement is certainly preferable to the slavish use of the limited material in a workbook or management system.

A third major departure from the basal approach that we would recommend is in the tempo of the program. Many observers are amazed at the amount of time that some teachers manage to devote to covering basal materials of trifling content. The spoon-feeding pace seems to arise from several faulty assumptions often unwittingly made by classroom teachers. Because the manual and the workbook are so highly organized, teachers fear to slight the most minute details and undoubtedly waste much time in implementing most of the suggestions of the manual and in ensuring that every pupil uses the entire workbook. While it is true that repetition is essential for overlearning, there is no real evidence that this present degree of overlearning is necessary for ultimate reading progress of pupils with average or high ability. If we may judge by the progress of pupils in other countries, particularly those in English-speaking lands, we realize that much more rapid progress is feasible. The crucial point that many classroom teachers have failed to recognize is that there is nothing particularly sacred or perhaps even essential in the vocabulary of any one preprimer or other basal reader. The repetition needed for eventual skill in sight vocabulary may also be achieved in breadth of reading materials, with the added advantages of interest and vitality. Rapid completion of the basal materials followed by individualized reading, with both being reinforced by judicious selection of workbook and teacher-made exercises, will accomplish the teacher's ultimate goals for average pupils.

When children have passed the primer stage, or have learned 100 to 200 words, they are quite capable of reading many of the easy-reading books now available. Routine reading of the basal, story by story, is no longer essential or even desirable at this stage. There is no magic in a particular reader's vocabulary and probably very little vocabulary that will not be encountered in most of the materials of suitable level of difficulty. Beyond the first 200 most frequent words in English, there is *no real basic vocabulary* essential for all children. Rather, the vocabulary of each reading series varies more and more from each of the other series with the list of words determined not by some mythical master list but by the nature of the content of the readers. For all these reasons, slavish story-by-story following of any reading series is naive. Other materials may be used alternately or substituted for the basal in a dozen ways, as we have already suggested. Children should be allowed to select stories of interest to them, both from the basal and their recreational books as often as possible.

If, as is probably the case, the teacher wishes to function with small groups, he or she may either order several copies of various trade books (preferably paperback editions since they are cheaper), or use such resources as the Easy Reading Books listed here and in the Appendix. In this manner, use of the basal reader becomes selective and the tempo of the reading program is accelerated, as we have urged.

These lists of books were drawn in part from George D. Spache's *Good Reading for Poor Readers* (copyright 1978 by Dr. George D. Spache). All of the books are of primary reading difficulty as determined in most cases by the Spache Readability Formula.

Easy reading books

Baker, Betty, *Little Runner of the Longhouse.* Champaign, Ill.: Garrard Publishing, 1972.

Blume, Judy, *Superfudge.* New York: Dell Publishing, 1980.

Brierley, Louise, *King Lion and His Cooks.* New York: Holt, Rinehart and Winston, 1982.

Brown, Marc, *Arthur's Halloween.* Boston: Little, Brown, 1982.

Bulla, Clyde Robert, *John Billington, Friend of Squanto.* New York: Crowell, 1956.

Bulla, Clyde Robert, *Squanto, Friend of the Pilgrims.* New York: Crowell, 1954.

Burningham, John, *Avocado Baby.* New York: Crowell, 1982.

De Leeuw, Adele, *Paul Bunyan Finds a Wife.* Champaign, Ill.: Garrard Publishing, 1969.

Douglas, Barbara, *Good as New.* New York: Lothrop, Lee and Shepard, 1982.

Felton, Harold, *Big Mose: Hero Fireman.* Champaign, Ill.: Garrard Publishing, 1969.

Friskey, Margaret, *Indian Two Feet and His Eagle Feather.* Chicago: Children's Press, 1967.

Funk, Tom, *I Read Signs.* New York: Holiday House, 1962.

Geisel, Theodore Seuss, *The Cat in the Hat.* New York: Random House, 1967.

Ginsberg, Mirra, *The Sun's Asleep Behind the Hill.* New York: Greenwillow, 1982.

Godden, Rumer, *The Mousewife.* New York: Viking Press, 1982.

Greene, Carol, *Hinny Winny Bunco.* New York: Harper and Row, 1982.

Hearn, Emily, *Around Another Corner.* Champaign, Ill.: Garrard Publishing, 1971.

Hoff, Sydney, *Chester.* New York: Harper and Row, 1961.

Hon-Tien, Cheng, *Six Chinese Brothers: An Ancient Tale.* New York: Holt, Rinehart and Winston, 1979.

Keats, Ezra Jack, *Whistle for Willie.* New York: Penguin, 1977.

Kennedy, Richard, *The Contests at Cowlick.* Boston: Little, Brown, 1975.

Kessler, Leonard, *Kick, Pass and Run.* New York: Harper and Row, 1978.

Keyser, Marcia, *Roger on His Own.* New York: Crown, 1982.

Kroll, Steven, *The Big Bunny and the Easter Eggs.* New York: Holiday House, 1982.

Le Sieg, Theo, *Ten Apples Up on Top.* New York: Random House, 1961.

McKellar, Shona, *The Beginning of the Rainbow.* Nashville: Abingdon Press, 1982.

McPhail, David, *The Great Cat.* New York: E. P. Dutton, 1982.

Margolis, Richard, *Big Bear Spare That Tree.* New York: Greenwillow, 1980.

Margolis, Richard, *Big Bear to the Rescue.* New York: Greenwillow, 1975.

(continued)

Meadowcroft, Enid, *Crazy Horse: Sioux Warrior*. Champaign, Ill.: Garrard Publishing, 1965.

Montgomery, Elizabeth Rider, *Seattle: Great Statesman*. Champaign, Ill.: Garrard Publishing, 1966.

Nixon, Joan Lowery, *The Mysterious Prowler*. New York: Harcourt Brace Jovanovich, 1976.

Oram, Hiawyn, *Angry Arthur*. New York: Harcourt Brace Jovanovich, 1982.

Ormerod, Jan, *Sunshine*. New York: Lothrop, Lee and Shepard, 1981.

Perkins, Al, *Don and Donna Go to Bat*. New York: Random House, 1966.

Rockwell, Anne, *Up a Tall Tree*. New York: Doubleday, 1981.

Say, Allen, *The Bicycle Man*. Boston: Houghton Mifflin, 1982.

Shapiro, Edna, *Windwagon Smith*. Champaign, Ill.: Garrard Publishing, 1969.

Showers, Paul, *Look at Your Eyes*. New York: Harper and Row, 1962.

Showers, Paul, *Your Skin and Mine*. New York: Harper and Row, 1965.

Shreck, Peter, ed., *Acorn Magic Readers*. New York: Macmillan, 1980.

Silverstein, Shel, *Where the Sidewalk Ends*. New York: Harper and Row, 1974.

Sleator, William, *Once, Said Darlene*. New York: E. P. Dutton, 1979.

Voight, Virginia F., *Red Cloud, Sioux War Chief*. Champaign, Ill.: Garrard Publishing, 1975.

Warner, Gertrude Chandler, *Mike's Mystery*. Chicago: Whitman, 1960.

Warner, Gertrude Chandler, *Mountain Top Mystery*. Chicago: Whitman, 1958.

Wildsmith, Brian, *Bear's Adventure*. New York: Pantheon Books, 1982.

Williams, Vera B., *A Chair for My Mother*. New York: Greenwillow, 1982.

Williamson, Stan, *No Bark Dog*. Chicago: Follett Publishing, 1962.

Wilkie, Katherine, *Pocahontas: Indian Princess*. Champaign, Ill.: Garrard Publishing, 1969.

Wright, Betty R., *I Want to Read*. Chicago: Western Publishing, 1965.

From "Good Reading for Poor Readers," by Dr. George D. Spache, reprinted with the permission of Garrard Publishing Company, Champaign, Illinois.

Another departure from the usual basal approach, which would inevitably follow if our earlier suggestions are accepted, is in the type and number of lesson preparations attempted by the teacher. It is our strong impression that one of the basic reasons for the small number of reading groups present in the average classroom is the teacher's concept of the role he or she must play with each group. Many teachers feel that they must conscientiously prepare a lesson for each group each day. Or, conversely, teachers believe that groups really cannot progress unless they have personally worked with them each time they engage in a reading activity. Some critics of the basal program would say that many teachers act as though they think children cannot learn unless the teachers sit and listen to them say the words, preferably in a round-robin reading circle.

If teachers attempt the type of program that is moving toward many small groups and individualization, they will have to abandon some of these illusions about their indispensability to child learning. If teachers diversify instruction according to needs, they will soon find that even in the first grade they are promoting the formation of a half-dozen groups and, eventually, perhaps even more groups than this. Obviously under these circumstances teachers cannot possibly prepare formal reading lessons for each group each day. At best, time will permit them to work intensively with only two or three such groups and to deal with the others only briefly. We have tried to suggest many ways in which teachers may move toward this more flexible program by listing alternatives to the oral reading circle, and by mentioning different ways of conducting group reading.

In today's publishing market, there are a wide variety of kits and boxes of varying types and merits. Many of these would lend flexibility to the reading program by fostering independent work by small groups of children. Among the more widely known are the *SRA Reading Laboratories* (Science Research Associates); the Merrill *Reading Skilltexts* and their accompanying *Skilltapes* (Charles E. Merrill), *New Reader's Digest Skill Builders* (Reader's Digest), and *Reading Theatre* (Economy Company). These are but a few of such available tools for independent work. Creative teachers will, of course, create their own supplementary practice materials and tapes in order to ensure relevance to their own instructional practices.

Dozens of other drill books, tapes, records, kits, paperbacks, computers, and the like could be mentioned. The authors have chosen to list only those aids which we or the teachers we work with have found effective. To some, this may appear to be a limited viewpoint, but since the authors spend more than half of their time working in and with clinics and classrooms throughout the country, we offer no apologies.

Although we have spoken of our combined program as a flexible plan, or an individualized program, it is apparent that we envision the use of basal readers for definite purposes, particularly with average and slow-learning readers. To promote the best possible use of this teacher tool, we have already suggested some deviations from the usual basal procedures. Among those discussed were the presentation of new vocabulary, the constant sequential following of the basal content, the preparation of reading lessons, and the tempo of the reading program. One final suggestion is now pertinent regarding the basal reading lesson itself.

In our judgment, the effective reading lesson, in which multiple copies of any type of reading material are employed, includes these components:

- Prereading discussion of related children's experiences (their schemata).
- Prereading questions to direct the thinking of the pupils.
- Silent reading to answer the prereading questions.
- Oral reading of these answers, as their discussion proves necessary.

- Evaluation of the material to elicit children's personal reactions, to discuss its point or purpose, etc. Review of meanings of difficult words.
- Applications—a follow-up activity providing reinforcement for the ideas, facts, vocabulary, or other necessary skills; or using these aspects of the material in a spontaneous, creative manner, as in planning a mural, play, puppet show, or creative writing to extend the story.

(The fifth and sixth components would not necessarily occur during the first approach to the material, but more often would provide the activity for small-group independent work.)

Grouping

A word about groups and grouping would be most appropriate here. We have already criticized the practices commonly utilized in the basal approach and should point out how these can be improved. A natural group is formed by children or adults because of a common interest or need. Goals are shared, members become more efficient in working toward these, and a hierarchy of leaders and followers soon appears. The cohesiveness of the group is fostered by developing interactions and influences among the members in their movement toward their goal. But ability grouping as employed in our classrooms tends to lack these normal group characteristics. In fact, studies show that this cohesiveness or group esprit with its inherent efficiency of achievement is present only in the top reading groups, perhaps because of their recognition of their superiority (1).

If we are to profit from these known facts about group dynamics and are to promote groups that are efficient, goal-seeking entities, it is apparent that teachers should be promoting group action on bases other than reading level alone. Temporary groups should be fostered to help children share a common reading interest, to work on projects, and to develop skills. Particularly in this last type of group, the members must see their work as meaningful and profitable for reading progress and class status. The work must also be recognized as valuable by members of other groups. Interaction among the members of a group should be stimulated when working with the teacher by skillful questioning and discussion in which all members are led to participate. Growth of cohesiveness will be stimulated by emphasizing cooperation and democratic leadership by both example and suggestion from the teacher. The authoritarian concept of the teacher, as shown in children's imitative play, may well be perpetuated in these groups, unless the teacher provides a more democratic model. The size of the group promoted should be relevant to the task or project in that all members can have responsibilities and contribute to the goal. Obviously these groups are not formed by arbitrary designation of the members by the teacher, for self-selection of members is most desirable. As the teacher identifies pupil needs for a certain skill, the nature and importance of this should be clarified for the pupils. A concrete goal permitting self-evaluation would then be established by discussion with the pupils and a way of sharing the outcomes with the rest of the class agreed upon. Finally, the pupils would be invited to form a working group or two by mutual selection.

In brief, the teacher plays the role of stimulating group formation by proposing projects and accepting those suggested by the children; by arranging for children to select helpers to aid them in skill development; by asking for volunteers to assist in a needed class activity; and by suggesting reading interest groups, providing materials, and sharing a goal, particularly in the second and third grades.

Boys Versus Girls

There is ample research to indicate that the difference between the reading achievement of boys versus girls is not simply a matter of psychological or physiological maturity. Rather, boys achieve less in reading because of lower teacher expectations for them, poorer relationships with female teachers, and because of their masculine interests, motivations, and goals that tend to make for poor adjustment to the routines of the school.

Boys get more negative admonitions and fewer opportunities to read to a group, and they seem aware of it. Both male and female teachers treat boys in this fashion (9). Undoubtedly these experiences effect the self-concept of many boys as to their learning ability. And there is ample evidence that teacher expectations and attitudes influence pupil success. For example, Good has shown that teachers show their attitudes toward low achievers (often the boys) in the following ways (17):

- Seating such pupils farther away from the teacher's desk.
- Paying them less attention, smiling and making eye contact less often.
- Calling on them less frequently than other pupils.
- Waiting less time for their answers to questions.
- Failing to provide clues or ask follow-up questions.
- Criticizing more often.
- Praising less often.
- Giving less feedback, less approval or correction of answers.
- Demanding less effort and less work.
- Interrupting such pupils more frequently.

Probably more than any other reading authority, Jo M. Stanchfield has explored this problem and tried to find solutions (47). Among the characteristics of boys that she identified are these in personality style: more aggressive; less conforming; lower frustration level for boredom and monotony; more inner-directed in reading to find out, not just to please the teacher; less adaptable and flexible to new situations. In language development, boys are poorer in fluency, articulation, auditory discrimination, and listening skills (except when really interested). They show a shorter attention span, and in terms of motivation are less anxious to please or to achieve, but more tenacious in trying to solve a problem. In terms of reading interests, they prefer unusual and dramatic, active and exciting stories, unlike those usually offered in the basal. Stanchfield has conducted a number of experiments intended to elicit greater achievement among boys by sex grouping, a basal series keyed to boy interest, and classroom instruction enriched by a variety of audiovisual aids and auditory discrimination training, as well as special reading materials. But although boys showed accelerated growth in these programs, it was equaled by the girls in the groups. In fact, very few experiments have overcome this differential achievement for any great length of time. However, there is the implication here that boys do respond to an enriched program with a masculine emphasis. (See the May 1976 issue of *Reading Teacher* for contrasting viewpoints on this interpretation of the reasons for differences in the achievement of boys and girls.) Even greater response is present when teachers are cognizant of their differences, acceptant of these deviations, but still hold high expectations for their male pupils.

To strengthen the concept that reading is a masculine activity, and to try to motivate boys, the Whitfields suggest using male pictures on the bulletin board, male visitors, male readers to children (or tapes done by males), parent involvement, community helpers such as male firefighters, policemen, letter carriers, and ministers invited for the sharing time (*50*). All would emphasize the need for reading in adult life, and by their model indicate reading as a masculine pursuit, a concept that many children lack.

There is no doubt of the superiority of girls, in general, in reading, in this country at least. Some attribute this to girls' greater verbal ability and to their faster rate of physical maturation. Girls continue to excel boys in reading even when boys are catching up to them in maturation in grades four to six. Even when boys are older than girls, the girls excel in reading. Yet girls do not excel in all subject areas, as they should if maturation were the sole explanation. The fact that the content of most basal readers is geared more to girls' interests plays a part in this difference (*10*).

As for the negative treatment that boys get from teachers, why doesn't this affect their achievement in areas other than reading and language arts? Perhaps the difference in verbal ability (girls talk earlier, talk more, talk faster) may be a partial explanation for girls' superiority in such areas as spelling, composition, grammar, and reading. Yet this difference is not present in other countries, such as Germany.

Doris V. Gunderson has pointed out that the reasons for the greater proportion of failures among boys (a ratio of about three to two) are still in need of intensive research. Fewer male than female teachers, lesser verbal facility, the effect of teacher expectations, and the perception of this attitude by boys probably do contribute to the failure rate among boys, althogh explicit proof is lacking. Practices that might change the picture, such as longer, more intensive readiness and language development programs for boys, special reading materials, a study of the differences in women's and men's use of language, the creating of a male role model for reading, and the exploration of a possible difference in learning style in boys and girls, all remain to be researched before we can find the causes and cures for this American problem (18).

The Primary Program with Slow Learners

Every classroom has a number of pupils who progress slowly in beginning reading. They may be handicapped intellectually or in verbal skills; they may be bilingual or lacking in some of the major aspects of readiness; or they may be simply more dependent. For this group, no completely satisfactory program of reading materials is yet available. But there is a realistic approach that utilizes the present tools in the best possible manner.

An extended readiness program is often essential for these pupils. Their visual, speech, auditory, listening, and language skills need considerable reinforcement if their efforts in beginning reading are to be attended with any degree of success. Although progress may be slow, we still believe that beginning reading instruction should utilize the experience chart with these pupils. Perhaps more so than for any other type of pupil, basing reading materials on the child's own language experiences is a realistic recognition of this child's readiness or capabilities for reading. Using the slow learner's own compositions, we can be fairly certain of moving into reading at an appropriate pace. We will probably not progress faster than the child's own speaking and auditory vocabularies permit. If these vocabularies are really quite limited, the child's compositions will tend to be repetitious and very simple, but meaningful. Overlearning of words may have to be ensured by careful teacher planning, but the child's own limited vocabularies help in achieving this need.

These pupils will be introduced to the basal materials as soon as the teacher judges that they are ready. This decision may be based upon the readiness characteristics outlined in the checklist in Figure 6–1. Meanwhile, during the children's experience chart stage, the teacher will continue efforts to increase readiness for success in early reading.

Although it is not specifically written in terms of their learning rates, the basal reading program is the only organized body of materials that is even remotely suitable for slow learners. These pupils need the carefully controlled introduction of new vocabulary, the simple concepts, and the high-frequency repetitions of the basal reader. Programmed instructional materials with their step-by-step, repetitive presentations and constant reinforcement of learning may eventually prove particularly valuable for this type of pupil. But until a variety of programs for primary readers is available, we shall have to do the best we can with the present basal materials.

Even when the basal reading program is pursued at a decelerated rate, the slow-learning group is in constant need of reinforcement, review, and reteaching. The basal workbook, teacher-made exercises, visual aids, and repetitive games are important aids in promoting learning in this group, perhaps even more than with average and above-average pupils.

Enriching the basal by including all the skill and other activities and materials recommended in the basal manual or otherwise available may delay the completion of the readers offered for a grade, but it definitely produces much greater reading development than using the reader and its workbook only. Simple parallel reading materials keyed to the vocabulary of the basal series—as available in some reading series—are needed for the slow-learning group. Materials emphasizing concrete words—nouns and transitive verbs rather than abstract words, such as adjectives, adverbs, prepositions, and conjunctions—must be provided for this relatively nonverbal group. Charts emphasizing concrete, pragmatic learning, such as the vocabulary of traffic and street signs, store signs, school and classroom rules, numbers, children's names, the calendar, and names of holidays, should be given special emphasis for this group.

The Primary Program with the Culturally Different Child

The basic facts needed to be able to teach reading effectively to the economically or language-handicapped child are just beginning to appear in the professional literature. At this time we cannot stipulate a best method or even a number of special activities for such children with certainty of their values. But we can overview those concepts of dealing with the problems of the disadvantaged child upon which there is relatively general acceptance.

Bilingual Education

We have mentioned earlier the divergence of opinion regarding the language of the minority groups in our culture. Some insist that there are deficits in the language and therefore in cognitive growth that must be repaired if schooling is to be successful. Another group points out that a dialect is an organized, effective language that differs from standard English but is not inferior or a handicap unless the school makes it so by its rejection of dialect speakers. A third group addresses itself to the problem of those pupils whose native language is a tongue other than English. These educators promoted the idea of bilingual education, that is, education in both the native language and English, and were successful in securing the Bilingual Education Act of 1968 (*13, 14*). They offered research to prove that children taught to read first in Spanish were later able to move into reading in English with greater success (*35*), and that learning to read in Spanish was easier than in English. The Act was ambiguously worded to imply that schooling could be continued in the native language into the secondary level, thus presumably producing students who were truly bilingual. However, pupils eligible for its benefits were defined by a poverty criterion, as though the special education was intended only for the economically disadvantaged, rather than to promote development of superior children from the Hispanic or other cultures.

Projects of great variety were undertaken in an effort to realize the benefits of the Act. But it soon became apparent that school administrators and some legislators interpreted the goal to be the development of programs to teach English to the pupils—not to develop or maintain the mother tongue or to employ members of ethnic groups in instruction. As Gaarder has pointed out, the only justifiable rationale for the Act, namely that every group has a basic right to rear its children in its image and culture, was inevitably lost in the implementation (12). First, our society is not pluralistic, but rather one in which the assimilation for the purpose of national unity means that the cultures and languages of minority groups must be eliminated. The power structure, both political and economic, as well as the prestige of the languages concerned, forces us toward monolingualism. True collective bilingualism, in which two languages are accorded equal status, does exist in a few countries, but even in some of these one language tends to dominate the other, as French over Flemish in Belgium, English over Afrikaans in South Africa, and English over Maori in New Zealand.

Second, all the preparatory steps essential to bilingual instruction were ignored by our school systems. Native speakers of Spanish who might have been expected to provide the instruction were not available or their educational qualifications were judged insufficient. Few training programs were initiated to equip teachers to function in a non-English tongue. Instructional materials in Spanish proved to be too difficult, both for the teachers and the pupils. Reading materials in dialect gave no real difference in reading achievement. Attempts to teach in both languages by switching back and forth demonstrated that the supposed quick learning of a language by young pupils either in conversation or in the reading act just did not happen. The difficulties with articulation, syntax, word recognition, sentence structure, and letter sounds were significant obstacles to acquiring bilingualism (21). Additional research in teaching English by grammar rules, English as a Second Language, intensive introduction to English before beginning schooling, dialect training, structural linguistics, aural–oral language training, linguistic readers, and specially created instructional materials gave no really positive results (12, 36, 39).

To test the efficacy of basal readers with culturally different pupils, Nicholas Criscuolo arranged to have one class do all the enrichment activities and supplementary reading recommended in the basal manual (7). A matched class completed only the few skill development activities suggested in the manual or workbook. The enrichment class gained twice as much and made as much gain as a normal class would, while the control group made only half as much growth in reading test scores. Children of the lower lower-class responded more than lower middle-class pupils. The skill development class finished two basal readers, compared with one for the enrichment class. This study seems to confirm our belief that a broader reading program produces better overall growth.

Even the identification by teachers of children who are bilingual is questioned by Zirkel (51). Using surnames, rating scales, and testing reading in English and Spanish (by tests that really aren't equivalent) just don't do an accurate job. We need special instruments to determine the dominant language of the children. Most such current tests are hardly standardized.

The bilingual education dispute continues to grow more bitter, according to William Trombley (48). Supporters of the program claim it is successful when adequate materials are available, teachers are well-trained, and classes are well-structured. But these conditions are not usually available. Opponents point out that there is very little research to support the initial teaching of reading in the pupils' native language, and that the intent of the Congressional Act of 1968 has been distorted by actions of the federal Department of Education, which has forced unproven programs upon school systems where there was little or no need and no readiness to implement the programs.

Our View

If we agree that these inconclusive experiments in some twenty-four languages and dialects and the social forces present in our society make collective bilingualism an impractical ideal, what steps can be taken to aid the economically disadvantaged and linguistically different pupils to succeed in school? Wilson (49) and others suggest that the solution lies in quality education —abundance of teaching materials in all media: stronger home–school relationships; extensive use of aides, parents, and community volunteers: strong staff development, and integration of the child's cultural heritage in the classroom activities. A number of writers stress use of the language experience technique with stories in the child's own words, with gradual introduction of idioms, inflections, and other elements of standard English, as we have suggested earlier. Follow-up activities emphasizing the child's cultural background (13), involving pictures, slides, foods, and native prose and poetry are also recommended. Attitude changes and reduction of prejudice toward minority groups can be promoted by using minority literature and multiethnic readers and stories (23). Some persons suggest using folk tales and materials grouped around a central theme, such as the art, music, poetry, or beliefs of a minority group, with intensive use of real materials from the culture. Reading to children and discussing the content has been shown to be a worthwhile contribution to language development.

It is unrealistic to expect that complete command of standard English or perfect articulation is readily achieved with bilingual or dialect speakers. The true goal of the emphasis upon language development is not "correct" English, but skill in communicating with others and achieving comprehension in reading. The proper goal of the teacher is not trying to teach the child to speak in his or her dialect, but providing opportunities for hearing and using language as a tool for self-expression and the exchange of ideas, and broadening experiences as a basis for the symbols (words) by which they are represented.

Discussion Questions

1. How does the program for primary grades attempt to combine characteristics of the individualized, the basal, and the language experience approaches?

2. What possible improvements could you suggest for this eclectic program?

3. Do you believe that this proposed program would be more successful than one based entirely on one of the common major approaches to reading? Why?

4. What is your reaction to the author's division of children into three types—gifted, average, and slow? Can you suggest other arrangements?

5. If you were a primary teacher following the program outlined here, about how much of your instructional time would you devote to the development and use of experience charts (in contrast to the time spent with readers and other books)? Why?

6. Make a tentative weekly plan encompassing elements of the individualized, basal, and language experience approaches. Be prepared to explain and defend your choice of activities and instructional sessions.

7. Visit several primary classrooms, particularly those using the language experience, the individualized, and the basal approaches. Try to include both a rural and an urban school. What similarities and differences do you recognize? Which situation would you prefer to follow in your classroom? Why?

References

1. Anderson, Linda M., Evertson, Carolyn M., and Brophy, Jere E., "An Experimental Study of Effective Teaching in First Grade Reading Groups," *Language Arts*, 56 (March 1979), 193–223.

2. Arnold, Helen, *Listening to Children Reading*. Kent, England: Hodder and Stoughton Educational, 1982.

3. Austin, Mary C., and Coleman, Morrison, *The First R*. New York: Macmillan, 1963.

4. Barry, Inez, "Paperbacks to the Rescue—Six Ways to Broaden, Freshen and Enrich Your Program Using Paperbacks," *Early Years* (May 1981), 74–75, 98.

5. Berglund, Roberta L., and Johns, Jerry L., "A Primer on Uninterrupted Sustained Silent Reading," *Reading Teacher*, 36 (February 1983), 534–539.

6. Cramer, Ronald L., "Dialectology—A Case for Language Experience," *Reading Teacher*, 25 (October 1971), 33–39.

7. Criscuolo, Nicholas P., "How Effective Are Basal Readers with the Culturally Disadvantaged Children?" *Elementary English*, 45 (March 1968), 364–365.

8. Dipon, Anne Haas, "Talking with Young Children: Writing," *Childhood Education*, 59 (September–October 1982), 30–36.

9. Dusek, Jerome B., "Do Teachers Bias Children's Learning?" *Review of Educational Research*, 45 (Fall 1975), 661–684.

10. Dwyer, Carol A., "Sex Differences in Reading: An Evaluation and a Critique of Current Theories," *Review of Educational Research*, 43 (Fall 1973), 455–468.

11. Ganz, Paul, and Theofield, Mary B., "Suggestions for Starting SSR," *Journal of Reading*, 17 (May 1974), 614–616.

12. Gaarder, A. Bruce, "Bilingual Education: Central Questions and Concerns," *New York University Education Quarterly*, 6 (Summer 1975), 2–6.

13. Garcia, Ricardo L., "Mexican American Bilingualism and English Language Development," *Journal of Reading*, 17 (March 1974), 467–473.

14. Garcia, Ricardo L., "Mexican Americans Learn Through Language Experience," *Reading Teacher*, 28 (December 1974), 301–305.

15. Gilbert, Luther C., "Functional Motor Efficiency of the Eyes and Its Relation to Reading," *University of California Publications in Education*, 11 (1953), 159–232.

16. Goldsmith, Virginia C., "Have You Disabled a Potential Read'n Dropout Lately?" *Elementary School Journal*, 70 (March 1970), 300–303.

17. Good, Thomas, "Teacher Expectations and Student Perceptions: A Decade of Research," *Educational Leadership*, February 1981.

18. Gunderson, Doris V., "Sex Differences in Language and Reading," *Language Arts*, 53 (March 1976), 300–308.

19. Harrison, Stephanie, "Open Letter from a Left-handed Teacher: Some Sinistral Ideas on the Teaching of Handwriting," *Teaching Exceptional Children* (Spring 1981).

20. Hammill, D., and Wiederholt, J. L., "Appropriateness of the Metropolitan Tests in an Economically Deprived Urban Neighborhood," *Psychology in the Schools*, 8 (1971), 49–50.

21. Hatch, Evelyn, "Research on Reading a Second Language," *Journal of Reading Behavior*, 6 (April 1974), 53–56.

22. Henk, W. A., "NIM Plus DRA—A Winning Combination," *Reading Teacher*, 36 (May 1983), 922–923.

23. Huitt, May, "Handwriting: The State of the Art," *Childhood Education*, 48 (January 1972), 219–220.

24. Jenkins, Esther C., "Multi-ethnic Literature: Promise and Problems," *Elementary English*, 50 (May 1973), 694–700.

25. Jenkins, Joseph R., and Larson, Kathy, Evaluation of Error Correction Procedures for Oral Reading. Technical Report 55, University of Illinois, 1978.

26. Johns, Jerry L., "Reading: A View from the Child," *Reading Teacher*, 23 (April 1970), 647–648.

27. Johnson, Richard, "Reading Aloud—Tips for Teachers," *Reading Teacher*, 36 (April 1983), 829–831.

28. Kaworski, Arleeta O., "Practicing Oral Reading Skills," *Reading Teacher*, 36 (March 1983), 690–691.

29. Laffey, James L., and Kelley, Donna, "Repeated Reading of Taped Literature—Does It Make a Difference?" in *Comprehension Process and Product*, George H. McNinch, ed. First Yearbook American Reading Forum, 1981, 80–82.

30. MacKinnon, A. R., *How Do Children Learn to Read?* Toronto: Copp, Clark, 1959.
31. Malmquist, Eve, *Research Report, No. 3.* Linkoping, Karlshamn, Sweden: National School for Educational Research, 1964.
32. Marquardt, Tom F., "Language Interference in Reading," *Reading Teacher*, 18 (December 1964), 215–218.
33. McCullough, Constance M., "Individualized Reading," *NEA Journal*, 47 (March 1958), 163.
34. Meltzer, N. S., and Herse, R., "The Boundaries of Written Words as Seen by First Graders," *Journal of Reading Behavior*, 1 (Summer 1969), 3–13.
35. Modiano, Nancy, "Bilingual Education for Children of Linguistic Minorities," *American Indigena*, 28 (1968), 403–414.
36. Morrison, Michael and Sue, "TESL: A Critical Evaluation of Publications, 1961–1968," *Elementary English*, 49 (January 1972), 50–61.
37. Nicholson, Tom, *An Anatomy of Reading.* Cammeray, Australia: Martin Educational, 1982.
38. Oliver, Marvin E., "The Effect of High Intensity Practice on Reading Achievement," *Reading Improvement*, 13 (Winter 1976), 226–228.
39. Pehrsson, Robert S. V., "How Much of a Helper Is Mr. Gelper?" *Journal of Reading*, 17 (May 1974), 617–621.
40. Rosen, Carl L., and Ortega, Philip D., "Language and Reading Problems of Spanish Speaking Children of the Southwest," *Journal of Reading Behavior*, 1 (Winter 1969), 51–72.
41. Rowell, E. H., "Do Elementary Students Read Better Orally or Silently?" *Reading Teacher*, 29 (January 1976), 367–370.
42. Schaudt, Barbara A., "Another Look at Sustained Silent Reading," *Reading Teacher*, 36 (May 1983), 934–936.
43. Simons, Herbert D., and Johnson, Kenneth R., "Black English Syntax and Reading Interference," *Research in the Teaching of English*, 8 (Winter 1974), 339–358.
44. Simpson, Adelaide W., and Erickson, Marilyn T., "Teachers' Verbal and Nonverbal Communication Patterns as a Function of Teacher Race, Student Gender and Student Race," *American Educational Research Journal*, 20 (Summer 1983), 183–198.
45. Smith, Lewis B., and Morgan, Glen D., "Cassette Recording as a Primary Method in the Development of Early Reading Material," *Elementary English*, 52 (April 1975), 534–538.
46. Southgate, Vera, Arnold, Helen, and Johnson, Sandra, *Extending Beginning Reading.* Exeter, N.H.: Heinemann Educational Books, 1981.
47. Stanchfield, Jo M., "Differences in Learning Patterns of Boys and Girls," in *Reading Difficulties: Diagnosis, Correction and Remediation*, W. K. Durr, ed. Newark, Del.: International Reading Association, 1970, 202–213.
48. Trombley, W., "The Bilingual Education Dispute Grows Bitter," *Sarasota Herald Tribune*, Section F, September 14, 1980, 1.
49. Wilson, Herbert B., "Quality Education in a Multicultural Classroom," *Childhood Education*, 50 (February 1974), 153–156.
50. Whitfield, Edie and Charles, "Sex Role Stereotyping and Reading Readiness," *Childhood Education*, 58 (May–June 1982), 298–299.
51. Zirkel, Perry A., "The Why's and Ways of Testing Bilinguality Before Teaching Bilingually," *Elementary School Journal*, 76 (March 1976), 323–330.

Professional References

Baskin, Barbara H., and Harris, Karen H., *Books for the Gifted Child*. New York: R. R. Bowker, 1980.

Carlson, Ruth Kearney, *Emerging Humanity: Multi-ethnic Literature for Children and Adolescents*. Dubuque: William C. Brown, 1972.

Ching, Doris C., *Reading and the Bilingual Child*. Newark, Del.: International Reading Association, 1976.

Clay, Marie M., *Reading: The Patterning of Complex Behavior*. Auckland, New Zealand: Heinemann Educational Books, 1979.

Cullinan, Beatrice, ed., *Black Dialects and Reading*. Urbana, Ill.: The National Council of Teachers of English, 1974.

Holdaway, Don, *Foundations of Literacy*. Sydney, Australia: Ashton Press, 1979.

Pialorski, Frank, ed., *Teaching the Bilingual*. Tucson, Ariz.: University of Arizona Press, 1974.

Polette, Nancy and Hamlin, Marjorie, *Exploring Books with Gifted Children*. Littleton, N.H.: Libraries Unlimited, 1980.

Polette, Nancy, *3 R's for the Gifted: Reading, Writing and Research*. Littleton, N.H.: Libraries Unlimited, Inc., 1982.

Shiman, David, ed., *Teachers on Individualization: The Way We Do It*. New York: McGraw-Hill, 1974.

Southgate, Vera, *Beginning Reading*. Mystic, Vt.: Lawrence Verry, 1972.

Spache, Evelyn B., *Reading Activities for Child Involvement*, 3d ed. Boston, Mass.: Allyn and Bacon, 1981.

Spache, George D., *Good Reading for the Disadvantaged Reader*. Champaign, Ill.: Garrard Publishing, 1975. (Annotated and graded books and instructional materials for minority pupils.)

Von Maltitz, Frances Willard, *Living and Learning in Two Languages*. New York: McGraw-Hill, 1975.

Zintz, Miles V., *The Reading Process: The Teacher and the Learner*. Dubuque: William C. Brown, 1980.

10 A Program for Intermediate Grades

In our opinion, the average basal reading system does not attempt to supply training for reading in the content areas. The systems are not entirely committed to developing the reading and study skills essential for middle and secondary school success, even though some have recently included an emphasis upon these areas. Reading instruction in the intermediate grades should begin to emphasize learning the special content field vocabularies, the organization and retention of facts, the structure of textual materials and the general types of presentation. The content vocabularies offer not only a number of essential words with new or limited meanings but also a second group of words already familiar with new meanings. These vocabularies are the idea or concept core of each subject area and are fundamental to the subject's comprehension. Strategies of reading and studying, ways of retaining facts, and the metacognitive act of monitoring one's own thinking are an integral part of content study. Children do not develop these behaviors spontaneously, for they need the stimulation of appropriate questions, discussion, practice, and other attempts by teachers to direct thinking.

Previous editions criticized basal reader programs for their failure to provide the special reading skills necessary for content fields. Most programs stressed narrative material heavily and only occasionally offered watered-down samples of science, social science, or other areas. Today's readers, speaking generally of course, have improved greatly in recognizing pupils' needs for training in study skills. But the materials representing various fields and the accompanying skill practice that can be presented within the framework of a basal program is necessarily limited. We could not expect a basal to do more than offer samples from various curricular fields and to initiate the study skill training. For these reasons, we emphasize development of flexibility, study skills, and essential reading behaviors in the content fields so strongly in the intermediate-grade program.

We suggest the following for training in the content reading skills: use the available content textbooks, as science, health, history, geography, and arithmetic, assuming of course that these are suitable for the reading levels of the various types of pupils. We recognize that many teachers are limited to a narrow range of textbooks in teaching the content fields. Some teachers will not have science books of different grade levels to match their pupils' reading abilities. In these cases, it is imperative that the teacher gradually secure a wide variety of booklets, pamphlets, brochures, maps, charts, and the like, of varying difficulty. To aid in finding these and securing them within a limited book budget, we have included a number of source lists of free and inexpensive materials. These sources offer a great variety of teaching materials on almost every topic normally touched upon in the intermediate-grade curriculum. In addition to this assumption that the teacher will have or will get varied content field materials, we are certainly expecting that much of the instruction and practice in content skills will occur in small groups, perhaps arranged according to reading levels and abilities. We cannot conceive of effective content skill teaching being conducted with a single piece of reading matter being used for all pupils regardless of their abilities. Exceptions to this might occur in the teaching of certain skills in map and chart reading or simple library skills.

There are a number of compelling reasons for the emphasis upon content reading skills in these grades (34). Any of the daily reading tasks in the classroom involves the study of content textbooks beginning in the third and fourth grades and continuing the rest of the school career. Not only must the pupil learn to use these materials effectively, but they must also learn that each area demands certain unique types of thinking, approach, and study habits. Even those pupils whose fundamental skills are well developed vary considerably in their effectiveness in reading in different fields. Some excel in science or in social science but are ineffectual in another field, such as mathematics. Good general reading ability such as that stressed in the basal program tends to support learning in the subject matter areas. But simply because pupils continue to develop in basic reading skills, we cannot assume that they will therefore also grow in subject matter achievement. Content fields differ too widely in vocabularies, fact relationships, types of reasoning, and background information to expect similar progress in all areas.

The manner in which the study of content fields is approached also determines the nature of the reading skills demanded. Some teachers use a single textbook and expect only direct recall with a minimum of interpretation. Other teachers use a variety of sources and reference materials, thus demanding that their pupils show some organizing ability as well as skill in comparing and combining sources. Some teachers utilize a great deal of independent work and small-group activity, expecting that their pupils will be able to collect and collate materials, organize them, and prepare reports based on a critical evaluation of the available resources. Still other teachers approach the content of a field through problem-solving activities that require the pupil to collect and organize facts, recognize principles, and discover and defend solutions.

It is true that most content textbooks are highly organized and offer a great many aids to learning. Texts commonly employ such devices as headings, summaries, illustrations, glossaries, indexes, diagrams, charts, and other graphic aids. Both the authors of these texts and the teachers who use them often assume that the textual aids simplify the reading task for the pupils and assist them in their learning. Unfortunately, this assumption is not true, for research shows that these visual and graphic aids do not ensure better understanding or retention for most pupils. Only when pupils are carefully trained to read and use them effectively do these aids function as intended. Without

such training, the average pupil finds common content textbooks more difficult because of the inclusion of a variety of so-called aids. No available basal
reading program offers complete training for these complexities of content
field reading.

Several writers have tried to discover what teachers understand and believe about reading in the content fields. Some of these reports are encouraging, for they seem to indicate that these authors are affecting teachers' thinking and practices in this area. Teachers who are now alert to student reading
problems (1) do recognize conceptual and experiential deficiencies; (2) contend with poor motivation and strive to develop pupil interest; (3) differentiate between general and technical vocabulary and try to establish conceptual
understanding beyond the mere recognition of the word: (4) differentiate levels of instructional materials to meet reading needs of the pupils; (5) find time
for individual work with pupils; (6) try to extend the extra-class reading of the
pupils; (7) use a variety of media to interest and instruct; and (8) adapt their
expectations to pupil's abilities. These are certainly hopeful signs that, when
teaching subject matter, teachers are more aware of the individual differences
in the reading abilities of pupils and the impact of these differences upon content learning.

Braam and Walker (4) conducted two surveys in 1973 of subject matter
teachers' awareness of reading skills needed for study in their areas. They
found that contemporary teachers downgraded critical reading as an important skill, in contrast to the teachers of eight years before who had named that
ability as second only to comprehension. In the two surveys, 28 and 27 percent
of the teachers, respectively, indicated that they had received any instruction
in reading methods. In pointing out the specific skills needed for reading in a
content field, the average teacher named only 2.4 skills, while principals and
reading teachers named more skills as important for content reading.
Apparently, reading specialists have not conveyed much information about
content area reading needs to subject matter teachers.

Other surveys show that teachers are beginning to believe that the teaching of reading skills can be incorporated into content presentations without
interfering with the learning of the field. A corollary opinion, that any teacher
who gives assignments should teach pupils how to read and study the assignments, is also gaining acceptance. Most teachers no longer believe that all the
reading training should be taken care of in the formal "reading lessons" or by
remedial teachers.

At the same time, there are gaps and weaknesses in the implementation of
these ideas, for many think their textbooks are suitable for most of their pupils,
without even knowing or trying to find out how difficult the textbooks really
are, nor how their readability levels compare with those of the pupils exposed
to them. Many still accept the publishers' labels for the levels of textbooks and
would be shocked to read the analyses of textbook difficulty, which almost
uniformly indicate that many, if not most, content textbooks are written at
reading levels much higher than the grade levels for which they are offered
(20).

Study Strategies

Before pupils may read efficiently in the content area, they must be skillful in a number of fundamental reading practices. Some of these are promoted by the training given in the average basal reading program, but most of them must be developed in realistic practice with content materials.

Paragraph Structure and Underlining

Some paragraphs are built like equilateral triangles. They begin with a minor point and then broaden out, adding more details until they reach a firm base, the main idea. Other paragraphs resemble an inverted triangle, that begins with a broad statement, or the main idea, and then add a series of details supporting the opening sentence. Some paragraphs can be compared with an arrangement of two triangles balanced on each other, point to point. Such a paragraph begins with a strong statement (the topic sentence), and then offers a series of details to support the main ideas. These details then build into a strong conclusion or statement, the summary sentence.

Children need to learn to distinguish the main types of paragraphs and to adapt their notetaking, outlining, or underlining to the manner in which the paragraph is arranged.

Enumerative or Listing Patterns. Some paragraphs simply enumerate or list a number of facts.

> *If you know some word parts, such as prefixes, suffixes, and stems, you have some help in vocabulary study. You will find external cues to the meanings of unfamiliar words in the sentences themselves. You may figure out the meanings from the internal cues within the words. Therefore, you analyze words in meaningful parts and then synthesize or put them together again to form whole words.*

If pupils were expected to learn this material, they probably should have noted, by underlining or some other technique, these facts:

external cues	*analyze—break up*
internal cues	*synthesize—put together*

Or, they should be able to summarize the main idea something like this: "Knowing word parts helps one to learn new, hard words because the parts have meanings."

Descriptive Patterns. Paragraphs of description are common in story-type materials. They help to give the reader some idea of the setting, and the traits of the characters as well as their appearance. In expository materials, descriptive paragraphs often show how some process or procedure works. If you were studying the following descriptive paragraph (7), what facts would you underline?

> Neuroscientists also believe that a short-term memory becomes a long-term memory via a consolidation process. A series of complex electrochemical and physical changes occur in the part of the brain called the hippocampus (specifically in minute structures called neurons, synapses and dendrites). Although the human brain weighs barely three pounds, it contains 30 billion nerve cells (neurons) hooked together like railroad tracks and interacting like a computer. When permanent changes strengthen the links in this neural circuitry, a thought becomes part of the long-term memory.

You might have underlined such facts as these:

short-term memory
consolidation process
electrochemical and physical changes in the brain
permanent changes in neural circuitry
long-term memory

If you were to draw a diagram to portray this paragraph, it might look like the two triangles, point to point, we described earlier. It opens with a strong statement, then offers a series of details, and ends with a strong statement summarizing the facts.

Time Order or Sequential Patterns. How-to books (such as for home repair), cookbooks, and detective stories often use a time-order or sequential pattern in their paragraphs. In a narrative or detective story, the sequence may be called the plot; in other types of books, the pattern may simply be a series of instructions or events.

How to Use the Spache Readability Formula

1. Count off approximately 100 words. Begin with the first word in a sentence and stop with the last word of the sentence containing the 100th word.
2. Count the number of sentences in the sample.
3. Check the separate words in the sample against the Revised Word List. Make a count of the words not found in this list. Use the rules if in doubt whether a word is counted as being on the list.
4. Divide the number of words in the sample by the number of sentences, to determine the average sentence length.
5. The number of hard words in a sample is the percent of hard words.
6. With the average number of hard words and the average sentence length, enter the table to find the grade placement of the sample (36).

Could you follow these directions in evaluating the reading difficulty of a sample from a child's book (presuming you had the word list and the table)? If so, you are ready to assign grade levels to primary books using the only formula based on American schoolbooks.

Cause and Effect Patterns. Some paragraphs explain how things came to be, or what caused certain results. Both cause and the outcome are illustrated in this type of writing.

> *There are many studies from animal literature supporting the critical-period hypothesis. German scientist Konrad Lorenz discovered many years ago that birds, such as duck and geese will follow the first moving object they see after they are hatched. Usually the first thing they see is that mother, of course, who has been sitting on the eggs when they are hatched. However, Lorenz showed that if he took goose eggs away from the mother and hatched them in an incubator, the fresh-hatched goslings would follow him around instead (23).*

What ideas would you have underlined if you were studying this portion of the textbook? Probably you would have noted critical-period hypothesis, follow the first moving object, took eggs away from the mother, goslings would follow him around instead. Can you now explain what happens to birds that makes them attached to their mothers?

Comparison and Contrast Patterns. Some paragraphs offer a comparison or contrast between before-and-after events or objects or persons. This brief excerpt from American history attempts to clarify the basic cause of the Civil War (*14*).

> *The negro became an issue only after a firm division of political ideas had started to separate the Union. Many Federalists had no particular love for the negro, and they had no objection to black subordination as it existed in this country. A great many leading men of their party had become rich out of the "slave trade," that is, bringing negroes to the Union and selling them to the Southern States. Laws in every state in the Union denied negroes equality with white people. The skilled worker in the north and the cool climate made it unprofitable to employ the negro as labor. The south with its largely agricultural based economy found the slave as a cheap and self-sustaining labor force. The next seventy years until the outbreak of war were filled with divisions over slavery, pressure from foreign relationships, and the intensified abolitionist movement. . . . The issue of slavery was to build and be accepted by many as the prime motivating factor of the inevitable war between the states.*

In studying this passage, what ideas would you have tried to remember by underlining or taking notes? Perhaps you would have included:

> *Negro became issue after political ideas divided*
> *No particular love for the negro*
> *Leading men of their party became rich out of the slave trade*

Laws in Union denied negro equality
Skilled workers and cool climate made negro unprofitable
Agricultural economy of South found slave cheap labor
Slavery, political ideas, foreign relationships and abolition causes
Many thought slavery prime motive for the war

Note the contrast between what the author considers the true causes of the Civil War and what most of us think caused it.

The authors have tried to illustrate these patterns of paragraph structure as they might occur in college reading, rather than using simple pieces from children's textbooks. Needless to say, the example teachers would choose to teach recognition of these patterns would be from children's materials.

Previewing

Essentially, previewing is an organized, rapid coverage of reading materials, such as a chapter in a book, a report, a newspaper article, or other source. In practice, it involves reading some or all of the following before deciding how or whether to read the entire selection: title, headings, and subheadings, summary or introductory statements, illustrative and graphic materials, and sometimes opening and closing sentences of each paragraph.

The purpose of previewing is to answer such questions as the following: What information may be obtained from this material? How is this information organized? Is this information significant to the readers' purposes? Should the entire selection be read? What are the main ideas presented? A large number of research studies show that previewing is an important initial step in reading almost any type of content material. When used before actual reading, comprehension and retention of the material is greatly increased, and the reader's time is conserved by eliminating irrelevant materials. After sufficient practice the reader learns to handle materials more rapidly and economically. Previewing should be taught as a preliminary step to all textbook study and as an effective device for reviewing for a test, as a quick brush-up before recitation, and for evaluating materials collected for a report. Since most narrative or basal material does not lend itself to this technique, it is apparent that this practice must be used extensively in content textbooks, reference, and resource materials.

Simple, repetitive practice of previewing, or other reading techniques that shall be discussed, is pointless unless the purpose of the training is apparent to the pupils. The teacher must not only demonstrate how to preview and provide practice, but also prove to the pupils the value of this device. The teacher may demonstrate these by testing pupil comprehension and retention in two halves of a chapter—with one half studied after previewing and the other studied without any previewing. The teacher may provide a number of possible resource materials on a topic for the children and then ask them to decide after a few minutes which of these are most important to the topic. The teacher may provide an unfamiliar textbook or other resource to the children and allow only a few minutes for them to find the main ideas of a certain chapter. Or, the teacher may provide two versions of a current event as found in different newspaper articles and ask the pupils to see how quickly they can find any facts present in one article but not in the other. These sample exercises will, with teacher guidance, demonstrate the values of previewing as contrasted with unplanned reading. From these introductory exercises the teacher may proceed to directed practice in previewing in the pupils' different textbooks and in other materials he or she commonly expects them to use. The Coronet film, "Reading with a Purpose," is particularly useful in introducing previewing to intermediate-grade pupils.

Four out of five sixth-graders and even many college students do not use previewing even when their purpose is simply to identify main ideas. The lack of development of this essential skill among mature students emphasizes two implications for the classroom teacher. This skill does not appear spontaneously merely because the pupil continues to mature in general reading skills. In addition, students do not learn to use this skill without extensive, realistic practice in content field materials.

The need for instruction in how to read and interpret subheadings when previewing is shown by the following investigation. The paragraph headings in newspaper articles were modified to repeat facts, or to be almost irrelevant, to be contradictory, or omitted entirely. The experimenter found that the variations had no differential effect upon the readers' recall of information given by them. In fact, less than half of the readers recognized that some headings were contradictory! In other words, headings of any of these types did nothing for the students to aid in previewing the material. The need for practicing reading subheads and discussing their meaning or implications is very real if pupils are to be successful in gaining an overview of the material before reading it thoroughly.

Before leaving discussion of this important basic skill, it would be wise to stress one other important facet of the training. Teachers often fail to realize that the manner in which their pupils handle reading tasks is a direct reflection of their structuring of the problem. The crux of the matter is not whether teachers pose "thought questions" or "memory questions." The significance of the practice lies in the way in which students are led to handle the answer, to organize the facts, to attack the reading materials. If teachers hope to teach children previewing and the other basic skills to be discussed, then their presentations of the reading task must impel pupils to use the particular skill they are stressing. In practicing previewing, for example, the assignments or questions they propose must be such that they can best be accomplished by previewing. Imposing time limits in these tasks, and asking for a variety of performances—rapid identification of main ideas, quick comparisons of sources, evaluation of relevance of a source to a given topic, discovery of the presence of a given fact or topic, quick reviews before recitation, rapid summaries of the content of a selection, frequent comparisons of retention with and without previewing—are reading tasks that push children in the direction of the desired practice. This purposeful practice is essential if students are to adopt and use effectively the technique offered to them.

Skimming and Scanning

These rapid reading techniques, like previewing, are fundamental to effective reading in the content fields. Skimming is actually a broadened previewing in which not only the main ideas are discovered but also some of the supporting details. When pupils have learned to preview, we suggest teaching them to skim by adding to their previewing the reading of some of the details within each paragraph. In previewing, pupils may read the opening and closing sentences of each paragraph, for in textbook materials these sentences commonly include the main ideas of the paragraph. To skim, pupils extend this to include the details within the paragraph as may be discovered by cue words or phrases. Having read the opening and closing sentences, pupils look quickly for such cues as italicized words, numbered sentences, or such words as *first, second, because, in addition to, also,* and *but.* These words serve as signals to point out the various supporting details that the author is offering. By reading these details, the pupils strengthen their understanding of the main ideas but save the time that would be needed for complete reading.

There are at least six ways of skimming mentioned by various writers (37).

1. Read the first few words and the last words of each sentence. This may or may not result in comprehension depending upon the sentence complexity and structure.

2. Having read the opening and closing sentences of each paragraph (previewing), the reader returns to pick up the facts by skimming rapidly through the main body of each paragraph.

3. The reader hugs the left (or right margin) reading only about a third of each line. The value of this method without extensive rereading is doubtful.

4. The reader reads only the central third of each line; thus reading only in the middle of the page.

5. Key words or phrases set off by numbers, quotation marks, italics, capital letters, etc., are read. This may result in fragmentary comprehension, and that mainly of details rather than main ideas.

6. The reader moves down the page in a more or less diagonal pattern. The reader may jump from the beginning of the line to the middle of the next line to the end of the next, and so on down the page. Occasionally the reader may read a complete sentence if it seems significant. This technique gives about as superficial a coverage as any.

The method we have suggested resembles the second just described. It has the advantage of a more adequate coverage than some of the other procedures.

Scanning is that type of reading used in quickly locating specific information in printed materials without reading the entire page. We use scanning constantly in such tasks as reading indexes, telephone directories, and dictionaries, and in finding a word, a date, a number, or a certain phrase. Three steps are involved in scanning: (1) knowing clearly what is being sought and the form in which it is likely to appear; (2) looking swiftly over the page, list, or column, expecting the fact to stand out from the rest of the page; and (3) verifying the answer when it is found by reading it carefully.

Skimming and scanning are not superficial types of reading that may result in weak comprehension. Rather, they are specific techniques for definite purposes in certain reading tasks. By learning to skim, pupils develop skill in strengthening the comprehension of main ideas that they might have grossly identified by previewing. Skimming ability promotes flexibility in reading; it increases skill in shifting to high speed in familiar material for quick exploration of an idea to determine its relevance; it promotes ability to select portions for more careful reading and to eliminate portions that are not related to the reader's purpose. By learning to scan, pupils read lists or columns intelligently or can find with ease a specific fact somewhere in the printed page. They learn that the single fact they are seeking can be found without reading the entire page.

As suggested earlier, practice in these skills should be carefully planned. Skimming may be practiced in timed reading tasks such as finding the number of details in a certain paragraph, finding the facts offered to support a certain main idea, deciding on the relevance of a certain portion, and comparing details found in two or more sources. Scanning may be practiced in finding a given fact in a textbook page or chapter, index, table of contents, dictionary, glossary, table or chart, street directory, and other sources. Imposing time limits and comparing the time required by various pupils helps keep these skills functioning as rapid reading techniques.

Skimming is not a type of random or casual reading, or just a "looking over" of materials. To prevent skimming from deteriorating into this unplanned, ineffectual approach, there should be a definite sequence in the training efforts. Having established the habit of previewing, begin practice in skimming a single paragraph to find such facts as a certain detail, the number of details, the nature of the author's proof or support to the main idea, the order of presentation of these proofs or details. Practice in a variety of materials from science, social science, and arithmetic, varying the practice according to the organization of the material. Gradually extend the skimming practice to several paragraphs, a whole page, a section, and finally a chapter.

Scanning is also a selective, not a random, type of rapid reading. Early practice should include only a paragraph or two of material in which the reader attempts to find a single fact—a name, a date, a number, or a phrase.

The length of the material to be scanned can be gradually increased and thus the readers' search made longer, with the result that they retain more of the desired information as well as incidental facts (16). Each practice exercise is introduced by a question clearly indicating the fact to be found. Multiple-choice or true–false questions are preferable at first, since they help to point out the form in which the answer is likely to be found. Children will be more successful in their early efforts if the form in which the answer is likely to appear is pointed out to them—in capital or italicized letters, in numbers, and so forth. The exact pattern of the movements of the eye in scanning is not very significant, provided it, in general, proceeds from the top to bottom of the page. The research studies which have been made of children scanning indicate that most employ a kind of Z-shaped movement over the lines and paragraphs. Both the amount and type of material in which scanning is practiced should gradually be increased from a paragraph or two, to a page, to several pages, to a whole chapter. In dealing with the longer selections, pupils should be helped to realize that the tasks will be done more quickly if they preview the material before scanning for the fact desired. By the previewing, they can quickly find the most likely section or page in which the fact will be and then scan only that portion.

All three of these techniques—previewing, skimming, and scanning —help pupils develop flexibility in rate and skill in adapting the form of reading to the reader's purpose. Flexibility results in greater comprehension, economy of study time, and greater enjoyment of work-type reading. As a result the flexible reader is more effective in handling study tasks, and more successful in retention and achievement in the content fields.

Reading Graphic Materials

There are relatively few studies clarifying the desirable sequence of training in such tasks as reading maps, graphs, charts, diagrams, and tables. Thus most of our suggestions for teaching pupils how to read these difficult materials must be based on logic rather than research. Studies give some clues regarding the map-reading abilities of pupils in the intermediate grades. The tests employed in these studies were used on a sufficient number of children to indicate the probable difficulties of various skills, and therefore some indications for the logical sequence in which they might be taught. The indications of these tests are combined in the order of difficulty from easier items to harder.

The accuracy with which sixth-grade children exercised these map reading skills varied considerably. The average scores on the tests ranged from 82 percent down to 57 percent. It was surprising to find that reading a key or legend, one of the first things we would teach, was so hard for these children. Of course, these data were derived from testing quite some time ago and may not represent the performances of today's children. But they may serve to remind

Map reading skills

A. Reading a key or legend to find

desert	products
capital of country	rivers
minerals	population
railroads	scale of miles
rainfall	seaports
swamps	flow of rivers
mountains, plateaus, lowlands	capital of states

B. Knowledge of globe
   Recognizing
      distance and direction
      distortion in polar equal-area projection
      distortion in any given map
      distortion in Mercator projection

C. General skills
   1. Longitude and latitude
      of a city
      naming city at given longitude and latitude
      reading latitude of given place
      reading longitude of given place

   2. Rivers
      recognizing junction of rivers
      identifying source and mouth
      recognizing a delta
      finding a tributary
      locating a city in reference to a river

   3. Coastlines
      identifying adjoining oceans
      finding city on coastline
      distinguishing regular and irregular coastlines
      finding protected harbor

   4. Directions
      on a globe
      on make-believe road map
      on Mercator projection
      in long and complicated journey
      use meridians and parallels
      on world or sectional map
      on polar map
      on partial, globular map

us that map reading skills need a good deal of attention during the primary and intermediate grades.

A bulletin, "Skills in the Social Studies," issued by the Board of Education, Prince George's County, Upper Marlboro, Maryland, offers a very helpful list of map and globe skills. The items listed under each skill correspond in number to their respective grades.

Map and globe skills

ABILITY TO ORIENT ONE'S SELF AND ONE'S POSITION IN RELATION TO THE ENVIRONMENT
1. Relationship of furniture, door, and windows to child.
2. Relationships of lunchroom, hall, office to own classroom.
3. Showing on community map relation of child's home to school and other community landmarks.
4. Locating one's community on country map in relation to other communities and landmarks.
5. Locating own town, county, and state on map of United States. Same for United States on a world map.
6. Locating home, community, county, state, and country to rest of the world in terms of cardinal directions.

ABILITY TO ORIENT ONE'S SELF IN TERMS OF THE CARDINAL DIRECTIONS— N, S, E, W
1. & 2. Distinguishing directions by own shadow in the AM and PM.
3. Locating directions in relation to the sun.
4. Locating north by a compass and thus identifying other directions, cardinal and intermediate.
5. Locating cardinal and intermediate (NE, SE, NW, SW) on a community map. Using compass to lay out community map.
6. Tracing route on map or globe, identifying each change of direction in terms of cardinal and intermediate directions, parallels, meridians, latitude, and longitude.

READING A MAP ACCORDING TO CARDINAL DIRECTIONS
1. Using cardinal directions on a street map. Tracing and telling directions in a route from the school to a landmark.
2. Using directions on a community map, or road map of the area. Reading directions for trip to nearest community.
3. Using a road map for directions on a simulated trip through several cities of the state or elsewhere.

(continued)

DEVELOPING A FEELING FOR DIRECTION AND DISTANCE
1. Walking to specified area of building, telling directions followed.
2. Giving directions for trip to school, store, fire house, etc., from home. Use picture map of community for similar activity.
3. Follow diagram of route for short field trip, as drawn by teacher. Telling directions of route from own to neighboring community.

FINDING GENERAL DIRECTIONS ON A GLOBE OR MAP
1. Discovering and discussing the north and south poles.
2. Discussing the poles and the equator.
3. Relating poles and equator to hot and cold lands.
4. Poles, equator, and earth's axis, network of lines on globe and rotation.
5. Locating positions using parallels, meridians, latitude, longitude, north and south poles. Locating SOS position with reference to latitude and longitude.
6. Locating cities, answering SOS when latitude and longitude are given. Using polar projection maps.

RECOGNIZING SCALE AND DISTANCES ON MAPS
1. Observing relative distances, time for travel on community maps.
2. Noting shortest distances between points on community map drawn to scale by teacher.
3. Noting distances between points on road maps, estimating time.
4. Recognizing linear units and their relative lengths: foot, block, mile, etc. Estimating distances and travel time between given points. Drawing to scale plan of such objects as desk, window, classroom.
5. Exploring ways of expressing scale: graphic, inches to miles, one-half inch to one foot, etc. Studying aerial maps and comparing with ground, linear units.
6. Drawing scale maps of the community. Using scale to measure distances on maps. Comparing map areas.

LOCATING DESIGNATED PLACES ON MAPS AND GLOBES
1. Comparing shape of globe to earth. Locating own community on globe. Comparing areas of land and water.
2. Comparing sizes of oceans and continents. Locating familiar states and communities.
3. Locating areas related to social studies content. Making large-scale community map. Using and coloring outline maps to show given areas.
4. Locating equator, hemispheres, parallels, latitude, longitude, Prime Meridian. Locating countries and states with reference to bordering land and water bodies. Making a relief map of given area, noting boundaries, terrain, etc.

(continued)

5. Locating points by latitude and longitude.
6. Using atlas grid to locate places on road map. Recognizing different grid systems.

UNDERSTANDING AND EXPRESSING RELATIVE LOCATION
1. Make model representation of school grounds. Using map terms to locate equipment, buildings, etc.
2. Using community map to show relative locations of school, home, and other landmarks.
3. Using large town and county map for relative locations.
4. Recognizing significance of physical features: bays, harbors, rivers, peninsulas, etc., for growth of a city. Expressing relative position by latitude, longitude, distance, and terrain.
5. Discussing growth effects of mountains, water bodies, distances, resources, etc.
6. City development in relation to trade routes, climatic conditions, physical features, resources and market areas, importance of great circle air routes.

DRAWING MAPS ORIENTED TO TRUE DIRECTION
1. Sketching a route.
2. Sketching rough map of town showing main streets.
3. Drawing maps to scale: room, playground, state.
4. Drawing maps using grids furnished by teacher. Comparing with wall map.
5. Drawing maps based on own grid of latitude and longitude.

READING AND USING MAP SYMBOLS, KEY, OR LEGEND
1. Using large-scale map of play area, placed in line with true cardinal directions, place cutouts of equipment, etc., to convey concept of symbolic representation. Devise key.
2. Introduce symbols for rivers, lakes, oceans, bays, continents, etc. Match these with pictures of same. Make pictorial map of community, later substituting with symbols.
3. Study firsthand differences in land and water forms. Make models of these and match with pictorial symbols.
4. Compare pictures of landscapes with aerial photographs and later with symbols on a large-scale map.
5. Using dots, lines, and color to show physical features, as streets, buildings, land forms, railroads, etc. Chart routes of explorers, discoverers, and other figures from social studies.
6. Constructing and reading transportation maps to show routes of steamships, railroads, airplanes, major highways, covered-wagon routes. Reading weather maps for atmosphere and climatic information.

(continued)

The types of exercises in map making and reading are fairly obvious from this list. Training might begin with an exercise or two from a lower grade level than your class to determine their readiness for the grade level skills. Adapt the skill descriptions to the exercises, or order a few of the different exercise books, as those by Dale, Job and Wolf, and Rushdoony, for ideas for the practice. In addition to these, intensive study of the maps in your textbooks is certainly desirable. Teachers' guides to teaching maps are available from several map-makers—Denoyer, Hammond, Rand McNally, and George F. Crum.

In learning to read maps of various types, children should be made aware of the inherent limitations in flat maps. Such maps inevitably distort areas, shapes, size, distances, and even directions. Recall, if you will, the size of Greenland on the usual classroom map of the Western Hemisphere. Other limitations of maps are their essential selectivity in the amount of detail any one map can offer: their variation in accuracy according to the information available in different parts of the world; and the use of representative or completely symbolic legends. Children (and the teacher) should be aware that certain projections introduce constant errors. For example, the Mercator map exaggerates size as distance increases from the equator; the Vander Grinten projection also exaggerates but to a lesser degree; while the Mollweide and other elliptical projections are correct in size but distort true shapes near the poles.

Chart and graph reading skills are outlined in the same bulletin in the brief fashion shown on page 360.

Make charts with the children of the daily number of books borrowed from the classroom or school library; subdivide the books into types and make other charts—biography, science, adventure, sports, etc. Have children make a survey of the soaps used in their homes. Construct a chart showing numbers of homes using such soaps as Dial, Dove, Ivory, etc.

Use these and other frequency charts to construct simple bar graphs, and later circle or pie graphs and line graphs using the same data. Construct two classroom thermometers (red ribbon in a piece of white cardboard) that will show the daily maximum and minimum temperature. Have children take turns adjusting the ribbons announcing the readings. Older children can construct charts to show wind speed and rainfall as given by the weather report on the local television station. Clocks can be made to show the time of sunset and sunrise. Children can survey the classrooms of the building with other teachers' permission to collect data on the relative number of pets owned; i.e., cats, dogs, hamsters, mice, etc. Mount the bar graph in the hall outside the room to share it with other classes.

Children can construct charts or graphs to show their successive test scores; or using the local newspaper, make a bar graph of the numbers of job openings in various occupations; e.g., plumbers, carpenters, office workers, computer programmers, etc. Other graphs can be made to show the number of want ads each day according to their type—jobs wanted, houses or apartments for rent, things for private sale, etc.

Begin studying tables with those in the children's textbooks, unless these are really too complex. Expand the study to include a collection of tables and diagrams that students bring in from newspapers and magazines. Take the graphs and charts that have been constructed and convert them to tables. Using the newspaper or shopping guide, students may construct tables of comparative prices for grocery items. With the Spiegel or Sears catalogues, it is possible to construct dozens of different tables (as well as charts and graphs).

Reading tables and diagrams

1. Read and interpret simple tables drawn from daily newspapers, such as guide to sections, index, TV and radio programs, etc.
2. Discuss structure of tables; their types; headings; marginal head or tail material.
3. Read and interpret railroad, airline, and bus timetables.
4. Read and interpret baseball or football records, shipping reports, weather forecasts.
5. Practice with various types of diagrams found in magazines, newspapers, and texts.
6. Make simple tables and diagrams to illustrate facts drawn from materials available.
7. Practice scanning in tables.
8. Make diagrams based on outlines or list of directions constructed by group.

One basic tool in reading many charts and tables, scanning, has already been described. In many instances, the reading of a chart or table is basically a scanning art. Readers quickly read the title and the column headings and then look within the material to find the facts they are seeking. Pupils should have practice in a variety of these items by following a systematic scanning, including the title, headings, and left-hand column of items, thus identifying the correct line and column in which to read.

As each type of chart or graph is introduced, having children execute a very simple example of it and adding these to the display areas reinforces reading skills with graphic materials. As implied in the lists of types earlier, the subject portrayed need not be complex. Almost any recurring phenomenon of life in the classroom or community will lend itself to graphs, charts, and diagrams. Almost any body of facts shown in a graph can be transmitted to a table, and most arithmetic problems can be represented by a chart or diagram (which also aids in understanding the problem). Almost any series of events can be represented by a time-line chart, as cause-and-effect relationships can be portrayed by drawings and charts. Even without extraordinary resources, the interested teacher who recognizes the importance of the development of these thinking–reading processes can supply a wealth of experiences for the pupils.

Single kits of practice materials for intermediate and upper elementary grades combined are available in the *SRA Graph and Picture Study Kits* and the *SRA Map and Globe Skills Kit*. Each of these kits offers a wide variety of exercises in different types of graphs or maps, respectively. Each exercise is an independent, brief task in reading and interpreting a type of graphic aid.

Practice materials in reading a variety of graphic, tabular, chart, and pictorial items are available in the *EDL Study Skills Library*. Other teaching aids are listed at the end of this chapter.

Teachers should develop learning centers that will involve students in using, interpreting, and creating these various types of graphic aids. See the detailed discussion of learning centers as a step toward individualization in Chapter 11.

Library Skills

Most teachers and reading authors agree that growth in effective use of the library is essential for success in reading in the content fields. However, there is little unanimity of opinion as to who shall assume the responsibility for this training. Some teachers attempt some training; others leave this task to the librarians. In the final analysis, the responsibility for training in library skills really rests upon both, according to the facilities, opportunities, and abilities they possess. When librarians are available and capable of offering such training, some division of responsibility must be agreed upon between the teaching staff and the librarian. When librarians are not available or their time is already completely occupied, the classroom teacher must assume complete responsibility for such training, with whatever guidance may be available from the professional librarian. Just how this ideal can be accomplished is very problematic when, as already noted, intermediate teachers allow only about an hour per week for library activities and independent reading in the room or school library.

Conferences at the University of Nebraska and the University of Miami have emphasized the role of the teacher in stimulating growth in library skills in these basic principles: the teacher must understand the nature and content of reference materials and their uses; the teacher must be interested in teaching the use of reference materials; such materials must be readily available; the skills of reference must be systematically taught; and the teacher must encourage independent exploration of a variety of sources of information. Principles such as these do not imply that children learn locational and library skills by doing a few simple exercises in a workbook (without ever actually using the reference tool for which they are presumably practicing). As in every other type of learning, practice in locational and library skills will have to be realistic, varied, and puposeful. At the end of the chapter we have listed a number of resources to aid in this teaching of library skills both of the audiovisual types and workbooks, including some to be used in actual library practice.

Teachers do not always make good use of the school library, even though they may do some teaching of library skills in their classrooms. Among the steps classroom teachers should take are (*13*):

1. Familiarize yourself thoroughly with the actual resources of the library before giving your children library assignments.

2. Make certain that the materials pupils need for their tasks are actually available in the library. Find out whether your pupils can find whatever resource materials they will need.

3. Make your library assignments explicit, "Go to the library, and from _____ find out _____."

4. Warn the librarian in advance that they are sending children with specific assignments.

5. Consider what degree of skill is necessary in completing the assigned tasks. In other words, they may ask for book reports, research papers, committee reports, summaries, etc. when they are certain their children are capable and experienced in such activities.

6. Ascertain the pupils' knowledge of the rules regarding quiet, movement, access to files and stacks, check out and return procedures, etc.

7. Realize that constant interchange of books in the classroom library by bringing in books from the local or school library will help promote the children's reading more than taking or sending them to the library. Ready accessibility promotes use.

8. Tell the librarians of your plans. Librarians are often accused of being uncommunicative, but all too often the problem is really the lack of teacher effort to keep the librarian informed. For example, the librarian should be told by the teacher of the functional reading levels of the pupils. With this information, the librarian can provide realistic help to children in choosing appropriate books. Before beginning a unit of study, the teacher should certainly visit the library or media center to apprise the librarian of the needs and plans, and to discuss the available relevant materials. Before sending a group of pupils or the whole class, the teacher should discuss with the librarian the nature of the assignments. There must be two-way communication between teachers and librarians to promote intelligent use of library or media center materials (22).

A fact about borrowing books from libraries that no one has seemed to follow up is the marked difference between the number of books borrowed compared with the number actually read (21). Robert Karlin interviewed 300 children of elementary and junior high status about the books they borrowed. The boys frankly admitted that they had not read 53 percent of the books, while girls had not read 59 percent of their choices. These data yield several implications. Obviously teachers and librarians should be giving pupils more help in selecting books for personal reading. It is true that an author may apparently intend a book for a certain age group and yet produce one that no child of that age can really read. But if children were taught how to presample their selections, these disappointments would diminish.

There are some naive selection techniques recommended to help children make book selections. One of these involves counting on the fingers of one hand the number of unknown words in a page. When five fingers have been counted (or five difficult words encountered) some say the book is too hard. Since the number of words per page varies by several hundred during the first six grades, this suggestion is obviously faulty. It reflects the inflated standards of those who build Informal Reading Inventories which consider any book that a child cannot read with 100 percent oral accuracy as too difficult. No one reads with that degree of accuracy in challenging material. No body of large-scale testing in oral reading shows that degree of accuracy to be common.

As a matter of fact, one study showed that up to 30 percent of the words in a grade level selection could be omitted (hence unknown) before comprehension was seriously disturbed. The only realistic prereading sampling technique we know is to read a portion of ten or twelve pages before deciding whether one will enjoy the book and its subject matter as well as its style.

Library and locational skills

PRIMARY LEVELS
1. Alphabetical sequence
2. Title, title page
3. Copyright page
4. Preface, foreword, tables of contents
5. Lists of tables, maps, illustration
6. Chapter headings or titles
7. Index
8. Graphic and pictorial aids
9. Picture captions
10. Introduction to the dictionary
11. Arrangement of the library

INTERMEDIATE GRADES
1. Sectional, side, and other headings
2. Chapter summaries
3. Card catalog—understand the three types of cards
4. Dewey Decimal System
5. Simple practice in finding a desired book by its classification
6. Glossary, appendix, footnotes
7. Almanac, yearbooks, atlas, encyclopedia
8. Picture and clipping files
9. Reader's Guide to Periodical Literature
10. Indexes
11. Simple projects in finding resources related to given topic
12. Projects involving: (a) compiling bibliography; (b) preparing outline of research paper; (c) summarizing various materials on given topic; (d) preparing brief paper incorporating quotations from several sources

---

Most of this training, if it is to be effective, should center around the resources available in the classroom or school library. If desired it can be supplemented by such aids as the *EDL Study Skills Library—Reference Skills* or some of the other resources listed in the bibliography for this chapter. Even more important than the teaching of library skills are the teacher's efforts to establish a good working relationship with the librarian and to motivate children to use the library.

Each of the following library skills should be individually practiced under teacher supervision. For example,

1. Given a list of words beginning with different letters, arrange them in alphabetical order.
2. Given a list of words beginning with the same letter, or the same first two or three letters, arrange them in alphabetical order.
3. Having given children an unfamiliar content area book (they may have the same or different books), use such exercises as:
   - Where can I find the title of a book or the name of the author? Open your new book and find the page that gives these facts.
   - How do I find out when a book was published? Be prepared to tell when your book was published.
   - How do I find out why the author wrote this book? Look in your book for a page that answers such a question. What is that page called?
   - Will you read what the author of your book says about his or her goals and intentions?
   - Where in your book does it tell you what maps, graphs, tables or pictures there are in the book? Can you find that list and read part of it to us?
   - What is the title of the first chapter?
   - What topics will be discussed in the second chapter in your book? What is the name of the page that tells you this?
   - If you want to find out whether your book has something about space, where will you look? What do you find?
   - What graphs are there in your book? Find one in the third chapter, if there is one. What is its title? What is it supposed to tell you? Can you explain it to us?
   - What does it say under any picture in the fourth chapter? What do we call this phrase beneath the picture?
   - Now let's go to the library and try to learn how we can find the books that we want to read.

These are the simplest kind of exercises in learning library and locational skills at the primary level. There are many other activities that can be devised or borrowed from some of the resources listed in the bibliography.

Particularly in the individualized reading program, motivating children to library use should develop naturally from the program. The library is the major source for replenishing the classroom library and is an obvious step to leading children to go to the library to seek other books that are like those they have enjoyed. Because of the heavy demands upon them and the frequent understaffing (only 17 percent have a full-time librarian), school libraries and media centers must often maintain what appears to be a rather rigid schedule for different grade levels. Children should know the schedule and, after having been introduced to the arrangement several times jointly by teacher and specialist, be permitted to avail themselves of these opportunities in small groups or even independently.

A very significant aspect of motivating children's reading is the example offered by teachers. They should demonstrate their own appreciation of reading by reading while the children are also so engaged in the classroom and center, by reading to them with obvious pleasure and expression, by familiarizing themselves constantly with children's books that may appeal and presenting them dramatically, by giving books as prizes for contests or exceptional achievement, by encouraging children to bring their own library books to loan to other pupils, and by keeping parents informed of children's reading needs and interests. When their class is scheduled for the library, as is the custom in some schools, many teachers seize the opportunity to disappear quietly to the teacher's lounge. In this and other instances, their negative attitudes may work against the primary goal of all reading instruction—the development of lifelong use and enjoyment of the ability to read. Even at the sacrifice of some personal free time, teachers' behavior must be consistent with their avowed intentions. Going to the library or center with children, and using its resources frequently in the classroom library, will produce significantly more reading among children than just sending them off on their own.

Organizing and Reporting

The research on organizing and reporting skills makes two points quite clear: (1) success in content field reading is improved by training in these abilities; and (2) many middle and senior high school students show great inadequacy in these important skills. On the other hand, the available research clarifies neither what the content of training in these skills should be nor the best sequence of steps. Very few prepared materials are available for this essential training.

A suggested sequence of steps is offered in the *SRA Organizing and Reporting Skills Kit*. This collection of short exercises is offered for intermediate and middle school and by its individualization permits students to progress at their own rates. The kit offers the following training in the skills of reporting.

Organizing and reporting skills

A. FORM OF THE REPORT
1. Identifying portions of a report as beginning, middle, or end.
2. Arranging parts of a report in proper order.
3. Recognizing which part of an incomplete report is missing.
4. Judging simple reports for completeness and order.

B. STICKING TO THE POINT
1. Finding irrelevant statements in reports.
2. Identifying statements of opinion or feeling.

C. ORDER IN THE PARAGRAPH
1. Correcting the sequence or time order of details in a paragraph.
2. Detecting the omission of opening or closing sentence.
3. Identifying topic sentences or recognizing omission of such.

D. QUALITY IN THE PARAGRAPH
1. Locating repetitious words or phrases.
2. Identifying repetition of ideas or contradictions.
3. Identifying paragraphs as objective or subjective opinion.

To each of these aspects of reporting, the experienced teacher will undoubtedly wish to add other kinds of practices. It is apparent also that training in reading, writing, and analyzing paragraphs, summaries, book reviews, and magazine and newspaper articles will have to precede and accompany the report training offered in this kit. Some of these applications are suggested in the kit.

Among the basic skills of note taking that should be taught are those shown at the top of page 368.

Practice, first at the chalkboard and later at the desk, in arranging main ideas and details in related groups should be provided. These may be simply key words or phrases derived from the reading. The words or phrases may be related by lines drawn, as from a main idea to the supporting details. Some call this technique an array or mapping and have pupils repeat the experience using strips of paper with words and phrases written thereon at their desks. Practice with arrays at the chalkboard or desk would probably precede notetaking training steps 6–10. Other sources of practice in notetaking are listed later in this chapter.

Note-taking skills*

1. Summarizing a paragraph with a single sentence.
2. Summarizing the main ideas or topic sentences of a group of paragraphs by single sentences.
3. Summarizing the answer to a specific question by a short note.
4. Summarizing successive paragraphs by single sentences.
5. Summarizing an entire passage by a paragraph.
6. Given a topic, choose relevant notes from a group of such.
7. Arrange these selected notes in logical sequence under the given heading.
8. Given a group of notes, select a possible topical heading and choose relevant items.
9. Arrange selected items in a sequence under a heading supplied by a student.
10. Given the topic and a number of relevant sentences, arrange the sentences in a pargraph, including a topic and summary sentence.

*Training in the concepts of main ideas, and topic and summary sentences, will precede this program.

This type of training in note taking and outlining can be expanded in a number of ways. The various steps can be practiced in the pupil's content textbooks of all types and in listening as well as reading situations.

Practice in taking summarizing notes while listening is an essential type of training. These notes can be improved by discussing them and comparing them with the teacher's outline of the lesson. Practice in varying the amount of detail taken in notes, as well as the degree of originality, should be given. Some areas demand more careful, detailed notes than do others; some require exact notes, while others may be freely paraphrased by the student. Notes including the summaries of main ideas, selected while reading or listening, should be practiced. The habit of revising or reorganizing notes shortly after they have been written, of combining notes from several sources into a single outline, and of evolving time-saving abbreviations that can later be readily interpreted should be given attention. Other types of practice and application of note-taking and outlining skills will suggest themselves as this training progresses.

As teachers know from their own experiences in high school and college, note taking tends to be a very personal kind of practice. Probably because of the lack of formal training, each student's system tends to have its own peculiarities. Some underline, some do not; some write a great deal, others have no systematic arrangement. Some copy the words of the text or speaker; others paraphrase ideas in their own words. Some can reuse their notes for review, while others find their notes too scanty or incomplete (or even unreadable). Some evolve abbreviations for frequently recurring terms, or even use incomplete writing of words to speed up the task. Are some of these practices ineffectual or even useless for retaining information? Should we give some sort of training in note taking to overcome these inefficient habits?

Unfortunately, most of the research on note taking does not give very definite answers to guide instruction. The studies are based largely on experiments with high school and college students who have already evolved their own peculiar systems. When these students are instructed in one type of note taking, and the retention is compared with another system, the results are often inconclusive. Possibly new note-taking systems conflict with their own systems and temporarily retard learning, or possibly the new system is not maintained long enough in these experiments to demonstrate its value.

Undoubtedly, disorganized, unsystematic notes are of less value than clearer arrangements. Reorganizing notes shortly after making them is profitable. But the other idiosyncratic variations in shorthand systems, or brevity versus direct quotations, do not appear to be significant, or, at least, have not been shown to matter (26). Recent studies have strongly supported the use of underlining as a note-taking device superior to outlining (8). We are not certain exactly how the student's previous habits might have affected these studies, but they are quite clear-cut in their results. Not only does this procedure seem to result in better retention, but the more extensive the pupils' underlining, the better the results. Other writers, however, continue to experiment with note taking, to defend it as a profitable study technique and to devise new systems (26).

Still another note-taking procedure is called the Herringbone procedure. As suggested by Tierney, et al. (41), it looks like this:

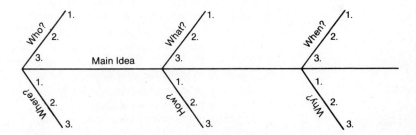

Children who need help in organizing are given this graphic aid to record their answers as they read. At first glance, the procedure would seem to be most feasible for use in semi-narrative materials.

One writer recommends a two-column arrangement with notes in the right-hand column and later labeling of the main ideas in the left-hand column. Other writers strongly recommend the formal outline—I., A., 1., a.—that few pupils eventually use. Another author would eliminate all the lettering and numbering and merely indicate the importance of each key word or phrase by the degree of indentation. Finally, some writers of the how-to-study books acknowledge that we haven't been able to prove any system superior to all others.

With this kind of research to guide us, we should probably compromise by introducing pupils to both note taking in various ways and to underlining, and let them evolve their own systems. We would, of course, review these systems from time to time to point out ways they could be improved in permanence, clarity, organization, and speed.

A more complete program of training in outlining would include the following steps.

Outlining skills

1. Group words under an appropriate given heading. Later practice same with children supplying the heading.
2. Group words under two headings.
3. Detect irrelevant words in a given classification.
4. Classify sentences under given heading.
5. Group words under three headings.
6. Arrange series of sentences as they appear in the reading material.
7. Arrange subtitles as in given material.
8. Arrange events in chronological order.
9. Select sentences that tell about the main idea.
10. Collect sentences bearing on a given question in a short selection.
11. Group such statements under one, two, or later, three headings.
12. Find subtopics in a paragraph.
13. Find subtopics in a longer selection.
14. Select main points to complete skeleton outline of given details.
15. Add main ideas and one or more subheadings to given skeleton outline.
16. Select main ideas for an outline.
17. Select main ideas and subheadings for an outline.
18. Outline more than one paragraph.
19. Organize notes from several sources under main ideas, subheadings, and details.

All of these study skills must eventually be woven into the fabric of instruction in the content fields. In other words, if these skills are to function realistically in the future, there must be ample opportunity for their use as a part of the class study of content materials. Thus, a typical content field lesson follows.

Plan for a Content Area Unit

Our suggestions for teaching content areas makes several assumptions. First, the presentation is of a unit of material in a series of lessons. Second, the instructional materials are relatively limited. Third, some of the pupils cannot read and comprehend the textbook.

Plan for a Content Area Unit

TEACHER PREPARATION

1. If a manual is provided, read this to make a list of the concepts to be taught, for teaching suggestions, and for teaching aids.
2. With the help of the librarian or media specialist, assemble pertinent materials, including books and other matter for supplementary reading. Preview these aids. Complete the selection and assembling of these aids at least several days before you are to present the unit to be certain of their availability.
3. Make a time schedule for the unit, indicating the major sections, approximate time required for their presentations, and for the use of the aids previously collated.
4. Preview the unit to identify general and technical terms probably new to your class. Add these to your overall plan, listing them in relation to the concepts they clarify.
5. If you will need any apparatus, maps, etc., for the unit, check their readiness for use and assemble them in a convenient place. Plan also, at least tentatively, for follow-up activities for each day's lesson.

PRESENTING THE UNIT

1. *Motivation*—Attempt to create interest by initiating a discussion of pupil-related experiences and knowledge about the topic. If unit is closely related to previous one, spend some time reviewing concepts already learned and the association between the units. In other words, try to establish the relevance of the unit concepts to the body of knowledge of this field, and, if possible, to life itself.

   If certain reading skills are to be demanded by the nature of the unit, point this out to the pupils in the unit in the textbook. With the relevant section before them, discuss the use of scanning, map reading, interpretation of chart or diagram, etc. Remind them or elicit from them the basic reading procedures to be used. Remind them to give full attention to these graphics during their previewing.

(continued)

---

2. *Vocabulary and concept development*—Using the chalkboard, present the new vocabulary and concepts to be gained from the first day's lesson on the unit. Repeat this at the opening of each subsequent lesson. In presenting new terms, elicit pupil definitions and related knowledge, as possible. Clarify structure, derivation, and meaning of each item, as well as pronunciation. Discuss the interrelationship of vocabulary and unit concepts.
3. Present your demonstration, experiment, or visual aids according to your schedule. Some, of course, will be done before pupil study, others after their reading, and still others at a strategic point during the lesson.
4. Preview the textbook material which is to be covered in that day's lesson. As pupils read silently the headings, subheads, graphic aids, etc., discuss possible interpretations or implications of these, as they relate to the group of concepts presented earlier. Ask pupils to suggest questions that seem likely to be answered in a full reading. Place these on the chalkboard in an order related to the organization of the textbook.

Other prereading activities for content area reading are suggested by Moore et al. (28):

1. *Asking and answering prereading questions*—Those dealing with the schemata of the pupils can, of course, be answered before reading. Those demanding facts or generalizations from the text can be answered after reading.

2. *Forecasting a passage*—The topic of the selection is written on the chalkboard and the pupils asked to suggest terms related to the topic. These, too, are written on the board. Then an outline under the title of the selection is attempted using the terms generated by the pupils. Each student writes a short paragraph using the terms and basing it on the outline. Then these paragraphs are rated by the teacher. After the passage is read, a second draft including the concepts offered in the text is constructed by the pupils and graded. This procedure incorporates reading, writing, speaking, and listening, the authors claim, and is suitable for content area topics that are of general interest to most students.

3. *Previewing new vocabulary*—An effective idea is placing a word giving the major idea or topic of the reading in the center of the blackboard and then mapping around it all the related words the pupils can suggest. The key words that will occur in the reading are woven into the map (probably by the teacher). All words are discussed in terms of their relevance to the main topic.

4. *Using graphic aids to preview*—The preview may take the form of relating an outline of the content of the selection to pupil knowledge. Other versions take the course of mapping cause–effect, comparison–contrast, problem–solution, and time order, and listing patterns that are present.

5. *Silent reading*—Have pupils read textbook paragraph by paragraph. As they finish each portion of one or several papagraphs, ask appropriate questions stressing interpretation, analysis, synthesis, and similar reading skills. (See detailed suggestions on questioning strategies in Chapter 13.) If certain material must be memorized, have pupils copy the principle, formula, or other item and point out various ways in which this might be memorized. As the answers to the questions on the chalkboard appear, discuss them.

Remember that some of your pupils cannot read this textbook easily. Spare them embarrassment by directing your questions to other pupils, unless the poor readers volunteer. Whatever these pupils learn about the topic will probably be through the medium of listening to the answers to your questions, the discussion of those answers, and the teaching aids or demonstration you use, unless you can supply some parallel easier materials for them to read.

As the new vocabulary terms appear during the silent reading, point them out; ask for definitions or interpretations. Ask how the text helped define these new terms.

Use oral reading only as needed to cite facts, clarify disagreements, show chronology, or to supply supporting facts in response to your questions—*not* for reading whole paragraphs.

As graphic aids such as charts, tables, and diagrams or pictures appear in the text, discuss these in terms of their clarification of the text, their relevance, and any additional information they offer.

Some subject matter teachers think that a difficult textbook is simplified by having pupils read it aloud bit by bit. They are unaware that the only pupils who might profit from this practice are those read to, not those reading. Some authors recommend that the class follow the oral reader by reading silently. This simultaneous oral and silent reading does not greatly benefit pupil comprehension of difficult material when it is the sole method of presentation. If discussion follows each brief reading, at least to identify the main idea, and the meanings of the new or technical words are clarified during each discussion, those pupils who really cannot read the text successfully will be helped to some degree.

6. *Application*—You will have been helping pupils apply such reading skills as comprehension, scanning, previewing, and vocabulary development as you presented each segment of the unit. Obviously you intended that some of the concepts presented were to be retained in long-term memory. For this to occur, some reinforcement, some application of the ideas and facts gained, must follow each presentation. Use any of the following, matching the task to pupil ability: outlining main facts and details; constructing a time line to show a sequence of events or cause-effect or enumerative relationships; group construction of a mural; individual drawings, charts, diagrams, or a simple map. Ask a group to plan a spontaneous role-playing session depicting one of the events in the lesson; suggest resources (from our list); allow pupils to select one to deepen their knowledge; plan for a sharing with the class. Distribute the supplementary books you borrowed from the library, trying to match their reading difficulty to pupil ability. Here again, permit pupils to make their

own selection and discuss with them their ideas about sharing the book with the class. If this supplementary material is nonnarrative, remind the pupils that this is another opportunity to practice their content reading skills, such as previewing, scanning, and learning new vocabulary.

Ask pupils to plan the presentation of one of the audiovisual aids you found at the media center. Ask a small group to show the film, or whatever, and lead the class discussion. Help them prepare for this interaction.

Have a small group take over the arranging of a trip to a local business that is engaged in activities related to the topic of the unit. They will be responsible for requesting permission from the business and from the school, as well as organizing the means of transportation for the class.

Initiate construction of a model or diorama illustrating the principles or concepts apparent in the unit.

7. *Review*—If it is essential for pupils to retain some of the concepts presented in a unit, then review of these must be planned. You can arrange some types of reviewing, such as discussing the concepts of the previous or other units, when introducing a new one. Group reviews can be accomplished by tests from time to time (as immediately after a unit, a few days later, and a few weeks later). Other types of review can be arranged by helping children repeat their previewing of all the segments to be included in a test; by aiding them in preparing an outline of the concepts and the supporting details. This is, in itself, a review, whether or not it is followed immediately by a test.

Keep in mind, in writing your review tests, that your poorer readers will have trouble reading these, too. Frame your questions as briefly and simply as possible; use true-false, completion, matching, and even multiple-choice questions in preference to essay types. Use open book questions requiring use of the text to find answers. You may still find that you will have to read or interpret your questions to the poor readers, if they are going to have a fair chance to show what they have learned.

Review your tests with your pupils by returning their papers to them and discussing why certain answers were correct or incorrect. This is an important means of correcting misconceptions and reinforcing learning.

In an earlier chapter we mentioned an experiment in which we were involved that attempted to teach content fields to middle-school pupils who could not read the usual textbooks. The teaching took the form of collating all the ideas and information pupils and the teacher could bring together on the chalkboard, somewhat as described in the previewing step of a content lesson above (except that the textbook was not the basic resource in these classes). These concepts were discussed, reorganized with the aid of the class, and, at the end of the day, duplicated to form, in effect, the textbook for the next day. Since the material was phrased by the pupils, even the poor readers could read and discuss the notes. Demonstrations and audiovisual aids were, of course, frequently used to reinforce the learning. Tests and quizzes were adapted to the content presented, and grades were utilized as usual. Thus, with the textbook serving only as an occasional resource book, practically the same content of English, science, social studies, and mathematics was taught to this disadvantaged group.

This is an oversimplified description of this successful attempt to teach content matter to poor readers. But the basic implication is true that content field learning can be taught to poor readers if teachers will make the adjustments in approaches and objectives that are necessary, and will lessen their dependence upon a textbook as the basic or only tool for instruction.

Studying a Textbook

It has been a widespread practice to teach students to follow a definite sequence of steps when they are studying a textbook. This system, often called *Survey Q3R* or *PQRST*, led students to frame questions through surveying or previewing (*Survey Q* or *PQ*), then to Read to answer these questions. Following these steps, the students would Recite to themselves the answers to the questions they proposed and Test themselves by reviewing answers without the text or their notes. Serious questions have been raised about this system by the research on the effect of reading to answer prereading questions. As pointed out in the discussion of ways to stimulate comprehension, detailed prereading questions tend to direct pupils to read only for the answers, and thus to achieve very limited comprehension. To overcome this hindrance to total comprehension, if students are to be urged to use a study method, it should probably take this form:

- *Preview*—Read title, headings, opening and closing of paragraphs, and introductory or summary paragraphs.
- *Summaries*—Begin to organize your comprehension of the material by making a rough outline of the main ideas as you were able to identify them by previewing. (Or, underline main ideas as you preview.)
- *Read*—Read through the chapter, either filling in your outline as you go or underlining the facts that support the main ideas.
- *Test*—Ask questions like those your teacher might ask, or quiz yourself. Check your answers by looking at the text or your outline.

This is a relatively idealistic plan for studying a textbook that students do not necessarily adopt just because the teacher recommends it. Moreover, brighter students eventually modify the system in terms of their experiences with it, as indeed they should. If the whole idea is worth teaching to students, and we believe it does aid in their organization, it will have to be presented, and practiced many times, step by step, under teacher guidance.

For those who question the rejection of the popular *SQ3R*, we may cite the research of Crewe and Hultgren (7), who have shown that, as logical as it may seem to be, there is little or no research to show that student learning is improved by adopting the system (8). Indeed, underlining has proved superior in several investigations of comparative study methods. The ineffectualness of reading to answer prereading questions has been demonstrated by a number of research experiments discussed in Chapter 14. This conclusion is reaffirmed by Goudey's comparison of directed reading. At all levels of reading ability among fourth-graders, retention of information was better under *nondirected* conditions (*17*).

The separate steps of the *Survey Q3R* or similar plans seem profitable to students, according to some research. In other words, when effective previewing is taught to students, and they use it, their comprehension is definitely improved. In isolated experiments, reciting to oneself or a friend, or reviewing after studying have also shown profit. But it has not been shown that adding all the steps of this study plan into one continuous act necessarily increases comprehension or retention as we add each additional step. The comprehension increases achieved by adding one of these steps to the reading is not quadrupled because the other steps are added. Yet many of the authors of how-to-study books recommend this study plan or some version of it.

Our experience in teaching the plan to high school and college students has been that over time they discover which of these steps is profitable to them and continue to use that step or two in addition to their reading. As in the area of outlining and note-taking, we have not been able to demonstrate a best method. Having been introduced to a variety of study techniques, students should be permitted to evolve their own procedures. This means, of course, that some will choose to use none of these aids or to use them only superficially and ineffectually. Hence, review of their personal study habits from time to time is very necessary.

In our reading clinic, the senior author discovered that, despite earlier instruction, many believed that a single reading of a text chapter would suffice. If this was questioned, the students would often suggest a second complete reading, and declare that that was certainly sufficient for test or recitations. However, a single reading without any note-taking or previewing does not yield adequate comprehension. A second reading will add about 5 percent more comprehension, too little to justify the time required for a complete careful reading. To retain the facts or concepts offered in a textbook chapter some sort of mediation (previewing, raising questions, discussing the ideas) and translation of the formal textbook language (note-taking, summarizing, outlining) are absolutely essential.

Although they object to our version of this study technique, Adams et al. recommend teaching intermediate grade children a very similar arrangement of steps (*1*): Preview, Recite subheads, form Questions from subheads, Read (to find answers to own questions), Rehearse by rereading subheads and recalling the related facts without consulting notes. They taught their system to fifth-graders in a four-day experiment. The pupils showed significant gains in retention from readings. But only about one half of the pupils were actually using the procedure at the end of the training period. On a delayed test, only 20 percent continued with this study strategy. Most of the pupils used some sort of rereading, reviewing of notes, etc., as compared to one third of the control untrained group. In other words, the attention to their study strategies alerted pupils to a need for some such steps, but not to those taught to them. Although Adams et al. were unsuccessful in inducing pupils to accept and use their version of the textbook study technique, most of the pupils exposed to the procedure responded by adapting some sort of study strategy.

Reading in Science and Social Science

The reading of science and social science materials presents an opportunity for the exercise of a variety of reading skills and techniques. Many writers have suggested that these skills be combined into a systematic approach to study-type reading. For example, *The EDL Study Skills Library* utilizes these steps in each science and social science lesson.

1. *Readiness*—The title, cover illustration, and a leading question under the illustration serve to stimulate the student's interest and curiosity and are discussed.
2. *Preview vocabulary*—A list of the technical vocabulary is also offered on the cover page. These terms will occur in the article. Their pronunciations and meanings are given. Pupil definitions are solicited and discussed.
3. *Survey*—The student is asked to survey or preview the selection by reading the headings and looking at the illustrations and the captions.
4. *Purpose*—A purpose-setting question is offered on the cover page. For example, the student is asked, "To read carefully to find out: 1. What makes magnets behave as they do? 2. Is a compass a magnet? 3. Why is the earth like a magnet?"
5. *Reading*—The student now reads the selection, presumably for the purposes previously defined.
6. *Comprehension*—Ten questions on general recall, main ideas, information from illustrations, and inferences are then answered.
7. *Study skill*—The back of the four-page folder offers further practice in a specific study skill such as outlining, summarizing, recognizing cause and effect, map reading, reading an experiment, a time line, or a diagram.

This particular sequence of steps is, of course, keyed to the format of the folders in the *EDL* kit. It is apparent, however, that the pattern of approach is adapted to transfer to the reading of other content field materials, such as the classroom textbooks. The steps of readiness, previewing vocabulary, survey or previewing the material, planning purpose, reading, and comprehension check can be used in the study of most science and social science materials.

General reading skills are important in reading in science and social science, but in addition there are a number of special skills that are demanded in these content fields. Some of the special reading skills and ways in which they may be promoted are listed as follows:

Reading skills in science and social science

Vocabulary. The technical terms and the general terms that are used with special meanings must be given strong emphasis. Their meanings may be approached by discussion, by teacher or pupil definition, by resorting to the glossary or dictionary, or the context, or by analysis of their structure and derivation. Similar attention must be given to terms involving concepts of distance, time, space, and the like.

Comprehension and interpretation
1. *Details*—Ability to recall details, to see relationships among them, to combine them into generalizations, concepts, or laws; to discriminate between significant and insignificant or irrelevent details; to be able to scan quickly to find specific details when needed; to follow detailed directions.
2. *Main Ideas*—ability to recognize, or formulate from details or observations; to select or make the best restatement of the main idea; to apply the main ideas in new contexts.
3. *Reasoning*—deducing generalizations from a series of observations, applying the generalization in new problems, recognizing cause-and-effect relationships among details or events. Using critical thinking such as evaluating sources, recognizing author's purposes, distinguishing opinion and fact, making inferences, forming judgments, and detecting propaganda devices.

Organization. Collating, summarizing, comparing materials from several sources; previewing; skimming, scanning, and careful reading. Using parts of a book, reference materials, and the library for own purposes. Taking notes and making outlines.

Use of graphic materials. Using common graphic and tabular materials with profit. Making such aids based on own reading. Reading, interpreting, and making maps.

In addition to these reading performances, some authors feel that pupils must learn to recognize and react to various patterns of writing in science and social science. Among the patterns commonly present are (1) directions for carrying out an experiment or creating a time line or map; (2) classification of main ideas versus details; (3) explanation of a technical process or a governmental structure by a diagram or chart; and (4) detailed statement of facts. In teaching a lesson in these contents; it would be feasible to help pupils recognize these patterns during the previewing step of the lesson, as outlined earlier.

The value in such an emphasis upon the structural organizational pattern of the textbook is that it helps to create a reading set or attitude. In other words, readers focus their attention on reading directions, or memorizing facts, or seeing relationships in a chart, etc. Speaking of memorizing, the teacher must be alert to detect pupils who constantly attempt to substitute memorization for real understanding. They have a constant set to try to learn all the facts, almost in a rote fashion, conceiving of this as the best type of studying. Of course, some teachers promote this set for memory of facts by their questions, which demand exact quotations from the printed material rather than reader reactions or interpretation. Two treatment approaches are appropriate: (1) pointing out the pattern of the segment of the material and discussing ways of understanding and retaining it during the previewing; and (2) focusing questions on analysis, synthesis, interpretation, and similar skills rather than sheer recital of facts. When readers who are overdependent upon sheer memory are detected by the teacher, and they are many, a few personal sessions with them in discussion of their set for reading will be profitable.

This prereading discussion of the structural characteristics of the study material helps organize the reader into a frame of mind that is receptive to learning. Like the other advance organizers we mentioned above, this preparation for reading or studying makes a direct contribution to comprehension and retention.

The experience children have in preparing language experience charts will be very useful in extending the learning in social and physical sciences. They can prepare large charts showing labeled collections of rocks, leaves, flowers, insects, pictures of trees, houses, community workers (and their duties); time lines of events in a certain period; descriptions of the events of a war or the chronology of explorations, inventions and discoveries, and the like. These charts may be mounted in the classroom and will serve as an aid in class discussions of a unit of study.

Some teachers expand this use of realia to include, as in the case of study of a certain culture, making models or dioramas of a village or other such population center; collecting objects (or making them) as tomahawks, headdresses, tepees, moccasins, beaded belts and headbands, peace pipes, blankets, and the like. These realia are collected, displayed, and used as props in the children's enactment of simple plays or pantomime. The playlet may be performed before other classes or parent groups (who have already been involved in helping to assemble or make the display). Making the content area realistic is often utilized in the study of foreign countries, occupations, the music and arts of a certain period, costumes, military uniforms, etc. In addition to the collection of realia and the construction activities, records, films, filmstrips, tapes, and related radio or TV broadcasts are integrated in the study with the assistance of the school media specialist and librarian. Obviously, these enriching, realistic experiences are carefully planned by the teacher before the topic is initiated.

Paul McKee, who wrote so well on reading in the content areas, objected strongly to make-believe construction activities in the attempt to expand or enrich social and physical science learning. It was his measured opinion that one-foot-high tepees, cardboard or clay castles on a table, or models made from shoe boxes with colored paper embellishments produced false and distorted concepts in children's minds. It would be difficult today to refute this opinion.

Reading in Mathematics

The introduction of what is termed the New Mathematics has created an acute problem in terms of pupil reading ability. Analysis of a number of these new curricula indicates that at each grade level the reading difficulty of the text is much above the average reading levels of children of that grade (12). Both in complexity of sentence structure and breadth of vocabulary, these new materials tend to be more difficult than normal instructional materials in the field of reading. It is obvious that their use will demand extraordinary efforts on the part of teachers to help pupils read and comprehend them.

In the primary grades, and to a decreasing degree, in the intermediate grades, the comprehension of arithmetic problems is largely a reading rather than a mathematical task. The simple arithmetic problem presents the basic reading tasks of word recognition, word meaning, and comprehension. Thus, in the lower grades, the improvement of fundamental reading skills reflects in improved reading in arithmetic. However, as arithmetic relationships and processes become more complex, good general reading ability becomes less significant and specific training in arithmetic reading skills is necessary.

Some teachers try to meet this problem of training for reading in arithmetic by teaching pupils a pattern of thinking in problem solving, involving such steps as: "What is given? What is to be found? What arithmetic steps shall I take? Approximately what will the answer be?" A number of research studies have shown that this logical type of training is not very profitable. The average pupil does not naturally follow a specific pattern of thinking such as this recommended procedure. Nor do the experiments show that training in trying to follow a pattern always results either in greater success in problem solving or a channeling of the student's thinking. A more general training in how to read in arithmetic is probably more effective.

Pupils should be taught a general pattern in problem solving: (1) a rapid first reading (or preview) of the problem for general understanding; (2) a second, slower reading to identify the details and relationships. After the first, or certainly after the second reading, pupils should be able to restate the problem in their own words, and should attempt this mental paraphrasing before beginning computation. If the problem involves several steps, students should be able, after the second reading, to visualize or express the computation steps they will take. These two types of reading should be practiced frequently with the pupils giving orally their restatement of the problem and their description of the computational steps they intend to take.

Some writers recommend making a sketch or diagram of the problem, as when measurement is involved. Others would have pupils use mental imagery to depict the problem. For some students, these aids work well; for others they do not, but all students should be encouraged to give them a sustained trial before discarding them.

Many reading skills are present in the reading of mathematical materials of expository, computational, and problem solving nature. When pupils are using these materials, the teacher must be alert to recognize the reading skills being demanded and do the direct teaching that will result in improved reading in arithmetic. Some of the significant arithmetic reading skills and supporting activities are these:

1. *Vocabulary*—By illustration, definition, analysis of structure or discussion, the technical vocabulary of arithmetic must be taught before the lesson, during the lesson, and in reviews. Anticipating the need for this instruction should be an integral part of the arithmetic lesson plan. Symbols such as $+$, $-$, $\times$, $\div$; abbreviations such as ft, in, yd, sq ft, % are an important part of the arithmetic vocabulary.

   One study of the mathematics vocabulary in eight series of books indicated that half of the 473 technical terms were not repeated as often as 50 times in all the books combined (35). As in many other textbooks, the authors do not recognize the limitations of their audience. We do not know whether 50 repetitions of a technical math term is enough or too much for elementary pupils. But we do know that special attention should be given to any new terms as soon as they occur and they should be reviewed and discussed again and again. There is ample evidence that stressing vocabulary is reflected in gains in understanding arithmetic concepts and in problem solving.

2. *Reading for details*—Pupils must be able to distinguish significant and insignificant details, and see relationships among details. They must also be able to scan quickly for details in order to begin computations and check correctness of their copy. Repeated practice in indicating the significant details and their relationships, and in detecting the insignificant, is essential for these skills.

3. *Interpretation*—Arithmetic problems make great demands upon deductive and inductive reasoning, upon children's ability to generalize a process from a group of details or to recognize a familiar type of problem by previewing it. Many problems demand the divergent reasoning that proceeds from a group of given facts to a visualization embodying these, as in problems of area, measurement, and the like. Practice in reading problems without numbers, or in interpreting them without attempting computation, and in attempting to visualize them on paper or to explain them in the pupil's own words promotes growth in the skills of interpretation.

4. *Use of graphic and tabular materials*—Charts, drawings, graphs, and diagrams are frequent in arithmetic and require special training. Practice in constructing and reading these proceeding from the simplest types to those testing the most complex situations that pupils are capable of handling is essential. As noted before, graphic materials without explanation in the text are not handled readily by most pupils. When this textual explanation is lacking, the

teacher's obligation is obvious. The making of sketches, diagrams, and other types of drawings in practicing visualization, as recommended above, is a realistic approach to learning to read the graphic materials encountered in texts and tests.

The reading of tables represents a task that differs from most conventional reading. The material is not necessarily arranged to be read from left to right. Sometimes tables are to be read vertically, sometimes both vertically and horizontally simultaneously. Headings may be at the top, side, bottom, or several of these places in the table. Observation of the habits of children, or even of adults, in reading tables often indicates a haphazard approach. Intermediate-grade children should be trained in an organized previewing and scanning of tables, which involves some of these steps: reading the title, reading the columnar headings, reading the left-hand headings or footings, as the case may be. This previewing of the organization of the table enables readers to identify the probable location of the fact they may be seeking. Then they are ready to run their eyes down or across (scanning) to find that fact.

To facilitate reading in mathematics, many other teacher efforts are recommended. The teacher must be cognizant of the pupils' reading test scores and give special assistance in reading text or problems as indicated. Pupils should be given an opportunity, when working in a group with the teacher, to ask questions about the problem—Earle recommends intensive study of the technical vocabulary at the chalkboard, with interrelationships shown by their arrangement or a sketch (12).

One article recommends that the teacher observe children's problem-solving efforts to detect such areas of difficulty as: (1) computation; (2) ability to plan solution when problem is read to them; (3) ability of children to describe steps in solution after having read the problem; (4) children's execution of their plan for solving the problem. Although time-consuming, this analysis would certainly aid the teacher in knowing where to begin in improving children's problem-solving skills (11).

Other teachers have suggested introducing manipulatives to be used in solutions, as the abacus, Cuisinaire rods, etc. Practice in having children formulate problems for the rest of the class also helps their thinking. There should be a wide variety of problems presented to the group, and new types should be related to those experienced previously. Small group work in discussing the process to be used and generalizing about common properties of problems is probably preferable to whole-class discussion.

The list of suggestions for teaching a content area unit given earlier in this chapter is relevant to this area when using a textbook as the basis for instruction. The steps outlined under Teacher Preparation, Motivation, Vocabulary and Concept Development, Silent Reading, and Application may be used with such a text. In mathematics, of course, much of the application will be the solving of problems that illustrate the relationships taught in the lesson or unit. Other detailed steps to be followed in teaching this content are given above.

One of the major problems faced in teaching science, math, or social science at almost every elementary school level is the high readability level of the textbooks. In Florida, one study pointed out that 55 percent of the almost 100 social science texts were by formula at least one grade level above the grade for which they were offered by the publisher. The material within these same texts varied from one to five grades above the average level of the book (*19, 20*). There are many other studies in these subject matter fields that give similar results.

Some question the use of a formula to estimate the reading difficulty of a book. They claim, and correctly so, that formulas do not evaluate such factors as child interest, reading background, writing style, or the like. However, no one has been able to evolve a method of estimation that would take all such factors into consideration. The choice is between a completely subjective guess as to readability, which varies greatly from one teacher or librarian to the next; or an examination of the sentence length and number of difficult words, two measures of readability validated in dozens of studies. Moreover, the research on the Spache readability formula, to mention only one such tool, proves that it reflects pupil oral reading errors and comprehension (*36*).

Reading in Literature

Sir John Herschel had the following to say about reading literature (*18*):

> Give a man a taste for reading and the means of gratifying it and you cannot fail to make him a happy, as well as a better man. You place him in contact with the best minds in every period of history, with the wisest and the wittiest, the tenderest and the bravest, those who really adorned humanity. You make him a citizen of all nations and a contemporary of all ages.

The Literature Program

Norine Odland has described the characteristics of various literature programs for the elementary school (*25*):

1. Periods are designated during which a book that has been read by the whole class is discussed. This practice constitutes the "literature program."
2. In some schools, providing access to the library is the program. There are scheduled periods for going to the library or media center, plus instruction in use of the library and some guidance by the

librarians. In some cases, the program is more informal in that children may go to the library at times of their choosing to achieve their personal reading needs.

3. In other schools, neither the faculty nor the curriculum is really responsible for instruction in reading. These schools seem to believe that since "fewer people are reading and none will be reading in the future" teaching about literature is impractical. Teacher aides, study-hall teachers, or volunteers do listen to children read and do take them to the library upon occasion, but these are not considered important activities.

4. In some schools, literature is secondary to reading, language arts, and even social science (somewhat the way reading is treated in some colleges that teach methods in one grand block). Book reports are made (often only on books related to social science); poetry may be analyzed (to study grammar or sentence structure); a story may be read (as a basis for drill with new vocabulary). Sometimes a bibliography is supplied. But this is merely a list of books related to the content fields. Children's books are studied in terms of the values or themes they illustrate—such as death, friendship, and courage—not as objects desired for their artistry or for personal enjoyment.

5. There is a type of literature program in which the main objective is personal enjoyment and continued interest in reading through developing sensitivity to literary artistry as well as to content. Evaluation of the program is based on how much is read by the pupils, what is read, and how their attitudes toward reading and life are modified. In this kind of school program, both teachers and pupils know that the literature being studied is the main goal, not just a supplement to some other subject matter area. Such a program is, of course, highly dependent upon the enthusiasm and literary knowledge of the teachers.

Odland goes on to list what she feels are the essential components of a literature program.

1. *Children's interests*—These need to be developed, brought to efficient levels and broadened in time. To accomplish these goals, there should be at least four books per child in the classroom library.
2. *Literary types*—Children should be introduced to myths, legends, folk tales, contemporary and historical fiction, fantasy, science fiction, biographies, biographical fiction, and nonfiction. There should be the opportunity to read and hear these types.
3. *Literary elements*—Pupils should be introduced to characterization, variations in diction, figurative language, the sincerity and

credibility of style, vividness of description, and awareness and understanding of plot structure and story themes.

4. *Creators of books*—The authors, editors, adapters, and illustrators of books, both of the past and present, should be introduced to pupils in a biographical perspective. The similarities and differences in art and writing styles should be approached.

Charlotte S. Huck, a recognized literature expert, makes suggestions for implementing and vitalizing the literature program. Among these are (*18*):

- Make books an integral part of each child's environment from pre-school ages on. Expose children to many books at home and in the classroom. Provide also a listening center in the classroom.
- Provide enthusiastic models (parents and teachers).
- Read to children daily. Select the books for their interest to children, not for their classic or moral values or relevance to some school subject. Read about four to five full books a year in third grade and above. In primary grades, read many short stories to students.
- Provide time for reading and sharing.
- Teach literary appreciation, perhaps as outlined by Odland above.

Many other writers have suggestions for the nature of the literature program. Among these, Ann H. Stoddard would emphasize the global perspective (*38*). She feels that this broad approach would promote good attitudes toward minorities or different ethnic groups, and help children to develop a sensitivity to cultural differences. The experiences with worldwide literature would facilitate an acceptance of self and others, the understanding of the similarities, differences, and interdependence among cultures, and increase the children's perception of the world.

Since she claims that 96 percent of good readers and 88 percent of poor readers read comics, Emma H. Swain would include these in the literature program (*39*). Other writers agree that comic books should play a role in the approach to children's literature. In listening to literature, Boothroy and Donham recommend a weekly television program *Reading Road Quiz* with teams of three pupils from two schools competing in responding to questions (*3*). In the all-school closed circuit listening situation, these authors suggest that children should choose the selections, that books should be varied from year to year, and that each book be followed by an instructional unit. This program would help the teaching staff increase its familiarity with children's literature; and children's book selections would be influenced and poor readers would gain familiarity with literature they might never have read.

Basal readers form the fundamental source of literature in many classrooms. Their manuals usually provide lists of suggested readings, a wide variety of reading selections, units of selections to stimulate child interest, and activities intended to promote understanding and appreciation of library materials. As commendable as this program is, it is a mistake to consider the reading series as a complete or even a broad literature program. Studies of teachers' implementation of this material as well as the quality of its content are not very encouraging. For example, the poetry in basal readers varies greatly both in quantity and quality. One series neither includes poetry nor even mentions it; another suggests its exploration but offers no examples or resources for the teacher. Most series offer one or two poems per unit, but these vary greatly from largely jingles or dull selections to sparkling, contemporary pieces accompanied by attractive illustrations (24).

Some basal authors consider the poetry they present as silent reading practice material, thus failing to realize the oral charactristics of melody, movement, rhythm, or rhyme. The poetry is also used to polish word analysis or phonic drills, a practice almost certain to destroy its appeal. Detailed analysis is suggested in some materials, desiccating the poem (as well as destroying its unique qualities). All of these criticisms imply that in approaching the poetry portion of the basal reader program at least, teachers should probably follow their own ideas in presentation.

Children's poetry preferences have been sampled by a number of studies. The usual procedure has been to read a wide variety of poems to the pupils and ascertain their choices by interview or questionnare. Several reports of this type seem to agree in their findings (24, 40).

- Primary children prefer narrative, rhymed, and metered poems with contemporary language expressing ideas about children or animals and with an element of humor.
- Primary children dislike free verse, lyric poetry, haiku, limericks, word play, and poems with metaphors or figurative language.
- Older elementary pupils prefer narrative poetry, limericks, and rhymed poetry, with sound elements; also humor and contemporary poetry.
- Older elementary pupils dislike free verse, haiku, and lyric poems, and metaphorical or descriptive and traditional words.

The reading of classics to pupils, with the excuse that they are "good" for children or will elevate their literary tastes, does not produce these desirable outcomes or promote reading interests (4). Leading stimulating discussions of their emotional and personal reactions to your presentations as well as to their own chosen readings stimulates their taste for literature. Arranging for many creative reactions through movement, writing, musical, and construction activities adds distinct values to the program. Assigning writing tasks or expecting creative writing after every experience, however, detracts from the positive attitudes (32). Oral responses to literature are more fluent and spontaneous than written responses. Students should be allowed to make their own choices from among the poems you have collected.

Teaching literary reading

WHAT WORKS	WHAT DOES NOT WORK
Selecting books according to expressed interests of pupils	Selecting books according to pupil ages or mental ages
Offering books in terms of pupil interest, not their exact difficulty	Offering low-level books to poor readers
Permitting self-selection	Offering books that children ought to read; books that you like
Allowing pupils to read very simple books, if they choose to	Expecting pupils to read only books at or above their reading levels
Recognizing that many books vary enough in interest level and in difficulty to be rejected	Expecting pupils to finish each book they borrow
Realizing that girls may read almost any type of book	Designating books as for boys or for girls
Offering children several books to choose from	Choosing a book for the child to read
Reading portions of interesting books aloud to class	Expecting children to develop fresh interests
Setting the example by reading while children do	Sending children to their seats to read while you do paper work
Permitting children to choose when and how they will share	Making sharing of books required each time
Arranging for children to sign up for a conference when they feel the need	Asking children to report to you personally on each book
Making a wide variety of books available in the classroom, by borrowing frequently from the school or public library	Sending children to the school or public library to bring back a book
Teaching children how to select a book they can read and thus perhaps enjoy	Permitting complete freedom of choice, as in the school library
Realizing that self-insight may not come spontaneously, without guidance and discussion	Expecting pupils to find answers to their own personal problems in books you select for them
Recognizing that many other media that bring ideas to children also strengthen their background for reading	Believing that only reading results in the improvement of reading ability

(continued)

WHAT WORKS	WHAT DOES NOT WORK
Arranging for use of the library resources for specific tasks related to classroom learning	Offering formal instruction in library usage and expecting this to promote it with children
Recognizing that many children feel very little need for reading, until they can learn to relate reading to their own goals	Expecting all children to want to read and to learn to read better
Perceiving the individual differences among pupils in verbal skills, as reflected in quantity and quality of their reading	Using stars, charts of the number of books read, presumably to motivate children
Offering better material in the areas of their interests and capitalizing on television presentations to evoke further reading	Warning children against excessive use of comic books, cheap magazines, and television
Encouraging reading by supplying many paperbacks as well as hardcover books	Expecting children to read and offering them only high-quality books
Understanding that some books are read for escape or fun, not for retention	Quizzing children for comprehension on each book they have read
Emphasizing development of racial identity and self-concept by offering children books on their own people	Offering a diet of books dealing with white middle-class family life
Influencing racial beliefs and prejudices by offering children books on many races and minority groups (and discussing the books)	Trying to affect prejudices by direct order or instruction
Strengthening learning in science and social science by biographies, stories of explorers, scientists, adventurers, etc.	Using library books only for recreational reading
Scheduling free reading time regularly to be spent in reading or preparation for sharing	Expecting children to read at home, and failing to provide time in class
Encouraging debates, panel discussions, mock interviews, choral reading, creation of plays as means of deepening appreciation	Emphasizing analysis of characters, writing forms and styles, memorization of teacher-selected poetry
Promoting enjoyment of the library by making it a center for book-related activities	Discouraging children by many library regulations about quiet, opening hours, number of books allowed, etc.

(*continued*)

WHAT WORKS	WHAT DOES NOT WORK
Promoting enjoyment of poetry by providing a wide selection; sharing children's choices	Choosing poetry for children to listen to or read
Reading aloud from many types of books to stimulate interest, relating your selection to contemporary events, time of year, holidays, weather, etc.	Limiting your selection for reading to children to "useful" books, as those related to social science (18)
Stimulating open discussion of author's intentions, feelings of the characters, realism of the book, etc. (18).	Discussing books in detail rather than in depth (18)
Making careful selection of book to read to children, based on their choice; reading only selected portion each day	Reading aloud an entire book, part by part, because it is "good for them"

These ideas presume that the teacher will have made the effort to bring a large number of poems to the classroom, and will provide opportunities for their sharing, in a planned program. Since no one really knows whether simply exposing children to interesting poetry or conducting lessons discussing and exploring them is better for promoting interest and enjoyment, the teacher will probably have to learn by trial and error and the reactions of the pupils which is most effective in the particular situation (30).

Remember that reading to children is a complex teaching skill. Appropriate materials, as guided by children's choices, must be selected; presentations rehearsed and performed well; and then time must be spent evaluating the selections with the children (14).

These suggestions assume that the teacher either knows or has ready means of determining pupils' reading interests to maintain a constant supply of appropriate materials. To accomplish this, some suggest the use of checklists of titles or questionnaires about the pupils' leisure-time activities. Responses to these are supposed to reflect the pupils' reading needs. But reading interests and free-time activities do not necessarily arise from the same motivations. Checking titles assumes a sophistication about the relationship of title to content not often present in elementary pupils. Reading interests are often motivated by desires for escapism, vicarious experiences, identification of self, information, and the like. These differ significantly from the need for peer recognition, physical prowess, and other motives for the participation in sports, hobbies, or the use of television. Rather, we suggest that the teacher be guided by the information obtained in individual and group conferences, pupils' reading records, and other spontaneous choices. Although we often generalize about the reading interests of children according to their ages or sex or intelligence, these are only rough guides, for reading interests tend to be highly individualized and even crystallized by about the fifth grade. Interests reflect socioeconomic status, sex, and the influence of the times, as in space travel, science, etc. The best source for teacher guidance in selecting books for the pupils is his or her own observations. The teacher must also be cognizant of the fact that peer choices are often more influential than his or her suggestions and capitalize on this in supporting and promoting interest groups.

Homework

In recent years, American schools, particularly the elementary school, have greatly changed in their attitudes toward homework. Many school systems have decided (1) correcting homework does not seem to produce more or better learning; (2) correcting homework involves too much work for teachers; (3) homework is often a pointless, unsupervised drill, often unrelated to the classroom lessons; and (4) teachers prefer to reteach and/or to review than to assign or correct homework.

However, there is positive evidence that homework can contribute to academic achievement. Jane M. Singh tested the effect of homework assignments over a sixteen-week period in intermediate grades. Both students and parents reacted favorably and there was a gain in test scores in reading, arithmetic, and social science but not in spelling or science. This trial with 400 students may not be conclusive for all students, but the results should certainly cause some schools to rethink their homework policy (29).

One problem seems to be pupil boredom with repetitive exercise drills such as those often assigned as homework. Teachers should be more creative in their assignments if they wish them to be effective. For example, if the social studies lesson is about agricultural products of the Midwest, students can be asked to search their kitchen cupboards at home, reading labels to find those products that contain Midwest produce such as wheat, corn, and pork. Any assignment that involves the student in search and recording, whether for social science, math, or whatever, will increase interest and promote retention. The information gathered should, of course, be shared and compared in class, enhancing the learning even more. In other words, homework should not be dull, dry, drill.

Nicholas Criscuolo suggests using the daily newspaper as a source for homework tasks (9). Among the assignments found there could be:

- *Sale items*—Practice writing your own sale ads.
- *Lost and found*—Write a story pretending that you have lost something.
- *Style*—Draw an inverted pyramid. Cut strips from an article to show how the information on who, what, when, where, why, and how are all clustered at the beginning of a newspaper article (the top of the pyramid). Paste strips on the drawing.

- *Comic strips*—Bring in samples of your favorites. Prepare to read or pantomime them to the class.
- *Local celebrities*—Try to arrange an interview with a local celebrity. Use a list of questions prepared with the class's help. Write up answers and report back to the class.
- *Celebrities*—Assemble a scrapbook on a favorite celebrity. Prepare a brief biographical sketch with the aid of the library.
- *Restaurants*—Find menus given in ads. Try to get your family to go to one of the restaurants. Write up your visit—atmosphere, prices, service, the food, specialities of the house—for the class Gourmet Review Book.
- *Reviews*—Write brief reviews of a book or movie and compare it with the newspaper reports.
- *Headlines*—Cut out some headlines, and group and classify them.
- *Holidays*—Cut out pictures symbolizing holidays and special occasions. Use these as the basis of a language experience story of your holiday.

Discussion Questions

1. What are your reactions to the deemphasis upon the basal reader and the substitution of reading instruction in content fields?

2. Prepare a unit in social science or science such as that illustrated in this chapter. Be prepared to explain your ideas on combining content and reading instruction for pupils of varying reading abilities.

3. Experiment in your class with instruction and practice in more efficient ways of reading and studying in a content area. Be prepared to report your observations and evaluation of the outcomes.

4. Discuss the possibilities of individualizing reading in the intermediate grades. For what types of pupils, in what kinds of materials would this be possible, in your opinion?

5. If you have witnessed any of the literature programs described by Odland, describe what the program was like.

6. What kind of a literature program did you experience when you were in elementary school? In secondary school? What is your evaluation of those experiences?

7. Visit the intermediate grades of a school during science, social science, math, or literature lessons. What changes, if any, would you make in the procedures you observe based on the ideas in this chapter?

References

1. Adams, Abby, Carnine, Douglas, and Gersten, Russell, "Instructional Strategies for Studying Content Area Texts in the Intermediate Grades," *Reading Research Quarterly*, 18 (1982), 27–55.

2. Anderson, Thomas H., *Study Skills and Learning Strategies.* Technical Report 104. Champaign, Ill.: Center for the Study of Reading, University of Illinois, May 1978.

3. Boothroy, Bonnie, and Donham, Jean, "Listening to Literature: An All School Program," *Reading Teacher*, 34 (April 1981), 772–774.

4. Braam, Leonard, and Walker, D. E., "Subject Teachers Awareness of Reading Skills," *Journal of Reading*, 16 (May 1973), 608–611.

5. Brown, Ann L., and Campione, Joseph C., *Memory Strategies in Learning: Teaching Children to Study Strategically.* Technical Report 22. University of Illinois. ED 136 234, 1977.

6. Brown, Ann L., Campione, Joseph C., and Day, J. D., "Learning to Learn: On Training Students to Learn from Texts," *Educational Leadership*, 10 (1981), 14–21.

7. Buys, Donna, "Memory: Why We Remember...Why We Forget," *Health Magazine* (June 1976).

8. Crewe, James, and Hultgren, Dayton, "What Does Research Really Say About Study Skills?" in *The Psychology of Reading Behavior*, George B. Schick and Merrill M. May, eds. Eighteenth Yearbook, National Reading Conference, 1969, 75–78.

9. Criscuolo, Nicholas, "Creative Homework with the Newspaper," *Reading Teacher*, 34 (March 1981), 921–922.

10. Cullinan, Bernice E., "Research Report—Teaching Children's Literature, " *Elementary English*, 49 (November 1972), 1028–1050.

11. Cunningham, James W., and Ballew, Hunter, "Solving Word Problems Solving," *Reading Teacher*, 36 (April 1983), 836–839.

12. Earle, Richard A., "Reading and Mathematics Research in the Classroom," in *Fusing Reading Skills and Content*, H. Alan Robinson and Ellen Lamar Thomas, eds. Newark, Del.: International Reading Association, 1969, 162–170.

13. Ehrhardt, Harryette B., "If We Don't, They Won't" *Reading Teacher*, 22 (January 1969), 377–381.

14. Farley, Paul, *Civil War Tales.* New Market, Md.: Daisy Publications, 1983.

15. Fenwick, G. and Evans, G., "An Analysis of Story Reading Skills," *Reading*, 12 (July 1978), 22–29.

16. Frase, Lawrence T., and Silbiger, Francene, "Some Adaptive Consequences of Searching for Information in a Text," *American Educational Research Journal*, 7 (November 1970), 553–560.

17. Goudey, Charles E., "Reading—Directed or Not?" *Elementary School Journal*, 70 (February 1970), 245–247.

18. Huck, Charlotte S., "Strategies for Improving Interest and Appreciation in Literature," in *Reaching Children and Young People Through Literature*, Helen W. Painter, ed. Newark, Del.: International Reading Association, 1971, 37–45.

19. Johnson, Roger E., "Can the Teaching of Reading Stop When Dick and Jane Are Put Away?" *Florida Reading Quarterly*, 6 (June 1970), 14–23.

20. Johnson, Roger E., and Vardian, Eileen B., "Reading, Readability and Social Studies," *Reading Teacher*, 26 (February 1973), 483–488.

21. Karlin, Robert, "Library-Book Borrowing vs. Library-Book Reading," *Reading Teacher*, 16 (November 1962), 77–81.

22. La Budde, Constance, and Smith, Richard J., "Librarians Look at Remedial Reading," *Reading Teacher*, 27 (December 1973), 263–269.

23. James V. McConnell, *Understanding Human Behavior*. New York: Holt, Rinehart and Winston, 1974.

24. Naturella, Margaret A., "Of Cabbage and Kings: Or What Kinds of Poetry Young Children Like," *Language Arts*, 56 (April 1979), 380–385.

25. Odland, Norine, "Planning a Literature Program for the Elementary School," *Language Arts*, 56 (April 1979), 363–367.

26. Palmatier, Robert A., "Comparison of Four Notetaking Procedures," *Journal of Reading*, 14 (January 1971), 215–240.

27. Paulin, Mary Ann. *Creative Uses of Children's Literature*. Hamden, Conn.: Library Professional Publications, 1982.

28. Rudie, Helen N., "Poetry in Basal Readers: Perished or Cherished?" *Elementary English*, 52 (January 1975), 136–140.

29. Singh, Jane M., "Research in Homework as the Motivating Factor in Reading Achievement," *Journal of Reading Behavior*, 3 (Summer 1970–71), 51–60.

30. Sloyer, Shirlee, *Reader's Theatre*. Urbana, Ill.: National Council Teachers of English, 1982.

31. Smith, C. C. and Bean, T. W., "The Guided Writing Procedure: Integrating Content Teaching and Writing Improvement," *Reading World*, 19 (1980), 290–294.

32. Smith, Richard, and Hansen, Lee H., "Integrating Reading and Writing: Effects on Children's Attitudes," *Elementary School Journal*, 76 (January 1976) 238–245.

33. Spache, George D., "Improving Reading in Subject Matter Areas," in *Seventh Annual Yearbook*, Southwest Reading Conference, Fort Worth, Texas, 1968, 30–38.

34. Spache, George D., "Types and Purposes of Reading in Various Curriculum Fields," *Reading Teacher*, 11 (February 1958), 158–164.

35. Spache, George D., "Effective Reading in the Content Fields," and "The Development of Work-Study Habits and Skills," in *Reading Attitudes and Skills Needed for Our Times*, Paul C. Berg, ed. Columbia, S.C.: School of Education, University of South Carolina, 1960, 15–16, 37–60.

36. Spache, George D., *Good Reading for Poor Readers*. Champaign, Ill.: Garrard Publishing, 1978, 189.

37. Spache, George D., and Berg, Paul C., *The Art of Efficient Reading*, 4th ed. New York: Macmillan, 1984.

38. Stoddard, Ann H., "Selecting Children's Books with Global Perspectives," *Florida Reading Quarterly*, 17 (June 1981), 7–9, 33.

39. Swain, Emma Halstead, "Using Comic Books to Teach Reading and Language Arts," *Journal of Reading*, 22 (December 1978), 253–258.

40. Terry, C. Ann, *Children's Poetry Preferences: A National Survey of Upper Elementary Grades*. Urbana, Il.: National Council of Teachers of English, 1974.

41. Tierney, Robert J., Readance, John E., and Dishner, Ernest K., *Reading Strategies and Practices: A Guide for Improving Instruction*. Boston: Allyn and Bacon, 1980.

42. Wilmon, Betty, "Reading in the Content Areas: A New Math Terminology List for the Primary Grades," *Elementary English*, 48 (May 1971), 463–471.

Professional References

Anderson, T. H., *Study Skills and Learning Strategies.* Technical Report 104. Urbana, Il., Center for the Study of Reading, University of Illinois, 1978.

Atwood, Beth S., *Building a Map Skills Program.* Belmont, Calif.: Pitman Learning, 1976.

Catterson, Jane H. ed., *Children and Literature.* Newark, Del.: International Reading Association, 1970.

Chambers, Aidan, *Introducing Books to Children.* Boston: Horn Book, 1983.

Cheyney, Arnold, *Teaching Reading Skills Through the Newspaper.* Newark, Del.: International Reading Association, 1971.

Christenbury, Leila, editor, *Developing Lifelong Readers.* Urbana, Ill.: National Council of Teachers of English, 1981.

Davis, Dorothy C., *Reading Through the Newspaper.* Geneva, Ill.: Paladin House Publications, 1980.

Earle, Richard A., *Teaching Reading and Mathematics.* Newark, Del.: International Reading Association, 1976.

Estes, Thomas H., and Vaughan, Joseph L. Jr., *Reading and Learning in the Content Classroom: Diagnostic and Instructional Strategies.* Boston: Allyn and Bacon, 1978.

Fenton, Edwin, ed., *New Social Studies for the Slow Learner.* New York: Holt, Rinehart and Winston, 1973.

Forgan, Harry W., and Mangrum, Charles T., *Teaching Content Area Reading Skills.* Columbus: Charles E. Merrill, 1981.

Gensler, Kennereth, and Nyhart, Nina, *The Poetry Connection: An Anthology of Contemporary Poems with Ideas to Stimulate Children's Writing.* New York: Teachers and Writers Press, 1978.

Gillespie, John, and Lembo, Diana, *Introducing Books: A Guide for the Middle Grades.* New York: R. R. Bowker, 1970.

Harms, Jeanne McLain, *Comprehension and Literature.* Dubuque: Kendall/Hunt, 1982.

Herber, Harold L., *Teaching Reading in the Content Areas.* Englewood Cliffs, N.J.: Prentice-Hall, 1978.

Hodges, Pauline, *A Resource Book for Teaching Reading in the Content Areas.* Dubuque: Kendall/Hunt, 1980.

Karlin, Robert, *Teaching Elementary Reading: Principles and Strategies.* New York: Harcourt Brace Jovanovich, 1980.

Koch, Kenneth, *Rose, Where Did You Get That Red?* New York: Random House, 1974 (a guide to presenting poetry and stimulating its production).

Lapp, Diane, and Flood, James, *Teaching Reading to Every Child.* New York: Macmillan.

Larned, Phyllis, and Randall, Nick, *Reading a Newspaper.* Hayward, Calif.: Janus Books, 1978.

Lunstrom, John, and Tayler, Bob, *Teaching Reading in the Social Studies.* Newark, Del.: International Reading Association, 1978.

McKee, Paul, and Durr, William K. *Reading: A Program of Instruction for the Elementary School.* Boston: Houghton Mifflin, 1966.

Mongillo, John, et al., *Reading about Science.* Manchester, Mo.: Webster Division, McGraw-Hill, 1975.

Moore, David W., Readance, John E., and Rickelman, Robert J., *Prereading Activities for Content Area Reading and Learning*. Newark, Del.: International Reading Association, 1982.

Piercey, Dorothy, *Reading Activities in the Content Areas*. Boston: Allyn and Bacon, 1982.

Plays, Inc. 8 Arlington Street, Boston, Mass. 02116 (a catalog of plays).

Readance, John E., Bean, T. W., and Baldwin, R. S., *Content Area Reading: An Integrated Approach*. Dubuque: Kendall/Hunt, 1981.

Readers' Theatre Script Service, P.O. Box 178333, San Diego, Calif. A catalog of plays.

Rembert, Emmato and Emma, *Alternative Strategies: Reading in the Elementary School*. Dubuque: Kendall/Hunt, 1979.

Robinson, H. Alan, *Teaching Reading and Study Strategies: The Content Areas*. Boston: Allyn and Bacon, 1978.

Robinson, H. Alan, *Strategies for Reading Paragraphs*. Boston: Allyn and Bacon, 1978.

Roser, Nancy, and Frith, Margaret, eds., *Children's Choices: Teaching with Books Children Like*. Newark, Del.: International Reading Association, 1983.

Sargent, Eileen E., *The Newspaper as a Teaching Tool*. Norwalk, Conn.: The Reading Laboratory, 1975.

Short, J. Rodney, and Dickerson, Bev, *The Newspaper: An Alternative Textbook*, Belmont, Calif.: Fearon Pitman Learning, 1980.

Sloyer, Shirlee, *Readers Theatre: Story Dramatization in the Classroom*. Urbana, Ill.: National Council of Teachers of English, 1982.

Stewig, John Warren, and Sebesta, Sam L., eds., *Using Literature in the Elementary Classroom*. Urbana, Ill.: National Council of Teachers of English, 1978.

Spache, George D., *Good Reading for the Disadvantaged Reader*. Champaign, Ill.: Garrard Publishing, 1975. Graded and annotated lists of books to promote reading and self-concept of minority groups.

Spache, George D., *Good Reading for Poor Readers*. Champaign, Ill.: Garrard Publishing, 1978. Tenth edition of a resource book in instructional and reading materials of all types.

Instructional Materials

This listing does not include the many collections of children's books, book clubs, or adapted and simplified books that form such a significant part of the reading program. See Spache, *Good Reading for Poor Readers* (above) for such lists.

Barnes, Donald L., and Burgdorf, Arlene, *Study Skills for Information Retrieval Series*. Boston: Allyn and Bacon, 1979.

Brown, Diane, *Notemaking*. Woburn, Mass.: Curriculum Associates. An exercise book for middle school pupils.

Clymer, Theodore, ed., *Read Better—Learn More*. Lexington, Mass.: Ginn, 1972. Three paperbacks for middle schools.

Dale, Level E., et al., *Reading Skills for Social Studies (Using Maps Charts and Graphs)*. Cleveland: Modern Curriculum Press, 1980. Four exercise books for grades three to six.

Dale, Level E., et al., *Reading Skills for Social Studies: Understanding Concepts*. Cleveland: Modern Curriculum Press, 1980. Workbooks for grades three to six.

Early, Margaret, ed., *Bookmark Reading Program: Skills Readers*. New York: Harcourt Brace Jovanovich.

EDL Study Skills Library. New York: EDL/McGraw-Hill. Separate kits for grades three to six.

Follett Student Atlas Worksheets. Chicago: Follett Publishing, 1979. Spiritmasters in map skills.

Furbush, Polly H., et al., *Thirty Lessons in Outlining, Level 1*. Woburn, Mass.: Curriculum Associates.

Hill, Herbert D. Jr., and McKenna, Joan, *The Outlining Kit*. Woburn, Mass.

Insel, Eunice, and Rabin, A. N., *How to Read in the Content Areas*. Freeport, N.Y.: Educational Activities. Cassettes, activity books, or ditto masters for grades three to four and five to six.

Job, Kenneth, and Wolf, Lois, *Skills for Understanding Maps and Globes*. Chicago: Follett Publishing, 1977. Exercise book.

Lapp, Diane, and Flood, James, *Clues for Better Reading*. Woburn, Mass.: Curriculum Associates. A kit of activity cards, spirit masters, and a teacher's guide to promote comprehension in the content areas in grades four to six.

Liddle, William, ed., *Reading for Concepts*. Manchester, Mo.: Webster Division, McGraw-Hill, 1970. Eight-book series in reading in science and social science.

Maney, Ethel, S., *Reading–Study Skills*. Elizabethtown, Pa.: Continental Press. Training in locating, evaluating, selecting, and organizing information.

Martin, Bill Jr., *Sounds of Language*. New York: Holt, Rinehart and Winston. Literature with emphasis upon rhyme, rhythm, and onomatopoeia for grades one to six.

Moore, George N., and Woodruff, G. Willard, *Writing Research Reports*. Woburn, Mass.: Curriculum Associates. Exercises in notetaking, organization, and reporting for middle schools.

Murray, Claire, *Library Reference Books*. Los Angeles: Bowmar/Noble. A four book series for middle schools.

Naslund, Robert A., et al., *SRA Graph and Picture Study Skills Kit*. Chicago: Science Research Associates, 1977.

Naslund, Robert A., et al., *SRA Map and Globe Skills Kit*. Chicago: Science Research Associates, 1977.

Naslund, Robert, A., et al., *SRA Organizing and Reporting Skills Kit*. Chicago: Science Research Associates, 1978. For elementary grades.

Reader's Digest Science Reader. Pleasantville, N.Y.: Reader's Digest Association. Reading selections and exercises for grades four to six.

Reading Skills for the Content Areas. New York: Holt Instructional Resources. Kits of activity cards and paperbacks for grades four to six.

Reference Skills. Chicago: Coronet. Cassettes and workbooks as well as teacher's guide for grades four to six.

Report Writing Workshop. New York: Holt Instructional Resources. For grades four to six.

Rushdoony, Haig A., *The Language of Maps*. Belmont, Calif.: Fearon Pitman Learning. Blackline master in reading, making and understanding maps, for grades four to six.

Scope/Reading Skills. New York: Scholastic. Exercises in study and reference skills for middle schools.

Skills Practice Books. Evanston, Ill.: McDougal, Littell. A nine-book series.

Smith, Nila B., et al. *Be A Better Reader*. Englewood Cliffs, N.J.: Prentice-Hall. A three-book series for middle schools.

Spargo, Edward, and Harris Raymond, *Content Skills Series—Middle Level*. Providence, R.I.: Jamestown Publishers, 1978. Separate workbook for each content area, probably for middle grades.

Tomei, Beatrice, *Reference Skills and Library Skills*. Elizabethtown, Pa.: Continental Press. Duplicating masters for intermediate grades.

Williamson, Ann Pollard, *How to Read a Newspaper*. Providence, R.I.: Jamestown Publishers. Three book series for middle schools.

Audiovisual Materials

Baker and Taylor Co. P.O. Box 230, Momence, Ill. A general source for all types of aids and books. Write for catalogs.

Basic Study Skills. Boulder, Col.: Learning Tree. Three strips.

Better Study Skills. Troy, Mich.: Educational Corp. of America. Ten tapes, each on a particular study skill.

Constructing Reports. Wilmette, Ill.: Encyclopedia Britannica Films Inc. Six strips for intermediate and upper elementary grades.

Developing Study Skills. Chicago, Ill.: Coronet. Eight cassettes or sound filmstrips for grades four to six.

Gordon, Sol, *Signs*. Freeport, N.Y.: Educational Activities. Four strips on reading store, food, street, etc. signs.

Library and Reference Skills. Big Spring, Tex.: Creative Visuals. Tapes for intermediate and upper elementary.

Library Skills. Santa Monica, Calif.: BFA Educational Media. Six strips plus records or cassettes for intermediate grades.

Map Competency. Chicago, Ill.: Coronet. Six sound filmstrips for grades six to eight.

Map Language. Chicago, Ill.: Coronet. Six sound filmstrips for grades four to six.

Map Mastery. Chicago, Ill.: Coronet. Ten cassettes and response books for grades seven to eight.

Study and Reading Skills. Jamaica, N.Y.: Eye Gate House. Series of strips for intermediate grades.

Teaching Map Reading Skills in Elementary Schools. Momence, Il.: Baker and Taylor. Strips, records, tapes, and cassettes. See catalog.

Wheeler, Helen R., *Learning the Library*. Freeport, N.Y.: Educational Activities. Four strips, records, and manuals plus a teacher's guide.

Reading Improvement for Culturally Different Pupils

Ballesteros, Octavio A., *Preparing Teachers for Bilingual Education: Basic Readings.* Washington, D.C.: University Press of America, 1979.

Barbe, Walter, B., *Reading Adventures in Spanish and English.* Columbus: Highlights for Children, 1977. Stories and exercises in Spanish and English for grades three to five.

Cabrera, Y. Arturo, ed., *Strategies for the Education of Chicanos.* San Jose, Calif.: Sierra Publications, 1978.

Cheyney, Arnold B., *Teaching Children of Different Cultures in the Classroom: A Language Approach.* Columbus: Charles E. Merrill Publishing, 1976.

Classroom Plays. Elizabethtown, Pa.: Continental Press. Duplicating masters for three original one-act plays.

Cordasco, Francisco, *Bilingual Schooling in the U.S.: A Sourcebook for Educational Personnel.* New York: McGraw-Hill, 1976.

Double Play and *Triple Play.* Los Angeles, Calif.: Bowmar/Noble Publishing Co. Each is a kit of two-three plays, worksheets and teacher's guide.

Durrell, Donald D. and Crossley, B. Alice, *Favorite Plays for Classroom Reading* and *Thirty Plays for Classroom Reading.* Boston, Mass.: Plays, Inc. One-act plays for intermediate and upper elementary students.

Oral Language Expansion. Long Branch, N.J.: Kimbo Educational Co. A kit of strips or cassettes, ditto masters, language games, for reading and creative dramatics, plus a teacher's guide.

11 Steps Toward Individualized Reading

Teachers who are familiar only with group instruction in reading find it difficult to conceive of other approaches or to visualize the ways in which they might begin to use these unfamiliar individualized procedures. Teachers accustomed to following the planned routine of a basal system or some other structured approach tend to doubt their ability to achieve a thorough skill-building program within the framework of an individualized program. For some these are probably legitimate doubts, for they have become so dependent upon the teacher's manual for planning.

Teachers who move toward individualization must show initiative and judgment in acquiring and familiarizing themselves with children's reading materials. In some instances they will even create some of these materials or stimulate the pupils to do so. The teachers must gradually learn how to utilize the information gained in individual and small-group conferences as a basis for planning for materials, for small-group instruction, and for individual pupil needs. Even before this, they must learn how to initiate, to schedule, and to conduct meaningful, profitable conferences with individuals or a small group. These teachers will gradually evolve record-keeping techniques that satisfy their needs, and teach their pupils how to maintain useful records of their reading and skill development.

No proponent of individualization suggests that such a program makes fewer demands upon teaching skill than other instructional approaches. But at the same time, practically all teachers who learn this approach find it a stimulating professional experience that they wish to continue.

Why Individualize?

As part of its Early Childhood Education program, the State Department of Education of California conducted a study of schools with increasing or decreasing reading scores. The study attempted to identify the positive and negative factors that contributed to changes in the reading achievement of children over a period of at least three years. Among the factors that seemed to result in reading gains were the following:

- The initial teaching of skills was done by the teacher, not by some media, material, or learning station, or commercial program of worksheets or workbooks.
- Learning stations were used to reinforce or practice skills already introduced by the teacher. The stations were not considered to be instructional devices.

- Diagnosis of pupil needs based on tests and pupil classroom performances was an integral part of teaching and learning; follow-up included re-teaching by the teacher or aide rather than assigning drill material.
- Children's ability to use new concepts or skills was monitored as part of the instructional program during follow-up activities.
- The heart of the program consisted of the teacher paying close and frequent attention to how each child responded to instruction. This involved a great deal of interaction between the child and the teacher (or aide) with an emphasis upon the teacher's listening to the student and checking upon his or her work at short intervals.
- In schools in which the curriculum consisted entirely or mostly of reading as in a management system, the reading scores were declining, whereas in schools in which pupils had opportunities to use and apply reading skills in a number of curricular areas, scores were increasing.
- Reading scores declined in schools in which a reading program was imposed upon teachers by order of the administration. Such programs were inconsistently and unenthusiastically implemented.
- Reading scores declined in schools that lacked a balanced variety of reading skills; e.g., in which there was overemphasis on decoding or phonic analysis and underemphasis upon story writing and comprehension. Pupils in such unbalanced programs scored well in phonic skills, but very low in comprehension in standardized tests.

Throughout this California study there was the constant theme that schools which produce good readers move toward flexible reading procedures. Instruction is not necessarily on a one-to-one basis, even with aides in the classroom. But there is obviously considerable interaction between the teacher or aide and individual pupils or small groups.

Organizational Steps

The primary problem for a teacher who is beginning to use individualized approaches is an adequate supply of reading and instructional materials. Some experienced teachers suggest a minimum class library of three to five trade books per child. In addition, there must be a continued flow of books borrowed from such sources as the school or public library, children's home libraries, or a school depository. Available materials should include not only a relatively constant supply of trade books but ample supplies of a wide variety of other materials. Among these are stacks of old child and adult magazines, an atlas or two, an almanac, an encyclopedia, several different dictionaries, a sampling of science and social science textbooks and reference books, a picture file, a clipping file, and a pamphlet or leaflet file. A variety of basal and supplementary readers and a selection of basal reader workbooks, both extending over several grade ranges, are highly desirable. Current subscriptions to children's newspapers and magazines and, perhaps, to an inexpensive children's book club are most useful. A variety of games for skill building may be selected from among those listed in this chapter or constructed according to the suggestions of Evelyn B. Spache. If the budget permits, the materials list may include an *SRA Reading Laboratory,* several of the *EDL Study Skills Kits,* and the other kits useful in content field reading mentioned earlier. Teachers may supplement the skill-building exercises present in their collection of basal reader workbooks by selections of phonics, word recognition, word attack, and vocabulary workbooks perhaps chosen from the list in *Good Reading for Poor Readers* or those listed in the next chapters.

To keep abreast of new trade books, the teacher should have access to such sources as the book reviews in *The Reading Teacher, Elementary English, The Horn Book, Bulletin of the Center for Children's Books* (Graduate Library School, University of Chicago), and the listings in the *Children's Catalog.*)

Even more readily available as sources of new books are the annual children's book review sections of leading newspapers, such as the following:

- *Book Week* (*World Journal Tribune, The Washington Post, Chicago Sun-Times*) The Fall Children's Issue of October 30 (Business Office, *Book Week,* 230 W. 41st St. New York, N.Y. 10036)
- *Boston Herald Traveler and Record American* Children's Book Fair Supplement of October 30 (Subscription Dept., *Boston Herald Traveler and Record American,* 300 Harrison Avenue, Boston, Mass. 02106)
- *Chicago Tribune* Books for Children Supplement of November 6 (Tom Tincher, Rm. 1212, *Chicago Tribune,* Chicago, Ill. 60611)
- *Christian Science Monitor* Children's Book Week Feature of November 3 (Circulation Dept., *Christian Science Monitor,* 1 Norway St., Boston, Mass. 02115)
- *Cleveland Press* Book Fair Supplement of November 1 (Public Service Counter, First Floor, *Cleveland Press,* 901 Lakeside Ave., Cleveland, Oh. 44114)
- *The Columbus Dispatch* Special Children's Book Section of November 6 (Circulation Dept., *Columbus Dispatch,* Columbus, Oh. 43216)
- *Denver Post* Children's Book Section of October 30 (Mail Subscription Dept., *Denver Post,* Denver, Colo.)
- *Detroit Free Press* Children's Book Section of October 30 (William Benson, Advertising Dept., *Detroit Free Press,* Detroit, Mich. 48231)

- *Louisville Courier-Journal* Children's Book Section of October 30 (Dispatch Room, *Courier-Journal*, Louisville, Ky. 40202)
- *The New York Times* Children's Book Section of November 5 (Subscription Mgr., *The New York Times*, 229 W. 43rd St. New York, N.Y. 10036)
- *San Francisco Chronicle* Children's Book Section of November 6 (Book Dept., *San Francisco Chronicle*, 860 Howard St., San Francisco, Calif. 94103)

It would be presumptuous to try to list the films, filmstrips, flat pictures, recordings, plays, and poetry collections that are an essential part of instruction in reading. Each teacher will use these devices according to the facilities and budget available. In the opinions of many observers, some teachers may use them too infrequently and haphazardly. They may even ignore those constructed as special aids to the basal materials, such as those offered by a number of basal reader publishers. Among other tools, these publishers offer free series of bulletins on reading, filmstrips correlated to their texts, newsletters, and monographs, and they should be utilized.

Lists of books recommended by various experts are given in Appendix I. Series books, epecially those of high interest and low vocabulary or easy readability, are listed in Appendix II. Most of these lists of books are compiled by committee opinion and offer annotations to enable the teacher to recognize the nature of each book's content. The groups of experts usually also offer an opinion as to the readability level of each book, or the ages of the children for whom they believe the book is suited.

Teachers should not be naive enough to believe that a materials collection such as outlined here will be waiting for them the first day of school. You will acquire these supplies slowly as a gradual approach to individualization makes them increasingly necessary. Even the ordering of new trade books during the first year may be delayed until you are asked to suggest a list for purchase for the classroom or the school library. Meanwhile you will depend on the existing materials in those and other sources. Your experiences during the year, however, will help you to learn the types of books and reference materials you should request.

A good part of the problem of selecting and grading the classroom library is being met by book collections offered by various publishers. Some of those listed at the end of the chapter have the advantages of graded books, prepared questions on vocabulary and comprehension, and suggestions for follow-up activities: ICT's *Reading Bookshelf* offers parallel books and tapes or records, for whatever value a two-way presentation has in learning to read.

These book collections, and others mentioned later, can be of great assistance to teachers moving toward individualization. None of them has enough variety or breadth to supply the total needs of an ordinary class of thirty or so pupils for an entire year. But, at the beginning of the individualized program, they do offer books of known reading levels, aid in assessing the pupils' reactions and learnings from the books, and help in planning related follow-up activities.

The teacher must have some estimate of the relative difficulties or grade levels of these books. If the books are part of the classroom library, the teacher may wish to paste colored stickers on them or make a secret mark somewhere in the book to indicate the grade level. The fact that children may recognize that the books with a pink sticker are more difficult than those marked with another color is not greatly important. They would soon evolve their own methods of estimating the difficulty of books in any event. They learn that the difficulty of a book is often an individual matter dependent, in a large degree, upon their interest in the content. Pupils are not overly concerned about the exact level of each book they read, for they do not progress directly from easy to more difficult books, but tend to alternate in levels. The major purpose of the labeling or grading of books is not to promote competition among the pupils but to facilitate the teacher's record keeping. This information is significant to the teacher to enable him or her to observe progress, guide children's choices, suggest other books of appropriate difficulty, select additional books for the classroom library, and the like.

In general, some basal readers are reasonably accurate in their labels, but unfortunately textbooks and trade books may often be incorrectly graded or even lacking in any indication of their grade levels. Estimates may be made by applying appropriate readability formulas such as the Spache formula for primary grades (49) or the Dale–Chall (13) for intermediate grades. These formulas or other methods of evaluation have been applied to a great many books in the lists by one of the present writers (50), Condit (10), Dees (16), Groff (22), and Sister Julitta (28). Cataloging and labeling of the classroom library, as well as suggestions for book orders, can be greatly facilitated by use of these evaluations.

Teacher Readiness for Individualization

Teachers are prone to plan in terms of pupil readiness for certain instructional procedures. Logically, teacher readiness should also be considered. You can't plunge into an approach to teaching reading without reviewing your readiness. An instructional approach differing from the structured basal system requires a teacher who has self-confidence and knowledge of reading behaviors. Answer these questions about yourself to help you determine whether you are ready to move toward individualization.

Personal Characteristics
1. Can I organize several activities that will function in various groups of children concurrently?
2. Do I feel comfortable with students moving between activities without my direct control?

3. Am I confident enough of my knowledge and management skills to convince others that I know what I am doing and why?
4. Do I have a working knowledge of word recognition and vocabulary and comprehension learning strategies that I will need to teach?

Skill Needs
1. Am I familiar with the materials that are available for my use?
2. Do I know how to go about securing additional materials?
3. Can I construct questions that will stimulate pupils to critical reading?
4. Can I diagnose pupils' errors, prescribe corrective steps, and plan for reteaching?
5. Do I have a system of recording student progress that will enable me to make evaluations and to report to parents?

How to Start Individualizing

Perhaps one of the chief advantages of the individualized approach is the flexibility with which it may be adapted to teacher or pupil readiness. Conferences may be introduced gradually into any type of classroom organization and thus eventually substituted for more conventional procedures. Some teachers are capable of planning and organizing the procedure rather readily. Other teachers find it difficult to adjust to a relatively large number of individualized or small-group activities. But it is quite feasible for all teachers to develop a personal program at their own pace beginning, as suggested earlier, with a few of the better readers. Later the approach may be extended to more of the superior group and then gradually to average pupils, as teacher skill in planning and directing the program increases.

Pupil readiness for individualized methods is second only in significance to teacher readiness. Pupils accustomed to basal reading procedures vary in their abilities to adjust to and profit from more individualized methods. Lack of experience with small-group or independent work or dependence upon constant teacher supervision and support may militate against initial adjustment to the new procedures for some pupils. Dependent pupils need constant support and encouragement, ask for assistance frequently, and show uncertainty and lack of adaptability in new situations. Withdrawn pupils lack initiative, persistence, and good qualities of attention. Our own research into the personalities of children who experience reading difficulties indicates that the number of depressed or withdrawn pupils is relatively small (49). But they do present problems that the teacher must attempt to solve for successful classroom management.

In planning the experiences necessary for introducing pupils to independent work, the importance of conveying to pupils some understanding of the reasons for the new procedures must be emphasized. Teachers should clarify the purposes of the individual conference, the reasons for the freedom of choice of materials, as well as the plans for the working procedures of small groups, teams, or committees.

The problem of providing leadership and direction for the small-group work that is characteristic of the individualized approach is often met by the training of pupil leaders. Initially, pupils who are qualified both by personality and reading skill may be selected by the teacher to function as team or group leaders. As the program expands, these positions are rotated among the other pupils to extend the leadership experiences to all. Among the responsibilities that pupil leaders may be helped to assume are the following:

- Helping the group to secure needed materials at the beginning of the work period and to replace them at the close.
- Answering the group's questions or relaying these to the teacher when convenient for the teacher.
- Helping the group to have a clear-cut idea of their purpose and of the directions outline earlier by the teacher.
- Checking progress of the group, giving assistance or directions where needed. Reporting special problems to the teacher.
- Helping members of the group to learn to function as leaders.

Teachers vary greatly in the manner in which they initiate the use of individual conferences. Some begin by substituting a small-group conference for the reading circle. The children assemble as usual but use silent reading in place of oral. Each child may be questioned privately on comprehension and reactions. A variant of this is the substitution of a book chosen by the child for the usual basal reader, followed by a group or teacher–pupil conference or both. Other teachers begin by using the parallel readings suggested in the basal reader manual as a substitute or supplement to the basal reader unit. Or, children are permitted self-selection of books related in content to the unit. These selections may then form the basis of small-group or teacher–pupil conferences. Another approach is the encouragement of self-pacing by the pupils in the basal material. As a result of self-pacing, simultaneous reading of the same story in the group rapidly becomes impossible and the group activity gravitates toward individualized conferences. Special reading assignments for an individual or a committee and projects involving self-selected reading, both of which are later shared with the class and with the teacher in conferences, are other initiating steps.

Pupil Readiness for Individualization

There are many indications and clues for the teacher who is attempting to initiate individualized reading with gifted or average pupils or, when it is feasible, with some of the slow-learning pupils. We have outlined our suggestions

Checklist for readiness for individualized reading

READING BEHAVIORS (Experience Chart Level)

Does the child

show recall or recognition of words and phrases on charts or in isolation, and almost daily learning of sight vocabulary?

ask for identification of words or letters he or she is interested in—as in signs, book titles, magazines—and identify some spontaneously with increasing frequency?

try to identify some words by spelling orally, and practice copying words, without demand; make some reversals in reading or writing, tending to correct them spontaneously or when queried?

enjoy books, pictures, picture sequences, scrapbooks, etc.; choose them during free time; select favorites and use them over again; ask the teacher to read from them; share findings with group?

READING BEHAVIORS (Primary and Intermediate Grade Levels)

Is the child able to

care for materials, borrow and return, take turns?

read, study, complete assignments independently or in small groups?

share materials, work cooperatively, wait turn with teacher, lead small-group work constructively and without undue friction, or follow another leader?

follow through on individualized reading assignments or group projects, and show realistic self-selection when given the opportunity?

show independence in word recognition skills, and reasonable command of sight and meaning vocabulary, insofar as these have been taught in the program?

show reasonable comprehension (60 to 70 percent) in materials at his or her instructional and independent reading levels?

evidence distinct reading interests or tastes; want to explore certain areas, to contribute or share findings with the group?

of criteria for judging pupil readiness for this type of program. The Checklist for Readiness for Individualized Reading outlines the characteristics and behaviors that the teacher would observe certainly differ with the grade placement and reading level of the pupil.

In later primary and intermediate grades, pupil readiness for individualized reading naturally demands different behaviors and skills. During the early reading stages in which experience charts are used, the teacher must again make judgments regarding pupils who may be ready for individualized reading. At this level, we have suggested a group of reading behaviors, evidences of learning and of interest, to help distinguish such pupils. Continually throughout subsequent grades, the teacher must make judgments before introducing pupils to individualized reading. These judgments require a slightly different group of criteria, for the children are no longer beginning readers nor in the very early stages. At these levels, the teacher's judgments will be based largely on children's demonstrations of independence in working habits and their command of fundamental or basal reading skills.

Some teachers would prefer a description of the exact type of behavior which satisfies each of the suggested criteria. But these descriptions would only succeed in spelling out the authors' peculiar ideas about child development and classroom management. No one can really dictate or even suggest to teachers precisely how they should operate, how much independent child activity they can successfully stimulate and direct, how many groups and subgroups they can instruct efficiently, how many effective conferences they need to or can give each pupil per week, etc. These are skills that vary greatly from one teacher to another, as teachers differ in competence, organizing ability, experience, and many related abilities. The Checklist provides some criteria for judgment, but teachers must interpret and apply these judgments and follow their implications as their own personal operational skills permit.

In speaking of class readiness for an individualized program, Betty Coody and Ben H. Harris considered essential characteristics of such teaching (11). Among those they mention are:

- Pupils can do advanced or enrichment reading.
- The arrangement of furniture promotes flexible grouping and freedom of movement.
- Materials are used at a number of levels of difficulty.
- Pupils lead a group of the class at times.
- Individuals and small groups receive a variety of assignments and reference materials. The groupings are flexible and need-oriented.
- Pupils work independently or in small groups of varying sizes with different needs, and help each other with peer tutoring.
- Routine classroom duties are shared in a planned manner.
- Many teacher-made materials are in use as well as library books, newspapers, pamphlets, and magazines.
- Pupils help in planning learning activities and with managing the learning stations.
- Pupils inspect their own work and try to correct their errors.
- Occasionally the teacher or aide works with individual pupils or the whole class. More frequently the interaction is with small groups.

It is obvious that the successful use of conferences includes adequate follow-up of the conference observations. In fact, lacking a manual to suggest appropriate follow-up activities, the teachers' effectiveness in devising applications is of crucial significance. Some would regard the lack of a manual as most fortunate, for this frees teachers to employ their own originality in creating follow-up activities. Many others, including the authors, are somewhat skeptical of the thoroughness of the average teacher's efforts to provide opportunities for the practice of various reading skills. It is for this reason that we have attempted in other chapters of this book to provide detailed outlines of the sequential development of various groups of skills. The phonics syllabus, the structural elements, the types of contextual clues, and the approaches to sight and meaning vocabularies offered in these chapters are intended to aid in planning the follow-up on skills training.

Teacher's manuals are an excellent source for ideas on how to teach various skills. They differ, of course, in their inclusiveness and sequences, but this is not a great handicap. Beginning teachers are well advised to try to make a collection of these guides and use them for teaching tips and procedures in skill development. The manuals will have to be previewed perhaps before each school week to select those ideas that are immediately relevant to the lessons the teacher plans to use for the pupil needs that have been observed. If the workbooks written to accompany these manuals have also been gathered, the appropriate parts may be used for independent, follow-up work if they are really relevant. The most efficient use of the workbooks would be to assemble them in a teacher-made kit that has been organized and indexed or color-coded, in the manner described earlier in discussing the individualized approach.

There are many helpful suggestions regarding grouping for teachers who are about to depart from a rigid three-group plan. Six types of intraclass grouping exist: (1) achievement group according to reading levels; (2) research grouping of two or three pupils to explore and answer specific questions; (3) interest grouping of pupils with similar or related reading tasks; (4) special needs grouping formed for development of a specific skill; (5) team grouping—three or four pupils, including a team leader and a recorder, who undertake a specific task resulting in materials and ideas that will be shared with the class; and (6) tutorial grouping, in which a particularly competent pupil helps one or several others in skill-building activities. Some writers speak of dyadic groups of two based on common interests or abilities. The pair of children read the same book, poem, or story, and question each other orally (or by written questions if the pupils are sufficiently mature). These writers emphasize such outcomes of this pairing as mutual enjoyment and empathy, as well as better comprehension and retention. Such interest grouping may readily arise from a class experience such as a movie, filmstrip, or trip. Following the class discussion, volunteers may be secured who will work together to answer some of the questions raised by the class. Guided by the questions and the teacher's suggestions regarding resource materials, the interest group (or research group or team) may prepare exhibits, a mural, a picture or book collection, graphic aids; present a formal, informational report or an entertaining pseudo-TV panel or debate; or share their findings in any of a multiplicity of ways (*36, 40*).

Individualizing with Learning Stations

A currently popular way of individualizing is the development of learning centers. Each center occupies a small area in the classroom and contains the basic equipment, furniture, directions, and work utensils for independent study and group interaction. Screens, mattress boxes, bookcases, or even a sheet hung from the ceiling act as dividers to set off the area from the rest of the classroom. Noisy areas (those with record players or typewriters or those intended for discussion purposes) are separated widely from quiet areas. Each center is intended to promote study in a particular skill area—word attack, comprehension, sustained silent reading, creative writing, decoding skills. Many teachers also eventually utilize science centers, math centers, art centers, music centers, etc.

Each center offers specific directions as well as written purposes or objectives for a variety of tasks that extend over a range of levels. Choices of activities intended to meet the same objective should be offered. These guidelines may be inscribed on a large chart or small cards in a file box or form the headings on worksheets. Manipulative activities beyond just paper and pencil work are most desirable and may be provided in the form of group games, puzzles, sorting and classifying, flannelboards and cutouts, and construction materials. It is not essential that all the tasks be completed at the center, for some may be done at the child's seat or elsewhere. All the materials needed for the planned activities, including such items as filmstrips and projector, kits, transparencies, tapes, records, typewriters, worksheets, etc., are filed at the learning center.

Criscuolo offers a number of options and alternatives in this approach to individualizing (12). Each center he describes is labeled with a catchy title: Peck Deck—creative writing; Tabletop Acres—plant care and study, etc.

Some idea of the appeal and acceptance of this step toward individualization can be gained from the lengthy bibliography on learning centers at the end of this chapter. Practically all these guides have been published in the last few years.

Basically a center should have something for the students to read, to write, to do at the center, and to take away for extension of their learning. All activities should be self-correcting, with some sort of arrangement for recording students' progress in the prescribed skills. Centers provide an opportunity for students to *do* instead of *read about* or just *answer questions.*

Remember that a learning center cannot replace a teacher or aide, nor can it be expected to teach children new skills. Its purpose is to provide individualized, interesting reinforcement, expansion, and enrichment of skills and concepts introduced by the teacher.

Perhaps a detailed description of a typical learning center will make this discussion more realistic.

Dictionary center

Materials—A variety of dictionaries, paper, and pencils; activity cards; a large writing area

Directions—In this center, you will practice (1) locating meanings of interesting words; (2) using guide words; (3) using a dictionary to find the pronunciation of a word; (4) finding some facts given in the dictionary.

Activity Card 1: Answering questions with the aid of the dictionary
1. What are duckpins? Do they fly?
2. Can you blow a conch?
3. How do you pronounce grandee?
4. Who is King Lear?
5. Does kilt mean dead? What does it mean?
6. What can you do with a molar?

Activity Card 2: Using guide words
1. If the guide words for the page are *mailbag* and *maize,* would *main* be found on this page? Would *mailman* be found on this page?
2. Write several words you can think of that might be on this page.
3. What do guide words tell you?

Activity Card 3: On page 59 of the dictionary, find
1. the name of a plant
2. something to eat
3. a tool for measuring
4. the name of a city
5. a word with many definitions

Activity Card 4: Go back to your desk and find five things in it. List them on your paper. Next, use your desk dictionary to locate the guide words for those items. Record the guide words to share later.

Preplanning for use of a learning station is essential (both for the teacher and for the children). Children need to be introduced to the concept, and to the circumstances under which they may use the center. They should be involved in setting the goals, devising new activities, and figuring out ways of evaluating their work at the station, as well as in formulating the rules regarding its use.

Learning centers need to be keyed to children's interests (pet center, personal reading, sports center, etc.) as well as to their skill needs (phonics, structural analysis, comprehension, etc.). The activities at the center will need (1) to be changed every so often; (2) to appeal to various modes of learning—visual, auditory, and kinesthetic; (3) to have specific, complete directions; and (4) to have duplicated answer sheets numbered to parallel the sequential order. The materials should be durable, and perhaps be covered with protective devices (plastic covers, lamination) so that the children cannot write on the directions sheets.

As in all efforts to individualize, this approach can develop no faster than the teacher's and the pupils' readiness for the idea. Teachers cannot try too many centers at once before their pupils are prepared for the flexibility of movement, maintenance of acceptable noise levels, and demand for independent study habits. Starting with one or two well-planned centers that the children become accustomed to using effectively before adding others is the sensible approach. The time and effort required for the preparation is well repaid in the growth of children's independent creative abilities. Learning centers take children beyond the repetitive use of commercial or teacher-made kits to a wide variety of purposeful, self-pacing, and highly motivated learning tasks.

Nurss recommends these types of centers (35): a story-reading center with book and parallel cassettes (we have reservations about the value of professional cassettes, and prefer those made by a child or the teacher); an alphabet center with alphabet cards, books, blocks, records; an oral language center with dress-up clothes, hats, puppets, masks; a writing center with pens, pencils, stationery, carbon paper, plastic letter and magnetic board, scissors, and colored paper; a word center with boxes of picture-word cards, small chalkboards, paper, crayons, etc. These supplies will, of course, reflect the activities of the class devised by the teacher.

Stewig emphasizes the possibility of incorporating materials for choral speaking in the oral language center mentioned by Nurss (53). He reminds us of the value of such practice in creating appreciation of literature; the social value in working together; the psychological value in a group experience without self-consciousness; the cognitive value inherent in the planning of the presentation; and the affective value, since choral speaking emphasizes the art of reading rather than the skills, plus the oral language practice in manipulating pitch, volume, juncture, and stress. Whether all these values are usually realized in the classroom practice of this activity is open to some question. But there is little doubt that there is potential for these outcomes.

Stewig recommends that the center contain some of the books suitable for choral speaking listed here. He notes also the special characteristics of some of the stories that make them particularly suitable for choral speaking.

Stewig speaks of these desirable arrangements for choral speaking: unison—avoid the sing-song monotony; antiphonal—two groups alternating at first, later more groups; cumulative—adding more voices as poem gathers momentum; single voices (after much experience)—all children at first, then singles, later alternating or group versus singles. He suggests beginning with repetitive poetry, then repeated rhymes; cumulative refrains, then simple unison; small groups; verbal obbligatos repeating certain phrases at certain intervals. He would, of course, include a tape recorder at the oral language center for polishing presentations and learning to modify them.

Stories suitable for choral speaking

Blegvad, Lenore, "Five Little Kittens," in *Mittens for Kittens.* New York: Atheneum Press, 1974 (for repetition).

Brewton, John E., et al., "What Night Would It Be," in *In the Witch's Kitchen.* New York: Crowell, 1980 (for obbligatos—a separate special voice accompanying the group).

Carroll, Lewis, *Jabberwocky.* New York: Frederick Warne, 1977 (for older students).

Ets, Marie Hall, *Jay Bird.* New York: Viking Penguin, 1974 (for repetition).

Fisher, Aileen, "Chirping," in *Out in the Dark and Daylight.* New York: Harper and Row, 1980 (for small group).

Gag, Wanda, *Millions of Cats.* New York: Coward McCann, 1928 (for refrains).

Hopkins, Lee Bennett, "5th of July," in *Moments: Poems About the Seasons.* New York: Harcourt Brace Jovanovich, 1980 (for small group).

Johnson, Sickles and Sayers, "A Farmer Went Trotting," in *Anthology of Children's Literature.* Boston: Houghton Mifflin, 1977 (for small group).

Kuskin, Karla, "Full of the Moon," in *Dogs and Dragons: Trees and Dreams* (for obbligatos).

Martin, Bill Jr., *A Ghost Story.* New York: Holt, Rinehart and Winston, 1970 (for unison reading).

Murray, Anthony, *The Thirteen Days of Yule.* New York: Crowell, 1968 (for cumulative effects).

Raskin, Ellen, *Ghost in a Four Room Apartment.* New York: Atheneum, 1969 (for cumulative effects).

Rogers, Joe, *The House That Jack Built.* New York: Lothrop, Lee and Shepard, 1968 (for cumulative effects).

Shekerjian, Haig and Regina, "Here We Come A-Caroling," in *A Book of Christmas Carols.* New York: Harper and Row, 1963 (for refrain).

Stanley, Diane, *Fiddle-I-Fee.* Boston: Little, Brown, 1979.

Stewig, John Warren, *Literature and Young Children: Classroom Approaches.* Urbana, Ill.: National Council of Teachers of English, 1976 (with cassette tape).

Sutherland, Zena, "Little Turtle," in *The Arbuthnot Anthology of Children's Literature.* Glenview, Ill.: Scott, Foresman, 1976 (for unison).

Sutherland, Zena, "Trains" in *The Arbuthnot Anthology of Children's Literature.* Glenview, Ill.: Scott, Foresman, 1976 (for obbligatos).

Sutherland, Zena, "The Baby Goes to Boston," in *The Arbuthnot Anthology of Children's Literature,* Glenview, Ill.: Scott, Foresman, 1976 (for obbligatos).

From John Warren Stewig, "Choral Speaking: Who Has the Time? Why Take the Time?" *Childhood Education* 58, 1 (September/October 1981): 29 (ref list). Reprinted by permission of John Warren Stewig and the Association for Childhood Education International, 11141 Georgia Avenue, Suite 200, Wheaton, MD. Copyright © 1981 by the Association.

Initiating Follow-Up Activities

Here are forty of the book-sharing activities that may be used as a follow-up to children's reading.

Book-sharing activities

1. Listen to a prepared tape with earphones. Good readers tape the informational material.
2. Make up new endings to stories. Children read their versions to the class.
3. Prepare a brief biography of the author. Present to class.
4. Prepare a monologue from a story. Putting themselves in others' places helps in understanding social relationships.
5. Children bring in objects made at home. They demonstrate step-by-step procedures to the group by either oral or written directions. This increases their ability to give and follow directions.
6. Have children read only dialogue in a story, while a good reader provides the narrative background material.
7. An excellent group project to provide opportunities for socialization, sharing ideas, and participation in simple drama is to allow the children who have read the same story, book, or play to give a performance based on their common reading.
8. Children enjoy tape recording a poem, episode, or story, which is then available to others for a variety of uses.
9. Collecting and reading newspaper articles related to social studies and science can be of great value. See later suggestions.
10. Reading stories to younger children is enjoyable for reader and listeners.
11. Preparing a report with accompanying questions for the listeners. Report should be brief.
12. A vivid oral description of a character in a book stimulates other children to want to become better acquainted with the character.
13. Reading the saddest part, the most exciting event, the part most enjoyed, or a very humorous incident helps children seek certain types of material.
14. Reading a story to the musical accompaniment of a tape or recording gives pleasure to the audience as well as skill to the performer in selecting music, controlling volume, etc.
15. Reading beautiful descriptive passages and displaying a painting or drawing of the scene stimulates imagery and enlarges vocabulary.
16. To stimulate interest in a book, the student may write, and share, a letter to the librarian or a friend recommending the book.
17. Several children reading the same book can check each other's comprehension by writing sets of questions and checking each other orally.

(continued)

18. Book reviews, given to a lower-level class, are an excellent experience in storytelling, especially when the book is displayed.
19. A book review broadcast over the school intercom requires careful reading and speech. This activity also provides opportunities for creative use of sound effects, background music, etc.
20. A commentator may narrate a story during the display of a tableau or series of paintings.
21. Writing and sharing letters asking for various types of information or materials from outside sources gives opportunities in writing and oral reading skills.
22. Oral reading of captions on filmstrips (after previewing it) as an illustrated lecture.
23. Choral reading of dramatic material or poetry can involve almost all the class. Children may conduct choral reading in unison, in two-part (high and low, boy and girl voices), by a line-a-child, with one solo part and the rest reading the refrain, and by arranging for a number of parts.
24. Using informational materials, notes, and pictures to make a scrapbook, which is then shared with others, stimulates interest in such projects.
25. Set aside a daily time for sustained silent reading. In some schools everyone—teachers, administrators, and pupils—reads a book of their choice at this time. The length of the reading period is, of course, adapted to the attention span of the pupils. But the attitude toward reading as a meaningful, enjoyable activity is certainly strengthened by this practice.
26. Invite the school librarian to visit your class and give a series of book talks. The librarian may bring several copies of each book discussed for children to borrow, or invite the pupils to come to the library to secure a copy, or to make their own choices. This idea will have to be adapted to the librarian's schedule.
27. Read to your class every day, at a time that seems appropriate. Perhaps let them choose the book that they would like to hear. Some groups prefer listening to successive parts of the same book; others will prefer a different book every few days. Make certain that a copy or several are available to those children who can read the book.
28. Arrange a schedule for pupil storytelling or reading orally to others. Preview their selections before they present the book. Suggest that they choose an exciting or interesting portion (as you would in reading to them). Promote group reactions to the story—not evaluation of the pupil reader.
29. Use various types of charts for pupil recording of the books they have read and their reactions. Small cards, for example, may be tucked in the back of the book, or mounted on a bulletin board, or displayed in any of a dozen ways. Thus the comments of those who have read a book may be shared with others. These will strongly influence other pupils' choices (*40*).

(*continued*)

30. Spontaneous dramatization of a story by one or several children with hand puppets or a more elaborate puppet theatre, or as a playlet, is both enjoyable for the class and highly motivating.
31. Make an illustrated book jacket with a summary of the book on the inside, as in commercial book jackets. Fit the jacket to the book and leave it there for other children to read.
32. Pantomime some of the actions of one of the book characters that you have already discussed with the class. Ask them to guess which character you are portraying.
33. If several of the class have already read a book, let them share in building a diorama or model that they will display and defend to the class.
34. Make sketches of your book characters. Cut them out and paste sandpaper or pellon to their backs. Use them to tell the story to your classmates, at the flannelboard.
35. Prepare a "movie" with scenes from the story. Paste the scenes in a long strip and pull them slowly across a hole cut in a box, to expose one picture at a time while you narrate.
36. Make models of your book characters from pipe cleaners, wire, colored paper, cloth, wood, cotton balls (for hair), etc. Display these as you tell the story.
37. Make a mockup of the first page of a newspaper with the headlines and text referring to incidents in your book.
38. Tell the class some of the things you learned from your story. Explain these, if you can.
39. Give a chalk talk at the chalkboard, writing the names of your characters and drawing lines between them to show relationships.
40. Make a book of sketches of scenes from your book. Put in your comments, and place your book on the shelf with the published book.

Gail Martin of Cleveland, Tennessee, has found a way of motivating children toward an appreciation of literature, authors, and illustrators. She begins by reading excerpts of a number of books to her class. Stimulated by the dramatic readings, some of the children are drawn to reading the books. If a book proves interesting, the child is helped to find others on the same subject or by the same author.

Mrs. Martin then initiates discussion about the author and illustrator and suggests that the child write to them. The letter is written on special stationery designed by the class, and includes such items as a bookmark, the child's picture, a form letter from the principal approving this activity, and the child's request for a photo and any materials related to the book that the respondent is willing to share. Addresses for the letters are obtained from standard references such as *Contemporary Authors*.

In most instances the author responds with a personal letter and often with a photo. Some send sketches of the book's illustrations, parts of the manuscript, copies of their latest book, or some other relevant realia. The correspondence may continue with a thank-you letter, a gift of a stuffed doll or puppet depicting a major book character, a photo of the mounted author's letter and picture, the child's drawing of a major incident of the book, perhaps several questions about the setting or the plot or even how the author happened to write this particular book.

The letters and photos received by the children are framed and mounted on the walls of the school library and the halls of the school building. Some of the realia donated by the author, such as posters, sketches, finished illustrations, and the like, are included as their size permits. Martin's collection, or rather the children's collections, serve as a constant motivation to continue to explore the world of children's literature. Many of the children attribute these experiences to initiating a lifelong enjoyment of trade books. The books, their story content, and the materials from the correspondence are, of course, shared with classmates and parents in many of the ways suggested above.

It should be remembered that these exercises would be prescribed after initial teaching and reteaching (if a need appears in conferences or class work) has been done. If a child cannot perform in a certain skill or area after it has been presented in lessons by the teacher, he or she certainly will not learn it by going off and doing worksheets alone. The collection of exercises is a source of reinforcement for those children who have had initial success in an area. For those who did not respond positively after the first teaching, the file is of very little value until they have been retaught by the teacher or aide.

Using Newspapers

Reading newspapers will be a lifelong application of reading ability. You can begin to prepare children for this use of their reading as early as primary grades. In attempting this training, several of the references at the end of this chapter under "Guides for Learning Centers" will be helpful. Eileen E. Sargent, for example, includes fifteen typical lesson plans in teaching pupils such elements of the newspaper as: news features and stories, editorials and opinion columns, letters to the editor, women's section, sports, human interest articles, reviews, weather, comics, classified advertisements, etc.

Burrus suggests that critical and creative skills can be fostered in using newspapers (6). Johns calls the newspaper a "new textbook every day" (26), and it certainly can be that. Other writers listed in the chapter bibliography give many other detailed suggestions for using newspapers as an instructional tool. The newspaper may be used to develop reading skills, such as using an index; finding the main idea; recognizing a sequence; outlining an article; learning to use graphs, charts, maps, and tables; and reacting critically to news reports, editorials, and advertisements, to mention only a few. Small groups (committees) or individuals may carry on such extended activities in the use of the paper as creating a map showing the travels of an important personage, such as the president or secretary of state, and attaching brief notes on the reasons for the trip; a weather chart showing daily changes; a record of the progress of a sports team; and a file of articles on a topic related to class study in social science or science. Other activities are planning a balanced menu and its daily cost from the information in store advertisements; screening the listing of television programs for features related to classwork and announcing these on a bulletin board; comparing the articles on a news item in several newspapers and leading a critical discussion of the contrasts; locating significant world events on a large world map; and making a calendar of local events of interest to the class. Still other uses of a newspaper are: comparing prices in the advertisements of competing stores and supermarkets; checking the For Sale columns for items of interest and for comparing prices; making a display collection of different maps or tables, or graphs or cartoons, to serve as a resource in children's own writing. Obviously, if this ready source of interesting and often vital information is explored, it may serve a wide variety of learning experiences.

Scheduling

The number of conferences and small-group sessions that a teacher can manage per week is an individual matter. The recommendation of two to four conferences per child per week suggested by some writers may be ideal but it is almost impossible for some teachers. If the daily time devoted to reading ranges from ninety to one hundred minutes in the first grade, to forty-five to sixty in the intermediate grades, a minimum of two ten-minute conferences per week per pupil would occupy all the time allotted to reading instruction in a class of twenty-five to thirty pupils. It is apparent that conferences must be less frequent than twice per week, extremely brief, or limited to one segment of the class—for example, to the superior readers. These are some of the reasons for having recommended that individualized reading be offered at first only to the better readers. Even with this arrangement, which assumes that about one third of the instructional time is devoted to this segment of the class, scheduling of the teacher's time is a problem.

Some teachers meet this situation by making a schedule which ensures that all pupils will have conferences in turn. Other teachers offer a schedule sheet on which children may write their names when they feel the need for a conference or wish to report on a book they have read. A third approach involves permitting children to ask the teacher for a conference at any time during the day that she is not otherwise engaged. As a fourth solution, some teachers conduct group conferences with pupil teams or committees. In our opinion the use of inventory and diagnostic conferences offers a real contribution to efficiency in scheduling conferences. Careful analysis of skill development will be made at planned intervals by this approach. Thus the teacher will be relieved of the impossible task of using most conferences for diagnostic purposes. The teacher will not feel pressured to have the child read orally each time under the mistaken illusion that this procedure is the best method of keeping a finger on the pulse of the child's reading development. Rather the teacher will devote the conferences to the more significant purposes of evaluating silent comprehension, stimulating interests, and planning follow-up and group activities with each pupil.

We are not implying here, as some might assume, that each child must be quizzed in detail on every book or selection read. Such a picayune attitude would probably help to destroy children's enjoyment of their reading rather than promote it. Evaluation of comprehension should occur often enough to create a set toward intelligent critical reading; thus the evaluative techniques will be used with varying frequency from pupil to pupil. Furthermore, this method is also promoted by those activities that require sharing or reporting to the group as much as by "telling" the teacher. In the final analysis, each teacher will have to work out solutions to the problems of frequency and content of individual conferences, perhaps with due recognition of the true purposes indicated.

Record Keeping

The Teacher

If the teacher follows the earlier suggestions, he or she will collect five basic types of records for each child. Whether these are placed in a notebook, a card file, or a folder is a matter of personal choice. The first records will include the facts acquired from the school's cumulative record-keeping system, and from informal discussions with the previous year's teacher. These should include the child's age, IQ, mental age, reading interests, and general comments on interests, progress, and difficulties. Recent reading test results from both standardized and informal testing may be included. Some teachers will want to add notes on the child's personality and needs, as well as any health problems and family conditions that are likely to affect schoolwork. A second record of the child's instructional, independent, and potential reading levels will be obtained during the initial inventory conferences. A third record will be that of oral reading behaviors. These observations will be based on a number of conferences and classroom notes.

A fourth record will contain an analysis of the pupil's oral reading errors as observed during the inventory conferences and several subsequent conferences during which the child reads orally. For the sake of securing a fairly reliable picture of the child's oral reading errors, the total number of errors analyzed in this fashion should probably be close to a hundred. This particular record would, of course, include a summary statement of the child's apparent needs for follow-up activities in word recognition skills and sight vocabulary.

The final set of records will include those notes that each teacher deems adequate for judging and guiding the progress of the pupils. These may include a page or card for each child on which he or she notes such items as titles of books read, degree of and types of comprehension shown, child's reactions to the book, books suggested to the child, plans for sharing the child's selections, plans for follow-up activities, and the like. The breadth and depth of these records will vary according to the teacher's concepts of their purposes and their values.

Some teachers tend to keep both individual and group records of pupil needs and progress. The individual records may note the particular skills in which the child shows weaknesses, such as contextual, structural, or phonic analysis, and breadth of sight vocabulary. The group records may note the skills to be stressed, the pupils forming the group, the materials used, and the dates upon which the group has met. Both group and individual records may

Table 11.1 Teachers' Progress Record

| Name: | John | Instructional: | 3.5 | Independent: | 4.5 | Potential: | 7.5 |

Date	Title of book Page number Level	Comments	Follow-up
2/2	*Jed Smith* by Lathan (Garrard) pp. 7–14 3	John is impressed by Jed's freedom and outdoor ability. Read aloud p. 10 and we discussed story. Expression excellent.	Suggested he add new words from each chapter to his word bank.
2/8	pp. 15–41	Help needed with long *a* as in we*i*ghing, wa*i*ted. Give definitions of words added to word bank.	Worksheets Nos. 14–17 phonics file A (*ei, ea, ue, ai*).
2/11	Finished book	Worksheets O.K. Supplied synonyms for several words. Needs some help. Wants book on Lewis and Clark.	File B: worksheets 60–61, synonyms. Marking map with Jed's route for talk to small group. Use *Scholastic Map Skills* for help.
2/15	*George Rogers Clark* by DeLeuw (Garrard) to p. 50 3.5	Excited about westward movement. Found filmstrip for class. Worked on compounds and inflectional endings. Easy reading—urge more difficult one next time.	Is making trail in different color on same map. Worksheets file A 23–24 plurals *s–es*.
2/20	Finished book	Found answers to questions— narrated filmstrip yesterday.	Alphabetize word bank by second letter.
2/24	*Jim Bridger: Mountain Boy* by Winders (Bobbs-Merrill) p. 20 4.4	Book difficult but interest high—reading carefully. Need conference again soon. Trouble recalling sequence of events.	Made comprehension questions to answer after next chapter. Keep word bank up to date. Worksheets B41–42, sequence.
2/27	p. 45	Questions answered O.K.— read orally exciting part. Asked questions about Mormons.	Library for reference on Mormons. Making model cabin. Writing short article to explain model for display.

Table 11.2 Teacher's Record for Small Group

Date: 10/9/76			*Book read:* Tuffy and Boots
Sherry	Read us an excerpt from her book.	Finished—*Green Eggs and Ham*	Suggested she present one of the humorous incidents to the class
Karen	Still absent		
Rosanna	Still anxious about status in group	Splash	Give individual help in preparing for sharing time
Paul	Still guessing wildly on new words	Animal riddles	Select exercises on contextual clues

be compared with the teacher's overall written plan for skills development outlined in the notebook or some such guide.

A typical individual record might resemble Table 11.1; a group record may be similar to Table 11.2.

Other teachers maintain an overall reference list of exercises for skill building in the available workbooks, exercise books, teacher-made exercise file, and similar sources. This catalog of skill training aids is consulted after diagnostic interviews and again from time to time after other conferences. The list permits quick prescription of an exercise or series that would correct the observed pupil weaknesses. If desired, these exercises may be cut from their sources, filed in folders or envelopes, or bound in manila folders to be drawn as needed.

Eucyle W. Spaulding, of Fort Lauderdale, Florida, accomplishes the recording of her pupils' skill progress in a unique fashion. She constructs a large wall chart depicting a number of satellites and space stations in orbit around the classroom. Each station is labeled in terms of a specific word recognition skill, such as sounds of initial consonants, consonant blends, long vowel sounds, vowel digraphs, and silent *e* rule. With the teacher's assistance each child draws materials from the exercise file to help practice these various skills. When the pupil has completed using the reinforcement materials, he or she asks the teacher to check the work. If he or she is successful, the pupil adds a drawing of his or her profile labeled with his or her name to the appropriate place on the space chart. Thus the children are kept aware of the skills they are attempting to master and their progress. The nature of this wall chart could, of course, be adapted to the particular level and interests of the class to depict a trip around the world, a time line of historical events, a wagon train, etc.

Record Keeping by the Children

Record keeping by the children is usually initiated by a class discussion of the needs for such records and by developing with the children the forms to be used. The pupil records, which may be kept in an easily accessible card file or in the child's own folder, commonly include a mimeographed form for listing titles, authors, dates of reading, and pupil comments. Some intermediate-grade teachers ask pupils to record also the types of books they are reading to encourage greater breadth and variety. This record may take the form of a large wheel in which the spokes represent various categories. As a child finishes each book, he or she writes its title or a key word on the proper spoke of the wheel. Other teachers have their pupils maintain a list of various categories and simply check each type as the pupil completes a book. A few teachers prefer their pupils to keep a list of unusual words or phrases, or unknown, interesting, or exciting words encountered in their reading. These lists may form the basis for vocabulary-building exercises, picture dictionaries, or various word games.

Older children may write short summaries of books and place these in a file to be consulted by any child who is considering a book. These peer comments are often significant influences upon pupil selection. At primary school levels when children's writing abilities are not highly developed, pupils often keep records of their reading in the form of art work. These records might include a painting or drawing of a particularly interesting incident, a series of drawings or pictures cut from old magazines depicting the chief characters of the book, or a make-believe cover of the book illustrated by the child. For these pupils, most of the record keeping will be in the form of teacher's notes on their follow-up activities, as book sharing by puppetry, dramatization, or oral report. Pupils at these levels can and should be expected to keep a list of the new words encountered in each book to stimulate their word consciousness. These lists may well be incomplete, for the average child or even college student does not know accurately with which words he or she is really unfamiliar. But keeping the list promotes a set toward learning words, an attitude or habit that is fundamental to continued vocabulary growth. If, as suggested earlier, these lists are used in a variety of ways by the child and teacher, this important set is strengthened.

If desired, individual records for each book read might take this form.

Individual records

Name _____

Date _____

1. Write the title of your book.

2. List the main characters and describe book.

3. Choose one character and tell what you liked most or least about him.

4. Make a list of some of the new words you met and learned.

Or, an individual's record might look like this:

Name _____

Date _____

Summarize the story.

How did this story make you feel?

Make a list of some of the interesting words that the author used.

Write a phrase that answers each of the following questions: Who? What? Where? When?

Individual records kept by the children may take a variety of forms, such as this example.

Child's record

Name: Sue				
Title of book	Begun	Finished	Comments	New words learned
Abigail Adams	April 29	May 2	Very good story about the girl growing up to be a fine lady	pinafore, petticoat

---

This type of record could be varied by using separate pages for different types of books, such as "Famous People," "Fun and Fancy," "Life in Other Places," etc.

Using the Conference for Evaluation

The individual conference between teacher and pupil is obviously the cornerstone of any approach to individualization of reading instruction. Teacher skill in the conference determines whether there will be effective diagnosis of the pupil's instructional needs or any continuous evaluation of overall reading development. The conference is a crucial opportunity for observation of the child's reading interests and skills in word recognition, comprehension, and oral and silent reading. In effect the recurring conferences become the major means of communication between the teacher and pupil in the area of reading instruction. On the one hand, the conference is the basis of teacher diagnosis, planning, and instruction; on the other, it is the prime pupil opportunity for receiving personal instruction, guidance, and support.

We are not suggesting that in the individualized approach no instruction is offered other than in the conference. Nor are we implying that there is no pupil–teacher interaction except that in the conference. Communication between teacher and pupil certainly occurs in a variety of settings. But for two significant reasons, the conference is the most important contact between teacher and pupil. First, the conference is the basis upon which most other contacts between teacher and pupil are planned. The nature, type, and frequency of the other kinds of teacher–pupil interaction are based on the teacher's findings in the conference. Second, the conference is the main opportunity for warm, personal communication between teacher and pupil, and hence a highly significant factor in the child's school adjustment and academic progress.

Elsewhere we have noted a number of interpretations of the purposes and conduct of the individual conference. To some writers, the conference is simply an opportunity for casual discussion of the child's reading selections, enjoyment of the material, and probable future choices. To other teachers, it is a substitute for the oral reading circle, for the teacher's major observation is the child's growth in sight vocabulary by having read to him or her. To still others, the conference involves a number of factors—diagnosis of the pupil's skill development, planning for related instruction, careful recording, review of the child's current and future reading—all occurring almost simultaneously during each brief conference.

Judging by the reports in most individualized reading literature, oral reading during the conference is the chief interaction between teacher and pupil. This type of oral reading is, often merely a substitute for the old oral reading circle. Like the oral reading in conventional classes, the practice is based upon two presumptions. It is obvious that many teachers and pupils believe that oral reading is the most important application or practice in reading, a very questionable assumption. It is equally obvious that teachers who depend heavily upon oral reading, either in the conference or the circle, believe that this practice affords a good opportunity for overall evaluation of reading progress. In several places of this book we have attempted to point out the errors in these beliefs.

In our opinion, oral reading is not an essential part of every individual conference. There are many other better reasons for conferences. The teacher could spend time discussing the child's current reading choice, determining readiness for sharing, discussing future choices, giving instructions regarding the child's role in small-group work, discussing the progress of research activities, reviewing reading records, checking comprehension of silent reading, and providing individualized instruction in reading skill, to mention only a few.

In assessing the child's comprehension in a conference, the questions should range over all of the book insofar as the child has read it, not just questions based only on that portion the child might read aloud in the conference (assuming that the teacher persists in using oral reading to observe the child's progress). Comprehension in oral reading is not efficient and is not indicative of the types or degree of understanding achieved through silent reading. These questions could be prepared early in the school year with relevance to each book in the classroom library and, as one of the commercial book collections has done, they could be placed on a small card and inserted in a holder on the back cover.

But if the supply of books is replenished from time to time, and the total number of books read by the pupils is quite large, and these conditions are very probable, there may be little teacher time to prepare a set of questions for each and every book. The teacher could, of course, just ask leading questions that would elicit a rehash of the story or the child's personal reactions. But these are useless as measures of comprehension despite their recommendation by several sources. Those who are accustomed to follow the questioning strategies outlined in a basal manual raise such doubts as: How does a teacher who has not read the book sample the child's comprehension? These problems can be solved by developing teacher skill in questioning, beginning perhaps with questions such as the following:

Questions for a Conference

Comprehension
1. Which character in the story did you like best? Why?
2. Would you like to trade places with any of the people in the story? If so, why?
3. What would you have changed in the ending of the story, if you had been the author?

4. If you close your eyes and think about the story, is there any part you can recall? What do you see or think of?

5. Which character in the story would you like to have as a friend? Why?

6. Do you believe that everything in the book could have happened? Why or why not? Was the story intended to be true to life?

7. What part of the story was hardest for you to understand? Let's turn to that part and talk about what puzzled you.

8. Who in our class do you think would like to read this book? Why? Will you tell him or her about it?

9. Would you like to meet the author? If you could, what would you talk about?

10. Is there any part of the story that you would have left out in order to make it more interesting? If so, what part?

11. Was there any person in the story whom you didn't like? What kind of person is he or she?

12. What other titles could you think of for this story?

13. What did you learn from this book? Something about people? Some new ideas? Something about the way people used to live?

Follow-up

1. Could you think of another way this story could have ended? Will you write down your ending and share it with me later?

2. You know that sometimes an author writes several stories about the same person. Could you pick a character in your story and write a short story about him?

3. Do you think that there is a part of the book that could made into a short play that the class would enjoy? What part? How would you like to ask some of your friends to help you present that part as a play? Let me know when you have practiced once or twice and I'll arrange a time for you to give the play.

4. Would you make a group of drawings showing some of the things that happened in the story? You could paste them together in a long strip and unroll them as you tell the class about the book.

5. Were there any funny parts to your book? Could you make a picture of that part, and write enough of the story so that others could enjoy the funny part? We could put it on our bulletin board.

6. Do you have a friend or a relative who is not in our class who might like to hear about this book? Will you write a letter telling why you think he or she would enjoy the book, and we'll arrange to mail it.

7. Was there a character in the book who was anything like you? Imagine that you were in the character's place in one part of the story, and write down what you would have done or said then.

8. Would you write a short paragraph telling why you liked this book and why you think others would like it? We'll put your review on the bulletin board.

9. Would you like to read another book like this? Or by the same author? Look through our library and let me know whether you find one you think you will like.

Skill Development

1. While you were reading you met some words you didn't know, didn't you? Did you make a list of these? Let's look at your list and talk about their meanings.

2. An author usually tells about characters by describing them, their looks, their behavior. Can you find a place in the book where the author is describing one of the characters? Let's see whether we can use other words to give the same ideas (synonyms) about that person.

3. Did your author use any large words in the story? Can you find some of them and divide them into syllables? Then we'll try to pronounce them and talk about their meanings.

4. Let's just pick a page from the book at random. On this page, try to find (adapt to pupil's previous training):

    a. Any compound words.

    b. Any with the short *i* sound.

    c. Any with prefixes.

    d. One with a soft *c*, and another with the hard *c* sound.

    e. Any with silent vowels.

    f. A sentence with two adjectives in it.

    g. Five words that have initial consonant digraphs.

    h. A three-syllable word.

    i. Two words with a vowel digraph.

    j. Any with suffixes.

    k. A word you cannot pronounce.

    l. A word that refers to clothing; a way of moving; a color word; one that tells time.

    m. A word that begins with each letter of the alphabet. (Write them down, beginning with one starting with *a*, then with *b*, and so on.)

5. Can you arrange all the words on this page that begin with *c* in the proper alphabetical order?

We have offered, of course, more questions than would be needed for a conference to show the types possible. Teachers would choose those questions they felt relevant, stress the area of the children's apparent needs, and soon enlarge this collection by adding their own questions.

We believe that the conference may take different forms and serve different purposes from time to time. One type of conference is diagnostic: it involves observation of children's skill development and planning for future instruction. Even before the diagnostic conference, some attempts to inventory children's initial status in various reading skills must be made. Thus the first individual conferences may serve the unique purpose of evaluating children's instructional, independent, and potential reading levels, and their present abilities in a number of reading skills. A third type of conference, mentioned most frequently in reading studies, involves the evaluation of children's growth in reading interests. This type answers questions regarding the development of new interests, the children's insights into the deeper meanings of their readings, their growth in informative background, their attempts at self-evaluation of their reading, and their groping efforts to explore new areas with their skills.

If these various types of individual conferences are to be effective in accomplishing their purposes, it is obvious that they must be carefully planned. The purpose of the conference must be clear-cut and the record keeping relevant and accurate. The form of the conference should certainly not be inflexible, for each is an opportunity for strengthening the relationships between teacher and pupil. But, on the other hand, neither is the conference a casual contact resulting in only incidental observations or information.

In the average-sized classroom, the opportunities for conferences are too infrequent and too brief for a casual approach or for a laissez-faire attitude that allows the conference to become a purely social contact. Because we believe that the individual conferences are extremely important in the success of individualized reading, we shall attempt to point out in detail our concepts of their organization and conduct.

Is this kind of inventory of reading skills a practical, economical device for determining children's reading performances? Why can't the results of a simple reading test accomplish the same goals in less time? These are some of the questions that will certainly arise in the minds of many teachers who are concerned with the amount of time demanded by our suggestions. Despite the extra teacher time required, there is little doubt in the minds of most reading authorities of the superiority of the inventory approach. Group tests, largely because of their brevity, fail to supply an adequate sampling of the skills the teacher is concerned about and thus fail in their primary purpose of supplying diagnostic information. Few commercial tests sample adequately the very skills the teacher will emphasize. Moreover, if their results are used to distinguish the working reading levels of pupils, as in preparation for tentative grouping, the scores are often greatly inaccurate and misleading.

One study compared several group tests and two versions of an informal inventory with teacher judgments of pupils' instructional levels. The *Gates Advanced Primary Reading Test* (Teachers College, Columbia University) provided adequate differentiation for planning for three or five reading groups but overestimated teacher judgment *constantly by two full grades*. The informal inventory, however, was superior in that it was equally efficient in indicating groups and in addition yielded significant diagnostic information. This inventory, incidentally, was scored in a modified manner rather than by the artificially high standards suggested by Betts or others, a necessary precaution already mentioned. Group tests have values for group studies, for school surveys, and the like, but most are inadequate for diagnosis, for pupil–pupil comparisons, or for classroom planning and grouping.

Taking Inventory in the Conference

At the beginning of the school year, in many classrooms the available records of pupil reading progress are scanty or inaccurate. The appropriate levels of reading materials needed for instructional purposes, the possible recreational or independent reading levels of the children, and the potential of the pupils for reading growth possibly may not be noted in the previous year's records. It is true that schools employing the more stereotyped basal reader approach often supply a list of the basal books read by each child. But to the current year's teacher, who intends to employ largely individualized procedures, such a list simply hints at the child's present reading status. The teacher still must discover the pupil's capacities for independent reading, estimate potential for the future, and evaluate reading skills. Despite the good intentions responsible for it, a list of basals previously read by each pupil gives no clues to present instructional needs.

Similarly, the score on a general reading test given near the close of the previous year is often of no real value to the current year's teacher. Aside from the inherent inaccuracy in group testing, which tends to result in misleading estimates of pupil reading status, the score on the average reading test is of little diagnostic significance. It is merely a gross sum of the pupil's performance in a half-dozen skills operating simultaneously with varying degrees of effectiveness, transmitted into a meaningless grade level.

Use of some diagnostic tests that sample pupil ability in significant subskills is much more useful than the usual end-of-year general reading test. Among those of merit are: Word Analysis—*McCullough Word-Analysis Tests* (Ginn); *Stanford Diagnostic Reading Test* (Harcourt Brace Jovanovich); and *The Diagnostic Reading Scales* (CTB/McGraw-Hill). These contain a fairly complete group of phonic measures that must be administered individually.

In many sources teachers are being urged to construct their own informal inventories. In brief, the directions suggest selecting samples from an unfamiliar basal reader series at successive grade levels. One such sample is used to test oral reading; another, to measure silent. In the oral reading, that level at which the child reads with no more than one error per twenty running words (95 percent accuracy) and at least 75 percent comprehension is called the *instructional level* and represents the level of reading matter to be used in classroom instruction. The sample in which the child reads with 99 percent oral accuracy and at least 90 percent comprehension is called the *independent level*, or that which may be used for supplementary and recreational reading. Some authories assume that the comprehension exhibited in the oral reading is also true for silent and give no test of this ability. Others use both silent and oral reading samples and average the percentages of comprehension to estimate these levels. Reading orally with more than ten errors per hundred running words and comprehension of 50 percent or less is supposed to represent the *frustration level*. The simplicity of this arrangement and the apparent realism of the testing material, as contrasted with that in many standardized tests, has given the Informal Reading Inventory (IRI) wide appeal.

But when we explore the history of the IRI and examine it for evidence of validity and reliability, its appeal diminishes markedly. The whole idea is based on a single study of forty-one children tested in reading selections *first silently, then orally*. With these two exposures to the same passages, their oral reading was, as we would expect, quite good, averaging 93 percent accuracy. This single study was accepted at face value by Emmett A. Betts, who then coined the terms and announced the standards for the three descriptive levels mentioned. Needless to say, the whole procedure has been severely criticized by a number of writers. Among the flaws they emphasize are (*28, 37, 38, 39, 41, 42, 51*):

1. Any basal series is not a good source of reading selections, for often the books are not graded accurately nor parallel from one series to another. A sample may or may not reflect the grade level designated by the publisher. Basals are certainly not the best source for sampling reading ability among children when they are being trained in non-basal programs. Bradley also found marked variations within books and between books of basal series supposed to be of the same grade levels (*5*).

2. One study compared samples from the Ginn 720 and Scott, Foresman unlimited series (*19*). In order to get two samples that would yield the same readability level, the authors found that they had to evaluate anywhere from five to fourteen selections at each level of the books. In fact, the readability estimates did not increase at successive levels in five of eight comparisons from one level to another in the Scott, Foresman series. In other words, the level designated by the publisher was often not significantly more difficult or different than adjoining levels. To reinforce this point, the mean number of oral errors of children reading successive levels of the Scott, Foresman were compared. They were found to show almost no increase as the levels progressed upwards.

3. Teacher judgment of the reading selections is not dependable, either. Jorgenson showed that the variability in teachers' estimates indicates a lack of a stable reference point for "grade level" (*27*). This affects their construction of an IRI or their notably inaccurate assignments of instructional materials.

4. When children were judged by the 95 percent oral accuracy standard that is so widely accepted, they were found to fail that criterion at a lower level in some selections than their highest successful performance (*19*). More than half of the pupils were inconsistent in this fashion when the Betts standard was employed.

5. The standards for oral accuracy in the IRI are completely arbitrary. A study by Powell and Dunkeld comparing these standards with actual child reading performances in the leading oral reading commercial tests and a sample of their own, showed a great divergence (*42*). Children just do not read as well as the IRI expects them to, particularly in reading orally at sight as in the

present-day procedure (not silently first, then orally as in the original study from which the IRI standards were derived). Their real oral accuracy ranges from about 80 percent at the first grade to between 85 and 90 percent at the second, and gradually increases to about 90 to 95 percent by the sixth grade (42). Table 11.3 expands the comparison between the original studies and the standards of the five leading oral reading commercial tests.

Obviously no wide-scale testing in standardized tests shows the constant percentage of accuracy that Kilgallon (on which the IRI standards are based) or Cooper claim. Combining these large-scale data shows an average of 78 percent oral accuracy at the first grade; 83 percent at the second; 88 percent for the third; 89 percent for the fourth; 91 percent for the fifth, and 92 percent for the sixth. These averages are depressed slightly by including the Gates–McKillop data, which are widely variant from the others at most levels. However, the gradual increase in oral accuracy is manifest, contradicting the rigid and unreal Betts standards for an IRI.

6. Kasdon has shown that the original testing method produced much higher oral accuracy than today's oral reading at sight, as well as a very different profile of errors, thus again challenging the IRI standards (29).

7. Limiting children's independent reading to a level below classroom instructional materials fails to recognize the influence of interest on children's choices. Many children read some harder materials with good comprehension. The fact that they may not be able to read these harder materials with the exaggerated degree of accuracy demanded by the IRI also ignores pupil ability to derive meanings from the context for words not in their sight vocabulary (51).

8. There is no real information about the reliability of a teacher-made IRI, or some of the commercial versions. Even trained reading specialists listening to a taped testing do not agree on the implications or scoring (38).

Table 11.3 Oral Reading Accuracy Standards*

Level	Kilgallon	Cooper	Powell	Spache	Durrell	Gilmore	Gray	Gates-McKillop
1–1	95	98	—	75	67	67	86	—
1–2	95	98	85	80	—	80	88	—
2–1	95	98	85	88	88	83	91	—
2–2	95	98	85	86	89	—	—	50
3–1	95	98	91	90	—	88	91	—
3–2	95	98	91	92	92	—	—	67
4	95	96	91	93	92	91	90	75
5	95	96	91	94	94	92	91	84
6	95	96	94	94	95	93	89	84
7	95	—	—	94	95	95	80	84
8	95	—	—	94	—	95	89	84

*After George D. Spache, Investigating the Issues of Reading Disabilities (Boston: Allyn and Bacon, 1976), p. 307.

9. In their college training, teachers are exposed to very different ideas about the standards for an IRI, or what errors should be counted or what the errors mean. Indeed, in some classes teachers are told to ignore the research data and use their own standards (perhaps because some will anyway).

10. The commercial IRI's either do not attempt to judge the reliability of their instruments (Silvaroli's Classroom Reading Inventory) even though their parallel forms would permit this evaluation. At the same time, Ekwall's Reading Inventory reports reliabilities, but we do not know how the correlations were done nor are they sufficiently high enough to permit the score to be used to judge individual pupils or to make comparisons among pupils (39).

11. The IRI is supposed to yield important information regarding the strengths and weaknesses of pupils and to tell the teacher what instruction the child needs. But the reading samples are too short and the collection of oral reading errors too small to accomplish this goal.

12. Different authors suggest conflicting ways of tabulating errors and have different ideas on what really are errors. Some count omissions, additions or insertions, substitutions, mispronunciations, and repetitions. Some do not count insertions, additions, or omissions because in their brief testing the number of these was quite low (14). Some count this error only when two or more words are involved. Besides, the fact that the types of errors reflect the method of instruction to which the child has been exposed is ignored (31).

13. Comparison of IRI instructional levels with teacher placement of pupils in readers ranged from 39 to 69 percent in various classes. The 95 percent standard gave a 61 percent agreement with teachers' judgments. In PP–II grade classes, an 85 percent standard gave better agreement (69 percent). In III–VI, the 95 percent standard was best in agreement (69 percent). (These findings tend to confirm the earlier statements about the gradual increase in oral accuracy.) In comparison with achievement test scores, the IRI instructional level showed 38 to 58 percent agreement. The 95 percent oral accuracy standard gave only 46.5 percent agreement (19).

14. Teachers are urged by those who promote the IRI to formulate their own questions on each selection. There is real doubt that such questions have real discriminatory power to differentiate between high and low scorers in comprehension. The percentage of children who answer each question correctly among those who score high or low in comprehension is usually not considered. Questions depending upon intelligence and/or background information and not upon the passage content are seldom detected or eliminated. Questions that can be answered without even reading the selection are not dropped, because that kind of testing just is not well known.

15. In counting oral reading errors to decide on corrective steps, many IRI users combine the errors from different levels. Yet many studies show that errors from easy or hard passages are not the same. They should not be combined, or the conclusions will be erroneous.

16. Some use multiple-choice questions with an IRI. These are easier than other types, and resulting estimates of pupils' reading ability are too high.

Teacher-Made Informal Tests

Since many classroom teachers do not have access to better oral reading tests, and there is some merit to trying to supply them with a suitable instrument, we offer the following suggestions for constructing a series of informal tests.

1. Draw reading selections requiring about 3 to 4 minutes reading time from the basal series you are using. The levels may not really represent what they are labeled by the publisher, but, realistically, they are what you and your children are going to live with. Apply a primary readability formula to the selections of primary level, as designated by the publisher (50), and an intermediate grade readability formula (13) to the remainder. McKenna makes the point that interest can seriously influence reading performance (33). Hence the reading selections you choose should reflect typical interests of your children.

2. Three sample selections should be drawn from each book and they should be within a few months of each other in readability according to the reading formula you employ. You may have to apply the formula to a number of selections at each level before you find at least three of reasonably equivalent difficulty. The formulas are essential because they are based on the analysis of a large number of classroom reading materials. Therefore, their estimates will resemble the difficulties of common textbooks. You will know what reading ability is required to read the selection with a reasonable number of errors and about 75 percent comprehension.

3. With older pupils, you may wish to assemble a similiar series of passages from your social science and science texts to evaluate pupil reading ability in these areas. For these and the basal selections, frame questions that appear to measure recall of the details, inferences, and main ideas, preferably in about equal numbers. For brief reading passages, 6 to 8 questions will suffice; 8 to 10 for longer passages. Do not try to count the number of each type of question that children answer correctly. The number they will attempt is too brief for any meaningful interpretation. Besides there is great doubt that the varied questions really measure different comprehension skills.

4. Try out your questions on 10 to 20 children to find those questions that can be answered without reading the passage. Drop those answered correctly by 30 percent or more of the pupils. Rewrite and try out new questions until you have a sufficient number.

5. Ignoring the questions you originally wrote and then decided to drop, score the children used in the tryout for comprehension. For each question, determine how many high scorers in comprehension answered it correctly compared with low scorers. The questions where the difference is small (under 30 to 40 percent) should be dropped, and others written to replace them.

6. Ditto or mimeograph a number of copies of the final passages and their questions, triple spacing between lines to permit recording of oral reading errors. Use the error recording system suggested later in this chapter.

7. Consider your students' performance adequate if they make no more than the average number of oral errors committed by children of your grade level. In oral errors, accept as satisfactory 75 percent or more in the first grade; 85 percent in the second; 90 percent in the third, fourth, fifth, and sixth. In other words, accept as satisfactory 20 to 25 mistakes in each 100 words in first grade reading; 15 in second grade selections; and 10 in third, fourth, fifth, and sixth grades. In comprehension, accept 70 percent as a minimum in oral reading and silent and auditory comprehension.

8. The three selections you have equated are for oral reading, silent reading, and reading to the child (auditory comprehension). In the last use, read the questions to the child, also. If necessary, the silent reading selection and that for auditory comprehension can be administered as a group test, provided you give the pupils some means of recording their answers. You may have to interview some pupils to determine exactly what they meant in their written answer.

9. Use the highest level selection in which both oral errors and comprehension are acceptable for instructional materials in your basal reader series. Use the highest level of success in silent reading to guide you in supplying supplementary and recreational books and magazines. Use the auditory performance as a rough estimate of children's language background and their potential for progress. In most middle-class pupils, this auditory estimate will be at least one to two years above the instructional level. When this difference is not present, recognize children's need for language and firsthand experiences to develop their capacities to deal with the reading program. Remember that these auditory estimates are temporary, true only at the time they were made. They will continue to advance as the children grow in schemata, language, and particularly vocabulary.

Some will say we are promoting the use of an informal reading inventory that has all the faults just enumerated for current formal tests. We agree with this criticism, for we do not believe that the IRI (even with all the additional steps recommended here) is a good way to evaluate children's reading ability and assign instructional materials, or a good way to group pupils. Test construction is really a very technical business. It took eight years for the senior author to complete the work on the Diagnostic Reading Scales, and they aren't perfect. But there is a solution.

The Cloze Procedure

The cloze procedure (46) is recognized as a true measure of comprehension comparable to a postreading questions test or a standardized test. It demands intelligent use of the semantic and syntactic constraints of the selection to identify the omitted words. It has been used as a test of reading ability or as a measure of the difficulty (readability) of many materials of unknown grade levels. Cloze eliminates all the problems of validity and reliability of a teacher-made test or the IRI. Cloze does not require, as do teacher-made tests, pretesting questions on a group of children; analysis of the percentage of children who can answer questions without reading the material; or revising the questions according to these inquiries—all of which are essential steps in building a teacher-made test (but usually ignored).

Using Cloze for Oral Reading

It is best to introduce young children to cloze by reading a story in which you leave out every fifth or tenth word. Stop each time and give the children the opportunity to tell what the word should be. It is wise to omit only nouns or verbs in this kind of introduction for the first few trials.

Other practice in cloze can be accomplished by masking out every fifth or tenth word when showing a story on the overhead projectors. Again, encourage the children to suggest a word for each blank space. Then remove the masks and discuss the substitutes offered for the actual words. A story may be used several times by masking a different sequence of words. Nursery rhymes, folk tales, and other very familiar material are good for the initial trials.

Another introduction to cloze may be initiated among intermediate grade pupils with multiple-choice answers, or what is really a sentence completion exercise, not true cloze. Put several one-word answers in the margin opposite the line with the blank space. At first only one answer is obviously correct; later, possible alternates can be offered to increase the difficulty of the exercise. Another version can be constructed by putting a synonym in the margin and asking pupils to supply a word for the blank with the same meaning as the given word. This will work well with synonyms for nouns, verbs, and adjectives, but not very well for prepositions or conjunctions. Hence the deletions may not be exactly every tenth word. But variations of this sort are not important at this time, for the purpose is to familiarize the pupils with the task of supplying the missing word, not to make a formal test of their reading ability.

Using Cloze for Silent Reading

This approach to estimating children's functional silent reading level eliminates the difficulty of creating comprehension questions that really function. Briefly, the steps are:

1. Use a set of passages selected as described above. (See earlier instructions regarding forming an IRI.) Each should be at least 500 words in length. Delete every tenth word, leaving constant blank

spaces of at least five or six letters in width. The deletions begin in the second sentence and should number at least fifty. Retype and mimeograph the material in multiple copies.

2. Give the passage to the pupils, in a group or individually, asking them to write a word for each blank space in the margin or, if they are mature enough, on numbered lines of a separate piece of paper. Make certain that they understand they are to leave a line blank if they cannot supply a word for a blank space in the passage.

3. Allow the pupils ample time to try all the items. Score for the total number of words *exactly* like those deleted that they can supply. Synonyms are not acceptable; misspelled words are. Multiply the score by two to find the percentage of correct answers if you have prepared fifty test items.

4. Those passages in which the children score 40 to 44 percent indicate their functional silent reading level, assuming that the passages actually reflect the various grade levels. For some children it will be necessary to administer several test passages to find their proper level. You may expect that this silent reading performance will often be higher than the instructional level found by the oral reading test.

Cloze can be used for determining whether your students can be expected to read a certain text with reasonable comprehension. Pretesting by cloze will reveal those pupils who can or cannot use the text.

Cloze can also be used to improve comprehension. Students given two or three pieces of cloze each week for five weeks showed significant gains in comprehension but not in vocabulary. The children's answers were read out,

---

A sample of cloze*

Earl Morris was three and a half years old when he dug up a prehistoric grave for the first time. His family lived in _____ log cabin near one _____ the ruins left by _____ people in New Mexico. _____ his father dug up _____ tools these vanished people _____ left behind. Of course, _____ wanted to help. One _____ his father gave him _____ short-handled pick of his _____. He whacked at the _____ and uncovered a beautiful _____ and black dipper. His _____ yell brought his mother _____. Together they loosened the _____, then with pick and _____ dug on and discovered _____ skeleton of the Old One, _____ ancient American with whom _____ pot had been buried.

*From Ruddell, Robert B., and Sebesta, Sam Leaton, *Time and Beyond*. Boston: Allyn and Bacon, 1978.

TEACHING FOR MAXIMUM SUCCESS

discussed, and critiqued for each cloze selection. As a result, the pupils grew markedy in the ability to supply a variety of answers for the deletions (47).

In this comprehension practice, use predictable or patterned books with rhyme to read to the group to give them the set for predicting the words that are omitted in the story. At first, accept reasonably sensible answers from them; gradually raising your standards until pupils are producing the precise word omitted.

This is a shortened piece of cloze. Your passages should be long enough to make about 50 deletions.

Open Book Testing

Before completing this discussion of how to conduct individual or group informal testing, another technique, once very widely used but today almost unknown, must be described. This is the open book test or practice. Briefly, it means that teachers ask pupils to perform any of a dozen or more reading acts in an open book. It tests such skills as: using an index; using a table of contents; finding a certain topic; reading and interpreting a graph or chart; reading a map or diagram; varying rate of reading as directed; skimming, scanning, previewing; using a dictionary; finding a fact in reference books; and using the card catalog, picture, or pamphlet file.

In other words, by using the actual text or other media in a structured way, the teacher can assess realistically children's progress in almost any significant skill. There is no question of the validity of the questions or the task. As for reliability, each type of testing can be readily repeated from time to time until children's mastery or need for reteaching are apparent.

When using their own informal open book tests, teachers must form their own standards and judgments of what is average performance in their classes and on their reading selections. The real purpose of this testing is not to assign a grade-level score in each major reading skill, or to determine how well children read in terms of some hypothetical normal population. The basic purpose of the tests is to yield diagnostic information: In what reading skills does this child perform poorest in comparison with other skills? What type of training does the child now seem to need most? Which one or two major skills should be emphasized in the instruction to help improve the child's overall reading growth?

It is true some teachers will evolve standards that are too low, while others will expect almost perfect reading. Some will tell the child almost every word on which he or she hesitates, even while testing to discover word attack and word recognition abilities. Others watch sternly, letting the child struggle alone, without offering any encouragement or assistance. But the teacher with common sense will try to elicit the child's best effort, compare the child's performances to determine weaknesses, and, using personal experience and the group's average performances as guides, try to make judgments and plans.

The Diagnostic Conference

Most individual conferences described in reading studies are intended to be diagnostic in that teachers determine children's needs for skill instruction by listening to their oral reading. This diagnostic effort appears to be the most common activity in the conference, if we may judge from current reports on individualized programs. There are several assumptions inherent in this approach to diagnosing pupil reading needs. First, there is the obvious belief that oral reading performances are good indicators of general reading ability. Second, there is, of course, the assumption that the average teacher is capable of judging each pupil's training needs by listening to oral reading—that the teacher can make appropriate judgments and accurate evaluations and then plan the best types of instruction for each pupil. Let us first explore the question of whether oral reading errors are a good indicator of other reading skills, such as silent comprehension. Preston's study of elementary school children considered retarded in reading by their teachers raises a number of doubts about teacher judgment (43). He found that from 40 to 60 percent of these children were not actually retarded when their silent reading levels were compared with the expected performance according to their mental ages. Teachers' judgments were most inaccurate at primary levels, not only because teachers ignored the children's mental ability, but also because the judgments were based largely on oral reading. Most teacher estimates of reading ability were related to the grade-level expectation and not to the true capabilities of the children. Preston decries the teacher habit of equating oral reading with silent reading and of drawing hasty conclusions about children's overall progress solely from observation of oral reading errors.

Gilmore's dissertation offers evidence that tends to substantiate Preston's complaints (20). He found that the correlations between oral reading errors and silent comprehension drop rapidly from a high level (.918) in the second grade to only moderate levels (.631 to .693) in the third to sixth grades and still lower levels (.572 and .561) in the seventh and eighth grades. Predictions of the pupil's silent reading ability from observing oral reading errors are about 36 percent better than a sheer guess in intermediate grades and about 25 percent better at the junior high school level. This trend toward an increasingly smaller relationship between oral and silent reading continues as skill in these two types of reading matures. In fact, among good first-year college readers one study found a high negative relationship between oral and silent comprehension. Good silent comprehenders tended strongly to score poorly in oral comprehension, whereas good oral comprehenders tended to be poor in silent comprehension. Among poor first-year college readers there was very little relationship between oral and silent comprehension.

The obvious implication of this research is that the teacher cannot judge the overall reading progress of pupils simply by observing their oral reading. Pupils may be significantly better (or worse) in such silent reading skills as rate, vocabulary, and comprehension than their oral reading implies. If teacher observation of oral reading has any useful purpose, it is certainly not that of overall evaluation. The proper function of an oral reading test is the observation of oral reading skills and word recognition skills, as we shall point out later.

For judging silent reading ability, only silent reading samples are appropriate. Comprehension may be evaluated by the quality and quantity of children's responses to such questions as those listed earlier; not by an oral informal inventory or an oral standardized test, as was previously emphasized.

Teacher observation of oral reading assumes accurate recording and interpretation of oral errors, as suggested earlier. Several studies cast serious doubt on these diagnostic skills of the average teacher. For example, in a broad cross section of elementary teachers, 96 percent were doubtful that even experienced teachers were able to diagnose their pupils' reading problems. Sixty-two percent were also doubtful of the teachers' ability to plan appropriate remedial steps, even when their pupils' problems had been diagnosed. After a three-month experience with individualized reading, Sartain's second- and third-grade teachers complained of their diagnostic inadequacies in the individual conference (48). A third study, by Eleanor M. Ladd, points up even more strongly these teacher difficulties in recording and interpreting oral reading errors (30). Ladd found that groups of untrained teachers recorded incorrectly 34 to 39 percent of the oral reading errors they were trying to observe. After thirty hours of training with recorded tests or actual children or both, teachers were still missing 33 to 37 percent of the errors. Collectively, these studies imply that diagnosis based on errors in oral reading in the individual conference is not made very accurately by the average teacher.

Most of the negative result, however, was due to teachers attempting to follow a recording system that was literally impossible. They had been asked to record hesitations of two seconds or more as well as apparent errors in ignoring punctuation. As the figures above show, scoring of these so-called errors was no more accurate after training than in the initial trial.

Seventeen reading specialists were asked to score the tape of a child's oral reading (36). Six of them said it was the child's Independent Level (100 percent accuracy), five rated the reading as the Instructional Level (95 percent accuracy), and six felt it to be the Frustration Level (90 percent accuracy). Obviously these specialists differed in their interpretation of various standards for oral reading, not to mention the difference in the correctness of their scoring of the child's reading. Studies of this type raise serious doubts about the ability of teachers (even specialists) to judge the reading abilities of their pupils. We hope it is possible to aid teachers in this diagnosis by outlining a more practical system for recording oral errors.

Teachers tend to listen differently to the oral reading of good and poor readers. Sometimes these differences become an obstacle to an objective evaluation of the children's reading ability. For example, when listening to poor readers, teachers tend to interrupt the children with corrections at the points of error much more frequently than they do with good readers. As a result the poor readers lose their concentration and any confidence they had, and probably read more poorly than they really could if undisturbed.

In correcting oral reading, teachers direct good readers to the syntactic and semantic information in the sentence. They are likely to ask, "What word would make sense here?" "What kind of a word—the name of something, or an action—would be good here?" "Now go back and read the sentence again and see if it sounds right."

Poor readers have their attention drawn to the graphemic or phonemic aspects of the word in error. The teacher is likely to say, "What sound does the first letter make? What word beginning with that sound would fit here?" Or, "What word beginning with the sound of _____ would make sense here?" Or, unfortunately she may say, "Sound out that word. Now what is it?" In these subtle ways, teachers push children toward two different modes of reading; one in which the words and sentences are supposed to make good sense, and one in which initial letters or all the letters of the word are the basic clue to word recognition and the sense of the sentence is secondary.

Recording Oral Reading Errors and Behaviors

A number of studies have made careful records of oral reading errors and skills. The authors of these used different checklists and hence recorded somewhat different patterns of errors and difficulties. Despite these differences it is possible to observe some trends in oral reading behaviors as children mature in this skill. Duffy and Durrell listened to the oral reading of a number of third-grade children and made certain general observations (18). A few years later Daw used the same checklist of difficulties in observing a number of fourth- and fifth-grade children (15).

These data are, of course, general observations of oral reading rather than a detailed analysis of oral errors. Although they are only crude diagnostic observations, they demonstrate certain definite trends. According to these studies, the average third grader tends to ignore punctuation and shows lack of sight word accuracy by many additions, omissions, and inaccurate guesses. The fourth- and fifth-graders may have been reading at sight in relatively difficult materials, for their difficulties were marked in word attack, phrasing, and expression. In the opinions of these observers, pupils of all three grades were guilty of poor enunciation, many mistakes on small words, and excessive head movements.

Using a much smaller number of pupils, but a similar checklist, Barbe et al. observed somewhat similar trends (1). They also noted the tendencies to poor sight vocabulary, guessing at words, and ignoring punctuation as characteristic of poor primary readers. Their upper-elementary-grade pupils, like those in the other studies, showed marked problems in phrasing, monotony of tone, frequent repetitions, and ignoring punctuation.

In her classic study of poor readers in grades one to six, Marion Monroe used a more diagnostic checklist of oral reading errors, for she was concerned about planning specific remedial steps (34). Madden and Pratt employed a somewhat similar checklist in observing the oral reading of over a thousand pupils in the third to ninth grades (32). The data collected in these two studies again permit us to observe significant trends in the patterns of oral reading errors as children advance in age and reading development.

Both studies show increasing omissions as children mature and their speed of oral reading increases. Madden and Pratt detected the same trend in additions of words. Both studies note the decrease in words aided or told to the child because of failure to analyze them successfully. This trend should appear as sight vocabulary grows and skill in word analysis improves.

Collectively, these studies indicate that the pattern of oral reading errors and children's general oral reading skills change in many respects as their reading development continues. It is apparent also that there are two distinct ways of approaching the observation of oral reading: one by noting general difficulties in fluency, word attack, and posture; the other, by carefully recording the exact errors made by children while they read. General observations, such as those that would be made by using the accompanying checklist, may represent the teacher's impressions accumulated during a number of individual conferences and other classroom activities. The detailed analysis of oral reading errors would, on the other hand, probably be made during one of the several conferences early in the school year and repeated perhaps at the middle and again toward the end of the school year. If the early conferences include taking an inventory of children's reading skills, as suggested earlier, a record of oral reading errors will be included.

Several relatively recent studies of oral reading errors have moved away from the detailed count of mistakes on vowels, consonants, and the like to other interpretations. One new emphasis is upon the graphic similarity between the printed word and children's responses (21, 54). In other words, each error is counted according to whether it resembles the given word in the beginning or ending letters. Another new trend is to interpret each error according to first, its graphic similarity to the printed word; second, whether the two words sound alike; third, whether the response is grammatically the same; fourth, whether the sentence produced by the child is syntactically correct; and fifth, whether the sentence is acceptable semantically (meaning). This type of analysis is exemplified in Goodman's *Reading Miscue Inventory* (21) Based on his studies of oral reading errors, Kenneth S. Goodman also emphasizes the need for a careful tabulation of the child's self-corrections.

However, we are not suggesting use of the procedure outlined by Goodman. As Joyce Hood has pointed out, the Inventory is much too time consuming (24). Scoring children's errors or miscues requires at least an hour per child. Besides, some of the deductions that the scorer is supposed to make have very questionable reliability. Performances in substituting a word appropriately for the context, for example, are not very similar from time to time and cannot be depended upon for planning corrective steps.

In this Inventory, stories used to test children are chosen more or less at random provided they are somewhat difficult for the children. With teacher inability to judge the actual difficulty of reading selections, this random choosing of the test material is not very realistic. Moreover, the children's experiential background as well as the subject matter of the selection may greatly influence reading in a particular selection.

Miscue analysis does not distinguish between inadvertent omissions and the skipping of hard words that many children do. The number of nonsense errors (unreal words produced by trying to sound out the letters of the word) depends upon the children's training. Those trained in a heavily phonic program make more such errors than do pupils trained by other approaches. Second-graders made more nonsense and no response errors on a story above grade level than one at grade level, even though their word recognition accuracy was 95 percent at both levels. In other words, the difficulty of the selection forced them into a pattern of errors that was untrue for their normal reading (*19*).

Several assumptions are inherent in the Miscue Inventory approach, as Leu notes (*31*). First, it is assumed that proficient readers use more contextual clues during reading than do poor readers. There is no proof of this belief. Second, it is assumed that good readers use less graphic information than do poor readers. Third, it is assumed that poorer readers should receive more frequent instruction in context-use strategies. There is no evidence that teaching to counteract a supposed weakness is a valid approach to instruction. Leu cites seven studies showing that good readers use the same or fewer contextual or graphic information as the less proficient readers. Fourth, it is assumed that the mistakes shown in oral reading are also present in silent reading, and that the instruction to correct oral errors will improve silent reading as well.

Leu criticizes the Miscue Inventory users for inconsistency in designating exactly what oral errors or miscues are. The variation from one writer to the next is disturbing, not only in their description of types of errors but also in the definition of each type. For example, does a miscue due to use of graphic information depend upon using the first, first two, last, or last two letters as a cue to word recognition?

Leu points out the same miscue may have graphic, semantic, or syntactic sources, making scoring completely arbitrary. Without knowing exactly what children tried to say, which is difficult for them to explain, there is no solution.

To get around the problem of no precise standards for judging children's performance, qualitative analysis rather than quantitative is recommended by some (*7*) without any proof of the meaningfulness of their idiosyncratic scoring systems.

Among the decisions that the teacher must make, without any real standards for guidance, when using the Miscue Inventory are (*23*):

1. When is a miscue fully semantically acceptable?
2. Before the child reads the story, the teacher is to outline its content with one hundred points being developed. Then when the child retells the story (as the measure of comprehension), the teacher is to check which of the hundred points the child recalls. The total number of recalls is the comprehension score. This parrot-like recall is the author's concept of comprehension, not what the child adds to his or her own background information from the author's

ideas as most other authorities say. Any questions asked by the teacher are not supposed to refer to anything the child *has not already mentioned*.

3. Although the teacher is supposed to determine whether the child knows the plot, comprehends unusual key words, understands the theme, names the characters, etc., no standards are suggested for any of these.

4. Miscues that change the syntax of a sentence are to be distinguished from those that change the meaning of the sentence. Yet a syntax change is unacceptable, according to the authors, thus making any such sentence semantically unacceptable. How then are these two miscues to be counted separately?

Other questions regarding the validity and reliability of this approach to observing oral reading that have been raised are:

- Selecting a story at random that is supposed to be harder than the child's functional level will not produce that child's typical classroom reading behavior. How then can the teacher plan corrective steps?
- The method by which the child has been trained will affect his or her pattern of reading errors. How does the teacher interpret this pattern?
- Will the miscues produced in reading the test selection be duplicated in basal reading? In reality, miscue patterns reflect the nature and content of the test selection and vary greatly from one reading to the next (25).
- Errors by good readers do not differ significantly from those by poor readers, except in quantity. Without any standards for types of errors, how does the teacher decide how to instruct a pupil after giving the Inventory?
- To insure the reliability of the sample, how many miscues must be analyzed? The Inventory provides for recording only twenty-five miscues. For a reliable diagnosis, about four times as many errors should probably be analyzed.

In summary, The Miscue Inventory lacks standardized directions and reading selections, criteria for interpreting patterns of reading, norms for interpreting scores, reliability or validity data, and supporting evidence for its prescribed strategies.

Interpreting Oral Reading

A doctoral study by Herlin attempted to establish contemporary norms for oral reading errors by testing children on Monroe's battery of tests and by the *Durrell Analysis of Reading Difficulty*, a fairly recent series (25). Surprisingly, Herlin found that today's children made the same proportions of errors in the Monroe tests as the children of forty years ago. At first, this seemed to imply that children's oral error tendencies had not changed in almost half a century. But when he compared the error profiles from the two tests, they were quite different. Moreover, the reading levels achieved in the two batteries differed by more than six months for the average child.

The most striking implications of this study are that, first, the kinds of reading errors that pupils seem to make are often peculiar to the particular test selections employed. Second, reading-level estimates from two tests, even though standardized, are very apt to differ significantly. How, then, does the teacher determine what the true errors of a child are and therefore what retraining procedures should be employed? Since no norms for proportions of errors are available, except those for several standardized tests, how does the teacher judge the children's profiles of errors to determine their needs? How does the teacher know whether the testing reveals an accurate estimate of the reading levels the children can deal with profitably?

The best answers to these problems are not very strong. We suggested that the teacher might employ an oral reading test in which the selections are at grade levels and the selections extend over a number of levels. Oral reading errors should be recorded in the manner described later. Lacking norms for proportions of errors, the teacher can identify probable needs by the frequency of each type of error. Della-Piana and Herlin have shown that this gives a reasonable indication of a pupils' error tendencies (17). Even though the profiles of errors may be peculiar to the test, if the teacher uses the same test with all the pupils to be evaluated, the results will, at least, be comparable from one child to the next.

Except for beginning readers, each reading selection should be close to two hundred words in length, for short samples do not yield an accurate profile. Sufficient test samples should be administered to permit collecting about seventy-five to one hundred errors, to ensure a reliable profile. The errors collected to form the profile should not be a combination of those from easy to difficult selections, since pupil errors vary with different levels of materials. The oral reading sample should be accompanied by comprehension questions for which some standard of accuracy has been established. Without such questions, good word callers will be judged to be good readers at levels they really cannot comprehend.

Standardized tests which meet most of these criteria are the *Diagnostic Reading Scales* (CTB/McGraw-Hill), the *Individual Reading Placement Inventory* (Follett), and the *Classroom Reading Inventory* (William C. Brown). If some measure of the breadth of sight vocabulary is desired, test lists are offered in the *Diagnostic Reading Scales* and the *Dolch Basic Sight Word Test* (Garrard). Oral reading errors in reading these word lists are sometimes added to those present in the reading selections, but this is a dubious procedure. Several studies show that children can recognize many words in context that they cannot on lists (21). Hence the judgment of which basic words children still need to learn is more accurately made from their performance with selections containing these words, such as those formed by the teacher or simple materials from basals or other sources. This difference in word recognition in lists and in context is less in the first grade than later primary grades because beginning readers vary so little from isolated words to contextual reading. Word lists at that level are therefore a reasonable sample of sight vocabulary. Above this beginning level, word lists tend to force the pupil toward phonic analysis, since other clues to the words are lacking. Thus, although students' performance does give some clues regarding their phonic skills, it does not reflect their actual word recognition or word analysis skills when reading in context. Above the first-grade level, sight vocabulary recognition must be tested both by list and contextual reading to secure an accurate picture.

We have regrouped and rephrased the checklists used in the studies described earlier to permit the teacher to make somewhat more detailed observations. With the checklist at hand, during conferences or classroom oral reading activities, the teacher may note the difficulties shown by each pupil. The category of speech difficulties provides an opportunity to note the child's needs for correction of such hindrances as stammering, lisping, or constant sound substitutions. The items losing place, skipping lines, or using finger to keep place are combined because they are related symptoms of poor directional attack.

Fluency

- Poor phrasing or word by word
- Speech difficulties
- Monotone, lacking inflection
- Pitch: too high or too low
- Volume: too loud or too soft
- Loses place, skips lines, uses finger
- Ignores punctuation

Word Attack

- Skips over unknown words
- Needs frequent prompting
- Substitutes by guessing from context
- Substitutes irrelevant words
- Spells or sounds letter by letter
- Blends poorly
- Mistakes mainly on small words
- Fumbles, repeats frequently

Posture

- Book too close, too far
- Moves head
- Cocks head or book
- Squints or frowns

The list of items under *Word Attack* is expanded to include more of the specific difficulties shown by primary schoolchildren and poor readers. Since the purpose of the checklist is to help the teacher plan corrective instructional steps, not simply to describe how well the pupils read, the list includes only symptoms of poor reading habits and skills.

If an inventory test, such as mentioned earlier, is given, the teacher will have a duplicate of the reading selection and can record the types of oral reading errors shown in the next chart.

If the pupils correct themselves in any type of error, do not count that error, unless the correction involves a repetition. For example, the child reads "a red house" for "a house." Realizing he or she has inserted a word, the child repeats the phrase correctly as "a house." Cross out or check the addition error as no error, but score the repetition by an arrow under the words repeated.

Do *not* attempt to record hesitations, phrasing, word stress, or the child's observation of punctuation. Ladd's study indicates that even after thirty hours of training, teachers could not record these accurately (30). Moreover, other research indicates that the tendencies to make these errors are inconsistent and unreliable.

Interpreting Errors

Attempting to assign an exact reason for each oral reading error or type of error that pupils make is literally impossible. The same type of error may occur several times during a reading, but for a different reason each time. Therefore, the diagnosis of pupils' instructional needs is not directly related to their pattern of oral reading errors. To make the best diagnosis, teachers can note the proportions of various errors, the types that are excessive, and the portion of the word in which errors are concentrated, and then assume certain explanations for the more frequent errors and begin the logical corrective steps. We can give only general suggestions of the meanings of various types of errors to aid the teacher in the interpretation of each pupil's pattern.

In general, when errors are concentrated on the beginnings of words, as they tend to be, they indicate either failure in sight vocabulary or difficulty with consonants and consonant blends. In the middle of words, vowel sounds may be the problem, whereas errors on endings may arise for several reasons, as shall be pointed out.

Do not interrupt the child's reading to make corrections. If the child stops to ask for help, tell him or her to skip the word in question and go on. When the pupil finishes, go back to his or her substitutions. Point to the word substituted for and ask the pupil to try the word again. If the child still miscalls it, ask him or her to read the sentence in which it occurs, first silently, then orally. If the child is still in error, count it as such. If he or she makes the correction in one of these steps, you can be certain that the initial error was momentary and that the pupil can recognize the word by phonic, structural, or contextual analysis.

Recording errors

	Examples
Additions. Insert a caret ∧ wherever the pupil adds a sound or a word. Write the addition above the line.	red s a ∧ house ∧
Omissions. Put a circle around each sound or word omitted.	a (red) house
Repetitions. Put an arrow under a repetition of two words or more. Ignore one-word repetitions.	<u>It was</u> difficult
Substitutions. Cross out any word that the pupil substitutes for or mispronounces. Write in the word as pronounced.	run Mary ~~ran~~ down the street.
Reversals. Show reversals of whole words or a letter sequence by a transposition symbol, ⎵⎴ .	John ⎸was⎸ a friend John was ⎸a⎸ ⎸friend⎸
Words aided. When pupil blocks on a word, wait five seconds. If the student says nothing, tell the word and cross it out.	Paul ~~Revere~~ was a

Before beginning analysis of the pupil's errors, Cohn and D'Allesandro suggest a review of the pupil's performance on the reading selections. These researchers would ask, "What are the first two letters? What sound do they make?" Then, "What do the letters _____ say?" (using the medial letters or syllable). "If I add a *b* to them, now what do they say? Now try the word again." With this review of the miscalled words, Cohn and D'Allesandro claimed that their pupils corrected their miscalls by 50 percent on the first try, and by 28.7 percent more on the second try. Only 21.4 percent of the pupils' errors could not be reviewed and corrected in this fashion. In their opinion, only one fifth of what appear to be decoding errors are really failures in the sound–symbol correspondence.

Reviewing the child's errors in this manner may help to give a more accurate picture of his or her needs for decoding training. But it may also convey the idea to the pupil that the best way of recognizing a word is to attack it by letter sounds—a very limited approach. As has been pointed out several times, even primary children can be helped to use contextual clues, the most permanent and enduring word recognition mode.

Do not follow these review procedures if you are using a standardized oral reading test such as the *Diagnostic Reading Scales*, the *Gray-Robinson Oral Reading Test*, or any other such test. The tests were not standardized under these types of inquiry, and if the reviews are added to the commercial test procedures the final results will be erroneous. If you think the review inquiry is desirable, and it certainly does help clarify a child's reading habits, then use it after you have finished scoring the formal oral test according to its author's instructions.

Interpreting Oral Errors

Additions. Additions of whole words may represent the pupil's attempt to embroider the author's ideas, as "the big old red house" for "the red house." This tendency is more common among intermediate-grade and older pupils, for it demands quick reactions, rapid reading, and a degree of verbal fluency. Other additions of this type tend to occur when, in trying to correct another error, the pupil adds a word or two to smooth out the phrase. When excessive, additions of whole words may represent superficial reading and an overdependence upon context with consequent loss of accuracy in comprehension of fine details.

Additions at the end of words that change the tense or number may well indicate lack of training in structural analysis, especially among primary-grade pupils.

Omissions. Omissions of whole words, particularly among intermediate-grade and older pupils, may indicate either excessive speed or a tendency to skip over unknown words. If the teacher asks the child to reread a list of the omitted words after finishing the reading selection, it is readily possible to distinguish between these two probable causes. Omissions of endings may also reflect poor structural analysis, or the influence of dialect.

Repetitions. Frequent repetitions may reflect poor directional attack, or lack of consistent left-to-right movement in reading. In some cases they represent the pupil's fumbling with recognition of a difficult word or thought occurring several words later in the sentence. While processing or attacking mentally the hard word, the reader repeats the preceding word or phrase, once or several times, meanwhile gaining time to recognize the difficult word. This mental fumbling, resulting in an error of repetition, is a frequent and normal part of the reading act. The overall estimate of the child's reading should not be unduly penalized by counting every single repetition made. After all, the habit of analyzing new, hard words while reading is a very desirable one. Therefore, count repetitions only when two words or more are involved to reduce the artificial frequency of this error. Another possible explanation of repetitions may be tension or nervousness of the child who is insecure in the threatening situation of reading aloud to another person, or the child's attempt to correct a miscue.

Substitutions. Substitutions of whole words take four forms: (1) The substituted word has the same shape or form and the same idea, as "house" for "home." This type implies that the reader is attending to the meaning of the context and word form, but probably not using phonics or syllabication for word identification. (2) The substitution is a whole word, same form, different idea, as "horse" for "house." This error may indicate overdependence upon gross word form as the chief means of word identification. It is the most frequent of the whole-word substitutions, especially among primary-grade readers. (3) The substitution is a whole word, different form, different idea, as "house" for "there." This implies little attention to word form, context, or any other method of word attack. (4) The substitution of a whole word, same idea, different form, as "can" for "will." This implies good use of context but little attention to word form or phonics.

Among primary grade and poor readers, the partial substitution error involving a letter or sound is the most revealing regarding the pupil's phonic and other word attack skills. As we have indicated earlier, the concentration of a high proportion of errors in one area of words may reveal the extent of the pupil's knowledge and use of consonants, consonant blends, vowels, and endings.

Reversals. If they occur in initial consonants or in other letter sequences, reversals may indicate lack of directional attack, especially among primary-grade or poor readers. If errors occur within certain letters, as *p* for *q*, *b* for *d*, they may show lack of knowledge of letter sounds or poor letter recognition. If reversals appear in word sequences, they may imply haste or carelessness, in some cases. They may also reflect the difference in word order in standard English and the child's mother tongue, as in the case of Spanish, in which adjectives follow the noun.

Reversals are seldom present among individuals who read above primary levels. Their frequency drops markedly as the reader matures, demonstrating that they are not due to handedness, mixed eye–hand dominance, or lack of cerebral dominance, as some writers suggest. If reversals were due to anatomical relationships, they would not disappear while handedness, eyedness, and the like persisted. In fact, most research studies show no consistent relationship between reversals and these physical factors. The error is characteristic of the beginning reader and it spontaneously disappears as skills improve.

Words Aided. A large proportion of errors of this type implies dependence in the reader. Lack of a habit of independent word attack or lack of training in phonics and word analysis is usually responsible for this error.

Graphic Similarity. Noting whether the response resembles the printed word in the first or first few or last letters is an indication of the child's use of phonic or graphic clues. Whether the word produced is similar in sound is an additional indication. Beginning readers use these cues in almost half of their oral reading errors. Gradually they begin to combine graphic and meaning cues, using such substitutions as *didn't* for *did not*, *blue* for *black*, and *many* for *most*. When combined with the error count on vowels, consonants, and the like, as in partial substitutions, the child's skill and knowledge of phonics is denoted.

To a degree the extent of errors in which there is a graphic similarity between the printed word and the response is influenced by the amount of phonics instruction. Children trained in a sight-word approach make relatively few errors of this type, substituting instead by configuration, word form, or using irrelevant words drawn from their reading or auditory vocabularies. Children trained in a phonics-oriented system make more errors of this type, as well as more mispronunciations, omissions, and repetitions, because of their emphasis upon phonemes as cues to word recognition.

Self-Corrections. As children mature in the reading act, their dependence upon the teacher lessens and their attempts to maintain meaning increases. Efforts at self-correction increase gradually with reading skill; thus the greater their number, the closer the child is toward meaningful reading. The repetitions that occur as a result of an attempt at self-correction would, of course, not be considered as oral reading errors, according to this interpretation. Much of the time these self-corrections either correct the initial miscue or involve substituting words of similar function, as a noun for a noun, a verb for a verb. This is the attempt by the maturing reader to maintain the syntax—the word order, tense, and word function—according to several observers (8, 21, 54). Only when the reader is not comprehending or the dialect interferes does he or she tend to violate syntax.

Dialect. What to do about dialect in oral reading testing becomes a very complex problem. If the teacher is not to downgrade the child's reading ability because the oral reading is delivered in dialect, he or she must be able to distinguish between what is a miscue due to lack of phonic skill or word recognition and a dialect pronunciation. Changes in word order, omissions of helping verbs and of word endings signifying tense or number, omissions of medial consonant sounds, as in *hep–help* and others involving *t, d, s, z, g,* and *k;* substitutions for vowel and consonant sounds, such as *pin–pen, breav–breathe, bref–breath* may characterize the black dialect reader. Spanish–English speakers may show many vowel confusions and substitutions, as *s* for *th, sh* for *ch, j* for *y,* as well as differences in word order, verb forms, and in dealing with negatives.

Teachers will have to familiarize themselves with these differences in time to make their decisions regarding the pupil's real needs. Until this ability is achieved, the judgments will have to be based on evaluations of the child's comprehension. Questioning will show whether the child has the message or, in the case of specific words, whether the child clearly understands the terms. As pointed out elsewhere, the teacher cannot jump to the conclusion that, because certain phonemes are missing or changed in the child's enunciation, the child needs further training in auditory discrimination or more phonics or exercises calculated to eradicate the dialect. If the child understands and can interpret the material, the fact that he or she reads it aloud in dialect is insignificant. The presence of dialect in oral reading is not evidence of a decoding failure but rather demonstration of successful decoding plus recoding into the child's own speech pattern.

Most teachers who speak English of a more or less standard nature have difficulty in scoring the oral reading of minority children who speak in dialect. It would be helpful for teachers who are not entirely familiar with the dialects of their pupils to know the common variations in speaking Black English or English with a Spanish accent.

Black English includes the following variations (55):

- *Omissions*—Of *r* and *l*, as *god–guard, hep–help;* of final consonants and consonant clusters, *pass–past, row–road,* of *s* in plurals; and of others involving *z, t, d, s, g,* and *k.*
- *Substitutions*—E becomes *i*, as *pin–pen, pinny–penny, bear–beer;* final *th* becomes *v*, as *breav–breathe;* unvoiced final *th* becomes *f*, as *bref–breath;* initial consonant *d* becomes *th;* and certain clusters are changed, as *skream–stream.*
- *Additions*—Certain plurals ending in *st* become *stes*, as *testes–tests;* pronouns are added to subjects—Angelo *he* told me.
- *Syntax*—Omission of final *s* in third person singular, as *run–runs;* of the *s* in possessives and plurals, and of prepositions, as "*He go to school.*" Omission of *ed* signifying past tense, *walk–walked,* of *s* in plurals. Use of a double negative, "I ain't got no"; and substitution for the copula, "He be my dog."
- *Word order changes*—Tranposition of the auxiliary verb, as "Why she won't come?" and faulty use of the "if" construction, as "I asked him did he do it."

Spanish–English speakers will be affected by many vowel confusions and these substitutions (57):

s for *th*, as in *sin–thin*	*c* for *g*, as in *coat–goat*
ch for *j*, as in *chudge–judge*	*d* for *th*, as in *dis–this*
s for *s* as *z*, as in *pleassure–pleasure*	*s* for *sh*, as in *soe–shoe*
p for *b*, as in *par–bar*	*sh* for *ch*, as in *shair–chair*
b for *v*, as in *bote–vote*	*j* for *y*, as in *jellow–yellow*
n for final *m*, as in *dine–dime*	*t* for *d*, as in *ten–den*
gw for *w*, as in *gway–way*	

The differences between Spanish and English sentence order may take the following form (57):

- *Negatives*—As "Mary no here." "He no go to school."
- *Verb forms*—"I go to sing," "I see you later," "I have twenty years," or "I have thirst"; dropping auxiliaries, as "This man works?" or "Works this man?"; omission of inflections, as "The boy eat."

- *Other variations*—Some English sounds and conventions are not present in Spanish: *z* sound for *s; ng, wh;* many vowel sounds; some consonant clusters, as *ts, lpt,* and *lkt* as in *bats, helped,* and *talked;* and irregular verbs, as *tear–tore, throw–threw (42).*

Indian children have difficulties with the distinction of number, gender, possessive, definite and indefinite articles, pronouns, verbs with inflections, negative questions, and many English idioms.

Gaining Skill in Recording Errors

The recording of the errors of an individual who reads to us is not a very simple matter. Most teachers, reading clinicians, and psychologists who are learning to perform this task require a good deal of training before they achieve a high degree of accuracy. Ladd's study indicates that this training is more effective if tape recordings are used at first, followed later by trials with live readers *(30).* The practice with taped readings is apparently easier for the teacher and more conducive to accuracy, probably because the teacher can give full attention to the recording rather than to the social interactions necessary in a live reading. The taped readings may also be reviewed as often as desired, and thus the accuracy of the recording of errors will be increased. Therefore, we suggest that wherever possible the teacher employ a tape recorder in initial attempts to record oral reading errors.

Summary

In this chapter we have tried to describe the various types of conferences intended to yield information regarding the child's needs for specific instruction. We have suggested that the first few conferences be used to make an inventory of the child's overall development. The use of an informal reading inventory or a standardized inventory will be essential to these evaluation conferences. By their careful application, the teacher may make judgments regarding the level of her instructional materials, the levels the child can read independently, and the child's potential for growth, as measured by listening comprehension. Other tests reviewing the child's word attack skills may also be employed.

Diagnostic conferences will serve two basic functions—observing the child's general reading behaviors in fluency, word attack, and posture; and making a record of the oral reading errors that the child characteristically makes. Checklists to guide these detailed diagnostic observations have been offered. With a little conscientious practice, most teachers can utilize these plans to guide decisions about pupils' instructional needs.

Some readers are concerned that the checklists do not give specific standards for error counts, comprehension level, word recognition counts, and other items. Such statistics were not supplied, for they could not possibly apply in all types of reading selections and school populations. If teachers construct their own informal inventories, or even if they use those published, they will find that the standards for average reading performances will vary from one group of selections to the next, certainly from one school to the next. When the teacher feels the need for standardized testing, we recommend our *Diagnostic Reading Scales* (51) for making comparisons with the general population.

The *Diagnostic Reading Scales* are a series of standardized reading selections and word lists for use from first grade to middle school. The first step is the use of a sight vocabulary list to estimate the child's probable reading level. The child then reads appropriate selections orally until he or she fails to achieve a satisfactory level in either oral reading errors or comprehension. This point is designated as his or her instructional or classroom working level. Continuing with the next most difficult reading selection silently, the limits of the child's independent reading ability are tested in successive selections until his or her comprehension fails. The next higher levels of selections are then read to the child to determine potential for reading performance through listening comprehension. Finally, a series of simple phonics tests are given to assess the pupil's skills in this area. The *Diagnostic Reading Scales* were constructed to give a fuller picture of pupil abilities than other oral reading tests by a group of measures that almost any classroom teacher could easily administer.

Discussion Questions

1. What do you think would be your greatest problem in making conferences an integral part of your teaching? How might you approach this problem?

2. If you were to begin using conferences, with what type would you start? Why?

3. Arrange a role-playing situation in which you will be the teacher conducting some definite type of conference. Use a pupil, or even another member of the class, if necessary. Discuss your strengths and weaknesses with the group.

4. How could you arrange for practice in recording and analyzing oral reading errors? How might a tape recorder contribute to improving your accuracy?

5. Is having the child read aloud to the teacher necessarily part of an individual conference? Why or why not?

6. Discuss the possibility of a series of conferences for purposes other than simply diagnosis. What might these be planned to accomplish?

7. In your experience, what are the characteristics of pupils who are ready for individualized reading? How would you approach this method with these pupils?

8. What do you think are the most difficult tasks for the teacher to learn when attempting to individualize reading?

9. Assuming that you have never attempted to individualize the teaching of reading, what do you foresee as problems for you?

10. Since individualized reading demands a wide variety of reading materials, how might this problem be attacked when school funds or library facilities are limited?

11. In what ways may a teacher who is accustomed to group instruction initiate individual and small-group conferences?

12. How do individualized reading teachers ensure and check on the sequential development of important reading skills?

13. Plan a role-playing session in which one member of your class defends the basal reading method while another supports individualized reading.

14. How does your readiness compare with the Teacher Readiness Checklist? What could you do to meet these standards?

15. Arrange to listen to a child reading several selections. Tape the reading if you can. Try the system of recording errors presented in the chapter and be prepared to criticize it in a sharing session with your classmates.

References

1. Barbe, Walter B., et al., "Types of Difficulties in Reading Encountered by Eighty Children Receiving Instruction at a Reading Clinic," *Journal of Educational Research*, 51 (February 1958), 437–443.
2. Beeler, A. J., "Teaching About the Newspaper in Elementary Schools," *Elementary English*, 49 (February 1972), 227–229.
3. Blanchard, Jay S., Borthwick, Paul, and Hall, Ann, "Determining Instructional Reading Level: Standardized Multiple Choice vs. I.R.I. Probed Recall Questions," *Journal of Reading*, 26 (May 1983), 684–689.
4. Bormuth, John R., "Literacy in the Classroom," in *Help for the Reading Teacher*, Wm. D. Page, ed. ERIC/CRIER and National Conference on Research in English, 1975, 60–90.
5. Bradley, John Michael, "Using Readability to Improve the Content Validity of Informal Placement Tests," *Reading Improvement*, 13 (Fall 1976), 182–191.
6. Burrus, Dorothy, "Developing Critical and Creative Skills Using the Newspaper," *Elementary English*, 47 (November 1970), 978–981.
7. Christie, James I., "The Qualitative Analysis System: Updating the I.R.I.," *Reading World*, 18 (1979), 393–399.
8. Clay, Marie M., "Reading Errors and Self-correction Behavior," *British Journal of Educational Psychology*, 39 (1969), 47–66.
9. Cohn, Marvin, and D'Alessandro, Cynthia, "When is a Decoding Error Not a Decoding Error?" *Reading Teacher*, 32 (December 1978), 341–344.
10. Condit, Martha O., "Trade Books for Beginning Readers," *Wilson Library Bulletin*, 34 (December 1959), 284–301.
11. Coody, Betty, and Harris, Ben H., "Individualization of Instruction Inventory," *Elementary English*, 50 (March 1973), 431–435.
12. Criscuolo, Nicholas, P., "Mag Bags, Peg Shed, Crafty Crannies, and Reading," *Reading Teacher*, 29 (January 1976), 376–378.
13. Dale, Edgar, and Chall, Jeanne S., "A Formula for Predicting Readability," *Educational Research Bulletin* (Ohio State University), 27 (January 21 and February 18, 1948), 11–20, 28, 37–54.
14. D'Angelo, Karen, and Mahliss, Marc, "Insertion and Omission Miscues of Good and Poor Readers," *Reading Teacher*, 36 (April 1983), 778–782.

15. Daw, Seward Emerson, "The Persistence of Errors in Oral Reading in Grades Four and Five," *Journal of Educational Research*, 32 (October 1938), 81–90.

16. Dees, Margaret, "Easy to Read for Beginning Independent Readers," *Elementary English*, 39 (May 1962), 418–420.

17. Della-Piana, Gabriel M., and Herlin, Wayne R., "Are Normative Oral Reading Profiles Necessary?" in *Improvement of Reading Through Classroom Practice*, J. Allen Figurel, ed. International Reading Association Proceedings, 9, 1964, 306–309.

18. Duffy, G. B. and Durrell, Donald D., "Third Grade Difficulties in Oral Reading," *Education*, 56 (September 1936), 37–40.

19. Fuchs, Lynn S., Fuchs, Douglas, and Deno, Stanley L., "Reliability and Validity of Curriculum-Based Informal Reading Inventories," *Reading Research Quarterly*, 18 (1982), 6–26.

20. Gilmore, J. V., "The Relationships Between Oral Reading Habits and Silent Reading Comprehension." Doctoral dissertation, Harvard University, 1947.

21. Goodman, Kenneth, "A Linguistic Study of Cues and Miscues in Reading," *Elementary English*, 42 (October 1965), 639–643.

22. Groff, Patrick J., "Recent Easy Books for First-Grade Readers," *Elementary English*, 38 (December 1960), 521–527.

23. Groff, Patrick J., "A Critique of an Oral Reading Miscue Analysis," *Reading World*, 19 (March 1980), 254–264.

24. Hood, Joyce, "Is Miscue Analysis Practical for Teachers?" *Reading Teacher*, 32 (December 1978), 260–266.

25. Herlin, Wayne R., "A Comparison of Oral Reading Errors on the Monroe Diagnostic Reading Examination and the Durrell Analysis of Reading Difficulty." Doctoral dissertation, University of Utah, 1963.

26. Johns, Jerry L., and Hunt, Linda, "Motivating Reading: Professional Ideas," *Reading Teacher*, 28 (April 1975), 617–619.

27. Jorgenson, Gerald W., "An Analysis of Teacher Judgments of Reading Level," *American Educational Research Journal*, 12 (1975), 63–75.

28. Julitta, Sister Mary, A List of Books for Retarded Readers," *Elementary English*, 38 (February 1961), 79–86.

29. Kasdon, Lawrence M., "Oral versus Silent-Oral Diagnosis," in *Reading Diagnosis and Evaluation*, Dorothy L. DeBoer, ed. International Reading Association Conference Proceedings, 13, 1940, 86–92.

30. Ladd, Eleanor Mary, "A Comparison of Two Types of Training with Reference to Developing Skills in Diagnostic Oral Reading Testing." Doctoral dissertation, Florida State University, 1961.

31. Leu, Donald J. Jr., "Oral Reading Error Analysis: A Critical Review of Research and Application," *Reading Research Quarterly*, 17 (1982), 420–437.

32. Madden, M., and Pratt, M., "An Oral Reading Survey as a Teaching Aid," *Elementary English Review*, 18 (April 1941), 122–126, 159.

33. McKenna, Michael C., "Informal Reading Inventories: A Review of the Issues," *Reading Teacher*, 36 (March 1983), 670–679.

34. Monroe, Marion, *Children Who Cannot Read*. Chicago: University of Chicago Press, 1932.

35. Nurss, J. R., "The Schedule: Organizing for Individual Instruction," in *The Kindergarten Child and Reading*, L. O. Ollila, ed. Newark, Del.: International Reading Association, 1977, 56–57.

36. Page, W. D., and Carlson, Kenneth, "The Process of Observing Oral Reading Scores," *Reading Horizons,* 15 (Spring 1975), 147–150.
37. Pikulski, John, "A Critical Review: Informal Reading Inventories," *Reading Teacher,* 28 (November 1974), 141–151.
38. Pikulski, John, and Shanahan, Timothy, "Informal Reading Inventories: A Critical Analysis," in *Approaches to the Informal Evaluation of Reading,* John Pikulski, ed. Newark, Del.: International Reading Association, 1982, 94–118.
39. Pikulski, John, and Tobin, Aileen Webb, "The Cloze Procedure as an Informal Assessment Technique," in *Approaches to the Informal Evaluation of Reading,* John Pikulski, ed. Newark, Del.: International Reading Association, 1982, 42–62.
40. Pillar, Arlene M., "Individualizing Book Reviews," *Elementary English,* 52 (April 1975), 467–469.
41. Powell, W. R., "Reappraising the Criteria for Interpreting Informal Inventories," in *Reading Diagnosis and Evaluation,* Dorothy L. DeBoer, ed. International Reading Association Proceedings, 13, 1970, 100–109.
42. Powell, W. R. and Dunkeld, Cohn G., "Validity of the I.R.I. Reading Levels," *Elementary English,* 48 (October 1971), 637–642.
43. Preston, Ralph C., "The Reading Status of Children Classified by Teachers as Retarded Readers," *Elementary English,* 30 (April 1953), 225–227.
44. *Report on the Special Studies of Selected ECE Schools with Increasing and Decreasing Reading Scores.* Sacramento, Calif.: California State Department of Education, 1980.
45. Rosen, Carl L., and Ortega, Philip D., "Language and Reading Problems of Spanish Speaking Children in the Southwest," *Journal of Reading Behavior,* 1 (Winter 1969), 51–72.
46. Rye, James, *Cloze Procedure and The Teaching of Reading.* Exeter, N.H.: Heineman Educational Books, 1982.
47. Sampson, Michael R., Valmont, W. J. and Van Allen, Roach, "The Effects of Instructional Cloze on the Comprehension, Vocabulary and Divergent Production of Third-Grade Students," *Reading Research Quarterly,* 17 (1982), 389–399.
48. Sartain, Harry W., "The Roseville Experiment with Individualized Reading," *Reading Teacher,* 13 (April 1960), 277–281.
49. Spache, George D., "Personality Patterns of Retarded Readers," *Journal of Educational Research,* 50 (February 1957), 461–469.
50. Spache, George D., *Good Reading for Poor Readers.* Champaign, Ill.: Garrard Publishing Co., 1978.
51. Spache, George D., *Diagnostic Reading Scales.* Monterey, Ca.: McGraw-Hill California Test Bureau, 1981.
52. Spache, George D., *Investigating the Issues of Reading Disabilities.* Boston, Mass.: Allyn and Bacon Inc., 1976.
53. Stewig, John Warren, "Choral Speaking—Who Has the Time? Why Take the Time?", *Childhood Education,* 58 (September–October 1981), 25–29.
54. Weber, Rose-Marie, "A Linguistic Analysis of First-Grade Reading Errors," *Reading Research Quarterly,* 5 (Spring 1970), 427–451.
55. Welty, Stella L., "Reading and Black English," in *Language, Reading and the Communication Process,* Carl Braun, ed. International Reading Proceedings, 1971, 71–93.

56. Wolk, Elsie, "Reading Disabilities of Children Learning English as a Second Language," *Elementary English*, 49 (March 1972), 410–414.
57. Zintz, Miles V., *The Reading Process*. Dubuque: William C. Brown, 1970.

Resources for Implementing Individualization

General References

Atwood, Beth S., *Building Independent Learning Skills*. Belmont, Calif.: Pitman Learning, 1975.

Bechtol, W., *Individualizing Instruction and Keeping Your Sanity*. Chicago, Ill.: Follett Publishing, 1975.

Champlin, Connie, *Puppetry and Creative Dramatics in Storytelling*. Austin: Nancy Renfro Studios, 1980.

Crutchfield, Marjorie, *Individualized Reading: A Guide for Teaching Word Analysis Skills*. Los Angeles, Calif.: Gramercy Press, 1975.

Holdaway, Don, *Independence in Reading: A Handbook on Individualized Reading*. Auckland, New Zealand: Ashton Press, 1977.

Howes, Virgil M., *Individualizing Instruction in Reading and Social Sciences: Selected Readings on Programs and Practices*. New York: Macmillan, 1970.

Jongsma, E.A., *Cloze Instruction Research: A Second Look*. Newark, Del.: International Reading Association, 1980.

Marcus, Marie, *Handbook for Individualized Reading*. Gretna, La.: Pelican Publishing, 1974.

McCaslin, Nellie, *Creative Drama in the Classroom*. New York: Longmans, 1980.

Musgrave, Ray, *Individualized Instruction: Teaching Strategies Focusing on the Learner*. Boston: Allyn and Bacon, 1975.

Rae, Gwen, and Potter, Thomas, *Informal Reading Diagnosis*. Englewood Cliffs, N.J.: Prentice-Hall, 1981.

Shiman, David ed., *Teachers on Individualization: The Way We Do It*. New York: McGraw-Hill, 1974.

Stahl, Dona and Anzalone, Patricia, *Individualized Teaching in the Elementary Schools*. West Nyack, N.J.: Prentice-Hall, 1970.

Veatch, Jeanette, *Reading in the Elementary School*. New York: John Wiley and Sons, 1978.

Guides for Learning Centers

Bennie, Frances, *Learning Center: Development and Operation*. Englewood Cliffs, N.J.: Educational Technology Publications, 1977.

Bielawski, J. G. and Pomerleau, L., *Reading Games Make Reading Fun*. Ridgefield, Conn.: R. D. Communications, 1973.

Borba, Craig and Michele, *The Good Apple Guide to Learning Centers*. Riverside, N.J.: The Library of Special Education, 1979.

Breyfogle, Ethel, et al., *Creating a Learning Environment*. Santa Monica, Calif.: Goodyear Publishing.

Crabtree, June, *Learning Center Ideas*. Cincinnati: Standard Publishing, 1977.

Davidson, Tom, et al., *The Learning Center Book: An Integrated Approach*. Santa Monica, Calif.: Goodyear Publishing, 1976.

Davidson, Tom, and Steely, Judy, *Using Learning Centers with Not-Yet Readers*. Santa Monica, Calif.: Goodyear Publishing, 1980.

Don, Sue, et.al., *Individualized Reading Instruction with Learning Stations and Centers*. Evansville, Ind.: Riverside Learning Associates, 1973.

Forgan, Henry W., *The Reading Center: Ideas, Games and Activities for Individualizing Reading*. Santa Monica, Calif.: Goodyear Publishing, 1977.

Forte, Imogene, et al., *Center Stuff for Nooks, Crannies and Corners*. Nashville Tenn.: Incentive Publications, 1973.

Forte, Imogene, and MacKenzie, Joy, *Kids' Stuff: Reading and Language Experiences*. Nashville, Tenn.: Incentive Publications, 1969.

Forte, Imogene and MacKenzie, Joy, *Nooks, Crannies and Corners: Learning Centers for Creative Classrooms*. Nashville, Tenn.: Incentive Publications, 1972.

Forte, Imogene, and MacKenzie, Joy, *The New Nooks, Crannies and Corners*. West Nyack, N.Y.: Parker Publishing, 1979.

Franklin, Marion P., *Classroom Centers and Stations in America and Britain*. Edison, N.J.: Mss. Information, 1973.

Godfrey, Lorraine Hunt, *Individualize with Learning Station Themes*. Menlo Park, Calif.: Individualized Books, 1974.

Graff, Kasper N., and Askov, Eunice N., *Learning Centers: An Ideabook for Reading and Language Arts*. Dubuque: Kendall Hunt, 1977.

Johnston, Hiram, et al., *The Learning Center Ideabook: Activities for the Elementary and Middle Grades*. Boston: Allyn and Bacon, 1978.

Langham, Martha A., and Peterson, Nancy M., *Open Your Cupboards to Learning Center Games*. Phoenix, Ariz.: Skills Reinforcement Systems.

Learning Centers: Children on Their Own. Washington, D.C.: Association for Childhood Education International, 1970.

Lee, Doris M., and Rubin, Joseph B., *Children and Language: Reading and Writing, Talking and Listening*. Belmont, Calif.: Wadsworth Publishing, 1979.

Marshall, Kim, *Opening Your Class with Learning Stations*. Belmont, Calif.: Pitman Learning, 1975.

Morlan, John, et al., *Classroom Learning Centers*. Belmont, Calif.: Pitman Learning, 1973.

Nations, Jimmy, *Learning Center in the Classroom*. Washington, D.C.: National Education Association.

Peterson, Gary T., *Learning Center: A Sphere for Non-traditional Approaches to Education*. Hamden, Conn.: Shoe String Press, 1975.

Petreshene, Susan S., *Complete Guide to Learning Centers*. Palo Alto, Calif.: Pendragon House, 1976.

Petreshene, Susan S., *Supplement to the Complete Guide to Learning Centers*. Palo Alto, Calif.: Pendragon House, 1978.

Reading Skills Centers. North Billerica, Mass.: Curriculum Associates.

Thomas, John, *Learning Centers Opening Up the Classroom*. Boston: Holbrook Press.

Voight, Ralph Claude, *Invitation to Learning I: The Learning Center Handbook*. Washington, D.C.: Acropolis Books, 1974.

Ward, Patricia S., and Williams, E. Craig, *Learning Packets: New Approaches to Individualized Instruction*. West Nyack, N.Y.: Parker Publishing, 1976.

Waynant, E., and Wilson, Robert, *Learning Centers: A Guide for Effective Use*. Paoli, Penn.: Instructo.

Using Newspapers

Cheyney, Arnold B., *Teaching Reading Skills Through the Newspaper*. Newark, Del.: International Reading Association, 1971.

Davis, Dorothy C., *Reading Through the Newspaper*. Geneva, Ill.: Paladin House Publications, 1980.

Larned, Phyllis, and Randall, Nick, *Reading a Newspaper*. Heyward, Calif.: Janus Books, 1978.

Sargent, Eileen E., *The Newspaper as a Teaching Tool*. South Norwalk, Conn.: The Reading Laboratory, 1975.

Short, Rodney J., and Dickerson, Beverly, *Newspaper: An Alternative Textbook*. Belmont, Calif.: Pitman Learning, 1980.

Instructional Materials — Activities and Kits

Adams, Anne H., *Reading for Survival in Today's Society*. Riverside, N.J.: Library of Special Education. Reproducible worksheets.

Archie Graphics Reading Kits. Huntington Stations, N.Y.: Instructional Communications Technology. Comic books, question cards, and spirit masters.

Burie, Audrey, A., and Heltshe, Mary A., *Reading with a Smile: Ninety Reading Games That Work*. Washington, D.C.: Acropolis Books, 1975.

Burns, Paul C., and Roe, Betty D., *Reading Activities for Today's Elementary Schools*. Chicago, Ill.: Rand McNally College Publishing, 1979.

Critical Reading Program. Huntington Station, N.Y.: Instructional Communications Technology. Selections, comprehension checks and skill development exercises. Separate kits for grade two to college levels.

Dorsey, Mary E., *Reading Games—Activities*. Belmont. Calif.: Pitman Learning, 1972.

Early Read Book/AV Ensembles. Huntington Station, N.Y.: Instructional Communication Technology. Books with filmstrips and cassettes.

Earlie, Elsie C., *Aims Reading Kits*. Elizabethtown, Pa.: Continental Press. Games for skill development in phonics, comprehension, and general reading.

Fowler, Flora C., *Reading Games for Middle and Upper Grades*. Edison, N.J.: Mss. Information, 1975.

Great Games. Palo Alto, Calif.: Creative Publications. One hundred games to teach reading skills.

Higley, Joan, *Activities Deskbook for Teaching Reading Skills*. West Nyack, N.J.: Parker Publishing, 1977.

Hollombe, Libby, *Reading Fun and Games: Beginning Reading Activities*. Riverside, N.J.: Library of Special Education.

I/CT's Reading Bookshelf. Huntington Station, N.Y.: Instructional Communications Technology. Five collections of twelve books each. Each collection offers a five grade range from fourth grade up.

Kaplan, Sandra, *The Teacher's Choice: Ideas and Activities for Teaching Basic Skills.* Santa Monica Calif.: Goodyear Publishing, 1978.

Kaplan, Sandra, et al., *The Big Book of Independent Study Games and Activities.* Santa Monica, Calif.: Goodyear Publishing, 1976.

Kemp, Alma, *Newspaper in Education.* Miami, Fla.: The Miami Herald. Materials for teaching uses of the newspaper.

Kromer, Thomas, and Bleecker, Joyce. *Learning Can Be Fun with Michigan Games.* Hillsdale, Mich.: Hillsdale Educational Publications.

Laird, Stan, *Individualized Reading Job Cards.* Sunnyvale, Calif.: Marie's Educational Materials, 1971. Each card describes a listening or reading activity for upper elementary.

Mallett, Jerry J., *Classroom Reading Games Activities Kit.* New York: Center for Applied Research in Education, 1975.

McIntyre, Virgil M., *Reading Strategies and Enrichment Activities for Grades 4–9.* Columbus: Charles E. Merrill.

Norton, Donna E., *Language Arts Activities for Children.* Columbus: Charles E. Merrill, 1980. In lesson plan format.

Raymond, Dorothy, *What You Can Do with a Word: 300 Classroom Activities.* Novato, Calif.: Academic Therapy Publications. For primary grades.

The SRA Skills Series. Chicago, Ill.: Science Research Associates. Kits for phonics, structural analysis, and comprehension. Each has lesson plan cards, skill cards, cassettes, spirit masters, and teacher's handbook.

Smith, Carl B., and Elliott, Peggy, *Reading Activities for Middle and Secondary Schools: A Handbook for Teachers.* New York: Holt, Rinehart and Winston, 1979.

Spache, Evelyn B., *Reading Activities for Child Involvement*, 3d ed. Boston, Mass.: Allyn and Bacon, 1982.

Thomas, Ellen L., *Reading Aids for Every Class: Four Hundred Activities for Instruction and Enrichment.* Boston, Mass.: Allyn and Bacon, 1980.

Thompson, Richard A., *Energizers for Reading Instruction.* West Nyack, N.J.: Parker Publishing, 1973.

12 Word Recognition Techniques and Skills

For most nonprofessionals writing on the subject of reading and for some teachers and authors of phonics materials, phonics skill is the most important area of all reading instruction. If we were to believe some of these writers, we would be led to think that the effectiveness of the entire reading program depended upon the manner and extent of phonics teaching. In reality, phonics is just one of several basic word recognition techniques. It is of only moderate importance in early reading success and must be replaced by more advanced, permanent skills, such as use of context, if overall reading development is to occur.

The recent research we have cited should help to clarify the proper role of phonics in the reading program. We now have objective evidence of the values of phonic generalizations during the first six years of schooling. Future phonics teaching should, therefore, be much more functional and pragmatic than formerly. We now know by reason of the overall results of the First-Grade Reading Studies and those extended into the second and third grades that no one system of teaching phonics is significantly better than any other, nor are reading systems based strongly on phonics superior. Furthermore, as we discovered in updating our analysis of the phonics in basals, such programs are introduced earlier and more intensively than formerly. This trend is directly parallel to the indications of the need for such a revision as found in the First-Grade Studies. These research studies and trends in phonics teaching should result in somewhat more effective primary reading programs in the future. Whether they will quiet the chronic critics or the ultra-phonic-minded authors, however, remains to be seen.

Phonics — How and When?

(It has become popular in recent years to call word analysis "breaking the code." Hence, some writers prefer the term *decoding* to *phonics*. We don't see any real difference in the terms.)

Since about 1910, the recognition program has been the subject of more heated debate than any other element of the entire reading program. Most of the arguments have centered around the question of the value of teaching phonic analysis, or, as it is more commonly but incorrectly termed, phonetic analysis. (Phonics, the practice of using letter sounds as an aid to word recognition, is a minor element of the field of phonetic analysis.) Reading instruction gradually shifted from a system that stressed phonics as the chief method of word recognition to a method involving practically no phonics at all in some schools. By the late 1920s, this trend was reversed and since then phonics has been presented in practically all American basal reading series as one of the significant word recognition skills. It is commonly taught not as the basis of learning to read but is introduced as one type of aid.

Before they are introduced to phonics, children spontaneously employ a variety of clues for word recognition. Among these are word shape, word length, context or sense of the sentence, pictorial clues, and details within the word. For example, once they have been identified in reading, such words as *elephant, Christmas,* and *rabbit* are subsequently easily recognized by their striking patterns or shapes, for example, ⌐_┌─┐ └───┘ ⌐──┘ . Other words, for example, *grandmother, automobile,* and *policemen,* offer clues to recognition not only by their distinctive shape but also by their unusual length. Many other words may be recognized by the inherent structure and thought of the sentence, particularly when the concept is supported by an accompanying picture. For example, few primary school children would be unable to supply the missing word in the sentence, "The cat likes to drink _____," if the adjoining picture shows a person pouring a fluid from a quart bottle into a pan placed in front of a cat. Finally, elements of a word, such as double letters, capitals, and details that lend themselves to a mental association between the word and its meaning—as "the two eyes in *look*," "the curly tail on *dog*"—contribute other clues to word recognition.

The intention of the authors of many basal reading programs was the promotion of the development of these quasi-spontaneous clues to word recognition. Beginning instruction was deliberately planned to stimulate the pupils' use of these means of word discrimination and recognition. The justifications offered for this *whole-word* method are the following:

- There is some evidence that early instruction in phonics is apt to be ineffectual with children under the mental age of six and one-half to seven.
- Too early introduction of phonics may tend to make children dependent upon letter sounds as their major or only technique of word recognition. Rapid recognition and, hence, rate of reading are impaired by this dependency.
- Too early or too great an emphasis upon phonics may make pupils read over-cautiously, slowly, and too analytically. These habits are difficult to overcome and may interfere with the normal development of rate and comprehension.
- The habit of rapid word recognition by a variety of clues is of permanent value in reading development. Therefore, it should be established early and none of the several clues taught, such as phonics, should be permitted to interfere with or displace this essential habit.

However, shape or length as a basis for word recognition promotes rapid initial learning but does not promote transfer to learning new words. It soon becomes a guessing game, as shown by the tendency to substitute for the printed word other words that are drawn from the child's auditory vocabulary or that were learned earlier. Today the early training directs the child's attention to the sounds of first letters, final letters, and middle letters, in that order of preference. Instruction that forces attention to more than a single-letter basis for discrimination aids the learning of new words. Color cues promote rapid learning at first but cannot transfer to ordinary print and, besides, they lead pupils to ignore the other cues present and hamper transfer of learning new words.

Letter name learning, although popular in a number of programs, does not facilitate learning to read, for names of letters are not functional in word recognition. It is true that some studies show that knowledge of letter names upon entering school is a good predictor of early reading success. But such knowledge obviously reflects the child's intelligence, socioeconomic and language backgrounds, and parental aspirations, for the learning is not present among economically disadvantaged or linguistically different children. The parents of such children do not usually teach their preschool youngsters the alphabet. Learning letter names does not foster learning new words, even when they are composed of the letters just learned (37, 44).

Many critics of current reading programs write as though there is a dichotomy between a phonics method and the whole-word method. They claim that the latter is the only word recognition skill offered in today's programs and that phonics is almost completely ignored. The analysis of the phonics content of several widely used basal programs in this chapter completely refutes this false argument. The teachers' manuals and other guides to training in word recognition clearly outline extensive programs in phonics. If these guides were followed carefully, every child would receive adequate training in this important skill. But, in the minds of some, there is doubt regarding the thoroughness and competence with which teachers follow the suggested program.

Disturbed by the attacks upon schools, a number of educators have reexamined the phonics program. Rather than assume that teachers understood the skills and were teaching phonics as outlined in the basal manuals, a number of investigators began to assess how much knowledge teachers had in this area. The results of these surveys were disturbing, for it became apparent that in the early 1960s teachers did not know much about phonics. Average scores on phonics tests in large samples were only about 50 to 60 percent correct, and apparently even this knowledge was gained only by classroom experience in teaching phonics to pupils (and learning it at the same time!) (48). The impact of these studies on preservice training of teachers was dramatic, and more intensive training of teachers in this area became common. Testing teachers with the generalizations listed later in this book, Fleming found that teachers could give examples of many of them, particularly those of superior validity, certainly an encouraging sign (18). This study does not, of course, prove that phonics is well taught everywhere, but the bulk of evidence in this and many other surveys at least supports the belief that it is being taught more effectively than twenty years ago.

One of the implications of the First-Grade Reading Studies was that the program of the basal readers of the late 1960s would be strengthened by a stronger, earlier functional phonics program. The children achieved better reading scores at the end of the first grade in those programs in which the basal was supplemented by an emphasis upon phonics. This result produced dramatic changes in the attention to phonics in basal readers published after the First-Grade Reading Studies reports became available in 1965–1967. These changes are noted in detail in our later discussion of the phonics content in the leading basal readers. Critical review of the early studies that supported a delay in phonics teaching until late first or early second grade has also cast doubts upon this practice.

A third series of questions concerning the current phonics program deals with its content and the proper programming of instruction. There is a tremendous diversity of opinion on these topics among reading authorities, authors of reading series, and popular writers on the subject. The diversity of practice in basal reading programs is apparent in a comparison of the generalizations in Table 12.2 (p. 474). Content in various phonics textbooks varies from teaching only the single sounds of seventeen consonants and nothing else regarding letter sounds to a program offering over five hundred letter sounds and combinations to primary school children. (We are quite aware that letters do not have sounds, but it is convenient to refer to the sounds we attach to our letters as "letter sounds.") Most of the popularized programs completely ignore the necessity for teaching pupils any rules that might guide their efforts and omit any training in blending sounds that might enable the children to produce some resemblance of the true word (45).

For many debated points, the research gives somewhat conflicting results. These include the questions of phonics before reading (49), of complex phonics programs versus simple or extra phonics versus the basal system (19), or the true importance of knowledge of the alphabet for early success in reading. Finally, although the research definitely does not support them, there are the current beliefs that phonics is particularly good for children of below-average mentality; that there is an exact sequence in which various letter sounds and combinations should be taught; that the ability to sound the letters of a word is equivalent to word recognition or even the complete reading act; and that the memorization of phonic elements will transfer automatically to the act of continuous reading, and the child will therefore read better.

Jeanne Chall's book *Learning to Read: The Great Debate* (New York: McGraw-Hill, 1967)* triggered a tremendous amount of attention to contrasting phonics systems that enlivened the field of reading for some time. After reviewing many studies of comparative methods, Chall reached the conclusion that intensive or systematic phonics, as she termed it, was superior to gradual phonics, as commonly taught in the basals. Actually, her definition

*See our review in *Journal of Reading Behavior*, 1 (Winter 1969), 71–74, and Rutherford, William, "Learning To Read: A Critique," *Elementary School Journal*, 69 (November 1968), 72–83.

was expanded to include a number of different phonics systems as well as the phonological approach of the linguists. In brief, she supported an approach which includes at least these characteristics:

- Letter–sound relationships before rhyming or alliteration.
- Teaching isolated letters and their sounds.
- Finding letters in words representing certain sounds; writing, pronouncing words by sounding letter after letter.
- Teaching a few prefixes and suffixes and a bit about the dictionary.
- Lots of letter naming, more letters, and more specific sounds.
- Little attention to deriving word recognition from context.

As we shall see, these practices contrast greatly with most basal programs (as well as with most linguistic programs). And many reviewers of her book did not feel that Chall had proved her theory, particularly when she depended so strongly upon studies over a long period of time from a wide variety of sources that often differed in their instructional practices from Chall's definition. Strangely enough, Chall did not refer to the 1965–1967 reports of the First-Grade Reading Studies, which contradicted much of her argument although she had copies prior to publication of her book.

But the book did stimulate many school boards and laypeople to turn to a type of phonics that apparently would make instruction more efficient. However, as in the past, the results were disappointing, for it was soon obvious that although a heavy emphasis upon phonics did produce better scores on word recognition tests, the system did not result in better comprehension, word meaning, or spelling, particularly among lower-ability pupils, nor did it appreciably reduce failures in reading. Harris et al. found no advantage in an intensive phonics system (Phonovisual) over each of three consecutive school years. In fact, their data show a negative correlation of $-.61$ between the time spent in phonics teaching and word knowledge and $-.75$ between phonics time and reading comprehension (27).

DeLawter's comparison of the reading miscues of children taught by a linguistic decoding system (Miami and Merrill readers) versus a sight-word approach (Chandler Language Experience) indicated dramatic differences after two years of instruction. The meaning-oriented children tended toward miscues that were real words while the decoding-trained children produced a high percentage of mispronunciations or nonwords. The errors of the latter showed strong graphic similarity between the miscue and the printed word, but many were semantically (meaning) inappropriate. Moreover, their self-corrections were usually on the basis of graphic cues, not meaning or contextual cues (12).

Phonics seems to be like a pendulum that swings our instruction from one extreme to another where the ultimate goal of comprehension often seems forgotten. Ignoring often the broader implications of the research, because of the temporary spurt in word recognition, we grasp at any new (?) phonics system that seems to offer solutions for our reading problems.

This brief review of its many debated or unsolved questions may help to show why phonics has received so much attention, even though it is probably not the most important word recognition skill. All these conflicting theories and experiments certainly imply that a careful review of our present program and methods is highly desirable.

As Emans has shown in his brief history of phonics (*15*), its teaching and rationale have been in and out of fashion repeatedly since the sixteenth century, and these differences in opinion and practice will probably continue to stimulate debate and interfere with progress in development of reading methods.

How We Now Teach Phonics

In each edition of this book we have attempted to summarize current practices in the teaching of phonics or decoding. A brief review of these summaries will illustrate the marked changes in content and instructional practices that have characterized this facet of the reading curriculum. In 1964 none of the leading programs attempted to teach pupils how to use letter sounds at the readiness or preprimer stages. Auditory discrimination of these sounds was all that was offered then. During the ensuing decade more and more emphasis was placed on the application of letter sounds in phonic analysis at these earliest stages of reading development. Today a child is commonly being taught to use the sounds of all twenty-one initial consonants, some final consonants, and perhaps some vowel sounds during the readiness–preprimer levels. (The reader should note that a number of current basal programs are substituting the term *levels* for such words as *readiness, preprimer, primer,* and the like. The development stages are similar, however, and we shall continue to use the more descriptive terms until they disappear from use.) This training is in addition to learning to name and match lowercase and capital letters and to recognize similarities and differences among letter sounds.

As a result of this downward shifting of the content of the decoding program, much less time is now spent on the prereading auditory training that many authorities believe is so essential. Just what effect this decrease in preparatory steps to phonic analysis will have on children's reading progress remains to be seen. There is, of course, the argument we have referred to earlier, that auditory discrimination training is not highly significant for early reading success, particularly among linguistically different children. It has been shown that these bilingual or dialectal speakers may not hear differences or observe these differences in their own speech, and yet they can comprehend standard English. Thus there may be some justification for the lesser emphasis upon auditory training in recent programs.

On the other hand, when the classroom instruction emphasizes hearing similarities and differences among letter sounds as the basic method of word recognition, the pupil must either have good auditory discrimination or be given adequate training in the hope of inducing this ability. The lessening attention being given to such training in current programs may prevent some children from coping with the situation when their natural auditory discrimination is weak.

A decade ago the instruction in phonics continued through the third grade and sometimes even into the fourth. Today practically all the content of the program, including consonant and vowel sounds, short and long vowels, consonant and vowel digraphs, and vowel diphthongs, has been taught by the end of the second grade. In most series, only a few of the more difficult letter–sound combinations are delayed until the third grade.

A third trend has been the tremendous increase in the presentation of word patterns, or phonograms as they once were called. These are largely two- to four-letter units of frequent occurrence in primary reading materials. A few years ago only a few of the basal reading programs presented any great number of these units. Today the number of word patterns being taught in most basal series is vastly greater than formerly. In fact, these letter combinations form the heart, if not the total content, of the decoding program in some series.

These word parts or spelling patterns as they are sometimes called, were largely derived from a computer analysis of the frequency of various letter combinations in our language. The linguistic analysis of these word patterns has shown that the sounds of vowels are often determined by the consonants preceding or following them. For example, the medial vowel in a consonant–vowel–consonant (CVC) unit is often a short vowel, while the vowel in a CVCe (consonant–vowel–consonant–silent *e*) is frequently a long vowel. Some basal series now emphasize the learning of these word patterns exclusively and offer no instruction in the sounds of individual letters or letter combinations. For example, the decoding objectives of the Merrill Linguistic Reading Program are:

- Decode words of the consonant–vowel–consonant (CVC) spelling pattern (preprimer through first half of second grade).
- Decode words of the consonant–vowel–consonant–silent *e* (CVCe) spelling pattern (second half of second grade through first half of third grade).
- Decode words of the consonant–vowel–vowel–consonant (CVVC) spelling pattern (second half of second grade through first half of third grade).
- Decode minor spelling patterns and irregular spellings (second half of second grade through third grade).

This, of course, is an extreme example of this trend. As shown in Table 12.1, most basal series are combining the emphasis upon word patterns with the usual training in individual letters and letter combinations that was once the entire phonics program.

Table 12.1 Decoding in the Basal Reading Program

Series	Word patterns	Consonants, blends, digraphs*	Short vowels	Long vowels	Vowel digraphs and diphthongs[†]
Preprimer and Primer Levels					
Allyn and Bacon					
Pathfinder					
D. C. Heath American Readers	CVC, CVCe, et, at, en, ot, st, op, y, ay, it, ing, all, in, ad, im, ig, ade, ag, ake, alk, ame, an, and, ap, ar, ark, art	d, g, h, w, y, m, f, l, p, s, t, c(k), n, b, g, l, p, n, j, v, r, k, ff, bl, br, dr, fr, pl, sl, sm, sp, sh, wh(hw), th, th	e, o, a, i		
Ginn 720	ill, ide, id, it, im, ike, ite, in, ine ip, ipe, en, ell, ed, et, eet, eel, eed, eek, eep, ead, eat, ean, ing, at, an, ack, ad, ake, ame, ade, CVC, CVCe, CVVC, CV, CVCC	b, l, r, h, j, c(k), f, y, n, d, g, t, v, m, s, w, p, d, ck, g, s, ss, z, l, ll, s(z)	i, e	i, e	ee, ea
Harper & Row: Design for Reading		h, n, y, f, l, k, b, v, z, t, n, g	i, a	y	
Houghton Mifflin	et, at, an, op, ay, ing, ick, un, ook, est, ack, er, ot, ell, ed, in, en, ake, qu, squ, ide, ight, all, ame, es, ock, ad	w, g, h, c, t, p, r, b, m, j, d, f, k, l, n, v, s, y, ck, tr, st, ch, sh, th, wh, z, pl, sm, c(s), fl, sc, fr, pr, gr, x, cr, nk, br, g, thr, ge, dge, sl, cl, sk, str	a, i, e, o, u	y	oo, ai, oy, oi, aw, oa, ee
SRA Basic Reading Series	an, ad, ag, at, ap, am, ab, al, it, in, ig, id, im, ip, CVC, CVCC, CCVC, CCVCC	c, d, f, m, r, n, p, v, b, s, d, w, g, h, t, l, j, k, z, y, x, ss, ff, ck, nd, nt, st, mp, ft, pt, xt, lf, lk, lp, bl, cl, fl, gl, pl, sl, sk, sn, sp, sw, tw, br, cr, dr, fr, gr, tr, sm, pr			
First Reader Level					
Allyn and Bacon	an, at, ame, and, id, ake, ave, ime, ed, em, et, eed, eet, eep, im, in, ot, op, ad, ike, ice, ine, ane, ide, ate, ear, eat, ade, ap, ob, op, ill, ell, ick, ack, un,	h, w, m, n, l, s, r, d, l, ll, b, j, p, s(z), k, t, c(k), f, y, g, ss(s), ff, z, k, fl, b, pl, th, sh, gr, tr, ch, cr, fr, pr, th, c(s), ce(s), cl, gl, sl, wh(hw), st, sm, sn, ld, lk, qu(kw), sk, sp	a, e, i, o, u, y	a-e, u, i-e, o-e, ee, ea, u-e, ai, ee, ow, ay, ie, oa, ow	ay, ow, oy, au, ow, oi, oy, oo

*Consonants—single letters produced by stopping and then releasing air. Blends—two or more letters that are blended in speech but are all heard in the pronunciation, as *bl, tr*. Digraphs—two letters joined into a single sound unlike either of them.

[†]Diphthongs—the sounds of two vowels in which the sound of one glides into the other, as *ou*. *(continued)*

Table 12.1 *(continued)*

Series	Word patterns	Consonants, blends, digraphs	Short vowels	Long vowels	Vowel digraphs and diphthongs
	ug, ive, ipe, it, ig, est, old, all, alk, ing, ink, ung, ust, ark, ound				
D. C. Heath	*CVVC*	*c(s), z, ck(k), nd, ce(s), ll(l), ss(s), nk(ngk), x(ks), mm(m), nn(n), nt, pp(p), tt(t), cl, fl, ch, fr, gl, gr, st, tr, sk, sn, str, thr, tw*		*u*	*ai, ay, ea, ee, oa, y-u, yu-u*
Ginn 720	*ook, all, ar, ang, ung, ink, ing*	*c(city), pl, sm, ch, nd, nt, bl*	*o(top), s(call), u*	*o-e(rope), o*	*oo(wood), aw, oo(moon)*
Harper & Row: Design for Reading	*er, ar*	*zz, sw, cl, pl, gl, br, fr, sn, str, scr, thr, nt, mp, nd, id, th, ch, tch*	*u*	*y*	*ai, ea, oa, oo, ew, ow, ay, oi, oy, ow*
Houghton Mifflin	*ir, ur*	*kh, wr, s(z), sh*			*ou*
SRA Basic Reading Series	*CCVCC, CVCCC*	*ng, nk, sh, th, ch, wh, qu, tch*			

Second Reader Level

Series	Word patterns	Consonants, blends, digraphs	Short vowels	Long vowels	Vowel digraphs and diphthongs
Allyn and Bacon	*ign, am, ont, ond, ock, ail, unk, ess, ook, ang, ank, oke, ead, eal, ight, ind, ong, ump, oil, ile, age, ale, ace, are, oat*	*ng, gl, kn, sk, rd, rk, ch(k), ft, g(j), wr, sp, spr, str, mm, tt, sw, squ(skw), thr, mp, x(ks), lt, ch(tch), gh(f), mb(m), ff(f), gg(g), nn(n)*	*ea, ir, or, er, ur*		*ou, au, ew, ow*
D. C. Heath	*CVV, CVVC*	*g(j), kn(n), wr(r), mp, gg(g), ge(j), gh(f), nch, scr(skr), ct(kt), lk, s(z), ze(z), zz(z), spr, shr, sl, cl(kl), ph(f), sw, ng, dge(j), bb(b), dd(d), ft, squ(skw), kr(cr), sc(s), ik(ic), ld, ch(tch)*		*i(igh), oe, i-y, ow, e-y, ey*	
Ginn 720	*ing, at, an, ack, ad, ake, ame, ade, CVC, CVCC, CVCe*	*tr, qu, v, x, st, wh, th, gs, sh, gr, fr, f, ff, th*	*a*	*a*	
Harper & Row: Design for Reading		*sh, th, wh, p, m, d, s, l, r, k, ss, ll, fl, sp, tr, sl, ck, ch, wr, kn, nk, ng, b, s(z), x, ff, cr, gr, sc, dr, sm, bl, sk, st, pr, spr, st, sh*	*e, o, u*	*a, e, i, o, u*	

Series	Word patterns	Consonants, blends, digraphs	Short vowels	Long vowels	Vowel digraphs and diphthongs
Houghton Mifflin	en, est, old	dr, sn, bl, sp, spr, gl	a, e, i, o, u	a, e, i, o, u	ow
SRA Basic Reading Series	CVCe, CVVC, CVVCe	c(city), gh(f), g(j), s(sh)	a(ball), o(cost), u(bush)		ee, ea, oo, ai, ay, oa, ou, ow, au, aw, oi, oy, oo, ea

Third Reader Level

Series	Word patterns	Consonants, blends, digraphs	Short vowels	Long vowels	Vowel digraphs and diphthongs
Allyn and Bacon		pp(p), sc(sk), scr(skr), dg(j), nk, nt, pl, pr, tw, ti(s), pt, s(z), si(z), ci(sh), gn, ph(f), gh(g)		ei	
D. C. Heath		on(en), pr, sc(sk) lt, scr(skr), ch(k), mb(m), sm, spl, qu(kw)		ie(e), ie(i)	
Ginn 720	igh, eigh	sp, ft, str, pt, squ, pr, spr, sw, lt, sc, scr, tw, mp, wr, gu, gue	o(dog), or, ar, u(bull), a(watch)	y, u	ea, ew, ie, ew, au, augh, ei, oi, oy, ou, ough, ou, ou(four)
Harper & Row: Design for Reading	gu, qu, squ, igh, ight, it, ur, or, ough, ought	g(j), c(s), tw, spl, sch, shr	y		ie, ey, aw, ea
Houghton Mifflin	or, ible, age, ally, ant, able, ous, ish, ate, ent, ive				

Fourth Reader Level

Series	Word patterns	Consonants, blends, digraphs	Short vowels	Long vowels	Vowel digraphs and diphthongs
Allyn and Bacon		s(z), si(z), ci(sh), gn, ph(f), gh(g)		ie(i), oe	ui, ough
Ginn 720		c(sh), ch(sh), ch(k), gn, gh, ph(f), t(fortune)	y	ue(clue)	ei
Harper & Row: Design for Reading	ai, aigh, ea, ei, eigh, es, ey, qu, uy, ear, ar, ie, arr, cqu	dg(j), ph, s(zh), sc(s), ss(z)			ui, ue, ie, oo, ew, ou, ough, au

Fifth Reader Level

Series	Word patterns	Consonants, blends, digraphs	Short vowels	Long vowels	Vowel digraphs and diphthongs
Harper & Row: Design for Reading	er, or, inc, ink	rh, x(gz), sc, cc(k), gn, bt, pn, ps, pt, mn			ae, ei, us

Sixth Reader Level

Series	Word patterns	Consonants, blends, digraphs	Short vowels	Long vowels	Vowel digraphs and diphthongs
Harper & Row: Design for Reading	ge, gue, ur, ien	ch(sh), ll			ough

The great variations among these decoding systems is another indication of the state of flux characteristic of this area of the reading curriculum. The basic research is lacking to tell us when to teach the sound of individual letters and letter combinations, or whether it would be better to teach these in the larger units called word patterns. The computer can tell us the frequency of occurrence of the letter sounds and the spelling patterns in which these variations occur. But it cannot tell us which phonemes (the sound of a letter or letter combination when we pronounce them) are most easily learned or the best sequence of presentation. Hence these decisions are often made on the basis of the words used in the reading selections of the basal series. As a result we see that the scope and sequence of decoding instruction varies from one series to the next and may extend over anywhere from two to six grade levels.

There is, of course, more content to this program than can be presented in tabular form. Practically all these basal series teach children to deal with compound words, contractions, silent letters, and such spelling conventions as doubling the final consonant, dropping a final *e*, and changing *y* to *i* when adding an ending.

The decoding or phonics content of six leading basal series is outlined in Table 12.1. The table does not include, of course, the details of methodology, the generalizations or rules presented, or a description of the readiness training that may precede these programs. This listing of the content of the average basal phonics program must be expanded by a description of the approach to convey an accurate picture. Letter sounds are usually not taught in isolation, but rather as an integral part of words. *B* is not *buh* but "the sound of the letter *b* as in *boy*." Initial consonant sounds are closely tied to the adjoining vowel and cannot readily be separated without distortion of the pronunciation of the word. Listen carefully to yourself as you say aloud the hard sound of *c*, then the phonogram *at*. Compare this with the distinctly greater resemblance to the true word as you say aloud the sound of *ca*, and then add the *t* sound.

Initial consonants, blends, and digraphs are stressed in the phonics program somewhat more than the final ones, and the final ones more than those occurring in a medial position. This emphasis reflects the known significance of these portions of words for word recognition. Because of the difficulty in pronouncing a single consonant sound without adding some sort of *uh* or vowel sound to it, a few of the most common short vowel sounds are usually taught with the first consonants. Again there is strong support for this practice because of the frequent occurrence of monosyllables containing the short vowel sound in most primary reading materials.

MacGinitie (33) has severely criticized the instructional procedures suggested in basal manuals for phonics lessons for their undue complexity and lack of research basis in the logic and concepts they demand. He also notes the lack of child understanding or cognitive clarity regarding the teacher's terms—letter, word, sound—that were referred to earlier. He describes several typical teacher presentations that are unreasonably difficult, particularly because of emphasis upon linguistic detail. For example, in such apparently simple tasks as recognizing and identifying the same phoneme present in the two words *now* and *nor;* or supplying a word that ends with *ed* and begins with the same sound, as in *be, but,* and *ball,* MacGinitie points out that we do not really know what process children use to do these tasks nor do we know how to advise them if they fail. Each of these common tasks and the terms they employ should be approached step by step, for the relation between the phonemic element and its sound is very complex. But we do not have the basic research to tell us how to present these concepts and analytic processes in the logical steps children can utilize. In a sense, the children are left to their own resources in learning and applying phonic analysis, except for the drill that so many teachers think solves all problems.

The vowel sounds are the most difficult to teach because of their many variations and combinations. Most basal programs try to aid children by leading them inductively to recognize that there are a number of basic rules that can assist them in recognizing the vowel sounds in unknown words. Unfortunately, there are a disturbing number of exceptions to almost any generalization that can be framed. As a result there is considerable debate about the values of these rules. The obvious answer to this question, of course, would be found by examining the vocabularies of a number of basal series for the number of applications and exceptions to each principle. But the authors of most basal series have been loathe to perform this analysis, perhaps for fear of what they might discover.

Theodore Clymer (*11*) and his students analyzed the manuals, workbooks, and readers of four basal series to determine the phonic principles taught. Amazingly, over 121 different statements were offered: fifty on vowels, fifteen on consonants, and twenty-eight each on endings and syllabication. The variation from one basal series to another was remarkable, ranging from thirty-three principles in one series to sixty-eight in another. Of the fifty vowel principles, only eleven were found in all four programs. Many principles were trite or repetitious and, as Clymer notes, almost useless as an aid to word recognition.

Clymer selected forty-five reasonably useful principles for evaluation and counted the number of examples and exceptions to each in the entire word list of the four combined basal series, plus the words in the *Gates Reading Vocabulary for the Primary Grades.* We have grouped his results from the data he has so kindly supplied, omitting for the moment those rules dealing with syllabication.

Two more recent studies have repeated Clymer's study by extending the analysis of the utility of phonic generalizations in reader vocabularies above the primary grades. Emans sampled 10 percent of the words beyond primary levels in *The Teacher's Word Book of 30,000 Words* by Thorndike and Lorge (*14*). Bailey's sample included words that were found in two or more of eight leading basal series for the first six grades (*2*). Thus one of the possible objections to Clymer's study, that his observations about phonic generalizations might not apply above the primary level, may be answered by these complementary studies.

Table 12.2 Phonic Generalizations

	Percent of utility		
	Clymer	Emans	Bailey

Vowel Principles

	Clymer	Emans	Bailey
1. When *y* is the final letter in a word, it usually has a vowel sound.	84	98	89
2. If the only vowel letter is at the end of a word, the letter usually stands for a long sound.	74	33	76
3. When there is one *e* in a word that ends in a consonant, the *e* usually has a short sound.	76	83	92
4. When a vowel is in the middle of a one-syllable word, ending in a consonant, the vowel is short.	62	73	71
5. When there are two vowels, one of which is final *e*, the first vowel is long and the *e* is silent.	63	63	57
6. When words end with silent *e*, the preceding *a* or *i* is long.	60	48	50
7. One vowel letter in an accented syllable has its short sound.	61	64	65
8. In many two- and three-syllable words, the final *e* lengthens the vowel in the last syllable.	46	42	46
9. The letter *a* has the same sound (*o*) when followed by *l*, *w*, and *u*.	48	24	34
10. When *a* follows *w* in a word, it usually has the sound of *a* in *was*.	32	28	22
11. When *y* is used as a vowel in words, it sometimes has the sound of long *i*.	15	4	11
12. When *y* or *ey* is seen in the last syllable that is not accented, the long sound of *e* is heard.	0	1	0

Vowel Digraphs

	Clymer	Emans	Bailey
13. When the letters *oa* are together in a word, *o* always gives its long sound and the *a* is silent.	97	86	95
14. Words having double *e* usually have the long *e* sound.	98	100	87
15. In *ay* the *y* is silent and gives *a* its long sound.	78	100	88
16. When *ea* come together in a word, the first letter is long, the second silent.	66	62	55
17. The first vowel is usually long, the second silent in the digraphs *ai, ea, oa, ui*.	66	58	60
18. When there are two vowels side by side, the long sound of the first one is heard and the second is usually silent.	45	18	34
19. *W* is sometimes a vowel and follows the vowel digraph rule.	40	31	33
20. In the phonogram *ie*, the *i* is silent and the *e* has a long sound.	17	23	31

Vowel Diphthongs

	Clymer	Emans	Bailey
21. The two letters *ow* make the long *o* sound.	59	50	55
22. When *e* is followed by *w*, the vowel sound is the same as represented by *oo*.	35	14	40

Vowels with *r*

	Clymer	Emans	Bailey
23. The *r* gives the preceding vowel a sound that is neither long nor short.	78	82	86
24. When *a* is followed by *r* and final *e*, we expect to hear the sound heard in *care*.	90	100	96

	Percent of utility		
	Clymer	Emans	Bailey

Consonants

25. When *c* and *h* are next to each other, they make only one sound.	100	100	100
26. When the letter *c* is followed by *o* or *a*, the sound of *k* is likely to be heard.	100	100	100
27. When *ght* is seen in a word, *gh* is silent.	100	100	100
28. When a word begins with *kn*, the *k* is silent.	100	100	100
29. When a word begins with *wr*, the *w* is silent.	100	100	100
30. When a word ends in *ck*, it has the same last sound as in *look*.	100	100	100
31. When two of the same consonants are side by side, only one is heard.	99	91	98
32. When *c* is followed by *e* or *i*, the sound of *s* is likely to be heard.	96	90	92
33. *Ch* is usually pronounced as it is in *kitchen*, *catch*, and *chair*, not like *sh*.	95	67	87
34. The letter *g* often has a sound similar to that of *j* in *jump* when it precedes the letter *i* or *e*.	64	80	78

Phonograms

35. When the letter *i* is followed by the letters *gh*, the *i* usually stands for its long sound, and the *gh* is silent.	71	100	71
36. When *ture* is the final syllable in a word, it is unaccented.	100	100	95
37. When *tion* is the final syllable in a word, it is unaccented.	100	100	100

The results of the three studies were combined in Table 12.2, since all three tested the value of the same phonic generalizations. The figures for each study represent the percent of utility, or the percent of the times that each principle actually held true in relevant words.

Clymer suggests that the validity of a phonic generalization should fall no lower than 75 percent utility: it should be true in at least three out of four words to which it is applicable. Perhaps another way of evaluating these principles would be to note the total number of words in which they function. Clymer's original table contains the number of examples and exceptions to each principle, and we shall use these facts in further evaluation.

It is apparent from Table 12.2 that the generalizations concerning the sounds of vowels and vowel combinations are not only more numerous but also more variable in utility. If we expect a principle to work three out of four times, only the first three of those dealing with the sounds of single vowels are valid. The second, however, applied to about 1 percent of the 2600-word basal vocabulary studied by Clymer. There is some disagreement between the figures of Emans and Bailey regarding this principle. But, since Bailey could find only thirty-eight examples in the vocabulary of the first six grades, it is apparent that the principle has no practical utility. The fourth in the list is widely taught in phonics and basal programs but functions in only 62 percent of 657 words. In other words, for every two words in which this principle works, there is one word which is an exception. We have modified Clymer's statement by adding the phrase "ending in a consonant" to distinguish from one-syllable words that end in *e*, as governed by principle 5. The fifth is also a very popular generalization, despite the fact that it works only two out of three times even in primary words. Thus, of the twelve phonic principles governing the sounds of single vowels in primary-grade vocabularies, only two appear to be functional and to justify teaching—the first and the third. The additional data from Emans and Bailey confirm Clymer's observations about these vowel phonic principles and offer no suggestion that they would function any more effectively above the primary level than they do there.

In a study by Burmeister (8), the fifth principle was again examined for its validity. The validity of the principle varies from 61.1 percent of the words with medial vowels to 100 percent for *y*. Burmeister suggests that if children were taught that the medial vowel may be long *or* short, the principle would function 85.6 percent of the time. Two exceptions should also be taught, she recommends, of *a–e* with the *a* having a short sound of *i*, and *i–e*, with the *i* having the short sound of *e*, as in *furnace* and *machine*, respectively.

Eight principles governing vowel digraphs, or double vowels forming a single sound, were analyzed by Clymer. Of these, only the first three meet his utility criterion of validity in three out of four applications.

The thirteenth and fifteenth principles apply in about 1 percent of basal words, which is hardly frequent enough to justify their teaching. On the other hand, the fourteenth of this group appears defensible since it has 148 examples during the first six grades.

Although it is very popular with the authors of basal and phonics series, principle 18 is very ineffectual, with more exceptions than examples. This result could readily be anticipated, for it makes no distinction between two adjoining vowels, which are simply a double vowel or digraph, and vowel diphthongs, which are the blending of two vowel sounds into a pair of new sounds, such as *oi*, *oy*, *ow*. None of the other vowel digraph principles appear to be justifiable.

The studies of Burrows and Zyra (*10*) and Burmeister (7) concentrated on these vowel pairs. Burrows and Zyra investigated their frequency and adherence to this principle among the first 5000 words of highest frequency in children's own writing. In the examples, 49 percent followed the principle, 51 percent violated it!

Burmeister counted the frequency of vowel pairs that yielded a single phoneme. She found that a vowel pair might have from one to nine common sounds! She distinguished four types of vowel pairs: long vowel plus a silent; a blend as in *au*, *aw*; a new sound, as *ou*'s most common sound being *schwa* (the unstressed, indefinite vowel sounds, as in *fir*, *fur*) and *ew* being *u*; and a type in which the vowel pair separates into two phonemes, as in *extraordinary*, *science*. To deal with these varying sounds, Burmeister suggests that *au*, *aw*, *oi*, *oy* and the two sounds of *oo* be taught as diphthongs; the second most common sounds of *ea* as short *e; ow* be taught with the most common sounds, as in *town* and *own*. *Ou's* most common sound, as we pointed out, is a schwa, with *ou* as in *out* being second in frequency for this pair. The combinations *ei* and *ie* are equal to so many sounds that any generalization is impractical, in her opinion (and ours).

The two vowel diphthong principles are relatively weak in validity and seem hardly worth teaching. Of the two principles on vowels with *r*, the first, a very popular version, shows high validity and functions in 484 words, according to Clymer. It works in four out of every five words to which it can be applied. Although it works well, principle 24 applies to only nine basal words and probably should be eliminated for this reason. Even in the six-grade vocabulary sampled by Bailey, it applied to only twenty-four words.

The ten consonant principles show, on the whole, much greater validity than those concerning vowel sounds, reflecting the greater consistency and fewer variants in English consonant sounds. Nine of the ten are completely justified by the utility criterion. However, principles 27, 28, 29, and 30 apply to very small proportions of words. In the interests of simplicity, it would seem more logical to teach these few words as sight words than by these generalizations. This evaluation of these four generalizations is not altered by our consulting Bailey's study, for each item is found to apply to less than 1 percent of the words.

Principle 35 concerns the *igh* or *ight* phonogram. In the form stated here, it applies to only thirty-one words, of which nine are exceptions. The small number of words in the basal vocabulary governed by this principle indicates that the phonogram *ight* can more profitably be taught as such, without burdening the pupil with another generalization with almost one exception for every two examples. Principles 36 and 37 refer to four and five basal words, respectively, and thus are hardly worth the effort of learning. The broader study by Bailey does not alter the picture of the relative infrequency of these three generalizations, for none of them applies to more than about 100 words in a six-grade vocabulary.

To summarize Clymer's highly significant study of phonic generalizations, we see that of the thirty-seven, only nine are sufficiently valid and widely applicable. Two of these, 1 and 3, concern vowel sounds; one deals with vowel digraphs, principle 14; one concerns vowels with *r*, principle 23; and five control consonant sounds, principles 25, 26, 31, 32, and 33. Neither of those regarding vowel diphthongs is acceptable. The additional data extending Clymer's type of study to a representative vocabulary of basal readers for the entire six grades, as offered by Emans and Bailey, do not change Clymer's implications in the slightest.

These studies also illustrate one of the factors contributing to the general confusion about the values of phonics teaching. Both teachers and pupils must certainly be confused: the teachers, by the great variations from one reading program to another in numbers of generalizations and the manner in which they are stated; the children, by the many exceptions to most of the principles they are being taught. Clymer's type of study has been most useful in clarifying this aspect of the phonics program, even though the implications will not be acceptable to some authors. But the onus of proof that other personal versions of phonics principles are more valid than Clymer's versions rests upon those who disagree with the implications.

How We Ought to Teach Phonics

Our concepts of the way in which phonics should be taught are neither very original nor revolutionary. Although we may not agree with many aspects of the present system, a research basis to support drastic changes is lacking. Our proposals will differ, however, from current practices in many details, such as sequence, time of introduction, and principles.

Suggested phonics syllabus

SIMPLE CONSONANTS
b, p, m, w, h, d, t, n, hard *g* (gate), *k,* hard *c* (cake), *y* (yet), *f* (for)

MORE DIFFICULT CONSONANTS
v, l, z (zoo), *s* (sat), *r, c* (cent), *q* (kw), *x* (ks), *j, g* (engine), *s* (as)

CONSONANT BLENDS AND DIGRAPHS
ck, ng, th (the), *zh, sh, th* (thin), *wh, ch*

SIMPLE CONSONANT BLENDS
with *l, r, p,* or *t,* as *bl, pl, gr, br, sp, st, tr, thr, str, spl, scr,* and others as they appear

SHORT VOWELS
a (hat), *e* (get), *i* (sit), *o* (top), *u* (cup), *y* (happy)

LONG VOWELS
a (cake), *e* (be), *i* (five), *o* (old), *u* (mule), *y* (cry)

SILENT LETTERS
k (knife), *w* (write), *l* (talk), *t* (catch), *g* (gnat), *c* (black), *h* (hour)

(continued)

VOWEL DIGRAPHS
ai (pail), *ea* (each), *oa* (boat), *ee* (bee), *ay* (say), *ea* (dead)

VOWEL DIPHTHONGS
au (auto), *aw* (awful), *oo* (moon), *oo* (wood), *ow* (cow), *ou* (out), *oi* (oil), *oy* (boy), *ow* (low)

VOWELS WITH *r*
ar (car), *er* (her), *ir* (bird), *or* (corn), *ur* (burn)
Same with *l* and *w*.

PHONOGRAMS (WORD PATTERNS)
ail, ain, all, and, ate, ay, con, eep, ell, en, ent, er, est, ick, ight, ill, in, ing, ock, ter, tion
Alternates—*ake, ide, ile, ine, it, ite, le, re, ble*

The order of presentation of our syllabus follows our knowledge of the development of the articulation of consonant sounds (39). All the simple consonants will have developed in the speech of the average child by the age of five-and-one-half. The more difficult consonants normally are not fluent or accurate in the speech of the average child until the ages of six-and-one-half to seven-and-one-half. This would seem to argue for their teaching and the relevant generalizations to be delayed until the latter half of the first grade or the beginning of the second, assuming that most children enter school at about the age of six. The order of the consonant blends and digraphs, which Groff suggests should be called consonant clusters (24), similarly follow the known order of their appearance in speech development. Groff suggests a sequence for teaching consonant clusters based on their ease of spelling, frequency of use, reading difficulty, and the total number of words in which they are found. The sequence he offers does not differ greatly, however, from that we give, although he includes a number of other clusters, such as *qu, nt, ss, ll, rm,* and the like, that are not commonly stressed in basal programs as significant phonemes. Most of those he would add would be more functionally taught, in our opinion, as phonogram elements, such as *ent, all,* and *ill.* Dependence upon frequency counts to suggest instructional sequences, as Groff (24) and Johnson (31) and a number of other writers have done, is unrealistic in our opinion. Frequency counts based on a large corpus of words tend to ignore first, the articulatory development of children; second, the abstractness or complexity of the combinations in which some letters are sometimes silent, sometimes sounded, sometimes blended, sometimes separate. Third, frequency of occurrence does not indicate learnability of the items, for we have practically no data on this important aspect. We cannot see the logic of a sequence which suggests teaching phonemes the child cannot yet articulate well, and thus probably cannot read, for their enunciation is not likely to be present in his auditory memory bank.

Phonics syllabi commonly include a list of rules which are to be taught inductively at various stages. Our review of the Clymer, Emans, Bailey, and Burmeister studies of the utility of these generalizations resulted in the reduction of such a list to a defensible minimum. We would eliminate the weaker or esoteric principles and suggest only the following:

Phonics rules

CONSONANTS

1. When *c* is frequently followed by *e, i,* or *y,* it has the sound of *s,* as in *race, city, fancy.*
2. Otherwise, *c* has the sound of *k,* as in *come, attic.*
3. *G* followed by *e, i,* or *y* sounds soft like *j,* as in *gem.*
4. Otherwise *g* sounds hard, as in *gone.*
5. When *c* and *h* are next to each other, they make only one sound.
6. *Ch* is usually pronounced as it is in *kitchen,* not like *sh* (in *machine*).
7. When a word ends in *ck,* it has the same last sound, as in *look.*
8. When two of the same consonants are side by side, only one is heard, as in *butter.*
9. Sometimes *s* has the sound of *z,* as in *raisin, music.*
10. The letter *x* has the sounds of *ks* or *k* and *s,* as in *box, taxi.*

VOWELS

11. When a consonant and *y* are the last letters in a one-syllable word, the *y* has the long *i* sound, as in *cry, by.* In longer words the *y* has the long *e* sound, as in *baby.* Some say this latter is a short *i* sound.
12. The *r* gives the preceding vowel a sound that is neither long nor short, as in *car, far, fur, fir.* The letters *l* and *w* have the same effect.

VOWEL DIGRAPHS AND DIPHTHONGS

13. The first vowel is usually long and the second silent in *oa, ay, ai,* and *ee,* as in *boat, say, gain, feed.*
14. In *ea* the first letter may be long and the second silent, or it may have the short *e* sound, as in *bread.*
15. *Ou* has two sounds: one is the long sound of *o*; the other is the *ou* sound, as in *own* or *cow.* The combination *ou* has a schwa sound, as in *vigorous.*
16. These double vowels blend into a single sound: *au, aw, oi, oy,* as in *auto, awful, coin, boy.*
17. The combination *oo* has two sounds, as in *moon* and as in *wood.*

We have adapted and simplified these generalizations from the forms in which they were offered by Clymer and Burmeister (*6, 7, 9, 11*). This attempted simplification is amply justified by MacGinitie's criticism of their unnecessary complexity. Yet the rules are still sometimes phrased for adults, not for children, as in the case of 11 and 15. Would that we knew how to simplify them further, and how to lead children through the logical steps that result in their understanding.

When we analyze the words in basal series or in larger samples by computer, these generalizations seem to be justified by the frequency of their appearance in such sources and by the infrequency of their exceptions. Mary Ann Dzama (*13*) has also tested them in a random sample of the sight vocabulary of first-graders in a language experience program. In general, she found similar results, except that fewer words fitted the generalizations in the children's sight vocabulary than in the Clymer study of a basal vocabulary, perhaps reflecting the breadth of the children's vocabulary resulting from use of the language experience method.

Inspection of our list of recommended phonics principles will show the exclusion of many generalizations commonly taught. Some reading teachers may feel that we have so drastically reduced the number of principles that children will be handicapped in attempting to apply phonics to word recognition. For example, it would seem that children taught in accordance with our syllabus and principles would have no clues in the following situations:

- Pronouncing the vowel sound in monosyllables, as *get, man, go*.
- Recognizing long or short vowel sounds, as in *pin–pine, cap–cape*, and the like.

It is certainly not our intention to deprive primary-grade children of any effective, functional aids to word recognition and thus to make the task of learning to read more difficult. On the contrary, we hope to make the process as painless, but also as pragmatic, as possible. Certainly, teaching children a number of generalizations that frequently fail to function or work only in a relatively small number of words cannot be justified. Phonics can be taught effectively without dependence upon such generalizations.

Our syllabus suggests the teaching of the long and short vowel sounds, the common and variant sounds of consonants, a number of vowel digraphs and vowel diphthongs, the effect of *r*, *l*, and *w* on adjoining vowels, and the recognition of silent letters. If these phonic elements are taught as outlined later, no pupil will actually be unable to deal with these when the word demands. But the question remains in the minds of some whether this knowledge will enable pupils to recognize the correct pronunciation of the vowels and vowel digraphs they encounter in primary words. For example, without some generalization to guide them, how do pupils know whether the vowel is long or short in *ate, five, get*, and *sit?* How will they approach such words as *seat, paint*, and *go?*

A study by Barbara P. Rosso and Robert Emans found that the 132 fourth-graders they tested did not need to learn the technical terms *vowel*, *consonant*, *digraph*, and *diphthong*, in order to apply the rules that govern these sound–symbol correspondences (43). As other studies have shown, most young children do not understand these terms, nor can they define them. Rosso and Emans used a test of thirty rules using nonsense words to exemplify the conventions. The children were asked to show their understanding by dividing the words into syllables or indicating the correct pronunciation of the nonsense words. In addition, the children were asked to state the generalization orally in fourteen rules. There were only slight relationships between the pupils' performances on this test and on the Stanford Diagnostic Test. Moderate relationships were found with the Stanford measure of syllabication (.43), sound discrimination (.60), and blending (.18). The students could generalize only two rules on the average, such as the *ee* and *ai–ay* combinations, even though they had pronounced the related nonsense words correctly. Seventeen of the children identified all the nonsense words but only two of them could state the relevant rule in nine of eleven generalizations. Rosso and Emans concluded that there is reason to question whether pupils need to know the rules consciously. Their inability to state the generalizations did not hinder their ability to analyze unfamiliar words.

Tovey, in a sense, replicated this study with a nineteen-item terminology test. Average scores ranged from 7 percent in the second grade to 33 percent in the sixth grade in defining terms. Yet these pupils were able to read nonsense words containing the test elements with performances from 55 percent to 83 percent in those grades. Did they need the terms to apply phonics (50)?

Steps to Word Recognition

Without actually teaching children to depend upon poor generalizations, we would teach children a system of approach, a series of steps that capitalizes upon the known vagaries of English pronunciation.

In effect, when meeting an unknown word, children should ask themselves:

1. What is the sound of the first letter or blend? (This may be sufficient to trigger off or recall the entire word, because of the contextual clues.)
2. What word beginning with this sound would make sense in this sentence?
3. How many vowels are there? Where are they?
   a. If there is one vowel in the beginning or middle, try the short sound of the vowel.
   b. If there is one vowel and *e* at the end, try the long sound.
   c. If there is one vowel at the end, try the long sound.

d. If there are two vowels in the middle or at the end, try the long sound of the first vowel, except in *oi, oy, ou, ew, au, aw, oo, ow.*

These four possibilities would result in an approximately correct pronunciation of the vowel sound in better than two out of every three words. If the first attempt does not result in a recognizable word, the child would simply try again as in steps 4 and 5.

4. Say the whole word. Do you know it? If not, try the other vowel sound.
5. Now do you know the word? If not, write it down and get help later from the teacher or your dictionary. Go on with your reading.

This systematic approach plus the generalizations we have recommended and the phonic facts suggested in the syllabus given earlier would, we believe, give the child sufficient phonics knowledge to be successful in this particular word recognition technique.

The syllabus and the generalizations are only the content of the phonics program. More significant by far than these are the principles that should guide the teacher in methods of presentation. Among these principles, we think the following are justified (46).

1. Precede and accompany phonics training by instruction in auditory discrimination as outlined elsewhere in this volume. Continue this auditory training as long as necessary, particularly for slow-learner groups, if profitable.

2. Begin informal phonics at the experience chart or preprimer level, teaching simple consonant sounds as they appear in a number of words in the pupil's reading vocabulary. Use games and, perhaps, M. Lucile Harrison's approach by auditory and context clues, as we describe later in this chapter. Make small cards for each letter in capitals and lowercase and picture cards for games in matching letters to beginning sound of pictured objects.

3. Although gifted pupils may not be learning a vocabulary identical with that in the basals used with other groups, they also need planned, small-group phonics instruction. If necessary use the chart vocabulary as the basis, if words known to all are needed. In other words, despite the fact that these pupils apparently learn many words very quickly, give them the same phonics training outlined in our syllabus.

4. For economy of time, introduce study of an element or a principle to a small group or the entire class. Follow up with workbook or teacher-made exercises, a phonics workbook, or several such applications. Place greatest emphasis upon promoting use of phonics skills during small-group reading or individual conferences. Ability to parrot sounds is useless. Constant use of the elements in attacking unknown words is the only purpose for their teaching. Try not to separate phonics learning from the act of reading by teaching phonics

only at certain periods. Help children to transfer their phonics knowledge by (a) using words drawn from their current reading materials in your phonics instruction; (b) refraining from telling children the unknown words when they are reading and instead urging them to try to use whatever phonics they know; (c) asking them to list new words they meet that contain a known phonic element, such as the initial consonant *m*, the long sound of *e*, etc.; and (d) using these children's lists in your phonics lessons.

5. In teaching each phonic element, deal only with words as units, not with sounds isolated from words. Approach each sound in a systematic fashion, perhaps in the manner suggested by Harrison, which will be described later. Remember that phonic analysis is only one type of clue to word recognition. Urge children to use others by asking questions about the significance of the word length, shape, details, probable contextual clue, and the like.

6. When teaching a particular phonic element, present it at first in only one part of the illustrative words. After it is easily recognized both visually and auditorily in its initial position, its function in medial or final positions may be taught.

7. Teach phonic elements in initial, medial, and final positions in words, except for those phonograms that normally do not occur in initial positions. In other words, after introducing *s* as an initial consonant, help children to recognize it anywhere in a word by using a variety of words containing *s* in your phonics lessons.

8. Teach children to utilize any or all other clues to word meaning simultaneously with phonics, such as word form, picture, context, and structure clues. The goal of phonics training is *not* to train children in a letter-by-letter, sound-by-sound approach to word recognition. Pupils should be taught to use as few phonic clues as possible in the effort to recall or recognize the word. In many instances, the simple sound of the initial consonant or blend should suggest a word that makes sense in that sentence. Ideally speaking, most of the practice with phonic elements should occur with words *in context* to stimulate the reading act and promote use of other clues. Unfortunately, most available teaching materials ignore this principle.

9. To be completely functional, phonics skill must operate in reading, spelling, and writing. Phonic elements must be readily recognized and translated from one medium to the other. Therefore, complete phonics training will result in these associations: (a) knowing name and common sound of element, (b) seeing and writing the element, (c) seeing and sounding while writing or tracing, (d) responding by sound when letter name of element is given, (e) responding by writing when letter name is given, and (f) responding by writing when sound and illustrative word are given.

Two fundamental phonics skills, often ignored in popular systems, are blending and substitution. Pupils must learn to recognize a phonic element, sound it, and then blend it with the rest of the word. Simple knowledge of phonic elements does not ensure successful blending so that the final pronunciation corresponds to the auditory memory of the word. Substitution involves recognition of an element present in an unknown word, as *ight* in *bright*, reasoning by analogy with a known word, *light*, substituting *br* for *l*, and pronouncing the word, *bright*. Both of these skills must be given ample attention and practice in order that other phonics learnings will function.

Railsback (*41*) questions strongly whether young children, particularly those below average in ability, have more difficulty than teachers or authors of basals realize in trying to use consonant substitution. The task demands having a good mental image of a word resembling the unknown word except for the initial letter; then mentally dropping the first letter of the known word and substituting the initial letter or letters of the new word. His observations of second-graders attempting to attack new and real and nonsense words (in which consonant substitution based on their known reading vocabulary was possible) showed that only one child used this technique in any words, despite training in it since the primer level. Again, our inadequacy in knowing how to teach these phonic skills so that they really function for children is manifest.

Steps in Teaching a Phonic Element (Such as Short *a* Sound)

Auditory Discrimination. Use a key word containing the new sound, preferably a word that can be illustrated by a concrete object (*apple, hat*). Use other objects for comparison, the names of which do not contain the short *a* sound (*eraser, pencil, light, seat*). Ask pupils to give the key word and compare it with the names of these classroom objects. Which has the short *a* sound?

Reproduction. Children repeat the names of objects in the classroom after the teacher in varied order. Repeat this, with teacher pointing to objects while children pronounce the names, without any auditory cue from the teacher. Make a game of the exercise by having children give the name of the object only when it contains the new sound. When the name does not contain the sound, the pupils respond by a greeting to the teacher.

Illustrative Words. Pupils look around the room to find items illustrating the short *a* sound (*map, Alice, bat, Jack, record rack*). These words are written on the chalkboard as children offer them. It is important, we feel, that these lists of words illustrating the new sound should *not* be prepared by the teacher or offered from a printed list. The words must be discovered and offered by the pupils as a result of discussion, observation, or their reading.

Reinforcement Activities. Items from home may be brought by the pupils and teacher, and arranged in a table display. Also, pictures from magazines may be used for charts illustrating a sound, or a picture–sound dictionary may be made by a group.

An exercise challenging the children's thinking is one in which the teacher asks questions leading to answers containing the new sound: "What could we use to hit a ball?" or "What is sticky and oozes from a tree?"

To promote transfer of the phonics learning to the reading act, ask the children to locate printed words illustrating the new sound. These words may be written on slips of paper as they are reading, and brought to the group session later, to be added to the list. The writing component of this activity helps pupils to match the sounds representing letters with their written forms, an essential phonics skill for spelling (an area even more demanding of phonics skill than reading).

While building these lists of illustrative words, it is essential to initiate discussion of these words, their multiple meanings, their opposites, and other associations related to them. Learning the pronunciation of these words and reacting to the presence of a certain phonic element is desirable, but not as important as understanding their meanings. Only by the building of many associations with each word can we be certain of their storage in long-term memory. (See Chapter 13 for techniques fostering growth of meaning vocabulary.)

For extended reinforcement, use teacher-made or commercial worksheets in such activities as:

- Answering riddles with words containing the new sound.
- Supplying missing words in a sentence with word containing the new sound.
- Circling words in a given list.
- Doing crossword puzzles composed of words with the new sound.
- Drawing a picture containing some objects whose names illustrate the sound; labeling those objects in the drawing.
- Classifying or grouping words, from the list already assembled, in such categories as foods, household items, toys, actions, etc.
- Adding words containing the new sound to spelling exercises or contests.

Alternative Approaches to Phonics

Two experiments by Hillerich in the first and second grades were concerned with teaching vowel sounds (28, 29). In the first grade, children taught the vowel rules were better in a test of nonsense words but not in a reading test. In fact, the nonvowel group showed better reading comprehension. In his second-grade report, Hillerich contrasted a group taught all vowel sounds with one trained in auditory perception and only the long and short vowels and a control group given no instruction on vowels. The second group, with minimal vowel training, achieved the highest reading scores; the group with complete vowel training had the lowest scores of all groups.

Hillerich's studies suggest that an emphasis upon phonics, particularly the more complex element of vowel principles, does not promote growth in comprehension. This is undoubtedly true, for many comparisons of phonics systems and more eclectic basal systems support this conclusion. (See the comparisons of the outcomes of basal versus other approaches in the earlier chapter on the basal method.) Phonic systems tend to produce better word recognition (word-calling?) but poorer comprehension. Basals are better with a definite phonics component than without, but phonics methods without the basal eclectic approach are inferior in their results.

Because of these outcomes of phonic methods of teaching reading, some writer suggest that we turn aside from all the generalizations and from sound-symbol correspondence teaching to teach beginning reading by the larger units called phonograms, word patterns, or syllables, (As we have noted, the recent editions of several basals do emphasize these word parts.)

For example, Wylie and Durrell have suggested another way of dealing with the difficulties inherent in the variable vowel sounds (53). They would stress teaching phonograms rather than vowel sounds and claim that it is easier for children to learn these than even the short vowel sounds. We have been emphasizing the values in teaching phonograms (three- to four-letter units of consistent pronunciation) since our original study of this field of phonics in 1939 and are glad to discover that there is now more evidence to support this viewpoint. Wylie and Durrell's first-grade pupils were able to identify whole phonograms by analogy with known words better than by having a knowledge of short vowels. In effect, most phonograms are closed syllables with a consonant or two following the vowel. A few involve a final *e* and a medial long vowel, but even these appeared to give little difficulty to these pupils. When the vowel was followed by *r*, *l*, or *w*, the change in the vowel sound did give some difficulty because the children, by this time, were expecting a short vowel sound.

Groff (25) and Gleitman and Rozin (21) independently recommend substituting syllables, as they call them, for phonemes. They do not mean the segments identified by the rules of syllabication, however, nor do they recommend teaching such rules. Rather, like the present authors, they are proposing the use of phonograms like those listed in the phonics syllabus in this chapter. The particular list here was selected by a number of criteria such as length, simplicity of pronunciation, frequency in basic vocabularies, few pronunciations, and position in initial or final part of words (45). This list is therefore shorter than most of the word pattern lists given in the description of the phonics content of basals in Table 12.1. Their lists ignore the relative frequency of combinations such as *oll*, *ose;* or the fact that the unit is usually part of a larger unit, as in the case of *ai, ar,* and *ea,* or the many pronunciations, as in *in*.

Groff argues that (1) children can learn syllables, as shown by Wylie and Durrell (53); (2) they learn to read as well as with the letter phonics approach; (3) they can read pronounceable trigrams better than unpronounceable ones; (4) several studies show that 85 percent of words were recognized by letter clusters or syllables, not individual letter sounds; and (5) single letter sounds produce more errors than the multiple-letter clues (25).

Glass justifies this idea a bit differently (20). He claims that decoding by clusters is supported by the concept of chunking (grouping information such as several single phonemes); and by Venezky's observation that English is organized in terms of graphemic sequences, not individual graphemes. Glass argues that because our language is not strictly phonetic in that each symbol does not stand for a single sound element, chunking soon becomes an efficient way of reading, Chunking helps reading speed (not comprehension). Hence, in international comparisons with German pupils, American children tend to excel in speed despite the fact that German is more phonetic than English. Because English is not strictly phonetic, some meaning is imparted by the variations in the sound–symbol correspondence; e.g., nation–nationality, principal–principle, civil–civilian, metal–metallic, and rebel–rebellion.

This procedure might well be a type of instruction given to those pupils who have difficulty reading vowel combinations and distinguishing the long from the short sound. If taught the three- to four-letter phonograms and practiced in generalizing from one word to another by initial consonant substitution, such pupils would indeed be enabled to recognize and pronounce many words, such as *band, sand, land, cake, make,* and *take,* without fumbling with the unpredictable vowel combinations.

This review of various methods of systematizing phonics teaching would include the approach suggested by M. Lucile Harrison and Paul McKee. This method has been tried out extensively with preschool, kindergarten, and primary-grade pupils. A television course addressed to parents of preschool children with a special manual, "Preparing Your Child for Reading," was prepared to promote wide use of the method in the Denver area. Preliminary results indicate that children taught by this system show marked success in early reading in the primary grades.

The program leads the child to make great use of initial consonant sounds and context for word recognition, through the following steps:

1. Begin training in auditory discrimination in kindergarten by emphasizing comparison of initial sounds of objects, children's names, and the like.

2. Teach children to relate name of initial consonant and its sound, for example, "Mary's name starts with an *M,* doesn't it?"

3. Develop a key word for each initial consonant sound. Select a drawing of an object beginning with a particular sound. Outline drawing with heavy lines, forming the initial letter. For example, an upright bat and an adjacent ball can be thus transformed into a lowercase *b.* In using the key word chart, refer to a letter by name only, not by its sound: for example, letter *b,* as in *ball,* not *buh* as in *ball.*

4. Practice recognizing words from context by allowing children to supply a word in a sentence of a story you are reading to the class. Select words beginning with a particular consonant in each story, thus practicing with only one consonant sound at a time, in words that are in the pupils' auditory and speech vocabularies.

5. Help children to associate both use of context and sound of initial consonant in act of recognizing words in oral context read to them.

6. Begin simple reading materials, experience charts. Urge children to use their two word attack skills for word recognition.

7. Expand usefulness of initial consonant approach by teaching the substitution technique: for example, "This boy's name is just like the word *back* except for the first letter. His name begins with the *j* sound like *jump*. Put the *j* sound in place of the *b* in *back*, and tell me the boy's name."

8. Do not attempt to teach vowel sounds.

Trial of this method in the Denver Public Schools shows that if taught at beginning or middle of kindergarten or beginning of the first grade, children are reading successfully, some even at the first reader level, after half a school year. Furthermore, these children show marked independence and skill in word attack.

It is apparent that certain steps in the selection and preparation of the reading materials, as well as further training in word attack skills, are necessary to ensure the ultimate success of this approach. Stories to illustrate contextual use of words beginning with a certain sound must be carefully selected. Beginning reading materials will certainly need stronger narrative and expository characteristics than are present in the preprimers and primers of many basal reading series to permit frequent successful contextual analysis. However, the many new easy-to-read books for beginners will be helpful in solving this problem, as will experience charts and teacher-made materials. Many teachers will feel the need to extend their pupils' knowledge of phonics to initial consonant blends, endings, phonograms, and the like (as Harrison probably does also) and perhaps to short and long vowel sounds (as Harrison apparently does not).

The strength of this approach to facilitating success in initial reading and independence in word attack lies in its provision for a two-pronged system of word recognition. The simultaneous use of rudimentary phonics and context strengthens the possibilities of accurate word recognition. Anticipation of a particular word from the sense of a sentence is completely natural and linguistically defensible. Success in the use of this logical approach to word recognition is further ensured when children confirm their contextual guesses by comparing them with the actual sounds of the beginning of the words. If the beginning reading materials are natural and resemble the sentence the children usually speak and hear (as they would in experience charts, teacher-made materials, and some trade books), successful word attack in the early stages of reading is greatly enhanced.

How Much Phonics Do Pupils Need?

The rationale for teaching decoding (phonics) varies from one author to the next. Some think of it as the most essential tool for learning to read, and that skill in this area should be manifest at all ages up to and including the college level. In truth, its justification lies in the fact that it helps *beginning readers only* to pronounce and thus recognize words for which auditory memories are already stored. In other words, decoding functions with simple, known words but not with harder or technical terms that are unfamiliar. It is a distinct aid in early reading stages but deteriorates as the normal reading vocabulary expands beyond the individual's auditory vocabulary. Decoding produces a pronunciation of a word that is helpful in its recognition—*if* the pronunciation is similar to the spoken version of the word and *if* some meaningful associations to that word have already been stored in the reader's memory. Without previous knowledge of the word, decoding produces only a meaningless group of sounds.

There is, of course, some question whether good auditory discrimination is essential to reading progress and even if it is somewhat related, whether all children can benefit or profit from auditory training. Dialect speakers do not normally show good discrimination in the common tests, for their dialect has not prepared them to make these distinctions. There is also evidence that these children can still learn to read reasonably well, when judged in terms of their intelligence and socioeconomic backgrounds. We also know that some children do not exhibit a preference for learning through auditory avenues, and, in fact, learn better when other facets are emphasized. In effect, we are questioning whether auditory training and phonics of the usual sorts are as important for some beginning readers as previously assumed.

It is fairly well accepted that phonics is not a great aid to children of less than average ability, or in some studies, for black pupils or other dialect speakers. For example, Hackney found that his high reading group was superior to the average, which, in turn, was better than the poor reading group in all eleven of the Doren phonics skills tests (30). Benz and Rosemier report a similar observation using the Bond–Hoyt–Clymer phonics skills battery (3). In general, then, good readers do seem to test better in phonics than do poor or average readers. But in both these studies it was noted that the correlations between phonics skills and reading were relatively low, with only a small part of the variation in reading scores being accounted for by the phonics skills. Furthermore, the variations in the phonics scores as measured by their standard deviation increased from high to average to poor readers. This implies that average and poor readers, in particular, vary greatly in their possession of phonics knowledge, and possibly even more in their application of these skills in the act of reading. Other studies indicate that not all phonics skills are mastered by normal readers even by the sixth grade (4).

Boyd's study showed that the most rapid growth on the fifteen phonic skills tested was in the second and third grades, but that their development thereafter was much slower (4). A similar testing in grades three to six found that phonic skills, such as recognizing phonic elements in a word, beginning sounds, rhyming sounds, and letter sounds grew progressively worse. Yet the children tested achieved expectancy levels in reading of 89 percent of the pupils in the third grade and 80 to 81 percent in the fourth to sixth grades.

When children achieve as well as those in Boyd's study despite lacking this or that phonic subskill, it may mean that trying to reteach a child any missing skill several years later does not make much sense. The diagnostic–prescriptive programs and management systems that insist on every child having command of all the subskills in order to read well are not very realistic in the face of such evidence.

These studies seem to indicate that the decoding skills first taught in the primary grades were deteriorating or falling into disuse in the intermediate levels. Moreover, the relationships among skill subtests and with reading comprehension were quite low by the middle grades (3, 29). Several inferences are possible in view of these facts: first, phonic skills are helpful or functional only in primary reading materials; second, other more relevant word analysis techniques should be stressed in the middle grades; and third, good readers, although generally better in phonics tests, vary in their knowledge and use of phonic skills beyond the second grade, whereas average and poor readers vary from skill to skill even more.

These studies are limited in scope and in the extent to that they can be generalized. But there is little doubt that there are some children who do not profit from much of our phonics instruction for a variety of reasons. If we grant this obvious fact, we are obligated to offer alternative types of training that will enable these children to deal with new or strange words and to read successfully. The alternatives we see as feasible are as follows:

1. If children can learn some of the initial consonant sounds, teach them these and use them as a clue to word recognition. Stress the thinking of "What word beginning with that sound would make sense in this sentence?" This is the most common word recognition technique used by children.
2. As a reinforcing method to word recognition (or as an alternative method for children who cannot distinguish initial consonant sounds accurately), substitute intensive training in contextual analysis by the cloze procedure and other exercises outlined later in this chapter.
3. If children respond favorably to that technique, teach them to use the kinesthetic procedure of tracing words in order to learn them. Reinforce this learning modality by providing ample practice in writing, as by the language experience approach.
4. Provide intensive practice for these pupils in classifying words to build depth of meanings, perhaps in the fashion described in earlier chapters. There is some evidence that this emphasis is effective for poor readers, and more so than training in phonics and syllabication for some.

There are, of course, a great many other approaches to phonics teaching. Many of these have their own coterie of devout followers who apparently feel that it is their mission to rescue the schools from the look–say method. Each group has its own rigid program that admits no merit in any other sequence, timing, or methodology than its own. The more attention given to these programs, the more confused anxious teachers become, for they find great contradictions and conflicting claims. The adherents of each phonics system are positive that they alone have the proper answers to all problems in this area.

Most reasonable American reading authorities are certain of only one fact—that they do not know the correct answers to all questions about phonics. Despite the best efforts, the available research does not prove any particular system superior to all others. Nor is our knowledge certain enough to determine the exact sequence, timing, methods, or content that is best. Since this is the true situation, any system offered to teachers that claims to have the answers to all the unsolved questions is likely to approach being a cult rather than a phonics program (45).

How We Teach Structural Analysis

Like phonics, training in structural analysis is founded upon the primitive recognition of words by configuration or shape as well as minor details. Young readers may identify words by a certain element, such as a curved letter at the end of *dog* reminding them of the dog's tail. Mature readers also use outlines of words but tend to recognize larger details, such as common syllables and affixes. The purpose of training in structural analysis is, then, the development of the habit of recognition by larger, more meaningful units within words. Among the units commonly included in a structural analysis program are inflectional endings, compound words, syllables, prefixes, roots, suffixes, and contractions. Most of the word elements taught in structural analysis are composed of several letters and have a pronunciation that does not depend upon the successive sounds of the letters present. Children trained in letter phonics alone are handicapped in attempting recognition by structural elements, unless they discard this approach and learn to deal with larger units. The necessity for this development of new word recognition skills is just another reason against overemphasizing letter phonics and a reason for the teaching of many phonograms in the word analysis program.

In Table 12.3, the structural analysis content of the primary levels of well-known basal reading series is presented. These are fairly representative of other basal programs.

In the teaching of these structural units, several principles that function also in spelling and writing are commonly emphasized. Among these are the following:

1. When a base word or accented last syllable of a word ends in a single consonant preceded by a single vowel, the final consonant is doubled when adding a suffix beginning with a vowel, for example, *hop–hopped*.
2. When a base word ends in *e*, the *e* may be dropped before adding an ending beginning with a vowel, for example, *hope–hoping*.

3. When a base word ends in *y*, preceded by a consonant, the *y* is changed to *i* before the ending (unless the ending begins with *i*), for example, *hurry–hurried–hurrying*.
4. When a base word ends in *f*, or *fe*, in which the *e* is silent, the *f* sometimes is changed to *v* before the ending, for example, *calf–calves, knife–knives*.

These principles are not phrased in the oversimplified versions preferred by most authors because the common versions are inaccurate and open to too many exceptions. The phrasing here is that proposed long ago by Wheat (52). Emphasis on full comprehension of the more accurate definitions probably should be postponed until intermediate grades. But they should eventually be understood in their entirety if they are to function in spelling and writing. Other structural relationships, learned more or less informally, include these: the formation of plurals of nouns by adding *s* or *es*, the use of the apostrophe and *s* to show possession in most words, the use of the apostrophe alone in words ending in *s*, the use of the hyphen in numbers and the combining form *self*, the use of the apostrophe to show the omission of a letter or letters in a contraction.

Table 12.3 includes, of course, only the inflectional endings, prefixes, and suffixes taught in these particular primary-grade programs. Compound words and contractions are also stressed in all these programs as they occur in the basal vocabulary. Roots or stems that are the core of polysyllabic words are also presented in these programs, beginning in about the fifth grade, as are rules for syllabication. These elements of a structural analysis program shall be discussed in greater detail later.

Even a casual inspection of the table reveals the marked variations from one series to another. Some do not stress any prefixes or suffixes until the second grade (Allyn and Bacon, Harper & Row); some teach only a few of these structural elements, as in the two-grade SRA Basic Reading Series. Suggestions for structural analysis extend into the intermediate grades, as in the Ginn 720 and Harper & Row programs.

The point is obvious that there is no constant sequence or content that can be observed in all these series. These word elements are taught, apparently, if and when they occur in the reading selections, rather than in any preplanned order. This basis of selection for the items in a structural analysis program can be justified, perhaps, on a practical basis. But, does the appearance of a suffix, prefix, root, or inflection once or even several times in a certain reading selection justify its instruction at that time? Are there no differences among these elements in learnability, difficulty, or meaningfulness? Should not their frequency in the total vocabulary encountered in the average child's reading, for example, in the first six years, be considered?

Beyond the primary levels, the selection of a syllabus of prefixes, suffixes, and roots is made in many ways. The possible criteria for choosing these items include their frequency in various word lists, such as basic reading or

Table 12.3 Structural Analysis in the Basal Program

Series	Prefixes	Suffixes and inflections
Preprimer–Primer Level		
Harper & Row Design for Reading		*s, ing, 's*
Houghton Mifflin		*s, ed, ing, ly, ful*
First-Reader Level		
Allyn and Bacon Pathfinder		*s, 's, ed, ing*
Ginn 720		*es, ed*
Harper & Row Design for Reading		*ed, er, est, ly, y*
Houghton Mifflin	*un*	*ness*
SRA Basic Reading Series		*ing*
Second-Reader Level		
Allyn and Bacon	*un*	*er, est*
Ginn 720		*er, est, ly, y*
Harper & Row Design for Reading	*un*	*n, en*
Houghton Mifflin	*re, ex, dis*	*tion, ment, less, al, ture*
SRA Basic Reading Series		*en, er, ed, est, ness, es, y, ies, ied, ly, ily, le, el, al, on, et, it, ic, ish*
Third-Reader Level		
Allyn and Bacon	*super, tele, dis*	*ish, ful, less, s', ous, fully, ness*
Ginn 720	*a, be, de, re, pre, un, under*	*ful, tion, sion, ion*
Harper & Row Design for Reading	*re*	*ward, some, ous, ship, ment*
Houghton Mifflin	*mis, de, pro, ad, pre, com, in*	*ance, en, ence*
Fourth-Reader Level		
Allyn and Bacon	*bi*	*ible, ity, ic, ion, able, ible, tion, ist, ment*
Ginn 720		*ment, ness, ful, fully*
Harper & Row Design for Reading	*mis, in, anti, inter, trans*	*al, ate, dom, ity, ure, ance, ion, ish, ty, ian, or, an, ism, ive*
Houghton Mifflin		*en, er, est, s, es, ies*

TEACHING FOR MAXIMUM SUCCESS

Series	Prefixes	Suffixes and inflections
Fifth-Reader Level		
Ginn 720	*over, fore, out, uni, bi, tri, ad, at, ex, pre, pro, sub, super, trans, com, con*	*miss, tract, less, scrib, spect, vis, port, ology, aud*
Harper & Row Design for Reading	*semi, co, im, ir, fore, il, mid, over, vice*	*ant, ic, ent, ee, ize, ster, age, ess, err, cy*
Sixth-Reader Level		
Ginn 720	*post, inter, intra, mono, octa, dec, duo, quad, quart, sex, centi, anti, counter*	*aqua, hydro, ward, ize*
Harper & Row Design for Reading	*en, non, sub, mal, a, pre*	

spelling vocabularies; their frequency in children's own writing; and their simplicity and infrequency of multiple meanings. Breen, for example, lists the thirty prefixes, fifty-four roots, and nineteen suffixes that were of greatest frequency in the Rinsland study of pupils' writing (5). This selection would seem to indicate those items pupils should learn in order to facilitate their writing. But the list ignores the question of multiple meanings. Are we to assume that children need to know most of the meanings of these affixes? Or are they simply elements that pupils recognize visually and by ear and thus can use them in writing? One writer, on the other hand, would eliminate all the roots suggested by Breen because they have multiple meanings. He includes in his syllabus only those structural elements that have single meanings, except for a few items. While simplicity of meanings is a practical criterion, it ignores the significance of the frequency of appearance in reading and writing vocabularies. Thus that list includes many items which function in only a few of the words the average elementary pupil will probably read or write.

In our opinion, two lists of these structural elements must be evolved. One list will include those items with singular meanings, the knowledge of which would aid pupils in word recognition and understanding word meanings. These elements would, of course, also function as familiar units in pupils' spelling and writing. The second list will include those items that would function as common units or syllables in reading, spelling, and writing, but without knowledge of their meanings. Pupils would learn to recognize visually these latter units, know their common pronunciations, but need not learn their multiple meanings. Both lists of meaningful and visual units, as they may be termed, must include only these items of reasonably frequent occurrence in pupils' learning experiences.

By combining a number of studies of frequency with a list of simple affixes, we can derive the list of meaningful units. Items of high frequency in reading materials, plus Breen's list of those frequent in pupil writing, may be combined into the second list of visual units in Table 12.4.

Syllabication

In addition to these structural elements to which we have referred, the structural analysis program includes the teaching of the principles and practices of syllabication. Syllabication functions as an aid in word recognition by

Table 12.4 Syllabus of Roots and Affixes

Meaningful units	Visual units	
Combining Forms		
auto- (self)	*aqua-*	
micro- (small)	*audio-*	
phono- (sound)	*bene-*	
poly- (much, many)	*cred-*	
tele- (far off)	*junc-*	
	mit-	
	pon-, pos-	
	scrib-, scrip-	
	vert-, vers-	
	vide-, vis-	
Prefixes		
circum- (around)	*a, ab-*	*per-*
extra- (outside, beyond)	*ad-*	*peri-*
in- (in, into)	*ante-*	*post-*
intra-, intro- (inside)	*anti-*	*pre-*
mis- (wrong)	*con-, com-, col-*	*pro-*
non- (not, the reverse)	*contr-*	*re-*
out- (more than, beyond)	*de-*	*sub-*
over- (too much)	*dis-, di-*	*super-*
self-	*e-, ex-*	*trans-*
syn- (together)	*inter-*	
under- (below)		
up- (up, above)		
Suffixes		
-self	Noun	

-wise (manner)	*-ance, -ence, -tion, -cion, -sion, -ism, -ment,*
	    -al, -ic, -meter, -scope, -fer, -ity, -gram,
	    -graph	

	Agent ("one who")	
	-eer, -ess, -ier, -ster, -ist, -stress, -trix	
	Adjectival	

	-est, -fic, -fold, -from, -wards, -less, -able,
	    -ible, -ble, -most, -like, -ous, -ious, -eous,
	    -ose, -ful, -way, -ways	

helping pupils break words into smaller units, pronounce these, blend, and thus recognize words in their auditory vocabulary. Syllabication helps pupils in spelling and writing. Moreover, as has been indicated, most normal readers, as they mature in reading in intermediate and upper elementary grades, become increasingly dependent upon their knowledge of syllables and less upon letter phonics.

In question in the teaching of syllabication is the utility of the various rules. Should pupils be taught a number of stable, consistent principles? If so, which principles? Is a knowledge of rules essential for reasonable success in syllabication or can the skill be learned by rule of thumb (36)? In other words, is precise syllabication needed for a functional use of syllables in reading, spelling, and writing? Is there evidence that mature readers use the rules they have been taught, or are they reasonably successful in discriminating syllables without such knowledge? Unfortunately, there are very few conclusive answers to these questions.

A number of modern researchers speak out against teaching these syllabication rules (30, 51). They point out that the rules were really created to aid printers in dividing words at the end of a line; and that the rules ignore our actual pronunciation of words, as *bu–ter or butt–er, not but–ter*. It is sufficient for pupils to learn that words can be broken into smaller parts in trying to pronounce them in the hopes of recognizing them. Pupils do not need to know a lot of complicated, artificial rules to do this. Nor do they retain the rules during their entire schooling. Hillerich, who makes this suggestion, also avers that in addition to this subdividing into pronounceable parts, children need to know that compound words are composed of two known words (30). These two techniques, plus contextual analysis, will suffice for word attack.

Our unpublished studies of the syllabication skills of first-year college students indicate little value in the knowledge of rules at this level. A comparison of the ability to complete the statements of thirteen principles showed very little relationship to a test of ability to indicate the number of syllables in fifty difficult words. Generalizing from these studies, we believe that most first-year college students and adults have probably long since forgotten the rules they once learned. Yet they are able to syllabify well enough for their own purposes. Perhaps syllabication would be of greater use and accuracy if they remembered the rules. But this is doubtful, since the correlation between knowledge of rules and accuracy in syllabication was very low in our studies.

This same question of the pragmatism of rules has been raised by a number of other authors who have made the observation that syllabication principles appear of decreasing value above elementary school levels because of the increase in exceptions. One writer also notes that teaching absolute rules makes the process an end in itself, for these are soon learned informally. In his experience, the use of context and the aid of the dictionary serve more effectively in word recognition than formal syllabication principles. After all, the aim of syllabication is an approximately correct pronunciation that may aid in recalling the auditory memories of the word in reading or writing. Therefore, he would teach only the principles that (1) each syllable has a vowel sound, (2) prefixes are separate syllables, and (3) doubled consonants may be split. All other rules are of doubtful value because of their exceptions.

Recent studies at the intermediate-grade levels tend to support this tendency to deemphasize rules as the most effective way of learning syllabication and other forms of word analysis. Children given practice in categorizing and grouping words showed good progress in word recognition skills and word pronunciation. Such pupils showed progress as great as those taught rules, and poorer readers showed even greater progress under this approach.

To turn to the objective studies of the utility of syllabication principles, we must refer again to the studies of Clymer (11), Emans (14), and Bailey (2). Among the principles they analyzed are those in Table 12.5.

Using Clymer's criterion of utility that a generalization should work at least three out of four times would definitely eliminate the fifth and eighth principles and raise doubts about the fourth principle. The second principle is unnecessarily complex and functions in a total of only ninety-nine words. It hardly seems justified. Similarly, the third principle applies to only 105 words, the sixth to sixty-four words, and the seventh to thirty words in the 2600-word vocabulary analyzed by Clymer. There is, of course, the possibility that if the entire reading, writing, and spelling vocabulary of the elementary grades were analyzed, certain of these principles might have much wider application and perhaps even greater utility. In the case of the second principle, Bailey's recent study does tend to alter the estimate of the functional value of this principle in basal vocabularies. In the six-grade vocabulary, this principle applies

Table 12.5 Utility of Syllabication Principles

	Percent of utility		
	Clymer	Emans	Bailey
1. In most two-syllable words the first syllable is accented.	85	75	81
2. If *a, in, red, ex, de,* or *be* is the first syllable in a word, it is usually unaccented.	87	83	84
3. In most two-syllable words that end in a consonant followed by *y,* the first syllable is accented and the last is unaccented.	96	100	97
4. If the first vowel sound in a word is followed by two consonants, the first syllable usually ends with the first of the consonants.	72	80	78
5. If the first vowel sound in a word is followed by a single consonant, that consonant usually begins the second syllable.	44	47	50
6. If the last syllable of a word ends in *le,* the consonant preceding the *le* usually begins the last syllable.	97	78	93
7. When the first vowel element in a word is followed by *th, ch,* or *sh,* these combinations are not divided and may go with either the first or second syllable.	100	100	100
8. In a word of more than one syllable, the letter *v* usually goes with the preceding vowel to form a syllable.	73	40	65

to 398 words with only sixty-two exceptions. Thus it would appear to have some significance if taught after the primary grades. In the remainder of the principles, the data of Emans and Bailey confirm the indications of the Clymer study.

Many authors writing on the teaching of syllabication would retain the fifth generalization because it functions more efficiently in the total vocabularies. It also is very useful as a complement to the fourth principle. The seventh, which suggests that consonant digraphs are not divided but rather move toward the syllable in front of or behind them, is often recommended because of its consistency and eventual wide applications.

Burmeister, in contrast, is inclined to follow the older system and teach that (6):

- Every single vowel or vowel combination means a syllable (except for final *e* in a *VCe* setting).
- Divide between prefix and root, between two roots, and between a root and a suffix. (If readers do not know the word, how do they know where these parts begin or end?)
- Divide at a consonant pair in *VCCV* but consider *ch, sh, ph,* and *th* as a single consonant.
- Divide before the consonant in a *Cle* pattern (*ble, tle,* etc.).

It may be interesting to note that the fourth rule above in Clymer's list, and Burmeister's third rule, contradict the phonic principle that two similar, adjoining consonants should produce only one sound. If we follow this syllabication principle, we would probably produce two identical sounds. Which is correct?

The problem of phrasing generalizations that are consistent and functional is still being attempted by many writers. Johnson and Merryman, for example, tried to rephrase the VCCV principle by suggesting that the syllabic division should be before the two consonants if they are the same, as *bu–tter* (32). This would produce a pronunciation closer to actual speech patterns, but so would dividing after the two similar consonants, as *butt–er.* McFeely has tested eight syllabication principles in a basal and social studies vocabulary and rephrased them in keeping with his findings (36). And this exploration will probably continue, for despite the difficulties with rules and exceptions, syllabication continues to be accepted as an important word analysis scheme by many.

In a comprehensive study of the usefulness of syllables, Groff concluded that the teaching of generalizations is not worth the effort because most of them are only spelling conventions, and besides, the syllable is almost indefinable (and by this time, the reader is probably inclined to agree with Groff) (25). Limits of syllables, Groff says, should be determined by the aural–visual perceptions of the word in units that seem logical, and seem to fit growing familiarity with the recurring patterns of spelling. Groff insists, and we are inclined to agree, that syllabication is largely intuitive, although he does seem to see some sense in helping children to distinguish open and closed syllables.

Groff believes that syllabication taught in this graphonemic fashion will help in both word recognition and spelling. Other writers reject syllabication on the grounds that the reader must know how to pronounce the word (or a great many rules) before dividing it into syllables, and that principles are too variable and difficult to remember (20). These legitimate criticisms would seem to be met by Groff's natural approach, particularly since special help is given children in blending syllables (rather than letter sounds).

Others are similarly critical of present practices in teaching syllabication. They point out that a syllable is a unit of speech (à la Groff), not a unit of letters. Moreover, the rules imply that consonants are significant in determining the boundaries of syllables (see rules 3 to 8 in Clymer's list or rules 3 and 4 of Burmeister's). In actuality, pronunciation ignores these artificial boundaries, as in the common reading of *butter*, *trample*, and many others. Even dictionary editors use pronunciation as a guide to syllabication, say these authors. Rather, these writers would stress the recognition of meaningful units in words as in our earlier list; deemphasizing syllabication to the goal of obtaining meaning for words; and teach only the principle that each syllable (part?) has a vowel sound.

Glass and Burton, who have criticized syllabication teaching before, tried to resolve the question by intensively interviewing and taping good readers of the second and fifth grades as they attacked thirty unknown words (20). Eighty-five percent of the pupils, as Groff predicted, used strategies falling into the general category of sound cluster analysis. If syllabication was used, it was employed only *after* decoding the words. Only one child attempted to decode any words letter by letter. In answer to the question of what they had looked for first, all the pupils said they looked immediately for familiar parts formed by letter clusters.

A recent study compared the gains in tests of syllabication with those in comprehension in a middle-school population. The correlation between the gains in syllabication and comprehension was extremely low ($r = .13$), indicating very little relationship between these reading skills. The authors conclude that there is hardly any justification for teaching syllabic rules (34).

We are much impressed with these objections to formal instruction in syllabication rules, which result in teaching pupils how to divide words at the end of the line rather than how to attempt their pronunciation. The concepts that we would try to convey to children in this area are:

1. Each important part of a word has a vowel or a vowel combination as part of it.

2. We call these parts of a word that we can recognize and pronounce, syllables.

3. Look at the word and try to say it slowly, part by part.

4. If a part seems to begin and end with a consonant, with a vowel between them, try the short sound for the vowel.

5. If a part seems to be only a vowel, or to end with a vowel, try the long sound of the vowel.

6. Do you now recognize the word?

7. If not, read the sentence all the way through again and try to guess what word that begins like the new word would make sense.

8. Try to say the word again, if you still have no clues, trying long vowel sounds instead of short in some of the parts. Now do you recognize it?

9. If not, mark it by underlining or a check in the margin. Go on and finish your reading.

10. If you still have not figured out the word, and you need it to understand the selection, go to the dictionary.

Clinical records of retarded readers clearly demonstrate the weakness of many such pupils in these word recognition skills. Many writers feel that the chief reason for this weakness is the failure of teachers to recognize the interdependence of auditory, phonic, and structural analysis skills. Another contributing case is the tendency to separate instruction in these successive skills into definite periods during the primary and intermediate grades—auditory training during the readiness period only, phonics in the first or second grades, syllabication in the intermediate grades, and so forth. This dichotomizing of related skills probably results in producing many reading failures among pupils in the intermediate and later school years. These pupils, despite their exposure to successive groups of skills, fail to develop the ability to relate their auditory discrimination to the recognition of letter sounds, do not base simple structural analysis and syllabication on letter sounds, do not abandon letter phonics gradually as familiarity with larger, syllabic and structural units grows, and do not learn gradually to use base words and affixes as a mature word recognition skill.

Another explanation for the failure of poor readers to develop word analysis skills is the unnecessary difficulty of the instruction. As any of a number of writers have shown, pupils seldom really understand the technical terms or rules. This complexity also explains why less intelligent pupils seem unable to learn and apply phonic and syllabication principles.

How We Teach Contextual Analysis

From the very beginning of their reading efforts, children spontaneously try to identify unknown words by the sense of the sentence. This process is known as contextual analysis and should be constantly strengthened by planned instruction throughout the elementary and secondary years. Linguists speak of this ability in somewhat different terms, as grammatical sense, or reaction to linguistic structure. They are disturbed that reading authors do not specifically refer to the significance of grammatical structure and its influences upon word function, word meaning, and comprehension. But this difference is simply a matter of semantics. No matter what we term the process or whether we describe examples in reading or linguistic terms, we are talking about the reader's ability to determine word recognition and word meaning by the position or function of a word in a familiar sentence pattern.

Contextual recognition of a word is accomplished by a number of clues. Constance McCullough, for example, distinguishes ideas and presentation clues (35). "Idea" clues give some help in recognizing the word: (1) Pictorial illustrations. (2) Verbal—The sentences before or after that sentence containing the unknown word give some indication of its probable nature and meaning. (3) Experience—Concrete experiences of readers enable them to assume or guess the difficult word. For example, "Sally gave the cat _____ to drink." Most children would recognize that the omitted word was *milk*, or perhaps *water*. (4) Comparison and contrast—"Mary was *happy* but John was *sad*." The implied contrast, plus knowledge of the word *happy*, enable readers to sense the meaning and probably identify *sad*. (5) Synonym—A sentence involves a repetition of the same idea and employs a synonym for the unknown word. "The girls were happy and *gay* at the party." (6) Summary—The strange word is a summary of several ideas already presented. "Oranges, limes, and lemons are some of the *fruits* grown in Florida." (7) Mood—The tone or mood of the sentence suggests the nature of the new word. "The happy boy's face was *wreathed* in smiles." (8) Definition—The unknown word is defined in the surrounding sentence or sentences. "A *triangle* is a closed figure with three straight sides." (9) Familiar expression—The word is recognized by its use in a familiar language pattern or verbal experience. "When he picked up the phone, he said, '*Hello*.' "

More mature readers are aided by what McCullough calls presentation clues, such as (35):

1. Position of word within a sentence
   "This portion of the _____ you are reading deals with contextual analysis." (book? chapter? obviously a noun)
2. An appositive phrase or clause
   "On her head she wore a *tiara*, a circlet of gold and precious stones, which complemented her beautiful hair."
3. A nonrestrictive clause
   "*Humus*, which is food upon which plant life depends. . . ."
4. Figures of speech
   "Such a *cyclopean* doorway could only have been built for the admission of a horse and carriage." (gigantic? huge?) "His argument was as *specious* as the words of the snake who beguiled Adam and Eve in the Garden of Paradise." (deceitful? untruthful?)
5. Inference
   "The pillars were almost immediately *contiguous*, with scarcely space enough between them for a hand to enter, much less a person." (adjoining? in contact?)

Other writers mention the contextual clues offered by typography: italics, capitalization, boldface type, parentheses, quotation marks, and footnotes. These serve to call attention to new words for which meaning may be derived from other contextual clues.

Apparently most context clues demand some degree of inferential thinking. As a result, some teachers assume that contextual analysis is not much more than guesswork and therefore should not be promoted. The truth is that such inferential thinking is an essential part of the reading process at all maturity levels and should be strongly encouraged. Pupils should not be burdened with learning the technical terms that might be employed to describe the types of context clues. Rather the emphasis should be placed upon helping readers use the sense of the sentence or the surrounding sentences as an aid in identifying the probable meaning of a difficult word. The goal of contextual analysis is not always an exact recognition of a word or its pronunciation. These may be approached by other means, such as phonic or structural analysis. But when these techniques are successful, they do not necessarily result in the derivation of the meaning of the word, for it may not be encompassed in the reader's auditory vocabulary. Thus contextual analysis takes the reader beyond pronunciation to meaning, which in many situations is more significant for ultimate comprehension.

Primary-grade children learn to use contextual analysis of simple types quite effectively, as Porter's experiments with good third graders show (40). When words were completely omitted from the context, these pupils correctly deduced the exact word omitted 23 percent of the time. They were able to deduce probable meanings of the omitted word 82 percent of the time. In other words, they were successful in contextual analysis for meanings in eight out of ten attempts. Contextual analysis is a very real help to comprehension among good readers, even when they have had no special training in its use. Since we cannot assume that skill in contextual analysis will increase spontaneously for all children, planned training is highly desirable.

Eventually, contextual analysis becomes one of the most frequently used methods of derivation of word meanings, as phonics and structural analysis decrease in use. Most college and adult readers use letter sounds or structural elements very little. They have discovered that although these help pronunciation, they do not aid in deriving meanings, unless the word is familiar auditorily. Since the reading vocabulary rapidly increases far beyond average students' auditory vocabulary during the secondary school years, pupils are constantly meeting terms they have never heard. Phonics and structural analysis that may aid in pronunciation are relatively useless in deriving meaning, for students just do not know the meanings of many of these words. Thus contextual analysis (or perhaps constant use of the dictionary) becomes readers' main tool for comprehending strange words.

Training in contextual analysis is part of the complete program in word recognition and word meaning skills. It should be begun during the early reading efforts of the child and continued indefinitely. Among primary school children, the following practices are appropriate:

Contextual analysis training

1. Read a sentence, rhyme, jingle, or predictable story in which obvious words are omitted. Encourage children to supply the missing word as you come to it. Discuss with them their reasons for selection of the words they offer. This practice may be combined with a given phonic clue, such as a constant initial sound, in the manner of M. Lucile Harrison described earlier.
2. Have children read a new selection silently. Then question them on the meanings of new words present in the story. Discuss reasons for their deductions.
3. Supply reading material with words occasionally omitted. Leave out every tenth word or a number of words of the same part of speech. Encourage children to infer the missing words and to defend their selections. Accept as correct any answers consistent with the sense of the sentence.
4. Insert a nonsense word in place of a certain noun or verb several times in a paragraph. Ask children to infer the word substituted for, to describe it, and to explain their selection.
5. Vary the nonsense word game by giving the correct initial sound, blend, or syllable present in the true word, thus promoting simultaneous use of phonic and contextual, or phonic and structural analysis. Use such games for oral or written responses by the children.
6. With children as young as first-graders, Mary K. Gove used such cloze procedures as deleting every fifth or tenth noun or verb; every fifth or tenth word; or portions of nouns, verbs at these intervals (22). Children's ability to deduce the omitted or incomplete word was practiced first while listening, later in reading the selections, as their reading ability permitted. Their answers and their reasons were discussed and answers synonymous, identical, or semantically correct were accepted.

Other examples of cloze exercises to be used in building meaning vocabulary are offered elsewhere in this book. For contextual analysis training at the intermediate-grade level, use similar exercises, but increase the difficulty of the material by using selections from content field textbooks. In these texts, wherever possible, also help children to use charts, maps, tables, and diagrams as contextual clues to word meanings and comprehension. Also, vary the types of contextual clues described earlier. Ask children to make lists of words approached by contextual analysis, and discuss their inferences and lists. Encourage the use of phonic and structural analysis in these lists, as well as contextual analysis, by questioning pronunciation as well as meanings. See also the games and exercises suggested by Evelyn B. Spache in her handbook of activities.

Based on the reading behaviors of a number of graduate students, Ames has offered a classification of contextual clues to meaning (1). He suggests that this process is supported by:

- experience with language and familiar expressions
- modifying phrases and clauses
- definition or description
- words connected in a series
- comparison or contrast
- synonym clues
- time, setting, and mood
- referents or antecedents
- association clues
- main idea and supporting details
- question–answer pattern of paragraph
- preposition clues
- nonrestrictive clauses or appositive phrases
- cause–effect patterns

The significance of this identifying of contextual clues by introspection of mature readers is not immediately apparent for our instruction of elementary pupils. Are these same clues used by children? If so, at what ages and with what degree of facility? Earl F. Rankin and Betsy M. Overholzer have done an initial study seeking answers to these questions (42). They tested Ames's series of contextual clues on fourth to sixth graders in cloze tests. The material was arranged so that each deleted word could be derived with the aid of one of these clues. The pupils were reasonably successful in supplying the expected words, with increasing scores from grade four to grade six. Most important of all, Rankin and Overholzer ranked the clues from easiest to most difficult as shown by the pupils' ability to supply the missing words in each type of context.

In order from easy to difficult, the clues are:

- words connected in a series
- modifying phrases or clauses
- experience with language and familiar expressions
- cause–effect patterns
- association clues
- referents or antecedents
- synonym clues
- definition or description
- preposition clues
- question–answer pattern of paragraph
- comparison or contrast

- main idea and supporting details
- nonrestrictive clauses or apposition phrases

The last four yielded less than 50 percent accuracy in supplying deleted words, a performance lower than normally expected.

Teachers could base instruction in using contextual clues on the implications of these studies. They might supply cloze exercises exemplifying each type of deduction, have children attempt to supply the missing words, and then discuss their reasons for their answers. Without giving the structures formal labels, teachers could follow the order suggested by Rankin and Overholzer from easiest to most difficult types, thus increasing children's skill in this most important of all tools for word recognition.

Arthur V. Olson queried a group of eleven-year-olds regarding the way in which they identified the meanings of test words they did not previously know (38). In order of frequency, they used:

- experience of familiar expression
- direct explanation in the text
- the mood or situation
- synonyms or restatements
- comparison and contrast
- the summary in the material

Thirteen percent of the thirty children identified 75 percent of the meanings of the difficult words; 97 percent of the children identified at least half of the words. The list of techniques used by these children is much shorter than all the types of context clues we would teach if we followed Rankin and Overholzer's list.

Emans has recommended several additional types of contextual analysis training based on his study of the information given by configuration and graphic clues to contextual derivation of words (16). Emans would employ the cloze and discussion steps suggested here and add to these exercises by (1) including pictures; (2) supplying the beginning letter in the blank space; (3) showing the length of the word by the size of the space; (4) giving the beginning and ending letters; (5) giving four words as possible answers from which children would select the best; and (6) printing only the consonants in the blank.

These types of practice, all using the cloze arrangement, do make use of pupils' phonics knowledge as well as their inferential thinking, and probably could be introduced earlier than the intermediate grades.

In constructing the practice exercises in training pupils in each type of contextual clue, a simple approach is to prepare dittoed or mimeographed reading selections, leaving out every tenth word. Variations following Emans' ideas would require leaving in the clue of the beginning or ending letter or all the consonants, etc. These cloze exercises may also be varied by omitting a particular kind of word as every fifth noun, verb, or adjective. Deleting every tenth word in this other kind of cloze would probably require too long a reading selection for a brief classroom activity.

Preparing training exercises to follow Ames's types of contextual clues would, of course, involve much more preparation and rewriting of the reading selections to ensure the repetition of each clue. Or, prior to deleting words, the teacher would identify the probable contextual clue by which every fifth noun or other type of word might be deduced by pupils. Then later the nature of the clue and the thinking necessary to employ it could be brought out in the class discussion.

Studies have been made of the contribution of various portions of a sentence to derivation of the meaning of an unknown word. It appears that the words following a strange word are more likely to aid in contextual analysis than those preceding it. These studies confirm the desirability of teaching pupils to read the entire sentence (and perhaps the rest of the paragraph) before attempting to derive the meaning of an unknown word. The use of a dictionary or any other aid to finding meaning should also be delayed until after the complete sentence or more has been read. This pattern of delayed attack in contextual analysis is also conducive to better overall comprehension, for it prevents interruptions in the continuity of the thinking process.

Discussion Questions

1. Is it possible that some pupils cannot learn to use phonics and yet can learn to read adequately? Discuss such types of pupils and their habits of word recognition.

2. Discuss the possible reasons for the often observed lack of word attack skills among retarded readers.

3. Would you emphasize phonics skills for a retarded reader of junior- or senior-high-school age who was functioning at the fifth- or sixth-grade level? Give reasons for your answer.

4. If you have observed or used any published systems of phonics teaching, describe them and compare them with the approaches suggested in the text or in other sources.

5. What are the implications of Porter's research on contextual analysis regarding the importance of this skill compared with other word attack skills?

6. Which of the word recognition skills contributes most to accurate pronunciation, to recognition of meaning, or to both? How do these outcomes of the various ways of analyzing words differ when the word is familiar or unfamiliar to the child's auditory vocabulary?

7. Discuss your opinion of the statement that phonics is of great value only at primary reading levels when the reading vocabulary includes only words already familiar to the child.

8. What is your reaction to the alternatives for phonics, such as the Harrison-McKee procedure, the elimination of syllabication rules, the teaching of phonograms or word patterns in place of letter sounds?

9. Using Table 12.2 examine the programs described in Table 12.3. Do some of these still try to teach phonic generalizations that really don't work? Which programs ignore the research? What conventions do they seem to agree upon that are relatively useless?

10. Try to arrange to visit a primary and an intermediate classroom to view the work in phonics. Compare the procedures with those suggested here.

References

1. Ames, Wilbur S., "The Development of a Classification Scheme of Contextual Aids." *Reading Research Quarterly*, 2 (Fall 1966), 57–82.
2. Bailey, Mildred Hart, "The Utility of Phonic Generalizations in Grades One Through Six." *Reading Teacher*, 20 (February 1967), 413–418.
3. Benz, D. A., and Rosemier, R. A., "Concurrent Validity of the Gates Level of Comprehension Test and the Bond–Hoyt–Clymer Reading Diagnostic Tests." *Educational and Psychological Measurement*, 26 (1966), 1057–1062.
4. Boyd, R. D., "Growth of Phonic Skills in Reading," in *Clinical Studies in Reading III*, Helen M. Robinson, ed. Supplementary Educational Monographs, 97 (1968), 68–87.
5. Breen, L. C., "Vocabulary Development by Teaching Prefixes, Suffixes and Root Derivatives." *Reading Teacher*, 14 (November 1960), 93–97.
6. Burmeister, Lou E., "Usefulness of Phonic Generalizations," *Reading Teacher*, 21 (January 1968), 349–356, 360.
7. Burmeister, Lou E., "Vowel Pairs," *Reading Teacher*, 21 (February 1968), 445–452.
8. Burmeister, Lou E., "Final Vowel-Consonant-*e*," *Reading Teacher*, 24 (February 1971), 439–442.
9. Burmeister, Lou E., "Content of a Phonics Program Based on Particularly Useful Generalizations," in *Reading Methods and Teacher Improvement*, Nila B. Smith, ed. Newark, Del.: International Reading Association, 1971, 27–39.
10. Burrows, Alvina Treut, and Lourie, Zyra, "When Two Vowels Go Walking," *Reading Teacher*, 17 (November 1963), 79–82.
11. Clymer, Theodore, "The Utility of Phonics Generalizations in the Primary Grades," *Reading Teacher*, 16 (January 1963), 252–258.
12. DeLawter, Jayne A., "The Relationship of Beginning Reading Instruction and Miscue Patterns," in *Help for the Reading Teacher: New Directions in Research*, W. D. Page, ed. National Conference on Research in English, 1975, 42–51.
13. Dzama, Mary Ann, "Composing Use of Generalizations of Phonics in LEA, Basal Vocabulary," *Reading Teacher*, 28 (February 1975), 466–472.
14. Emans, Robert, "The Usefulness of Phonic Generalizations Above the Primary Grades," *Reading Teacher*, 20 (February 1967), 419–425.
15. Emans, Robert, "History of Phonics," *Elementary English*, 45 (May 1968), 602–608.
16. Emans, Robert, "Use of Context Clues," in *Reading and Realism*, J. Allen Figurel, ed. Proceedings of the International Reading Association, 13, 1969, 76–82.

17. Emans, Robert, and Fisher, Gladys M., "Teaching the Use of Context Clues," *Elementary English*, 44 (March 1967), 243–246.

18. Fleming, James T., "Teachers' Understanding of Phonic Generalizations," *Reading Teacher*, 25 (February 1972), 400–404.

19. Gates, Arthur I., "Results of Teaching a System of Phonics," *Reading Teacher*, 14 (March 1961), 248–252.

20. Glass, Gerald G., and Burton, Elizabeth H., "How Do They Decode? Verbalizations and Observed Behavior of Successful Decoders," *Education*, 94 (September–October 1973), 58–64.

21. Gleitman, Lila R., and Rozing, Paul, "Teaching Reading by Use of Syllabary," *Reading Research Quarterly*, 8 (Summer 1973), 447–483.

22. Gove, Mary K., "Using the Cloze Procedure in a First Grade Classroom," *Reading Teacher*, 29 (October 1975), 36–44.

23. Groff, Patrick, *The Syllable: Its Nature and Pedagogical Usefulness*. Portland, Ore.: Northwest Regional Laboratory, 1971.

24. Groff, Patrick, "Sequences for Teaching Consonant Clusters," *Journal of Reading Behavior*, 4 (Winter 1971–1972), 59–65.

25. Groff, Patrick, "Teaching Reading by Syllables," *Reading Teacher*, 34 (March 1981), 639–663.

26. Hackney, Ben H., "Reading Achievement and Word Recognition Skills," *Reading Teacher*, 21 (March 1968), 515–518.

27. Harris, Albert J., et al., "Comparing Approaches in First Grade Teaching with Disadvantaged Children Extended into Second Grade," *Reading Teacher*, 20 (May 1967), 698–703.

28. Hillerich, R. L., "Vowel Generalizations and First Grade Reading Achievement," *Elementary School Journal*, 67 (March 1967), 246–250.

29. Hillerich, R. L., "Teaching About Vowels in Second Grade," *Illinois School Research*, 7 (1970), 35–38.

30. Hillerich, R. L., "Syllabication," *Ohio Reading Teacher*, 14 (January 1980), 12–14.

31. Johnson, Dale D., "Suggested Sequences for Presenting Four Categories of Letter–Sound Correspondences," *Elementary English*, 50 (September 1973), 888–896.

32. Johnson, Dale D., and Merryman, Edward, "Syllabication: The Erroneous VCCV Generalization," *Reading Teacher*, 25 (December 1971), 267–270.

33. MacGinitie, Walter H., "Difficulty with Logical Operations," *Reading Teacher*, 29 (January 1976), 371–375.

34. Marzano, Robert J., Case, Norma, De Booy, Anne Prochoruk, "Are Syllabication and Reading Ability Related?" *Journal of Reading*, 19 (April 1976), 545–547.

35. McCullough, Constance M., "Context Aids in Reading," *Reading Teacher*, 11 (April 1958), 225–229.

36. McFeely, Donald C., "Syllabication Usefulness in a Basal and Social Science Vocabulary," *Reading Teacher*, 27 (May 1972), 809–814.

37. Muller, Douglas, "Phonic Blending and Transfer of Letter Training to Word Reading in Children," *Journal of Reading Behavior*, 5 (Summer 1972–1973), 212–217.

38. Olson, Arthur V., "Use of Context Clues in Science and Social Studies," in *The Quest for Competency in Teaching Reading*, Howard A. Klein, ed. Newark, Del.: International Reading Association, 1972, 222–231.

39. Poole, I., "Genetic Development of Articulation of Consonant Sounds in Speech," *Elementary English Review*, 11 (1934), 159–161.

40. Porter, Douglas, "The Instrumental Value of Sound Cues in Reading," Paper read at the AERA Convention, Atlantic City, N.J., February 17, 1960.

41. Railsback, Charles E., "Consonant Substitution in Word Attack," *Reading Teacher*, 23 (February 1970), 432–435.

42. Rankin, Earl F., and Overholzer, Betsy M., "Reaction of Intermediate Grade Children to Context Clues," *Journal of Reading Behavior*, 1 (Summer 1969), 50–73.

43. Rosso, Barbara Rak, and Emans, Robert, "Children's Use of Phonic Generalizations," *Reading Teacher*, 34 (March 1981), 653–658.

44. Samuels, S. Jay, "Modes of Word Recognition," in *Theoretical Models and Processes of Reading*, Harry Singer and Robert B. Ruddell, eds. Newark, Del.: International Reading Association, 1976, 270–282.

45. Spache, George D., "A Phonics Manual for Primary and Remedial Teachers," *Elementary English Review*, 16 (April–May 1969), 147–150, 191–198.

46. Spache, George D., "Limitations of the Phonetic Approach to Developmental and Remedial Reading," in *New Frontiers in Reading*, J. Allen Figurel, ed. Proceedings of the International Reading Association, 5, 1960, 105–108.

47. Spache, George D., Andres, Michaela C., Curtis, H. A., et al., *A Longitudinal First Grade Reading Readiness Project*. Cooperative Research Project No. 2742. Florida State Department of Education, Tallahassee, Fla., 1965.

48. Spache, George D. and Baggett, Mary E., "What Do Teachers Know About Phonics and Syllabication?" *Reading Teacher*, 19 (November 1965), 96–99.

49. Sparks, Paul E., and Fay, Leo C., "An Evaluation of Two Methods of Teaching Reading," *Elementary School Journal*, 57 (April 1957), 590–596.

50. Tovey, Duane R., "Children's Grasp of Phonic Terms vs. Sound–Symbol Correspondence," *Reading Teacher*, 33 (January 1980), 431–437.

51. Wardhaugh, Ronald, "Syl-lab-i-ca-tion," *Elementary English*, 43 (November 1966), 785–788.

52. Wheat, Leonard B., "Four Spelling Rules," *Elementary School Journal*, 32 (May 1933), 697–706.

53. Wylie, Richard E., and Durrell, Donald D., "Teaching Vowels Through Phonograms," *Elementary English*, 47 (October 1970), 787–791.

Resources for the Teacher

Professional References

Artley, Sterl, *Word Perception for Teachers*. Columbia, Mo.: Micas Bros. Publishing, 1978.

Burmeister, Lou, *Words from Print to Meaning: Classroom Activities*. Menlo Park, Calif.: Addison-Wesley, 1975.

Durkin, Dorothy, *Phonics, Linguistics and the Teaching of Reading*, New York: Teachers College Press, 1972.

Ewing, John M., *Word Analysis for Teachers*. Danville, Ill.: Interstate Printers, 1974.

Gray, W. S., *The Teaching of Reading and Writing*, 2d ed. Ralph C. Staiger, ed. Glenview, Ill.: Scott, Foresman, 1974.

Heilman, Arthur W., *Phonics in Proper Perspective*. Columbus: Charles E. Merrill, 1976. A rational view of phonics.

Hull, Marion A., *Phonics for the Teacher of Reading*. Columbus: Charles E. Merrill, 1976. Programmed self-instruction.

Ives, Josephine P., *Word Identification Techniques*. Chicago, Ill.: Rand McNally, 1979.

Rinsky, Lee Ann, and Griffith, Barbara, *Teaching Word Attack Skills*. Dubuque: Gorsuch Scarisbrick, 1978.

Robinson, H. Alan, *Strategies for Reading Words in Context*. Boston, Mass.: Allyn and Bacon Inc., 1978.

Schell, Leo M., *Fundamentals of Decoding for Teachers*. Chicago, Ill.: Rand McNally, 1980.

Spache, Evelyn B., *Reading Activities for Child Involvement*. Boston, Mass.: Allyn and Bacon Inc., 1982.

Trela, Thaddeus M., *Sensible Phonics: A Self-Teaching Guide for Teachers*. Belmont, Calif.: Pitman Learning, 1975.

Wilson, Robert M. and Hall, Mary Anne, *Programmed Word Attack for Teachers*. Columbus: Charles E. Merrill, 1979.

Instructional Materials

Barsch, Ray, *Configurations*. Novato, Calif.: Academic Therapy Publications. A three-book spirit master series for visual recognition skills.

Cory, Beverly, *Word Structure*. Belmont, Calif.: Pitman Learning. Exercises for intermediate grades.

Crossword Puzzles for Phonics. Elizabethtown, Pa.: Continental Press. For grades one to four, liquid duplicating edition.

Durrell, Donald D., and Murphy, Helen A., *Sound Start*. North Billerica, Mass.: Curriculum Associates. Decoding program in beginning reading and writing.

Edson, Ann, and Insel, Eunice, *Phonics in Context*. Freeport, N.Y.: Educational Activities. Cassettes, activity books or dittoes and games for grades two to four and four to six.

Edson, Ann, and Insel, Eunice, *Reading/Language Learning Games*. Freeport, N.Y.: Educational Activities. Ten games for phonics and language development.

Ervin, Jane, *Phonics Workbooks*. Cleveland: Modern Curriculum, 1977.

Feldman, Shirley C., and Merrill, Kathleen K., *Learning Ways to Read Words*. New York: Teachers College Press, 1978. A four-book series.

Games Power for Phonics. Pleasanton, Calif.: Spin-A-Test. A kit of directions for 210 games.

Glass-Analysis Decoding Kit. Garden City, N.Y.: Easier-to-Learn. Teaches names of letters, vowel clusters, and stories containing words that include the clusters.

Hay, Julie, and Wingo, Charles E., *Reading with Phonics*. New York: J. B. Lippincott, 1978.

Henninger, Dorothy Grant, *Words, Sounds and Thoughts*. New York: School Book Service, 1977.

Insel, Eunice, and Edson, Ann, *Reading–Structural Analysis Creature Features*. Freeport, N.Y.: Educational Activities. Records or cassettes for grades three to five.

Ireland, John, *Word Attack Skills*. Milwaukee, Wis.: Raintree Children's Books, 1977.

Johnson, Donald, et al., *Word Analysis Kit*. North Billerica, Mass.: Curriculum Associates. Four kits for primary grades in categorizing sets of words.

Mangrum, Charles T., and Messmore, Peter B., *Phonic Plus*. Englewood Cliffs, N.J.: Prentice-Hall, 1981. A seven-workbook series.

Mangrum, Charles T., Messmore, Peter B., and Logan, Richard, *Letter Sounds All Around*. Los Angeles, Calif.: Bowmar/Noble Publishing Co. Thirty filmstrips and three groups of workbooks to teach sound–symbol correspondence.

New Phonics and Word Analysis Skills. Elizabethtown, Pa.: Continental Press. Three workbooks each for grades one to six, plus teacher's guide.

Phonics. Palo Alto, Calif.: Creative Publications. Ten duplicating masters for primary grades.

Phonics Comics: Word Probe. Chicago, Ill.: Coronet. Ten cassettes and parallel response books to introduce letter sounds.

Phonics Kits. Chicago, Ill.: Science Research Associates. Three kits for kindergarten to third offering games, exercises and short stories.

Phonics Program. New York: Holt Instructional Resources. A kit for primary pupils.

Phonics from Symbol to Sound. Long Branch, N.J.: Kimbo Educational Co. Filmstrips and accompanying cassettes, fifteen in all.

Ruchlis, Hy, *Phonic Word Builder*. Brooklyn, N.Y.: Book-Lab, 1972. For grades one to four.

Schoolhouse: A Word Attack Skills Kit. Chicago, Ill.: Science Research Associates. Two kits for grades one to three and three to four in phonics and structural analysis.

Scott, Louise Binder, *A New Time for Phonics*. Manchester, Mo.: Webster Division, McGraw-Hill. A six-book series for primary grades.

Star Words. Freeport, N.Y.: Educational Activities. Two filmstrips, two cassettes, six ditto masters to promote use of context clues.

Weinstein, Marcia, *Sounds and Stories*. Brooklyn, N.Y.: Book-Lab, 1975. Four page units of stories introducing vowel sounds. Teacher's manual.

Word Family Fables. Elizabethtown, Pa.: Continental Press. Each of the three duplicating masters introduces more than 20 phonograms.

Like many other facets of reading instruction, the task of vocabulary development is undergoing reexamination and reevaluation. The drill procedures, the dependence upon sheer repetition, even such criteria of success as word calling or matching words and definitions are being questioned. The factors that influence vocabulary growth most significantly may lie in the classroom or school climate, the language experience in the family or community setting, as well as in the directed teaching efforts of the teacher. For all these reasons, classroom development of sight and meaning vocabularies in reading is undergoing change.

New concepts about vocabulary include the realization that there are a number of different vocabularies. To mention only a few, there are distinctly different groups of words in children's speaking, listening, writing, and reading vocabularies. Promotion of each of these vocabularies requires differing experiences that must be presented in the medium in which new terms are to be used. Knowledge of words does not readily carry over from reading or listening to speaking or writing, or from any one medium to the other.

Another basic concept beginning to influence vocabulary training is the recognition that words are not learned as of a certain date because of a certain number of repetitions. Rather, words are thoroughly understood only as a group of associations is built around each word, associations that include multiple meanings and visual, auditory, and perhaps kinesthetic imagery. Accepting this concept of vocabulary growth makes the teacher's task one of providing multifaceted experiences with words—their meanings and their usage—in a variety of settings and contexts, rather than a task of providing drill and massive repetitions. All of this can perhaps be expressed in a quotation from G. H. Bower (3). "... No word is an island unto itself. It rather occupies the intersection of a vast number of classifying features."

Many writers and teachers use the term "vocabulary" as though it referred to a single kind of learning with words. They may be speaking of the children's speech—sentence length, choice of words, and fluency. Or, if children are in the primary-grade reading stages, they may be discussing the number of words they recognize without analysis or help—sight vocabulary. The same general term is also used to describe the variety of words that pupils use in their spontaneous writings—writing vocabulary—or those words whose meanings they ultimately understand in reading—meaning vocabulary. At other times the term "vocabulary" is used to mean the words that children can hear and understand—listening vocabulary. But every teacher knows that pupils have these several vocabularies which differ in breadth, accuracy, and the fluency with which the children use each.

514

These various vocabularies are not equivalent or synonymous at any time in children's development. Before they learn to speak, they often demonstrate a sizable listening vocabulary, and even after they have begun talking, their ability to comprehend auditorily exceeds their own speech vocabulary markedly. In fact, the most people can listen to and understand more words and more complex language patterns than they use in ordinary speech probably throughout their entire lifetime. Similarly, their listening vocabularies exceed their meaning and sight vocabularies in reading until they reach secondary school age. At this point, if they have developed good reading abilities, they begin to read more complex material than they can listen to. At the same time, their writing vocabularies lag far behind their speaking, reading, and listening vocabularies, and probably continue to be inferior indefinitely. Thus at no time in their lives are their growth precisely similar in the various types of vocabulary.

Just what is the significance of our interpretation of the term "vocabulary"? It is important to recognize the differences among various kinds of vocabulary growth simply to avoid the loose thinking and faulty teaching practices based on the assumption that pupils have a "vocabulary." Understanding and use of words does not transfer readily from one language medium to another. Children do not easily write the new words they have learned by listening or reading, and they do not tend to incorporate these same words into their daily speech. New words learned from reading or listening are often only imperfectly understood. Moreover, the school climate is not conducive to oral experimentation with new words, for such attempts are likely to meet with ridicule from peers. Pupils and adults tend to depend upon commonplace, conversational terms rather than on the more precise words they learn from reading or listening. Because of these almost universal tendencies, classroom practices which assume that vocabulary is a unitary trait or that pupils will use in speech or writing the words they are taught by certain reading exercises fail to accomplish their purposes. Classroom practices that attempt to teach children to write or spell most of the words they learn in reading or listening or to use these in their speech are not realistic. Listening to a teacher explain new terms, looking up lists of new words in the dictionary, completing artificial exercises in workbooks, and similar common practices do not necessarily help to increase children's reading vocabularies. This is a matter of concern when we are discussing methods of improving reading ability.

In the activity of reading, there are two basic vocabularies—sight vocabulary and meaning vocabulary. Sight vocabulary includes those words that primary-grade pupils recognize visually and by the aid of their auditory memories for each word. Their recognition is aided by their training in phonics and structural and contextual analysis. Meaning vocabulary includes those words for which children have a number of meaningful mental associations. The word may not be in their listening vocabulary, and they may not be able to pronounce it correctly. Knowledge of the meanings of roots and affixes, and recognition of a known base word may aid in clarifying the meaning. But they finally recognize the meaning of the word as used in each particular reading context. When we speak of children's reading vocabularies at the primary-grade levels, we usually mean their sight vocabularies. When we refer to their reading vocabulary in the intermediate and upper elementary grades, we are really referring to their meaning vocabularies.

We make these distinctions between sight and meaning vocabularies deliberately, because in many classroom practices, particularly in primary grades, they are assumed to be synonymous. If children can recognize and name a printed word, it is often presumed that they must be familiar with its meanings. For this reason, observers since the time of Horace Greely have been disturbed by the fluent word naming of many children that is not accompanied with the comprehension of the message. Word calling is rampant in our schools at all educational levels and in every field of learning. Teachers and some reading experts who attempt to judge comprehension by the fluency, phrasing, and expression of the oral reader are similarly misled. As pointed out in the discussion of oral reading, very good oral performances are not proof of comprehension. In other words, lists of words are not a true measure of reading. Being able to read lists of words at sight does not prove that these same words are correctly interpreted in the context of a passage. The performance is evidence only that these words have become familiar visually and auditorily as printed symbols, not necessarily as meaningful ideas. For these reasons, we will emphasize the differences between these two types of reading vocabulary throughout this discussion of vocabulary development.

Influences upon Reading Vocabulary Growth

The school is certainly not the only or even the major influence upon children's development of sight and meaning vocabularies. The ability of primary school children to develop sight vocabularies in early reading is highly dependent upon their auditory memories for words. If they are limited in verbal intelligence or in experiences with words because of bilingualism, poor family or different cultural background, narrow preschool verbal experiences, and the like, the children will lack auditory background for acquiring adequate sight or meaning vocabularies. The intellectual interests of their families and the level of their verbal intercommunication also condition the children's readiness for reading vocabulary growth. Throughout the elementary years the pupils' play and reading interests, hobbies, and pastimes influence their vocabulary development. Although in general they tend to lag behind girls, boys' vocabularies show distinct breadth in their areas of interest such as sports and science. Girls tend to show greater overall development in vocabulary and less tendency to excel in specific areas of high interest. Thus we see that a number of factors other than the school's efforts influence the development of meaning vocabulary both before and after children enter school.

Direct efforts to promote vocabulary development begin almost the day children enter school. By providing many verbal and visual experiences, and listening and speaking opportunities, the school attempts to strengthen the average children's auditory readiness for reading. The vitality and spontaneity of the curriculum offered to the pupils as well as the very atmosphere of the classroom exert powerful influences upon vocabulary development. The freedoms to explore, to be curious, to question and discover determine ultimately the breadth and depth of this development, or by their absence stifle and restrict it. Other classroom efforts to promote sight vocabulary at the primary-grade levels—acquiring a broad classroom library, training in word recognition skills, language activities that reinforce the reading vocabulary, and the prolific use of word games and audiovisual aids—are reasonably effective in supporting early sight vocabulary development. Training in the use of the dictionary, varied exercises in manipulating word meanings, workbooks and games emphasizing word study probably make a small contribution to growth of meaning vocabulary. But in our opinion these planned efforts on the part of the school have much less effect than the cultural and socioeconomic backgrounds. Some children respond to the school's planned and indirect influences upon vocabulary development but probably are more conditioned by extra-school factors to function close to a level commensurate with their cultural and social backgrounds. A few are driven by their own efforts or by the school's training to function on distinctly higher linguistic levels than those from which they started. On the other hand, most eventually learn to read about as well as might be expected in view of their verbal intelligence and sociological backgrounds, a level probably adequate to their ultimate vocational and cultural interests.

How Pupils Learn Words

The bases for all early vocabulary learning are children's firsthand experiences. For example, hundreds of tactile, visual, and psychomotor observations underlie the words *rough* and *smooth*. These nonverbal contacts must also be reinforced and associated with a number of auditory and speech experiences with the same words in varying language patterns and contexts. Collectively, these multisensory concepts determine and are essential to understanding the tools we call "words." Contrast this variety of experiences, if you will, with the common five-minute prereading chalkboard or flash card drill that primary school teachers sometimes offer in the naive belief that they are teaching the group the new sight vocabulary of the reading lesson. How effective can this superficial presentation be in the absence of multisensory experience with these words? The presentation of these words is pointless unless the children already know the words from previous auditory or firsthand experiences. Since they usually do know the words, what is accomplished by the prereading presentation, other than associating the visual and auditory images which might be better accomplished in the context of the story?

However, direct teaching of vocabulary probably produces superior growth to incidental methods. Intensive emphasis at primary-grade levels pays dividends in increased sight and meaning vocabularies and improved comprehension. In fact, at these early stages of development such training may appear to produce quite dramatic gains, insofar as these are measured by common vocabulary and reading tests. With older elementary school pupils and at secondary and collegiate levels, intensive vocabulary programs show gains but usually of a much less striking nature. Improvement is often linked to verbal intelligence, with the brighter pupils showing the greater gains.

But careful review of much of our direct training for meaning vocabulary shows there is still much to be desired. Drills with synonyms and antonyms, matching, categorizing, and the like ignore the multiplicity of meanings of many words and the basic fact that the meaning intended is often dependent upon the context. For example, many exercises tend to emphasize only the commonest meaning of a word such as *fast*, a word for which most dictionaries offer six or eight different definitions. These word drills also assume that there is a direct transfer of the learning to the reading situation. How do exercises with singular or common meanings help pupils to interpret the uncommon, multiple meanings they encounter in their reading? Despite these limitations and weak assumptions, these planned efforts probably produce more development and transfer to various language media than the incidental learning resulting simply from casual classroom word activities or general reading. Extensive or intensive reading undoubtedly also makes some contribution to reading vocabulary but probably less than planned, direct teaching.

There are many natural ways in which pupils learn correct or incorrect meanings of words by their auditory or visual similarity to other words: assumption of total meaning from recognition of one major part of the word—*earnest* means earn something; the influence of a figure of speech —*brawny* means smart because of confusion with the common expression "brains and brawn"; and associations with familiar experiences—"that boy dawdles." Certainly most reading authorities agree in recognizing these naturalistic contributions to vocabulary development, but favor direct, inspirational teaching. Teachers, on the other hand, tend to prefer those vocabulary activities involving little or no direct teaching—dictionary use, context, and incidental and informal attention. These same teachers consider vocabulary card files, lists given by the teacher or from the textbook, exercises in writing words in sentences as least effective, an opinion shared by many reading experts. To sum up this discussion of how pupils learn words, the foundations of vocabulary are (1) vital firsthand experiences, (2) direct teaching that provides many meaningful associations, and (3) incidental learning from casual contact with words through one or several language media.

Marie M. Clay of New Zealand conducted a year-long study of first-grade (five-year-old) pupils' efforts at learning to read (4). The children drew pictures, created captions for the pictures, read them, and then went on to readiness books and preprimers. In their efforts to write, they first reacted to words and letters by scribbling, and later inventing letter and word shapes. After that, they were able to copy with personal variations. This progressed to correct copying and later still to the ability to write correct letters and word forms spontaneously.

Their compositions at first were largely repetitive short sentences—"This is me." The sentences would be reasonably appropriate to the picture, but not to the exact caption they had offered. Gradually they progressed to word-by-word reading that was more or less accurate. In writing, they tended first to make an oral statement, then to check to see whether it was correct and matched the words they had written. There were distinct differences between the high and low groups in the amount they read, the proportion of errors in oral reading, and the proportion of self-corrections.

In effect, Clay used what some would call a language experience approach in teaching pupils to read and write simultaneously. Other writers who have carefully observed how children learn in the very beginning steps have discovered that when left to their own resources, first-graders develop their own word attack strategies. MacKinnon found they helped themselves recognize words by noting double letters and outstanding letter clusters (phonograms), and by using context, to mention only a few of their spontaneous learnings (17).

We know that children's oral reading errors show the tendency to substitute at first by visual or graphic similarity or by drawing upon words previously learned or words in their auditory vocabularies. Gradually the proportion of errors of these types are replaced by those reflecting attention to the meanings of words. As phonics is taught, children learn to attend to the first letters of words and their sounds. Shape and configuration are early clues that are soon replaced by others because so many of the beginning words are similar in shape. But more research at this beginning level is needed, if only to discover what other strategies and concepts children spontaneously employ with success. Much of what is known in this area has been reviewed in the earlier chapter on reading in the primary grades.

Learning Sight Vocabulary

The Experience Chart

Our approach to beginning reading emphasized the use of experience charts as the initial reading medium. Such charts form the basis of common language experiences for the gifted readers until they are ready for individualized reading and thereafter serve as a type of group reading activity. In the average and slow-learning groups, the chart approach would serve as a group activity during the readiness period and thereafter as a supplement to the basal program. The experience chart can continue to be useful in a variety of purposeful group activities during the intermediate grades.

Before and after formal reading activities have begun, the chart is a prime means of promoting growth in sight vocabulary. In the fast-moving group, it helps provide a common core of words among those pupils pursuing their own reading interests. In all the reading groups, the chart offers the teacher an opportunity to observe pupils' knowledge of sight words and their use of word recognition skills. Charts offer also an opportunity for repetition and reinforcement that is necessary for permanent learning. The teacher can arrange for reinforcement in interesting ways by emphasizing sensory appeals such as repetitive sounds, rhythm, rhyme, and words stressing color. This principle can be kept in mind and approached carefully without stifling the spontaneity and creativity of the pupils' compositions. Similarly, the important service words, as listed by Dolch (6), will be repeated frequently in children's charts. These lists tend to include the connectives, conjunctions, prepositions, and the like that play so large a part in all written materials. These words are more difficult to learn than the nouns, verbs, and even many of the polysyllabic words that find their way into the charts. Because of their frequency, difficulty, and significance for comprehension, these service words should (and probably will be) frequently repeated in the charts but not at the expense of stultifying their content.

Words that should be learned are best approached in meaningful pairs, as "the *boy* chased the *ball*" or "the *girl* catches the *ball*." This linking is more effective using verbs and prepositions than conjunctions, as "the *boy* and the *ball*." Grouping words to be learned according to common experiential bases, as *moon–night–dark* or *sun–light–day* are effective presentations. Also, grouping and learning words that have related meanings, as *talk–speak–shout*; or in rhyming, as *I–eye* is more effective than grouping based on structural or spelling patterns, as *age, ago, fat, pat*.

Sight vocabulary learning will also derive from pupils' self-help efforts, such as keeping lists or notebooks or card files of new words. With the aid of other pupils, the children may use these words for the basis of reviews, games, a picture dictionary, a resource list for writing, exercises in categorizing or classifying words according to their type (name of something showing action or description—for example, vegetable, animal, mineral, or zoo, farm, school) or sorting word cards by the number of syllables or phonic elements, suffix, prefix, or root elements, and other activities. There is recent evidence that these inductive self-help exercises in analyzing and sorting words are very effective, especially for poorer readers. In some instances this approach is even more effective than exercises in learning vocabulary based upon knowledge of phonic and syllabication rules.

Many teachers are concerned whether their pupils are learning the "basic" words that they will need. Even those teachers using the language experience or individualized approaches often share this concern. As a result many turn to the Dolch Word List of the 220 most frequent words (6). When also used as a test, it is possible to measure the pupils' progress in this area. Elton G. Stetson used the earlier data of Maude McBroom and her fellow workers at the University of Iowa to form what might be called norms for the word list (29). The scale is in Table 13.1.

These figures give an aura of exactness that, of course, is not true. They are estimates of what some children accomplish in learning this list of words. They do not represent expected performances for children. Rather, they show the relationship between the list of very common words and reading progress at the very beginning stages. Learning these words helps reading development.

However, there are a number of cautions to be observed when using this or any similar word list. Sound and unsound procedures are listed at the end of this chapter that should guide your teaching of sight vocabulary. The Dolch Word List and others tell us the most frequent words in our language. It is desirable that children become very familiar with such words, for they constitute most of the words in any reading matter. But, as pointed out later, these important words are not learned simply by repetition, drill, or rote memory. Words are learned only when a number of associations become attached to them—several meanings and the way they function in the sentence structure of our language. Despite the fact that most of these very frequent words are short, they are not easy to learn. Many of them are quite difficult because of visual similarity, as *where–when*, *there–then*, or because their meanings and functions are quite complex, as in the case of *too–to*, and *for*, *by*, and *as*. Use the suggestions in the chart at the end of this chapter when teaching these words. Consult also books on activities (25) and basal reader manuals for many ideas to enliven the reinforcement of the learning of these basic words.

Table 13.1 Stetson's Norms for the Word List

Score	Reading level	Score	Reading level
Preprimer		*Second Reader*	
0–20	1.1	170–171	2.0
21–40	1.2	172–175	2.1
41–60	1.3	176–180	2.2
61–75		181–185	2.3
		186–190	2.4
Primer		191–195	2.5
76–80	1.4	196–199	2.6
81–100	1.5	200–202	2.7
101–120	1.6	203–206	2.8
		207–210	2.9
First Reader		210–220	3.0
121–140	1.7		
141–160	1.8		
161–170	1.9		

Learning Aptitudes

The evidence regarding the value of determining learning modality of a child is very weak. The Mills Learning Aptitude Kit that was formerly recommended for this purpose is apparently no longer available. We know of no good substitute for that instrument, although several current devices are claiming to make these distinctions. Yet it is apparent that some children learn better by an emphasis upon one learning channel than another. Some appear to profit, at least temporarily, by an auditory, or a visual or a kinesthetic approach. This impression is widespread, at this moment, and a great many materials are being created that appeal to one or several channels of learning. We mentioned some of these earlier, as Echo Reading, the Neurological Impress Method, and simultaneous reading and listening to a taping of the reading matter. It appears that the makers of parallel books and tapes are quite certain that many children will learn to read better with that kind of help.

As remarked earlier, the effectiveness of these multi-modal methods for a large proportion of children is not so convincing. But to be fair, when children show a lack of progress under usual classroom instruction, it may be desirable to try the parallel reading–listening. If the children respond with better progress, then we have discovered something that works for them. It may well be that the novelty of the treatment produces the apparent progress, but this will become obvious if that progress diminishes. Moreover, our experience in clinical and classroom work has taught us that the effectiveness of emphasis upon one modality does not persist after a few months. If children are learning to read reasonably well, they soon demonstrate that they are using several types of clues to word recognition, and no longer are so dependent upon the modality that is being stressed. At that time, it is sensible to support and promote an eclectic approach to word recognition and analysis.

John Paul Jones has written a comprehensive review of the research on modality testing and teaching (13). Several of the studies he cites followed the Mills technique, with various results. Among the conclusions possible are (1) that the Mills test can identify the preferred modality for some children, (2) modality preference does not seem as significant for good readers as for poor readers, and (3) modality preference is an individual matter, not a group or class phenomenon. In a group situation, the individual differences tend to cancel each other, so that one method does not seem more efficient than another based on group results (4).

Modality preferences seem to vary over time among both good and poor readers. Thus we have very little evidence that teaching the apparently preferred modality over a long term is profitable. Another problem in interpreting the effectiveness of modality teaching is the fact that children may be translating the approach and learning through other channels than we intend. Because words are not a unimodal experience as simply a visual memory, or an auditory memory, or a kinesthetic gestalt, or a tactile sensation, children may actually be learning the words by some combination of cues that may or may not include the modality stressed in the lesson (30).

Changing from the previous method to the modality apparently preferred by the children will provide a degree of success, at least temporarily, if for no other reason than because of the newness of the method. The sense of failure that the children may be experiencing can thus be relieved. As this Hawthorne effect wears off and the initial success diminishes, other modality cues may be introduced (or appear spontaneously in the children's learning) to restimulate progress. We believe it is most essential to explore new, stimulating approaches in this fashion to try to maintain children's positive self-concept as readers.

In the opening chapter on reading as a perceptual process, we emphasized the variety of ways in which children learn sight vocabulary. Because some authors of reading materials for primary-school children ignore these natural word recognition techniques, we think it important to review their implications again. Some writers tell us that our current methods are faulty; they say that children do not recognize words by their shape, their context, and such clues. They believe that children read the letters, recognize the sounds for which they stand, translate the letter sounds into words, and thus recognize words. To these authors, the clues given by a familiar sentence, the outline of the word formed by the ascending and descending letters, the stimulus of the recognition of sounds of the first letter or two plus the sentence, the recognition of two familiar words in a compound, and similar perceptual stimuli just do not matter, or do not even exist. Only the recognition of the separate letters or the sounds of all of these are significant, they say. In keeping with this particular reasoning, we see primary-grade reading materials offered that carefully control the appearance of letters, doling these out, as it were, a few at a time. Other readers offer sequences of words one group at a time, each of which contains the same vowel sounds or a particular two- or three-letter combination. Still others offer a complete new alphabet in which each new symbol represents all the possible spellings of a sound, such as the long sound of *i*. All of these, and others still to appear, depend exclusively upon the assumption that letter–sound recognition is essential before word recognition can occur.

A few minutes spent in the average American primary-school classroom observing children's spontaneous efforts to identify words should dispel this absurd assumption. Every day, children who do not know one letter of the alphabet from another, or any of the variant sounds for which one letter may stand, or any of the many ways in which a sound or phoneme may be represented orthographically, learn to read. Children recognize words by a wide variety of clues ranging from one extreme—an inspection of some letters and details—to the other extreme—simply guessing that so-and-so would make sense in the sentence. Numerous experiments in analyzing the word recognition techniques of older students and adults confirm the persistence of this variety of word recognition techniques. Even pupils trained in a method emphasizing recognition solely by letter sounds gradually abandon this technique and adopt a variety of approaches. Studies of the eye-movement photographs of readers of all ages and of the elements and parts of words perceived when words are exposed for a fraction of a second unmistakably prove these facts. The values for word recognition and spelling of mechanical training by tachistoscopes, filmstrips, and other devices which expose words too rapidly for a letter-by-letter translation again demonstrate that the true nature of the word recognition process is not a letter-by-letter or a sound-by-sound recognition.

One group of reading specialists keeps claiming that knowledge of the names of the letters is very significant in beginning reading. It is supposed to be highly predictive of early success in reading, to show marked growth among good beginning readers, and to be a primary aid to word recognition. We have disputed these claims earlier by pointing out that letter naming reflects first of all the socioeconomic status of the family and its identification with the school's goals, insofar as it understands them. Second, this early learning of letter names is certainly characteristic of pupils of better than average intelligence, but not of dull children. Third, gains in letter naming are not significantly related to gains in reading ability (28).

It is true, of course, that letters stand for speech sounds. Even the primary-school child eventually recognizes that reading is simply talking written down. We did not have to wait for linguistics to discover that reading is an extension of speech. But we should not attempt to explain the entire process of word recognition as a matter of translating words letter by letter into the speech sounds they represent. Children can learn to read by a letter-by-letter sounding approach but almost every objective study of the results of this method shows that it delays or prevents the very goal it claims to accomplish—rapid, facile word recognition and comprehension.

These divergent interpretations of the true nature of word recognition are the basis for the current conflict between the "sight-word" and "phonics" schools. More recently, the disagreement has been used as the basis of an attack upon current reading instruction by certain groups of linguists, as was pointed out in reviewing the thinking of these groups. The heart of the argument lies in the interpretation of the significance of the alphabet. The phonics and linguistic schools argue that since letters represent speech sounds they must be the basis of every act of word recognition. We believe, in company with many other reading specialists, that this is *confusing the reading process with the reading unit.* Certainly, letters represent speech sounds and reading is, in one sense, a process of recognizing the meanings of speech sounds set down in symbolic fashion. But we have proven that word recognition is not often accomplished by a unit translation of the symbols for speech sounds into mental words or spoken sounds. This is not to say that children need never learn the alphabet or its many sound equivalents, for these skills are essential to phonic and structural analysis, which in turn are fundamental to full development of word recognition skill. But the translation of written letters into sounds is not *the* basis of early or mature word recognition, however useful it may eventually become as a supplementary skill.

Early Cues to Word Recognition

Children spontaneously discriminate among words by similarities and differences in the following ways:

- Unusual length—as *grandmother*.
- Shape—as ⌐⎍⎍⌐ *beautiful*.
- Base words—as *smile* in *smiled*.
- Context—The kitten likes to drink _____.
- Picture clues.
- Compounds—as *milkman*.
- Initial letters or sounds—as *boy, box, ball*.
- Internal details or cluster analysis—as in *apple, look*.

One other word recognition technique is used by primary-school children and sometimes mistakenly promoted by teachers. This is the attempt to recognize small words within other words, and use these small words as a guide to pronunciation. Unfortunately, the lack of consistent relationship between sounds and symbols in our language makes this technique impractical. The common little words that appear to be present in larger words vary considerably in their ponunciation within different contexts. For example, contrast the sounds of *in* when it appears in *line, tin, ring, singing, drink*, and other such words. The small words—*on, an, is, it, at, are, be*, and the like—are not sound guides to the pronunciation and recognition of the words within which they may be found.

The eight other word recognition techniques comprising the sight-word approach should be strengthened as much as possible in the daily reading lesson. In promoting sight vocabulary from experience charts, basals, or trade books, these recognition clues should constantly be emphasized. Children should be urged to compare lengths, shapes, details, base words, and other characteristics of words visually, auditorily, and kinesthetically. The last of these comparisons may include drawing word outlines, laying them upon or next to or under others, tracing outlines through transparent paper, and trying to read words when only the outline, or the outline and the initial letter or two, are given *in a sentence*. Speed in recognition of familiar words is desirable and may be promoted through judicious use of games (25) and far-point or hand tachistoscopes, provided that speed of presentation is emphasized only after a high degree of accuracy is obtained.

These sight-word recognition techniques naturally lead to and blend with phonic, contextual, and structural analysis as outlined earlier. But these clues are never completely displaced by the more structured technique. The clues are refined and made more discriminative by the formal training in other word recognition skills, but they are still present in mature, adult reading.

Other strategies to promote word recognition are: (1) The use of pictures to provide the association with the printed word. Several studies indicate that it is not essential to have the actual object in the classroom since both boys and girls learn as well with pictures alone. (2) The use of pictures should be discontinued soon after the words are introduced, or actual word recognition is delayed because of the attention to the picture. (3) Children should be given explicit help in identifying inflected forms of known words, for recognition of such does not come automatically (*10*).

Virginia W. Jones has evolved an approach that differs from most common ways of teaching sight words. She has her pupils look through the word from left to right and underline clusters (phonograms) that begin with vowels. The pupils are also taught that closed syllables without an *e* ending are pronounced differently than those that end in *e* (*14*). This last idea is, of course, an extension of the generalization regarding the effect of the final silent *e* on the medial vowel in a word. As the studies cited earlier indicate, this rule is too vague, for it works only about 63 percent of the time.

George H. McNinch was in the habit of teaching his students to reinforce vocabulary development with activities and games (*19*). After repeated contacts with his teachers, he felt that this approach was inadequate. As a result, he devised this more successful program:

1. Present the word in oral context; ask the children to try to do the same.
2. Use the word in sentences or phrases on the chalkboard; underline important clusters, and outline the shape of the word.
3. Write the word in isolation; discuss its features, such as the sound of the first letter or any phonogram present.
4. Have children read the words in the phrases or sentences; correct any errors.
5. Have the children read the word in context in the book.
6. Achieve mastery by activities dealing with the features of the word (as length, beginning letter sounds, rhyming words, its place in categorizing or classifying exercises).

Learning Meaning Vocabulary

Anderson and Freebody point out that there are at least three philosophies of teaching vocabulary (*1*). One they call the Instrumentalist Hypothesis, by which teachers employ lists and drills mainly on isolated words. In other words, those who ascribe to this concept teach "words."

A second concept is called Verbal Aptitude, in which the teachers try to promote vocabulary development through wide reading and emphasis upon language development. Other techniques stressed are introducing and practicing with words in logical contexts, integrated with subject matter, not in isolation or in lists. This belief probably arises from the recognition that high scorers in vocabulary know more of words and have better informational backgrounds. These individuals also have greater fluency in most verbal tasks, probably because of the high relationship between vocabulary knowledge and measured intelligence.

A third way of thinking about vocabulary development is called the Knowledge Hypothesis. This implies that vocabulary words represent in each case a whole mass of related information.

S. Jay Samuels offers his own model of word recognition (23). He believes that the process occurs (1) by using the information contained in the reading passage; (2) by the reader generating hypotheses of what the next word will be; (3) by testing those hypotheses by cues that give at least partial perceptions of letters, word length or configuration; and (4) by accepting or rejecting the hypotheses.

It is apparent that these and other models of word recognition generate relevant teaching approaches. The number and variety of these models tends to account for the diversity of practices in our classrooms. Unfortunately, some of these practices are not productive, yet until we have a universally acceptable model we can expect to see both good and bad vocabulary teaching.

The goals of meaning vocabulary training as suggested by reading textbooks, workbooks, and professional articles are apparently very diverse. Judging by the exercise materials offered in some sources, the primary goal would seem to be the memorization of the meanings of a certain list of words collected by a teacher or author. How realistic is a specific list of a certain number of words that are supposed to be taught at each grade level? Beyond the first thousand or so commonest words in printed or handwritten materials, who really knows just what words most pupils need to learn during a particular school year? In the authors' opinion many lists are offered on very questionable grounds, for there is no agreement among their authors upon the proper sources for compiling such lists. Some lists are drawn from the study of child or adult writing, some by sampling a certain dictionary, others by sampling the textbooks and teaching materials used at a certain grade level. A few lists seem to represent simply the author's concepts of pupils' needs, without reference to any objective criterion. Are the words used in the spontaneous writings of adults, or even those of children, the words most necessary for reading comprehension, or are they really the words children should learn to spell in order to express themselves in writing? While there is an overlap in these two vocabularies, the one that functions in reading must obviously be much larger than the writing vocabulary. How does sampling every *nth* word from a dictionary prove that these are essential for reading success? Of these various sources of words for meaning vocabulary study, only current textbooks and other reading materials would appear to be related realistically to pupil needs for reading development.

Much of the research and training materials seem to be predicated on the assumption that simply enlarging the reading vocabulary by any means is the desired goal. Little attention is paid to the breadth of concepts to which the words are linked. In our opinion, this common approach to vocabulary building can result only in word calling or verbalism, not in the development of words (or ideas) with which the individual thinks.

There is another conflict of opinion among the authors of meaning vocabulary exercises concerning the aims of the exercises. Some authors apparently think that the goal is for pupils to learn the commonest meanings of a certain number of words which may be drawn from a questionable source. Other writers, ourselves included, believe that the training is intended to equip pupils with efficient methods of attacking, analyzing, and comprehending word meanings. This latter group has grave doubts about the validity of most lists of words and about exercises that tend to deal with words apart from meaningful contexts.

Studies from reading clinics and other sources offer strong support for the emphasis upon word analysis skills. The difficulties of poor readers are frequently observed to be due to their lesser skill in word attack, rather than to less exposure to lists of words. Weaknesses in phonic, structural, and contextual analysis are often the basic explanation of the poor sight and meaning vocabularies of these pupils.

Approaches to Training

Olive S. Niles, a secondary school reading specialist, and many others (20) have suggested that meaning vocabulary training must (1) be interesting and challenging to pupils; (2) provide positive reinforcement for learning; (3) be self-pacing or otherwise individualized to pupil needs; (4) stress a wide variety of activities with words, most frequently in contextual settings; and (5) emphasize words of permanent value. These authors also stress the need to teach the multiplicity of meanings of most words, the need to provide for application of the learning in other language activities such as writing and speech, and the need to teach word meanings by a variety of visual, auditory, and kinesthetic experiences with each word.

Probably the best sources of the words to be stressed in meaning vocabulary training are the daily reading and study materials of the classroom, if there is reasonable breadth in these materials. Words from the experience charts, the basals and trade books, as well as the technical vocabularies of the texts are appropriate. Teachers who are unsure of the significant technical terms to be stressed in each content field may make temporary lists based on the glossaries and indexes of their pupils' textbooks and by inspection of the classroom textbooks. To these primary sources may be added children's own lists of the difficult and interesting words they have encountered. It is true that many pupils, even college students, may be unaware of their inability to define or use accurately many of the difficult words they meet. They often just don't know what words they don't know well and fail to add such to their personal lists. But this ignorance may be combated by emphasizing words of permanent value as drawn from readers, textbooks, and the like. Despite their limitations, personal lists provide a necessary element of interest and individuality to word study. Teachers must try to develop an interest in words and stimulate independent study. Teachers should ensure frequent opportunities for pupils to report on findings and progress in building personal lists and for sharing these lists with others.

Several writers stress, and properly so, the desirability of training pupils for a more-or-less systematic approach to new, difficult words. Niles suggests that pupils should be helped to recognize that practically all polysyllabic words fall into one of these types (20):

1. Compound words, as *honeydew, Yellowstone.*
2. Known words with affixes, as *unsystematic, unbreakable.*
3. Familiar syllable is largest recognizable element, as *laboratory, foundation.*
4. Sufficiently nonphonetic to need dictionary, as *louver, ricochet, quay.*

In effect, Niles is suggesting that pupils should analyze a word first by its major elements or most recognizable part; second, by adding to this base word the variations given by their knowledge of the meanings of the affixes; and third, if this analysis plus the context does not lead to recognition of the word, by turning to the dictionary. One author offers a series of steps by which pupils should approach a word for its meaning:

1. Check or underline it. Try to get the meaning from context. Go on reading.
2. Break it up. Try to recognize parts, guess at total meaning.
3. Sound it out. Perhaps then the word may be recalled.
4. Look it up in the dictionary. Pronounce it, note its parts and various meanings. Select the appropriate meaning for the context.

Bernard P. Floriani provides practice in dealing with multiple versions of each new word by (1) adding prefixes and suffixes and using each form of the word in sentences; (2) categorizing the word as a word of action, place, mood, etc.; (3) using the word in multiple-choice sentence completion exercises; and (4) using the word in sentences of varying form—i.e., declarative, interrogative, passive (8).

We should recognize that there is marked support for teaching associations to new vocabulary in the studies contrasting the oral responses of good and poor readers. Good readers give significantly more related associations in response to a group of words even in the first grade. One of the best ways of providing or stimulating associations is through activities in classifying words in as many categories as possible (2).

We must remember that words taught in isolation result in significantly better scores on tests of *words in isolation*. Teaching words with pictures or contexts does not produce such scores. If we were to encounter words in isolation in our reading, then training with isolated words would make sense. But since we do not deal with words apart from contexts, it is apparent that our training should emphasize learning vocabulary in meaningful settings, a practice strongly supported in any of a number of studies (7, 9).

Schwartz explored the strategies that young readers need to acquire meaning vocabulary (26). He found that previewing new words prior to a reading lesson did not help comprehension. The flashcards or chalkboard introduction of the new words so commonly used by teachers did not emphasize the meanings or build the necessary associations. Instead, he suggested that children be taught to rehearse the meanings of words, to categorize them in several ways, and to elaborate on their meanings by free association. These steps would be a deliberate attempt at remembering.

Kaplan and Tuchman ask their pupils to read the titles and headings and then to predict the words that will probably be used in the selection (15). After reading, the pupils compare the accuracy of their predictions and justify their choices. Another strategy is to have the teacher start a period of free association by making a statement such as, "When I think of environment, I think of pollution. What does pollution make you think of?" This continues until ten to twelve words have been explored. The practice can be varied by writing an abstract term from the class reading on the chalkboard and asking for related words. These are written on the board and pupils are asked to use as many of them as they can in a paragraph. A third technique is to ask the pupils to fold their paper into four columns and label the columns in this fashion:

New Words	Predicted Meaning	After Reading	Clue Words
ruler	something used to measure	one who controls	king, crown

Dale D. Johnson has recommended three new strategies for vocabulary development (12):

1. *Semantic association*—Have the children choose two words from today's reading. Write these on the chalkboard and add all the related words they can think of. Discuss the relationships and the meanings.
2. *Semantic mapping*—Select a word central to the story or subject and write it on the chalkboard. As children suggest related words group them in categories labeled with the aid of the class.
3. *Semantic feature analysis*—Begin with a list of words that share some feature, such as tools, written on the chalkboard. Ask children for their features, or things to do with them, such as pound, and cut. Under these as headings, put a plus or minus opposite each word that has or does not have that feature. Ask for other words that have these features, add them to the list and enter pluses or minuses under each categorical heading. Help the children to realize that although many of these words have much in common, none are really synonyms. Thus *synonym* means "something

like," not "the same as." Concrete terms, such as words related to games, occupations, plants, toys, vegetables, etc., are good for the beginning trials in this activity. Later abstract terms such as moods, sizes, shapes, feelings, and the like can be used in similar practice.

Among young pupils, Evelyn B. Spache has suggested another way of approaching semantic mapping (27). She writes the letters H O R S E on the chalkboard. The children are then asked to give words beginning with each letter that are related to a horse, in this fashion.

H	O	R	S	E
heavy	*ornery*	*roan*	*swift*	*elegant*
high	*old*	*rearing*	*sturdy*	
			stallion	

Jenkins et al. reports that short periods of training for poor readers resulted in the acquisition of some word meanings, and more with more training (*11*). Some gain in sentence comprehension appeared, but there were no real gains in comprehension of passages. Perhaps this study is telling us that a single approach or kind of training in vocabulary does not really produce significant reading growth.

Cunningham and Cunningham suggest practice in what they call contextual redefinition (5). The pupils are to try to define a new word; read the sentence again and try again, then verify their definition by the dictionary. We would extend this type of practice to ask pupils to try to tell how they were helped by the context in their definition, and then initiate class discussion of the various answers.

Use of the Dictionary

It is apparent that these systematic habits of word analysis are built upon phonic, structural, and contextual training such as has been outlined earlier. In addition, these approaches imply that pupils have been trained in effective use of the dictionary. This reference tool involves at least two real problems—the vitality of the teaching and the number of subskills involved. Many studies show that stereotyped training in use of the dictionary fails in its purposes. Simply looking up teacher-made or personal lists of words for their meanings does very little to improve vocabulary. Such words are divorced from their contexts and their connotative associations in reading. Furthermore, the practice limits the child's concepts of the values of a dictionary by failing to help him to realize that it may also be a source for assistance in pronunciation, derivation, spelling, and usage. Once the skills needed to handle a dictionary effectively have been taught, further practice should be varied among these possible uses.

Dictionary skills

NEEDED TO LOCATE WORDS

*1. Knowledge of alphabetical order, from A to Z.
*2. Knowledge of alphabetical sequences or relative position of each letter in the entire order, for example, *D* is in the first quarter, *M* is in the middle, *V* is in the last quarter, etc.
*3. Ability to alphabetize by first, first two, or first three letters.
 4. Knowledge of the value of thumb indexes.
*5. Ability to interpret guide words and their clues to alphabetic position, for example, the word *strong* would be found somewhere between the guide words *strange* and *structure.*
 6. Knowledge that derived or inflected forms do not necessarily immediately adjoin the root word, for example, *streaky* may not immediately follow *streak.*
 7. Knowledge that complete meanings may not be given for all inflected or derived forms of root words and that it may therefore be necessary to consult the entry under the root word.
*8. Ability to use cross references.

NEEDED TO DERIVE PRONUNCIATION

*1. Knowledge of consonant and vowel sounds and their combinations, and ability to recognize the symbols for each in the pronunciation key.
 2. Ability to blend letter sounds into syllables or pronunciation units, and these, in turn, into complete words.
*3. Recognize the meanings of common diacritical marks as used to indicate vowel sounds.
 4. Recognize the syllabic divisions and the effect of primary and secondary accents.
 5. Ability in reading phonetic respelling.
 6. Willingness to pronounce word aloud in order to create an auditory memory for it.
 7. Recognition of the possible effect upon pronunciation of words that vary in usage, or in pronunciation of inflected forms, for example, *ac'cent* versus *accent'uate, pro'gress* versus *pro gress'.*

NEEDED TO DERIVE APPROPRIATE MEANING

 1. Ability to comprehend the definitions offered.
 2. Ability in using illustrations, pictures, diagrams, or examples given in comprehending the meaning.
*3. Recognition that a word may have many meanings, that the first definition is neither necessarily relevant to given context nor the most common meaning in some dictionaries.

(continued)

*4. Ability to try several definitions in the given context and to select the most appropriate.
*5. Ability in adapting the appropriate definition to the context in which the word occurs.
*6. Comprehension of the approved usage of the word, as a noun, verb, etc.
  7. Ability to utilize information regarding synonyms and antonyms.

NEEDED FOR USE OF DICTIONARY FOR SPELLING
*1. Knowledge of variant spellings of common sounds.
  2. Knowledge of common silent initial letters, such as *kn, gn, wr, pn.*
  3. Recognition of dictionary's method of handling compounds, separates, hyphenated words, and plurals.
*4. Ability to recognize dictionary's method of indicating syllabic division.
*5. Ability to locate and form plurals.
  6. Ability to understand the treatment of homographs.

NEEDED FOR USE OF DICTIONARY FOR USAGE
*1. Knowledge of meanings of usage terms and abbreviations, for example, *n, t, v.*
  2. Knowledge of functions of various parts of speech, for example, transitive verb denotes action.
  3. Understanding of possibility of multiple functions of a word, as one which may function both as a noun and a verb, for example, *progress.*
*4. Understanding of abbreviations used to indicate standards of usage, for example, *obs (olete), arch (aic), rare, slang.*
  5. Ability to interpret information on idiomatic usages, for example, "pick a bone with."

NEEDED FOR COMPREHENSION OF DERIVATION
*1. Knowledge of meaning of common abbreviations used to indicate etymology, for example, *Lat., Engl.*
  2. Knowledge of meaning of abbreviations used to indicate words or meanings of technical nature, for example *Mus., Chem., Bot., Zool.*

NEEDED FOR PERMANENT LEARNING
  1. Interest in the details of the derivation of the word, its source and history, and variety of meanings.
  2. Forming of several mental associations with known words derived from the same root or bearing some other structural relationship.
  3. Recognition of the effect of the affixes present upon the root word.

(continued)

4. Attention to any unusual orthographic details, such as words that are examples or exceptions to common spelling rules, or that present uncommon spellings of common sounds.

*5. Recognition that a dictionary is a guide, not a rulebook. Also that it reflects and records contemporary usage.

*The starred items were considered most important by a panel of experts according to Mower, M. L. and Barney, L., "Which Are the Most Important Dictionary Skills?" *Elementary English,* 65 (April 1968), 468–471.

Our research with a dictionary test for secondary school pupils indicates that these various skills overlap and interrelate markedly. The abilities to use a dictionary for pronunciation and spelling, and for spelling and derivation, are particularly related, for obvious reasons. Skills in dealing with meanings and derivation are only slightly less interdependent. Perhaps the implication here is that related uses might be taught simultaneously.

A recent article suggests that children prepare their own brief dictionaries, as a slang dictionary, and in so doing learn more about how a dictionary functions. Other interesting variations on this idea are preparing a dictionary with pictures cut from magazines and grouped to illustrate a sound, a setting (a farm), or a theme (transportation). A dictionary may represent a collection of words from the child's personal reading or interests, such as the Civil War, baseball, dog training, or some other subject, with or without pictures. The arrangements within the child's collection of words may be alphabetical or as in many beginning dictionaries, thematic (words that name things, express action). The formality of these dictionaries will, of course, be related to the maturity of the pupils and will range from simple picture collections to productions offering meanings, derivations, and illustrative sentences.

Use of the Context

Earlier we offered an explanation of the role of contextual analysis in word recognition. When the unknown word is within the listening vocabulary of the reader, context analysis functions as an aid in word recognition. When the word is not within the reader's auditory experiences, contextual analysis may continue to be helpful by revealing the probable meaning. Thus even when the reader does not know the word by ear, context may reveal enough of the word meaning to permit comprehending reading.

In the intermediate grades and increasingly thereafter as reading vocabulary exceeds listening vocabulary, context analysis becomes more significant in the development of meaning vocabulary and reading comprehension. It functions not, as some critics of the whole-word or sight method think, as sheer guessing but as a constant tool to inferential derivation of deeper meanings. Among intermediate-grade pupils, exercises such as the following promote greater facility in contextual analysis.

1. Select a half-dozen difficult words from a future reading assignment. Have pupils write their definitions of these words without any exchange of ideas or discussion. After the reading has been completed, permit pupils to correct or revise their earlier definitions. Discuss their reasons for their revisions and their justifications for their final definition. Ask pupils to discuss the ways meanings were clarified by the context.

2. Give a series of sentences using a word in several contextual meanings. Ask pupils to explain the exact meaning of the key word as used in each sentence. For example:

    a. We made the boat *fast* to the dock.

    b. In the morning, we broke our *fast* before beginning the journey.

    c. The horses ran a very *fast* race.

Use the dictionary as a source of these contrasting meanings. If pupils have any difficulty in deriving the various meanings, allow them to use their dictionaries.

3. Vary the second exercise given above by requiring students to attempt to supply a synonym appropriate to the meaning of the key word in each sentence.

4. Duplicate an explanatory or descriptive paragraph from some uncopyrighted teaching materials. Advertisements are almost ideal for this exercise. Choose a paragraph in which a word is used several times. Delete this word in your reproduction. Ask pupils to read the paragraphs and to attempt to supply the missing word. Discuss the various answers offered, their accuracy, and the tendency to introduce synonyms. Ask for explanations of the ways in which they deduced the unknown word.

5. Vary the fourth exercise by inserting a nonsense word in the paragraphs at each point where the key word originally appeared. Before attempting to identify the true word, ask pupils to describe and tell the functions of the nonsense term: What does it look like? What does it do? What action does it have? How do you know? How did the paragraph support these ideas?

6. Give pupils a series of sentences in each of which a key word is underlined. Give also three or four words, one of which means the same as the underlined word. Have the pupils choose the best synonym, and defend their choices.

7. Vary the preceding exercise by supplying a group of sentences in which the underlined word is to be replaced by a synonym supplied by the pupil. Compare and discuss their answers. Use the same exercise in the pupil's own sentences.

These and other exercises in contextual analysis suggested by Spache (27) are intended to strengthen the deductive thinking characteristic of successful use of contextual analysis. Exercises such as the fourth and fifth given above strengthen pupil efforts to deduce probable meanings of an unknown word. The sixth and seventh exercises promote the searching for mental associations, for synonyms, for probable meaning from context which are the heart of this skill.

Learning vocabulary

WHAT WORKS	WHAT DOES NOT WORK
Categorizing or classifying words according to type, function, rhyme, sounds, etc. (7)	Attempting to learn lists of words
Recognizing that the needed writing vocabulary is much smaller than in reading; teaching spelling only of those words children need to communicate	Expecting transfer from one medium to another, e.g., from reading to spelling
Recognizing that words are symbols for ideas or experiences that must often precede the learning of the word	Teaching "vocabulary" or teaching "words"
Fostering vocabulary development by permitting children to read widely and in depth in their areas of interest (1)	Structuring or planning a similar reading program for all
In nontechnical materials, encouraging children to work out new words in each piece of reading, and then reviewing their deductions	Presenting new words by having children pronounce them prior to attempting to read them in context
Presenting, gradually, a word in many contexts that emphasize its many meanings (9)	Teaching a word and its meaning
Recognizing that different children show varying aptitudes in learning modality as visual, auditory, or kinesthetic (13)	Presenting new words in a repeated, static fashion to all the group
Realizing that some children are confused by multisensory impressions of words and would learn better if only one avenue was employed, at least at one time	Assuming that a multisensory presentation of a word is superior to use of a single medium
Helping children to recognize which strategies work best for each of them and then strengthening their use of this technique (15)	Placing dependence for vocabulary growth upon one strategy, as phonics or dictionary use
Recognizing that small words in large words are often not true words and that their pronunciation differs widely from the true word	Teaching children to look for known small words within a new word

(continued)

Stimulating interest in words, collecting interesting words, displaying and discussing them, finding opportunities to use them	Limiting word study to the list offered in a reader or some such source
Offering pictures and actions and relevant adjectives to reinforce lexical words: teaching structural words only in phrases: *to the store, in my desk* (24)	Teaching lexical words (nouns and verbs) in same fashion as structural words (prepositions, conjunctions, etc.)
Trying to build relationships among the words, as *cows* eats *hay*, the *rope* is around the *jug;* including related words, as *moon–night–dark* to strengthen retention of the desired word (24)	Teaching several unrelated new words
Using pictures only in the initial presentations, then practicing without pictures (22,23)	Using pictures as a constant reinforcement to word recognition, as with picture word cards
Strengthening word recognition by variety of exercises in classifying same words (i.e., according to size, color, shape, setting, common word elements, etc.) (2)	Reviewing word recognition largely by workbook exercises emphasizing matching of word and picture
Encouraging children to use only the sound of the first letter and the context to derive the word	Expecting children to react to pattern of separate letters, e.g., spelling patterns
Realizing that word recognition is much more successful in context than in lists (6)	Using a test on a list of words as a final indication of a child's recognition of these
Being aware that a list of commonest words demands differentiated instruction for nouns and verbs than for conjunctions and prepositions, for which a variety of associated meanings is very difficult to assemble	Teaching some list, such as the Dolch, as essential to all future reading (6)
Realizing that long-term learning of words necessitates forming generalizations and associations, as suggested above in this column (16)	Repeating words over and over again as primary strategy for learning
Recognizing that associations are stimulated better when words are heard than when they are seen, as in reading to children, then discussing (21)	Relying on chalkboard presentation of new words as basic technique

(continued

Stimulating deduction from context by the cloze procedure, by discussing their reasons for their choices (24)	Discouraging children from guessing what a word is
Postponing practice in quick recognition until much practice in classification and forming associations has occurred	Moving quickly to rapid drill on words with flash cards, or some machine soon after their initial presentation

Discussion Questions

1. What is your reaction to the current emphasis upon language development in preschool and primary-grade federal and state programs for culturally and linguistically different children? Why is language development thought so significant for reading and school success?

2. How do the authors' basic concepts of pupil learning of words contrast with common classroom methods of stimulating growth in reading vocabulary?

3. Is there really a core or basal vocabulary that children need to know in order to read adequately? What is the best source of such a list—a particular reading series, some word count, the Dolch or Barbe lists, or some other source?

4. Select types of word recognition exercises from workbooks and textbooks that agree or disagree with the viewpoint expressed in this text. Compare and justify these various approaches.

5. What sources should be used for words to be added to the meaning vocabulary of the average pupil in intermediate and upper elementary classrooms?

6. When can it be said that a child "knows" a word? When he or she can read it in context or isolation, or use it in speech and writing, or interpret its multiple meanings, or all of these? When is this process of learning a word completed?

7. Visit a classroom to observe the instruction in vocabulary development. What practices that you see would you question? Why? Share your comments with your classmates.

References

1. Anderson, Richard C., and Freebody, Peter, "Vocabulary Knowledge" in *Comprehension and Teaching: Research Reviews*. Newark, Del.: International Reading Association, 1981, 77–117.
2. Bickley, A. C., Dinnan, James A., and Jones, J. P., "Oral Associates and Reading Readiness," in *Reading: The Right to Paticipate*, Twentieth Yearbook National Reading Conference, 1971, 14–16.

3. Bower, G. H., "Organizational Factors in Memory," *Cognitive Psychology*, 1 (1970), 18–46.
4. Clay, Marie M., "Emergent Reading Behavior." Doctoral dissertation, University of Auckland, New Zealand, 1966.
5. Cunningham, J. W., Cunningham, P. M. and Arthur, S. V., *Middle and Secondary School Reading*. New York: Longman, 1981.
6. Dolch, E. W., *The Dolch Word List*. Champaign, Ill.: Garrard Publishing.
7. Ehri, Linnea C., and Wilce, Lee, "Do Beginners Learn to Read Words Better in Sentences or in Lists?" *Reading Research Quarterly*, 15 (1980), 451–476.
8. Floriant, Bernard P., "Word Expansions for Multiplying Sight Vocabulary," *Reading Teacher*, 33 (November 1979), 156–157.
9. Gipe, Joan P., "Use of a Relevant Context Helps Kids Learn New Word Meanings," *Reading Teacher*, 33 (January 1980), 398–402.
10. Hillerich, Robert L., "Recognition Vocabularies: A Research-Based Caution," *Elementary School Journal*, 81 (May 1981), 313–318.
11. Jenkins, J. R. et al. "Vocabulary and Reading Comprehension: Instructional Effects." Technical Report 100. University of Illinois, 1978, ED 160 999.
12. Johnson, Dale D., "Three Sound Strategies for Vocabulary Development," *Ginn Occasional Papers*, No. 3.
13. Jones, John Paul, *Intersensory Transfer, Perceptual Shifting, Modal Difference and Reading*. ERIC/CRIER and International Reading Association, 1972.
14. Jones, Virginia D., *Decoding and Learning to Read*. Portland, Ore.: Northwest Regional Laboratory, 1970.
15. Kaplan, Elaine, and Tuchman, Anita, "Vocabulary Strategies Belong in the Hands of Learners," *Journal of Reading*, 24 (October 1980), 32–35.
16. Lane, John Manning Jr., "Verbalization and Learning of Paired Associates," in *Reading: The Right to Participate*. Twentieth Yearbook National Reading Conference, 1971, 272–282.
17. MacKinnon A. R., *How Do Children Learn to Read*. Toronto: Copp/Clark, 1959.
18. Manzo, A. V. and Sherk, John K., "Some Generalizations and Strategies for Guiding Vocabulary Learning," *Journal of Reading Behavior*, 4 (Winter 1971–1972), 78–89.
19. McNinch, George H., "A Method for Teaching Sight Words to Disabled Readers," *Reading Teacher*, 35 (December 1981), 269–272.
20. Niles, Olive S., "Improving General Vocabulary," *High School Journal*, 39 (December 1955), 147–155.
21. Reynolds, Richard J., "Effects of Modality on Response in Word Association Tasks," in *Reading: The Right to Participate*. Twentieth Yearbook National Reading Conference, 1971, 300–303.
22. Samuels, S. Jay, "Attentional Process in Reading: The Effect of Pictures on the Acquisition of Reading Responses," *Journal of Educational Psychology*, 58 (1967), 337–342.
23. Samuels, S. Jay, "Effects of Pictures on Learning to Read, Comprehension and Attitudes," *Review of Educational Research*, 40 (June 1970), 397–407.
24. Samuels, S. Jay, and Chen, C. C., "Comparison of Word Recognition in Strategies of Adults and Children," in *Reading: The Right to Participate*. Twentieth Yearbook National Reading Conference, 1971, 73–77.

25. Schubert, Delwyn G., "Reading Games: Why, How, When," *Elementary English*, 36 (October 1959), 422–423.
26. Schwartz, Robert M., "Strategic Processes in Beginning Reading," *Journal of Reading Behavior*, 9 (Spring 1977), 17–26.
27. Spache, Evelyn B., *Reading Activities for Child Involvement*. Boston, Mass.: Allyn and Bacon, 1982.
28. Spear, Olga B., and Lamb, George S., "First Grade Reading Ability and Fluency in Naming Symbols," *Reading Teacher*, 29 (March 1976), 572–576.
29. Stetson, Elton G., "Rating Scale for the Dolch List of 220 Basic Sight Words." Unpublished paper, Diagnostic Learning Center, University of Houston.
30. Wolpert, Edmund M., "Modality and Reading: A Perspective," *Reading Teacher*, 24 (April 1971), 640–643.

Resources for the Teacher

Professional References

Dale, Edgar, O'Rourke, Joseph, and Bamman, Henry A., *Techniques of Teaching Vocabulary*. Palo Alto, Calif.: Field Educational Publications, 1971. An extensive collection of illustrative activities and exercises.

Dale, Edgar, Glanze, Walter D., and O'Rourke, Joseph, *The World Book Complete Word Power Library*. Chicago, Ill.: World Book–Childcraft International, 1981. A guide to writing and speaking, a treasury of quotations are offered in the first volume. Second volume contains a word-builder guide of self-help exercises and a word finder thesaurus.

Johnson, Dale D., and Pearson, P. David, *Teaching Reading Vocabulary*. New York: Holt, Rinehart and Winston, 1978. Includes instructional activities and discussion of sight and meaning vocabulary, phonics, structural analysis, contextual analysis, and types of vocabulary.

Instructional Materials

Sight Word Vocabulary

Dolch, E. W., *Basic Sight Word Cards*. Champaign, Ill.: Garrard Publishing.

Dolch, E. W., *Group Word Teaching Games*. Champaign, Ill.: Garrard Publishing.

Dolch, E. W., *Match*. Champaign, Ill.: Garrard Publishing.

Dolch, E. W., *Picture Word Cards*. Champaign, Ill.: Garrard Publishing.

Dolch, E. W., *Popper Words*. Champaign, Ill.: Garrard Publishing.

Dolch, Marguerite P., and Astrofsky, Lillian, *My Puzzle Books, I and II*. Champaign, Ill.: Garrard Publishing.

Essential Sight Words Program. Hingham, Mass.: Teaching Resources Corp. Two kits of pre- and posttests by hand tachistoscope, worksheets, mastery tests, and books with vocabulary parallel to their basic word list.

Other Way Words. Long Branch, N.J.: Kimbo Educational. An LP and guide to help children with opposite concepts. Ditto masters are available.

Prime Vocabulary Lessons for Dolch Sight Words. Port Washington, N.Y.: Prime Learning.

Wordplay Vocabulary Program. Long Branch, N.J.: Kimbo Educational Co. Film-strips, cassettes, and two storybooks to teach basic vocabulary.

Meaning Vocabulary

Building Word Power. Chicago, Ill.: Coronet. Cassettes and worksheets on word origins and word parts. For upper elementary.

Carney, John et al., *Words We Use.* Chicago, Ill.: Benefic Press. An eight book series for kindergarten to sixth grade to build word attack, word meaning and dictionary skills.

Crossword Puzzles for Reading–Thinking Skills. Elizabethtown, Pa.: Continental Press. One workbook for each of first six grades in duplicating master edition.

D'Abre, Therese, *Vocabulary Classification Exercises.* North Billerica, Mass.: Curriculum Associates. A spirit-master book for grades six to nine.

Forest, Robert G., *Learning Words by Classifying.* North Billerica, Mass.: Curriculum Associates. A spirit-master workbook using the dictionary to define words, and in writing sentences explaining word relationships. For grades five to nine.

Forest, Robert G., *Precise Word: Multi-Meaning.* North Billerica, Mass.: Curriculum Associates. Activity cards presenting words similar in meaning that can be distinguished by the definitions.

Forest, Robert G., *Word Squares and Word Opposites.* North Billerica, Mass: Curriculum Associates. Word puzzles stressing synonyms or opposites.

Forte, Imogene, and Pangle, Mary A., *Vocabulary Magic.* Nashville, Tenn.: Incentive Publications, 1977.

Friedland, Joyce and Kessler, Rikki, *Lessons in Vocabulary Development.* North Billerica, Mass.: Curriculum Associates. Groups of words with related meanings, tests, and teacher's guide.

Reading–Thinking Skills. Elizabethtown, Pa.: Continental Press. Two workbooks or duplicating masters for each grade one to six. Emphasize classification, word meanings, inferences, relationships, and organization.

Reading Vocabulary Laboratories. New York: Holt Instructional. Five kits of exercises for grade three to junior high.

Scinto, Joyce, *Context Phonetic Clues.* North Billerica, Mass.: Curriculum Associates. Approaches vocabulary building by grouping words by their phonograms and meanings. For grades three to six.

Taylor, Stanford E., Frackenpohl, Helen, and McDonald, Arthur S., *EDL Word Clues.* New York: McGraw-Hill/Educational Developmental Laboratories. Programs in vocabulary development through context clues for grades seven up.

Useful Words II. North Billerica, Mass.: Curriculum Associates. Forty spirit masters to stress functional vocabulary related to the telephone, driving, applications, health services, and labels.

Vocabulary Mastery. Chicago, Ill.: Benefic Press. Duplicating masters for grades three to eight with variety of exercises.

Vocabulary Skills Center. North Billerica, Mass.: Curriculum Associates. A kit of skillbooks, activity cards and spirit masters for intermediate grades.

Word Learning Stories. Chicago, Ill.: Coronet. Cassettes and workbooks for primary grades emphasizing core vocabulary in a narrative setting.

Dictionary

Cory, Beverly, *Word Meaning.* Belmont, Calif.: Pitman Learning. Dictionary and vocabulary exercises for intermediate grades.

Dictionary Skills Series. Englewood Cliffs, N.J.: Scholastic Book Services. Books for each two grades from two to six with activities and puzzles.

Lucken, Jean Albrecht, *Activities for Dictionary Practice.* North Billerica, Mass.: Curriculum Associates. A spirit-master thirty-page book.

Morley, Stevan-Adele, *Dimensions of a Word.* North Billerica, Mass.: Curriculum Associates. Word study based on the dictionary emphasizing the many functions words can have.

Moquin, L. Doris, and Nunes, Agnes, *Dictionary Skills.* North Billerica, Mass.: Curriculum Associates. Fifty-five self-directing exercises in use of a dictionary for intermediate grade pupils. Available in spirit-master form.

Rosenbauer, Donna, *Explaining Language with the Dictionary.* Englewood Cliffs, N.J.: Prentice-Hall. A four book series for grades three to six emphasizing location, function, application, and extension.

14 Developing Comprehension Strategies

The term "comprehension" is one that is used glibly by many teachers and reading experts. Yet the meaning given the word differs greatly from one user to the next. Despite the research analyses of the process, comprehension is often hypothesized as a long list of subskills. The logical assumption is then made that each of these skills must be practiced separately—that eventually all the skills will function simultaneously while the individual is reading. Some teachers stress a certain few of these subskills; other teachers emphasize others. Both are quite sure, however, that they are promoting the development of comprehension.

Recent studies by tests and interviews are beginning to raise questions about this multiplicity of comprehension subskills. It appears that what the readers retain while reading reflects such influences as (1) their purpose in reading or what they intend to retain; and (2) the instructions they are given before reading, which may lead them to find only the precise answers to specific questions or to secure a broader comprehension if the questions are more general (3). Comprehension is affected even more, however, by the pattern of questions the children learn to anticipate. They learn to read with only those types of thinking that the teacher's questions demand. Since teachers' questions appear to be limited in type and depth, children's thinking (or comprehension) tends to be superficial and stereotyped, and lack critical thinking.

Interviews of students with good and poor comprehension reveal one other significant element. This is the degree of involvement of the readers, their interaction with the author's ideas, the depth and variety of the associations they react with to the material. Active reacting to reading is, again, a habit promoted by classroom practices that foster stimulating, interesting follow-up to children's reading. Thus, again, it seems that the comprehension achieved by pupils is largely determined by what associations the teacher stimulates.

Defining Comprehension

Since the fourth edition of this book, there has been a tremendous development of interest in comprehension. Dozens of authors have offered definitions or models of comprehension varying widely in their interpretation of this reading behavior. There is still a group of experts who define comprehension in terms of what are supposed to be separate reading skills. Indeed the number of these skills has apparently grown in some management systems far beyond the thirty to fifty that were popular in the literature of the mid 1970s. Other writers seem to have consolidated their lists of comprehension skills. For example, Wayne Otto, one of the authors of the Wisconsin Design for Reading Improvement, enumerates only forty-one comprehension tasks for the first six grades in his textbook.

Dolores Durkin described comprehension simply as something the teacher does to aid children in dealing with more than a single word (9). But this behavior is still defined by reading tests largely in such outcomes of reading as main ideas, conclusions, details and inferences, etc. Tests do not attempt to sample the cognitive or thinking processes of readers, despite all the emphasis upon this aspect of comprehension in the current literature. They do not try to separate the influence of experiential background from the measurement of information gained from the reading, as some writers feel they must in order to sample readers' true comprehension ability. Some definitions of comprehension are very lengthy and complex; others use the oversimplified cliché of what students understand or can retell when they finish.

But the important questions that we should be reviewing are what teachers believe about comprehension; what basal reader manuals that guide the instruction of a great many teachers say about learning comprehension; and what teachers actually do to promote comprehension development.

What Do Teachers Believe?

Jean M. Greenlaw and Ruth J. Kurth reported an attempt to sample teachers' beliefs on the nature of comprehension (15). By questionnaire, graduate teachers were asked to rank eight simplified definitions of comprehension. Elementary and secondary teachers were involved and offered similar opinions. First choice in the total group of teachers was the substrata factor model—reading is a reasoning process in which thinking skills interact in a hierarchical pattern. The second choice was the intellectual functions model—reading is an intellectual process much akin to thinking and a way of making predictions based on evidence presented. The teachers surveyed rejected strongly the communication model—reading comprehension is the same as language comprehension.

Several other models, including one emphasizing the chunking of information, the psycholinguistic model, and the skills model were all ranked poorly. An information processing model (reading is a precise processing of information with exact, detailed sequential perception and identification of letters, words, spelling patterns, and large language units) was a second choice of elementary teachers.

It is apparent that the current emphasis upon the thinking or cognitive aspect of comprehension has been absorbed and accepted by today's teachers. The low ranking of the skills model is quite surprising in view of its total acceptance in present management systems, now extant and, of course, in the basal reader manuals used by the majority of elementary teachers. Perhaps the information processing model as defined by Greenlaw and Kurth has displaced the quite parallel skills model.

With regard to teacher attitudes toward a skills development definition of comprehension, Sterl A. Artley's article is quite apropos. Like the present authors, Artley decries the overemphasis in many instructional materials upon picayune skills promoted by the behaviorist school of learning. Artley feels this concept and practice has reinforced the ideas of accountability, management systems, and the like. As his interviews with children demonstrate, reading has become in many quarters the act of completing exercises, the purple monsters (dittoes) and worksheets until "reading isn't fun" (any more) (1). Apparently many teachers are beginning to share this viewpoint of skill development programs which so monopolize the reading period that no actual sustained reading is possible.

A quotation from Mason, Osborn, and Rosenshine seems relevant here (26): "General reading comprehension cannot be reliably subdivided into subskills, not even into the skill of deriving implicit meaning and the skill of deriving explicit meaning." Yet the bulk of what is considered training in comprehension in our classrooms consists of teacher questions, worksheets, or workbooks that stress specific comprehension "subskills."

What Do Teachers Teach?

The crucial question that arises from this exploration of teachers' apparent rejection of the skills model and acceptance of the intellectual aspects of comprehension is whether their instructional practices follow their beliefs. In looking for the answer, there are several dramatic studies of teachers' comprehension instruction practices. Dolores Durkin and her assistants observed fourth-grade teachers during their reading periods (9). They tried to categorize teacher time spent on comprehension and study skills. They made the shocking discovery that the greatest amount of class time was concerned with assessment by questions or worksheets (17.7 percent of the period). Such practices as review of instruction, application, prediction, and study skills instruction *were completely missing* from the teachers' practices. Less than 6 percent was spent, on the average, on help to children with the worksheets or on the preparation of the group for understanding the reading selection. Any application of the assignment occupied less than 1 percent of the period. Some silent and oral reading was present in small proportions, but even then the oral reading alone took more time than anything to do with comprehension except for the postreading assessment. Comprehension instruction (how to read) was deemed seldom sustained, or coherent, or well organized. Learning behaviors were defined to the children or mentioned in passing, but seldom illustrated, explained, or practiced. In social studies lessons, the situation was much the same—more time listening to oral reading than any comprehension activity except help with the assignment; e.g., clarifying the mechanics or directions.

One reviewer of Durkin's study objected to her definition of comprehension instruction and claimed that when her data was rearranged according to his definition, 23 percent of the teacher lesson was spent on comprehension instruction. He agreed, however, with Durkin's observation that instructional procedures were scanty and that questioning by the teacher was the most time-consuming practice.

Kurth and Greenlaw conducted a parallel study of teachers' comprehension activities in a broader sampling of elementary grades, kindergarten, second, fourth, and sixth grades (22). These researchers used categories paralleling Durkin's but somewhat more broadly defined. They found an average of 33 percent of the period spent in some form of comprehension instruction, 35 percent on phonics and structural analysis, 8 percent on silent reading, 4 percent on oral reading, 19 percent on transitional and non-instructional activities (preparing for a new lesson, distributing and collecting materials, etc.). Comprehension assessment occupied 20 percent of class time, and was the most time-consuming single activity, as Durkin found. This assessment practice plus checking assignments plus aiding children with the assignment took up 47 percent of the total class time. They certainly must be deemed important reading activities by teachers.

Jana M. Mason observed in third and fourth grade classes (27). In only five of 110 classroom lessons was there introduction to the text, oral or silent reading, plus discussion of the text—elements Mason feels are essential. Most lessons included only one or two of these basic components of a reading lesson. Seventy-five to 80 percent of the instruction included such minutiae as giving directions for, supervising, or checking the accuracy of the pupils in worksheets, skillsheets, or workbooks. She did not try to identify what portion of a lesson was given to what the other researchers called comprehension training. But obviously it was a minor element of the lessons.

These observational studies show that despite their claimed belief in comprehension as an intellectual or thinking task, elementary teachers do almost nothing to promote their children's cognitive skills. The comprehension activities, such as they are, are almost exclusively the answering of teachers' questions and the completing of worksheets or pages in workbooks. Teachers may claim that they are stimulating their children's thinking by the questions they ask. However, teachers are not skilled in questioning nor in stimulating higher level thinking such as evaluation, explanation, or translation.

By taping teachers' questions in classrooms, Guszak tried to categorize their types, the proportions answered correctly by the pupils, and the sequences of questions and responses that were common (16). He found that recall of memory questions formed 66.5 percent in second grade, 48.4 percent in fourth grade, and 47.6 percent in sixth grade. Other types of questions, such as translation, explanation, and evaluation, were not used more than about once in every five questions. Moreover, the evaluation questions were quite superficial, for they usually demanded no more than a "yes" or "no" answer.

Pupils' accuracy in answering questions was greatest in the second grade, perhaps because so many questions demanded only recall of details. In the intermediate grades, teachers often accepted incorrect answers from the children because they themselves could not recall so many details from the selections. The most frequent pattern of question–response was simply a direct, correct answer to the teacher's question, accounting for more than half of the pupil–teacher interactions. Other common interactions were those in which a teacher offered a guiding remark or question and then, without waiting for a response, asked a second direct question. Sometimes teachers asked for verification of an answer from the textbook, or justification of a response by the pupil or by other pupils. Guszak concluded his observations of teacher questioning strategies with the remark, "About the only thing that appears to be programmed into the students is the nearly flawless ability to anticipate the trivial nature of the teachers' literal questions...the students have learned well to parrot back an endless recollection of trivia" (*16*, p. 234).

How Are Teachers Guided by Basal Manuals and Textbooks?

Some, particularly the authors of basal reader manuals, would insist that more diverse, more challenging questions are offered to teachers, if they would only follow the manuals. Two studies of the comprehension instructional advice in basal series have been made. Using the same definition as in her observational study, Durkin analyzed the manuals of five widely used basal reading series (*10*). She discovered that actual instruction to teachers on how to teach comprehension comprised the smallest number of suggestions in these manuals. Advice regarding reviewing assignments was very irregularly, almost randomly, offered, but appeared five times as often as directions for teaching comprehension in some series.

Application suggestions were two to five times as frequent as techniques of teaching comprehension, largely, Durkin thinks, because the authors thought that was instruction rather than assessment. Practice was suggested four times as much as application in some manuals. Preparation of the pupils to understand the readings and to be able to relate their former learnings to the ideas to be read was very variable from one basal to the other, although it was mentioned three or four times as often as application. Assessment received the greatest emphasis, which may explain why teachers overemphasize this practice. The instructions in the manuals dealt with graphic signals most, then sentences and smaller word groups, then signal words, language functions, and passage comprehension. They dealt least with possession and anaphora (referents). Most of these suggestions to teachers were about a sentence long:

- *Graphic signals*—Exclamation mark suggests emotion or excitement. A period is something that shows where a sentence ends.
- *Signal words*—*As* and *like* suggest a comparison.
- *Language functions*—Details are for the purpose of conveying a clear idea or picture.

- *Sentence*—Adding *not* to a sentence gives it opposite meaning.
- *Smaller word groups*—Differently worded phrases may have the same meaning.
- *Passage comprehension*—The first sentence in a paragraph may express its main idea.

The authors of basals apparently consider these terse pronouncements to be instructions to the teacher, even though the teacher hasn't taught the pupils what a sentence is! Durkin concluded that the connection between what is being taught in instruction and how to read is almost entirely overlooked in basal reader manuals. Who can blame teachers for the paucity of their comprehension instruction?

The second analysis of the instructional practices in basal reader systems was reported by Johnson and Barrett (20). Using their own checklist of important comprehension behaviors or tasks, they found that those starred in the list below were practically nonexistent in four basal reader series at the third and fifth grades.

*Paraphrase	Fact and opinion
*Association	Bias
Main idea, details	Author's craft
Comparison	*Mental images
*Figurative language	Study skills
*Ambiguous statements	Reality and fantasy
Causal relations	*Punctuation
Sequences	Literary form
*Anaphora	

Some of their terms need definition: *association* means discerning and discarding irrelevant statements; *paraphrase* means that children can recognize the equivalence in meaning in two or more sentences, or can summarize in their own words; anaphora implies that pupils can realize the relationship between an anaphoric term (substitute) like a pronoun, and its antecedent. The remaining reading tasks are self-explanatory.

The unstarred comprehension tasks were mentioned, but hardly implemented. Unfortunately for comparison with the Durkin study, this report did not discriminate between direct teacher instruction in these tasks and worksheet exercises. Johnson and Barrell's general conclusion was that the teacher's questions can be just assessment, as Durkin observed, or instructional strategy to help pupils read more critically (although this last half of the conclusion can hardly be justified by their data).

From basal manuals, Johnson and Barrett turned to reading textbooks to determine what instructions were being given teachers from this source. They found that the textbook authors emphasized main ideas and details, sequences, causal relations, and comparison and making judgments. Two authors mentioned paraphrasing and processing anaphoric relations. Only one spoke of sentence ambiguity. All five recommended teaching study skills; four of the five spoke of literary form and the author's craft. To Johnson and Barrett's chagrin, none of the textbook authors referred to association, figurative language, fact and opinion, bias, mental images, reality and fantasy, or punctuation. If Johnson and Barrett's seventeen comprehension tasks are important, and there may be some doubt of this, it is apparent that neither the authors of basal manuals or textbooks agree with them, or with each other.

Strategies to Improve Comprehension

The study of how to teach comprehension has turned aside almost completely from noting the characteristics of the reader such as the degree of response or involvement with the material read; the reader's beliefs, attitudes, and prejudices; the use of inappropriate rate for the difficulty of the reading matter and the effect of the overemphasis upon word analysis. The studies cited earlier reveal that most classroom emphasis and the manuals that accompany basal reader systems stress assessment of pupil comprehension almost entirely by teacher questioning or worksheets. Actual classroom instruction in how to achieve comprehension is quite deficient according to these studies.

Lacking this kind of information, we formerly believed that the problem was a lack of variety and depth in teachers' postreading questions. Hence in earlier editions of this text, we tried to stimulate teachers in their assessments and thus aid children's development of their cognitive skills. Today we know that this approach is inadequate and, in fact, may have contributed to the overuse of questioning as the major classroom activity related to comprehension.

Recent experimental studies of instruction in comprehension may be grouped into three categories: background knowledge or schemata, as it is currently called; reasoning skills; and organizational strategies during reading (19).

Background Knowledge or Schemata

A *schema* (the new "buzz word") may be described as a data structure for representing the general concepts stored in memory. Or, after Rumelhart, a schema is all the ideas (words) related to a single word or concept, as *buy* (purchase, sell, merchandise, money, trade, bargaining, etc.) (34). Schemata are constantly being revised and adjusted as the reader receives and stores new information about the world.

According to current theory, teachers should assess schema availability (sample children's related memories and experiences) before reading. Then they should help the pupils to relate to and make sense of the text by making analogies, comparisons, recognizing principles, giving related examples, etc.

Association and categorization tasks should be used to aid pupils to focus on relevant schema (to bring their background into consciousness). Semantic mapping or a visual outline of the main ideas will enable the readers to recognize the implicit relationships. This whole idea of prereading preparation of pupils for comprehension was once called reading readiness and was supposed to be an integral part of every reading lesson. Perhaps the current emphasis and the many detailed suggestions being offered will stimulate teachers to resume their prereading activities.

Organizational Strategies. Many writers have stressed the importance of background information for comprehension, for reading is a matter of integrating the textual and the background data. Among the techniques that have been used to promote this integration are "advance organizers," or material intended to relate what readers already know to what they need to know to learn from the reading matter. Often these organizers take the form of an overview of the content of the reading passage, or a summary of what readers might know that is relevant to comprehending the passage. Results with this technique have been inconsistent. Perhaps the organizers failed to aid the readers because the instructor did not help them to relate the new knowledge to the old; or the readers may not have had the knowledge that the organizer was providing and hence the technique did not augment comprehension. Or, perhaps readers did not always see the relevance of the advance organizer to the concepts of the passage. For whatever reasons, advance organizers are not now thought to represent an important aid to comprehension (*19*).

Reasoning Skills. Other efforts to influence comprehension have been based on a model of generative learning (*24*). The model suggests that when readers build relationships, first between the text and their schemata, and second among the parts of the text, comprehension is enhanced. Pupils are stimulated to generate associations, abstractions, inferences, text relevant summary sentences, headings, main ideas, critical comments, and evaluations. The question that arises about this model and its implementation is not whether all these teacher-directed activities would produce better comprehension. Rather we wonder whether pupils will spontaneously continue to employ these procedures and show long-range growth in comprehension.

Another approach to utilizing pupils' schemata to predict events in a story was explored by Hansen (*17*). She included practice in answering questions that required inference between the text and the readers' schemata before the reading. In other words, pupils were asked to predict events in the story based on their previous experiences. Although this practice was successful in dealing with simple basal stories, the improvement in comprehension did not transfer to more difficult readings.

The pupils made specific predictions of the probable concepts or events in the reading. Choosing two of these more difficult concepts, Hansen proposed two questions about each focused on children's previous experiences, and then asked for a second prediction from the children. These prereading activities improved the pupils' performances in both literal and inferential post-reading questions. Was it the prereading questions or the discussion of related children's experiences that promoted better comprehension? Both are known to have positive effects.

Pictures. Pictures closely related to the text may serve to provide schemata and hence enhance comprehension (*19*). Pictures may be helpful in acquiring information, but do little to aid children in learning to read. Used before or during reading as a basis of class discussion, pictures can help prepare pupils to gain information and to anticipate story concepts or events.

Speeded Decoding. Several authors agree that a high level of speed or automaticity in decoding is a strong aid to comprehension (*11*). Whereas it is true that good and poor comprehenders differ in the speed with which they decode single words, this difference has not been shown to be a significant influence upon comprehension. Speeded isolated word training does not affect comprehension, nor does word drill on all the words of a selection, according to several studies.

Repeated Reading. Rereading of the same selection as practiced in one study for a full year did appear to produce greater fluency, better oral reading, and quicker word recognition, as well as significantly better comprehension. The reading in context as well as the duration of this study may have helped the children to achieve better organizational skills in handling complex sentences as well as fluency.

Vocabulary. Whereas factor analyses of the reading process show word knowledge to be almost as significant as the reasoning factor, it is very difficult to show that vocabulary instruction affects comprehension. For example, experiments in teaching contextual analysis, roots and affixes, concept development, meanings of specific words in context, telling word meanings to children when they are reading orally, relating words to common experiences, and providing practice in applying word meanings have not been shown to affect passage comprehension, although some of these procedures do influence sentence comprehension (*28*).

In contrast, drilling on synonyms or practicing generating meanings for a word newly learned in oral reading seemed to produce better inferential comprehension, but not better literal comprehension. An approach involving a known key word that has a sound or clang association with a new word, such as *supply–surplus*, seemed to be quite effective with young children. But whether this technique will effect comprehension remains to be shown (*8*).

Cloze. The task of deducing omitted words in a continuous context called cloze has grown to have a number of classroom applications. It has become an informal measure of several types of comprehension, a technique for vocabulary development, and a way of teaching contextual clues. More recently it has been explored as a means of improving comprehension. The results of these studies are not consistent in indicating comprehension expansion. But one group of studies in predicting words that could logically follow in a sentence, called hypothesis-test training, reported improved comprehension in most cases. This is the basic task in using cloze.

Among third-grade students, an instructional cloze center was substituted for various reading centers for a fifteen-week period. The pupils read and responded to cloze selections and then discussed and compared answers in terms of their semantic and syntactic fitness in the context. An experimental group did significantly better than the control group in posttests of comprehension and in divergent production of answers to a final cloze test. No differences appeared in vocabulary development (35). In all probability, the interaction between teacher and pupils was a major contributor to the pupils' development.

Chunking. Practice in combining sentences to learn how to deal with those of increasing complexity and unscrambling sentence anagrams have been tried with mixed results in improving comprehension. These activities were intended to facilitate "chunking" of information while reading. Students' awareness of larger linguistic units and fluency in dealing with language are supposed to be improved by this training, according to this theory of the reading process (38, 40).

Teaching Subskills. Today most of the classroom activities are devoted to subskill instruction, which is really practice, not instruction. Pupils are supposed to learn "finding the main idea," "drawing inferences," etc., for hundreds of such concepts. Repeated practice in the management worksheets or the workbooks, it is believed by most teachers and basal authors, will produce learning of these tasks. But none of the studies that report success in their experiments offer any evidence that these subskills improve comprehension in general reading. Children can and will learn these specific "comprehension skills" but without any effect on their overall comprehension.

Imagery. Teaching children to employ imagery, to draw stick figures or cartoons to depict action, and to discuss their imagery with peers and the teacher seems to have some effect upon comprehension above the fourth grade for some pupils. However, in one study the pupils did not spontaneously continue to employ the strategy after training unless reminded to do so. Other limitations to this practice are the lack of concrete references in some selections, the difficulty some students have in calling forth imagery, the negative effect of mental retardation, and the interference of decoding problems. Even when practiced while reading, the effects were quite small (19, 23).

Summarizing. Another effort to aid children in elaborating on the text involved writing summary sentences after each paragraph in a story. The practice appeared to improve comprehension in a reading posttest and a cloze test, particularly for lower ability students. We think the efficacy of this strategy could be improved by feedback from discussion with peers and teacher regarding the paraphrasing. Certainly this approach should be attempted with a wide variety of pupil ages and abilities to explore its value more thoroughly. Moreover, an attempt should be made to determine whether pupils adopt the summarizing as a permanent aid to study.

Top-structure. A series of studies have explored the values of teaching students to recognize the structure of authors' schemata (paragraph structure) (3, 24). Ninth-grade students were taught to identify the "top-level structure," as it is now termed, in expository texts and to use the structures to organize their own written recall. The students soon learned to recognize the structures (problem-solution, comparison, cause–effect, description, listing) and they recalled twice as much information as untrained students. Good readers were particularly successful in recognizing the authors' strategies and using the same strategies in their recall. In another study, this type of training was extended downward to elementary children (*14*). Their comprehension as well as the writing of their own stories was improved, as they learned about the structures underlying types of stories.

Pupil Questions. One author proposes what he calls "active comprehension," by which he means questions by the children deliberately promoted by the teacher. After a question such as "What question could you ask from the title?" this writer would have the teacher say, "Who would like to answer that question? Does anyone have a different answer?" Or the class could take turns pretending to be the teacher, to initiate questioning. The writer claims that pupils who ask each other questions in this fashion score significantly higher in achievement.

In one study at the third grade, pupils were taught to ask *wh* (who, when, where, what, why) questions. They began with the question, "What is the story about?" They read to answer and then tried to generate two more *wh* questions. The teacher felt that most of the children learned this strategy and improved in comprehension (5).

This self-questioning technique is not a new idea, for some version of it has long been taught to secondary and college students (the *SQRRR* or *PQRST*). Anderson modified it by asking his students to frame a question demanding the main idea of each paragraph (*1*). As we might guess, this technique proved to be too time-consuming and boring. Other variations were having students ask each other questions, and forming pairs or teams to question each other. The author did not offer any evidence that these self-questioning practices improved comprehension among elementary pupils.

Story Problem. In attempting to improve comprehension in reading fiction, one teacher tried to teach her pupils to recognize the central story problem (main idea) that she feels is present even in basal stories. The pupils' schemata are stimulated by discussion of problems and solutions in their experiences, or inferred from other stories. These ideas are categorized as wanting or needing, feelings, thinking the wrong thing, thinking something different. Models from similar stories are then cited. The pupils give their interpretations of what or who wants, feels, needs, or is thinking, and these responses are discussed. Then a chalkboard chart is drawn:

Central Story Problem	Solution
Ways of acting that were part of the problem	Ways of acting that were part of the solution

This chart is completed as the group reads. By this approach, the author believes that children learn to recognize the central story problem, to evaluate central characters, to recognize ways of solving problems and types of solutions, and to recognize stories with single or multiple problems (30).

Story Grammar. Nancy Marshall uses what is called story grammar to evaluate pupil reading comprehension (25). She makes the checklist shown below, and allows one pupil to retell the story while the group adds to his or her account as she asks the appropriate questions.

Results with this highly detailed probing of story organization are mixed, and Marshall does not give any supporting evidence of its benefits for comprehension, or of the transfer of such analytic thinking to nonfiction materials.

Story grammar checklist

- *Theme*—What is the major point? What is the moral point? What did _____ learn at the end?
- *Setting*—Where does the story happen? When did it happen?
- *Character*—Who is the main character? What is he like?
- *Initiating events*—What is _____'s problem? What does _____ have to try to do?
- *Attempts*—What did _____ do about? What will _____ do now?
- *Resolution*—How did _____ solve the problem? What would you do to solve _____'s problem?
- *Reactions*—How did _____ feel about the problem? Why did _____ do _____? How did _____ feel at the end? Why did _____ feel that way? How would you feel about _____?

Critical Reading. A three-day study is reported of an attempt to teach certain aspects of critical reading to fifth-graders. The pupils were given three rules to guide their judgments:

1. Just because you know about the part doesn't mean you know about the whole thing.

2. Just because two things happen together doesn't mean that one causes the other.
3. Just because an important person in one area says something is good in another area, you can't be sure it's true.

Our readers will probably recognize these statements as the propaganda devices commonly called overgeneralization, post hoc ergo propter hoc, and testimonials.

After direct individualized instruction, the pupils' ability to read critically was significantly better than a control group exposed to the same training through the medium of a workbook (31). Just what the authors hoped to accomplish of a permanent nature in three days of tutoring is quite obscure. There is little doubt that intermediate-grade and older students can be taught to recognize and deal with a number of the "tricks of the trade" present in advertisements, political speeches and elsewhere. But such improvements take extended training in a wide variety of readings.

Another study using television commercials as lesson content also claimed success in increasing critical reading (6). The author claims that the children were able to transfer their critical attitudes to other media such as comic books and newspapers.

Anaphora. Several authors have emphasized the need for helping pupils to understand anaphoric relationships; i.e. the use of a word such as a pronoun or adjective to refer to a person or concept introduced earlier (an antecedent). Johnson and Barrett distinguish six basic types of anaphora (20): pronouns, locational pronouns (here, there); adjectives (few, several); arithmetic anaphora (former, latter, the two); a superordinate substitute (animal for dog); inclusive anaphora (this, the idea, the reasons). Other authors, of course, identify different types of anaphora or give them different names. In any case, some children need special help in dealing with these relationships in order to achieve good comprehension, particularly since examination of basal reader manuals and reading textbooks reveals that few pay any attention to this language structure (20).

Think-time. The tendency for teachers to ask one question after another of a group is widely recognized. The typical interaction is question–response, then if no response, question to another child, all within a few seconds. Gambrell has shown that when the time allowed for pupil thinking is increased to five seconds, better and longer answers are elicited, more answers are correct, and speculative thinking by the students is increased (13). Expectation of immediate response cuts the thinking time of the student and produces shorter, poorer answers.

As teachers practice allowing long think-time, they tend to use higher level questions and to follow these with high-level questions. Gambrell cautions that both teacher and pupils may feel uncomfortable at first when longer think-time is allowed. Don't react by rewording your questions or starting another. Wait the full five seconds (counting silently—1000, 2000, and so on). Prepare students for your change of pace by explaining what is happening. Tell them they don't have to answer immediately anymore. We believe that Gambrell's suggestion cannot help but improve pupil–teacher interaction.

Helfeldt and Lalik have offered an interesting variation in teacher questioning (18). When a student responds correctly to a teacher question, he or she is permitted to address one to the teacher or to another pupil. This approach produced better comprehension than teacher questioning followed by verbal reinforcement in a simple two-week experiment.

The development of any real depth of comprehension or the faculty of intelligent, critical reading is impossible if teachers depend upon drill books, workbooks, dittoes, and other stereotyped, repetitive materials. Our goals will be reached only by direct teacher instruction on how to read.

Comprehension instruction

WHAT WORKS	WHAT DOES NOT WORK
Providing direct instruction on meanings of words in the reading (11)	Chalkboard prereading presentation of new words
Learning multiplicity of word meanings by categorizing words	Teaching commonest meanings of words
Asking pupils to attempt to define new words, eliminating study of those already known (11)	Previewing all new words in the selection
Teaching meaning and effect of signal words. (11)	Teaching connectives and signal words as sight words
Using cloze to promote development of contextual analysis; following with discussion of choices and training in hypothesis testing	Teaching contextual analysis as a group of terms
Teaching interpretation of paragraph types above fourth grade (34)	Assuming that author's style is not significant
Beginning assessment with factual questions—who, what, when, where (39)	Following basal manual in questioning
Moving from factual to explanatory questions—how, why (39)	Mixing questions to test thoroughly
Moving then to higher level questions—generalization, evaluation, inferences (39)	Covering facts read as completely as possible

(continued)

Confining imagery questions to grades above primary, expecting that some pupils cannot use it (19)	Teaching children to use imagery
Spending time relating pupil knowledge to content of selection by discussion, pretests, spelling out purposes, and previewing (20)	Getting into the reading as soon as possible
Reinforcing recall by writing pupil concepts on chalkboard, reorganizing this with aid of pupils (30)	Testing comprehension by questioning only
Discussing pictures in the text may help recall (19)	Failing to discuss and react to pictures
Teaching post-primary children to write a summary sentence after each paragraph in content material (19, 23)	Using teacher questioning and printed exercises for assessment
Recognizing that main ideas include most important idea, ideas related to theme, and what could be expressed in a new title (23)	Teaching main ideas as central thought
Direct teaching of these comprehension strategies (22)	Using printed exercises to practice main ideas, details, etc.
Realizing that a comprehension difficulty may require indirect treatments, as vocabulary, informational background, word analysis, etc. (23)	Curing comprehension difficulty by direct teaching of comprehension strategies
Using tests and discussion of correct answers, information feedback and reviews (23)	Giving tests to measure comprehension.
Using children's prior experiences as related to selection as a basis for predicting probable ideas in the selection (17)	Talking with children about their experiences as they might be related to the title of the selection
If children answer a question correctly, they may ask one of the teacher or other children (17)	Having all questions come from the teacher
Teaching pupils how to summarize, outline, raise questions to be answered in the reading; providing practice in these skills (4)	Reserving study skills instruction only for subject matter lessons
Recognizing that comprehension is not really promoted by oral reading.	Expecting oral readers to show more than bare, literal recall

(*continued*)

Using inferential prereading questions that require a good deal of reading before answering, above primary grades	Using factual prereading questions
Supplying glosses or marginal headings on ditto sheets before reading to guide students	Assuming pupils can use present headings
If content of selection is beyond pupil informational background, helping them by prereading preparation with explanation and discussion (23)	Using an audiovisual aid to prepare students for new, difficult materials
Allowing at least five seconds after each question for think time (13)	Continuing to expect rapid responses to your questions
Recognizing that there may not be correct answers to some questions because they are a matter of opinion or judgment (7)	Expecting and demanding correct answers
Giving feedback asking for elaboration or explanation or by pointing out why answer is correct (37)	Recognizing answer is correct by saying so.

Discussion Questions

1. What is your concept of comprehension and of appropriate ways of stimulating it?

2. Would more intelligent children be more likely to develop deeper comprehension and more evidence of critical thinking spontaneously, regardless of the classroom practices?

3. Suggest ways in which a teacher can promote more active reacting and associating while reading among pupils who read with poor comprehension.

4. Which comprehension skills do you think are most important? Why? What evidence can you give that these skills really involve different intellectual or reading behaviors than are supposedly present in other skills?

5. In your opinion, is critical reading a type of comprehension, a separate group of skills, or something else?

6. In your opinion, what would be an optimal combination of some of the instructional strategies mentioned in this chapter?

7. You may recall that some of the instructional strategies are best only at certain ages. Which that you can recall are best for primary children? Which for older children? Why does this distinction exist?

8. Visit several primary and intermediate classes to observe reading lessons. What real instruction in comprehension strategies do you note? What are your comments? Share your observations with your classmates.

References

1. Anderson, Thomas H., "Another Look at the Self-Questioning Study Technique." Reading Education Report No. 6. University of Illinois, Sept. 1978, ED 163 441.
2. Artley, A. Sterl, "Reading Skills or Competencies?" *Language Arts*, 57 (May 1980), 546–549.
3. Bartlett, B. J., "Top-Level Structure as an Organizational Strategy for Recall of Classroom Text." Doctoral dissertation, Arizona State University, 1978.
4. Brown, Ann L., et al., "Learning to Learn: On Training Students to Learn From Texts." Technical Report #189, Center for the Study of Reading, University of Illinois, Urbana, Ill. 1980.
5. Cohen, Ruth, "Self-Generated Questions as an Aid to Reading Comprehension." *Reading Teacher*, 36 (April 1983), 770–775.
6. Cook, J. E., A Study in Critical Listening Using 8–10 Year Olds in an Analysis of Commercial Propaganda Emanating from Television, 1972. ED 076 944.
7. Davidson, Roscoe, "Teacher Influence and Children's Levels of Thinking," *Reading Teacher*, 22 (May 1969), 702–704.
8. Drum, Priscilla A., Calfee, Robert C., and Cook, Linda K., "The Effects of Surface Structure Variables on Performance in Reading Comprehension Tests," *Reading Research Quarterly*, 16 (1981), 486–514.
9. Durkin, Dolores, "What Classroom Observation Reveals About Reading Comprehension," *Reading Research Quarterly*, 14 (1978–1979), 481–533.
10. Durkin, Dolores, "Reading Comprehension Instruction in Four Basal Reader Series," *Reading Research Quarterly*, 16 (1981), 515–544.
11. Eeds, Maryann, "What to Do When They Don't Understand What They Read —Research-Based Strategies for Teaching Reading Comprehension," *Reading Teacher*, 34 (February 1981), 565–575.
12. Frase, Lawrence T., "Boundary Conditions for Mathemagenic Behavior," *Review of Educational Research*, 40 (June 1970), 337–348.
13. Gambrell, Linda E., "Think-Time: Implications for Reading Instruction," *Reading Teacher*, 34 (November 1980), 143–146.
14. Gordon, C. J., "The Effects of Instruction in Metacomprehension and Inferencing on Children's Comprehension Abilities." Doctoral dissertation, University of Minnesota, 1980.
15. Greenlaw, M. Jean, and Kurth, Ruth J., "Current Research and Analysis of Definitions of Comprehension," in *Comprehension: Process and Product*, George H. McNinch, ed. First Yearbook American Reading Forum, 1981, 36–38.
16. Guszak, Frank J., "Teacher Questioning and Reading," *Reading Teacher*, 21 (December 1967), 227–234.
17. Hansen, Jane, "An Inferential Comprehension Strategy for Use with Primary Grade Children," *Reading Teacher*, 34 (March 1981), 665–669.
18. Helfeldt, John P., and Lalik, Rosemary, "Reciprocal Student–Teacher Questioning," in *Reading Comprehension at Four Linguistic Levels*, Clifford Pennock, ed. Newark, Del.: International Reading Association, 1979, 74–79.
19. Jenkins, Joseph R., and Pany, Darlene, "Instructional Variables in Reading Comprehension," in *Comprehension and Reading: Research Review*, John T. Guthrie, ed. Newark, Del.: International Reading Association, 1981, 163–202.

20. Johnson, Dale D., and Barrett, Thomas, C., "Prose Comprehension: A Descriptive Analysis of Instructional Practices," in *Children's Prose Comprehension: Research and Practice*, Carol M. Santa and Bernard L. Hayes, eds. Newark, Del.: International Reading Association, 1981, 72–102.

21. Kuchinskas, Gloria, "It's a Matter of Organizational Pattern: Problems Detecting Author's Organizational Pattern," *Florida Reading Quarterly*, 18 (December 1981), 17–20, 43.

22. Kurth, Ruth J., and Greenlaw, M. Jean, "Research and Practice in Comprehension Instruction in Elementary Classrooms," in *Comprehension: Process and Product*, George H. McNinch, ed. First Yearbook American Reading Forum, 1981, 38–41.

23. Levin, Joel R., and Pressley, Michael, "Improving Children's Prose Comprehension: Selected Strategies That Seem to Succeed," in *Children's Prose Comprehension: Research and Practice*, Carol M. Santa and Bernard L. Hayes, eds. Newark, Del.: International Reading Association, 1981, 44–71.

24. Linden, Michael, and Wittrock, M. C., "The Teaching of Reading Comprehension According to the Model of Generative Learning," *Reading Research Quarterly*, 17 (1981), 44–57.

25. Marshall, Nancy, "Using Story Grammar to Assess Reading Comprehension," *Reading Teacher*, 36 (March 1983), 616–621.

26. Mason, J. M., Osborn, J. H. and Rosenshine, B. V., "A Consideration of Skill Hierarchy Approaches to the Teaching of Reading." Technical Report 42. Champaign, Ill.: University of Illinois, 1977.

27. Mason, Jana M., "An Examination of Reading Instruction in Third and Fourth Grade," *Reading Teacher*, 36 (May 1983), 906–913.

28. Mezyuski, Karen, "Issues Concerning the Acquisition of Knowledge: Effects of Vocabulary Training on Reading Comprehension," *Review of Educational Research*, 53 (Summer 1983), 253–279.

29. Meyer, Bonnie J. F., Brandt, David M., and Bluth, George J., "Use of Top-Level Structure in Text: Key for Reading Comprehension of Ninth-Grade Students," *Reading Research Quarterly*, 16 (1980), 72–103.

30. Moldofsky, Penny Baum, "Teaching Students to Determine the Central Story Problem: A Practical Application of Schema Theory," *Reading Teacher*, 36 (April 1983), 740–745.

31. Patching, W., et al., "Direct Instruction in Critical Reading Skills," *Reading Research Quarterly*, 18 (Summer 1983), 406–418.

32. Piekarz, Josephine, "Getting Meaning From Reading," *Elementary School Journal*, 56 (March 1956), 303–309.

33. Ruddell, Robert B., "The Effect of Oral and Written Patterns of Language Structure on Reading Comprehension," *Reading Teacher*, 18 (January 1965), 270–275.

34. Rumelhart, David E., "Schemata: The Building Blocks of Cognition," in *Theoretical Issues in Reading Comprehension*, Spiro, R.J., et al. eds., New York: Lawrence Erlbaum, 1980.

35. Sampson, Michael R., Valmont, W. J., and Van Allen, Roach, "The Effects of Instructional Cloze on the Comprehension, Vocabulary and Divergent Production of Third-Grade Students," *Reading Research Quarterly*, 17 (1982), 389–399.

36. Samuels, S. Jay, "Effect of Word Associations on Reading Speed and Recall," in *Proceedings*, American Psychological Association, 1966, 255–256.

37. Schwartz, Elaine and Sheff, Alice, "Student Involvement in Questioning for Comprehension," *Reading Teacher*, 29 (November 1975), 150–154.
38. Searls, Evelyn F., and Neville, Donald D., "Sentence-Combining Exercises to Improve Reading Comprehension of Content Texts," *Florida Reading Quarterly*, 19 (June 1983), 8–15.
39. Taba, Hilda, "The Teaching of Thinking," *Elementary English*, 42 (May 1965), 534–542.
40. Weaver, P. A., "Improving Reading Comprehension, Effects of Sentence Organization Instruction," *Reading Research Quarterly*, 15 (1979), 129–146.
41. Wiesdanger, Katherine D., and Wollenberg, John F., "Prequestioning Inhibits Third Graders' Reading Comprehension," *Reading Teacher*, 31 (May 1978), 892–895.

Resources for the Teacher

Professional References

Bower, G., ed., *The Psychology of Learning and Motivation.* New York: Academic Press, 1975.

Danks, Joseph, and Pezdek, Kathy, *Reading and Understanding.* Newark, Del.: International Reading Association, 1980.

Gerhard, C., *Making Sense: Reading Comprehension Improved Through Categorizing.* Newark, Del.: International Reading Association, 1975.

Griese, Arnold A., *Do You Read Me? Practical Approaches to Teaching Reading Comprehension.* Santa Monica, Calif.: Goodyear Publishing, 1977.

Guthrie, John T., ed. *Comprehension and Teaching: Research Reviews.* Newark, Del.: International Reading Association, 1981.

Harms, Jean McLain, *Comprehension and Literature.* Dubuque: Kendall/Hunt, 1982.

Hittleman, D. R., *Developmental Reading: A Psycholinguistic Perspective.* Chicago, Ill.: Rand McNally, 1978.

Lamb, Pose, and Arnold, R., ed., *Reading: Foundations and Instructional Strategies.* Belmont, Calif.: Wadsworth Publishing, 1976.

Lapp, D., and Flood, J., *Teaching Reading to Every Child.* New York: Macmillan, 1978.

Levin, Joel R., and Ailen, V.L., eds., *Cognitive Learning in Children: Theories and Strategies.* New York: Academic Press, 1976.

McNinch, George H., ed., *Comprehension: Process and Product.* First Yearbook American Reading Forum, 1981.

Otto, Wayne, Chester, R., McNeil J., and Meyers, S., *Focused Reading Instruction.* Reading, Mass.: Addison-Wesley, 1974.

Pearson, P. D. and Johnson, Dale D., *Teaching Reading Comprehension.* New York: Holt, Rinehart and Winston, 1978.

Sanders, Norris M., *Classroom Questions: What Kinds?* New York: Harper & Row, 1966.

Santa, Carol M., and Hayes, Bernard L., eds., *Children's Prose Comprehension: Research and Practice.* Newark, Del.: International Reading Association, 1981.

Smith, F., *Comprehension and Learning: A Conceptual Framework for Teachers.* New York: Holt, Rinehart & Winston, 1975.

Sund, Robert B., and Carin, Arthur, *Creative Questioning and Sensitive Listening Techniques: A Self-Concept Approach.* Columbus: Charles E. Merrill, 1978.

Instructional Materials*

Comprehension. Palo Alto: Creative Publications. Four duplicating masters providing practice in a variety of skills.

Comprehension Laboratories. New York: Holt International Resources. Eight kits, each for a two-grade range, from first grade up.

Counterpoint Reading Programs. Chicago, Ill.: Coronet. Two multimedia skill development kits for 2.5 to 4.0 and 4.4 to 5.4. Nonfiction materials with parallel sound filmstrips and workbooks.

Fox, Bernard, and Weiner, Audrey, *Comprehension Critical Reading.* Chicago, Ill.: Benefic Press. Kits for four to six, five to seven, and six to eight of activity cards, pre- and posttests, answer booklets, and teacher's guide.

Gold Dust Books. Los Angeles, Calif.: Bowmar/Noble Publishing. Two collections of three copies of six titles each with teacher's guide. Books range from 2.0 to 2.9 in readability by Spache formula.

Primary Reading Series. Los Angeles, Calif.: Bowmar/Noble Publishing. Six kits containing three copies each of twenty-five four-page story cards with comprehension checks. Teacher's guide available.

Quicksilver Books. Los Angeles, Calif.: Bowmar/Noble Publishing. High-interest stories with comprehension checks and open-ended questions at reading level of 3.0 to 4.5. Multiple copies of twenty-five selections with teaching guide.

Reading Comprehension Labs. New London, Conn.: Croft Educational Services. Kits at primary and intermediate levels of pre- and posttests, teaching plans, guide, and student worksheets for twelve comprehension skills.

Reading Comprehension Series. Los Angeles, Calif.: Bowmar/Noble Publishing. Brief stories of 3.0 to 4.4 of high interest with comprehension checks in kits of seventy-five story cards each. Eight kits offered for grades four to eight.

Reading Skills Program: Real People at Work. Washington, D.C.: Changing Times Education Service. Offers fifteen modules at fifteen levels from low second grade to high sixth grade. Each contains ten books, ten cassettes, ten spirit masters, a teaching guide, and a skills chart.

Skillpacks. New London, Conn.: Croft Education Services. Kits of exercises in literal and interpretive, analytic or critical reading for primary and intermediate levels.

Sports Reading Series. Los Angeles, Calif.: Bowmar/Noble Publishing. Each of three kits contains three copies of 50 sports stories at 2.0 to 4.0 levels, with comprehension checks and teacher's guide.

Starting Line. Los Angeles, Calif.: Bowmar/Noble Publishing. Each of four kits offers an introductory filmstrip, six copies of a forty-eight-page book, duplicating masters, and a teacher's resource book.

*Most of these still emphasize drills, rather than teacher instruction.

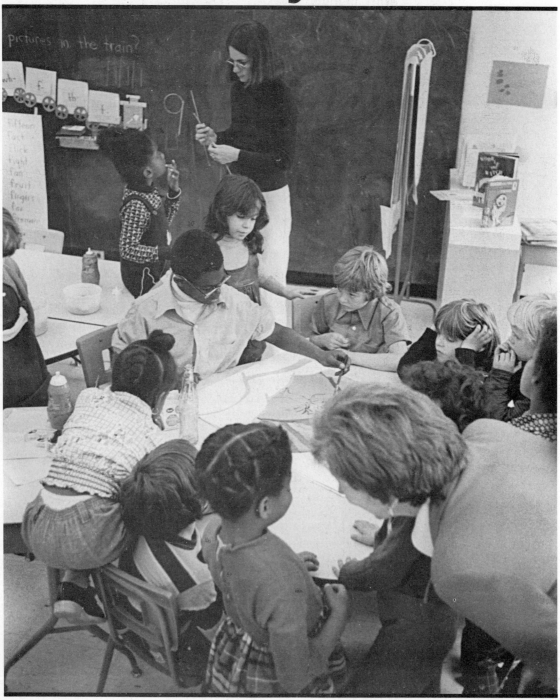

We have been experimenting with patterns of classroom management ever since the first school was built in America. Even in the past half-century we have had two periods of great interest in grouping schemes, first in the 1920s to 1930s and again in the past two decades. At each peak in this cycle we sought solutions to our educational problems in trying many types of arrangements without finding all the answers. Currently we are drawing upon some hitherto unused community resources in using parents, other adults, and pupils as tutors. Other new developments in the past two decades are team teaching, cluster grouping, the open school, pupil teams, and the like.

There are a number of problems both recognized and hidden in adopting a new grouping scheme for a classroom or a school. While most such changes are justified by the persons involved as attempts to provide differentiated instruction keyed to pupils' needs and abilities, this laudable goal is often lost among the new problems created. New patterns of classroom management often fail because:

1. There is not sufficient or significant information about pupils to warrant a new arrangement. Pupils may be grouped in this or that arrangement on the superficial grounds of the results of a single general test, or that plus a mental test. As a result, there are only slight differences between the groups and hence no differential results.

2. The available instructional materials may be inappropriate or inadequate to the new arrangement, as in shifting from basal groups to individualized reading or cluster grouping without changing greatly the variety and quantity of reading materials.

3. Many patterns of grouping make the assumption that the children assigned to a unit are at the same point in reading development, use their reading skills about the same way, have similar interests, need the same kind of instruction, and will progress similarly. And all these assumptions are, again, often based on a test or two of overall reading or mental ability. Categorically speaking, this group of assumptions is almost never true in ordinary school situations.

4. New grouping schemes depend for success on the efforts of the teacher, perhaps more than any other variable, for a competent teacher can make any system look good. Yet teachers are not always consulted about their opinions of

the grouping arrangement nor are teacher assignments often related to teacher interest, experience, or even willingness to experiment. Individual teachers may fail in trying a different arrangement because their concept of a teacher's proper role conflicts with the procedures demanded in the new plan. For example, they find they cannot endure the noise, movement, pupil freedom, and constant personal demands of cluster grouping or individualized reading as in the open-school concept.

5. Changes within a school or even within a classroom imply that the teachers involved have administrative support and encouragement, as well as in-service training in the new procedures. Some grouping arrangements depend heavily upon the help of the librarian, special teachers, the reading supervisor, and others of the school staff. Even with the best efforts and intentions, a new plan may well be defeated by the lack of teacher preparation and support.

6. Experiments in classroom management often turn out to be social class stratification because of the relationship between reading success and language and cultural backgrounds. Minority, economically disadvantaged, and bilingual children tend to be channeled into certain groups, with consequent negative attitudes toward the scheme (and the school) of the pupils, their parents, and some of the teachers.

Whether we are considering a new way of grouping within one classroom, or a major change in the school organization, these are a few of the factors that limit its success. We are not negative to changes, for they are excellent experiences in promoting classroom competence, flexibility, and deeper self-insights. But each shift has its own peculiar disadvantages, as well as advantages, as shall be pointed out.

Homogeneous Versus Heterogeneous Groups

Probably the commonest type of grouping in many schemes is the attempt to bring together pupils of similar ability—in other words, a homogeneous population. Pupils of similar reading ability or mental capacity or both seem to be a unit lending itself to maximum effectiveness of teaching and minimum teacher effort. Since the pupils are all starting at about the same level and are supposed to learn at about the same rate, whole group instruction with perhaps only one type of material and one lesson plan preparation appears quite feasible.

But pupils grouped by reading level still vary in various important reading skills. The range of reading levels is only reduced about 20 percent in homogeneous elementary classes according to one survey. In other words, rather than having a range of four to five grade levels in the classroom, a homogeneous fourth grade may now have a three- to four-grade range. And using mental test results also in selecting the pupils would further reduce the range only by about another half-year. Unless the number of pupils at a grade level is very large, and performances in a number of reading skills, plus intelligence, plus interests, plus learning modality, plus academic motivation are the criteria for the formation of the groups, the experimentation with homogeneous grouping is not feasible. If these factors are not considered, the group formed is not really homogeneous, and one of these factors may be as responsible for the results as the grouping itself.

The Research. A quick review of the voluminous research on the achievement of homogeneous versus heterogeneous classes uncovers just about an equal number of reports favoring either approach. Most studies reached no definite conclusions because the groups compared differed only in one trait, as high versus low reading or mental ability. There is some indication that homogeneous grouping is inclined to be advantageous for high-ability pupils in increasing their achievement. At the same time, the segregation by mental or reading ability or both reduces the competition present in groups of mixed ability. As a result, the high self-ratings of gifted students drop, self-assessments of slow pupils increase, and average pupils are unaffected. Motivation appears to decrease, particularly for the high and low students in homogeneous grouping. These undesirable side effects should certainly be considered as significant as the unsure effects upon achievement (46).

Homogeneous grouping is often attempted in some systems when pupils leave self-contained (mixed) classes to enter a departmentalized arrangement at intermediate or middle school ages. There is very little research exploring the effects of this shift to the pattern in which each subject area is taught by a different teacher and the class usually moves as a body from one room to another. Lamme has shown that teaching reading as a separate subject, in this arrangement, has a distinct effect upon children's reading practices (22). The influence of the teacher was markedly lessened, as shown by the fact that the departmentalized pupils read fewer books, used the classroom library very little, and depended upon self-selection, not the teacher or their peers, for their choices, which were more often paperbacks than books.

Intraclass Patterns

Earlier, the most common three-reading-group plan observed so often in basal reading instruction was described and criticized. We emphasized its inadequacy in dealing with the actual range of reading levels in using only three or four levels of instructional materials, and stressed particularly its failure to provide for the full capabilities of gifted students. We claimed that teacher-organized reading groups violate all that we know about how natural groups operate, develop leaders and followers, and show cohesiveness in working toward a self-selected goal. Pupil relationships and interests, and the possibilities in self-motivation, group esprit, and growth in independence are all ignored (28).

Teachers who utilize this type of intraclass grouping by reading levels with the avowed intention of meeting individual differences were challenged.

It was shown that their selections of children for the groups was based on very weak grounds or no real evidence of diagnosis of pupil strengths or weaknesses. Moreover, the arbitrary nature of these selections is demonstrated in that, after the first few weeks of school, very few changes in placement of the children are made, no matter how the pupils progress. Finally, although the evidence is not strong, there is certainly an effect upon pupil self-concepts when they are segregated and labeled according to their abilities (13).

Perhaps we are overconcerned with the stereotyping of pupil self-concepts. But there are other significant effects that are undesirable. When a teacher uses a single textbook for each reading group, as usually happens, the possibilities of teacher–pupil interaction, pupil spontaneity, and pupil mobility are reduced. The teacher also makes less provision for individual differences, and like the children, offers fewer positive verbal remarks than if using multilevel texts (30). Moreover, how realistic in terms of the actual reading levels of the children is this use of one reader for each group? The low reading group often actually extends over a two- to three-year range, while the high group has an even greater range of reading levels in almost any grade from the third grade on. When the instructional procedures are adapted to a recognition of the diversity of abilities in each group by the use of multilevel texts and supplementary reading materials, we find more positive teacher and pupil behavior, fewer negative interactions among pupils, more independent and creative activities initiated by teacher or pupils, and quicker assumption of responsibility and of leadership in the group by the pupils (30). Does the three-group plan appear to be a defensible practice?

Richard P. Holland reminds us that teachers must consider certain personal characteristics of pupils as well as their reading abilities in assigning them to reading groups (16). For example, the teacher should consider the child's ability to interact with varying numbers of peers in a group. Some children are intimidated in a large group and fail to contribute or even to grow in response to the instruction. This decision can be based on the teacher's observations of a child's behavior at various times in group work. The amount of authoritative structure—directions, rules, teacher talking, assistance to pupils, rigidity of scheduling, etc., should vary in accordance with children's responses rather than be determined by a teacher's habits. Some groups of motivated, responsible learners do not need a great deal of teacher regimentation. They can often function quite well with a minimum of supervision. Finally, the project experiences for the children should be adjusted to their individual abilities, needs, and preferences, Holland reminds us.

Interest Groups

A pair of authors sampled teachers' techniques for stimulating reading interests. Their responses included an auction of books with play money; arranging reading to or with a partner; taping portions of interesting books for use in group guessing games; writing one's own book; arranging to share books by posters; bulletin boards; reading selected portions to peers; puppet shows; and role playing (40). Obviously, the conditions must be favorable to permit this development of interest groups. Freedom of choice, time to enjoy, lots of books and related materials, as well as such teacher practices as reading carefully selected, interesting books to children, discussing them in depth rather than in detail, and enthusiasm for reading are all essential (18).

Interest grouping or allowing pupils to form their own reading groups on the basis of friendship, a common reading interest, mutual admiration, age, or whatever would seem a very realistic approach. If the teacher feels this is impractical because he or she wants to give instruction to pupils in a group with similar needs, such arrangements can be formed at other times. But any type of silent reading (assigned or supplementary), project or creative activity, class newspaper, mural, diorama, or other project should be done by a self-selected group. Even study exercises should be similarly arranged, as will be pointed out later in our discussion of pupil teams, for the learning will be better and the work done more efficiently. Or are we to continue to think that pupils learn best by teacher-directed activities with which the group does not identify and whose goals they never discuss or understand?

Interclass Grouping

Cross-class or interclass grouping involves parallel scheduling of reading lessons among several sections of one or several grades. The pupils go to different rooms at the appointed time according to their general level. Thus teacher A teaches all the fourth graders who read at third-grade level, teacher B instructs the fourth graders of fifth-grade ability, and so on. There is present in this arrangement the assumption that the range of abilities is thus reduced in each classroom, and the teacher's job is made easier. In actuality, these goals are not achieved, for the range of differences in major reading skills is not appreciably lessened since the selection criteria are so superficial.

Some advocates of the Joplin plan, as it was commonly called, seem to find merit in the arrangement in short-term experiments. But, in longer studies, any favorable results in achievement tend to disappear after one semester. Several studies have shown that, in the majority of trials, superior results were obtained in the self-contained classroom (26), particularly for better-than-average readers.

Interclass grouping ignores age and maturity in combining pupils from several grade levels upon many occasions. It also separates reading from all other language activities as though it were a nonlanguage type of learning. The information derived from observation and personal experience with children is often not transmitted from teacher to teacher. The particular problems of the poorest readers may be unknown by the teacher assigned those pupils.

Thus reading instruction becomes less efficient and more difficult because of the compartmentalizing of pupils as well as the related facets of language development. As a result, it has been shown that the poor readers developed less favorable attitudes, unhappiness with their placement, and poorer personal relations with the other pupils. Their parents were negative to the interclass grouping.

Nongraded or Ungraded Primary

Arrangements of classes with a wider than usual age span and no regard for academic performance, or nongraded classes, are in use in elementary and secondary schools. It is claimed that such groups promote interaction of different age levels and are therefore stimulating to achievement.

Ungraded primary programs emphasize informal grading and grouping by achievement levels. Children are regrouped each year by rough reading levels, or even more frequently if multiple levels are recognized. The pupils sometimes may continue with the same teacher for the three-and-one-half or four years allotted for this program.

The research on nongraded classes is almost nonexistent, but the claim persists that this plan adapts instruction to pupil rate of growth. Such a result could, of course, be obtained in any classroom by individualizing instruction and materials. A recent study indicated unfavorable effects upon the peer status of younger pupils when mixed ages were combined for instruction (1).

Nongraded classes offering an individualized curriculum are based on the belief that repeating a grade, as it often occurs in graded schools, does not improve academic achievement and has poor effects on a pupil's self-concept. In contradiction, some studies show that nonpromotion has a beneficial effect upon immature children's marks, school behavior, and home behavior. But the spread of various versions of a nongraded program has continued and the majority of recent comparative studies support its favorable effects upon achievement and mental health, particularly for poorer achievers (37).

There is a version of nongraded arrangements presently called continuous progress. In this plan there are no formal promotions from grade to grade, and children are encouraged to progress academically at their own rate of learning. McLoughlin's study of the effect of the continuous progress approach indicates that the grouping plan required several consecutive years to make an impact upon pupil achievement (29). One-year trials were inconsistent in their results; changing teachers each year and grouping heterogeneously appeared the most effective procedures, in comparison with the usual graded schools, in producing acceleration in achievement.

The studies regarding ungraded primary groups are much greater in volume since the idea has been in use in schools since the 1940s. Most of the reports show higher reading achievement in instances when the plan extended over several years. Parental and pupil attitudes also tend to favor the ungraded scheme. The ungraded primary has the advantage over nongraded classes of avoiding the complications of differing ages and maturity, and of widely varying levels of reading ability. With the groups formed on the criterion of reading progress, the division into ten to fifteen stages during the primary grades does reduce the demands on the teacher for instruction on many levels, does tend to encourage progress at the child's own rate, and approaches individualization of instruction more than ordinary classrooms. Most important, it tends to push teachers toward the recognition of individual differences, a trend reacted to favorably by both parents and pupils.

Pupil Teams and Pupil Tutors

In the early 1960s, several studies by students of Donald D. Durrell described successful experiments with pupil pairs or teams working together in reading (8). The more competent pupil would help the classroom peer, or three or four would work together as a team. The research confirmed the opinions of many teachers who had used the arrangement, and the idea of using other pupils to assist or tutor poor readers spread widely. We now find dozens of reports of trials with older pupils tutoring younger. Some of these are very simple arrangements, as in Lawrence's article on sixth-graders helping first graders with their language experience stories (23). Typically, the tutors gained in their own writing mechanics as a result of the relationship. Other reports show more carefully planned arrangements, in which the tutors receive some training in how to relate to a younger child, and in how to respond and support (40). Often the tutors are selected because they, too, are poor readers, and, as expected, their skills improve significantly in helping a younger pupil. Sometimes tutors and tutees are carefully matched, as black with black, Chicano with Chicano. A few schools have used a reading specialist to diagnose the young child's needs and prescribe the remedial materials. Others keep the relationship more spontaneous and informal and simply provide the tutor with a choice of materials and some ideas on how to chart progress. Even teacher-training institutions have recognized that a tutoring experience is a realistic introduction to classroom practices, particularly during a course in reading methods (40), and may even result in some reading improvement for the college student.

Using peer tutors has led to some freedom to experiment with methods of teaching reading. Learning disabled third-grade children gained more from the tutoring when the teacher circulated, praised, modeled behavior for the tutor, or assisted if needed. Tutoring at the back of the classroom or in another room did not affect the results. Another variation was arranging for middle school volunteers to tutor primary children during the summer vacation. They used low level books, lots of praise, short sessions, and activities suggested by the remedial teacher who was available in the library where the tutoring took place (15).

Oakland and Williams experimented with one group being taught reading and spelling by peer tutors while a second group practiced oral reading ten minutes a day, alternating with listening to the tutor's reading and the two reading aloud together (35). A third group received regular instruction as the control group. Just why these writers would expect that progress in reading and spelling might be better under a tutor than a teacher is not very clear. Despite continuing these programs for a full year, there were no real differences in the final reading scores for the three groups. Tutoring is probably most effective as an adjunct, not as a substitute for teacher instruction, in the minds of most teachers who employ it.

A somewhat similar study was conducted by Hoskisson (17). The child was read to, then asked to repeat after the tutor. After a while the pupil was supposed to point to and read the words that were seen frequently. Later the child was expected to want to do the reading, with the assistance of the tutor. Sixth-graders were used with first-graders of high risk, but no test results were reported. It is apparent that this author conceives of learning to read as a rote learning through repetition, rather than as an act that has meaning.

If we were to use older pupils with first graders, we would expand Hoskisson's procedure by teaching the tutors how to help the young ones to use effective word recognition techniques. The context, word order or sense of the sentence, the presence of common phonograms or clusters, the inflections of base words, picture clues and compound words can be utilized by beginning readers with the help of the tutor (assuming that the latter knows them).

Mavrogenes and Galen suggest an almost idealistic training program for tutors. They include teaching positive relationships, supportive rapport, role playing, how to schedule, how to write books for their tutees, using puppets and pantomime, making games, and keeping a daily log recording comments on the tutee's reactions and progress (26).

In the many reports of success in using peer tutors, we find that some schools gave some sort of preparatory training, whereas others did not. Purely on a common sense basis we would expect the tutoring to be more effective in stimulating reading growth if the tutor had some training in reading strategies. Moreover, the gains that tutors themselves often show as a result of the experience implies that their insights into the reading process have been deepened by trying to help someone who reads poorly. These gains would perhaps be increased by some preparatory training and both tutors and tutees would benefit. Obviously our concept of what tutors should know is concentrated in the act of reading. The psychological training outlined by Mavrogenes and Galen may be very desirable. But omission of the emphasis upon how to read more efficiently by many tutor preparatory programs may explain why some may not profit from the experience.

A review of the implications of the research on peer tutoring yielded these conclusions (6):

- Results from programmed tutoring are favorable with one, not two, sessions per day, and particularly with poorest readers.
- Long-range results four years later did not show sustained gains.
- Using either underachievers or overachievers to tutor is profitable. They tend to improve the academic achievements of their tutees, and some of them also gain.
- Self-concept and attitudinal changes are not regularly affected.
- Low achievers as tutors for young children seems to work well, but tutees do not always gain.
- The sex of the tutor is not significant.
- The effect of the socioeconomic status and race of the tutor is inconclusive.
- The difference in ages of the tutor and tutee has not been found important.
- The length of the tutoring session has not been found significant.
- Training of tutors has not been shown to affect the academic gains.

A recent description of the practices of good and poor comprehending tutors is pertinent here (11). Sixth-grade tutors, including good and poor comprehenders, worked with fourth-graders. It was observed that the good comprehenders helped their tutees to look back for answers, to look back selectively, according to the question, and to sample rather than reread the entire passage. Poor comprehenders were apparently unfamiliar with these strategies and did not teach them to their tutees. The implications from this study would seem to strengthen the argument for training of tutors in reading strategies.

Nevi has tried to answer the question of why cross-age tutoring often helps the tutors to improve in reading (31). He found at least ten theories in the literature that tried to explain this fact. They included such concepts as the tutors' feelings of prestige and authority; their reinforcement by the tutees' success and the approval of their supervisors; their increase in insight into the reading and learning processes and their importance for them; their relearning of skills and materials helpful to their reading; the greater amount of time they were devoting to reading. Perhaps some day we will know exactly what causes this outcome.

While we believe in some sort of preparatory training for tutors, Nevi points out that it can be too much of a good thing. In one study he cites tutors failed to gain in reading, perhaps because of considerable training and a highly structured relationship with their supervisors. The observers felt that the relationship between tutors and tutees lost its friendliness and flexibility because of all the training and supervision. There is certainly the implication that too much training and too close supervision may interfere with the processes that result in reading gains for the tutors, an observation to be remembered in initiating tutoring programs.

Team Teaching, Cluster Grouping, and the Open Classroom

The arrangements of team teaching and cluster grouping are almost identical in that two or three classes are combined in one oversized area with a staff of several teachers. One teacher may instruct the entire class or a group in an area of particular competence, while the other teachers work with individuals or other groups. Teachers may alternate as instructor or resource person in various subjects, and relate their areas more closely by mutual planning. The shifting of teacher responsibilities tends to make for flexibility in grouping, for more opportunity for teacher–pupil interaction, and a wider variety of instructional activities, according to its supporters.

Most reports on team teaching or cluster grouping are not research evaluations. It has yet to be demonstrated whether the schemes result in better academic progress, or the other advantages in recognition of individual differences that appear to be present. It is apparent, however, that these plans demand more than usual creativity, competence, and compatibility among teachers, as well as motivation, independence in work habits, and adaptability to different teaching styles among pupils.

It may be that longer studies in comparing the self-contained classroom with a team-teaching arrangement are needed to clarify the values of the latter approach for pupil achievement. For example, Lambert found the self-contained classroom better in gains after the first year; the team teaching better after the second year (21). The arrangement creates certain problems for teachers, as we have suggested, and also has effects upon pupil peer relationships. Perhaps because of the number of children present, the pupils in one study experienced increased difficulties in finding friends and relating to classmates (5). Conceivably, this trend could affect the morale and cohesiveness of the class and thus reduce its progress.

The lack of formal research on the effects of combining classes and teachers, or simply placing them in a large undivided area, as in the open school, as it is called, has not deterred a current trend in this direction. Many American schools were designed to operate in this way, in what was intended to be a model of the British open primary school. A physical resemblance is easily constructed, with art, music, work, or study centers, easily accessible libraries, group and individual work areas, and the like. But some observers doubt that some of the more subtle elements of the British open school can be as readily substituted for traditional American school practices.

To illustrate, British children do not all enter school the same day, but rather upon their fifth birthday or four designated admission dates during the year. As a result, the first-year program is characterized by much greater flexibility than most American primary teachers offer. This flexibility extends to the choice or even creation of instructional materials, which, unlike so many American schools, are the prerogative of the teacher. Freedom of choice of materials, management procedures, and curriculum permeates the elementary grades. Reading tests are not highly valued and their use is infrequent, possibly because of their irrelevance to what are considered the major goals of the reading program. The goals are not development of reading skills for their values per se; indeed, hardly any teacher manuals or workbooks are issued for the readers to guide the teacher in skill development. Rather the emphasis is placed upon development of maturity in the uses and applications of reading, the appreciation of and interest in literature, and permanent reading interests keyed to one's life goals. For example, it is considered much more important to be able to talk and write about what one has read than to report on its details or to do worksheets.

Several authors have been very critical of the impetuous rush of American schools to imitate the British open school. They point out that American educators have failed to recognize that the British system is not revolutionary but has evolved slowly over a period of twenty-five to thirty years to serve its own closely knit society and its philosophy of education (7). The British people are characterized by stability, strong family life, lack of mobility, and by courtesy and respect for other people. Its education is child-centered with emphasis upon the here and now of children's abilities and interests (36). The first aim is to produce people who read and want to read; the secondary aim is to help them to read effectively. If the secondary aim were given priority, as it is in American schools, Vera Southgate of Manchester points out that the first goal would probably never be achieved (41).

John Downing says that the open school has become a fad with open space buildings going up all over to contain the same conventional closed education practiced in the old buildings (7). Perhaps this explains why the few research studies we have on the outcomes of this new mode tend to be negative. After two-and-one-half years in the open school, the achievement of fifth-grade pupils was inferior to that in traditional schools in all areas and subjects except spelling and language (47). In another study, pupils' attitudes toward school, teachers, reading, and the freedom in the classroom became less and less favorable as their years in the open school increased.

It remains to be proven that an educational system so different from our own in rationale, goals, materials, and classroom procedures can be transported in toto to an oversized American classroom and made to function with advantage.

Since the previous edition of this book was published in 1977, the open classroom has continued to serve as an alternative classroom management system. Many of these classrooms have been reconverted to traditional self-contained units, perhaps because schools have become discouraged at the failure of their open classrooms to produce real differences in pupil achievement. A recent study indicated that perhaps open classrooms often did not provide the individualized instruction that had been intended (39). In Rogers's report, one half to two thirds of the units still used basal readers, and two thirds used workbooks, worksheets, and other exercise materials. Despite the goals, 66 to

78 percent of the teachers still set specific times of the day for reading instruction, although this was commonly done in small temporary groups, rather than the traditional three-group plan.

The outcomes of the open classroom were reported in test results by Lukasevich and Gray (24). Reading achievement was less than in conventional classrooms, as was mathematics. There was a better self-concept in relation to school subjects in open space classrooms. Wright found that open classroom pupils were poorer after four-and-a-half semesters in that environment in word meaning, paragraph meaning, arithmetic concepts, arithmetic application, social science, and science (47). Only in spelling and language were the differences insignificant, but even then they favored the traditional classes. There were no differences in tests of cognition or personality.

A third report comparing open area classes with traditional classes again found the former inferior in reading achievement in the first grade (3). As a result of these and other basically negative findings, Marshall questions whether the term and concept may have outlived its usefulness (25). The definition of this form of classroom organization and, as Rogers has observed, the implementation of the idea have differed greatly. The negative studies are as numerous or more so than the positive in terms of achievement, self-concept, attitudes toward school, creativity, problem solving, and independence, and results are as yet inconclusive. The major problem was and continues to be the fact that some administrators who instituted this concept in their systems did not distinguish between a way of teaching and the mere use of a large classroom.

Open classrooms were intended to promote individualization of instruction, like the British schools, with the teacher acting as facilitator, the student responsible for learning, with more small-group than large-group work, with student choice of activity, with richness of materials and the integration of curriculum areas. Often these goals were expected when teachers had no inservice training or trained supervision to assist them in making the transition from conventional practices. Perhaps, like so many idealistic educational experiments, open classrooms will gradually disappear without ever having really been implemented often enough to be objectively evaluated. Their decreasing numbers would seem to support this conclusion.

Parents and Paraprofessionals

We are witnessing a growing practice in the use of parents and other adults as paid or volunteer assistants to the teacher. The programs take many forms: aides or parents working with an individual or small group while the teacher conducts a lesson for the others; tutoring by parents after school hours; aides or parents simply helping with clerical work, marking workbooks, making displays or other audiovisual materials, and performing many of the tasks inherent in the operation of a school.

Once they have overcome their fears of interference from the nonprofessional adults, or from the demands on their time to train their aides, many teachers have reacted positively to this new source of assistance. And a few small studies of the results of tutoring by adults seem to indicate improved academic motivation and achievement for the pupils involved (44).

When volunteer or paid aides are used to assist in instruction, it has become apparent that they need a modicum of professional training in how to relate to children positively, how to teach a simple skill, and how to judge pupil progress. The length and content of the training program that will help produce effective aides is gradually being evolved. Many manuals for parents, or paraprofessionals as they are called, offering various training programs are listed in the bibliography of this chapter.

Another approach to employing adults in reading instruction has developed from the experiments of Ellson in devising a practical, programmed sequence in word recognition. His scheme has changed from using an automatic flash-card machine with verbal reinforcement to a programmed tutor's guide. Using common readers, all the interaction of the pupil and the adult is spelled out step by step. Thus presumably someone untrained in reading methods can work with a beginning reader with profit for the pupil, following training sessions on the guide and in emulating the teacher's role, and after a short period of supervision. Ellson's programmed guide for adults has been tried in many school systems and the initial reports are favorable (45). Some of the results have been a reduction in nonpromotions, and good performances on tests based on the readers used, which are rather dramatic outcomes from daily fifteen-minute tutoring sessions added to the regular basal instruction. Such results might be due to the motivation imparted by the individual attention of the tutor as much as by the exact nature of the programmed guide. We recall that similar outcomes were mentioned above as the result of pupil teams of an older and a primary child, without using such detailed instructions. It will be profitable for us to learn eventually exactly how much direction the adult or pupil tutor needs to conduct profitable sessions. Meanwhile, it would seem desirable to continue using adults as aides or tutors for pupils who need individualized help.

There remain to be answered such questions as the number of aides that proves effective, or whether having several aides in the classroom may prove to be too much of a good thing. Only one study has attempted to attack this problem. One, none, and up to five aides per class were contrasted. Using one aide produced superior readiness scores for kindergarten children to using no aide, but no significant gains above this were noted as more aides were added.

Those evaluating the National Head Start program's use of untrained adults as aides concluded that:

1. Learning is an intensely personal thing, depending directly on human interaction. Aides can increase this interaction.
2. Successful aides have an interest in children and a supervising teacher who knows how to utilize the aides well.

3. Learning by doing, at least for young children, is a reality of life supported by firsthand experiences. Aides can help provide this essential variety of experiences.

Teachers who attempt to use parents or aides must not lose sight of these observations in their emphasis upon skill development. As in the case of peer tutors, the friendliness, support, and encouragement of the parent or aide is largely responsible for the child's growth.

Parents and Reading

The liasion between parents and the school has grown markedly in the past decade. It has been extended to inviting or even urging parents to help their children learn to read. As the bibliography at the end of this chapter shows, dozens of books have been written extending the idea of parents teaching reading.

First steps in enlisting parents in the effort to improve children's reading may take the form of (42):

1. Visits to parents to show them how to initiate reading training for preschoolers, plus the distribution of literature on readiness.
2. Orientation with parent groups to describe the forthcoming program at particular grade levels.
3. Planned classroom demonstrations of small group and individual instruction.
4. Providing reading lists for children at strategic times such as Christmas, Easter, birthdays, national holidays, and the summer vacation.
5. Urging parents to take their children to the library regularly; to help them with research projects; to let them make their own choices of books; to share books with them, perhaps by reading portions alternately (2).
6. Taking the children to the supermarket to let them find the products matching the coupons; to play rhyming games with product names; and, in the case of preschool children, to have them try to find products that begin with each letter of the alphabet.

With young children in the family, the advice to parents often includes taking them up on the lap to read Mother Goose, alphabet books, Dr. Seuss, cumulative stories, stories with a refrain, and the like. Alternating telling the story in a wordless picture book, such as Bahr's *Blizzard at the Zoo* (Lothrop, Lee and Shepard, 1982), and finding books that relate to life experiences, such as being sick, moving, getting glasses, caring for pets, are other desirable practices. Reading multiethnic books like Carle's *Do You Want To Be My Friend?* (Crowell, 1971), books with a predictable phrase like Lee's *Garbage Delight* (Macmillan, 1977), or a nonfiction book such as Srivasta's *Spaces, Shapes and Sizes* (Crowell, 1980) help broaden the child's listening experiences.

Parents are advised by some schools to teach their children to listen by:

- Encouraging them to focus attention on you as you read or speak to them.
- After reading, give practice in recalling the story and in answering questions.
- Read simple rhymes and have the children supply some of the rhyming words.
- Ask the children to try to recall the events of the story in sequence.
- Sing songs and play records for children.
- Give simple directions to children, at first one at a time, about the jobs they should do.

In encouraging parents to teach children to read, we need to show them how to write children's stories on large pieces of paper, saying each word as it is written, then sliding their hands slowly underneath while reading each sentence aloud. They must not censor the children's expressions, but rather write as they dictate. Later they can read the story together. The stories will be brief, perhaps no more than a few sentences at first, and the parents should have their children read the stories on subsequent days. The parents can cut the stories into sentence strips and have their child rearrange them as in the originals. Finally, parents can cut the strips into single words and ask their children to rearrange the entire story from them. Parents should spend perhaps as much as four or five short sessions on each story, varying the reading activities. They should spend more time on the words that seem hard to learn, presenting them again in sentences, not in isolation.

In learning words, parents should not present similar or confusable words at the same time, as *was–saw*. They should teach each one with dissimilar words, at different times, and should take the same caution for letters, as *b–d*, *b–p*, *p–q*, etc. Words should be presented in context, in sentences, with alternates, as

this
We read every day
was

Word recognition can be practiced by circling one word each time it can be found in a newspaper column (*17*). Or, parents can read sentences to the children, leaving out words that begin with a certain letter: *boy, box, baby*. Let children guess what the missing word is.

When parents work with their teenagers, Childrey offers these suggestions (*4*):

- Structure the family reading time and place.
- Bargin for a time. For one hour of television, ask for one hour of family reading.

- Try to share your reading with your children. Discuss the books you have read.
- Read with teens, a piece they choose, for a comfortable time. You may want to practice first.
- Strengthen listening and reading abilities by asking questions —Why? Would you? Do you believe?
- Read a variety of materials—fiction, nonfiction, poetry, plays, and short stories.
- Don't expect your teenager to give up his peer activities, but do set a schedule and stay with it.

James F. Kerfoot says that parents need to understand comprehension (20). Among the facts to be presented are: (1) the purpose for reading is comprehension; (2) there are different types of comprehension—literal, inferential, evaluative—to be sampled by the parent's questions; (3) several factors influence comprehension: decoding skills (at primary levels only), breadth of vocabulary, intelligence, life experiences, and language development. Several strategies can be used to develop comprehension, as varying the content of the reading, preparing the reader for the concepts to be read, perceptive questioning, postreading questions, and above third grade reading level, prereading, nonfactual questions.

James F. Flood studied fourteen aspects of parent-child interaction during reading and their effects on ten prereading tasks (9). The facts should be told to parents. Contributing to prereading abilities were: warm-up questions as preparation for reading, ability of the child to relate the content to past experiences through verbal interaction with the parent, reinforcement of the child's efforts and postreading evaluative questions. It is interesting how closely Flood's findings parallel Kerfoot's suggestions.

W. H. Teale has tried to consolidate what we now know and what we need to know about parents and their child's reading (43). He claims that it has been demonstrated that reading to children helps with language development, with vocabulary development, with the child's eagerness to read, and with success in early reading. Many children who are read to actually learn to read, or learn to read easily after entrance to school. In attempting to read the books that have been read to them, children practice reading behaviors such as self-regulation, self-correction, and orientation to the organization of a book. They also evolve some spontaneous methods of word recognition.

Research studies find important: (1) the total number of words spoken by the child; (2) the number of questions answered by the child; (3) the warm-up questions; (4) the postreading evaluative questions; (5) the number of relevant questions asked by the child; and (6) the give-and-take, question–answer feedback between child and parent (40).

A study of parent practices indicates that reading most often precedes the nap or bedtime. In a black community, reading was rare and hence the children lacked skill in reporting on their reading in school. Teale points out that we need more studies of parent–child interaction; more facts regarding the extent of causal relationships between elements of being read to and subsequent development in reading, and more information on cultural patterns and what they do to the child's concepts of books and reading.

With this much attention to parents and children's reading, with several states promoting "Parents and Reading Partners" programs, with hundreds of schools initiating efforts to promote the involvement of parents, we may expect this activity to spread worldwide in those countries concerned about ways and means of involving families in the effort to improve literacy. Such programs have already started in New Zealand, Africa, Asia, and Malaysia (32).

Discussion Questions

1. What classroom arrangements have you witnessed or participated in? Share your reactions with the class.

2. Why do you suppose that so many experiments in grouping fail to give very definite results? Is it because of their length, the Hawthorne effect, the lack of differentiation in instruction and materials, the criteria for selecting children for grouping, or some other reason?

3. The variable of teacher competence and enthusiasm seems to be significant in many grouping trials. How could this influence be controlled to give greater significance to the experimental results?

4. Is it conceivable that a trial of a type of grouping will create more problems than it might solve? How might the difficulties in initiating a new type of grouping be overcome?

5. What is the true goal of any organizational pattern, in your opinion? Do some attempts lose sight of this goal? How and why?

6. Have you witnessed the use of parents as aides in the classroom? What is your opinion of the value of this assistance? Could it have been improved?

7. When parents become active in the teaching of reading to preschoolers and to schoolchildren, what problems would you anticipate?

References

1. Ahlbrand, William P. Jr., and Reynolds, James A., "Some Social Effects of Cross-Grade Grouping," *Elementary School Journal*, 72 (March 1972), 327–332.
2. Alongi, Constance, "Taking Your Child to the Library," in *Developing Active Readers: Ideas for Parents, Teachers and Librarians*, Dianne Monson, DayAnn K. McClenathan, eds., Newark, Del.: International Reading Association, 1979, 52–57.
3. Bell, Anne E., et al., "Open-Area Education: An Advantage or Disadvantage for Beginners," *Perceptual and Motor Skills*, 39 (August 1974), 407–419.
4. Childrey, John A. Jr., "Home Remedies for Reluctant Readers," in *Motivating Reluctant Readers*, Alfred J. Ciani, ed., Newark, Del: International Reading Association, 1981, 13–25.

5. Cooper, Dan H., and Sterns, Harvey N., "Team Teaching: Students Adjustment and Achievement," *Journal of Educational Research*, 66 (March 1973), 323–327.

6. Devin-Sheehan, Linda, et al., "Research on Children Tutoring Children: A Critical Review," *Review of Educational Research*, 46 (Summer 1976), 355–386.

7. Downing, John, "Language Arts in Open Schools," *Elementary English*, 52 (January 1975), 23–29.

8. Durrell, Donald D., "Pupil Team Learning Objectives, Principles, Techniques," in *Changing Concepts of Reading Instruction*, J. Allen Figurel, ed. Proceedings of the International Reading Association, 6, 1961, 75–78.

9. Flood, James F., "Parental Styles in Reading Episodes with Young Children," *Reading Teacher*, 30 (May 1977), 864–867.

10. Frazer, Stanley, and Stern, Carolyn, "Learning by Teaching," *Reading Teacher*, 23 (February 1970), 403–406, 417.

11. Garner, Ruth, Wagoner, Shirley, and Smith, Terrie, "Externalizing Question Answering Strategies of Good and Poor Comprehenders," *Reading Research Quarterly*, 18 (Summer 1983), 439–447.

12. Green, Donald Rosse, and Riley, Hazel Walter, "Interclass Grouping for Reading in the Middle Grades," *Journal of Experimental Education*, 31 (March 1963), 273–278.

13. Hawkins, M. L., "Mobility of Students in Reading Groups," *Reading Teacher* 20 (November 1966), 136–140.

14. Hill, C. H., and Tolman, R., "Tutoring: An Inexpensive Alternative," *Journal of Reading Specialist*, 10 (1970), 19–23.

15. Himmelsteib, Carol, "Buddies Read in Library Program," *Reading Teacher*, 28 (October 1975), 32–35.

16. Holland, Richard P., "Learner Characteristics and Learner Performance: Implications for Instructional Placement Decision," *Journal of Special Education*, 10 (Spring 1982), 7–20.

17. Hoskisson, Kenneth, "Successive Approximation and Beginning Reading," *Elementary School Journal*, 75 (April 1975), 443–451.

18. Huck, Charlotte S., "Strategies for Improving Interest and Appreciation in Literature," in *Reaching Children and Young People Through Literature*, Helen W. Painter, ed., Newark, Del.: International Reading Association, 1971, 37–45.

19. Jolly, Hayden B. Jr., "Teaching Basic Function Words in Reading," *Reading Teacher*, 35 (November 1981), 136–140.

20. Kerfoot, James F., "What Parents Should Know About Reading Comprehension," in *Parents and Reading*, Carl B. Smith, ed., Newark, Del: International Reading Association, 1971, 87–92.

21. Lambert, Phillip, et al., "A Comparison of Pupil Achievement in Team and Self-Contained Organization," *Journal of Experimental Education*, 33 (Spring 1965), 217–224.

22. Lamme, Linda Leonard, "Self-Contained to Departmentalized: How Reading Habits Changed," *Elementary School Journal*, 76 (January 1976), 208–218.

23. Lawrence, Dolores, "Sparta Revisited," *Reading Teacher*, 28 (February 1975), 464–472.

24. Lukasevich, Ann, and Gray, Roland F., "Open Space, Open Education and Pupils' Performance," *Elementary School Journal*, 79 (November 1978), 108–114.

25. Marshall, Hermine H., "Open Classrooms: Has the Term Outlived Its Usefulness?" *Review of Educational Research*, 51 (Summer 1981), 181–192.
26. Mavrogenes, Nancy A., and Galen, Nancy D., "Cross-Age Tutoring: Why and How," *Journal of Reading*, 22 (January 1979), 344–359.
27. Mayhall, W. F. et al., "Supervision and Site of Instruction as Factors in Tutorial Programs," *Exceptional Children*, 42 (November 1975), 151–154.
28. McGinley, Pat, and McGinley, H., "Reading Groups as Psychological Groups," *Journal of Experimental Education*, 39 (1970), 35–42.
29. McLoughlin, William P., "Continuous Pupils' Progress in the Non-Graded School," *Elementary School Journal*, 71 (November 1970), 90–96.
30. Morrison, Virginia B., "Teacher–Pupil Interaction in Three Types of Elementary Classroom Reading Instruction," *Reading Teacher*, 22 (December 1968), 221–225.
31. Nevi, Charles N., "Cross-Age Tutoring: Why Does It Help the Tutor?" *Reading Teacher*, 36 (May 1983), 892–898.
32. Nichols, Nancy J., "Interclass Grouping for Reading Instruction: Who Makes the Decisions and Why?" *Educational Leadership*, 26 (1969), 588–592.
33. Nicholson, Tom, "Why We Need to Talk to Parents About Reading." *Reading Teacher*, 34 (November 1980), 19–21.
34. Niedemeyer, Fred C., and Ellis, Patricia, "Remedial Reading Instruction by Trained Pupil Tutors," *Elementary School Journal*, 71 (April 1971), 400–405.
35. Oakland, Thomas, and Williams, Fern C., "An Evaluation of Two Methods of Peer Tutoring," *Psychology in the Schools*, 12 (April 1975), 166–171.
36. O'Brien, Thomas C., "Some Comments on British Education," *Elementary School Journal*, 75 (October 1975), 42–49.
37. Pavan, Barbara Nelson, "Good News: Research on the Non-Graded Elementary School," *Elementary School Journal*, 73 (March 1973), 333–342.
38. Roeder, Harold H., and Lee, Nancy, "Twenty-five Teacher-Tested Ways to Encourage Voluntary Reading," *Reading Teacher*, 27 (October 1973), 48–50.
39. Rogers, Janette Staton, "Reading Practices in Open Education," *Reading Teacher*, 29 (March 1976), 548–554.
40. Schoeller, Arthur W., and Pearson, David A., "Better Reading Through Volunteer Reading Tutors," *Reading Teacher*, 23 (April 1970), 625–630, 636.
41. Southgate, Vera, "The Language Arts in Informal British Primary Schools," *Reading Teacher*, 26 (January 1973), 367–373.
42. Spache, George D., *Toward Better Reading*. Champaign, Ill.: Garrard Publishing, 1966.
43. Teale, W. H., "Parents Reading to Their Children: What We Know and Need to Know," *Language Arts*, 58 (November–December 1981), 902–912.
44. Vellutino, F. R., and Connolly, C., "The Training of Paraprofessionals as Remedial Assistants in an Inner-City School," *Reading Teacher*, 24 (March 1971), 506–512.
45. White, Jean, "The Programmed Tutor," *American Education*, 7 (December 1971), 18–21.
46. Williams, Mary Heard, "Does Grouping Affect Motivation?" *Elementary School Journal*, 73 (December 1973), 130–137.
47. Wright, Robert J., "The Affective and Cognitive Consequences of an Open Education Elementary School," *American Educational Research Journal*, 12 (Fall 1975), 449–468.

Resources for the Teacher

Professional References

Dunn, Rita and Kenneth, *Educators Self-Teaching Guide to Individualized Instruction*. West Nyack, N.Y.: Parker Publishing, 1975.

Good, T. L., and Brophy, J. E., *Looking in Classrooms*. New York: Harper & Row, 1973.

Gordon, Ira J., and Brevogel, W. F., *Building Effective Home–School Relationships*. Boston, Mass.: Allyn and Bacon, 1977.

Harris, Larry A., and Smith, Carl B., *Reading Instruction: Diagnostic Teaching in the Classroom*. New York: Holt, Rinehart and Winston, 1976.

Johnson, L. W. and Bany, M. V. *Classroom Management: Theory and Skill Training*. New York: Macmillan, 1970.

Lombardo, Victor S., *Paraprofessionals Working with Young Children: Infancy Through the Third Grade*. Springfield, Ill.: Charles C. Thomas, 1981.

Lapp, Diane, ed., *Making Reading Possible Through Classroom Management*. Newark, Del.: International Reading Association, 1980.

Monson, Dianne, and McClenathan, DayAnn K., *Developing Active Readers: Ideas for Parents, Teachers, and Librarians*. Newark, Del.: International Reading Association, 1979.

Olson, Joanne, and Dillner, Martha, *Learning to Teach Reading in the Elementary School*. New York: Macmillan, 1976.

Sartain, Harry W., ed., *Mobilizing Family Forces for Worldwide Reading Success*. Newark, Del.: International Reading Association, 1981.

Wallen, C. J. and Wallen, L. L., *Effective Classroom Management*. Boston, Mass.: Allyn and Bacon, 1978.

Wilson, Richard C., and James, Helen J., *Individualized Reading: A Practical Approach*. Dubuque: Kendall/Hunt, 1972.

Guides for Parents and Aides

The Alphabet Connection: A Parents' and Teacher's Guide to Beginning Reading and Writing. New York: Shocken Books.

Blanchet, Eileen, *When Your Child Can't Read*. San Rafael, Calif.: Academic Therapy Publications, 1972.

Brosnahan, JoAnne, and Milne, Barbara, *A Calendar of Home/School Activities*. Santa Monica, Calif.: Goodyear Publishing.

Butler, Dorothy, and Clay, Marie, *Reading Begins at Home*. Exeter, N.H.: Heinemann Education Books, 1979.

Carter, E., and Dapper, A., *School Volunteers: What They Do and How They Do It*. New York: Citation Press, 1971.

Chan, Julie M. T., *Why Read Aloud to Children?* Newark, Del.: International Reading Association, 1974.

Children's Book Committee, *Reading with Your Child Through Age Five*. Washington, D.C.: Child Study Association, 1976.

Clough, Dick B., and Clough, Bonnie M., *Utilizing Teacher Aides in the Classroom.* Springfield, Ill.: Charles C. Thomas, 1978.

Cohn, Marvin, *Helping Your Teen-Age Student.* New York: E. P. Dutton, 1980.

Danish, Steven J., and Hauser, Allen L., *Helping Skills: A Basic Teaching Program.* New York: Behavioral Publications, 1973.

Dorsey, Mary E., comp. *Language Arts Tutorial Handbook.* Tallahassee, Fla.: State Department of Education, 1975.

Eberly, Donald, *How Does My Child's Vision Affect His Reading.* Newark, Del.: International Reading Association, 1972.

Egan, Gerard, *The Skilled Helper: A Model for Systematic Helping and Interpersonal Relating.* Monterey, Calif.: Brooks-Cole Publishing, 1975.

Elder, Rachel Ann, et al., *Minicourse in Tutoring in Reading.* San Francisco: Far West Laboratory for Educational Research and Development, 1973.

Erickson, Ruth, and Erickson, Edsel, *Children with Reading Problems: A Guidebook for Parents.* Kalamazoo, Mich.: Learning Publications, 1979.

Ervin, Jane, *Your Child Can Read and You Can Help.* Garden City, N.Y.: Doubleday, 1979.

Hadley, Gary D., *The Three R's: A Handbook for Teachers, Tutors and Parents.* Washington, D.C.: Acropolis Books, 1977.

Hansen, Hazel A., *Parents: Teach Your Child Phonics.* Ardmore, Pa.: Dorrance, 1978. Beware of authors who offer a single panacea.

Harrison, C. V. *Structured Tutoring.* Englewood Cliffs, N.J.: Educational Technology Publications, 1980.

Humphrey, James H., and Humphrey, Joy N., *Help Your Child Learn the 3 R's Through Active Play.* Springfield, Ill.: Charles C. Thomas, 1980.

Illinois State Office of Education, *Teaching Children to Read: A Parent's Guide.* Springfield, Ill. CS 003 849.

Kusnetz, Len, *Your Child Can Be a Super Reader.* Roslyn Heights, N.Y.: Learning House.

Larrick, Nancy, *Encourage Your Child to Read: A Parents' Primer.* New York: Dell Publishing, 1980.

Lee, Barbara, and Rudman, Masha Kabakow, *Mind over Media: New Ways to Improve Your Child's Reading and Writing Skills.* New York: Seaview Books, 1982.

Margolin, Edythe, *Teaching Young Children at School and Home.* New York: Macmillan, 1982.

Matthes, Carole, *How Children Are Taught to Read.* Lincoln, Neb.: Professional Educators Publications.

McDiarmid, Norma J., et al., *Loving and Learning.* Don Mills, Canada: Longman Canada Ltd., 1975.

McEathron, Margaret, *Phonics Primer for Teens and Adults* (for the *Reading Helper*). Seal Beach, Calif.: The Reading House, 1980. In view of the lack of comprehension in phonics after the fourth grade, I doubt the relevance of teaching phonics beyond this reading level.

McIlroy, Ken, *School Failure and What to Do About It.* Palmerston North, New Zealand: Dunmore Press, 1979.

McKeown, Pamela, *Reading: A Basic Guide for Parents and Teachers.* Boston, Mass.: Routledge and Kegan, 1974.

Nedler, Shari, and McAfee, Oralie, *Working with Parents: Guidelines for Early Childhood and Elementary Teachers.* Belmont, Calif.: Wadsworth Publishing, 1979.

Ornstein, Allan C., *Paraprofessionals Handbook*. Belmont, Calif.: Pitman Learning, 1975.

Parent/Paraprofessional Kit. Oklahoma City, Okla.: Economy. Activity and game cards for individualizing instruction in seven areas

Pickering, C. Thomas, *Helping Children Learn to Read: A Primer for Adults*. New York: Chesford Publishing, 1977.

Rogers, Ruth E., et al., *Reading Tutor's Handbook for Grades 2-6*. Kalamazoo, Mich.: Learning Publications, 1977.

Rudman, Jack, *Auxiliary Teacher—Elementary School*. Syosset, N.Y.: National Learning.

Siegal, Ernest, *Teaching One Child*. Freeport, N.Y.: Educational Activities.

Shank, Paul, and McElroy, Wayne, *Paraprofessional or Teacher Aides*. Midland, Mich.: Pendell Publishing, 1980.

Spache, George D., McIlroy, Ken, and Berg, Paul C., *Case Studies in Reading Disability*. Boston, Mass.: Allyn and Bacon, 1981. Contrasting tutoring styles—one-on-one, parent–child, wife–husband, professional–child.

Sparkman, Brandon, and Saul, Jane, *Preparing Your Preschoolers for Reading*. New York: Schocken Books, 1977.

Spiegel, Dixie Lee, *Reading for Pleasure*. Newark, Del.: International Reading Association, 1981.

Teacher Aides. Center for Research, Service and Publications, College of Education, University of Wyoming, Laramie, Wyo. 82071.

Your Child's Reading: What You Can Do. Boston, Mass.: Allyn and Bacon.

Wiesendanger, Katherine D., and Birlem, Ellen, *Parents: Help Your Child Become a Better Reader*. Palo Alto, Calif.: R & E Research Associates, 1982.

Working with Schools: A Parent's Handbook. Washington, D.C.: Government Printing Office, 1979.

Peer Tutoring Guides

Allen, Vernon L., *Children Are Teachers: Theory and Research on Tutoring* New York: Academic Press, 1976.

Bloom, Sophie, *Peer and Cross Age Tutoring in the Schools*. Washington, D.C.: Department of Health, Education and Welfare, 1976.

Bremmer, Barbara L., *Students Helping Students Program*, 1971–1972. Washington, D.C.: U.S. Office of Education, 1972.

Klaus, D. J., *Patterns of Peer Tutoring*. ERIC/CRIER ED 117 695.

Koskinen, Patrick S., and Wilson, Robert M., *Tutoring: A Guide for Success*. New York: Teachers College Press, 1982.

Koskinen, Patricia S., and Wilson, Robert M., *A Guide for Student Tutors*. New York: Teachers College Press, 1982.

Lippitt, P., et al., *Cross-age Helping Program: Orientation, Training and Related Materials*. Ann Arbor, Mich.: University of Michigan, 1971. Accompanied by record and filmstrip.

McClellan, Billie Frances, *Student Involvement in the Instructional Process*. ERIC/CRIER ED 055046.

Melargno, R. J., *Tutoring with Students: A Handbook for Establishing Tutorial Programs in Schools.* Englewood Cliffs, N.J.: Educational Technology Publications, 1976.

Morrissey, P. A., *Guide for Teachers: How to Set Up a Peer Tutoring System in Your Classroom.* ERIC/CRIER ED 163 684.

Newmark, G., *This School Belongs to You and Me.* New York: Hart Associates, 1976.

Stewart, E., and Larsen, Steven C., *Peer Tutoring for Individualized Instruction.* Boston: Allyn and Bacon, 1980.

Book Lists for Parents

American Library Association, *Let's Read Together: Books for Family Enjoyment*, 4th ed. Chicago: American Library Association, 1981.

Children's Book Committee, *Reading with Your Child Through Age Five.* Washington, D.C.: Child Study Association, 1976.

Cianciolo, Patricia Jean, *Picture Books for Children.* Chicago: American Library Association, 1981.

Hearne, Betsy, *Choosing Books for Children.* New York: Delacorte Press, 1981.

Kimmel, Margaret Mary, and Segel, Elizabeth, *For Reading Out Loud: A Guide to Sharing Books with Children.* New York: Delacorte Press, 1983.

Appendixes

Appendix I

Book Lists

We offer this selected list of indexes and booklists to aid the teacher in book selection. Perhaps with these aids the teacher will find it possible to promote a degree of individualized, pleasureful reading.

National Council of Teachers of English, 1111 Kenyon Road, Urbana, Ill. 61804

Adventuring with Books. A list for preschool and first to sixth grade of 2500 books selected for literary merit, interest, and equitable treatment of minorities (1981 edition).

Learning to Love Literature. Theory and practice in bringing books to primary children plus a list of many books of strong appeal (1981 edition).

Reading Ladders for Human Relations. Five themes beginning with the self and extending to groups, cultures, and the world are used to list books of value from preschool through high school (1981 edition).

Literature By and About the American Indian. Almost 800 books of American Indian literature and culture (1979 edition).

H. W. Wilson & Co., 950 University Avenue, New York, N.Y. 10052

The Children's Catalogue. An annotated list of books with estimated reading and interest levels. Annual supplement available.

R. R. Bowker & Co., 1180 Avenue of the Americas, New York, N.Y. 10036

Growing Up with Books. An annual list of 200 of the best children's books.

Growing Up with Paperbacks. A guide to 200 of the best paperbacks of the year for children.

Growing Up with Science Books. A list of 250 of the best books in science.

Large Type Books in Print. A list of 200 books in oversize type for the visually handicapped.

Paperbound Books in Print. A quarterly index of paperbacks arranged by author, title and subject.

Best Books for Children: Preschool Through the Middle Grades. Outstanding books published from 1966 to 1972.

Association for Childhood Education International, 3615 Wisconsin Avenue, N. W. Washington, D.C. 20016

Bibliography of Books for Children. An annotated list of about 200 books arranged by age and subject. Particularly good for preschool and primary selections.

Children's Book Council, 67 Irving Place, New York, N.Y. 10003

Children's Choices. Offers an annual list of the books selected by children in *The Reading Teacher* of the International Reading Association. Reprints available from the Council, as well as a variety of materials for promoting reading—posters, mobiles, display materials, certificates for children, etc.

Children's Books—Awards and Prizes. A list of the award-winning books of each year, as selected by adults, not children.

University of Chicago Press, 5801 Ellis Avenue S., Chicago, Ill., 60637

The Best in Children's Books. Annotates and critiques about 1500 books for children published in 1973–1978 (1980 edition).
Bulletin of the Center for Children's Books. A monthly in which books are thoroughly evaluated as they are published.

Dell Publishing Co., Inc., 245 East 47 Street, New York, N.Y. 10017

Paperback Books for Young People. An annotated and descriptive list to aid teachers and librarians.

American Library Association, 50 E. Huron Street, Chicago, Ill. 60611

Books for Children. A compilation of the reviews of about 1000 books recommended in the bimonthly magazine *Booklist.*
Books on American Indians and Eskimos. A selected guide for children and young adults.

Garrard Publishing Co., 1607 N. Market Street, Champaign, Ill. 61820

Spache, George D., *Good Reading for the Disadvantaged: Multi-Ethnic Resources.* Lists books by and about seven American minority groups, as well as relevant instructional materials and audiovisual resources for working with such groups (1975).
Spache, George D., *Good Reading for Poor Readers.* Discusses problems in book selection and gives annotated graded lists of trade books, textbooks, workbooks and games, magazines and newspapers, series books, book clubs, reading lists, programmed materials, materials for auditory and for visual perception training, and resources for the teacher of the disadvantaged (tenth edition, 1978).

Government Printing Office, Washington, D.C. 20402

The Best of Children's Books, 1964–1978 (1980).
Children's Books, 1981 (1982).

Other very helpful sources are the reviews given in such publications as:

The Horn Book Magazine, Park Square Building, 30 St. James Avenue, Boston, Mass. 02116.
Language Arts, National Council of Teachers of English, 1111 Kenyon Road, Urbana, Ill. 61801.
Childhood Education, Association for Childhood Education International, 3615 Wisconsin Avenue N.W., Washington, D.C. 20016.
Elementary School Journal, University of Chicago Press, 5801 S. Ellis Avenue, Chicago, Ill. 60637.
The Reading Teacher, International Reading Association, 800 Barksdale Road, Newark, Del. 19711.
Junior Libraries, American Library Association, 50 E. Huron Street, Chicago, Ill. 60611.
Booklist, American Library Association.

Appendix II

Series Books and Collections

These books were, for the most part, written at higher levels of interest, action, and adventure than their reading levels. Most were scaled by the Spache or the Dale-Chall Readability formulas. Hence the reading levels indicated are parallel to books used in our schools at the given levels. This and other such lists present a sampling of series books rather than a complete roster.

Benefic Press, 10300 West Roosevelt Road, Westchester, Ill. 60153

Animal Adventures. Preprimer and first reader level stories of action and adventure are offered in these nine books.

Butternut Bill. Eight books, preprimer to first on activities of a mountain boy and his friends.

Buttons Family Adventure. Twelve family stories at preprimer to third grade.

Cowboy Sam. Fifteen very popular western stories about a young boy, at preprimer to third level.

Cowboys of Many Races. Adventures of multi-ethnic cowboys, written at preprimer to fifth grade.

Dan Frontier. Early life in the Midwest is depicted in this eleven-book series written at preprimer to third grade.

Easy To Read. A series at preprimer to fourth-grade level offering a variety of stories.

Emergency Series. Adventures of paramedics in six books of second- to fourth-grade level.

Exploring and Understanding. Thirteen-book series on science, all at grade four level.

Helicopter Adventure Series. Six adventure books of young people at first- to third-grade levels.

Find Out About. Simple science books in a twelve-book group at first- to third-grade levels.

Inner City Series. Five titles in urban setting at second to fourth grade.

Horses and Heroines. A girl and her horse are the main characters in this six-book series at second to fourth grade.

Moonbeam Series. Ten space age adventures of a monkey and his human friends at preprimer to third grade levels.

Mystery Adventure. Eight-book series of young people solving mysteries, at reading levels two to six.

Racing Wheels. Twelve titles of exciting auto racing stories at second to fourth grade.

Sailor Jack. Sea stories of action written at preprimer to third grade levels in this ten-book group.

Space Age. Space travel and contacts with alien creatures are featured in this eight-book series at second to sixth levels.

Sports Mysteries. Adventures of inner city athletes of various ethnic backgrounds are told in this four-book group, at fourth to ninth grade levels.

Tom Logan. Western action portrayed in this eight-book series at preprimer to third grade material.

World of Adventure. Explorations by young people are the themes of this eight-book series written at second to sixth grade.

Addison-Wesley Publishing Co., 2725 Sand Hill Road, Menlo Park, Calif. 94025

Checkered Flag. Exciting car racing is the subject matter for this eight-book series at second to fourth grade.

Deep Sea Adventure. Twelve dramatic deep-sea diving stories are offered at high first to fifth grade.

Jim Forest Series. Outdoor adventures of a teenager and his forest ranger uncle are presented in this six-book series written at first to third grade.

Happenings. Pop music and rock bands are featured in this four-book group written at fourth grade.

Morgan Bay Mysteries. Three teenagers combine to solve mysterious events in this nine-book group written at second to fourth grade.

New Kaleidoscope. An eight-book series on such topics as sports, cars, and careers, written at second to ninth grade.

Top Flight. Young people of varied ethnic backgrounds experience action in different flying machines in this six-book collection at second to third grade.

Wildlife Adventure. Animal adventures are the themes of this six-book set written at second to fourth.

Garrard Publishing Co., 1607 N. Market Street, Champaign, Ill. 61820

American Folktales. America's superheroes are features of this nineteen-book series offered at third-grade level.

Americans All. Biographies of great Americans are presented in this fourth-grade twenty-five book set.

Around the World Holidays. Holidays in seven foreign countries in this fifth-grade collection.

Basic Vocabulary. True animal stories and folklore in this seventeen-book set are written at second grade within the words of the Dolch Word List.

Discovery. Simple biographies of American figures in this thirty-book collection, at third grade.

Famous Animals. A seventeen-book group of the actions of noted animals, written at grade three.

First Holiday. Second grade stories of favorite holidays in these five books.

Folklore of the World. Fourteen books within the Dolch vocabulary for third grade.

Good Earth. Easy books on environmental education written at third grade constitute this thirteen-book series.

Holidays. Celebrations in America and other lands are the themes of this ten-book set of third-grade materials.

Indians. Stories of the great American Indian chiefs are presented in this thirteen-book third-grade collection.

Jimmy and Joe. First-grade level stories about a pair of boys of mixed ethnic background in this nine-book set.

Junior Science. Physical and natural science are the subject of this nine-book group at third grade.

Pleasure Reading. Thirteen stories of old classics adapted to fourth grade.

Sports. Stories of sport figures and histories of sports are featured in this twenty-two book collection at fourth-grade level

Fearon-Pitman Learning Publishers Inc., 6 Davis Drive, Belmont, Calif. 94002

Adventures in Urban Reading. A four-book set in comic book format on inner city life at second- to third-grade reading levels.

Americans West. Factual stories about famous and infamous Western figures at fifth-grade level are featured in this three-book group.

Bestsellers. Three sets of ten titles each offer mysteries, romance, science fiction, and other topics at second to third levels.

Galaxy 5. Science fiction stories at third grade are offered in this six-book set.

International Folktales. Ten stories from other lands in this group, at second to fourth grade.

First Reading. Animal folklore for beginning readers written at first grade reading level within the Dolch vocabulary comprise this seventeen-book group.

Jim Hunter. Twelve books on the adventures of a secret agent in this first- to third-grade series.

Pacemaker Classics. Famous stories adapted to second grade are presented in this eight-book collection.

Pacemaker Stories. Four sets of six books each offer adventure or mystery tales at second to fourth grade.

Pacemaker True Adventure. Eleven stories of historical figures at second grade.

Fearon Racing Series. Five books on car racing at fifth to sixth levels.

Regions of the World. Twelve social science easy-reading books at fifth grade.

Space Police. Police officers in space are featured in this six-book series at third grade.

Specter. Mystery-horror stories offered at third grade in this eight-book group.

Random House Inc., 201 East 50 Street, New York, N.Y. 10022

Allabout Books. Nonfiction on a wide variety of topics at fourth to sixth grades.

Beginner Books. Easy books on a variety of subjects for second grade.

Landmark. Almost seventy titles devoted to historical events at fourth to sixth grade.

Step-Up Books. Action and adventure in this four-book series written at second to third grade.

Raintree Publishers Ltd., 205 W. Highland Avenue, Milwaukee, Wis. 53203

A Book About. Each of sixteen books is devoted to a science topic, at second grade.

Great Unsolved Mysteries. Twenty-four famous mysteries at fifth grade level.

Myths, Magic and Superstitions. Ghosts, haunted houses, and the like are the subjects in a twenty-book group at fifth grade.

Read About Science. Fifteen different science topics are treated at second to third grade difficulty.

Globe Book Co., 50 West 23 Street, New York, N.Y. 10010

Adapted Classics. These classic stories are adapted to fourth- to eighth-grade levels in a twenty-three book set. Five others are offered in paperback.

This publisher also offers more than twenty one- and two-book groups on a wide variety of topics—action, biography, adventure, sports, mystery, etc. All are written at third- to sixth-grade levels.

Follett Publishing Co., 1010 West Washington Boulevard, Chicago, Ill. 60607

Outer Space Stories. A three-book series at fourth to fifth levels about other planets.

Mystery Books and Dragon Series. Four mysteries and four horse stories written at fifth-grade level.

Supplementary Reading Sets. Each set offers six books at first or second grade plus a poster and teacher's guide. Fourteen such sets available.

Venture. Twelve books, each on a separate sport, offer action stories and information at fourth to sixth grade. A student exercise book and a filmstrip parallels each book.

Vocational Reading Series. A six-book group on as many vocations, at fourth to sixth grade, with exercises.

Bowmar-Noble Publishing Co., 4563 Colorado Boulevard, Los Angeles, Calif. 90039

Play the Game. Eight biographies of famous athletes at second to fourth grade.

Reading Incentive Series. Twenty books offering facts about sports such as surfing, motorcycles, go-car and dune buggy racing, at third to fourth grade.

Search Books. Twelve informational books on topics such as dolphins, bird migration, weather, skin diving, written at second-grade level.

Young Adventurers. Six books on the actions and outdoor activities of teenagers written at fourth to sixth grades.

Freedom Book Series. A ten-book group on America offered in sets of six copies each with activities, cassettes, and guide.

Scholastic Magazines Inc., 904 Sylvan Street, Englewood Cliffs, N.J. 07632

Action Libraries. A variety of mystery, romance, and adventure stories are offered in these forty books written at second to third grade.

Contact. Four books on the media, five concerned with individuals, and eight on social problems comprise this package library written at fourth to sixth grade, for upper elementary children.

Double Action Libraries. Ten stories of teenage romance, mystery, and adventure comprise this series written at third grade.

Firebird. An American history group offering books on the contributions of ethnic minorities at fifth to sixth grade.

Sprint Libraries. Forty books on sports, mystery, and adventure comprise these two kits of second- and third-grade reading levels.

Individualized Reading Libraries. Each of six collections of 100 books covers a three- to five-grade range, from first grade up.

Plus Reading. Five book collections of 25 books each with a readability range of two or more grades.

Text Extenders. Collections of books paralleling the content of ten leading basal reading series. Offer six copies of three titles and thirty-seven others at primary, and six copies of four titles and thirty-seven others at fourth to sixth reading levels.

Pleasure Reading Libraries. Each is a collection of thirty or fifty titles. Two or three such libraries are offered for each grade, kindergarten to sixth, plus two each for junior and senior high, amounting to eighteen different groups.

Scholastic Bookshelf. Eight copies each of four "core" books, sixteen copies of a workbook, a library of 28 additional titles and a number of spirit masters are included in each bookshelf of the three collections for fourth, fifth, and sixth grades.

Sprint Starter Libraries. Three book collections for middle grades at first grade reading level. Each library contains four copies each of five titles plus spirit masters and teaching guide.

Reluctant Reader Library. Each contains fifty books, two each of twenty-five titles and a teaching guide. These collections are offered for grades five to nine, two per grade. Each set is one or two grade levels lower in readability than the grade for which it is offered.

Tune-in To Books. Each group offers two copies each of twenty-five titles for each grade from two to nine.

Basic Reading Collection. Two collections each for grades one to ten contain forty on-grade books. Seventeen such libraries available.

King Features, 235 East 45 Street, New York, N.Y. 10017

Comics Reading Libraries. Each of two libraries offers twelve copies of eight titles, posters, spirit masters and teacher's guide, for middle grades.

King Classic Libraries. Twenty-four classics adapted for upper elementary grades. Library has six copies each of eight titles plus spirit masters and teacher's guide.

Cypress Publishing Co., Glendale, Ca.

City Kids. One of dozens of paperback sets on a wide variety of topics. This is a twelve-title collection at primary levels. Others offered for all elementary grades.

Educational Activities Inc., P.O. Box 392, Freeport, N.Y. 11520

Interesting Careers of Interesting People. Biographies of five different workers in each of four books for fifth-grade reading.

Robb Family Adventures. Two series ranging from first to third grade with four books and accompanying cassettes in each. Exciting family activities are the theme.

Biographies from American History. Six books and teacher's guide for grades two to three. Cassettes also available.

Just Right Stories. Two books of short stories at third grade intended to help readers develop positive attitudes toward life.

Sea Hawk. Ten-book set ranging from mid-first to fourth grade in reading level on sea adventures of two teenagers.

Griffin Readers. A twelve-book series at primary levels on pirates, buried treasure, and storms at sea, with accompanying workbooks. A supplementary set of eight books, *Griffin Pirate Readers*, is offered for third to fourth grade.

The Dragon Books. Two groups of books, one of six titles for first grade, the other comprising four sets of five books each for primary grades, are offered. Content emphasizes dramatic search and danger episodes. Workbooks available.

Flightpath to Reading. Four groups of suspenseful adventures of a teenager, eight titles in each, at second to fourth grade.

Buccaneers. An eight-book series of a boy's adventures in another world. Written at fourth-grade level.

Time Out Stories. Three books of short stories of actions of young people, written at fourth to sixth levels.

Action Reading Series. Nonfiction sports books giving information, rules, etc. on eight different sports. Written at third to fourth grade.

I Hate to Read Series. Offers six sets of four books each, with filmstrips, and cassettes at primary levels. Most titles indicate they deal with personal and social issues pertinent to intermediate or upper elementary pupils.

Science Research Associates, 259 East Erie Street, Chicago, Ill. 60611

SRA Lunchbox Libraries. Offers sixty-four eight-page selections for primary grades on variety of topics, with teacher's guide.

SRA Pilot Library Series. Each kit contains seventy-two brief booklets. Separate kits for grades 3 to 5, 6 to 7 and 8 to 9.

ABC Books*

Anno, Mitsumasa, *Anno's Alphabet.* New York: Crowell, 1975.

Asimov, Israel, *ABC's of the Earth.* New York: Walker Publications, 1971.

Carle, Eric, *All About Arthur (an absolutely absurd ape).* New York: Franklin Watts, 1974.

Delaunay, Sonia, *Alphabet.* New York: Crowell, 1972.

Emberley, Ed, *Ed Emberley's ABC.* Boston: Little, Brown, 1978.

Grant, Sandy, *Hey, Look at Me.* Scarsdale, N. Y.: Bradbury, 1973.

Rockwell, Anne, *Albert B. Cub and Zebra.* New York: Crowell, 1977.

Picture Books

Ahlberg, Janet and Allan, *Funnybones.* New York: Greenwillow Books.

Alexander, Martha, *Bobo's Dream.* New York: Dial, 1970.

Brown, Margaret Wise, *The Steamroller.* New York: Walker Publications, 1974.

Carroll, Ruth, *What Whiskers Did.* New York: Walck, 1965.

Delton, Judy, *Two Good Friends.* New York: Crown, 1974.

Goodall, John, *Creepy Castle.* New York: Atheneum, 1975.

Goodall, John, *Naughty Nancy.* New York: Athenum, 1975.

Hazen, Barbara Shook, *The Gorilla Did It.* New York: Atheneum, 1974.

Hoban, Lillian, *Arthur's Honey Bear.* New York: Harper & Row, 1974.

Kent, Jack, *The Egg Book.* New York: Macmillan, 1975.

Krahn, Fernando, *The Mystery of the Giant Footsteps.* New York: E. P. Dutton, 1977.

Krahn, Fernando, *A Funny Friend from Heaven.* Philadelphia: J. B. Lippincott, 1977.

Prelutsky, Jack, *Circus.* New York: Macmillan.

Provenson, Alice and Martin, *Our Animal Friends at Maple Hill Farm.* New York: Random House, 1974.

Provenson, Alice and Martin, *An Owl and Three Pussycats.* New York: Atheneum.

Rayner, Mary, *Mrs. Pig's Bulk Buy.* New York: Atheneum.

*The following four lists were collated with the assistance of Dr. Betty Ruth Raygor, formerly of Hamline University.

Rice, Eve, *Benny Bakes a Cake*. New York: Greenwillow Books.

Sendak, Maurice, *Outside Over There*. New York: Harper & Row.

Wells, Rosemary, *Timothy Goes to School*. New York: Dial Press.

Spatial and Relational Concepts

Anno, Mitsumasa, *Anno's Counting Book*. New York: Crowell, 1975.

Barton, Byron, *Building a House*. New York: Greenwillow Books.

Carle, Eric, *I See a Song*. New York: Crowell, 1973.

Crowther, Robert, *The Most Amazing Hide-and-Seek Counting Book*. New York: Viking Press.

Freschet, Bernice, *The Ants Go Marching*. New York: Charles Scribner's Sons, 1973.

Hoban, Russell, *Ten What?* New York: Charles Scribner's Sons, 1974.

Hoban, Tana, *Take Another Look*. New York: Greenwillow Books.

Hoban, Tana, *Circles, Triangles and Squares*. New York: Macmillan.

Ichikawa, Satomi, *Friends*. New York: Parents Magazine, 1976.

Krahn, Fernando and Maria, *The Life of Numbers*. New York: Simon and Schuster, 1976.

Lionni, Leo, *A Color of His Own*. New York: Pantheon, 1975.

Maestro, Betsy and Guilio, *Traffic: A Book of Opposites*. New York: Crown.

Ormerod, Jan, *Sunshine*. New York: Lothrop, Lee and Shepard.

Reiss, John J., *Shapes*. Scarsdale, N.Y.: Bradbury.

Wildsmith, Brian, *What the Moon Saw*. Fairlawn, N.J.: Oxford University Press, 1978.

Yolen, Jane, *An Invitation to the Butterfly Ball*. New York: Parents Magazine, 1976.

Rythmic Verse or Repetitive Patterns (Predictable Books)

Aadema, Verna, *Bringing the Rain to Kapiti Plain: A Nandi Tale*. New York: Dial Press.

Aliki, *A Mary's Bloom*. New York: Puffin Books, 1978.

Caldone, Paul, *The Little Red Hen*. New York: Scholastic Book Service, 1973.

Farber, Norma, *Where's Gomer?* New York: E. P. Dutton.

Hogrogian, Nonny, *One Fine Day*. New York: Macmillan, 1971.

Kellog, Steven, *There Was an Old Woman*. New York: Four Winds Press, 1974.

Kent, Jack, *The Fat Cat: A Danish Folktale*. New York: Parents Magazine, 1971.

Langstaff, John, *Oh, A-Hunting We Will Go*. New York: Atheneum.

Lee, Dennis, *Alligator Pie*. Toronto: Macmillan of Canada, 1974.

Lee, Dennis, *Garbage Delight*. Toronto: Macmillan of Canada, 1977.

Lexau, Joan M., *That's Good, That's Bad*. New York: Dial Press, 1963.

Martin, Bill Jr., *Brown Bear, Brown Bear, What Do You See?* New York: Holt, Rinehart and Winston, 1970.

Mizumara, Kazue, *If I Were a Cricket*. New York: Crowell, 1973.

Seuss, Dr. *The Cat in the Hat*. New York: Random House, 1957.

Sonneborn, Ruth, *Someone Is Eating the Sun*. New York: Random House, 1974.

Viorst, Judith, *Alexander and the Terrible, Horrible, No Good, Very Bad Day*. New York: Atheneum, 1972.

Zolotow, Charlotte, *If It Weren't for You*. New York: Harper & Row, 1965.

Zolotow, Charlotte, *Do You Know What I'll Do?* New York: Harper & Row, 1968.

More Easy Books* (and Series Books)

Adoff, Arnold, *Big Sister Tells Me That I'm Black*. New York: Holt, Rinehart and Winston, 1976.

Adoff, Arnold, *Black Is Brown Is Tan*. New York: Harper & Row, 1973.

Austin, Mary, ed., *Discovery Books*. Champaign, Ill.: Garrard Publishing.

Bate, Lucy, *Little Rabbit's Loose Tooth*. New York: Crown, 1975.

Baylor, Byrd, *Hawk, I'm Your Brother*. New York: Charles Scribner's Sons, 1976.

Beginning-to-Read Books. Chicago: Follett Publishing.

Beginner Books. New York: Random House.

Breinberg, Petronella, *Shawn's Red Bike*. New York: Crowell, 1976.

Breinberg, Petronella, *Shawn Goes to School*. New York: Crowell, 1974.

Chandler, Edna Walker, *Boxcar Children Mystery Stories*. Chicago: Benefic Press.

Chandler, Edna Walker, *Cowboy Sam Series*. Chicago: Benefic Press.

Chandler, Edna Walker, *Tom Logan Series*. Chicago: Benefic Press.

Choma, Michael, *The Robb Family Adventures*. Freeport, N.Y.: Educational Activities.

Coerr, Eleanor, *The Big Balloon Race*. New York: Harper & Row.

Dolch, E. W. and M. P., *Basic Vocabulary Books*. Champaign, Ill.: Garrard Publishing.

Dolch, E. W. and M. P., *First Reading Books*. Champaign, Ill.: Garrard Publishing.

Easy-to-Read Series. New York: Random House.

Glendinning, Sally, *Jimmy and Joe*. Champaign, Ill.: Garrard Publishing.

Gramatky, Hardie, *Little Toot*. New York: E. P. Dutton, 1978.

Harwood, Pearl Augusta, *Mr. Bumba Books*. Minneapolis: Lerner Publication.

Hoban, Lillian, *Arthur's Funny Money*. New York: Harper & Row.

Hurley, William J., *Dan Frontier Series*. Chicago: Benefic Press.

I Can Read Books. New York: Harper & Row.

Johnson, Charles E., *Holiday Books*. Champaign, Ill.: Garrard Publishing.

Keats, Jack, *Louie*. New York: Greenwillow Books, 1975.

Keats, Jack, *Whistle for Willie*. New York: Penguin Books, 1977.

Larrick, Nancy, *Junior Science Books*. Champaign, Ill.: Garrard Publishing.

Let's Read and Find Out. New York: Crowell.

Marriott, Alice and Rachlin, Carol K., *Indian Books*. Champaign, Ill.: Garrard Publishing.

McCall, Edith, *Butternut Bill Series*. Chicago: Benefic Press.

McCall, Edith, *Button Books*. Chicago: Benefic Press.

McCullagh, S. K., *The Griffin Readers*. Freeport, N.Y.: Educational Activities.

Pacemaker Classics. Belmont, Calif.: Fearon Pitman Publishers.

Palazzo, Tony, *Animal Books*. Champaign, Ill.: Garrard Publishing.

Parish, Peggy, *Amelia Bedelia and the Baby*. New York: Greenwillow Books.

Simon, Norma, *All Kinds of Families*. Chicago: Albert Whitman.

*These books range from first to third grade according to the Spache Readability formula.

Step-Up Books. New York: Random House.
Van Leeuwen, Jean, *More Tales of Oliver Pig.* New York: Dial Press.
Walt Disney Story Books. Wayne, N.J.: Golden Press.
Wasserman, Selma and Jack, *Helicopter Adventure.* Chicago: Benefic Press.
Wasserman, Selma and Jack, *The Moonbeam Series.* Chicago: Benefic Press.

Index